CRIMINAL BEHAVIOR
Text and Readings in Criminology

CRIMINAL BEHAVIOR

Text and Readings in Criminology
Second Edition

DELOS H. KELLY
California State University, Los Angeles

ST. MARTIN'S PRESS
New York

Editor: Debra Nesbitt
Project Management: Caliber Design Planning, Inc.
Cover design: Judy Forster

Library of Congress Catalog Card Number: 88-63049

For information, write:
St. Martin's Press, Inc.
175 Fifth Avenue
New York, NY 10010

ISBN: 0-312-02131-3

Acknowledgments
Acknowledgments and copyrights are continued at the back of the book on pages 573–575, which constitute an extension of the copyright page.

Gwynn Nettler, "Definition of Crime." Reprinted with permission from *Explaining Crime*, second edition, by Gwynn Nettler. Copyright © 1978 by McGraw-Hill, Inc.

Howard S. Becker, "Moral Entrepreneurs: The Creation and Enforcement of Deviant Categories." Reprinted with permission of The Free Press, a Division of Macmillan, Inc. from *Outsiders* by Howard S. Becker. Copyright © 1963 by The Free Press.

Richard C. Hollinger and Lonn Lanza-Kaduce, "The Process of Criminalization: The Case of Computer Crime Laws." Reprinted by permission from The American Society of Criminology and the authors from *Criminology*, 26:1, 1988, pp. 101–113.

Robert Tillman, "The Size of the 'Criminal Population': The Prevalence and Incidence of Adult Arrest." Reprinted by permission from The American Society of Criminology and the author from *Criminology*, 25:3, 1987, pp. 561–579.

Richard McCleary, Barbara C. Nienstedt, and James M. Erven, "Uniform Crime Reports as Organizational Outcomes: Three Time Series Experiments." © 1982 by the Society for the Study of Social Problems, Inc. Reprinted from *Social Problems*, vol. 29, no. 4, April 1982, pp. 361–372, by permission.

James D. Orcutt and Rebecca Faison, "Sex-Role Attitude Change and Reporting of Rape Victimization, 1973–1985." Reprinted with permission of JAI Press Inc. from *Sociological Quarterly*, 29:4, pp. 589–604.

To Russ

Preface

The study of criminal behavior is in many respects the study of the society that defines it and attempts to control it. Criminologists have, traditionally, been interested in why crime exists in a social system, as well as why people may be motivated to violate laws. Recently, however, more attention has been given to the ways in which interactions between social actors and institutional agents can affect such interrelated concerns as the production of crime data; the measurement of criminal activity and its explanations; and the identifying, processing, and control of those designated as criminals. *Criminal Behavior*, with its integration of classic and current approaches to the study of crime, offers a framework — *the interactional-organizational* — that helps to clarify interactions such as these. A guiding tenet is that interactions (e.g., these occurring between a citizen and a police officer) become more meaningful when evaluated against an institution's underlying organizational structure and approach to crime (e.g., a police department's *theory of the office*, range of *diagnostic stereotypes*, and existing career lines).

A body of law is not constant. New laws evolve and old ones change over time. It is important, therefore, to understand how and why changes may occur. Part 1 of this book describes the evolution of laws and how various historical forces — primarily legislative and political — influence their creation. The selections demonstrate how those with vested interests, power, and resources often affect the prevailing definitions of crime, decide who the potential criminals are, and determine how they should be treated. The selection from Hollinger and Lanza-Kaduce's article on the criminalization of computer abuse offers a particularly excellent account of this.

Part 2 examines the measurement of crime. It begins with a description of the strategies that are used to assess the nature and extent of criminal activity and then moves to an analysis of some of the correlates (e.g., race, class, and gender) that frequently characterize the study of crime. A major theme of this section is that not only should the production of crime data be evaluated, cautiously, from an organizational frame of reference, but that the potential impact of any presumed correlate of crime is best assessed by an examination of how it is mediated through organizational structures and components.

Explanations of why crime exists and why people violate laws are dealt with in Part 3. The selections present several of the classic and current sociological and social-psychological theories that have been advanced to explain motivation. It concludes with a piece that illustrates how theories can be tested in terms of their explanatory power.

Part 4 explores how people become exposed to crime and learn criminal values and traditions. The initial selections discuss the socializing experiences that may give rise to criminal activities and perhaps, ultimately, a criminal career. A range of crimes, from personal (e.g., marital rape and child abuse) to government and corporate, is then examined.

The effects of criminal involvement on an actor's personal and public identity are also examined.

Part 5 describes how those agents who act in the name of social-control institutions attempt to control crime and the criminal. The readings illustrate how institutional-bureaucratic representatives, influenced and constrained by the official positions they occupy, go about finding, identifying, processing, and sanctioning criminals. Throughout this part especially, one can obtain an excellent "feel" for how an individual's traits articulate with organizational components and processes to produce selected organizational outcomes (e.g., the filing of felony charges, or the rendering of a guilty verdict)—which is a major thrust of this book. The effects of legal processing on the accused person's personal and public identity are also considered.

Finally, Part 6 examines various attempts that may be used to change crime and the criminal. The initial pieces address some of the basic issues in corrections (e.g., the retribution versus rehabilitation argument); this is followed by selections that describe how institutions and guards may operate. The part concludes with materials illustrating how changes in existing structures (e.g., enhancing opportunities), laws (e.g., criminalizing selected acts while decriminalizing others), and enforcement strategies (e.g., focusing more attention on white-collar and government crime) could affect the picture of crime that is produced.

Many people have helped in the preparation of the second edition of this book, and I would like to acknowledge their efforts. Special thanks go to my editors Don Reisman and Debra Nesbitt, as well as to my colleagues Tim Diamond and Steve Gordon, particularly for their ongoing help and encouragement. I would also like to thank my reviewers for the many valuable comments and suggestions they offered. Finally, a special debt is owed to the authors represented in the book, for without their fine contributions this book would not have been possible.

Delos H. Kelly

Contents

CRIMINAL BEHAVIOR
Text and Readings in Criminology

GENERAL INTRODUCTION

Definitions of crime and the criminal are not absolute but emerge out of interactions taking place among people. Understanding these interactional processes requires an awareness of how individual attributes interact with social control institutions vested with the authority to apply criminal labels to lawbreakers. Ultimately a person may be officially judged criminal by the court. In this event, an evolving or precriminal career may become solidified, and the person may be thereafter cast into the role of criminal.

The study of crime, then, entails an understanding of the society that defines it. Other concerns also fall into the purview of criminology. For the purposes of this volume, six major topics are addressed: (1) defining and creating crime, (2) measuring crime, (3) explaining crime, (4) becoming criminal, (5) controlling crime and the criminal, and (6) changing crime and the criminal. All of these topics are interrelated.

DEFINING AND CREATING CRIME

How one conceptualizes crime has a direct bearing on all the major topics covered in this book. If, for example, crime is defined according to the legalistic model—that is, the criminal is one who violates a law and is thereafter judged guilty by a court—then lawbreakers become the major object of scrutiny and the basis for the collection of official data. From the analysis of such data, certain factors will emerge as "causes" or correlates of crime. These correlates are, in turn, used not only to explain crime but to justify various types of control, treatment, and prevention strategies. If the official crime data indicate that social class and race are important factors in crime, then certain groups will probably be singled out for special treatment—a strategy that, as we shall see, is frequently unfounded or ill-conceived. Suffice it to say here that reliance on the legalistic model of crime—and especially the data it generates—is associated with serious difficulties.

Criminologists have generally accepted laws as givens and have then proceeded to examine their violation and enforcement. Such an approach masks the fact that new laws are evolving, old laws are changing, and as laws change, so too must the picture of crime and the criminal. Thus it is necessary to examine those processes by which *acts* become defined as criminal; how historical, legislative, and political factors affect the *content* of the law; and how the powerful endeavor to influence the definitions of crime as well as how criminals are to be processed, sanctioned, and treated.

It is equally important to analyze how *actors* become defined as criminals – that is, how the police, the courts, and the correctional institutions perceive and respond to different offenders (hence the *interactional-organizational* perspective of this book). However, for a criminal to come into being, three conditions must be met: (1) a law must exist, (2) a person must violate the law, and (3) someone must demand enforcement of the law.

MEASURING CRIME

Efforts to assess the nature and extent of crime use two sources of data: official and unofficial. Official data are those collected by some law enforcement agency. However, each of the various agencies of the criminal justice system produces its own data. We are thus confronted with a variety of police, court, and correctional statistics. The best-known data are contained in the FBI's *Uniform Crime Reports*, a summary of national crime statistics released at the end of each year. Although heavily relied upon, official statistics are deficient in many ways. First, much criminal activity is unreported and unrecorded. Second, official crime data are best viewed as an *indication of enforcement activity*. Therefore, not only must official statistics be approached with caution, but an effort must be made to analyze how law enforcement agents go about producing their statistics – especially how stereotypes and preconceptions may affect the labels they apply to people.

Dissatisfaction with official data has led to the development of other, unofficial techniques of crime measurement. Most notable is the self-report method, which examines statements of those who have committed crimes, and the victimization survey, which asks people to report on crimes committed against them. Regardless of the strategy used, any data base generated will have a bearing on other criminological concerns. For example, if race, gender, and poverty emerge as strong correlates of crime, then attempts to explain motivation should acknowledge these factors. Unfortunately, many of the well-known statements advanced to explain crime lack grounding in empirical reality or the real world; this situation no doubt partially accounts for the low level of theorizing that plagues the study of crime.

EXPLAINING CRIME

Why people choose to violate the law has long been a subject of debate. Some investigators have been concerned with how actors become exposed to and learn criminal values and traditions. Some have stressed biological or psychological factors, while others have concentrated on societal conditions. Still others have invoked a combination of individual and structural variables. Few, however, have analyzed how individual traits articulate with organizational structures and processes to produce crime. Part 3 presents a sampling of primarily sociological and social-psychological perspectives on crime.

BECOMING CRIMINAL

Most people are not only aware of what the law is, but they have, in many cases, also made a conscious decision to violate it. This suggests that people *learn* to become criminals.

The process of becoming a criminal is not necessarily straightforward. Various influences are involved. Most of us, at some time, have committed illegal acts. Yet few of us would consider ourselves as criminals. But there are those who do view themselves as criminals and who act in accordance with their profession and its associated labels. The professional fence, the street hustler, the prostitute, the check forger, the con artist, and the hit man are examples.

Becoming a career criminal involves a socializing process, and some individuals become successes while others do not. To succeed in crime, a person must gain exposure and entry to criminal activities and careers. The novice must become familiar with the content of the profession's culture and traditions; failure to live up to its dictates can result in sanctioning or outright expulsion. Throughout the training period, would-be criminals also learn the appropriate techniques and rationalizations associated with their chosen activity. These rationalizations help them to legitimate their involvement in crime and shield them from threats to their identity and self-image. A classic case of such training is contained in *Oliver Twist* in the description of how Fagin recruited and trained young boys in the art of becoming successful street hustlers and criminals.

At some time in the socialization process, a person may decide to pursue the chosen profession as a career. Such a decision is often associated with significant *identity* and *behavior* changes. The person, for example, may not only come to view himself as a professional fence but may change his behavior, mannerisms, dress, and acquaintances to accord with his new identity. Ultimately, the criminal may become entangled with the criminal justice system and even be sentenced to a correctional facility. If this occurs, the criminal is often cast into a passive role—a role with limited choices. (There are of course some notable exceptions to this generalization. The Watergate criminals were, predictably, treated and often allowed to respond much differently than common street criminals.)

On the other hand, one might question whether young runaways, male or female, who become prostitutes consciously decide to pursue such a profession or are coerced, however subtly, into it. Selections in Part 4 document those interactional processes and related decisions that may give rise to the early stages of a criminal career.

While some people systematically pursue criminal activities as the source of their livelihood and accept a criminal identity, others who commit illegal acts do not accept the label. They may commit crimes sporadically, such as stealing office supplies or assaulting someone. Or, on a far larger scale, they may be government officials or corporation executives who engage in a pattern of sustained illegal activities. What this suggests is that not only do criminal activities take various forms, but that in terms of identity states and behavioral manifestations, participants respond differently to their involvement. Readings in Part 4 explore contingencies such as these.

Involvement in criminal activities is frequently not without its personal and social costs. Publicly a person may be viewed as a law-abiding citizen; privately, however, he may view himself as a hit man or con artist. To maintain his public image and, of course, to avoid detection by the police, he must conceal his private identity and act according to accepted behavior norms. Some people can accomplish this feat, while others, for various reasons (e.g., a lack of significant contact with others), cannot. In some cases the constant need for monitoring one's behavior, as well as the concomitant lack of genuine interaction, can lead to an identity crisis. The affected person may attempt to resolve the crisis, but this is not an easy matter. The hit man can "come clean," but the cost of his admission would most assuredly be prosecution for murder and a criminal label affixed to him.

CONTROLLING CRIME AND THE CRIMINAL

Being publicly branded as a criminal can serve as a precursor to a criminal career. Whether or not this happens, if a person is formally branded, such as through court processing, and if a specific label, such as that of convicted murderer, is attached to a person, we can speak of the social construction of the criminal. It is in this sense, then, that the criminal can be viewed as a social construct.

The major catalyst in the *status-conferring ceremony* (i.e., the movement of a person from a noncriminal to a criminal status) is *audience reaction* to violations of the law. Observers may ignore the lawbreaker, or they may demand that the law be enforced. Thus predicting audience response is often problematic. If, however, we know something about the audience's values, the actor's attributes, and the nature of the act, we are in a better position to predict the reaction. Elsewhere (Kelly, 1979, 1984, 1989), I have developed two paradigms that can be used to illuminate interactional-organizational processes that may lead to labeling as a social deviant; these same tools can be applied to the study of crime and the criminal. Stated differently, interactions become imminently more meaningful when evaluated against an organizational backdrop.

The Interactional Paradigm

A prostitute (the social *actor*) is observed soliciting males (the *act*, a violation of the law in most places) by a police officer (a social *audience*, an enforcer of the laws against prostitution) and is arrested and booked. The prostitute's behavior thus becomes a matter of official record, and, if not released, she may be officially tagged as a criminal. A similar incident is witnessed by another officer who, because he has different values or enforcement priorities, ignores the prostitute's activities. In the first instance, an official, or *institutional*, career may be initiated, while in the second it is not. On the other hand, both officers would probably respond to a liquor store holdup or a case of physical assault. Audience response, then, is in part a function of the type of criminal act being observed. Obviously, not all police officers – or judges or attorneys – will respond to the same event in the same way. They have different opinions about what constitutes "crime" and how the "criminal" should be treated. Thus audience response provides meaning to the actions of others. In short, crime lies in the eye of the beholder.

The beholders of an act may also include *third parties*, or witnesses – the final element in the interactional model. One citizen seeing a prostitute soliciting customers may be offended and attempt to have her arrested; another may be indifferent and ignore the matter. The offended citizen may, moreover, bring still other parties into the picture in an attempt to develop consensus about the seriousness of the offense. As a result, public pressure may be brought to bear to effect a crackdown on prostitution, and the prostitutes caught up in the sweep become, once again, subject to social control and criminal processing.

Although social control agents operate in part on the basis of their own volition and values, they are subject to various constraints. These controls are embedded in the *theory of the office* that an agent occupies. Analyzing how the institution impinges on an agent is critical to an understanding of why a police officer or judge acts the way he or she does. The "organizational paradigm" can help us make such an analysis.

The Organizational Paradigm

Any institution set up to process and change people has a working ideology based on its function and how it carries out its mission. The police exist for the enforcement of the law, and they must have ways of going about their business. Associated with their mandate and enforcement strategies are what Scheff (1966) terms "diagnostic stereotypes"; these are the criteria used to identify and select clients for processing or changing. Through formal or informal socializing experiences, such as in police academies and at social gatherings, the police become familiar with their agency's diagnostic stereotypes. They learn, for example, how to recognize the "typical" street hustler or criminal (Sudnow, 1965). Once identified, the clients are placed into one of the institution's existing slots, or *career lines*, and are thereafter processed in accordance with the expectations associated with the specific career. Similarly, in a correctional facility, sex offenders, "minor" offenders, and "hard core" offenders are each differently typed, processed, and treated.

An institution's diagnostic stereotypes are basic to the *rate production process*, or the application of labels and their subsequent aggregation to form a body of statistics. If, for example, a police officer conveys to others the idea that minorities constitute the "real" crime problem, these groups will become more susceptible to processing as criminals. The statistics generated will, in turn, exhibit a heavy concentration of minority offenders. The statistics can (and frequently do) become a self-fulfilling prophecy. The police may concentrate their surveillance efforts in minority communities, and minority groups may come to expect such treatment. This sort of activity breeds disrespect and hostility on both sides.

In the study of crime, then, we must not only dissect the ideology of social control agencies, but we must also examine how they process clients and produce crime data. Like laws, statistics and institutional functioning should not be accepted as givens. The selections in Part 5 offer further insight into how various types of "criminals" are identified, processed, and sentenced.

Legal processing, like the process of becoming a professional criminal, can necessitate changes in a person's identity and behavior. The accused may not only be officially stamped as a criminal but, if sent to prison, is perceived as a convict and is expected to act according to the behavior patterns associated with his or her crime. The inmate, on the other hand, may not accept the identity of criminal. Once again the two competing definitions—this time the institution's and the inmate's—can cause serious identity problems for the person in question.

CHANGING CRIME AND THE CRIMINAL

At some point, a convicted criminal may decide to go straight, or a known street hustler may attempt to curtail his illegal activities. Each can expect to encounter significant individual and structural barriers that often mitigate against the successful transformation of a criminal identity and career. Such a transformation entails not only desisting from illegal activities but changing one's view of self from criminal to noncriminal. The process is often hardest for the officially stamped criminal. Ex-cons and ex-delinquents are effectively discriminated against in the world of work. Their rejection by society at large drives home the fact that even though they have presumably atoned for their crimes, they must still bear the stigma of criminal. This realization may send them back into a life of crime.

The American corrections system needs to recognize two important principles. First, the desire to reform must come from *within* the individual. Second, efforts to help the individual reform must be meshed with efforts to change the social conditions that encourage criminal activities. Failure to alter such factors as discrimination, injustice, and inequality will only guarantee the continued production of criminals. The burden of reducing crime must be shared by the individual and society alike.

One step that needs to be taken arises from the fact that while institutions are adept at bestowing stigmatizing labels on people, they make no effort to remove such labels. There are no "status-return ceremonies" (Trice and Roman, 1970) that delabel the criminal and return him or her to a noncriminal status in society. The selections in Part 6 deal with this concern and other theoretical issues in corrections, as well as treatment, or rehabilitative, programs that have been mounted to change the criminal's behavior.

In addition to manipulating conditions responsible for crime and finding ways to delabel criminals, other strategies have been advanced to change the picture of crime. One is to change the laws. For example, decriminalizing "victimless crimes"— activities like prostitution and gambling in which people willingly participate—would give crime and its statistics a different appearance. The last two selections in this work recommend specific changes in the law.

SUMMARY

This book aims to help students understand the dynamic and ongoing manner in which crime and the criminal are constructed socially. A main concern is how criminal careers and identities evolve, are perpetuated, and may be transformed. Two other underlying themes are how institutional components and processes interact with individual attributes (the interactional-organizational perspective) and how the powerful and powerless perceive and relate to each other. In the latter sense, it is hoped this collection makes a partial contribution to the sociology of power or conflict.

References

Kelly, Delos H., ed. *Deviant Behavior: A Text-Reader in the Sociology of Deviance.* New York: St. Martin's Press, 1979, 1984, 1989.

Scheff, Thomas J. "Typification in the Diagnostic Practices of Rehabilitation Agencies." In Marvin B. Sussman, ed., *Sociology and Rehabilitation.* Washington, D.C.: American Sociological Association, 1966.

Sudnow, David. "Normal Crimes: Sociological Features of the Penal Code." *Social Problems,* 12 (Winter 1965), 255–270.

Trice, Harrison M. and Paul Michael Roman. "Delabeling, Relabeling, and Alcoholics Anonymous." *Social Problems,* 17 (Spring 1970), 538–546.

PART 1

DEFINING AND CREATING CRIME

As discussed in the introduction, several conditions must be satisfied before a person becomes publicly typed as a criminal: (1) a law must exist, (2) the person must violate the law, and (3) someone must enforce the law. If the enforcement is successful, the wrongdoer takes on the identity of criminal in the eyes of society. The selections in this part deal primarily with the laws themselves. The first reading considers the definitional components of crime, particularly those based on a *legal* conception of crime. This is followed by selections that introduce some of the major concepts and processes involved in the making of laws and provide accounts of how specific laws came into being.

In "Definition of Crime," Gwynn Nettler points out that "crime" derives its meaning from the interpretation of others. If, for example, crime is defined by moral or personal beliefs, then definitions will vary from one person to another. Such personalized conceptions, however, make it difficult to identify criminal acts with any degree of certainty. Thus we rely on the law for needed specificity. Nettler elaborates upon the various notions underpinning this legal conception of crime. Crime, he says, does not exist (1) without law, (2) where an act is justified by law, (3) without intention, and (4) without capacity. He concludes by discussing the justifications or ends served by criminal law, for example, the idea that law has a deterrent effect.

Although the law is at the heart of the study of crime, most criminologists have traditionally skipped over the subject of how laws develop and change. They have taken existing laws as givens and concentrated their attention on the lawbreakers. But it is important to understand how laws evolve, how people and processes interact to determine what constitutes a criminal offense.

One way in which laws come into being is at the instigation of crusaders who seek to reform society. Howard S. Becker considers their roles in "Moral Entrepreneurs," a term he applies to two groups of people: those who see an evil in society and believe that it can only be corrected by legislation; and those who are charged with enforcing the law. To illustrate his analysis, Becker describes how specific legislation—such as the prohibition and sexual psychopath laws—originated and how both the reformers and special interest groups influenced their preparation and final form. Turning to the enforcers, particularly the police, Becker suggests that they typically see the law not

9

as a means of stamping out evil but as a justification for the existence of their jobs. Their attitude is professional and entails winning the respect of the public. Hence they enforce the law selectively, thereby incurring the indignation of the reformers at whose behest the law was made.

Richard C. Hollinger and Lonn Lanza-Kaduce, in "The Process of Criminalization: The Case of Computer Laws," extend the concern for law formation or construction by providing a contemporary account of how various types of computer abuse have become criminalized. In describing the criminalization process, they focus particularly on the impact of three main factors: (1) the role of the media, (2) the interest groups and individuals involved (i.e., the "moral entrepreneurs"), and (3) the existing normative climates. As an example, they describe in some detail the role that August Bequai, a noted expert on white-collar crime, played in the enactment of several state and federal crime statutes.

1. Definition of Crime

GWYNN NETTLER

"Crime" is a word, not a deed. It is a word that describes deeds, of course, but as long as it is used only to express moral condemnation, no one will be able to identify a criminal act with certainty. The meaning of the word varies with the morality of the user. Thus people use "crime" variously, as when they say, "It's a crime the way he treats her," "Private property is a crime," or "It's a crime to have to live like that."

Attempts to define crime more rigorously look to the law for help. Crimes, we have seen, are wrongs judged to be deserving of public attention through application of state power. It has been felt, therefore, that crimes are best defined as acts which are harmful to social welfare and which carry the possibility of a penalty imposed by the state. This definition helps a little, but not enough. It does not mark a clear boundary between criminal acts and other wrongs, since the state attends legally to many attacks on public welfare that are not considered criminal. Thus there is no clear line between those wrongs which are regarded as crimes, those personal injuries which are treated as civil actions (torts), and those numerous violations of regulatory laws to which penalties are attached, even though these violations are not called "crimes."

In short, *there is no essence of criminality.* No quality can be found in acts called "criminal" that distinguishes them from noncriminal injuries, breaches of contract, violations of regulations, and other disappointments (G. Williams, 1955).

The question, then, is why we should bother trying to define crime. There are, of course, different reasons for clarifying our terms.

Functions of definition: Defining words serves several purposes. One purpose is to gain our audience's attention. When we define a term in a particular way, we are saying, "Look here. Attend to what I'm talking about."

Definition also has a personal function. Defining terms for ourselves helps us ascertain whether we know what we're talking about. We use many words automatically, and we often think we know what they mean until we are asked to define them. Defining a word tells us whether we are using it emotionally—to arouse a particular feeling—or denotatively—to refer to something.

A third function of definition is that of aiding communication. It derives from the second function, but here definition is an attempt to assure that two or more people attribute the same meaning to a word. If we are interested in communicating our ideas accurately, we need clear definitions. If, on the other hand, we wish to use words merely persuasively, we need be less clear about their definitions.

Legal definition of crime: The closest *approximation* to a clear definition is that given by law. As defined by law, *a crime is an intentional violation of the criminal law, committed without defense or excuse and penalized by the state* (Tappan, 1947).

Without further interpretation, this definition draws a circle. It says that a crime is a certain kind of breach of those laws called "criminal laws." However, we can use this unsatisfactory definition for the purposes of gaining attention and aiding communication if our questions are clear. We should keep at least the following questions separate so that we can think more calmly about their answers:

1. Why does this society treat certain acts, but not others, as crimes? This is a question for the sociology of law; it is beyond the scope of this book.

2. Why does a certain society have more or less of those wrongs universally regarded as crimes—those more serious wrongs such as treason, murder, forcible rape, assault, and theft? This is a question for theories of criminogenesis. It is the kind of question raised by *public concern* with crime; the attempts to answer it are the subject of this book.

Wrongs universally regarded as serious violations have been called *mala in se* (wrong in themselves). Public concern with such offenses narrows our attention. Such concern means that we need not ask why people commit those minor infractions which are crimes only because a local jurisdiction has prohibited them—crimes called *mala prohibita*. Social concern about crime is not with such sometime "delinquencies as that of a housewife who shakes her doormat in the street after 8 A.M., or a shopkeeper who fails to stamp a cash receipt, or a guest who fails to enter his name, nationality, and date of arrival in the hotel register, or the proprietor of a milk bar who allows his customers to play a gramophone . . . without an entertainment license from the justices" (G. Williams, 1955, p. 112). Few people want to spend time explaining why such ordinances are violated.

The context of the question asked about crime causation is that of public anxiety about the serious offenses as these have been widely regarded. In this context, it seems most reasonable to employ a legal definition of crime such as that cited by Tappan. This definition regards a "crime" as an intentional act that violates the prescriptions or proscriptions of the criminal law under conditions in which no legal excuse applies and where there is a state with the power to codify such laws and to enforce penalties in response to their breach. This definition says several things that require amplification. It holds that (1) there is no crime without law and without a state to punish the breach of law; (2) there is no crime where an act that would otherwise be offensive is justified by law; (3) there is no crime without intention; and (4) there is no crime where the offender is deemed "incompetent," that is, without "capacity." Each of these elements has its own history, its peculiar difficulties, and a range of implications.

NO CRIME WITHOUT LAW

The legal idea of a crime restricts its meaning to those breaches of custom that a society has recognized in either its common or its statutory law. As it is applied in Western countries, this restriction carries with it four characteristics that define "good" criminal law: politicality, penal sanction, specificity, and uniformity.

"Politicality" refers to the idea that there can be no crime without a *state* to define it. "Penal sanction" refers to the power of a state to punish violations of its law. This definition says that the legal meaning of crime requires a state, an organization with a monopoly of power, to enforce the law and to attach penalties to its breach. Laws that are not backed by force are less than law and more like agreements or aspirations. Laws without penalties are hollow. By this token, the term "war crimes" is a figure of speech, since such crimes are not legally constituted.

Law and Liberty

The conception of crime that places it within the boundaries of *law* has strong implications for civil liberties. The maxim that there can be "no crime without a law" means that people cannot be charged with offenses unless these have been defined. The protection of citizens against vague charges depends upon this ideal—that there must be a clear statement setting the limits of one's conduct in relation to others and defining the limits of the state's power to interfere in our lives.

This ideal has promoted other considerations having to do with the formulation of "good law" as opposed to "poor law," particularly as good and poor laws are conceived in the Anglo-American tradition. These additional ideals are that the criminal law must be *specific* and that it must be *applied uniformly.*

Good laws *specify actions* that are criminal and *specify penalties* for each breach. Poor laws are omnibus condemnations, such as one from a dead German code which prohibited "behaving in a manner contrary to the common standards of right conduct." This kind of phrasing lacks the specificity that is an ideal of Western criminal jurisprudence.

Similarly, it is an objective of modern jurisprudence that laws be framed and enforced so as to guarantee their *uniform application.* The ideal of uniform application does *not* require that each person and each crime be dealt the same sanction. People, and their crimes and circumstances, vary. Our law therefore allows consideration of individual cases and discretion in judicial response. The ideal of uniform application does require that *extralegal* characteristics of the offender not affect arrest, conviction, or sentence. Extralegal characteristics are those features of the offender that are *not* related to the purposes of the law—characteristics such as race and religion. . . . This ideal is easier to express in general terms than it is to assess in particular instances. It is easier to express than to assess because some extralegal factors are entangled with legally relevant considerations, as is the case when ethnic differences are associated with differences in patterns of criminal activity.

Not All Wrongs Are Crimes

The legal conception of crime as a breach of the criminal law has an additional implication. It narrows the definition of wrongs. Not all the injuries we give each other are recognized by law, nor are all the injuries recognized by law called "crimes."

For example, United States, Canadian, and European law recognizes *breaches of contract or trust,* so that people who feel themselves thus harmed may seek a remedy from the law. Similarly, the law acknowledges other injuries to person, reputation, and property, called "torts," which, while not breaches of contract, may entitle one person to compensation from another. There is an overlap between the ideas of crime and tort. The same act can be both a crime and a tort, as in murder or assault. However, we can distinguish between the wrongs defined by contract and tort law and the wrongs defined by criminal law in terms of the procedures employed in response to these different categories of wrong. The procedural difference lies in "who pursues the offense." A crime is deemed an offense against the public, even though it may have a particular victim and a particular complainant. It is the state that prosecutes crime, but it is individuals who "pursue" offenders against tort and contractual laws.

NO CRIME WHERE AN ACT IS JUSTIFIED BY LAW

A second category of "defense or excuse" against the application of the criminal law consists of legally recognized justifications for committing what otherwise would be called a crime. Both literate and preliterate societies recognize the right of individuals to defend themselves and their loved ones against mortal attack. The injury or death that may be inflicted against one's assailant in self-defense is thereby excused.

Similarly, all states accord themselves the right of self-defense. With the French philosopher Sorel (1908), states distinguish between *force*, the legitimate use of physical coercion constrained by law, and *violence*, its illegitimate use. The damage that occurs through the state's application of force is excused from the criminal sanction. Thus homicide committed in the police officer's line of duty may be deemed "justifiable," and the injury defined as noncriminal.

NO CRIME WITHOUT INTENTION

As a result of our moral and legal history, the criminal law tries to limit its definition of criminal conduct to intentional action. "Accidents" supposedly do not count as crimes. As the American jurist Oliver Wendell Holmes, Jr., put it, the law attempts to distinguish between "stumbling over a dog and kicking it." If "a dog can tell the difference between being kicked and being stumbled over," as Justice Holmes believed, so too can judges and juries.

This assumption seems plausible, but it gets sorely tried in practice. It gets tested and disputed because, in real life, some "accidents" are still defined as the actor's fault. "Negligence" may be criminal.

All criminal laws operate with some psychological model of man. According to the model prevalent in Western criminal law, the "reasonable person" ought to use judgment in controlling his behavior in order that some classes of "accidents" will not occur. For example, the reckless driver may not have intended to kill a pedestrian, but the "accident" is judged to have been the probable consequence of his or her erratic driving. Persons licensed to manipulate an automobile are assumed to know the likely results of their actions. They are assumed, further, to be able to control their actions, and they are held accountable, therefore, regardless of lack of homicidal intent.

Western criminal law is based upon this changing, and challenged, set of assumptions. It therefore qualifies its desire to restrict "crime" to intentional breaches of the criminal code. This qualification is accomplished by distinguishing between classes of crime – impulsive rather than premeditated, accidental rather than intentional. Since the law wishes to hold able, but negligent, people to account, it includes the concept of "constructive intent," a term that stretches "intent" to cover the unintended injurious consequences of some of our behavior. The penalties for doing damage through negligence are usually lighter than those for being deliberately criminal; yet the term "crime" covers both classes of conduct.

Intention and Motivation

Motivation is sometimes used by lawyers to prove intention. The two concepts are not the same, however.

An *intention* is that which we "have in mind" when we act. It is our purpose, the result we wish to effect. The criminal law is particularly concerned to penalize illegal intent when it is acted upon.

A *motive* is, strictly speaking, that which moves a person to act. The word may apply to an intention, but it need not. Intentions are but one of the many motors of action.

Intention is narrow and specific; motivation is broad and general. A jewel thief may *intend* to steal jewels; the *motive* is to become richer. The motive is widespread and does not distinguish one thief from many others. His intention, to steal jewels, is more specific, and it is only one possible way of satisfying his motivation.

An intention may or may not move a person. It may remain a wish, a plot, a dream. *A criminal intention, without the action, is not a crime.*

Motives, on the other hand, may move us haphazardly, purposelessly, without the focus of intent. A motive may be purely physiological and variously gratified. It may even be "unconscious," if we believe the psychoanalysts. *An intention, however, is only something cognitive.* The word "intention" is reserved for thoughts, for verbalizable plans. It does not refer to those subterranean urges or those physiological fires that may have kindled the ideas.

Since "intent" is part of the definition of crime, prosecutors in Western countries must establish such purpose in the actor, and they sometimes try to do this by constructing "the motive." The strategy of demonstrating intention from motivation calls for showing the "good reasons" why a person might act as the accused is alleged to have done. The good reasons, the alleged motives, may all have been there, however, without the actor's having formed the criminal intent which the prosecutor is attempting to establish. This is simply because "good reasons" are not always the real ones.

The distinction between the movers of action and intentions becomes important as criminal law takes heed of another qualification in its definition of crime, the qualification that people shall be held responsible for their actions, and hence liable to the criminal law, *only if* they are mentally competent. The legal meaning of "intention" is embedded in the concept of competence.

NO CRIME WITHOUT CAPACITY

The condemnation that is implicit in calling actions "criminal" is based on moral premises. It is part of our morality to believe that a person ought not to be blamed for actions that are beyond his or her control. The notion that behavior is within or beyond one's control rests upon conceptions of "capacity" or "competence." These conceptions, in turn, are cultural. They vary in time and with place, and they remain disputed today. The dispute concerns the criteria of competence, but it does not challenge the legal and moral principle that people must be somehow "able" before they can be judged culpable.

Among modern states, the tests of competence are cognitive. They look to *mens rea*, the "thing in the mind," as definitive of the ability to form a criminal intent and as the regulator of one's actions. *Until* "the mind"[1] is sufficiently well formed to control the actor's behavior, and *unless* it operates in normal fashion, Anglo-American criminal law *excludes* the agent from criminal liability. Actors are considered "not responsible" or "less responsible" for their offenses if the offense has been produced by someone who is (1) acting under duress, (2) under age, or (3) "insane."

Crime under Duress

The first exclusion consists of criminal deeds performed "against one's will." The law recognizes circumstances in which a person may be forced into a criminal action under threat. Since intent and the capacity to act freely are diminished when this is the case, so too is legal responsibility.

Age and Capacity

A second application of the moral principle that people must have some minimal mental capacity before they ought to be held legally accountable has to do with limitations of age. Laws of modern nations agree that persons below a certain age must be excluded from criminal liability. The number of years required to attain legal responsibility varies by jurisdiction, but the legal principle persists in declaring individuals who are "under age" to be "incompetent" or "legal infants." They may be protected by laws, but they are not subject to the criminal law. In most Anglo-American jurisdictions a child under the age of seven years cannot be held responsible for a crime. . . .

Insanity as a Defense

A third excuse by which one may reduce or escape the application of the criminal law is the claim that the offender's capacity to control his or her behavior has been damaged. The locus of the damage, the "place" in which one looks for this incapacity, is, again, the mind.

Defects of the mind seem clear in the extremities of senility, idiocy, and the incapacitating psychoses. They are clear, too, as one is able to link abnormal performance to lesions of the central nervous system. However, it is in the gray area between these extremities and more normal behavior that citizens, lawyers, and their psychiatric advisers dispute the capacity of offenders.

It bears repeating that this dispute rests upon moral considerations. The quarrel is stimulated by the belief that only people who "choose" their conduct deserve punishment for their crimes, that "accidents" and "irresistible impulses" do not count, and that other classes of behavior beyond one's control should not be penalized. The philosophical questions opened by this debate range beyond our present concern. These questions include, at a minimum, the ancient issues of free will and determinism, of the justice and the value of praise and blame, and of the proper ends of the criminal law.

These questions intrude upon the law and ensure that attempts to define mental competence are all imperfect. They are less than perfect because moral conceptions of the "causes" of behavior color the assignment of responsibility to actors. They are less than perfect, also, because the boundaries of the defense of insanity move with the justifications of the criminal law. That is, who we believe to be "incompetent" before the law varies with what we want the law to do. . . .

CAPACITY AND JUSTIFICATIONS
OF THE CRIMINAL LAW

The guidelines for judging the capacity of offenders are imperfect. They continue to be debated because our moral beliefs find the causes of human behavior in different locations. These beliefs move responsibility between the actor and his or her environment so that "who is to blame" and who deserves punishment are points endlessly disputed. Dispute is fostered, too, by the fact that *justifications* of the criminal law are supported by assumptions about the conditions under which human beings can control their own behavior. What we want the law to do and what we believe it does have bearing upon whom we are willing to excuse from criminal liability.

The criminal law is justified by what it supposedly does. If the law is to be respected for what it does, it must be applied in ways that achieve specific ends—or, more accurately, it must be applied in ways that are *believed* to achieve these ends.

The law serves a changing mixture of objectives, however, and this instability of its objectives encourages the continuing quarrel about which people should and which people should not be held responsible for their conduct.

The criminal law is commonly considered to be useful in achieving six ends, some of which are in conflict. These objectives have been described in various ways, but we can classify them as efforts to (1) restrain offenders, (2) deter criminals and others, (3) reform offenders, (4) revive communion symbolically, (5) achieve justice through retribution, and (6) achieve justice through restitution. All these functions are relevant to the issue of who should and who should not be excused for "incompetence."

1. Restraint

The word "arrest" is derived from the Latin word meaning "to stop." A principal function of the criminal law is to stop a person from injuring others. An arrest may involve restraining the miscreant for some time.

The need to restrain a bad actor does not rest upon a desire to punish or correct. Restraint attends only to controlling an offender. Whether the law should also punish or treat the person being restrained is another issue.

Definitions of capacity enter into the problem of achieving restraint principally in terms of determining *how* the lawbreaker is to be repressed. In recent years it has been our practice to restrain sane criminals in prisons and insane ones in mental hospitals. The growing emphasis upon the rehabilitative function of "correctional institutions" has meant, however, that some prisons now have as many psychotherapeutic facilities as mental hospitals (A. S. Goldstein, 1967). It is an open question whether incarceration in prison is more or less painful than incarceration in hospital (A. S. Goldstein, 1967; Kesey, 1964).

2. Deterrence

The criminal law is commonly justified as having a deterrent effect. The notion of deterrence is not a simple one, however, and it is possible to discern many meanings in the concept (Cousineau, 1976). Most criminologists, but not all of them (Zimring and Hawkins, 1973, pp. 224ff.), distinguish between *specific deterrence* and *general deterrence.*

The idea behind specific (or individual) deterrence is that the arrested person is less likely to commit a similar offense in the future as a result of the legal penalty suffered. This concept is similar to that of reforming the offender, although, as we shall see, some people who wish to reform convicts think that their criminal ways ought to be changed by some means other than the threat of punishment.

The assumption underlying the idea of general deterrence is that application of the criminal law to others will reduce the probability that you and I will commit the crimes for which they have been punished. This justification assumes that we are sufficiently normal to get the message. It is further assumed, with some good evidence, that the more closely you and I identify with the miscreant, the more clearly we will get the message. It is believed that the more we resemble the punished person, the more forcefully his or her penalty threatens us and deters us. It is assumed that, if we have felt the same desires as the punished person and have come close to committing similar crimes, the punishment provides us with a deterrent example. If, however, we healthy people observe "sick minds" being punished, then, presumably, the law's lesson is lost on us; in such cases the deterrent example is diluted because we perceive the offender as different from ourselves.

The determination of capacity is considered to be important, therefore, as a means of increasing the efficacy of the law as a deterrent. It is not *known* how effective this determination is in increasing deterrence, but some jurists *believe* it to be very important.

Morals seem more important here than *consequences.* Our moral beliefs find it cruel and unjust to punish persons who are "not responsible for their actions," regardless of the societal ends that such punishment might serve. The test of capacity tries, in a fumbling manner, to define persons who are sufficiently different from us that they may be excused from accountability under the criminal law.

3. Rehabilitation

It is popularly assumed that the criminal law is applied, or ought to be applied, to correct the offender. If the law is employed to improve the criminal's conduct, then it is believed that the candidate for rehabilitation must be capable of recovery with the attention the law provides. This means, to the conventional way of thinking, that the offender must have a mind capable of guiding behavior and amenable to education. The idea implicit in this justification of the law is that just as one does not pummel hydrocephalic idiots for failing at mathematics, so one does not penalize criminals who "can't help themselves."

Does rehabilitation work? It may be humane to refrain from punishing people who seem mentally defective. It may also be humane to refrain from punishing people – period. The ethics of this issue aside, however, some facts ought to inform conceptions of rehabilitation.

A first fact is that arrest "reforms" some offenders, in the sense that their behavior is "corrected." The offensive behavior stops. This change in conduct is seen most notably among some more intelligent criminals, such as embezzlers, and some impassioned offenders, such as murderous spouses. . . .

Despite this fact, many observers do not regard a change of conduct after arrest and upon the threat of additional penalty as "rehabilitation." What they seek is not just a change in behavior, but a change of heart that leads to the change in behavior.

Whether or not one requires that a change of character accompany a change in conduct before a person can be deemed to have been "rehabilitated," a second fact deserves reporting: *Efforts to rehabilitate offenders do not work well.*

There is no science of personality change which has yet been verified or which, in its experimental phases, has proved successful. There is counseling, of course, and some people are helped by advice. In particular, *self-selected* groups – those that people join voluntarily, like Alcoholics Anonymous and Synanon – have a better record of successful counseling. *But there is no science of corrections.*

The demonstration of this fact can be found in many places. Martinson (1974) and Lipton et al. (1975) have summarized the evidence on this point.

4. Symbolism

A neglected, but important, function of the criminal law is symbolic. Exercise of the criminal law reaffirms what we are for and what we are against. Thus the courtroom becomes one of the various educational theaters every society uses.

Capacity is part of this legal drama because, again, the drama depends upon identification. One must be able to identify with the roles portrayed if the dramatic lesson is to be learned. The symbolic and the deterrent functions of the law use capacity in the same way: it is, presumably, the "normal mind," not the defective one, that can appreciate the threats and the symbolism of the law.

5. Retribution

"Retribution" means "to give in return." It may refer to recompense for merit or for evil, although in criminology only the return of harm to the evildoer is implied.

Retribution is the oldest conception of justice. It is the moral demand that evil not go unpunished, that the harm a person does be returned to him or to her in equal degree, if not in kind. Retribution assumes that justice requires a *balance* between the wrong that was done and the penalty the wrongdoer is made to suffer.

Today retribution is not popular as a stated objective of the criminal law, partly because it has become confused with the idea of revenge.

Retribution Is Not Revenge. Revenge is the emotional impulse to wreak havoc on a person who has injured us. Revenge knows no balance.

It may seem difficult to disentangle revenge and retribution in any particular demand that a wrong be punished. However, the balancing principle of retribution distinguishes it from revenge (Atkinson, 1974; Gerstein, 1974). Retribution sets limits to punishment. It seeks a punishment *proportional* to the wrong done. Its standard of punishment is the law of talion *(lex talionis)*, the law of "like for like" (Kant, 1965, p. 101). This principle is to be found in the laws of many cultures, notably in Mosaic and Roman law. It is expressed in the code of the Babylonian King Hammurabi (1760 B.C.), which recommended "an eye for an eye, a tooth for a tooth."

Justice and Retribution. Although the idea of retribution runs counter to some facets of the Christian ethic and is opposed by "enlightened" opinion (Long, 1973), the demand for a balancing of wrongs remains a major component of our sense of justice. This conception of justice has been defended on practical grounds (Gerstein, 1974; Kant, 1965; J. G. Murphy, 1971). However, whether or not one agrees with these appeals to the concrete effects of retribution, satisfaction of this motive remains a justice-dealing function of the criminal law.

For example, the moral requirement that evil not go unpunished is well put by the philosopher Hannah Arendt in her study of the trial of the Nazi Eichmann by the Israelis. Arendt justifies the trial and the hanging of Eichmann by saying, "To the question most commonly asked about the Eichmann trial: What good does it do?, there is but one possible answer: It will do justice" (1964, p. 254).

It bears repeating that the criminal law is not merely practical; it is also symbolic. *It expresses morals as well as it intends results.*

Competence and Retribution. It is part of the morality being expressed by the law that people should be held accountable only for what they have "chosen" to do. If Eichmann had been defined as an idiot or a lunatic, justice would not have required his execution. The same sense of justice that calls for retribution also demands some quality of capacity in the offender.

6. Restitution

Restitution is restoration—righting a wrong by returning things to their original state. The idea of restitution is more readily understandable in connection with property offenses, where we can calculate the cost of the damage. However, even in the case of attacks against persons, we often arrive at a price to be paid that may compensate for the injury. In fact, the anthropologist Lowie reports a case in the last century of a North American Indian woman who asked that the murderer of her son be "given" to her as a substitute for her lost boy.

Restitution is recognized in the criminal law of some lands as a proper penalty against the offender and also as a possible means of rehabilitation. The Canadian Criminal Code, for example, recognizes restitution as a form of sentence, but it is a sentence that has rarely been applied. The Law Reform Commission of Canada (1974) found that in 4,294 criminal convictions handed down between 1967 and 1972, the sentence of restitution was given in only six cases.

It is now being urged that restitution be more frequently used as a sentence and that property offenders in particular be given the option of working out their debt to their victims instead of going to prison. This has been recommended in Britain by K. J. Smith (1965), in the United States by Laura Nader (1975), and in Canada by A. J. Katz et al. (1976), directors of the Alberta Restitution Project.

Relevance: The idea of justice through restitution is related to conceptions of competence in several ways. First, it is assumed that only offenders who can understand the restitutive contract and who are able to fulfill it are properly eligible for this sentence. Second, it is assumed that a contract between a thief and his or her victim will restore some sense of the humanity of both. This objective depends, too, on the emotional and intellectual capacities of the contracting parties.

The restitutive contract is an interesting experiment in the uses of the criminal law—one that may save citizens the expense of imprisonment, help in the rehabilitation of wrongdoers, and, at the same time, satisfy a sense of justice. The results are yet to be tallied.

Note

1. Placing the word "mind" in quotation marks indicates its vagueness. Like many other useful terms, "mind" has many meanings. It may be interesting to consider how you use the word.

References

Arendt, H. 1964. *Eichmann in Jerusalem: A Report on the Banality of Evil.* New York: Viking.

Atkinson, M. 1974. "Interpreting retributive claims," *Ethics,* 85:80–86.

Cousineau, D. F. 1976. *General Deterrence of Crime: An Analysis.* Edmonton: University of Alberta, Department of Sociology, Ph.D. dissertation.

Gerstein, R. S. 1974. "Capital punishment: 'Cruel and unusual'?: A retributivist response," *Ethics,* 85:75–79.

Goldstein, A. S. 1967. *The Insanity Defense.* New Haven, Conn.: Yale University Press.

Kant, I. 1965. *The Metaphysical Elements of Justice.* Trans. by J. Ladd. Indianapolis: Bobbs-Merrill.

Katz, A. J., et al. 1976. *Progress Report: The Pilot Alberta Restitution Centre.* Calgary: The Centre.

Kesey, K. 1964. *One Flew over the Cuckoo's Nest.* New York: Compass Books.

Law Reform Commission of Canada. 1974. *Restitution and Compensation.* Working Paper No. 5. Ottawa: Information Canada.

Lipton, D., et al. 1975. *The Effectiveness of Correctional Treatment: A Survey of Treatment Evaluation Studies.* New York: Praeger.

Long, T. A. 1973. "Capital punishment: 'Cruel and unusual'?" *Ethics,* 83:214–223.

Martinson, R. 1974. "What works?: Questions and answers about prison reform," *The Public Interest,* 35:22–54.

Murphy, J. G. 1971. "Three mistakes about retributivism," *Analysis*, 31:166–169.

Nader, L. 1975. Address at the First International Symposium on Restitution, Minneapolis (November 10–11).

Smith, K. J. 1965. *A Cure for Crime.* London: Duckworth.

Sorel, G. 1908. *Reflections on Violence.* Reprinted 1950. Glencoe, Ill.: Free Press.

Tappan, P. W. 1947. "Who is the criminal?" *American Sociological Review*, 12:96–102.

Williams, G. 1955. "The definition of crime." *Current Legal Problems*, 8:107–130.

Zimring, F. E., and G. J. Hawkins. 1973. *Deterrence: The Legal Threat in Crime Control.* Chicago: University of Chicago Press.

2. Moral Entrepreneurs: The Creation and Enforcement of Deviant Categories

HOWARD S. BECKER

RULE CREATORS

The prototype of the rule creator, but not the only variety as we shall see, is the crusading reformer. He is interested in the content of rules. The existing rules do not satisfy him because there is some evil which profoundly disturbs him. He feels that nothing can be right in the world until rules are made to correct it. He operates with an absolute ethic; what he sees is truly and totally evil with no qualification. Any means is justified to do away with it. The crusader is fervent and righteous, often self-righteous.

It is appropriate to think of reformers as crusaders because they typically believe that their mission is a holy one. The prohibitionist serves as an excellent example, as does the person who wants to suppress vice and sexual delinquency or the person who wants to do away with gambling.

These examples suggest that the moral crusader is a meddling busybody, interested in forcing his own morals on others. But this is a one-sided view. Many moral crusades have strong humanitarian overtones. The crusader is not only interested in seeing to it that other people do what he thinks right. He believes that if they do what is right it will be good for them. Or he may feel that his reform will prevent certain kinds of exploitation of one person by another. Prohibitionists felt that they were not simply forcing their morals on others, but attempting to provide the conditions for a better way of life for people prevented by drink from realizing a truly good life. Abolitionists were not simply trying to prevent slave owners from doing the wrong thing; they were trying to help slaves to achieve a better life. Because of the importance of the humanitarian motive, moral crusaders (despite their relatively single-minded devotion to their particular cause) often lend their support to other humanitarian crusades. Joseph Gusfield has pointed out that:

The American temperance movement during the 19th century was a part of a general effort toward the improvement of the worth of the human being through improved morality as well as economic conditions. The mixture of the religious, the equalitarian, and the humanitarian was an outstanding facet of the moral reformism of many movements. Temperance supporters formed a large segment of movements such as sabbatarianism, abolition, woman's rights, agrarianism, and humanitarian attempts to improve the lot of the poor. . . .

In its auxiliary interests the WCTU [Women's Christian Temperance Union] revealed a great concern for the improvement of the welfare of the lower classes. It was active in campaigns to secure penal reform, to shorten working hours and raise wages for workers, and to abolish child labor and in a number of other humanitarian and equalitarian activities. In the 1880s the WCTU worked to bring about legislation for the protection of working girls against the exploitation by men.[1]

As Gusfield says,[2] "Moral reformism of this type suggests the approach of a dominant class toward those less favorably situated in the economic and social structure." Moral crusaders typically want to help those beneath them to achieve a better status. That those beneath them do not always like the means proposed for their salvation is another matter. But this fact—that moral crusades are typically dominated by those in the upper levels of the social structure—means that they add to the power they derive from the legitimacy of their moral position, the power they derive from their superior position in society.

Naturally, many moral crusades draw support from people whose motives are less pure than those of the crusader. Thus, some industrialists supported Prohibition because they felt it would provide them with a more manageable labor force.[3] Similarly, it is sometimes rumored that Nevada gambling interests support the opposition to attempts to legalize gambling in California because it would cut so heavily into their business, which depends in substantial measure on the population of Southern California.[4]

The moral crusader, however, is more concerned with ends than with means. When it comes to drawing up specific rules (typically in the form of legislation to be proposed to a state legislature or the federal Congress), he frequently relies on the advice of experts. Lawyers, expert in the drawing of acceptable legislation, often play this role. Government bureaus in whose jurisdiction the problem falls may also have the necessary expertise, as did the Federal Bureau of Narcotics in the case of the marihuana problem.

As psychiatric ideology, however, becomes increasingly acceptable, a new expert has appeared—the psychiatrist. Sutherland, in his discussion of the natural history of sexual psychopath laws, pointed to the psychiatrist's influence.[5] He suggests the following as the conditions under which the sexual psychopath law, which provides that a person "who is diagnosed as a sexual psychopath may be confined for an indefinite period in a state hospital for the insane,"[6] will be passed.

First, these laws are customarily enacted after a state of fear has been aroused in a community by a few serious sex crimes committed in quick succession. This is illustrated in Indiana, where a law was passed following three or four sexual attacks in Indianapolis, with murder in two. Heads of families bought guns and watch dogs, and the supply of locks and chains in the hardware stores of the city was completely exhausted. . . .

A second element in the process of developing sexual psychopath laws is the agitated activity of the community in connection with the fear. The attention of the community is focused on sex crimes, and people in the most varied situations envisage dangers and see the need of and possibility for their control. . . .

The third phase in the development of those sexual psychopath laws has been the appointment of a committee. The committee gathers the many conflicting recommendations of persons and groups of persons, attempts to determine "facts," studies procedures in other states, and makes recommendations, which generally include bills for the legislature. Although the general fear usually subsides within a few days, a committee has the formal duty of following through until positive action is taken. Terror which does not result in a committee is much less likely to result in a law.[7]

In the case of sexual psychopath laws, there usually is no government agency charged with dealing in a specialized way with sexual deviations. Therefore, when the need for expert advice in drawing up legislation arises, people frequently turn to the professional group most closely associated with such problems:

In some states, at the committee stage of the development of a sexual psychopath law, psychiatrists have played an important part. The psychiatrists, more than any others, have been the interest group back of the laws. A committee of psychiatrists and neurologists in Chicago wrote the bill which became the sexual psychopath law of Illinois; the bill was sponsored by the Chicago Bar Association and by the state's attorney of Cook County and was enacted with little opposition in the next session of the State Legislature. In Minnesota all the members of the governor's committee except one were psychiatrists. In Wisconsin the Milwaukee Neuropsychiatric Society shared in pressing the Milwaukee Crime Commission for the enactment of a law. In Indiana the attorney-general's committee received from the American Psychiatric Association copies of all the sexual psychopath laws which had been enacted in other states.[8]

The influence of psychiatrists in other realms of the criminal law has increased in recent years.

In any case, what is important about this example is not that psychiatrists are becoming increasingly influential, but that the moral crusader, at some point in the development of his crusade, often requires the services of a professional who can draw up the appropriate rules in an appropriate form. The crusader himself is often not concerned with such details. Enough for him that the main point has been won; he leaves its implementation to others.

By leaving the drafting of the specific rule in the hands of others, the crusader opens the door for many unforeseen influences. For those who draft legislation for crusaders have their own interests, which may affect the legislation they prepare. It is likely that the sexual psychopath laws drawn by psychiatrists contain many features never intended by the citizens who spearheaded the drives to "do something about sex crimes," features which do however reflect the professional interests of organized psychiatry.

RULE ENFORCERS

The most obvious consequence of a successful crusade is the creation of a new set of rules. With the creation of a new set of rules we often find that a new set of enforcement agencies and officials is established. Sometimes, of course, existing agencies take over the administration of the new rule, but more frequently a new set of rule enforcers is created. The passage of the Harrison Act presaged the creation of the Federal Narcotics Bureau, just as the passage of the Eighteenth Amendment led to the creation of police agencies charged with enforcing the Prohibition Laws.

With the establishment of organizations of rule enforcers, the crusade becomes institutionalized. What started out as a drive to convince the world of the moral necessity of a new rule finally becomes an organization devoted to the enforcement of the rule. Just as radical political movements turn into organized political parties and lusty evangelical sects become staid religious denominations, the final outcome of the moral crusade is a police force. To understand, therefore, how the rules creating a new class of outsiders are applied to particular people we must understand the motives and interests of police, the rule enforcers.

Although some policemen undoubtedly have a kind of crusading interest in stamping out evil, it is probably much more typical for the policeman to have a certain detached and objective view of his job. He is not so much concerned with the content of any particular rule as he is with the fact that it is his job to enforce the rule. When the rules are changed, he punishes what was once acceptable behavior just as he ceases to punish behavior that has been made legitimate by a change in the rules. The enforcer, then, may not be interested in the content of the rule as such, but only in the fact that the existence of the rule provides him with a job, a profession, and a *raison d'être.*

Since the enforcement of certain rules provides justification for his way of life, the enforcer has two interests which condition his enforcement activity: first, he must justify the existence of his position and, second, he must win the respect of those he deals with.

These interests are not peculiar to rule enforcers. Members of all occupations feel the need to justify their work and win the respect of others. Musicians . . . would like to do this but have difficulty finding ways of successfully impressing their worth on customers. Janitors fail to win their tenants' respect, but develop an ideology which stresses the quasi-professional responsibility they have to keep confidential the intimate knowledge of tenants they acquire in the course of their work.[9] Physicians, lawyers, and other professionals, more successful in winning the respect of clients, develop elaborate mechanisms for maintaining a properly respectful relationship.

In justifying the existence of his position, the rule enforcer faces a double problem. On the one hand, he must demonstrate to others that the problem still exists: the rules he is supposed to enforce have some point, because infractions occur. On the other hand, he must show that his attempts at enforcement are effective and worthwhile, that the evil he is supposed to deal with is in fact being dealt with adequately. Therefore, enforcement organizations, particularly when they are seeking funds, typically oscillate between two kinds of claims. First, they say that by reason of their efforts the problem they deal with is approaching solution. But, in the same breath, they say the problem is perhaps worse than ever (though through no fault of their own) and requires renewed and increased effort to keep it under control. Enforcement officials can be more vehement than anyone else in their insistence that the problem they are supposed to deal with is still with us, in fact is more with us than ever before. In making these claims, enforcement officials provide good reason for continuing the existence of the position they occupy.

We may also note that enforcement officials and agencies are inclined to take a pessimistic view of human nature. If they do not actually believe in original sin, they at least like to dwell on the difficulties in getting people to abide by rules, on the characteristics of human nature that lead people toward evil. They are skeptical of attempts to reform rule-breakers.

The skeptical and pessimistic outlook of the rule enforcer, of course, is reinforced by his daily experience. He sees, as he goes about his work, the evidence that the problem is still with us. He sees the people who continually repeat offenses, thus definitely branding themselves in his eyes as outsiders. Yet it is not too great a stretch of the imagination to suppose that one of the underlying reasons for the enforcer's pessimism about human nature and the possibilities of reform is the fact that if human nature were perfectible and people could be permanently reformed, his job would come to an end.

In the same way, a rule enforcer is likely to believe that it is necessary for the people he deals with to respect him. If they do not, it will be very difficult to do his job; his feeling of security in his work will be lost. Therefore, a good deal of enforcement activity is devoted not to the actual enforcement of rules, but to coercing respect from the people the enforcer deals with. This means that one may be labeled as deviant not because he has actually broken a rule, but because he has shown disrespect to the enforcer of the rule.

Westley's study of policemen in a small industrial city furnishes a good example of this phenomenon. In his interview, he asked policemen, "When do you think a policeman is justified in roughing a man up?" He found that "at least 37 percent of the men believed that it was legitimate to use violence to coerce respect."[10] He gives some illuminating quotations from his interviews:

> Well, there are cases. For example, when you stop a fellow for a routine questioning, say a wise guy, and he starts talking back to you and telling you you are no good and that sort of thing. You know you can take a man in on a disorderly conduct charge, but you can practically never make it stick. So what you do in a case like that is to egg the guy on until he makes a remark where you can justifiably slap him and, then, if he fights back, you can call it resisting arrest.
>
> Well, a prisoner deserves to be hit when he goes to the point where he tries to put you below him.
>
> You've gotta get rough when a man's language becomes very bad, when he is trying to make a fool of you in front of everybody else. I think most policemen try to treat people in a nice way, but usually you have to talk pretty rough. That's the only way to set a man down, to make him show a little respect.[11]

What Westley describes is the use of an illegal means of coercing respect from others. Clearly, when a rule enforcer has the option of enforcing a rule or not, the difference in what he does may be caused by the attitude of the offender toward him. If the offender is properly respectful, the enforcer may smooth the situation over. If the offender is disrespectful, then sanctions may be visited on him. Westley has shown that this differential tends to operate in the case of traffic offenses, where the policeman's discretion is perhaps at a maximum.[12] But it probably operates in other areas as well.

Ordinarily, the rule enforcer has a great deal of discretion in many areas, if only because his resources are not sufficient to cope with the volume of rule-breaking he is supposed to deal with. This means that he cannot tackle everything at once and to this extent must temporize with evil. He cannot do the whole job and knows it. He takes his time, on the assumption that the problems he deals with will be around for a long while. He establishes priorities, dealing with things in their turn, handling the most pressing problems immediately and leaving others for later. His attitude toward his work, in short, is professional. He lacks the naive moral fervor characteristic of the rule creator.

If the enforcer is not going to tackle every case he knows of at once, he must have a basis for deciding when to enforce the rule, which persons committing which acts to label as deviant. One criterion for selecting people is the "fix." Some people have sufficient political influence or know-how to be able to ward off attempts at enforcement, if not at the time of apprehension then at a later stage in the process. Very often, this function is professionalized; someone performs the job on a full-time basis, available to anyone who wants to hire him. A professional thief described fixers this way:

> There is in every large city a regular fixer for professional thieves. He has no agents and does not solicit and seldom takes any case except that of a professional thief, just as they seldom go to anyone except him. This centralized and monopolistic system of fixing for professional thieves is found in practically all of the large cities and many of the small ones.[13]

Since it is mainly professional thieves who know about the fixer and his operations, the consequence of this criterion for selecting people to apply the rules to is that amateurs tend to be caught, convicted, and labeled deviant much more frequently than professionals. As the professional thief notes:

> You can tell by the way the case is handled in court when the fix is in. When the copper is not very certain he has the right man, or the testimony of the copper and the complainant does not agree, or the prosecutor goes easy on the defendant, or the judge is arrogant in his decisions, you can always be sure that someone has got the work in. This does not happen in many cases of theft, for there is one case of a professional to twenty-five or thirty amateurs who know nothing about the fix. These amateurs get the hard end of the deal every time. The coppers bawl out about the thieves, no one holds up his testimony, the judge delivers an oration, and all of them get credit for stopping a crime wave. When the professional hears the case immediately preceding his own, he will think, "He should have got ninety years. It's the damn amateurs who cause all the heat in the stores." Or else he thinks, "Isn't it a damn shame for that copper to send that kid away for a pair of hose, and in a few minutes he will agree to a small fine for me for stealing a fur coat?" But if the coppers did not send the amateurs away to strengthen their records of convictions, they could not sandwich in the professionals whom they turn loose.[14]

Enforcers of rules, since they have no stake in the content of particular rules themselves, often develop their own private evaluation of the importance of various kinds of rules and infractions of them. This set of priorities may differ considerably from those held by the general public. For instance, drug users typically believe (and a few policemen have personally confirmed it to me) that police do not consider the use of marihuana to be as important a problem or as dangerous a practice as the use of opiate drugs. Police base this conclusion on the fact that, in their experience, opiate users commit other crimes (such as theft or prostitution) in order to get drugs, while marihuana users do not.

Enforcers, then, responding to the pressures of their own work situation, enforce rules and create outsiders in a selective way. Whether a person who commits a deviant act is in fact labeled a deviant depends on many things extraneous to his actual behavior: whether the enforcement official feels that at this time he must make some show of doing his job in order to justify his position, whether the misbehaver shows proper deference to the enforcer, whether the "fix" has been put in, and where the kind of act he has committed stands on the enforcer's list of priorities.

The professional enforcer's lack of fervor and routine approach to dealing with evil may get him into trouble with the rule creator. The rule creator, as we have said, is concerned with the content of the rules that interest him. He sees them as the means by which evil can be stamped out. He does not understand the enforcer's long-range approach to the same problems and cannot see why all the evil that is apparent cannot be stamped out at once.

When the person interested in the content of a rule realizes or has called to his attention the fact that enforcers are dealing selectively with the evil that concerns him, his righteous wrath may be aroused. The professional is denounced for viewing the evil too lightly, for failing to do his duty. The moral entrepreneur, at whose instance the rule was made, arises again to say that the outcome of the last crusade has not been satisfactory or that the gains once made have been whittled away and lost.

Notes

1. Joseph R. Gusfield, "Social Structure and Moral Reform: A Study of the Women's Christian Temperance Union," *American Journal of Sociology*, LXI (November, 1955), 223.

2. *Ibid.*

3. See Raymond G. McCarthy, editor, *Drinking and Intoxication* (New Haven and New York: Yale Center of Alcohol Studies and The Free Press of Glencoe, 1959), pp. 395–396.

4. This is suggested in Oscar Lewis, *Sagebrush Casinos: The Story of Legal Gambling in Nevada* (New York: Doubleday and Co., 1953), pp. 233–234.

5. Edwin H. Sutherland, "The Diffusion of Sexual Psychopath Laws," *American Journal of Sociology*, LVI (September, 1950), 142–148.

6. *Ibid.*, p. 142.

7. *Ibid.*, pp. 143–145.

8. *Ibid.*, pp. 145–146.

9. See Ray Gold, "Janitors Versus Tenants: A Status-Income Dilemma," *American Journal of Sociology*, LVII (March, 1952), 486–493.

10. William A. Westley, "Violence and the Police," *American Journal of Sociology*, LIX (July, 1953), 39.

11. *Ibid.*

12. See William A. Westley, "The Police: A Sociological Study of Law, Custom, and Morality" (unpublished Ph.D. dissertation, University of Chicago, Department of Sociology, 1951).

13. Edwin H. Sutherland, editor, *The Professional Thief* (Chicago: University of Chicago Press, 1937), pp. 87–88.

14. *Ibid.*, pp. 91–92.

3.   The Process of Criminalization: The Case of Computer Crime Laws*

RICHARD C. HOLLINGER AND LONN LANZA-KADUCE

During the past three decades computers have become an indispensable tool of our technologically dependent society. This greater societal dependency has also generated heightened criminological attention, as computers have been involved in the commission of an assortment of unethical and deviant acts. In response, 47 states have enacted "computer crime" legislation in an attempt to prevent unauthorized activities by computer users (BloomBecker, 1986; Soma et al., 1985).[1] In addition, Congress in 1984 and 1986 enacted two pieces of computer crime legislation, U.S. Public Laws 98-473 and 99-474 (18 U.S.C. 30). All of this legislative activity has occurred since 1978, when Florida and Arizona became the first states to pass specific laws against computer abuse (Scott, 1984: 8.17). In less than a decade an entirely new body of substantive criminal law has evolved that is specifically focused on criminality related to the computer. The rapid criminalization of computer abuse represents an exception to the gradual and reformist nature of typical law formation in common law jurisdictions.

This paper analyzes the process by which recent computer crime laws were formed.[2] It begins by summarizing the nature of computer abuse. Then, it describes the criminalization process, specifically (1) the role of the media in the definitional process, (2) the interest groups and individuals advocating criminalization, and (3) the normative climate of public and computer-user opinion during enactment. The paper concludes with a discussion of the implications of the findings for theory and research on the study of criminal law formation.

COMPUTERS AND THE CRIMINAL LAW

Since the advent of the digital electronic computer, there has been increasing concern regarding its inherent vulnerabilities to deviant and criminal behavior (McKnight, 1974). Computer criminality is generally classified as an "occupational" form of white-collar crime that benefits the perpetrator by victimizing an individual or organization and is usually committed during the course of one's occupational activity (Clinard and Quinney, 1973). Parker (1976: 17–21) has delineated four distinct types of criminal behavior in which a computer can be involved. In the first type, the computer is the direct "object" of the illegal act. Examples include instances of physical abuse, sabotage, vandalism, or arson directed against the computer "hardware" itself. The second type involves the "symbolic" use of the computer and data processing output "to intimidate, deceive, or defraud victims." These offenses, such as the false invoice scam, rely partially on the perceived infallibility of computer-generated information. In the third type the computer is used as the "instrument" of the offense. These are offenses in which electronic data processing equipment is used to perpetrate theft and trespassing offenses that in the past could not have been committed without physically removing something or entering the premises of the victim.

Most of the above types of "computer crime" are not new forms of criminality and, as such, can usually be prosecuted under traditional theft, embezzlement, fraud, property, or privacy statutes (Nycum, 1976a; Parker, 1983: 240). For example, Nycum (1976b) has documented at least 40 federal statutes that could be applied directly to many computer-related violations. A number of legal scholars have argued that most examples of "computer abuse" (Parker, 1976: 12) are neither unique forms of behavior nor crimes (Ingraham, 1980). Kling (1980) warns that those who define a particular act as computer abuse or crime based solely on the fact that a computer was tangentially associated with a victimization risk "banalizing" the concept.

A fourth type of computer criminality, however, concerns an entirely new class of intangible property, which can become the "subject" of criminality. It is this final type of computer crime that presents virtually all the unique legal questions (Parker, 1976: 19). In the new "paperless office," proprietary information stored in a computer memory or on an electronic medium can be accessed, altered, stolen, and sabotaged without the perpetrator's being physically present or resorting to the use of force. Thus, it is the intangible, electronic-impulse nature of computerized information that has caused the greatest concern in the legal community over possible loopholes in criminal law.[3]

One of the most novel legal problems associated with computer crime involves whether the mere unauthorized access or electronic "browsing" in another user's computer files constitutes trespassing, theft, or some other form of criminal activity. The earliest enactment of computer crime legislation, Florida's 1978 Computer Crimes Act (Chap. 815.01–815.08), defined *all* unauthorized access as a third-degree felony regardless of specific purpose. At first, subsequent state legislatures elected instead to adopt California's less punitive approach to browsing. The California statute (Sec. 502) criminalized unauthorized access to a computer file made under false pretenses, but excluded actions that were not "malicious" in nature (Scott, 1984: 8.16–17). Interestingly, in response to a widely reported case of computer browsing by a student at the University of California, Los Angeles, in late 1983 (Hafner, 1983), the California legislature subsequently amended its computer crime statute to include nonmalicious, intentional, unauthorized access as a misdemeanor offense (Bloom-Becker, 1985). Virtually every state with computer crime legislation has now also incorporated this nonmalicious "illegal access" provision, typically as a misdemeanor (Soma et al., 1985).

Given the intangible nature of "electronic property" and the legal ambiguity surrounding malicious intent, we should not be surprised to find states amending extant criminal law to cover abuse by computer. A few states (e.g., Alabama, Alaska, Maine, Maryland, Massachusetts, and Ohio) initially responded to the objective or perceived realities of computer-related abuses within the extant legal framework by incorporating crimes committed by computer into existing theft, trade secrets, or trespass laws (see Soma et al., 1985). Most jurisdictions, however, adopted a very different tactic. They defined computer crime as a unique legal problem and thereby created separate computer crime chapters in their criminal codes.

THE CRIMINALIZATION PROCESS

Our understanding of the process of criminalization depends on the important legacy of case studies regarding laws on theft (Hall, 1952), vagrancy (Chambliss, 1964), juvenile law (Platt, 1969), alcohol prohibition (Gusfield, 1963), marijuana (Becker, 1963), opiate use (Lindesmith, 1967), and sexual psychopathy (Sutherland, 1950, 1951). Many theoretical and empirical issues, however, remain unresolved. Hagan's (1980) review of over 40 case studies of mostly twentieth century criminal law formation is one of the most thorough attempts to systematize findings across various criminal enactments.

Hagan emphasized that the media usually played a critical role in criminalization efforts, noting that extensive media attention accompanied most successful enactments. He also reported that, counter to common wisdom, economic elites and interest groups generally did not dominate the actual criminalization process. Instead, Hagan frequently credited moral reformers or entrepreneurs as being the causal agents behind enactments, observing that many of these crusaders converted their moral fervor into personal, professional, or occupational benefits. Finally, Hagan found there was generally little polarized disagreement over criminal enactments (with the exception of alcohol prohibition). Given the importance of Hagan's review to the study of criminalization, his observations are used here as a framework for analyzing the criminalization of computer abuse.

Media Give and Take

The media have played both a direct and indirect role in the formation of computer law. To know about the nature and incidence of the computer crime phenomenon is to rely essentially on the media. Indeed, this is exactly what the best-known expert on computer crime, Donn Parker, has done. He has been amassing a data base on all forms of computer "abuse" for over a decade (Parker, 1976, 1983). Collecting information almost exclusively from newspaper clippings, Parker has documented over 1,000 reported instances in which computers have in some way been abused. It is this data base from which virtually all estimates reported in the media regarding the incidence of computer crime have been made (Parker, 1980a).

Although Parker has been careful to point out that no one can possibly know the true extent of computer crime and abuse, he concluded from his collection of news accounts in 1976 that "the growth in this file appears to be rapid and exponential" (Parker, 1976: 25). Parker suggested that we are seeing only the "tip of the iceberg" because so many cases have been discovered purely by accident (U.S. Congress, Senate, 1978: 57). Thus, the "actual" level of computer abuse must be substantially higher. Although Parker claims that the media have misconstrued or inaccurately reported statements made by him and his associates regarding their data (Parker, 1980b: 332), he and many other experts have regularly responded to reporters' requests for incidence estimates with merely educated guesses. For example, one computer crime expert obviously guesstimated that "95% of all computer crime is never discovered" (Rutenberg, 1981). Unfortunately, many of these educated guesses (which are based almost entirely on press accounts in the first place) are then reified as fact when these experts are quoted later by the press.

Among other "experts" there is not unanimous agreement that computer crime is reaching epidemic proportions. For example, Taber (1980) has critically examined Parker's data base and has concluded that the actual incidence of computer crime has been grossly exaggerated. He cites instances of both misclassification and poor verification procedures by Parker. Taber claims that a number of the more prominently cited computer crimes have been found not to be crimes directly perpetrated by computer.[4] He argues that Parker's heavy reliance on newspaper accounts without independent verification has allowed his data set to become contaminated with a number of apocryphal events. After specifically comparing Parker's computer crime data with the substantially lower levels of victimization reported in a U.S. General Accounting Office (1976) study, Taber concludes there is no doubt that some computer crimes occur, but he seriously questions the incidence estimates made by Parker and repeated by the media. This critique has had some effect on estimates made earlier. Even Parker now regrets claiming that his data base is a representative sample of computer abuses (1983: 25).

Although the actual incidence and degree of harm associated with computer crime are unknown, the number of feature articles appearing in the mass media increased dramatically throughout the late 1970s and early 1980s (see *New York Times Index* and *Reader's Guide to Periodical Literature*). Regardless of whether this increase is attributable more to heightened media attention than to actual behavior, these reports have had an impact on the perceived incidence of computer crime. In the absence of verifiable and reliable data, it is the perception of serious computer crime as presented in the popular media that seems to have catalyzed computer law enactments. The effect of media attention has been evident for over a decade, as exemplified by the front-page attention given to the 1977 computer crime incident at the Flagler Dog Track in Miami, Florida, which led to the passage of the country's first state computer crime statute in 1978 (Miami Herald, 1977).

The direct effect of the media is best illustrated in the evolution of post-1983 federal and state computer crime legislation. Two media events, in particular, have had the most significant effect on recent criminalization efforts. The first incident was the discovery of the "414 hackers." So named because of the area code for their hometown of Milwaukee, the "414 hackers" were young computer aficionados arrested in 1983 for using their home computers and telephone modems to access illegally approximately 80 rather notable computer installations (including the Sloan Kettering Memorial Cancer Institute, Security Pacific National Bank, and the Los Alamos National Laboratory) (Newsweek, 1983a). Except for some files that were accidentally damaged at the Sloan Kettering Institute, no material harm was done. The activities of the "414 hackers" could best be characterized as instances of computer browsing. (In fact, only two members of this group eventually pled guilty, each to two misdemeanor counts of making harassing telephone calls [New York Times, 1984b].)

At approximately the same time, the country was captivated by *WarGames*, the movie in which a fictitious young computer genius gained control over the North American Air Defense (NORAD) Command in Wyoming and almost triggered a nuclear world war by accident. The screenplay of this movie was loosely based on real NORAD computer hardware and software failures that had occurred a number of years earlier (U.S. General Accounting Office, 1981); however, little else in the movie was even remotely plausible (see *Newsweek*, 1983b). Nevertheless, during the late summer and fall of 1983, the media began to fixate on the prospect of young computer hackers creating international mayhem from their bedrooms using home computers and telephone modems (e.g., ABC News Nightline, 1983).

In late August and early September 1983, *Newsweek* (1983a, 1983b), *People* (1983a, 1983b), and *Time* (1983a, 1983b) all featured stories on these juvenile hackers and the perceived threat of computer crime. Virtually all of the reports in the popular press during this period painted an alarming picture of highly vulnerable private and public computer installations. The combined dramatic effect of the "414" case and *WarGames* was illustrated in subsequent congressional hearings. In September 1983, Neal Patrick, one of the now infamous "414 hackers," was brought to Washington to testify regarding his unauthorized computer activities. Immediately before Patrick's testimony a segment from the movie *WarGames* was shown to the subcommittee as evidence "of what real hackers do" (U.S. Congress, House, 1983c).

These 1983 media events ensured that both the public and its elected representatives "knew" that computer crime was a major problem and that something had to be done quickly. This was the emotional climate in which about half the states and the federal government passed initial computer crime legislation. It also was during this period that most earlier computer crime statutes were amended to criminalize nonmalicious browsing. Even before the above incidents (and especially after), many articles and news reports about computer crime focused on two so-called facts. First, the media told us there was a whole generation of young hackers who were involved in epidemic levels of computer crime (e.g., Business Week, 1981; Shea, 1984). Second, many articles pointed out that the criminal justice system was ill-trained and almost legally powerless to respond to this new threat (e.g., Minneapolis Star, 1978; Time, 1982; New York Times, 1983).

An Interest Group Analysis and the Role of Reformers

Pluralistic accounts of law formation direct us to look for specific interest groups and moral reformers who might have been instrumental in bringing about computer crime legislation. Accounts like Gusfield's (1963) suggest social movements may be at the base of criminalization. Although social movements can frequently rely on pressure groups (see Useem and Zald, 1982), no consistently active interest groups or identifiable social movements were behind efforts to criminalize computer abuse. The only organized group to mount an early lobbying effort for computer crime legislation was the American Society for Industrial Security (ASIS), a professional organization for private security professionals and the security industry. It is difficult, however, to separate the impact of ASIS from that of its counsel, August Bequai, whose role as reformer is discussed below.

One other organized special interest group that may have had some influence was the American Bar Association (ABA), but its impact was primarily on the recent federal legislation. The ABA released a survey purporting to show significant business and government victimization from computer crime immediately prior to the vote in 1984 on the first federal law (New York Times, 1984c). The impact of the ABA was probably due more to its authoritativeness than to specific entrepreneurial efforts. The ABA does not appear to have played an important role in the formulation of earlier state computer crime legislation.

Although representatives of some economic and organized interest groups (e.g., data processing professional groups, equipment manufacturers, computing service companies, insurers, and computer consulting firms) testified before legislative committees, there is little evidence of their spearheading an intense lobbying effort on behalf of computer crime legislation. In fact, some computer manufacturing and services interests were conspicuous by their absence or tardiness. For example, it was only recently that the Data Processing Management Association and the Videotex Industry Association drafted model legislation to criminalize various unauthorized computer uses, after virtually every jurisdiction had already enacted similar statutes (Conroy, 1985, 1986).

The most visible legislative input from economic interest groups at the federal level occurred by way of response to interrogatories requested by Senator Joseph R. Biden (Del.) while the Senate was considering an early computer crime bill (S. 1766). Inquiries were also sent to various law enforcement and legal agencies. The responses offered suggested provisions and language changes (U.S. Congress, Senate, 1978) and some minor wording changes were incorporated into the subsequent federal laws. Examples include the elimination of nonmalicious and petty offenses by setting a minimal jurisdictional amount of loss and the definition of "computer" to exclude the hand-held calculator.

Individual reformers, rather than widespread grassroot social movements or economic interest groups, have been the principal forces behind the passage of computer crime legislation. However, these reformers have not been the "moral entrepreneurs" (Becker, 1963) of previous criminalization efforts. Instead, those who were most influential in the formation of computer crime laws have been computer abuse "experts" and legislators.

Without doubt the single most important expert has been Donn Parker. His data base was instrumental in convincing legislators that an objective problem exists. For example, after Parker's invited special presentation to the joint Florida House and Senate, those bodies passed the Computer Crimes Act unanimously with only two definitional amendments. Parker has made similar presentations to numerous state and federal legislative committees during the past decade. In these formal presentations he provides legislators with a summary of his data, which he argues document the widespread prevalence and increasing incidence of computer crime and abuse (e.g., U.S. Congress, Senate, 1978: 52–69; U.S. Congress, House, 1982: 45–53, 1983a: 23–31). From the separate states to the U.S. Congress, Parker has had a profound impact on the proliferation of legislation, and in the process he has earned a national reputation as the premier computer crime expert.

Another important reformer is author and attorney, August Bequai. Already an established expert on white-collar crime (Bequai, 1977), he quickly developed expertise on the subject of computer crime (1978, 1983, 1987). Bequai was instrumental in efforts to enact both state and federal computer crime statutes, and he was one of the authors of the first piece of proposed federal legislation, S. 1766, Federal Computer Systems Protection Act (Taber, 1980: 302). Additionally, in his role as counsel for the American Society for Industrial Security, Bequai was the acknowledged principal author of ASIS's prepared statement submitted in support of S. 1766 in 1978.[5] In this document Bequai argued that computer crime was dramatically increasing and that new federal legislation with "large fines and lengthy prison terms" would be required to stem the tide (U.S. Congress, Senate, 1978: 113–20). In 1983 Bequai testified before Congress in support of H.R. 3075, Small Business Computer Crime Prevention Act. In his formal remarks Bequai maintained that computer crime is rapidly outpacing the criminal justice system's ability to respond to the threat (U.S. Congress, House, 1983a: 4–12). In his writings and public speeches, and without much more than anecdotal data to support his case, Bequai has continued to lobby both legislatures and the general public for a tougher response to the myriad of "dangers" presented by our recently computerized and cashless society.

In the political arena a number of legislators have played a key role in the efforts to pass federal legislation on the computer crime phenomenon, principally former Senator Abraham Ribicoff (Conn.), Senator Biden, and Representative Bill Nelson (Fla.). Senator Ribicoff introduced S. 1766, a bill that would have made virtually all crimes committed by computer a federal offense. The earliest testimony was in the Senate Judiciary Subcommittee on Criminal Laws and Procedures, chaired by Senator Biden, who, as noted, specifically requested industry comment on the proposed legislation (U.S. Congress, Senate, 1978, 1980). In their testimony on this bill and a subsequently introduced legislative revision (S. 240) Parker and others generally agreed that a problem existed, but there was not consensus in the Senate that computer crime was a federal matter. Although Senator Biden and his subcommittee retained interest in computer crime, with Senator Ribicoff's retirement much of the momentum in the Senate for passage of S. 240 soon dissipated and the focus of legislative activity then shifted to the House of Representatives.

During the 97th and 98th Congresses, Representative Bill Nelson became the advocate of a federal computer crime statute. Having been the principal author of Florida's computer crime act while in the state legislature, Nelson viewed computer crime as one of his areas of personal expertise, as evidenced by its prominent mention in his list of personal legislative accomplishments (Nelson, 1985). Nelson soon sponsored several computer crime bills in the House (i.e., H.R. 3970 and H.R. 1093) (U.S. Congress, House, 1982, 1983b). Adopting the strategy he successfully used in Florida in 1978, Nelson invited a broad range of experts (including Donn Parker) to testify in support of the bills.

Until 1984 the primary impact of House and Senate testimony on federal computer crime legislation was to provide the states with model legislative wording (Sokolik, 1980). While state computer crime statutes were proliferating, however, legislative initiatives continued to be delayed in the Congress, due primarily to concerns about federal jurisdictional overreach and redundancy. Despite the impressive array of testimony supporting a federal statute, no House or Senate committee could be convinced that the federal government should play a specific role in controlling computer crime.

What little opposition to computer criminalization efforts that can be found has been relatively minor and is most relevant to federal legislation. The FBI, for example, initially expressed reservations about the jurisdictional scope of legislation that would make the FBI responsible for investigating all instances of computer crime (U.S. Congress, Senate, 1978: 34). Colorado's Attorney General, J.D. MacFarlane, argued before a Senate committee that the issue of computer crime could better be handled at the state level (U.S. Congress, Senate, 1980: 5–16). Further, in 1982 Milton Wessel, a lawyer and computer law instructor at Columbia University, testified in the presence of Representative Nelson that a federal computer crime statute was not necessary given the fact that the Florida statute had not been used since its enactment. (Concerned by this allegation, Nelson later introduced documents showing that Florida's statute had been utilized, albeit only twice in four years [U.S. Congress, House, 1982: 39–43].)

The first piece of federal legislation passed by both the House and Senate that addressed computer crime was incorporated into H.R. 5616, Counterfeit Access Device and Computer Fraud and Abuse Act of 1984 (U.S. Congress, House, 1984). Much of the wording from Representative Nelson's proposed legislation was incorporated into H.R. 5616 – a bill that primarily addressed credit card fraud and the abuse of credit information. Thus, the first federal computer crime bill was passed by attaching it to a related banking and finance bill (U.S. Public Law 98-473, 1984), a subject over which there is clear federal jurisdiction. In addition, federal jurisdiction was limited and petty cases were excluded by mandating a minimum dollar amount of $5,000. Due to its banking emphasis, the bill assigned most enforcement duties to the Treasury Department's Secret Service rather than to an already overburdened and somewhat reluctant FBI.

The most recent addition to federal computer crime law was passed in the waning days of the 99th Congress. The Computer Fraud and Abuse Act of 1986 provides additional penalties for fraud and related activities in connection with access devices and computers (U.S. Public Law 99-474, 1986). This legislation extends federal privacy protection to computerized information maintained by financial institutions and clarifies unauthorized access of computers used by the U.S. government. Three new offenses are defined: unauthorized computer access with the intent to defraud, malicious damage via unauthorized access, and trafficking in computer passwords with the intent to defraud (e.g., placing such information on computer bulletin boards). In sum, P.L. 99-474 tightened, extended, and clarified the earlier 1984 legislation.

The Normative Climate during Enactment

Based on the substantial media and legislative attention being directed to computer crime, one would expect to find widespread public debate over the relative merits of criminalization. No significant organized opposition to criminalization was mounted, however. In fact, the minimal opposition that did surface was primarily at the federal level, and some of it was raised for reasons other than normative disagreement. The absence of normative conflict or "segmented dissensus" (Rossi and Berk, 1985) over criminalization, however, does not mean there was a public consensus that demanded the criminalization of certain computer activities, especially before the media events of late 1983. Even in the wake of the movie *WarGames* and the "414 hackers" case, computer criminalization did not result from grassroots popular politics. In fact, before 1983, there is evidence that the public was rather ambivalent about reports of embezzlements and thefts via computers. A Roper Poll found these computer crimes to rank 8th on a list of 11 concerns (Roper, 1982b). In 1982, the public was more unified about protecting "privacy" interests in personal data stored in large computer files. Over 80% of those polled favored a variety of laws to protect private information in this regard (Roper, 1982a). Legislative bodies did not begin to emphasize the privacy themes in computer crime enactments until relatively late in the process.[6]

Another aspect of the normative climate surrounding computer crime concerns the computer user. Specifically, do computer users consider the various types of prohibited computer activity to be acceptable or deviant? Are they likely to support or resist criminalization? In what may be the only study addressing this issue, 200 undergraduates enrolled in upper-division computer science courses at a major Midwestern university were anonymously surveyed during the fall of 1982 to determine their propensity toward involvement in crime by computer (Hollinger, 1984). Each respondent was presented with scenarios that depicted four types of computer abuse—computer as "object," "symbol," "instrument," and "subject" of crimes (based on Parker, 1976). Hollinger found a high degree of normative consensus among users for the first three types of computer deviance; 90% of the respondents (in a state that at the time did not have a computer crime statute) indicated they would not engage in behaviors in which computers were the "object," "symbol," or "instrument" of crime. For the last type, computer as "subject" of the abuse, there was more ambivalence. Twenty-two percent of the respondents indicated that they "definitely" or "probably" would examine or modify confidential information stored in a computer account if they had the opportunity, and only 3% said they definitely would not.

This receptivity to browsing and modifying electronically stored information seems to reflect the informally established subcultural norms and customs found among some dedicated computer users. The unauthorized access of computer accounts is often not perceived as being either deviant or criminal by computer aficionados (Markoff, 1982, 1983). Some users accept a subcultural "hacker ethic," which is based on the philosophical position that all data files placed on telephonically linked computers are essentially in the public domain and should be free and accessible to all (see Levy, 1984: 26; see also McCaghy and Denisoff, 1973, who found a similar ethic justifying music piracy). Some pioneering users of computers argue that the free and unrestricted use of computers is a human "right" that in recent years has become far too constrained and limited. There is evidence that this "high-tech norm" may actually predate the microcomputer revolution. For example, some of the famous "phone phreaks" of the 1970s (i.e., those in the "blue-box" free long-distance telephone subculture) later combined their telephone fascination with the new computer technology (Landreth, 1985: 28–34).

An increasing number of contemporary examples suggests that both malicious and nonmalicious computer hacking may be explicitly or implicitly encouraged during the process of becoming computer literate. In the extremely competitive environment of computer science, system hacking is viewed by some instructors and peers as an indicator of excellence. Students of computer science sometimes dare each other to break into computer systems as a test of programming prowess (e.g., Harrer, 1985). Parker (1976, 1983: 134–36) and others have expressed concern that computer training may be criminogenic in that computer pranksterism generally is not negatively sanctioned and is sometimes even encouraged. The example of the California Institute of Technology students who reportedly received course credit for taking control of the computerized scoreboard during the 1984 Rose Bowl game (New York Times, 1984a) helps to confirm the contention that computer science students are sometimes encouraged to attack computer systems as an educational activity (Parker, 1979: 54).

Because computer science is a relatively new profession, professional or occupational norms are still developing (e.g., Parker, 1983: 196–203). Only recently have there been efforts to institutionalize norms regarding the unacceptability of certain types of acts (Johnson, 1985). Professional associations are now rapidly moving to develop codes of ethics and model penal codes relating to computer crime and abuse (see Johnson and Snapper, 1985). Since computer crime legislation preceded active involvement by professional associations in establishing occupational norms, computer crime laws were not the result of the occupation's attempting to regulate itself (see Akers, 1968).

DISCUSSION

Summarizing the criminalization process is relatively easy. Public opinion neither called for nor opposed the criminalization of computer abuse. In fact, there was very little direct pressure on legislators from any interest group—moral or economic. Nor were there any "moral entrepreneurs" zealously seeking to legislate morality. Instead, individual state and federal lawmakers took the initiative. "Computer crime" presented activist legislators with an ideal issue with which to maximize personal media exposure without offending any major constituency. To legitimize their campaign, the legislators enlisted technical experts on computer abuse, who also gained recognition for themselves and their work.

Both the experts and the legislators relied heavily on the media in their efforts to advance criminalization. Legislators would not have received so much publicity and the experts could not have assembled the supporting data were it not for extensive media coverage of computer abuse. Unlike the experts and activist legislators, however, the media did not play a direct advocacy role in criminalization. It was the media's reporting, and not their advocacy, that was most indispensable to the criminalization process. . . .

Notes

*An earlier version of this paper was presented at the annual meetings of the Academy of Criminal Justice Sciences on March 19, 1986, in Orlando, Florida. This research was funded in part by a grant from the Division of Sponsored Research, University of Florida. The authors wish to thank Ronald L. Akers, Donna Bishop, Jay BloomBecker, Pamela Richards, Charles W. Thomas, and the anonymous reviewers for their helpful comments on drafts of this paper.

1. The only states currently without computer crime statutes are Arkansas, Vermont, and West Virginia.

2. This analysis is necessarily an interpretation of a series of legislative actions at both the state and federal levels. Accordingly, the objective was to document the available record on the computer crime legislative process over the past 10 years with as many sources as possible. Legal accounts (e.g., *Index to Legal Periodicals*) were sought to document the evolution of the specific statutes in the various states and in the Congress (e.g., BloomBecker, 1985 and 1986; Scott, 1984; Soma et al., 1985). The *Congressional Information Service* and CompuServe's *Online Today Electronic Edition* Computer Legislation Database were used to follow specific pieces of proposed legislation. Popular media were systematically reviewed by using several indexes, including the *Reader's Guide to Periodical Literature*, the *New York Times Index*, the *Wall Street Journal Index*, and the *NewsBank Index*. Although various other regional newspapers were consulted, the *Tallahassee Democrat* and *Miami Herald* were examined intensively because Florida was the first state to pass a separate computer crime statute (1978). Other media coverage, including television and film, also was surveyed in a less systematic way. Various computer-related business and professional periodicals were examined (using the *Business Periodicals Index*) for references to legislative input by the private sector and statistical information on the growth of the computer industry. The social science literature was also examined via *Sociological Abstracts* and *Criminal Justice Abstracts* for relevant academic sources to build a comparative appreciation of past criminalization efforts. Finally, various experts and informants who have carefully followed the evolution of computer crime legislation were interviewed. The most helpful was Jay BloomBecker, director of the National Center for Computer Crime Data. Undoubtedly, there are sources that were inadvertently overlooked, but nevertheless, an accurate and thorough account of the computer criminalization process has been assembled.

3. Three cases in particular raised early questions about the legal status of this intangible electronic property. In Ward v. Superior Court (3 CLSR 206, California Superior Court, 1972), the judge advanced *dicta* that telephonic impulses are not tangible items and therefore do not in and of themselves satisfy the common law asportation (i.e., physical removal) requirement of theft (Ingraham, 1980: 432–433). In Lund v. Commonwealth (217 Va. 688, 232 S.E.2d 745 [1977]), Virginia failed in attempts to prosecute the theft of software and computer services because of the common law requirement of a physical carrying away or taking. In U.S. v. Seidlitz (589 F.2d 152 [4th Circuit, 1978]), a former employee of a computer company used a telephone and modem from both his Maryland home and Virginia office to obtain computing services and a proprietary program. The movement of magnetic impulses did not satisfy the traditional common law interpretations of stealing or taking under Maryland's property theft laws. Consequently, Seidlitz had to be charged under a federal wire fraud statute and was convicted only because he placed two interstate phone calls (Volgyes, 1980).

4. John Taber (1980: 310) has meticulously critiqued the data base assembled by Parker and concludes that it is unreliable because it is based on poor documentation, unacceptable methods, and unverified (indeed unverifiable) losses. For example, Taber points out that the famous $10.2 million bank embezzlement by Stanley Mark Rifkin was actually a wire transfer deception conducted verbally over telephone lines and did not involve a Trojan horse attack. He also demonstrates that round-off error crimes arithmetically cannot yield multimillion dollar violations. Even the famous Equity Funding case was not uniquely a computer crime.

5. Jay BloomBecker, personal conversation with the authors in San Diego, California, November 15, 1985.

6. Connecticut offers a case in point. One of the proponents of Connecticut's 1984 computer crime statute was the state Civil Liberties Union because of the law's privacy protection provisions (Lavine, 1984).

References

ABC News Nightline
1983   *WarGames* scenario: Could it really happen? July 8.
Akers, Ronald L.
1968   The professional association and the legal regulation of practice. Law and Society Review 2: 463–482.
Becker, Howard S.
1963   The Outsiders. New York: Free Press.
Bequai, August
1977   White Collar Crime, Lexington, Mass.: Lexington Books.
1978   Computer Crime. Lexington, Mass.: Lexington Books.
1983   How to Prevent Computer Crime: A Guide for Managers. New York: John Wiley and Sons.
1987   Technocrimes. Lexington, Mass.: Lexington Books.
Berk, Richard, Harold Brackman, and Selma Lesser
1977   A Measure of Justice: An Empirical Study of Changes in the California Penal Code, 1955–1971. New York: Academic Press.
Best, Joel and Gerald T. Horiuchi
1985   The razor blade in the apple: The social construction of urban legends. Social Problems 32: 488–499.
BloomBecker, Jay
1985   Computer crime update: The view as we exit 1984. Western New England Law Review 7: 627–649.
1986   Computer Crime Law Reporter: 1986 Update. Los Angeles: National Center for Computer Crime Data.
Business Week
1981   The spreading danger of computer crime, April 20, 86–92.
Chambliss, William
1964   A sociological analysis of the law of vagrancy. Social Problems 11: 67–77.
Clinard, Marshall B. and Richard Quinney
1973   Criminal Behavior Systems: A Typology (2nd ed.). New York: Holt, Rinehart and Winston.
Conroy, Cathryn
1985   Computer crime law drafted. Online Today, June: 8.
1986   States cool toward computer crime laws. Online Today, November: 14.
Gusfield, Joseph R.
1963   Symbolic Crusade. Urbana: University of Illinois Press.
Hafner, Katherine
1983   UCLA student penetrates DOD network. InfoWorld 5(47): 28.
Hagan, John
1980   The legislation of crime and delinquency: A review of theory, method, and research. Law and Society Review 14: 603–628.
Hall, Jerome
1952   Theft, Law and Society. Indianapolis, Ind.: Bobbs-Merrill.
Harrer, Tom
1985   Hackers try to outsmart system . . . as software producers work to foil "pirates." Gainesville (Florida) Sun, July 7, Supplement: 6.
Hollinger, Richard C.
1984   Computer deviance: Receptivity to electronic rule-breaking. Paper presented at the annual meetings of the American Society of Criminology, November 7, Cincinnati, Ohio.
Ingraham, Donald G.
1980   On charging computer crime. Computer/Law Journal 2: 429–439.

Johnson, Deborah G.
1985   Computer Ethics. Englewood Cliffs, N.J.: Prentice-Hall.
Johnson, Deborah G. and John W. Snapper
1985   Ethical Issues in the Use of Computers. Belmont, Calif: Wadsworth.
Kling, Rob
1980   Computer abuse and computer crime as organizational activities. Computer/Law
          Journal 2: 403–427.
Landreth, Bill
1985   Out of the Inner Circle: A Hacker's Guide to Computer Security. Bellevue, Wash.:
          Microsoft Press.
Lavine, Douglas
1984   New measure defines abuse of computers. New York Times Sunday Magazine, May
          20, sec. xxiii: 1.
Lindesmith, Alfred R.
1967   The Addict and the Law. New York: Vintage.
Levy, Steven
1984   Hackers: Heroes of the Computer Revolution. New York: Doubleday.
Markoff, John
1982   Computer crimes: Lots of money, little ingenuity. InfoWorld 4(46): 27–28.
1983   Giving hackers back their good name. InfoWorld 5(48): 43.
McCaghy, Charles H. and A. Sergio Denisoff
1973   Pirates and politics: An analysis of interest group conflict. In A. Sergio Denisoff and
          Charles H. McCaghy (eds.), Deviance: Conflict and Criminality. Chicago: Rand
          McNally.
McKnight, Gerald
1974   Computer Crime. London: Joseph.
Miami Herald
1977   Dog players bilked via computers, September 20: 1.
Minneapolis Star
1978   Crime's knowledge of computers far outstripping law enforcement, December 5: 1.
Nelson, Bill
1985   Highlights of Bill Nelson's legislative accomplishments. Handout from Represent-
          ative Nelson's congressional office, photocopy.
Newsweek
1983a   Beware: Hackers at play, September 5: 42–46, 48.
1983b   Preventing "WarGames," September 5: 48.
New York Times
1983   Laws in U.S. called inadequate to block abuse of computers, September 18: 1.
1984a   Low Tech, January 5: 26.
1984b   Two who raided computers pleading guilty, March 17: 6.
1984c   Survey outlines computer crimes, June 11: 16.
Nycum, Susan
1976a   The criminal law aspects of computer abuse: Part I – state penal laws. Rutgers Jour-
          nal of Computers and Law 5: 271–295.
1976b   The criminal law aspects of computer abuse: Part II – federal criminal code. Rut-
          gers Journal of Computers and Law 5: 297–322.
Parker, Donn B.
1976   Crime By Computer. New York: Charles Scribner's Sons.
1979   Computer Crime: Criminal Justice Resource Manual. Washington, D.C.: Govern-
          ment Printing Office.
1980a   Computer-related white collar crime. In Gilbert Geis and Ezra Stotland (eds.),
          White Collar Crime: Theory and Research. Beverly Hills, Calif.: Sage.
1980b   Computer abuse research update. Computer/Law Journal 2: 329–352.
1983   Fighting Computer Crime. New York: Charles Scribner's Sons.

People
1983a   Computers can be robbed, tricked or sabotaged, warns an expert, and their power, if abused, could cause havoc, September 12: 49–54.
1983b   The FBI puts the arm on hacker Neal Patrick, September 12: 54.
Platt, Anthony
1969   The Child Savers. Chicago: University of Chicago Press.
Roper
1982a   Roper Report 82–6, June 5–12.
1982b   Roper Report 87–2, July 10–17.
Rossi, Peter and Richard Berk
1985   Varieties of normative consensus. American Sociological Review 50: 333–347.
Rutenberg, Sharon
1981   In 10 minutes almost anyone can rob a bank via computer. Indianapolis Star, April 5, sec. 4: 19–20.
Scott, Michael D.
1984   Computer Law. New York: John Wiley and Sons.
Shea, Tom
1984   The FBI goes after hackers. InfoWorld 6(13): 38.
Sokolik, Stanley L.
1980   Computer crime–the need for deterrent legislation. Computer/Law Journal 2: 353–383.
Soma, John T., Paula J. Smith, and Robert D. Sprague
1985   Legal analysis of electronic bulletin board activities. Western New England Law Review 7: 571–626.
Sutherland, Edwin H.
1950   The sexual psychopath laws. Journal of Criminal Law, Criminology and Police Science 40: 543–554.
1951   The diffusion of sexual psychopath laws. American Journal of Sociology 56: 142–148.
Taber, John K.
1980   A survey of computer crime studies. Computer/Law Journal 2: 275–327.
Time
1982   Crackdown on computer crime, February 8: 60–67.
1983a   Playing games, August 22: 14.
1983b   The 414 gang strikes again, August 29: 75.
Useem, Bert and Mayer N. Zald
1982   From pressure group to social movement: Organizational dilemmas of the effort to promote nuclear power. Social Problems 30: 144–156.
U.S. Congress, House
1982   Hearing before the Subcommittee on Civil and Constitutional Rights of the Committee on the Judiciary on H.R. 3970: Federal Computer Systems Protection Act. 97th Cong., 2nd Sess. (September 23). Washington, D.C.: Government Printing Office.
1983a   Hearing before the Subcommittee on Antitrust and Restraint of Trade Activities Affecting Small Business of the Committee on Small Business: Small Business Computer Crime Prevention Act, H.R. 3075. 98th Cong., 1st Sess. (July 14). Washington, D.C.: Government Printing Office.
1983b   Hearing before the Subcommittee on Civil and Constitutional Rights of the Committee on the Judiciary: Computer Crime. 98th Cong., 1st Sess. (November 18). Washington, D.C.: Government Printing Office.
1983c   Hearing before the House Subcommittee on Transportation, Aviation and Materials of the Committee on Science and Technology: Computer and Communications Security and Privacy. 98th Cong., 2nd Sess. (September 26). Washington, D.C.: Government Printing Office.

1984   Counterfeit Access Device and Computer Fraud and Abuse Act of 1984 (H.R. 5616). Report 98-894, 98th Cong., 2nd Sess. (July 24). Washington, D.C.: Government Printing Office.

U.S. Congress, Senate
1978   Hearings before the Subcommittee on Criminal Laws and Procedures of the Committee on the Judiciary on S. 1766: Federal Computer Systems Protection Act, 95th Cong., 2nd Sess. (June 21 and 22). Washington, D.C.: Government Printing Office.

1980   Hearing before the Subcommittee on Criminal Justice of the Committee on the Judiciary on S. 240: Federal Computer Systems Protection Act. 96th Cong. 2nd Sess. (February 28). Washington, D.C.: Government Printing Office.

U.S. General Accounting Office
1976   Computer related crimes in federal programs. Reprinted in Problems Associated with Computer Technology in Federal Programs and Private Industry, Computer Abuses. Senate Committee on Governmental Operations, 94th Cong. 2nd Sess. 71–91. Washington, D.C.: Government Printing Office.

1981   NORAD's Missile Warning System: What went wrong? GAO Report MASAD 81-30 (May 15). Washington, D.C.: Government Printing Office.

U.S. Public Law 98-473
1984   Counterfeit Access Device and Computer Fraud and Abuse Act of 1984. Amendment to Chapter 47 of Title 18 of the United States Code (October 12).

U.S. Public Law 99-474
1986   Computer Fraud and Abuse Act of 1986. Amendment to Chapter 47 of Title 18 of the United States Code (October 16).

Volgyes, Mary R.
1980   The investigation, prosecution, and prevention of computer crime: A state-of-the-art review. Computer/Law Journal 2: 387–402.

PART 2

MEASURING CRIME

In Part 1 we saw how legislative and political processes affect the creation of definitions of crime. Obviously, how crime is defined will have a bearing on how criminal involvement is measured. If, for example, a researcher takes an *official*, or legalistic, approach to the study of crime, then the emphasis will be on the violators of the law, particularly those who have come into contact with the criminal justice system. Traditionally, statements and generalizations about the nature and extent of crime have been based on two categories of official data: (1) crimes known to the police and (2) arrests.

Official data, however, are incomplete and hence often misleading. This occurs in part because of differential law enforcement policies. If, for example, the police believe minorities to be a major crime problem, they will maintain heavy surveillance in the minority community. This, in turn, may mean that members of minority groups are overrepresented in the crime statistics. In this way, official data can promote and perpetuate myths about crime and the criminal.

Enforcement policies are not the only problems that plague crime statistics. Another is that the police do not report and record events uniformly. Still another is that victims frequently fail to report criminal acts to the police.

Because of the inadequacies of official data, other ways have been devised to measure crime. Chief among these are the *self-report* methods and the *victimization* survey.

Researchers have primarily used the self-report strategy to measure delinquency. A sample group of juveniles is given a questionnaire and asked to check, in confidence, those illegal acts they have committed and the number of times they have committed them; this information is then used to make inferences about the nature and extent of delinquent involvement. The weaknesses of the technique are that respondents are not always able to recall offenses they have committed; they may exaggerate their involvement; and many of the questionnaires itemize only minor offenses. Still self-reports do provide useful information on the volume of crime and delinquency. When self-report data are compared with official statistics, it becomes clear that a substantial amount of criminal and delinquent activity goes unreported.

Victimization surveys attempt to measure the extent of unrecorded crime by asking people what offenses were committed against them and whether the offenses were reported. The data collected are then compared with official statistics. Although widely used, victimization surveys also suffer from problems, such as people's inability to remember events or their reluctance to report them.

The initial selections in this part describe and evaluate some of the strategies and methods that are employed to study the nature and extent of criminal activity and involvement. These are followed by studies that examine some of the traditional correlates of crime — such as social class, race, and sex — that have been used in explanations of crime. These latter pieces also help to underscore the need for examining how specific correlates become mediated through organizational structures (e.g., tracking systems) in such a way as to give rise to the beginning stages of a range of criminal careers and identities.

MEASUREMENT PROBLEMS AND ISSUES

As noted, traditionally a heavy focus has been placed on those individuals who have experienced some type of contact with law enforcement officials; this has often meant, logically, that a rather strict reliance has been placed on the use of official data (e.g., arrests). Hence, out of an existing population of law violators, a portion, due to some type of law enforcement activity, becomes available for scrutiny. Robert Tillman, in "The Size of the 'Criminal Population': The Prevalence and Incidence of Adult Arrest," offers an excellent illustration of how official data bases may be used to make observations about selected aspects of crime. He is concerned with examining several recent conclusions that a small subset of "chronic offenders" or "career criminals" contribute disproportionately to existing crime rates. Tillman also notes that this concentration on chronic offenders has produced a noticeable shift away from a concern for social-structural explanations of crime to more of a focus on individualistic, reductionist statements. Tillman proposes to shed some light on this trend by examining the *prevalence* (i.e., the proportion of a population ever arrested) and *incidence* (i.e., the number of arrests of those ever arrested) of arrest for a group of males and females. The actual data base was drawn from California's Adult Criminal Justice Statistics System, and it contains the arrest histories of people born in 1956 and who were later arrested between 1974 and 1985 (i.e., between the ages of 18 and 29). Some interesting findings emerge. In terms of prevalence, these data indicate that, contrary to the expectations based on past research, the phenomenon of being arrested is not limited to a small subset of chronic offenders but is, rather, distributed widely throughout the study population. As an example, 40 percent of black males, as compared to 3 percent of white females, were arrested for an index offense. The information on incidence is equally revealing, with these data indicating that a substantial number of offenders experienced multiple arrests over the period of the study. Tillman ends his analysis by examining the contributions that chronic offenders make to the crime rate. He concludes that "getting arrested and obtaining a criminal record are not limited to small groups of 'criminals' but are common experiences for many young adults in California."

Although Tillman and others make use of official data, it needs to be recognized at the outset that many factors go into the production of a body of organizational statistics — factors that can reflect directly on the validity, reliability, and utility of such data. Richard McCleary, Barbara C. Nienstedt, and James M. Erven, in "Uniform Crime Reports as Organizational Outcomes: Three Time Series Experiments," provide us with an outstanding analysis of how changing organizational structures can impact on the body of statistics that is produced. Their focus is placed on the *Uniform Crime Reports* (UCRs) that are published annually by the FBI. They comment initially on some of the shortcomings that characterize the UCRs (e.g., ignoring or not reporting offenses that do not fit into existing "index" categories). Most city and state governments do, however, rely heavily on the UCRs, particularly in terms of assessing whether or not crime rates are going up or down. And fluctuations can occur because of differences in real crime or because of structural changes in the way complaints are processed. Differential organizational processing can thus produce alterations in the crime rate. The researchers then describe how incidental or unplanned changes in the structures of police departments can affect the crime-UCR reporting link. Their guiding thesis is that "the official crime rate in a jurisdiction is a function of the organizational structure of the crime-processing agency, that is, the local police department." Three natural experiments (i.e., instances of unplanned or incidental change) are described. In Case One, the researchers, operating on the assumption that UCR rates are a function of the relationship between the complaint investigators and processors (i.e., the coding clerks), examine the dramatic shifts that occurred in City A during a 21-month period. Specifically, prior to this period, complaints were not investigated beyond the filing of a field report; however, during the period studied, all complaints were formally investigated, resulting in an abrupt drop in the level of burglaries. In their accounting for the rather precipitous decline in UCR burglaries, the authors locate and describe how the formal investigations actually reduced three main types of errors (i.e., those relating to definitional distinctions, discretionary decisions, and double-counting) that had been incorporated into prior recording and reporting practices. In Case Two, the researchers describe how changes in hierarchical structure (i.e., the planned retirement of the incumbent police chief and associated personnel changes) can also produce a UCR "crime wave." They conclude their analysis by describing how, in Case Three, various types of screening, especially by sergeants, affected the resulting crime rate. As an example, calls from ghetto areas were not only heavily screened but were less apt to produce a service call. The authors end by emphasizing the fact that UCRs are "official statistics" and, as such, they should be used primarily for studying organizational processes. They also underscore the need for more qualitative studies of single police departments.

James D. Orcutt and Rebecca Faison, in "Sex-Role Attitude Change and Reporting of Rape Victimization," offer another piece of research illustrating how selected changes may impact on the production of a body of organizational statistics. They are concerned with examining whether or not changes in sex-role attitudes have produced any noticeable shifts in definitions and reporting of rape victimization. A portion of their research is concerned specifically with analyzing how changes in sex-role attitudes may be linked more closely to changes in the reporting of *nonstranger* rapes than to the reporting of *stranger* rapes to police. They analyze data obtained from three surveys conducted between 1972 and 1985. Some interesting findings emerge. Their preliminary data indicate that even though the reporting of both stranger and nonstranger rape has increased during the study period, the rate of increase for nonstranger reporting is over twice the rate for reporting stranger rape. Subsequent analyses also reveal, for example, that the threat or use of force in terms of a weapon increases the probability that women will report stranger rapes to the police.

CORRELATES OF CRIME

In the attempt to understand why people become criminals, a host of variables has been studied. Some researchers study poverty and urbanization, while others explore the effects of racial, familial, and educational factors. The pieces in this section introduce a few of the more common themes.

In "Is Violent Crime Intraracial?," William Wilbanks introduces a correlate that traditionally has been given much attention: race. He notes that not only is violent crime, with the possible exception of robbery, often assumed to be intraracial, but that interracial crime is also viewed as being relatively infrequent. He cites numerous existing sources in support of these assumptions and then, through use of a national victimization survey, proceeds to examine the nature of selected forms of violent crime (i.e., robbery, assault, and rape) from the "perception (of race) of the victim perspective." His initial data indicate that "more whites are victimized by whites (77 percent) than by blacks (17.1 percent) and more blacks are victimized by blacks (81.9 percent) than by whites (14.4 percent)." These observations suggest that crime is intraracial; however, when examined from a "choices of victim" perspective, some interesting findings emerge. Specifically, although violent crime by whites is primarily *intraracial*, with white offenders most often selecting white victims (96.9 percent), violent crime by blacks is predominantly *interracial*, with blacks choosing white victims (55.2 percent). This general pattern holds separately for each of the three crimes of violence selected for study. Hence, the use of overall or summary statistics, Wilbanks warns, can mask the interracial character of violent crime by blacks. Wilbanks concludes by discussing some of the reasons why black offenders may choose white victims (e.g., the notion that robbery is primarily an economic crime and whites, as a group, tend to have more money). He also takes to task those criminologists who, in their reliance on arrest and homicide data, have concluded that violent crime is intraracial. Victimization data can, as his evidence suggests, produce a different set of results. In further support of this, Wilbanks notes that if one examines *Uniform Crime Reports* for murder, women usually kill men and not women; however, if one examines the victimization data for assaults viewed as unsuccessful murders, 85 percent of the victims of female assaulters were other females.

Sex is another variable that has been emphasized. Carol A. Whitehurst, in "Women and the Commission of Crime: A Theoretical Approach," notes that theories of deviance generally have ignored the subject of women's crime; this oversight, moreover, underscores the need for a feminist analysis of crime, one that is not based on the traditional white, middle-class male model. Whitehurst proposes to offer such an analysis. She is concerned specifically with examining how our present sociological theories can be used to explain women's crime, especially in view of two basic facts: (1) women's reported crime is but a small proportion of men's reported crime, and (2) the proportion of total reported crime by women has increased substantially since 1960. Whitehurst provides some arrest data in support of these trends and then discusses numerous limitations of official data. She also comments on some of the trends in female crime that have been produced by self-report studies (e.g., the gap between male and female crime is smaller for self-report data than for official arrest records). Whitehurst proceeds to examine several theories that have been advanced to explain the changes noted in women's crime (e.g., subcultural, social learning, and socialization theories). She then concludes that such crime is probably "best seen as an expression of structural changes in the economy, opportunities, societal values, and changing roles and relationships."

Some researchers and theoreticians, in their search for correlates of crime that can help explain it, have looked more closely at institutional components and processes. And frequently the family and the schools have been given scrutiny. In "Societal Change and Change in Family Violence from 1975 to 1985 as Revealed by Two National Surveys," Murray A. Straus and Richard J. Gelles document some of the changes that have occurred over a span of ten years. They begin by providing a historical overview of child abuse and wife beating and then move to an assessment of whether or not there currently exists an epidemic of child abuse and spouse abuse. If examination is given to "official statistics" on child abuse, one might conclude that such abuse is on the rise; however, this may be incorrect because, conceivably, the true incidence of child abuse may actually be on the decline. How, then, can such an apparent anomaly be explained? Straus and Gelles cite two factors behind the apparent increase in cases of reported child abuse: (1) all states now have compulsory reporting laws and, hence, millions of previously unreported cases have come to the attention of the authorities, and (2) the definitions of child abuse have broadened to include acts that previously were not viewed as child abuse, and thus a wider range of acts has been reported to social-control agents. A somewhat similar situation exists with respect to wife beating; however, unlike child abuse, very few good data bases exist. In fact, Straus and Gelles suggest that the perceived epidemic in this area may be more of a function of increased media coverage, as well as a growing awareness on the part of family members that a problem exists. The researchers use two national surveys to explore concerns such as these. They observe, for example, that with very few exceptions violence against children has declined over the period from 1975 to 1985. The material on marital and couple violence also exhibits a similar trend. The researchers conclude by discussing various factors that could affect their findings (e.g., differences between the two surveys and reluctance to report). Straus and Gelles note that in spite of these apparent reductions, child abuse and wife beating remain very high.

In "School Crime and Individual Responsibility: The Perpetuation of a Myth?," William T. Pink and I focus attention on the educational system. We initially comment on the *interactional* and *organizational* paradigms (see General Introduction) and then move to an analysis of the role that *diagnostic stereotypes* and associated typing ceremonies can play in the beginning stages of deviant and criminal careers and identities, particularly for those who are drawn from the lower or disadvantaged reaches of American society. It is noted here that attempts to explain school crime continue to focus on low-income children, even though tests of such notions have been less than kind. What the bulk of research does suggest, however, is that school factors such as academic failure, independent of social class, are linked significantly to school crime, dropout, delinquency, and a range of other "deviant" outcomes. Evidence of this type directs us, necessarily, to a beginning examination of the structure and process of schooling, and it is at this juncture that we describe how the educational system is actually geared organizationally, particularly in terms of its existing student stratification systems (i.e., ability groups and track systems). Once the basic underlying organizational structure has been described, we move to an examination of how students are selected out for placement in available career lines (e.g., the college-prep track versus the noncollege-prep track). And it is during this process of track assignment that we can begin to obtain an understanding of how correlates such as race, gender, and ethnicity may influence the placement decision. As an illustration, Schafer and Olexa observed that, even controlling for "ability" (i.e., IQ and previous achievement), low-income students and blacks were more apt to be situated in the basic or noncollege-prep tracks. And such students, once placed, will be required to align their attitudes and behaviors with the existing normative/subcultural system. Demanded conformity and subsequent socialization may — in terms of the particular *content* of the values of a normative system — require the commission of illegal, deviant, or criminal acts. We conclude by describing how, in structural-organizational terms (e.g., doing away with student stratification systems), school crime can be reduced. We also emphasize the need for moving beyond the rather strict fascination with notions of individual pathology to a broad investigation of the structural roots of such crime. Many of the observations and notions contained in this article, I should add, have direct relevance for the study of crime in general, and I will be applying them in many places throughout this book.

At this point, and prior to moving into Part 3, it must be recognized that not only are many of the traditional correlates of crime important in the production of crime, but as suggested especially by the Kelly-Pink article, they must be conceptualized, both analytically and empirically, as operating in rather specified ways. In this model, selection factors such as race, class, gender, ethnicity, and so on, become *mediated* through organizational structures; this further suggests that attempts to understand the rise of criminal behavior should, as an initial and basic requirement, locate and describe the underlying organizational structure of all of those institutions invested with a mandate for the identifying and processing of clients. The existing organizational apparatus thus becomes the *backdrop* against which interactions can be analyzed, evaluated, and assessed. This necessary focus on the institutional identifying and processing of clients gives us a more solid footing from which to examine how a body of statistics is organizationally produced, and it also provides us with a context that can be used to analyze how criminal careers and identities are created, perpetuated, and perhaps, ultimately, transformed.

4. The Size of the "Criminal Population": The Prevalence and Incidence of Adult Arrest*

ROBERT TILLMAN

Recent longitudinal studies of criminal careers have drawn attention to the existence of what are referred to as "chronic offenders" or "career criminals" who appear to contribute disproportionately to the crime rate. The well-known finding of Wolfgang, Figlio, and Sellin (1972) that among a birth cohort of young males in Philadelphia 6% of the cohort was responsible for over half of the cohort's total "police contacts" has become a benchmark for subsequent studies of criminal careers. The findings from these studies have led to an increasingly wide acceptance of the premise, stated succinctly by Boland, that "crime rates are high not because large numbers of people commit one or two crimes in a lifetime but because a relatively small number of people are habitual offenders" (Boland, 1980: 94).[1]

   This premise is also reflected in a recent shift in criminological theory away from social structural explanations and towards more reductionist, individual-level theories of the etiology of crime and delinquency. This shift in thinking is evident in the recent works of several well-known criminologists including Wilson who, with Herrnstein, has argued that "the causes of crime lie in a combination of predisposing biological traits channeled by social circumstance into criminal behavior" (Herrnstein and Wilson, 1985: 31). The much-publicized Rand study of selective incapacitation (Greenwood, 1982) also lends tacit support to this perspective. While not strictly concerned with explaining the sources of all criminal behavior, the authors focused on offender's employment history, drug use, and prior juvenile convictions as indicators of future criminal behavior and recommended policies that explicitly weigh these factors in imposing sentences. The implication in both works is that the roots of serious crime are to be found in the individual personalities, constitutions, and circumstances of small groups of "chronic offenders," not in the social structural factors that affect large numbers of potential law breakers.

   Despite the contributions of recent studies to this issue, the empirical grounds for conclusions regarding the concentration of criminality among "chronic offenders" remain tenuous. These studies have fallen short of adequately answering two questions central to theoretical explanations of crime: first, how many persons will at some point in their lives become involved in crime and, second, for those who do become involved, how often will they commit criminal acts? The importance of these questions for an understanding of the etiology of crime lies in the fact that if crime is indeed concentrated among a relatively small group of repeat offenders, then the origins of criminal behavior may well reside in the "constitutional factors" (Wilson and Herrnstein, 1985) that individual-level theories focus on. On the other hand, the widespread participation in crime by large numbers of persons in the general population, or within specific sociodemographic subpopulations, would require a macro-structural theory of deviance for an adequate explanation. Answering these empirical questions will not completely resolve these theoretical issues, but either type of theory must be able to account for observed patterns of criminality within the general population.

The findings of several recent studies showing the concentration of crime among small groups of offenders have been limited by a number of methodological factors, notably sampling designs, that prohibit the application of their results to the general population. The majority of longitudinal studies have focused on samples taken from a single jurisdiction (Wolfgang et al., 1972; Shannon, 1982) or have drawn their samples from populations of prison inmates (Chaiken and Chaiken, 1982; Greenwood, 1982). Cross-sectional studies, based on self-report data, have tended to focus on juveniles. All of these sampling designs exclude from their analyses large numbers of offenders within the general population and thus prevent an adequate answer to basic questions concerning the distribution of criminality within American society.

In an effort to overcome the methodological limitations encountered by previous research, the present study employs a recently developed longitudinal data base to estimate the distribution of arrests among young adults. The analysis indirectly addresses Boland's (above) assertion by answering the question: are adult arrests concentrated among a small group of habitual offenders or are arrest rates largely the product of one- or two-time offenders? To do this, the prevalence of arrest—defined as the number of persons ever arrested—among a cohort of males and females between the ages of 18 and 29 is estimated. Next, the incidence of arrest—the number of arrests incurred by those persons ever arrested—is estimated. Based on these estimates of incidence, the contributions of "chronic offenders" to the aggregate arrest rate are then calculated.

While the data employed in this study are innovative, the results should be interpreted in relation to the findings of previous studies. Therefore, the discussion next turns to a brief review of previous work in this area.

PREVIOUS RESEARCH

Prior to the publication of Wolfgang et al.'s *Delinquency in a Birth Cohort*, estimates of the prevalence of criminality in the United States were based largely on aggregate arrest and court data.[2] Studies of incidence were most often studies of recidivism among samples of former correctional inmates. The Philadelphia study was the first to provide measures of the prevalence of delinquency within the general population of juveniles and the rates of recidivism for those with recorded "police contacts." It was this latter measure that garnered the most attention from criminologists and policy makers, for with it Wolfgang and his colleagues were able to demonstrate that individual rates of criminality varied considerably and to argue that a relatively small portion of all "delinquents" was responsible for a large portion of all reported crimes. Their data show that 6% of the total birth cohort, or 18% of those with a "police contact," were responsible for 51% of the cohort's total number of "police contacts." The presence of these repeat offenders, termed "chronic offenders," was documented in a second cohort born in 1958, where they comprised only 7.5% of the cohort's male members but accounted for 61% of the total "police contacts" among the males in the cohort (Tracy, Wolfgang, and Figlio, 1985). A follow-up study of a 10% sample of the 1945 cohort followed their criminal careers to age 30 and found that by that age, 47% of the original cohort had incurred at least one "police contact" and 22% had been arrested for one of the serious crimes known as an index offense (Wolfgang, 1983: 77; Petersilia, 1980: 342–345).

A similar cohort study conducted by Shannon (1982) recorded the number of "police contacts" among three cohorts of males and females in Racine, Wisconsin. The oldest cohort, born in 1942, was followed to age 32. By that age, 57% of the males had at least one recorded "police contact" (excluding traffic offenses, status offenses, and suspicion arrests), and 8% had been arrested for a felony offense (Petersilia, 1980: 342–345).

Both the Philadelphia and the Racine studies were limited by the fact that their results for adults were based on relatively small samples drawn from single jurisdictions.[3] By contrast, Blumstein and Graddy (1981–82) have presented estimates of the prevalence and incidence of index arrest among urban males in one of the few attempts to calculate the distribution of criminality among large segments of the adult population. Based on a variety of data sets (including the Philadelphia study), they estimated that one in four urban males is at some point arrested for an index offense – defined in their study as murder, rape, robbery, burglary, aggravated assault, larceny-theft, motor vehicle theft, and arson. The differences between blacks and whites, in their calculations, were startling. They estimated that 51% of all urban black males, as opposed to 14% of all urban white males, are arrested at least once for an index offense. Sophisticated as their methods may have been, however, the validity of Blumstein and Graddy estimates rests on a number of assumptions about the compatibility of the various data sets they employed. Combining arrest histories for 971 males under the age of 30 from Philadelphia with the arrest histories of 5,364 males over 30 years of age from Washington, D.C., and extrapolating those findings to all urban areas in the U.S. raises a number of methodological questions. Aside from these issues, their results are confined to males living in urban areas who are arrested for index offenses, and thus exclude females, less serious offenders, and persons living in nonurban areas.

These and other studies that estimate the prevalence of arrest among both juveniles and adults have recently been surveyed in a report to the National Academy of Sciences on criminal careers (Blumstein, Cohen, Roth, and Visher, 1986). That review led to the conclusion that "the most striking finding about criminal participation is the pervasiveness of involvement in serious crimes" (Visher and Roth, 1986: 287). Taken together, the results of previous studies indicate that among urban males, 60% will have been arrested (or have a recorded "police contact") for a nontraffic offense and 25% will be arrested for an index offense at some point during their lifetimes. As the authors note, however, these estimates are based on data that are historically as well as geographically limited and may not apply to other places and other points in time (Visher and Roth, 1986: 290).

DATA AND METHODS

Overcoming the limitations in previous analyses requires a longitudinal data base of criminal histories, for both males and females, drawn from the general population in a large number of diverse jurisdictions. Until recently, such a data base did not exist. The Adult Criminal Justice Statistics System (ACJSS) longitudinal file, created by the California Bureau of Criminal Statistics, meets these requirements and allows one to accurately estimate the distribution of adult arrests. The ACJSS data base consists of the criminal histories of persons whose first adult (18 years or older) arrest in California occurred in 1973 or later. The data trace each individual's history from first to last (or most recent) reported arrest. The file contains information on arrests for all "retainable offenses" – both misdemeanors and felonies – and their dispositions.[4] Because the file consists of the adult arrest histories of persons whose first reported California arrest occurred in 1973 or later, it includes, by definition, the criminal histories of all persons in certain age groups who were arrested as adults in California. Thus, it contains the arrest records for all persons, born in 1956, who were later arrested in California between the years 1974 and 1985.

At the outset it must be recognized that the application of the present findings to the question of the concentration of criminality is limited by at least two factors. First, arrests cannot simply be used as proxy measures of crime; the well-known problems of underreporting and changing recording practices by law enforcement agencies prevent such an interpretation of the data. Yet, previous research (Hindelang, 1978, 1981) has demonstrated that arrest data do provide rough, and undoubtedly conservative, measures of the involvement of individuals in criminal activities. Second, by excluding arrests for juveniles and those adults over age 29, the analysis cannot address questions of the prevalence and incidence over a lifetime. Nonetheless, since a large proportion of all arrests are of persons in the 18-to-30 age bracket, the analysis provides reasonable estimates of the distribution of arrests among those persons responsible for a large proportion of crime in the United States.

Using the ACJSS longitudinal data, this analysis will estimate the *prevalence* and *incidence* of arrest among a cohort of adults born in 1956. The analysis addresses three main questions: (1) what portion of young adults in California are arrested (prevalence), (2) for those arrested, how many arrests do they incur (incidence), and (3) how many arrests are "chronic offenders" responsible for?

THE PREVALENCE OF ARREST

To measure the prevalence of arrest the researchers took advantage of the fact that the ACJSS file indicates the age at first arrest for each individual in the file. By counting the first arrests of persons born in 1956 for successive years, 1974–1985,

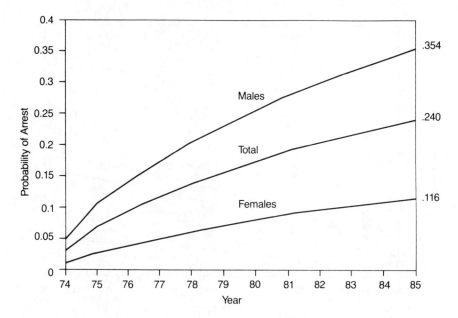

Figure 1.   Cumulative Probability of Arrest Total, Males and Females, 1974–1985

researchers were able to calculate the age at first arrest for a cohort of persons who were 18 years old in 1974. Each year's sum total of first arrestees was then divided by the number of persons in the total population who were the same age. That measure indicated what proportion of the 1956 age cohort was arrested for the first time in each successive year following 1974. In order to show the increasing probability of adult arrest for the Population Cohort, each year's totals were summed and transformed into cumulative probabilities. Using this technique, the probability of arrest over a 12-year period for all 18-year-olds living in California in 1974 was estimated.

It should be emphasized that the prevalence of arrest is estimated among an artificially created age cohort, not an actual age cohort. Were it not for in and out migration, the procedure would track the arrest experiences of a true cohort. However, because of migration into and out of the state, the composition of the at-risk population changes over time; an individual's first California arrest may not represent his or her first-ever arrest, since he or she may have been arrested in another state before migrating to California. Similarly, individuals leaving the state may have no California arrests but may incur an arrest elsewhere. Calculations of the potential bias caused by migration indicate that migration rates for the target population would have to be unrealistically high to significantly distort the estimates provided here. Nonetheless, the reader is cautioned to be aware of the potential error caused by these factors that the model cannot control for.[5]

Using the technique described above, the probability of arrest for an age cohort of 18-year-olds was estimated. The 1974 18-year-old population in California is estimated at 435,438. The cumulative probabilities displayed in Figure 1 show that 24%

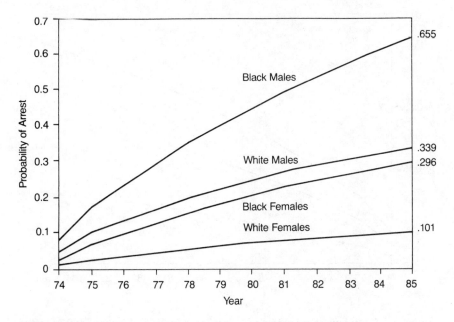

Figure 2.   Cumulative Probability of Arrest, Black and White Males and Females, 1974–1985

of the cohort experienced at least one arrest during the 12-year period 1974–1985. As previous research on age and crime would predict, most of those "first arrests" came in the early years of adulthood; 57% of those ever arrested as adults were arrested for the first time between the ages of 18 and 22. Also as one would expect, significant differences in the likelihood of arrest were evident between males and females. Thirty-five percent of the males as compared with 11% of the females were arrested.

When these data are disaggregated by race, dramatic differences are revealed. For this analysis, race was dichotomized as black and white, with Hispanics (an "ethnicity" category) included within the white category.[6] Figure 2 shows that white females had the lowest probability of arrest with one-tenth (10.1%) arrested during the period. Black males, by contrast, had a very high probability of arrest; nearly two-thirds (65.5%) were arrested at least once by the end of 1985. Interestingly, despite the differences in their social circumstances, white males and black females showed similar rates of prevalence—33.9% versus 29.6%, respectively.

Taken together, the data displayed in Figures 1 and 2 indicate that being arrested was not an uncommon experience among young adults in California in the 1970s and early 1980s. In fact, within some groups, the majority of persons could expect to be arrested at some point in the first 12 years of their adult lives. Even among that group with the lowest aggregate rates of arrest—white females—one out of ten was arrested at least once.

Many of the arrests in the above data were for relatively minor misdemeanor offenses or "victimless" crimes such as drug possession. Most research on "chronic

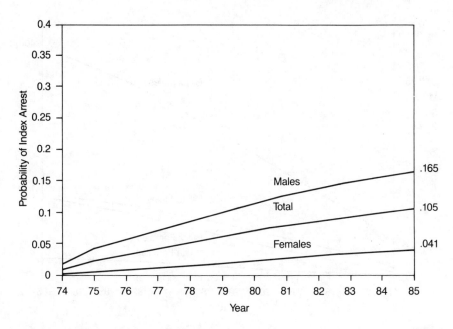

Figure 3. Cumulative Probability of Index Arrest Total, Males and Females, 1974–1985

offenders," however, is concerned with the more serious offenses referred to as Part I or index offenses. Arrests for these offenses—in this analysis, murder, manslaughter (nonvehicular), rape, robbery, burglary, felony assault (excluding simple assault), felony theft/larceny, and motor vehicle theft[7]—were isolated and prevalence rates were calculated, as displayed in Figures 3 and 4. While certainly less prevalent than arrests for all offenses, index arrests were surprisingly common among the age cohort. As Figure 3 indicates, one out of ten (10.5%) members of the group was arrested and charged with an index crime. Among males, one out of six (16.5%) was arrested for one of these offenses. Translated into absolute numbers, this means that approximately 37,644 of the estimated 228,148 males in the original age cohort were arrested for a serious felony offense between the ages of 18 and 29.

More dramatic variations are observed in Figure 4 where race and gender differences are compared. While only 3% of the white females were arrested for an index offense, fully 40% percent of the black males were estimated to have been arrested for one of these offenses between the ages of 18 and 29. Even considering the potential for error created by undercounts of black males in the population data,[8] the magnitude of this rate is startling given the severity of these offenses. Startling as this figure might be, however, it is not inconsistent with the estimates made by Blumstein and Graddy (1981–82).

In sum, whatever the contributions of "chronic offenders" to the crime rate, the ACJSS data reveal that the phenomenon of arrest is not limited to a small group of offenders, but is widely distributed throughout the population of young adults, albeit with extreme, but expected, differences in the likelihood of arrest experienced by

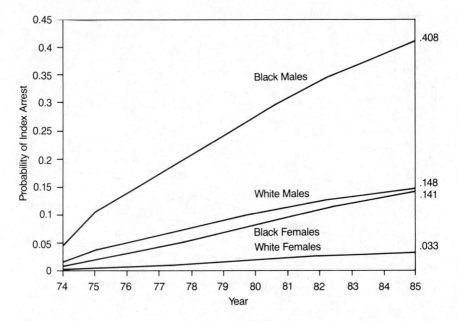

Figure 4. Cumulative Probability of Index Arrest, Black and White Males and Females, 1974–1985

various subgroups. Even with these relatively high rates of prevalence, however, arrests might still be concentrated among repeat offenders who, over time, contribute disproportionately to aggregate arrest rates. Determining the extent of this concentration requires an estimate of the incidence of arrest among the cohort.

THE INCIDENCE OF ARREST

Calculating the incidence of arrest—defined as the number of subsequent arrests for those members of the age cohort ever arrested during the period—is a fairly straightforward procedure. The arrest histories for all persons in the ACJSS file born in 1956 and arrested between 1974 and 1985 were selected and their total number of arrests during the period tabulated.

With these data on recidivism, the researchers were able to calculate the proportion of one-time offenders among the arrestee population. It should be noted that the category "one-time offender" is being applied here to persons in the cohort with a single recorded arrest and no subsequent arrests after December 31, 1985. It is likely that some of these individuals were or will be arrested after that point in time and thus the proportion of "one-time offenders" estimated here would be smaller if calculated over the individuals' lifetimes.

The proportions for the various recidivist subgroups within the arrestee population are displayed in Table 1. For all arrestees, the chance of a subsequent arrest was almost one in two; 45.9% of the arrestees were rearrested by the end of 1985. While

Table 1.   Incidence of Arrest

	One Arrest (%)	Multiple Arrests (%)	Mean	Median
All Arrests				
White Males	52.3	47.7	2.7	.95
Black Males	39.7	60.3	4.0	1.47
White Females	67.0	33.0	2.1	.75
Black Females	52.9	47.1	3.1	.94
Total	54.1	45.9	2.7	.92
Index Arrests				
White Males	62.5	37.5	2.0	.80
Black Males	47.9	52.1	2.8	1.11
White Females	74.4	25.6	1.6	.73
Black Females	66.1	33.9	1.9	.76
Total	62.3	36.7	2.1	.80

recidivism rates are clearly affected by race and gender, the magnitude of the differences between those groups is not as great as the differences in prevalence rates. Among males, 40% of the blacks and 52% of the whites were one-time arrestees. Similar differences are observed for females.

Despite the relatively large number of one-time arrestees, the mean number of arrests was 2.7, reflecting the presence of a substantial number of offenders with numerous arrests over the period. Similarly, differences in the mean number of arrests for blacks and whites are strongly influenced by small numbers of blacks at the upper end of the arrest distribution. These differences are greatly reduced when the medians for all groups are compared.

As one would expect, recidivism rates for index offenses are lower than for all offenses. The bottom half of Table 1 shows that of those members of the age cohort arrested for an index offense, less than two-fifths were rearrested for another index offense by the end of 1985 (although nonrecidivists may have been arrested for a nonindex offense). Here, again, differences between blacks and whites are not dramatic, at least when compared with prevalence rates. Among males who were ever arrested, 62% of the whites and almost 48% of the blacks were one-time arrestees. Combining this finding with earlier estimates of prevalence confirms the earlier estimates of Blumstein and Graddy (1981–82) that the differences in the aggregate rates of index arrest between young adult blacks and whites is largely the result of higher probabilities of arrest for blacks and not higher rates of recidivism.

CHRONIC OFFENDERS

To determine the contribution of "chronic offenders," one needs to know more about the concentration of arrests within the total population of arrestees. Arranging the data on incidence in a cumulative format, one may ask: of the total number of arrests

Table 2. Concentration of Arrests

Arrestees with x or More Arrests	Comprised Percent and Number of Arrestees		Accounted for Percent and Number of Total Arrests	
All Arrests	%	n	%	n
1	100.0	110,475	100.0	301,344
2	45.9	50,713	80.2	241,582
3	28.3	31,240	67.2	202,636
4	19.6	21,599	57.6	173,173
5	14.5	15,988	50.2	151,269
6	11.2	12,421	44.3	133,434
7	8.9	9,886	39.2	118,224
8	7.3	8,034	34.9	105,260
9	5.9	6,558	31.0	93,452
10	4.9	5,393	27.5	81,967
Index Arrests				
1	100.0	49,227	100.0	101,095
2	37.7	18,552	69.7	70,420
3	20.7	10,181	53.1	53,678
4	13.4	6,606	42.5	42,953
5	9.1	4,503	34.2	34,541
6	6.4	3,172	27.6	27,886
7	4.9	2,305	22.4	22,684
8	3.5	1,707	18.3	18,498
9	2.5	1,251	14.7	14,850
10	1.9	916	11.7	11,835

incurred by the members of the age cohort over the 12-year period, how many were "chronic offenders" responsible for? The definition of a "chronic offender" is not fixed. However, a reasonable starting point is with Wolfgang et al.'s criterion of five or more police contacts. Table 2 indicates that 14% of the arrestees (those members of the age cohort arrested at least once) were "chronic offenders" and that they accounted for 50.2% of the group's total arrests. Conversely, "one-time" offenders, that 54.1% of the group with only one arrest, accounted for only 19.8% of all the arrests. It would appear, then, that a relatively small group of offenders is responsible for a highly disproportionate share of all adult arrests.

One should bear in mind, however, that Wolfgang et al.'s "chronic offenders" were those with five or more "police contacts" and that, for the entire cohort, less than 40% of these "police contacts" resulted in a formal arrest (Wolfgang et al., 1972: 219). Thus, the criterion for "chronic offenders" might reasonably be lowered to three or more arrests. Under this definition, the data in Table 2 indicate that 28.3% of those ever arrested during the period could be designated as "chronic offenders," and they accounted for 67% of the group's total arrests. The significance of these numbers can perhaps best be appreciated when expressed in terms of absolute numbers. Among a population of 435,488 18-year-olds (in 1974), it is estimated that 24%, or 104,505, would be arrested at least once before they turned 30 years of age. Of these, 28%, or 29,261, eventually became "chronic offenders." Thus, applying these definitions of chronicity to the population of all young adult arrestees reveals the presence of a group of "chronic offenders" who contribute disproportionately to the arrest rate, but their numbers are much larger than has previously been recognized.

Table 2 also displays the results from the same analysis of index offenses only. Those data show that index arrests were less concentrated among repeat offenders than were all arrests. Among those members of the age cohort ever arrested for an index offense, over 60% were not rearrested for an index offense before they turned 30 years of age. That group of "one-time offenders" was responsible for 30% of all index arrests. Slightly over half (53%) of all index arrests were incurred by those persons with three or more index arrests, a group comprising 20 percent of the subcohort of persons with index arrests. That relatively small group (9%) of offenders with five or more index arrests was responsible for 34% of the group's total number of index arrests.

These results suggest that while index arrests are spread unevenly among arrestees, the levels of concentration of serious arrests among small groups of offenders discovered by Wolfgang and his colleagues are not in evidence here. These differences could be due to the different responses by the criminal justice system to the juveniles studied by Wolfgang and the adults under study here. The system may respond much more harshly to adults convicted of serious crimes, incarcerating them for relatively long periods of time, thereby reducing their time "at risk" for future arrests. First- and second-time juvenile offenders may receive much more lenient sentences, allowing them to incur more arrests in the future.

IMPLICATIONS

This study was undertaken with an interest in comparing common assumptions, both lay and expert, regarding the size of the "criminal population," the dimensions of which are crucial to current debates concerning the role of "chronic offenders" in the production of aggregate crime rates. If that population is defined in terms of arrest (recognizing the difference between crimes and arrests), then the estimates obtained in this analysis show that population to be very large indeed. Nearly one-quarter of all persons, over one-third of all males, and almost two-thirds of all black males in an age cohort of 18-year-olds in California were arrested at least once before they were 30 years old. Apparently, getting arrested and obtaining a criminal record are not limited to small groups of "criminals" but are common experiences for many young adults in California.

The data on recidivism — referred to here as the "incidence" of arrest — shed light on the contributions of "chronic offenders" to aggregate arrest rates. The analysis did locate a group of repeat offenders whose numerous arrests over the 12-year period added disproportionately to the cohort's total number of arrests. However, the size of this subgroup of repeat offenders may be much larger than previously thought. While the analysis can only provide estimates and not precise numbers, it appears that approximately 7% of the 435,438 18-year-olds in California in 1974 were arrested three or more times before they turned 30. If this proportion remains constant over the years, this means that, annually, California's criminal justice system must absorb 29,000 new "chronic offenders." These facts suggest the limits that a strict incapacitation policy would face in a state where approximately 17,000 new felons are committed to an over-crowded prison system every year.

It might be argued, from a policy perspective, that incapacitation focuses on more serious offenders, whose numbers are much smaller than the "all arrests" figures indicate, since many of those included in those estimates were arrested for relatively minor offenses. It is true that when only index offenses are counted, the number of "chronic offenders" is reduced significantly. Table 2 shows that a little over 10,000 of those members of the age cohort arrested for an index offense were arrested three or more times for index offenses. However, the main problem for incapacitation policies lies in determining which offenders, out of all potential candidates, will go on to repeat their crimes. The fact that 60% of the index arrestees were one-time offenders makes this task all the more difficult. Furthermore, the data on incidence do not reflect a bimodal distribution that clearly differentiates between one-time arrestees and those with large numbers of arrests. The relatively smooth decline in the number of arrestees with increasingly large numbers of index arrests suggests that it may be difficult to make sharp distinctions between low-rate and high-rate offenders.

It should be recognized that these findings regarding the relative contributions of chronic offenders to the arrest and crime rates are suggestive rather than conclusive. The analysis is limited to recidivism by age 29. It is possible that among the cohort studied, a small proportion of offenders continued to commit crimes at high rates after the age of 29, representing, as others have argued (Blumstein and Cohen, 1979), an ideal target group for selective incapacitation. The existence of such a group and the consequences of their incarceration are by no means settled matters (Gottfredson and Hirschi, 1986) and will undoubtedly be the topics of future empirical work. Despite these limitations, the findings presented here make it clear that chronic offenders and their criminal activities must be viewed within the broader context of all offenders and the total distribution of offenses.

Notes

*The research for this study was made possible by a fellowship from the California Attorney General's Office, California Department of Justice. The opinions, findings, and conclusions are the author's and do not necessarily reflect those of the Department of Justice.

1. At least one prominent policy maker has accepted this premise. Consider the following statement by a former head of the Office of Juvenile Justice and Delinquency Prevention (Regnery, 1985):

> The bulk of our crime—probably 75 percent of all serious offenses—is committed by someone like our profiled youngster. Known as chronic offenders, these people comprise fewer than 10 percent of the population. . . . Yet because of the high rate at which they commit felonies. . .they

are responsible for a great proportion of robberies, burglaries, muggings and aggravated assaults, car thefts, rapes, and even a significant number of murders.

2. Most earlier studies used a "lifetable technique," similar to the method used here, to estimate prevalence rates. Monahan (1960) used the age at first juvenile court appearance in Philadelphia to calculate the likelihood of at least one court appearance by age 18. Ball, Ross, and Simpson (1964) utilized a similar methodology to estimate that in 1960, 20.7% of the boys and 5.2% of the girls in Lexington, Kentucky, had appeared in juvenile court. In a report to the President's Commission on Law Enforcement and the Administration of Justice, Christensen (1967) combined juvenile court data from Philadelphia with data on age-specific first-adult-arrest rates from Washington, D.C., to estimate that 50% of all U.S. males and 12% of all females would be arrested (for nontraffic offenses) during their lifetimes.

3. The results of Wolfgang's follow-up of the 1945 cohort to age 30 have not yet been made available in a form that allows one to focus exclusively on adult arrests. Likewise, descriptions of the adult careers of the oldest Racine cohort (tracked to age 32) are not available in a published form.

4. Retainable offenses consist of most felonies and misdemeanors in which defendants are booked and fingerprinted. The major offenses excluded are driving under the influence of drugs or alcohol, public drunkenness (unless under the influence of drugs), possession of not more than 28.5 grams of marijuana, violations of local ordinances, and offenses for which incarceration is not a possible punishment. Also excluded are incidents in which individuals are detained but not formally booked.

5. The biases introduced by in and out migration on cohort studies of crime and delinquency are discussed by Gordon (1976).

6. In the data used in this report, "Hispanics" could have been separated from "white-not-Hispanics" and it would have been very useful to do so. However, audits conducted by the Bureau of Criminal Statistics have discovered that "Hispanics" are frequently miscoded by law enforcement agencies as "white-not-Hispanic" on their fingerprint cards and therefore appear as "white-not-Hispanic" in the ACJSS data. One audit found that for a random sample of arrests occurring in 1980, 21% of the Hispanics were coded as "white-not-Hispanic." For this reason, in this analysis Hispanics were included in the "white" category. Technically, this is correct since "Hispanic" is an ethnicity code that can be attached to either a "white" or a "black" racial code.

7. This categorization differs somewhat from the FBI's definition of index offenses, which includes arson and *all* thefts and larcenies. In California, felony-level arrests for theft and larceny must involve amounts of $200 or more, prior to 1983, and in 1983 or later, amounts of $400 or more. Thus excluded are most petty thefts, except those charged as a felony where a prior conviction is charged. Arson was excluded because that offense was not included in the FBI's list of index crimes until 1979.

8. The U.S. Census Bureau has estimated that the census systematically undercounts adult black males. The Census Bureau estimates that the 1980 census data undercount 18-year-old, black males by 1% and the level of undercounting increases steadily for each year of age so that 29-year-old, black males are undercounted by 12% (Passel, Siegel, and Robinson, 1982). This problem is discussed in more detail in Tillman (1987).

References

Ball, John, Alan Ross, and Alice Simpson
    1964   Incidence and estimated prevalence of recorded delinquency in a metropolitan area. American Sociological Review 29: 90–93.
Blumstein, Alfred and Jacqueline Cohen
    1979   Estimation of individual crime rates from arrest records. Journal of Criminal Law and Criminology 70: 561–585.

Blumstein, Alfred, Jacqueline Cohen, Jeffrey Roth, and Christy Visher (Eds.)
  1986   Criminal Careers and "Career Criminals." Washington, D.C.: National Academy
          Press.
Blumstein, Alfred and Elizabeth Graddy
  1981   Prevalence and recidivism in index arrests: A feedback model. Law and Soci-
  –82   ety Review 16: 265–290.
Boland, Barbara
  1980   Fighting crime: The problem of adolescents. Journal of Criminal Law and Crimi-
          nology 71: 91–97.
Chaiken, Jan and Marcia Chaiken
  1982   Varieties of Criminal Behavior. Santa Monica: Rand.
Christensen, Ronald
  1967   Projected Percentage of U.S. Population with Criminal Arrest and Conviction
          Records. In President's Commission on Law Enforcement and Administration of
          Justice, Task Force Report: Science and Technology. Washington, D.C.: U.S.
          Government Printing Office.
Gordon, Robert
  1976   Prevalence: The rare datum in delinquency measurement and its implications for
          the theory of delinquency. In M. Klein (ed.), The Juvenile Justice System. Beverly
          Hills: Sage.
Gottfredson, Michael and Travis Hirschi
  1986   The true value of lambda would appear to be zero. Criminology 24: 213–234.
Greenwood, Peter
  1982   Selective Incapacitation. Santa Monica: Rand.
Herrnstein, Richard and James Q. Wilson
  1985   Are criminals made or born? New York Times Magazine (August 4).
Hindelang, Michael
  1978   Race and the involvement in common law personal crime. American Sociological
          Review 43: 93–109.
  1981   Variations in sex-race-age-specific incidence rates of offending. American Socio-
          logical Review 46: 461–474.
Monahan, Thomas
  1960   On the incidence of delinquency. Social Forces 39: 66–72.
Passel, Jeffrey, Jacob Siegel, and Gregory Robinson
  1982   Coverage of the National Population in the 1980 Census, by Age, Sex and Race.
          Bureau of the Census. Washington, D.C.: U.S. Government Printing Office.
Petersilia, Joan
  1980   Criminal career research: A review of recent evidence. In Norval Morris and
          Michael Tonry (eds.), Crime and Justice: An Annual Review of Research, Vol. 2.
          Chicago: University of Chicago Press.
Regnery, Alfred
  1985   Getting away with murder: Why the juvenile justice system needs an overhaul.
          Policy Review 34: 1–4.
Shannon, Lyle
  1982   Assessing the Relationship of Adult Criminal Careers to Juvenile Careers: A Sum-
          mary. Rockville, MD: Office of Juvenile Justice and Delinquency Prevention.
Tillman, Robert
  1987   The Prevalence and Incidence of Arrest Among Adult Males in California.
          Sacramento: California Bureau of Criminal Statistics.
Tracy, Paul, Marvin Wolfgang, and Robert Figlio
  1985   Delinquency in Two Birth Cohorts: Executive Summary. Rockville, MD: Office of
          Juvenile Justice and Delinquency Prevention.
Visher, Christy and Jeffrey Roth
  1986   Participation in criminal careers. In Alfred Blumstein, Jacqueline Cohen, and

Christy Visher (eds.), Criminal Careers and "Career Criminals." Washington, D.C.: National Academy Press.

Wilson, James Q. and Richard Herrnstein
1985   Crime and Human Nature. New York: Simon and Schuster.
Wolfgang, Marvin
1983   Delinquency in two birth cohorts. American Behavioral Scientist 27: 75–86.
Wolfgang, Marvin, Robert Figlio, and Thorstein Sellin
1972   Delinquency in a Birth Cohort. Chicago: University of Chicago Press.

5. Uniform Crime Reports as Organizational Outcomes: Three Time Series Experiments*

RICHARD McCLEARY, BARBARA C. NIENSTEDT, AND JAMES M. ERVEN

The oldest, most comprehensive source of crime statistics in the United States is the Uniform Crime Reports (UCRs), published annually by the Federal Bureau of Investigation. UCRs are not the only source of crime statistics, nor are they more valid or reliable than alternative statistics. The shortcomings of UCRs as measures of "real" crime have been widely noted. UCRs ignore crimes which do not fit neatly into established "index" categories, for example, as well as crimes which are not reported to local police agencies (Hindelang, 1976; Skogan, 1974, 1976). Federal, state, and local governments nevertheless rely heavily on UCRs to monitor crime control programs; when politicians complain that crime rates are up or brag that crime rates are down, they invariably mean that UCR crime rates are up or down. UCRs in this most important sense represent the *status quo*: they provide the official crime statistics for most U.S. cities and states.

This paper examines organizational structures which threaten the validity of UCRs, a problem which has been referred to as the "production of crime rates" (Black, 1970; Maxfield et al., 1980). Kitsuse and Cicourel provide the best general statement of this problem:

> [Crime] rates can be viewed as indices of organizational processes rather than as indices of the incidence of certain forms of behavior. For example, variations in the rates of deviant behavior among a given group (e.g., Negroes) as reflected in the statistics of different organizations may be a product of the differing definitions of deviant behavior used by those organizations, differences in the processing of deviant behavior, differences in the, ideological, political, and other organizational conditions which affect the rate-making process (Kitsuse and Cicourel, 1963:137).

Two jurisdictions may thus have different UCR rates because of differences in real crime or, as Kitsuse and Cicourel suggest, because of differences in the way the jurisdictions process complaints.

Using an organizational theory model, "real" crime can be viewed as an input to the police department and UCRs as the output. The relationship between organizational structure and input-output chains could ordinarily be inferred from static cross-sectional designs or controlled experiments. Since "real" crime inputs are unknown, however, traditional cross-sectional analyses must be ruled out. And since researchers cannot ordinarily manipulate the structure of a police department, classical experiments must also be ruled out. The structures of police departments do change over time, of course, though not experimentally and usually not by conscious plan. These incidental or unplanned changes constitute a class of "natural experiments" (Campbell, 1969) which may be analyzed to reveal relationships between structural variables and the crime-UCR chain. In this paper we present the results of three such "natural experiments" which provide insight into this relationship. After describing the results of these three experiments, we develop a minimal theory of crime rates as organizational outcomes. Put simply, the official crime rate in a jurisdiction is a function of the organizational structure of the crime processing agency, that is, the local police department.

CASE ONE: INVESTIGATION AS A MEDIATING VARIABLE

We suggest that UCR rates are a function of the structural relationship between complaint investigators (detectives) and complaint processors (UCR coding clerks). Figure 1 shows monthly UCR burglaries in a major southwestern city (identified here only as "City A") from January 1975 to May 1981. Burglary complaints in City A were not normally investigated beyond the simple field reports filed by uniformed officers as part of the formal complaint procedure. For a 21-month period, however, all burglary complaints in City A were formally investigated by detectives. The level of the UCR burglary series dropped abruptly with the onset of this program and then rose abruptly with its termination. We conclude from this evidence that the program effectively reduced UCR burglaries in City A, but of course the reason for this reduction is unknown.

The two most obvious explanations for the reduction can be ruled out immediately. First, the program was expected to increase the rate of burglary "clearances." Had this goal been realized, one might expect an eventual reduction in burglaries but not the immediate reduction shown in Figure 1. A second, more cynical explanation—that the detectives reduced UCR burglaries by "cheating"—may also be ruled out. If this effect were due to a simple conspiracy, one would expect a coincidental effect on burglary clearances. Since clearances did not increase during this period, we can rule out both of these explanations.

A less obvious explanation is that the experimental program somehow changed the procedures by which burglary complaints become UCR burglaries. The three events which constitute complaint-processing are an official complaint taken from the victim by uniformed officers, an investigation by detectives, and a coding decision by UCR coding clerks. Under normal circumstances (i.e., before and after the experimental program), uniformed officers are dispatched to the scene of a burglary to take a formal

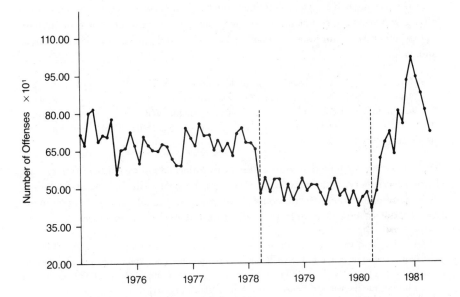

Figure 1.   Monthly UCR burglaries for City A from January 1975 to May 1981. The vertical dotted lines indicate onset and termination of an experimental program.

complaint from the victim. The uniformed officers conduct a *pro forma* investigation at that time, securing descriptions of stolen property, checking for physical evidence, and so forth. If the site investigation produces no investigative leads, which is ordinarily the case, there is no follow-up investigation by detectives.

The next event in the complaint-processing flow is a UCR coding decision. Coding decisions are made directly from the field reports filed by the uniformed officers at the scene. Our interviews with UCR coding clerks suggest that it is this aspect of complaint-processing which changed during the experimental program.[1] As it turns out, the field reports are unreliable. Errors fall into three common categories: definitional misunderstanding, discretion, and double-counting.

1) *Definitional misunderstanding*: The UCR burglary category has a complex definition. According to coding clerks, many complaint report errors were due to simple misunderstandings of this definition by uniformed officers:

> A burglary has the element of breaking and entering a *building*. In a lot of cases, the thief breaks through a fence and steals something. That's not a burglary, but a lot of officers don't know that. They code those as burglaries and if the report narrative isn't real clear, which is usually the case, I don't catch the mistake. An enclosed garage *is* a building but an open shed or a carport or a covered patio isn't. Officers don't like to show their ignorance by asking questions, I guess. If they're not sure what it is, they code it as a burglary (Interview: coding clerk).

Coding clerks agreed that misunderstanding of the burglary definition was the greatest source of error.

2) *Discretion*: UCR burglary definitions often require discretionary decisions of the officer who takes the complaint. Errors may be due to honest differences of opinion as to whether a structure was a garage or shed, a covered patio or an enclosed porch, and so forth.

> Here's a case where the building was under construction. The officer [who took the complaint] claimed it was a burglary and the detectives claimed it wasn't. There's not too much we can do here. I guess it depends on how far along the construction was. We don't know that and we don't have enough time to check it out, so we take the officer's word (Interview: coding clerk).

Discretion may be limited to some extent by the informal policies of beat supervisors. Some beat supervisors, for example, may reward officers who exercise discretion in order to minimize the burglary count. In all cases, discretion may be limited by the demands of victims. One uniformed officer described this contingency:

> You don't want to be the one who tells an irate citizen that they weren't burglarized. Citizens don't want to hear about [the UCR burglary definition]. They know they were burglarized and if you try to tell them different, they'll think you're trying to downgrade the crime. On a borderline decision, it's easiest to call it a [UCR burglary].

If time permits, the coding clerk may check the validity of the officer's decision. Discretion is discretion, however, so if the decision is not obviously a discrete error, it stands.

3) *Double-counting*: There are many circumstances which lead to double-counting of burglaries.[2] All of these circumstances involve the filing of two or more complaint errors. For example:

> Lots of times the victim doesn't know what was taken. A week later when they have a complete list of what was taken, they call up and ask to have an officer sent out. If an officer is dispatched, another report comes in here and the burglary gets counted again (Interview: coding clerk).

> If the original report doesn't call it a [UCR burglary], the insurance company won't pay off, but a lot of victims don't know that. When they find out, they want to change the report. That's not possible, of course. Once the report's filed, it's all over. So what they do is call the crime in again. We'll dispatch an officer and, in most cases, a new complaint report comes in here (Interview: coding clerk).

Few officers admitted deliberately filing redundant complaint reports. Victims who want to file a second complaint are not always forthright, so officers may not know that a complaint report has already been filed. But in some cases, depending on informal beat-level contingencies, officers may knowingly file redundant reports rather than argue with the victim.

There is no independent measure of these coding errors, but coding clerks reported finding several errors each day. All agreed that most errors were never caught. More important, each of these three types of errors inflates the UCR burglary rate.

Under the experimental program, the normal complaint-processing flow changed in two important respects. First, all burglary complaints were investigated. Second, investigations preceded UCR coding decisions and, as a result, errors in complaint reports were more likely to be corrected prior to the UCR coding decision. In simplest terms, the program re-ordered the flow of events by which complaints become UCRs. The program reduced the number of personnel filing complaint reports, making the policies on complaint reports more enforceable. Discretionary decisions and double-counting which inflate the UCR burglary rate were minimized. The personnel filing reports, moreover, were experts who appreciated the fine definitional distinctions between UCR burglary, UCR theft, vandalism, trespass, and so forth. Since errors tended to inflate the UCR burglary rate, restructuring of the process affected a reduction in UCR burglaries.

The experimental program also affected feedback from the detectives to the UCR coding bureau. Under normal circumstances, most burglary complaints are not investigated by detectives. Detectives review all burglary field reports, however, and bring errors to the attention of the UCR coding bureau:

> The [detective] sergeant calls me every three or four days with a list of revisions. I try to check them out. I don't always have time for that, so sometimes I have to let them pass. And a lot of them *can't* be checked out. If the original report says one thing and the sergeant says something else, I have to go with the original report. That's the rule and I can't break it (Interview: coding clerk).

When detectives discover errors during routine reviews, feedback follows the UCR coding decision by as much as a week. These later data do not have the practical weight as the original complaint report. More important, most of the feedback from detectives is aimed at correcting clearance counts and credits:

> No, there's no pressure from the detectives [to correct the UCR rate]. They're really not concerned about their UCR statistic. They're only interested in their clearance statistic. That's where I get what you might call "pressure" (Interview: coding clerk).

> Sometimes individual [detectives] call down to make sure they got credited with a case clearance. That's pretty common. They'll raise the roof if someone else gets credited [by mistake] (Interview: coding clerk).

Our interview data are consistent on this point: burglary detectives are more interested in clearances than in the UCR burglary rate. They have no incentive to make the UCR burglary rate more reliable or accurate.

Under normal circumstances, investigative feedback plays no role in the complaint-processing flow. Under the experimental program, on the other hand, investigative feedback became routine. Overall, each of these factors associated with the program increased the reliability of coding decisions, and the data in Figure 1 reflect this change. The level of the UCR burglary series dropped profoundly, but monthly variation (which, presumably, reflects unreliability in the reporting process) also decreased. Further, the drop in level for this time series was abrupt.[3] Since restructuring in this case was itself abrupt, this too is expected.

CASE TWO: HIERARCHICAL CONTROL

Crime rates are a function of the police department's internal goals (Seidman and Couzens, 1974). The ability of any department to realize its goals, however, is a function of hierarchical control. Figure 2 shows monthly UCR burglaries in City B, another large southwestern city, from January 1975 to May 1981. Until July 1979, this series follows a slight downward trend. Thereafter, the series rises dramatically. Total UCR burglaries for the last six months of 1979 was 20 percent higher than the total for the first six months.

The most obvious explanation for the increase in UCR burglaries shown in Figure 2 is that "real" crime increased correspondingly. But our data support another explanation. The onset of this UCR "crime wave" coincided with retirement of an incumbent police chief. The administrative shake-up which followed the retirement had a direct effect on the UCR coding bureau, with the results shown in Figure 2.

By all accounts, the incumbent chief had been considering retirement for several years. In early 1979, he was offered an executive position in state government. According to the state government official who recruited the chief for this position, a formal job offer was tendered in June 1979. A search of newspaper files during this period turned up no report of this recruitment process. When questioned about this discrepancy, the official explained that negotiations had necessarily been kept secret. Interviews with other government officials confirm not only the date, but also the agreement to keep the impending retirement a secret for as long as possible.

While news of the impending retirement was successfully withheld from the public until January 1980, department insiders learned of it almost immediately. The departmental chain of command includes five assistant chiefs who are not protected by civil service. Since these incumbents would be replaced by the incoming administration, the chief immediately informed them of his impending retirement. They in turn informed their subordinates and news of the retirement spread rapidly through the department.

In a study of "getting the crime rate down," Seidman and Couzens (1974) focused on the discretionary decisions of patrol officers. Given discretion at the street level, a police chief can "wish" crime rates down by rewarding district commanders who produce low UCR rates; they in turn can pass this "wish" down the ranks until it reaches the patrol officer. Hierarchical control of street-level discretion is essential to this process and, of course, four of the five incumbent assistant chiefs were replaced by the incoming administration. Because these positions were filled from within, the retirement had a "domino effect," resulting in as many as three dozen personnel changes at and above the rank of captain.

In this case, one need not focus on street-level discretion to explain the increase in official crime rates. The UCR coding bureau was not immune from the "domino effect." The coding bureau staff, three officers and four civilians, were supervised by a sergeant. The sergeant reported to the commander of the research and planning division who in turn reported to an assistant chief. The sergeant, commander, and assistant chief were all replaced in the administrative shake-up. Although these changes did not occur officially until late 1979 and early 1980, their impact on the routine operation of the UCR bureau was felt immediately:

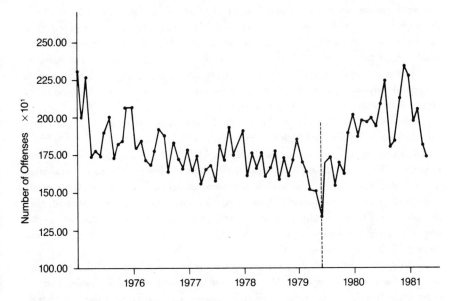

Figure 2.   Monthly UCR burglaries for City B from January 1975 to May 1981. The vertical dotted line indicates the month in which an incumbent chief resigned.

[The commander] wasn't here much during the summer [of 1979]. It was pretty well known that he was leaving the department in the fall. There was some talk that he was gone because he was out looking for a new job. I don't know if that was true or not, but he was gone quite a bit of the time. Even when he was here, he didn't spend as much time in the office as he usually did (Interview: coding clerk).

This point was verified in several interviews. The breakdown in hierarchical authority during the summer of 1979 had real implications for the coding of UCRs:

[The commander] was a perfectionist. He had a certain way of doing things and he demanded that you do it his way. Some of the [coding] guidelines he used were probably wrong. He knew that but he didn't care. If you didn't do things his way, he'd let you know about it. And if you were in doubt, you had to go to [the sergeant]. He'd go to [the commander] to find out the right way to do it (Interview: coding clerk).

As hierarchical authority disintegrated, the sergeant began to make decisions that had previously been made by the commander. When the sergeant was replaced a few months later, the disintegration process continued:

Not everyone was disappointed to see [the sergeant] go. For one thing, the work around here was more enjoyable with him gone. You have the opportunity to make some decisions on your own for a change. When he was in charge, you had to okay every minor decision with him (Interview: coding clerk).

Coding decisions for UCR burglaries are seldom made by mechanically applying written guidelines. As demonstrated in Case One, the field reports from which UCR coding decisions are made do not always make facts clear. Crimes that appear to fit the UCR burglary definition on the basis of field reports are often better categorized as "no crime," theft, vandalism, or trespass. Since UCR coding decisions always involve discretion, even a slight change in the decision-making process can result in a profound increase in a UCR rate. The increase shown in Figure 2 represents a change of only two or three UCR burglaries per day, well within the range one could expect from a slight change in the decision-making process.

The genesis of this "crime wave" is not unlike several others reported in the literature. In Chicago (Campbell, 1969; Glass et al., 1975), Kansas City (Guyot, 1976), and Washington, D.C. (Seidman and Couzens, 1974), changes in police department administrations led to changes in hierarchical authority. The precise nature of change in each case was idiosyncratic and, hence, unpredictable. Nevertheless, since crime rates were controlled by means of hierarchical authority, the changes in structure led to changes in UCR rates. Our findings are entirely consistent with the literature in this respect, although, as noted, we trace the cause not to street-level contingencies but directly to the UCR coding unit.

Analysis of this UCR burglary series uncovers an important aspect of this phenomenon. In Case One, complaint #7 processing was restructured abruptly, and we expected to find an abrupt drop in UCR burglaries. In Case Two, on the other hand, the time series did not change abruptly with the chief's retirement but, instead, increased gradually to reflect the gradual disintegration of a hierarchical authority structure. This is exactly the sort of effect one would expect.

CASE THREE: PROTECTION AND FRONT-END SCREENING

The literature describes two distinct types of "unreported" crime. The first type consists of crimes which, for whatever reason, citizens do not report to the police. Skogan (1976) estimates that over 50 percent of all serious crimes fall into this category. A second type of "unreported" crime consists of crimes which citizens report to the police but which, for whatever reason, the police refuse to treat as "real" crimes (Black, 1970; Waegel, 1981). The literature gives us no measure of the proportion of total crime which falls into this second category, but it is undoubtedly a significant proportion.

One obvious factor in this phenomenon is the nature of the initial dispatching action. Pepinsky (1976) has shown, for example, that patrol officers are most likely to report an incident as a crime when the dispatcher designates the call as crime (Maxfield, 1981). In light of this, we hypothesize that UCR rates are a function of dispatching routines and, in particular, that UCRs increase as dispatched "calls for service" increase. The interesting question, of course, is which organizational structures affect the rate at which citizen complaints are dispatched as "calls for service."

Figure 3 shows monthly "calls for service" dispatched by the City A police department. A "service call," for our purposes, is a citizen call for assistance which results in the dispatch of an officer to the scene. Any official crime (Part I UCR or otherwise) must begin with a "service call," but not all "service calls" result in an official crime.

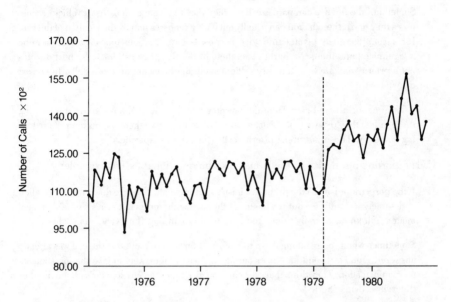

Figure 3. Monthly "calls for service" in City A from January 1975 to December 1980. The vertical dotted line indicates the month in which sergeants were removed from supervisory positions in the dispatch bureau.

If a call for police assistance does not result in the dispatch of an officer, the event is not a "service call." This is an important point because, clearly, a police department can increase or decrease its official crime rate by increasing or decreasing the likelihood that a call for assistance will result in a dispatched "service call."

Prior to April 1979, all shifts in the City A dispatch bureau were supervised by sergeants. Thereafter, sergeants were removed from most shifts. The result of this administrative change was an increase in the number of "service calls" dispatched and an increase in crime due to a decrease in "unreported" crime. Judging from the effect shown in Figure 3, the proportion of "unreported" crime in City A was relatively large, perhaps 20 percent or higher.

Our interpretation of this phenomenon rests on an understanding of the work performed by dispatchers. Dispatchers write records, answer telephones (sometimes), and, if necessary, dispatch officers to answer citizen calls for assistance.[4] Sending officers to the scene requires a decision, but only a small proportion of decisions involve real discretion. More than half of the calls to the dispatch bureau, for example, are "wrong numbers," such as requests for non-police services (sanitation, public health, etc.) and requests for general information. Other calls report threats to safety such as crimes in progress or public disturbances. The decision in both of these cases is obvious to the dispatcher.

In some cases, however, the dispatcher must exercise discretion. Some incidents, such as auto theft reports, may be crimes in a technical sense but are nevertheless questionable:

Sometimes the finance companies call us when they're going to repossess a vehicle. Sometimes they don't, though. You can usually tell if it's a repossession by the location of the call. If it's from [the ghetto], you can bet it's a repossession. . . . Sometimes it turns out to be a legitimate [auto theft]. No harm done, though, because they call back the next day. It's not a priority call anyway. You very seldom send an officer out on those calls (Interview: dispatcher).

A lot of cars get towed away from the downtown parking lots. You try to avoid answering those unless they're sure that it's not a tow-away. You can give them the number of the towing company. Those just aren't priority calls (Interview: dispatcher).

Calls reporting burglaries or thefts may also be questionable. For example:

If the perpetrator isn't on the premises, it isn't a priority call. You take down the information and sometimes you find out it's bogus. If they know the perpetrator, it's probably a civil matter. You know, a family thing. You have to tell them that (Interview: dispatcher).

Sometimes when you're taking down the information, you find out that the call was already answered. You can't send an officer out again. Usually they want to give the investigators more information. They think that's urgent. You give them the investigator's phone number (Interview: dispatcher).

There is no apparent threat to public safety in any of these examples. More important, these "crimes" are marginal, unimportant, or not serious. They are not "real" crimes in the eyes of police officers. This is an important aspect of the phenomenon. As uniformed officers, the sergeants made normal distinctions between "real" crimes and complaints that appeared not to be "real" crimes. The sergeants discouraged their dispatchers from sending officers to answer these calls. When the sergeants were removed from supervisory positions in the dispatch bureau, of course, dispatchers were no longer rewarded for making such distinctions. But there is another aspect to this phenomenon.

Under normal circumstances, the dispatcher is reluctant to send an officer to the scene of questionable calls. This dispatcher will often try to negotiate a compromise, such as directing the complainant to some other public agency. If this compromise is not possible, an officer will be sent to the scene. Before capitulating, however, the dispatcher will ordinarily seek a higher authority, the sergeant:

That's what the sergeant's there for. When the caller gets abusive or unreasonable, you can give the call to the sergeant. That's [protection]. If something comes down later on, you don't have to worry. You're following procedures, so there's nothing they can do to you. Also, you've got the sergeant as a witness (Interview: dispatcher).

By bringing the sergeant into the process, the dispatcher is protected from such consequences as civil suits and internal investigations. When the sergeants were removed from the dispatch bureau, the dispatchers lost this most important source of protection. In a similar context, record-writing, McCleary (1977:585) defined "protection" as ". . . the writing of records . . . to demonstrate *absolute* compliance with *minimal* rules in every case . . . for example, a report format . . . demonstrating . . . *literal* compliance with rules and regulations." In the present context, we define "protection" analogously as a literal compliance with regulations; the dispatcher sends an officer to the scene of a call without questioning the call's validity. Many calls for police assistance may not be entirely valid, of course, and sending officers to answer such calls wastes resources. But dispatchers are rewarded only for seeing that calls are answered, not for conserving resources. By sending officers out on all calls, dispatchers "protect" themselves, optimizing personal rewards at the expense of departmental resources.

The sergeants acted as an informal screening mechanism at the front end of the complaint-processing system. Screening has no direct effect on UCR coding decisions, of course, but when a call goes unanswered, a UCR crime cannot result. If the call did represent a UCR crime, it goes unreported. When an officer is sent to the call, on the other hand, there is an unknown but nonzero probability that a UCR crime will result. Increasing the number of "calls for service" by removing the informal screening mechanism is thus expected to increase the rate of such UCR crimes as burglary, larceny, and auto theft.

UCR crime in City A increased substantially during this period and the police department interpreted this as an increase in "real" crime. Our alternative interpretation is more plausible, however: "calls for service" increased when sergeants were removed from the dispatch bureau. The rate at which crimes were reported increased, but not as a result of an increase in "real" crime.

CONCLUSION

UCR rates are commonly believed to be so unreliable as to be useless for research. Seidman and Couzens (1974:463) argue that "crime statistics are basically non-comparable across jurisdictions," and hence, that cross-sectional analyses of UCRs are not possible. Our findings support this conventional wisdom on one level. Any researcher who analyzed these series without knowing about the interventions would arrive at nonsensical conclusions. But on another level, our findings support a more optimistic view. Since each of our three cases involves a clearly defined organizational variable, research into the structural determinants of official crime rates, as originally suggested by Kitsuse and Cicourel, is promising.

Any organizational outcome theory of crime rates must begin with a model of the organizational process. The following model, in our opinion, describes most police departments in large cities:

Complaint → Investigation → Coding Decision

The process is initiated by a citizen complaint, and any organizational structure which affects the propensity of citizens to seek police assistance is called a "screen." Because system outputs are proportional to system inputs, screening structures that reduce the level of inputs, making it harder for citizens to complain, reduce the official crime rate.

Case Three illustrates a typical screening structure. Sergeants in one dispatch bureau routinely screened complaints that they understood to be "marginal." It is not surprising that the sergeants relied on complainant characteristics, especially race, to calculate the expected "marginality" of a complaint. Complaints from ghetto areas were heavily screened and were less likely to result in dispatched service calls.

The basis of this phenomenon is a conflict between public perceptions and the street-cop ethos (Black, 1970; Wilson, 1975). While the nature of screening may vary from case to case, we expect the degree of screening to be a function of how strongly the process reflects a street-cop ethos. In particular, where the dispatch function is controlled by street cops, we expect a vigorous screening function.

We see two crucial factors here: civilianization and automation. In both of the departments we studied, uniformed officers spoke disparagingly of civilian employees: civilians do not appreciate the practicalities of street work, so civilians should not control the dispatch function. Where civilians do have some control over the dispatch function, however, we expect to find weaker screening structures and, by implication, higher official crime rates. Automation has a similar effect. Discretionary decisions become less important. The most important decisions are made by mainly civilian telephone operators; as the dispatch function is automated, the ratio of civilian employees to uniformed officers in the dispatch bureau increases.

Complaints that pass through the screening structure are investigated. Case One illustrates the difference between a general investigation, conducted by patrol officers, and a specific investigation conducted by detectives. Specific investigations are relatively more bureaucratized than general investigations. Detectives may not be more adept at investigation than patrol officers, but they are certainly more adept at applying formal definitions to cases. The effect of mandating specific investigations of all burglary complaints in City A was an increase in the reliability of UCR coding decisions (as shown by a decrease in monthly variance), and because coding decision errors tended to inflate the UCR count, a decrease in the UCR burglary rate. Generalizing this result, we expect official crime rates to vary inversely with the relative use of formal, specific investigation. Certain crimes (homicide, armed robbery, etc.) are more likely to be subjected to specific investigation, of course, so we expect that these UCR rates will be relatively reliable.

Finally, given the specified effects of screening and investigation, the official crime rate will be a function of organizational goals. In Case Two, retirement of an incumbent police chief led to an increase in UCR burglaries. The general principle here is that police departments have abstract goals operationalized in terms of a crime rate. To achieve its goals, however, a department must be able to exercise hierarchical control over its complaint-processors. Other things being equal, the more effective the hierarchical organizational structure, the lower the UCR crime rate.

A minimal theory of crime rates as organizational outcomes requires a cross-sectional study of dependent variable crimes explained by three independent structural variables. The theory is not easily tested, however. An obvious weakness is that not all relationships are fully specified. For screening structures, the relationship is clear: screening reduces the official crime rate, especially UCR assaults, auto thefts, burglaries, and larcenies. But for investigative structures, the relationship is more complex. While investigation structures reduced the UCR burglary rate in City A, these structures could increase the UCR burglary rate in other cities or under other circumstances. Elaborating on this point, any theory must recognize three possible process outcomes. After screening, that is, a citizen complaint may result in an official crime or not; but a complaint of a specific crime – burglary, for instance – may also be displaced or downgraded to a nonburglary category such as theft, vandalism, or trespass. We suspect that investigative structures are more likely to displace complaints rather than to divert them entirely. Finally, for hierarchical control structures, we cannot assume that all police departments follow the same simple-minded goal of reducing crime rates across the board. Goals are more likely to be operationalized as complicated mixtures of increases, decreases, and displacements.

Lacking adequate specification, we agree with the conventional view that UCRs are noncomparable across jurisdictions; or at least, that there is little theoretical basis for their comparison. Given the relatively constant nature of structures, longitudinal analyses appear to be more valid, but this may be only an appearance. In either case, we advise a return to the understanding that UCRs are "official statistics" which may be "used" validly only for the study of organizational processes (Kitsuse and Cicourel, 1963). Research following this tradition must emphasize qualitative studies of single police departments. We are clearly not yet at the stage where theory will support broad statistical generalizations across many departments.

Notes

*An earlier version of this paper was presented at the November 1981 meeting of the American Society for Criminology in Washington, D.C. Correspondence to: Center of Criminal Justice, Arizona State University, Tempe, AZ 85281.

1. We regularly visited the police departments in Cities A and B in various official and unofficial capacities during the 1978–80 period. All quotations in this paper are typical of the interviews we conducted with over 30 supervisory personnel, sworn officers, and civilian employees. Given the sensitive nature of this material, all interviewees remain anonymous.

2. Ann L. Schneider (personal correspondence) has discovered that apartment burglaries are under-counted in a city in the northwestern United States. In cases where several apartments in a single building are burglarized, the apartment manager is listed as the complainant and a single report is filed. UCR coding clerks then incorrectly count these several crimes as one UCR burglary.

3. We analyzed each of the time series using the procedures described in McCleary and Hay (1980) and McDowall et al. (1980). Details of these analyses are reported in McCleary et al. (1982).

4. In most large cities, dispatching work is divided into two distinct functions. Operators answer phone calls and forward all requests for service to dispatchers. Operators are typically civilian employees and dispatchers are typically uniformed officers, but both are supervised by the sergeant. Most of the dispatchers in City A had experience answering telephones. See Antunes and Scott (1981) for an excellent description of dispatching.

References

Antunes, George and Eric J. Scott
    1981   "Calling the cops: Police telephone operators and citizen calls for service." Journal of Criminal Justice 9:165–179.
Black, Donald J.
    1970   "Production of crime rates." American Sociological Review 35:733–747.

Campbell, Donald T.
1969   "Reforms as experiments." American Psychologist 24:409–429.
Glass, Gene V., Victor L. Willson, and John M. Gottman
1975   The Design and Analysis of Time Series Experiments. Boulder: Colorado
        Associated University Press.
Guyot, Dorothy
1976   "What productivity? What bargain?" Public Administration Review 36:341.
Hindelang, Michael J.
1976   Criminal Victimization in Eight American Cities: A Descriptive Analysis of Com-
        mon Theft and Assault. Cambridge: Ballinger.
Kitsuse, John I. and Aaron V. Cicourel
1963   "A note on the use of official statistics." Social Problems 11:131–138.
Maxfield, Michael G.
1981   Service time, dispatch time, and demand for police services: Helping more by serv-
        ing less. Unpublished paper, School of Public and Environmental Affairs, Indiana
        University, Bloomington.
Maxfield, Michael G., Dan A. Lewis, and Ron Szoc
1980   "Producing official crimes: Verified crime reports as measures of police output."
        Social Science Quarterly 61:221–236.
McCleary, Richard
1977   "How parole officers use records." Social Problems 24:576–589.
McCleary, Richard and Richard A. Hay, Jr.
1980   Applied Time Series Analysis for the Social Sciences. Beverly Hills: Sage.
McCleary, Richard, Barbara C. Nienstedt, and James M. Erven
1982   "Interrupted time series analysis of crime statistics: The case of organizational
        reforms." Chapter 2 in John C. Hagen (ed.), Methodological Advances in Crimino-
        logical Research. Beverly Hills: Sage.
McDowall, David, Richard McCleary, Errol E. Meidinger, and Richard A. Hay, Jr.
1980   Interrupted Time Series Analysis. Volume 21, University Papers Series: Quantita-
        tive Applications in the Social Sciences. Beverly Hills: Sage.
Pepinsky, Harold
1976   "Police patrolmen's offense-reporting behavior." Journal of Research in Crime and
        Delinquency 13:33–47.
Seidman, David and Michael Couzens
1974   "Getting the crime rate down: Political pressure and crime reporting." Law and
        Society Review 8:457–493.
Skogan, Wesley G.
1974   "The validity of official crime statistics: An empirical investigation." Social Science
        Quarterly 54:25–28.
1976   "Crime and crime rates." Pp. 105–120 in Wesley G. Skogan (ed.), Sample Surveys
        of the Victims of Crime. Cambridge: Ballinger.
Waegel, William B.
1981   "Case routinization in investigative police work." Social Problems 28:261–275.
Wilson, James Q.
1975   Varieties of Police Behavior. New York: Basic Books.

6.   Sex-Role Attitude Change and Reporting of Rape Victimization, 1973–1985

JAMES D. ORCUTT AND REBECCA FAISON

Feminist writers argue that rape is culturally learned by both victims and offenders (Brownmiller 1975; Clark and Lewis 1977; Russell 1975). That is, women learn to be "legitimate victims" (Weis and Borges 1973) and consequently fail to define or react to many instances of sexual violence and aggression as rape. This learning takes place through conventional sex-role socialization in a gender-stratified society, and traditional sex-role attitudes serve as the basis for stereotypic beliefs about sexual aggression – "rape myths" (Schwendinger and Schwendinger 1974) that rationalize or even justify such behavior. Wilson, Faison, and Britton (1983) argue that rape myths affect situational definitions of sexual assault in several ways: (1) when the assault does not correspond to the cultural stereotype of rape by a violent stranger, it may be denied that a sexual offense has occurred; (2) victims may be blamed for the occurrence of sexual offenses; and (3) rape may be rationalized in terms of stereotypic notions of male-female sexuality that characterize males as aggressive and females as passive or even masochistic. Thus these myths constrain women's definitions of sexual assaults as rape and contribute to underreporting of rape victimization. As Cherry (1983, p. 252) puts it, "in some instances, rapes literally 'don't exist' because the victim sees the coercive sexual experience as natural and legitimate in the context of a structured power relationship between a man and a woman."

A number of cross-sectional studies indicate that adherence to traditional sex-role attitudes is related to acceptance of rape myths and restrictive definitions of rape. For instance, Klemmack and Klemmack (1976) show that women with traditional, stereotypic views of women's roles are less likely than nontraditional women to define situations of forced intercourse as rape. Similarly, Feild (1978) finds that men's and women's endorsement of various "pro-rape" attitudes is correlated with traditional attitudes toward women's roles. Krulewitz and Payne (1978) report that favorable attitudes toward feminism affect one's perception of a situation as rape and attribution of cause to the assailant rather than to the victim. Finally, Burt (1980, p. 229) concludes from her survey data that "many Americans do indeed believe many rape myths," and that their views about rape are strongly connected to other, deeply held attitudes such as sex-role stereotyping, distrust of the opposite sex, and acceptance of interpersonal violence. Thus, rape myths are part of a more general attitude structure that supports sexual violence and aggression against women. These findings clearly imply that adherence to traditional sex-role attitudes, being associated with more restrictive definitions of rape, would inhibit reporting of rape victimization.

In this study, we attempt to go beyond previous cross-sectional research to examine whether broader variations in sex-role attitudes over time are related to corresponding shifts in definitions and reporting of rape victimization from 1973 to 1985. Several longitudinal studies document a marked decline in support for traditional sex-role attitudes beginning in the 1960s and continuing through the 1970s (Cherlin and Walters 1981; Mason, Czajka, and Arber 1976; Thornton, Alwin, and Camburn 1983). While there are some indications that the pace of this change may have slackened recently in some groups for some sex-role dimensions (e.g., college-educated women's attitudes toward women working; see Cherlin and Walters [1981]), a general pattern of cultural change away from traditional views of women's roles is apparent among both men and women surveyed in these studies. The rise of the women's movement in the late 1960s was followed by a strengthening of the consistency of sex-role attitudes and heightened public awareness of women's issues (Cherlin and Walters 1981; Thornton et al. 1983). During the 1970s, feminists' attacks on sexist conceptions of violence against women and efforts to define rape as a serious social problem began to have a widespread institutional and public impact (Rose 1977). However, no investigation has attempted to examine the articulation of trends in sex-role attitudes with changing reactions to rape and other acts of violence against women over this crucial period.

These historical patterns coupled with cross-sectional evidence on sex-role attitudes and rape definitions serve as the basis for several hypotheses we assess in this study. First, we expect that declining support among women for traditional attitudes toward female sex roles will be related to an increasing rate of reporting rape victimizations to police during the 1970s and early 1980s. This prediction follows directly from research showing that nontraditional sex-role attitudes are consistently linked with broader definitions of sexual assaults as rape.

Second, and more important from a definitional perspective, we expect changes in women's sex-role attitudes to be more closely related to changes in reporting of *nonstranger* rapes than to reporting of *stranger* rapes to police. A prominent rape myth is the stereotype of the rapist as stranger (Burt and Estep 1981; Klemmack and Klemmack 1976; Weis and Borges 1973). Williams (1984) shows that women are less likely to report sexual assaults to police when these incidents depart from the "classic rape" by a stranger after a break-in or in a public place (also see Lizotte [1985]). Therefore, sexual violence that does not fit this conventional stereotype (i.e., assaults by an acquaintance) should be particularly subject to redefinition and increased reporting if sex-role attitude change is eroding the influence of rape myths on victims.

Third, we expect changes in men's attitudes toward female sex roles to have similar but less pronounced effects than women's attitudes on trends in reporting of rape victimizations by females to police. The reasoning for this hypothesis is based on the fact that reporting of a sexual assault, and the definitional process that precedes it, are often (if not typically) *interpersonal events* involving the female victim and male officers or confidants (Holmstrom and Burgess 1978). The receptiveness of these men—both actual and as perceived by the victim—to a definition of an assault as rape should increase her willingness to follow through with a criminal complaint. Because research has shown that nontraditional attitudes toward female sex roles are correlated with broader definitions of rape among men, we expect to find evidence of this "receptiveness effect" in a longitudinal relationship between men's sex-role attitudes and women's victimization reports.

To highlight our definitional arguments and to rule out alternative explanations of the predicted patterns of relationship between sex-role attitude change and reporting of rape victimization, we incorporate measures or controls for other forms of victimization and social change into our time-series analysis. Because we are proposing that reports of rape incidents are a specific function of women's (and men's) redefinition of sexual assault, we would *not* expect to find a significant relationship between sex-role attitudes and reports of other nonsexual personal crimes. To address this point empirically, we relate sex-role attitudes across the 1970s and early 1980s to trends in women's reports of *nonstranger and stranger robberies* to police. We also consider the possibility that trends in reporting of rape victimization might be influenced by another relevant variable—attitudes toward crime—whose effects over time may be confounded with or independent of sex-role attitudes (see Stinchcombe and Associates [1980]). Time-series measures of *punitiveness toward criminals* from two different sets will allow us to assess whether changing reactions to criminality in general, versus redefinition of sexual assault, might better account for victims' reports to police.

Our victimization data also permit a partial appraisal of how offenders' threats or use of force affected victims' reports of rape. If the level of threat in sexual assaults increased over time (e.g., if a greater proportion of offenders used a weapon) this in itself might account for a substantial increase in women's tendency to define and report such incidents as rape (cf. Lizotte 1985; Williams 1984). Owing to limitations in our data for nonstranger rapes, we focus mainly on whether *offenders' use of weapons* relates to victims' reports of stranger rapes across the time series. Finally, we introduce the annual rate of *women's participation in the labor force* as a control variable in several of our analyses. This variable serves two functions: (1) given its generally upward trend from 1973 to 1985, it is a rough proxy for cumulative structural changes over the time series; and (2) it provides an indirect measure of increased risk of victimization outside the home for a population—employed women—that tends to hold relatively nontraditional sex-role attitudes (Thornton et al. 1983).

MEASURES

Our analysis of trends in sex-role attitudes and levels of rape victimization reporting is based on secondary data obtained from published reports of three major survey projects conducted between 1972 and 1985. Our most complete time series on sex-role attitudes and attitudes toward crime is taken from reports by the Cooperative Institutional Research Program (CIRP) of annual surveys of U.S. college freshmen from 1972 to 1984 (Astin and Associates 1972–1984). These reports present national norms—weighted marginal distributions—for items on questionnaires mailed in the fall of each year to the freshman classes of participating undergraduate institutions. The numbers of CIRP respondents during the years considered here range from 215,890 (from 393 institutions) in 1976 to 182,370 (from 345 institutions) in 1984. Aside from providing the most complete annual series of attitudinal measures available for the relevant period, the CIRP data offer another advantage for the purposes of our study. That is, freshman samples coincide in age to the population of women at highest risk of rape victimization (U.S. Department of Justice 1974–1985, pp. 16–17).

Our primary measure of *sex-role traditionalism* is the percentage of students *agreeing* with the following item, which was included on the CIRP questionnaire for each year from 1972 to 1984: "The activities of married women are best confined to the home and family."[1] Despite the unavoidable limitations of this single-item measure of a complex construct, it is important to note that the CIRP measure of sex-role traditionalism does reflect the notion of restricting women to the "private sphere" of home and family that has been central to feminist critiques (see Gerson and Peiss [1985]) and cross-sectional research on sex-role stereotypes and rape myths (Burt 1980).[2] The percentage *agreeing* with the following item, which appeared on the student questionnaires from 1972 to 1983, constitutes our CIRP measure of *punitiveness toward criminals:* "There is too much concern in the courts for the rights of criminals."

To broaden the base of our investigation, we also employ alternative measures of attitudes toward sex roles and crime from the NORC General Social Surveys (GSS) for certain years from 1972 to 1984 (Davis and Smith 1985; also see Cherlin and Walters [1981]). The GSS included two female sex-role items (FEWORK and FEPRES) for seven years considered in this analysis (1972, 1974–1975, 1977–1978, 1982–1983). We combined nontraditional responses to these items to form an additive scale, the *GSS nontraditionalism index.*[3] The GSS also included the following item on punitive treatment of criminals for 11 years of our study (1972–1978, 1980, 1982–1984): "In general, do you think the courts in this area deal too harshly or not harshly enough with criminals?" The percentage responding "not harshly enough" constitutes our measure of *GSS punitiveness toward criminals.*[4] We use the GSS measures to assess the validity of comparable items in the CIRP freshman data and to replicate our time-series analysis of the CIRP data.

Data on reporting of rape incidents to police were obtained from the National Crime Survey (NCS) results reported in the 1973 to 1985 volumes of *Criminal Victimization in the United States* (U.S. Department of Justice 1974–1985). These data are based on continuous surveys in a nationally representative sample of households in the United States. Our analysis focuses on the percentages of females in households who, during a given year, (1) experienced an incident of rape or robbery victimization, and (2) reported the incident to the police. Central to our study, of course, is the NCS distinction between reports of incidents where the offender was a *nonstranger* versus those involving a *stranger.* We also make use of data on the percentage of NCS rape incidents in which nonstranger or stranger *offenders used weapons*, although the estimates for nonstranger rapes involving weapons are based on small numbers of cases for each year of the time series.[5] Our data on *women's labor force participation* (i.e., civilian women employed as a percentage of the noninstitutional population) for 1973 to 1985 are from the *Statistical Abstract of the United States* (U.S. Department of Commerce 1980, p. 396; 1986, p. 375).

In the analyses that follow, the attitudinal measures are lagged one year behind victimizations reported to police (e.g., we correlate CIRP data gathered in the fall of 1972 with 1973 NCS victimizations). We begin by presenting descriptive statistics for each of our measures, including estimates of linear trends across the time series. Then

Table 1.   Descriptive Statistics and Annual Trends for Time-Series Measures

Data Set and Measure	N	Mean	SD	Annual Trend b^a	r
A. NCS Female Victimizations Reported to Police					
Nonstranger rapes	13	45.0	8.1	1.16	.56
Stranger rapes	13	56.5	6.8	.42	.24
Nonstranger robberies	13	57.8	7.3	.87	.46
Stranger robberies	13	67.2	3.1	.27	.34
B. CIRP Sex Role and Crime Attitudes (by Gender)^b					
Traditional sex role (females)	13	19.3	2.3	−.40	−.65
Traditional sex role (males)	13	36.4	4.2	−.99	−.91
Punitive crime (females)	12	55.6	8.6	2.28	.96
Punitive crime (males)	12	66.0	7.1	1.87	.94
C. GSS Sex Role and Crime Attitudes (by Gender)^b					
Nontraditional index (females)	7	76.2	4.2	.83	.82
Nontraditional index (males)	7	75.8	4.5	1.04	.94
Punitive crime (females)	11	79.8	6.6	1.35	.84
Punitive crime (males)	11	80.2	5.6	.89	.66
D. Control Variables					
Nonstranger rape weapon^c	13	14.1	6.8	−.81	−.46
Stranger rape weapon	13	28.7	4.2	−.09	−.08
Women's labor force participation	13	46.1	2.9	.72	.96

Notes: ^{a}Unstandardized bivariate regression coefficient.
   ^{b}Attitude variables (1972–1984) lagged one year behind victimizations (1973–1985).
   ^{c}Estimates of nonstranger rapes with weapon are based on small numbers of cases and should be interpreted with great caution.

we assess the concurrent validity of the CIRP student data by correlating these measures of sex-role traditionalism and punitiveness toward criminals with comparable measures from the GSS. Finally we present bivariate and multivariate analyses of the hypothesized patterns of relationship between these attitudes and NCS victimizations reported to police.

RESULTS

Descriptive Statistics and Trends

Table 1 presents the means, standard deviations, and regression and correlation coefficients for annual trends for each of our measures. Of particular interest here are the differences in means and trends for females' reports of nonstranger versus stranger rapes to police. The mean level of reporting of rape incidents involving nonstrangers for the entire time series is 45.0% as compared to 56.5% for stranger rapes. As the regression coefficients and correlations for trends indicate, reporting of both nonstranger and stranger rapes has tended to increase from 1973 to 1985. However, the estimated rate of increase for nonstranger rape reporting is over twice as great as that for stranger rapes ($b = 1.16$ versus $b = .42$). Similarly, while women were generally more likely to report stranger robberies to the police, women's reports of nonstranger robberies have increased at a higher rate than reports of stranger robberies ($b = .87$ versus $b = .27$).

Turning to the student data in Panel B of Table 1, the mean level of endorsement of the CIRP measure of sex-role traditionalism is higher among freshman men than among women (36.4% versus 19.3%). While a negative trend in sex-role traditionalism over the 1970s and early 1980s is apparent for both sexes, the regression coefficients indicate that this decrease is steeper among males. In contrast, the marked upward trend in agreement with the CIRP measure of punitiveness toward criminals from 1972 to 1984 is somewhat steeper among college women than among men.

The trends in the GSS sex-role index and crime item in Panel C of Table 1 closely resemble the parallel measures in the CIRP data. As Cherlin and Walters (1981) report, males' endorsement of nontraditional attitudes (i.e., support for women working and for a woman for president) increased at a slightly higher rate than females' support across the seven years these items were included in the GSS. The positive trends for agreement with the GSS statement that "courts are not harsh enough" for both gender groups replicate the CIRP trends in agreement that there is "too much concern in the courts for the rights of criminals."

Finally, the descriptive results on the percentage of all NCS rape incidents that involved the use of weapons suggest that (1) weapons are about twice as likely to be used in stranger than in nonstranger rapes, and (2) the use of weapons in rape incidents may have decreased slightly over the time series. As expected, the annual increase in women's labor force participation is virtually monotonic across the time series ($r = .96$).

CIRP Attitudes and Rape Reporting

To assess the concurrent validity of the CIRP measures of sex-role and crime attitudes, we correlated these variables with corresponding measures from the GSS data. In every case, the CIRP items are strongly and significantly correlated with comparable measures of attitudes among the adult population. On the one hand, the CIRP measure of sex-role traditionalism is negatively related to the GSS nontraditionalism index for both female ($r = -.76$, $p < .05$) and male ($r = -.96$, $p < .01$) respondents across the seven years the sex-role items were included in the GSS. On the other hand, strong positive correlations exist between the CIRP and GSS measures of punitiveness toward criminals among females ($r = .91$, $p < .01$) and males ($r = .82$, $p < .01$) for ten years of comparable data. In sum, the student measures cross-validate quite well with the attitudinal measures based on NORC surveys of the adult U.S. population.

Table 2 presents zero-order correlations and selected ordinary least squares (OLS) slope coefficients relevant to the hypothesized relationships between CIRP attitudes and females' reports of rape and robbery victimizations to police. As predicted by our first hypothesis, endorsement of sex-role traditionalism among college women is

Table 2. Zero-Order Correlations and Unstandardized Coefficients of CIRP Sex Role (N = 13) and Crime Items (N = 12) with NCS Female Victimizations Reported to Police[a]

| CIRP Item and Gender | Female Victimizations Reported to Police | | | |
| | RAPE | | ROBBERY | |
	Nonstranger	Stranger	Nonstranger	Stranger
Females				
Traditional sex role	-.76** (-2.61)	-.52* (-1.50)	-.39	-.42
Punitive toward criminals	.47	.06	.16	.11
Males				
Traditional sex role	-.72** (-1.38)	-.37 (-.60)	-.37	-.27
Punitive toward criminals	.42	-.01	.14	.11

Notes: [a] Unstandardized slope coefficients in parentheses.
  * $p \leq .10$.
  ** $p \leq .01$.

inversely related to the proportion of stranger and, especially, nonstranger rapes reported to police from 1973 to 1985. Whereas the relationship for reports of stranger rapes is only marginally significant ($p = .07$), the more crucial bivariate relationship between women's sex-role traditionalism and nonstranger rape reporting is substantial and highly significant ($r = -.76, p = .003$). The latter finding, of course, is in line with our second hypothesis, which emphasized the special importance of women's redefinitions of sexual assault for recognition and reporting of nonstranger rapes to police. The unstandardized slope estimates in Table 2 indicate that the effect of females' sex-role traditionalism on nonstranger rape reporting is over half again as strong as its effect on stranger rape reporting ($b = -2.61$ versus $b = -1.50$).

We also find some support for our third hypothesis that *men's* attitudes toward female roles would have some effect on women's willingness to report rape incidents to police. While the predicted negative relationship for stranger rape is not significant ($r = -.37$), the level of male endorsement of the CIRP measure of sex-role traditionalism is strongly related to reporting of nonstranger rapes ($r = -.72, p = .005$). However, a comparison of unstandardized slopes suggests that levels of nonstranger rape reporting are more closely linked to women's sex-role attitudes than to men's ($b = -2.61$ versus $b = -1.38$).[6]

The relatively modest correlations in Table 2 for reports of robbery incidents indicate that sex-role attitude change has had little impact on women's definitions or reports of these nonsexual victimizations. Also, the CIRP measures of punitive attitudes toward criminals are not strongly related to reporting of either rape or robbery victimization. Thus, at least in bivariate analyses of the CIRP data, sex-role attitude change stands out as an especially influential predictor of nonstranger rape reports from 1973 to 1985.

To provide a more adequate assessment of our definitional arguments relative to other possible explanations of changing reactions to sexual assault, we conducted a series of multivariate analyses of the CIRP data. First, we reexamined the relationships between sex-role traditionalism and reporting of rape victimizations while controlling for the CIRP crime item. We calculated estimates for the 1984 missing value on the CIRP crime item from prediction equations that regressed the CIRP time series on the parallel GSS crime attitudes for women and men.[7] Our control for CIRP crime attitudes in three out of four regression analyses (sex of CIRP respondents by form of rape) had little effect on the zero-order relationships between sex-role traditionalism and rape reporting shown in Table 2. None of the partial relationships between crime attitude and rape reporting was significant. However, the first-order partial correlation between men's sex-role traditionalism and reports of stranger rapes increased to $r = -.57$ ($b = -1.33, p = .05$). Whereas a high degree of collinearity between the sex-role and crime measures among CIRP male respondents (zero-order $r = -.72$) complicates interpretation of the latter result, it is evident that the CIRP data offer little support for the argument that growing punitiveness toward crime in general across the 1970s and early 1980s influenced changing levels of rape reporting.

However, our analyses of the other control variables – use of weapons and women's labor force participation – yielded more interesting results. Somewhat surprisingly, the limited measure of weapon use by nonstranger offenders has a modest negative correlation with women's reports of such rapes to police ($r = -.29, p = .340$). More important, we find a significant positive relationship between strangers' use of weapons and reporting of stranger rapes ($r = .63, b = 1.01, p = .022$). The upward trend in women's labor force participation is moderately associated with increasing reports of nonstranger rapes ($r = .47, p = .106$), but it is virtually unrelated to reports of stranger rapes to police ($r = .16, p = .591$).

Table 3 presents some findings of our multivariate analyses of these predictors and the CIRP measures of sex-role traditionalism. First, note that controls for use of weapon and women's labor force participation do not markedly affect the crucial negative relationship between female sex-role traditionalism and reports of nonstranger rape (second-order partial $r = -.68, p = .023$). Second, the negative relationship between male sex-role traditionalism and nonstranger rape reports also remains strong and significant when both control variables are included (second-order partial $r = -.74, p = .009$). However, CIRP sex-role traditionalism among males is strongly correlated with the trend for women's labor force participation (zero-order $r = .88$), and serious problems of multicollinearity are reflected in the second-order partial correlations (i.e., reversal of sign) between women's labor force participation and rape reporting.

Finally, the most important new findings in Table 3 emerge in the analyses of stranger rape reports. The use of weapons in assaults by strangers is consistently related to higher levels of stranger rape reports. In contrast, none of the negative effects for sex-role traditionalism are significant after we control for use of weapons. Owing largely to the contribution of weapon use to explained variance, both stranger rape equations remain marginally significant overall even with the addition of the trend for women's labor force participation (female equation adj. $R^2 = .34, p = .081$; male equation adj. $R^2 = .37, p = .069$). Thus, while changes in sex-role traditionalism continue to account for most of the temporal variation in reports of nonstranger rape, our multivariate analyses shift attention to the threat or use of force in the form of a weapon as an influential predictor of women's reports of stranger rapes to police.

Table 3. Partial Correlations for CIRP Sex-Role Traditionalism and Control Variables with Rapes Reported to Police by Gender of CIRP Respondent

	Nonstranger Rape Reports		Stranger Rape Reports	
	1ST-ORDER	2ND-ORDER	1ST-ORDER	2ND-ORDER
Predictors and Variance Explained	PARTIAL r	PARTIAL r	PARTIAL r	PARTIAL r
A. *Analyses Based on CIRP Females' Sex-Role Traditionalism*				
Traditional sex role	−.74**	−.68**	−.43	.30
Use of weapon	−.14	−.12	.57**	.56*
Labor force participation		.06	.	.09
Multiple R	.76	.77	.71	.71
Adjusted R^2	.50***	.45**	.41**	.34*
B. *Analysis Based on CIRP Males' Sex-Role Traditionalism*				
Traditional sex role	−.69***	−.74***	−.45	−.35
Use of weapon	−.14	−.12	.66**	.60**
Labor force participation		−.53*		−.17
Multiple R	.72	.81	.72	.73
Adjusted R^2	.43**	.54**	.42**	.37*

Notes: * $p \leq .10$.
  ** $p \leq .05$.
  *** $p \leq .01$.

GSS Attitudes and Rape Reporting

Before turning to the implications of our analysis of the CIRP data, we must consider the alternative measures of attitudes toward women's roles and crime gathered in the GSS from 1972 to 1984. Whereas the advantages of a two-item index of nontraditional sex-role attitudes are more than offset by the limitations of a sporadic series of seven data points, the GSS time series for punitive attitudes toward crime is almost as complete as its CIRP counterpart. Table 4 presents the zero-order correlations between the GSS measures and women's reports of victimizations.

The GSS nontraditionalism index for both female and male respondents shows the expected positive correlations with reports of nonstranger and stranger rape, but none of these zero-order relationships attain statistical significance. However, contrary to our line of argument, a similar pattern of positive correlations is evident between the nontraditionalism index and women's reports of robbery victimizations. Moreover, the GSS measures of female and male respondents' punitiveness toward crime are strongly and significantly related to women's reports of nonstranger rapes ($r = .72$, $p = .012$ for females; $r = .67$, $p = .025$ for male respondents). Thus, among other things, these unexpected results reopen a question we addressed earlier: Are nonstranger rape reports to the police more closely linked to increasing punitiveness toward crime than to changing attitudes toward women?

To reassess this issue with a complete time series in a multivariate framework, we reversed the strategy employed in our earlier analysis and used the CIRP time-series

Table 4. Zero-Order Correlations of GSS Sex-Role Index (*N* = 7) and Crime Item (*N* = 11) with NCS Female Victimizations Reported to Police

	Female Victimizations Reported to Police			
	RAPE		ROBBERY	
GSS Measure and Gender	Nonstranger	Stranger	Nonstranger	Stranger
Females				
Nontraditional sex role	.52	.42	.59	.52
Punitive toward criminals	.72**	.24	.15	.07
Males				
Nontraditional sex role	.65	.34	.22	.58
Punitive toward criminals	.67*	.24	.03	−.05

Notes: * $p \leq .05$.
        ** $p \leq .01$.

measures of punitiveness toward crime to estimate the missing 1979 and 1981 values for the corresponding GSS measures.[8] Then we regressed nonstranger rape reports simultaneously on the complete set of estimates for GSS crime attitudes and the CIRP measures of sex-role traditionalism. Although the control for GSS crime attitudes reduced the effect of CIRP sex-role attitudes, traditionalism among female respondents was still significantly related to nonstranger rape reports (partial $r = -.58$, $b = -2.18, p = .045$). Likewise, in the analysis of male attitudes, CIRP sex-role traditionalism also had a diminished but significant effect after the control for GSS punitiveness toward crime (partial $r = -.57$, $b = -1.52, p = .054$). On the other hand, the simultaneous control for CIRP sex-role traditionalism dramatically reduced the effect of the GSS crime measure on nonstranger rape reports in equations for both female (partial $r = .20$) and male (partial $r = -.08$) respondents.

DISCUSSION AND CONCLUSION

The mixed results of the GSS replication are a sobering reminder of the hazards of basing inferences about complex cultural and situational processes on aggregate-level estimates of attitudes and behavior from different national surveys. Whereas the CIRP national norms offer a more complete and, perhaps, more relevant assessment of attitudinal changes that may have affected victims' definitions of sexual assault during the 1970s and 1980s, it is important to bear in mind that key links in our concluding arguments rest primarily on the frequency distributions for single items from surveys of college freshmen.

Nonetheless, we feel that our analysis of the CIRP time series complements and extends the cultural explanation of rape definitions that has been advanced by feminist theorists (Brownmiller 1975; Clark and Lewis 1977; Russell 1975) and supported in numerous cross-sectional studies (Burt 1980; Feild 1978; Klemmack and Klemmack 1976; Krulewitz and Payne 1978). Our major findings suggest that, over time, a devaluation of constraining views of "women's place" in society—as in the CIRP statement that "women are best confined to the home and family"—has been closely related to broader definitions of rape among potential victims and increased reporting of certain sexual offenses to police. More specifically, the robust negative relationship between sex-role traditionalism among CIRP females and reporting of nonstranger rapes indicates that shifts in the cultural basis for rape myths have been most conse-quential for women's reactions to "date rape," assaults by relatives, and other acts of sexual violence by acquaintances whose criminal status has been blurred or denied by "classic" rape stereotypes (Williams 1984; also see Schwendinger and Schwen-dinger [1974]).

The finding that declining traditionalism among young men in the CIRP surveys also relates to increased reporting of nonstranger rape is in line with our hypothesis about the implications of men's potential receptiveness to a wider range of rape defini-tions. As Holmstrom and Burgess (1978, pp. 30–34) have shown, rape reporting is typically an interpersonal process in which the victim seeks advice and support from others in her social network. In many cases, family members or friends actually initi-ate the contact with police. Therefore, men as well as other women may have a decisive influence on victims' definitions of sexual assaults and subsequent reactions to such incidents. Our analysis of declining sex-role traditionalism among men, coupled with evidence from cross-sectional research on rape myths (e.g., Burt 1980), suggests that victims have become increasingly likely to receive consensual support for broader definitions of nonstranger rape and for formal complaints among male (and female) members of their social networks.

Of course, the increased receptiveness of significant others is only one of many con-textual changes that may have affected victims' willingness to define and report rapes to police during the 1970s and early 1980s. For instance, this study has not directly assessed various institutional developments—such as the proliferation of rape crisis centers (Gernick, Burt, and Pittman 1985)—or policy changes designed to make law enforcement agencies, medical treatment centers, and judicial systems less threaten-ing and more responsive to victims of sexual assault (Rose 1977). At best, the weak effects of our control for the upward trend in women's labor force participation provide only an indirect measure of the cumulative impact of these organizational develop-ments and other structural changes on victims' reactions to rape incidents.

While our evidence points to a progressive redefinition of nonstranger rapes over the 1970s and 1980s, a rather different picture emerges in the trends and relation-ships for victims' reports of stranger rapes. The level of stranger rape reporting has increased only modestly across the time series, and its relationship to longitudinal var-iations in CIRP sex-role traditionalism appears to be tenuous. Instead, our multivari-ate analyses reveal that stranger rape reports are more closely connected to offenders' use of weapons—a situational contingency that occurs at a relatively constant rate over time. Although this pattern of results departs somewhat from our initial expectations, it is quite consistent with Williams' (1984) finding that the threat or use of force was associated with higher levels of reporting to the police when a "distant relationship" existed between rape victims and offenders. Williams concludes that these circum-stances correspond to the stereotypic "classic rape situation [that] provides the victim with the evidence she needs to convince both herself and others that she was indeed a rape victim" (1984, p. 464). Accordingly we conclude that the relatively high rate at which stranger rapes with a weapon were reported to police from 1973 to 1985 reflects the persistence and salience of the "classic rape" stereotype in victims' situational definitions of this particular form of sexual violence.

Despite serious limitations in the yearly estimates for the NCS measure of weapon use in nonstranger rapes, its downward trend over time and its modest negative relationship with women's reports of nonstranger rapes to the police deserve some additional attention. Taken at face value, these results raise doubts about the possibility that increased reporting of nonstranger rapes across the period of our study was prompted by more threatening or violent behavior among nonstranger offenders. In fact, when we combine the yearly estimates from earlier (1973–1979) and later (1980–1985) victimization surveys, nonstranger rape incidents mentioned in the NCS interviews were significantly *less likely* to involve the use of weapons in the 1980s than in the 1970s. For the seven NCS surveys conducted during the 1970s, the mean estimate of nonstranger rapes involving use of weapons was 17.3%, whereas the comparable average for nonstranger rapes mentioned in the six NCS surveys during the 1980s was only 10.5% ($t = 1.99$, $p = 0.36$).

There are two ways of looking at this last result. On the one hand, it might be taken as an indication of *change in the behavior of nonstranger offenders* (i.e., they are now less likely to threaten violence or use a weapon in the course of a sexual assault). On the other hand, it might reflect a *change in the kinds of sexual assault that respondents define and mention as "rape incidents" during NCS interviews.* The former interpretation seems questionable in light of the lack of change in strangers' use of weapons in the 1970s (mean = 28.0%) versus the 1980s (mean = 29.4%). However, the latter interpretation raises an important methodological implication of our theoretical approach to victims' definitions of rape. That is, if cultural change and less constraining definitions of rape have contributed to increased reporting of nonstranger rapes to police, these same processes should also *increase the range of sexual assaults that respondents mention as rape incidents during the NCS interviews.* Assuming that rape myths would tend to narrow respondents' definitions of what constitutes a rape incident in early NCS surveys, an erosion of these stereotypic definitions through the 1980s should increase the overall proportion of "date rapes" and other nonstranger assaults without a weapon that NCS respondents mention as rape incidents. As a greater share of these "less threatening" incidents "show up" in the NCS surveys, the relative proportion of "more threatening" rapes with a weapon would tend to decline over time.

This line of reasoning not only makes sense of the diminishing proportion of nonstranger rapes with a weapon that appear in victimization surveys during the 1980s, but it also implies that our analyses of the NCS data may *underestimate* the rate of increase in reports of nonstranger rapes to police over time and, perhaps, the strength of its relationship to sex-role attitude change. If respondents increasingly mention less threatening and, presumably, less "reportable" nonstranger rape incidents in later years of the NCS survey, the heavier overall weight or representation of such incidents would tend to (1) expand the base of total NCS rape victimizations, (2) exert a downward bias over time on NCS sample estimates of the proportion of rapes reported to police, and (3) attenuate linear estimates of longitudinal increase in reports of nonstranger rapes. Thus, if anything, our estimates of relationships between sex-role attitude change and reports of nonstranger rapes to police may be on the conservative side.

However, here as elsewhere in our analysis, we lack direct measures of the definitional processes that lie at the core of our explanation of changing patterns of rape reporting from 1973 to 1985. Consequently we have based our case mainly on indirect inferences and on evidence against alternative explanations of the longitudinal relationship between sex-role attitudes and women's reports of rape. Whereas previous research on the close articulation between acceptance of rape myths and sex-role traditionalism provides some important links in our chain of inference, only victims themselves can offer the kind of evidence that is necessary for a sociologically adequate and experientially grounded account of what it means to be raped.

Acknowledgments.   This is a revision of a paper presented at the 1984 annual meeting of the Society for the Study of Social Problems, San Antonio. We are grateful to the anonymous reviewers and to numerous colleagues for valuable comments on earlier drafts. The order of authorship was determined randomly.

Notes

1. Only percentages of students agreeing with attitude items, rather than full response distributions, are presented in the CIRP reports. Therefore we do not know what percentages of students disagreed with the CIRP items or simply did not respond. Rather than assuming that disagreement is the complement of agreement in these data, we have treated agreement with the sex-role item as a measure of sex-role traditionalism in contrast to the GSS measures described below, which are scored to reflect *non*traditional sex-role attitudes.

2. The CIRP measure of sex-role traditionalism is very similar to items included in Burt's (1980, p. 222) scale of sex-role stereotyping—for example, "There is something wrong with a woman who doesn't want to marry and raise a family"; "It is acceptable for a woman to have a career, but marriage and family should come first." Burt's multivariate analyses show that this scale is one of the strongest predictors of rape myth acceptance among both women and men in her sample of Minnesota adults.

3. The GSS item FEWORK is worded as follows: "Do you approve or disapprove of a married woman earning money in business or industry if she has a husband capable of supporting her?" (nontraditional response is "approve"). The second GSS item, FEPRES, is worded as follows: "If your party nominated a woman for President, would you vote for her if she were qualified for the job?" (nontraditional response is "yes"). The intercorrelation across years between the marginal percentages of female GSS respondents who gave nontraditional responses to these two items is $r = .83$ ($p = .022$), whereas the comparable intercorrelation across seven GSS surveys for male respondents is $r = .92$ ($p = .003$). To construct our index of sex-role nontraditionalism for GSS females, we simply took the mean of the nontraditional marginal percentages for these two items among female respondents for each year of the survey. The GSS nontraditionalism index for males is based on the yearly mean of these two marginal percentages among male respondents.

4. We took the time-series data for the GSS measure of punitiveness toward criminals from the *Sourcebook of Criminal Justice Statistics* (Hindelang, Gottfredson, and Flanagan 1981, pp. 196–197; Jamieson and Flanagan 1987, pp. 86–87).

5. We are especially grateful to an anonymous reviewer for *The Sociological Quarterly* who suggested the addition of a control for "the use of physical violence by assailants." This reviewer also raised the important issue of possible race differences in rape reporting and its relationship

to sex-role traditionalism. While the annual reports of NCS data include a breakdown of non-stranger and stranger rapes reported to the police for white versus black victims, the latter estimates are often based on very few cases and fluctuate widely from year to year—for example, black victims' reports of nonstranger rapes range from 100 percent in 1975 and 1982 to 0 percent in 1980. It is also worth noting that the race breakdowns do not exclude male rape victims, although this is a negligible share of NCS rape victimizations in any given year. Nonetheless, we did examine the key relationships between CIRP sex-role traditionalism and reporting of non-stranger and stranger rapes in separate analyses of the data for white and black victims. The results for white victims are virtually identical to the longitudinal relationships we report in Table 2 for all female victims. As might be expected in light of the instability of yearly estimates for black victimizations, none of the zero-order relationships between CIRP sex-role traditionalism and black victims' reports to police are statistically significant; however, all of them are in the predicted negative direction. Given these results and the fact that our sources for the CIRP attitudinal measures and the NCS controls for weapon use do not provide separate breakdowns by race, we base the remainder of our analysis on the NCS data for all female victims.

6. The confidence intervals ($p < .05$) for these slope estimates overlap, and thus we cannot conclude that they are significantly different. Durban-Watson tests for serial correlation in our OLS estimates of the relationships between nonstranger rape reporting and women's (DW = 2.72) and men's (DW = 2.29) sex-role traditionalism allow us to reject the hypothesis of positive autocorrelation but are inconclusive for negative autocorrelation. An additional check for serial correlation using the nonparametric runs test (Siegel 1956) indicated that the hypothesis of randomly distributed runs in the residual errors could not be rejected at the .05 level for either of these regression equations.

7. The bivariate regressions of the CIRP crime item on the GSS crime item were based on data (for each sex) from those 10 years in which these items were both included on the respective surveys. The resulting equations that we used to estimate the missing value for the CIRP crime item from the 1984 value for the GSS crime item is as follows:

Female respondents: $Y_{CIRP} = -39.9 + (1.19) \chi_{GSS}$

Male respondents: $Y_{CIRP} = -16.6 + (1.02) \chi_{GSS}$

8. The equations for estimating the 1979 and 1981 missing values for the GSS crime item from the corresponding observed values for the CIRP crime item are as follows:

Female respondents: $Y_{GSS} = 41.5 + (.70) \chi_{CIRP}$

Male respondents: $Y_{GSS} = 37.3 + (.66) \chi_{CIRP}$

References

Astin, A.W. and Associates. 1972–1984. *The American Freshman: National Norms.* Los Angeles: Cooperative Institutional Research Program.

Brownmiller, S. 1975. *Against Our Will: Men, Women and Rape.* New York: Bantam Books.

Burt, M.R. 1980. "Cultural Myths and Supports for Rape." *Journal of Personality and Social Psychology* 38:217–230.

Burt, M.R., and R.E. Estep. 1981. "Apprehension and Fear: Learning a Sense of Sexual Vulnerability." *Sex Roles* 7:511–522.

Cherlin, A., and P.B. Walters. 1981. "Trends in United States Men's and Women's Sex-Role Attitudes: 1972–1978." *American Sociological Review* 46:453–460.

Cherry, F. 1983. "Gender Roles and Sexual Violence." In *Changing Boundaries: Gender Roles and Sexual Behavior,* edited by E.R. Allgeier and N.B. McCormick. Palo Alto, CA: Mayfield.

Clark, L., and D. Lewis. 1977. *Rape: The Price of Coercive Sexuality.* Toronto: The Women's Press.

Davis, J.A., and T.W. Smith. 1985. *General Social Surveys, 1972–1985: Cumulative Code-book*. Chicago: National Opinion Research Center.

Feild, H.S. 1978. "Attitudes Toward Rape: A Comparative Analysis of Police, Rapists, Crisis Counselors and Citizens." *Journal of Personality and Social Psychology* 36:156–179.

Gernick, J., M.R. Burt, and K.J. Pittman. 1985. "Structure and Activities of Rape Crisis Centers in the Early 1980s." *Crime and Delinquency* 31:247–268.

Gerson, J.M., and K. Peiss. 1985. "Boundaries, Negotiation, Consciousness: Reconceptualizing Gender Relations." *Social Problems* 32:317–331.

Hindelang, M.J., M.R. Gottfredson, and T.J. Flanagan (eds.). 1981. *Sourcebook of Criminal Justice Statistics—1980*. Washington, DC: U.S. Department of Justice, Bureau of Justice Statistics.

Holmstrom, L.L., and A.W. Burgess. 1978. *The Victim of Rape: Institutional Reactions*. New York: Wiley.

Jamieson, K.M., and T.J. Flanagan (eds.). 1987. *Sourcebook of Criminal Justice Statistics—1986*. Washington, DC: U.S. Department of Justice, Bureau of Justice Statistics.

Klemmack, S.H., and D.L. Klemmack. 1976. "The Social Definition of Rape." In *Sexual Assault: The Victim and the Rapist*, edited by M.J. Walker and S.L. Brodsky. Lexington, MA: Lexington Books.

Krulewitz, J.E., and E.J. Payne. 1978. "Attributions About Rape: Effects of Rapist Force, Observer Sex and Sex Role Attitudes." *Journal of Applied Social Psychology* 8:291–305.

Lizotte, A.J. 1985. "The Uniqueness of Rape: Reporting Assaultive Violence to the Police." *Crime and Delinquency* 31:169–190.

Mason, K.O., J.L. Czajka, and S. Arber. 1976. "Change in U.S. Women's Sex-Role Attitudes, 1964–1974." *American Sociological Review* 41:573–596.

Rose, V.M. 1977. "Rape as a Social Problem: A Byproduct of the Feminist Movement." *Social Problems* 25:75–89.

Russell, D.E.H. 1975. *The Politics of Rape*. New York: Stein and Day.

Schwendinger, J.R., and H. Schwendinger. 1974. "Rape Myths: In Legal, Theoretical, and Everyday Practice." *Crime and Social Justice* 1:18–26.

Siegel, S. 1956. *Nonparametric Statistics for the Behavioral Sciences*. New York: McGraw-Hill.

Stinchcombe, A.L. and Associates. 1980. *Crime and Punishment—Changing Attitudes in America*. San Francisco: Jossey-Bass.

Thornton, A., D.F. Alwin, and D. Camburn. 1983. "Causes and Consequences of Sex-Role Attitudes and Attitude Change." *American Sociological Review* 48:211–227.

U.S. Department of Commerce. 1980. *Statistical Abstract of the United States, 1980*. Washington, DC: U.S. Bureau of the Census.

U.S. Department of Commerce. 1986. *Statistical Abstract of the United States, 1987*. Washington, DC: U.S. Bureau of the Census.

U.S. Department of Justice. 1974–1985. *Criminal Victimization in the United States*. Washington, DC: Bureau of Justice Statistics.

Weis, K., and S.S. Borges. 1973. "Victimology and Rape: The Case of the Legitimate Victim." *Issues in Criminology* 8:71–114.

Williams, L.S. 1984. "The Classic Rape: When Do Victims Report?" *Social Problems* 31:459–467.

Wilson, K., R. Faison, and G.M. Britton. 1983. "Cultural Aspects of Male Sex Aggression." *Deviant Behavior* 4:241–255.

7.   Is Violent Crime Intraracial?

WILLIAM WILBANKS

One of the most commonly accepted facts of criminology is that violent crime, with the possible exception of robbery, is intraracial. Interracial violent crime, whether it is whites victimizing blacks or blacks victimizing whites, is assumed to be relatively infrequent. This fact is so well established that some texts do not even discuss the intraracial versus the interracial nature of crime (e.g. Nettler, 1984; Inciardi, 1984; Sutherland and Cressey, 1970). Some texts simply assert that violent crime is gener- ally intraracial without specifying particular crimes that are considered intraracial (Reid, 1976: 62; Sanders, 1983: 172). Other texts make specific mention of the intraracial character of such crimes as homicide (e.g., Conklin, 1981: 301; McCaghy, 1980: 96; Barlow, 1978: 113; Glaser, 1978: 209), assault (e.g., Conklin, 1981: 301; Bartol, 1980: 216; McCaghy, 1980: 102; Barlow, 1978: 120; Sykes, 1978: 136), and rape (e.g., Conklin, 1981: 301; Bartol, 1980: 250; McCaghy, 1980: 120; Barlow, 1978: 346; Carey, 1978: 269; Haskell and Yablonsky, 1974: 76). At least one author has gone beyond reporting the fact of intraracial violent crime to suggest that whites misperceive violent crime as interracial and thus fear blacks more than whites, and that when interracial crime does occur, it is more likely to involve whites victimizing blacks than blacks victimizing whites (Reid, 1976: 62).

Two types of data are generally cited to support the view that violent crime is intrara- cial. First, several authors cite arrest studies (or crimes reported to the police with or without an arrest) such as the 17-city survey of arrest reports by Curtis (1975: 21) that indicate that interracial events are infrequent. Similarly, Amir's (1971) study of rapes reported to the police, which is widely cited in texts (e.g., Conklin, 1981: 301), found few cases of black on white or white on black rape. One early review of the literature on interracial rape found no arrest study indicating a predominance of black on white rape (Agopian et al., 1974). However, two more recent reviews have found that studies in some cities report that rapes involving blacks victimizing whites constitute as many as 60% of total incidents (LaFree, 1982; Katz and Mazur, 1979). LeBeau (1984) maintains that interracial rape (of blacks against whites) has increased in recent years. Second, victimization surveys are widely believed to support the intraracial character of violent crime and are often cited by authors of textbooks in support of this position.

This article examines the victim's perception of the race of the offender in victimiza- tion reports so that the racial characteristics of offenders (apprehended and not appre- hended) can be examined, along with the race of the reporting victim. The use of perception of race data is not without problems (see Hindelang, 1978; Laub, 1983). Perhaps the most serious problem is the assumption that the victim's perception of the race of the offender is accurate.[1] It may be that some victims are mistaken in their racial identification of the offender or that some are untruthful. In addition, percep-

Table 1. Percentage Distribution of Single-Offender Victimizations for Crimes of Violence by Race of Victims and Perceived Race of Offender[a]

Race of Victim	Number of Victimizations	Perceived Race of Offender		
		WHITE	BLACK	OTHER
White	3,740,000	77.0	17.1	5.9
Black	635,000	14.4	81.9	3.7

[a] From 1981 U.S. Victim Survey.

SOURCE: U.S. Department of Justice, *Criminal Victimization in the United States* (1981: Table 44, p. 49).

tion of offender data from victimization surveys can only be used to produce rates of incidence as opposed to rates of prevalence. Multiple offenders may inflate a group's rate and multiple or series offenders may be more likely to be black (see LeBeau, 1984). Moreover, the perception of race of offender data used in this study includes only incidents involving single offenders (N = 4,375,000 for 1981) as opposed to incidents involving multiple offenders (N = 1,935,000) because multiple offender incidents may not always involve offenders of the same race.[2] Another limitation of the perceived race of the offender information is that the sample size used in the survey did not reveal enough incidents for some table cells for the national estimates to be statistically reliable. For example, [U.S. Department of Justice] Table 44 for 1981 indicates an estimate of 0.0% for incidents of white offenders raping black victims. So that comparisons could be made, I went back to the latest year (1979) when the estimate of white on black rapes was statistically reliable. Finally, the national victim sample cannot reveal city and regional variations for interracial rape and thus the results reported here may not be applicable to all jurisdictions. LeBeau (1984), LaFree (1982), and Katz and Mazur (1979: 103) report that several studies of western cities found much higher rates of interracial rape than cities elsewhere in the United States.

A limitation of the victim survey reports that has not been discussed is the fact that only one set of probabilities—the chance of being victimized by someone of a different (or the same) race—are presented in victimization reports. The probability that an offender will select a victim of another (or the same) race is left unexamined. This reliance on the probabilities reported from the perception (of the race) of the offender perspective has led to the commonly accepted view that violent crime is almost always intraracial. However, an examination of the probabilities from the choice (of race) of victim perspective indicates that whites tend to choose white victims (intraracial) while blacks also tend to choose white victims (interracial).

ASSESSING THE INTRARACIAL AND INTERRACIAL NATURE OF VICTIMIZATION

The data in Table 1, taken from the 1981 national victimization survey (U.S. Department of Justice, 1983), illustrates the victimization survey approach. The format of the table provides percentages only from the perception (of race) of the victim perspective. One can readily see that more whites are victimized by whites (77.0%) than by blacks

Table 2.   Race and Victim/Offender Relationship for Criminal Violence (Robbery, Assault, and Rape) for United States According to 1981 Victim Survey Figures

Race of Offender	White Offender Incidents	Black Offender Incidents	Other Race or Unknown[a]	Total Incidents
WHITE VICTIMS				
Number of incidents[b]	2,879,800	639,540	220,660	3,740,000
Perception of offender perspective				
Percentage	77.0	17.1	5.9	100
Choice of victim perspective				
Percentage	96.9	55.2	90.4	
Percentage of total victimizations[c]	69.7	15.5		
BLACK VICTIMS				
Number of incidents[b]	91,440	520,065	23,595	635,000
Perception of offender perspective				
Percentage	14.4	81.9	3.7	100
Choice of victim perspective				
Percentage	3.1	44.8	9.6	
Percentage of total victimizations[c]	2.2	12.6		
TOTAL VICTIMS				
Total incidents	2,971,240	1,159,605	244,155	4,375,000
Choice of victim perspective				
Percentage	100	100	100	100

[a] Some victims could not identify the race of their assailant. (The question was: Were the offenders white, black or some other race?) Approximately two-thirds of this category involved "other race" responses (the remaining being unknown).

[b] Total incident figures for white and black victims are taken from Table 44, page 49. Incident figures involving white and black offenders are derived by multiplying the percentage of incidents by the total incidents (e.g., 77.0% of 3,740,000 = 2,879,800).

[c] Percentage of all incidents (4,130,845) where race of victim and offender was known and was white or black (not "other race").

SOURCE: U.S. Department of Justice, *Criminal Victimization in the United States* (1981: Table 44, p. 49).

(17.1%) and more blacks are victimized by blacks (81.9%) than by whites (14.4%). The format does not focus on the choice (of race) of victim—that is, the extent to which white and black offenders are more likely to choose victims of their own race. However, since the total number of victimizations are given by race of victim, a more elaborate table can easily be constructed that provides percentages for the choice of victim and for the perception of race of offender (see notes at bottom of Table 2).

Tables 2 through 5 are reconstructions of the victimization data to reflect both sets

Table 3. Race and Victim/Offender Relationship for Robbery for United States According to 1981 Victim Survey

Race of Offender	White Offender Incidents	Black Offender Incidents	Other Race or Unknown[a]	Total Incidents
WHITE VICTIMS				
Number of incidents[b]	225,094	201,744	40,162	467,000
Perception of offender perspective				
Percentage	48.2	43.2	8.6	100
Choice of victim perspective				
Percentage	91.7	63.9	80.2	
Percentage of total victimizations[c]	40.1	36.0		
BLACK VICTIMS				
Number of incidents[b]	20,304	113,760	9,936	144,000
Perception of offender perspective				
Percentage	14.1	79.0	6.9	100
Choice of victim perspective				
Percentage	8.3	36.1	19.8	
Percentage of total victimizations[c]	3.6	20.3		
TOTAL VICTIMS				
Total incidents	245,398	315,504	50,098	611,00
Choice of victim perspective				
Percentage	100	100	100	100

[a-c] See Table 2.

SOURCE: U.S. Department of Justice, *Criminal Victimization in the United States* (1981: Table 44, p. 49).

of percentages. A third percentage figure—that of the percent of cell events of all victimizations—is presented as this figure is commonly found in the literature as an indication of the extent of intraracial crime.[3]

Determining whether the three (combined) crimes of robbery, assault, and rape are intraracial or interracial is seen as a more complicated question when Table 2 is examined. On the one hand, it appears that 82.3% of the incidents where race of the offender was known involved either whites victimizing whites (69.7%) or blacks victimizing blacks (12.6%) and thus these three crimes could be viewed as being predominantly intraracial. Likewise, as reported in Table 1, the percentage figures showing the relative frequency with which victims of one race have been victimized by someone of the same or different race also suggest that violent crime is intraracial—77.0% of white victims perceived their offender to be white and 81.9% of black victims perceived their offender as black.

Table 4.   Race and Victim/Offender Relationship for Assault for United States According to 1981 Victim Survey

Race of Offender	White Offender Incidents	Black Offender Incidents	Other Race or Unknown[a]	Total Incidents
WHITE VICTIMS				
Number of incidents[b]	2,578,452	410,280	167,268	3,156,000
Perception of offender perspective				
Percentage	81.7	13.0	5.3	100
Choice of victim perspective				
Percentage	97.3	51.8	92.3	
Percentage of total victimizations[c]	74.9	11.9		
BLACK VICTIMS				
Number of incidents[b]	70,984	382,006	14,010	467,000
Perception of offender perspective				
Percentage	15.2	81.8	3.0	100
Choice of victim perspective				
Percentage	2.7	48.2	7.7	
Percentage of total victimizations[c]	2.1	11.1		
TOTAL VICTIMS				
Total incidents	2,649,436	792,286	181,278	3,623,000
Choice of victim perspective				
Percentage	100	100	100	100

[a-c] See Table 2.

SOURCE: U.S. Department of Justice, *Criminal Victimization in the United States* (1981: Table 44, p. 49).

It is only when one examines the choices of victims that the predominance of interracial crime for black offenders appears. Though violent crime by white offenders appears to be strongly intraracial in that 96.9% of the white offenders choose white victims, violent crime by black offenders appears to be predominantly interracial with 55.2% of the black offenders choosing white victims. It is for this reason that the use of an overall statistic, such as the 82.3% figure cited above, to represent the extent of intraracial versus interracial crime, as well as the use of percentages showing the proportion of victims of one race who have been victimized by a person of the same race, mask the interracial character of violent crime by black offenders from the choice of victim perspective.

Tables 3 through 5 indicate that the pattern found for the three crimes of violence as a group holds for each of the crimes when considered separately. Black offenders

Table 5. Race and Victim/Offender Relationship for Rape for United States According to 1979 Victim Survey

Race of Offender	White Offender Incidents	Black Offender Incidents	Other Race or Unknown[a]	Total Incidents
WHITE VICTIMS				
Number of incidents[b]	92,560	27,950	9,490	130,000
Perception of offender perspective				
Percentage	71.2	21.5	7.3	100
Choice of victim perspective				
Percentage	94.5	58.6	83.4	
Percentage of total victimizations[c]	63.5	19.2		
BLACK VICTIMS				
Number of incidents[b]	5,346	19,764	1,890	27,000
Perception of offender perspective				
Percentage	19.8	73.2	7.0	100
Choice of victim perspective				
Percentage	5.5	41.4	16.6	
Percentage of total victimizations[c]	3.7	13.6		
TOTAL VICTIMS				
Total incidents	97,906	47,714	11,380	157,000
Choice of victim perspective				
Percentage	100	100	100	100

[a-c] See Table 2.

Source: U.S. Department of Justice, *Criminal Victimization in the United States* (1979: Table 43, p. 49).

chose white victims in 63.9% of robberies (Table 3), 51.8% of assaults (Table 4), and 58.6% of rapes (Table 5). By contrast, white offenders chose black victims in 8.3% of robberies, 2.7% of assaults, and 5.5% of rapes. These percentages suggest that each of the three violent crimes is strongly intraracial for white offenders but predominantly interracial for black offenders.

DISCUSSION

The fact that black offenders tend to choose white victims is not so surprising in robbery because this offense is primarily economic—whites tend to be the racial group most likely to have money, and there are more whites in the population. The choice of white victims by black assaulters is more surprising since assault has generally been considered to be similar in pattern to homicide (Pittman and Handy, 1964), which is largely intraracial from the choice of victim by the black offender perspective. In the absence of further analysis of the victimization data, it is possible that assaults as reported by victims in the surveys are quite different from assaults that result in arrests (which do not show the interracial character). This may be because black on white assaulters are more likely to be strangers and thus less likely to be arrested; or because white victims tend to overreport any threatening contacts with blacks as assaults; or because the assaults by blacks against whites are more trivial than the assaults that result in arrests.

The fact that black rapists tend to choose white victims is even more surprising and difficult to explain. Though Eldridge Cleaver's (1968) comments about raping white women to "get back" at white society are widely quoted, there is no suggestion in the literature that rape is interracial in that black rapists tend to be more likely to choose white rather than black victims—except in prison (Lochwood, 1980). Without suggesting that black rapists choose white victims more often, Curtis (1976: 128) does suggest that interracial rape may be increasing due to increased social contacts between blacks and whites and/or to reduced inhibitions against attacking whites due to an emerging sense of identity and confidence in the black community. If those who work with rapists (Groth, 1979) are correct, and rape is an expression of hostility to women, it would appear from the victimization data that black men are more often angry and hostile toward white women than at black women. LaFree (1982) did find some empirical support for the conflict explanation. Certainly more work needs to be done with convicted rapists to discover the dynamics behind their choice of victims.

Little explanation is needed as to why white offenders choose white victims and why both white and black victims more often report that their offender was of their race. However, the "discovery" of violent crime as interracial when the choice of victim of black offenders is examined as opposed to intraracial when the choice of victim of white offenders is examined may suggest that the motives behind black assault and rape are different from the motives behind white assault and rape. It may be that black assaulters are largely strangers who are expressing hostility toward whites in general whereas white assaulters are largely persons known to the victim who are involved in some more personal or familial dispute. Likewise, it may be that black rapists are expressing hostility toward whites as well as women through rape while white rapists are simply expressing hostility toward women.

The failure of the literature to discuss the partially interracial character of violent crime may be because of a reluctance on the part of criminologists to discuss so sensitive an issue. It seems unlikely that those who formulated the tables for the publications of the victimization survey did not recognize the partially interracial character of crime that would have been revealed if column percentages as well as row percentages were presented and discussed. Perhaps a conscious decision was made to simply avoid this issue. Fred Graham (1970) suggested a decade ago, without referring to interracial crime, that high black crime rates have been hidden from public view because of the failure of the FBI, the press, and the black community to discuss the problem. He further suggests that the "long-standing national myopia about Negro crime has been a remarkable public exercise in whistling past a graveyard" (1970: 64). If that is the case, certainly the myopia about interracial crime is even more subject to this characterization.

Or perhaps criminologists who maintain that violent crime is intraracial have relied upon arrest studies rather than on an analysis of data from victimization surveys. Arrest studies do appear to suggest that violent crime, with the exception of robbery, is intraracial from all four perspectives. A recalculation of Curtis's (1975: 21) arrest data for 17 cities indicates that blacks chose blacks as victims in 88.7% of aggravated assaults and 85.0% of rapes. Robbery was interracial however in that 54.2% of unarmed robberies and 55.0% of armed robberies by blacks were against whites. Conklin (1981: 301) cites other arrest studies to support the view that crimes of violence, with the exception of robbery, are intraracial.

The belief that violent crime is almost always intraracial may also have developed from the wide dissemination of homicide statistics, which do indicate that black offenders largely victimize black victims (Wolfgang, 1958; Wilbanks, 1984). As murder appears to be intraracial from all four perspectives and data has not been as readily available for assault and rape, many may have assumed simply that the intraracial pattern of murder also existed for rape and assault. A similar conclusion with respect to the intersexual versus the intrasexual nature of assaults by women was previously drawn from a reliance upon murder figures. Because the *Uniform Crime Reports* figures for murder indicated that women almost always killed men rather than other women, it was assumed that the same pattern held for assaults that are considered to be simply unsuccessful murders. However, victimization data demonstrated that 85% of the victims of female assaulters were females (Parisi, 1982: 120). The failure of others to recognize this fact before Parisi was probably a result of the format of the table by Hindelang (1979: 151) that reported only one set of percentages.

Notes

1. Hindelang (1978) says that some victims may adhere to popular stereotypes of criminals and thus may report Latino offenders as black. Sagarin (1977) suggests that some victims of interracial rape become confused as to the race of the offender.

2. However, an analysis of the choice of victim perspective for black offenders for incidents involving multiple offenders suggests that this type of event is also interracial in the choice of victim by black offenders. Of the incidents in the 1981 survey where the groups of offenders were perceived as all white or all black, the all-black groups chose white victims in 58.4 percent (413,135) of their total incidents (707,919). By contrast, all-white groups chose white victims in 95.6 percent (921,369) of their total incidents (963,105).

3. The most common statistic found in the literature to measure intraracial versus interracial crime appears to be the percent of all events that involve either whites victimizing blacks or blacks victimizing whites. Katz and Mazur (1979) point out rather high overall percentages of blacks raping whites but then conclude that rape is intraracial.

References

Agopian, M.W., D. Chappell, and G. Geis
    1974   "Interracial forcible rape in the North American city: An analysis of sixty-three cases," pp. 93–102 in I. Drapkin & E. Viano (eds.) Victimology. Lexington, MA: D.C. Heath.

Amir, M.
    1971   Patterns in Forcible Rape. Chicago: Univ. of Chicago Press.
Barlow, H.D.
    1978   Introduction to Criminology. Boston: Little, Brown.
Bartol, C.R.
    1980   Criminal Behavior: A Psychosocial Approach. Englewood Cliffs, NJ: Prentice-Hall.
Carey, J.T.
    1978   Introduction to Criminology. Englewood Cliffs, NJ: Prentice-Hall.
Cleaver, E.
    1968   Soul on Ice. New York: McGraw-Hill.
Conklin, J.E.
    1981   Criminology. New York: Macmillan.
Curtis, L.A.
    1975   Criminal Violence: National Patterns and Behavior. Lexington, MA: D.C. Heath.
    1976   "Rape, race and culture: Some speculation in search of a theory," pp. 117–134 in M.J. Walker & S.L. Brodsky (eds.) Sexual Assault. Lexington, MA: D.C. Heath.
Glaser, D.
    1978   Crime in Our Changing Society. New York: Holt, Rinehart & Winston.
Graham, F.
    1970   "Black crime: The lawless image." Harper's Magazine 241:64–71.
Groth, A.N.
    1979   Men Who Rape. New York: Plenum.
Haskell, M.R. and L. Yablonsky
    1974   Criminology: Crime and Criminality. Chicago: Rand McNally.
Hindelang, M.J.
    1978   "Race and involvement in common law personal crimes." Amer. Soc. Rev. 43:93–109.
    1979   "Sex differences in criminal activity." Social Problems 27:143–156.
Inciardi, J.A.
    1984   Criminal Justice. Orlando, FL: Academic.
Katz, S. and M.A. Mazur
    1979   Understanding the Rape Victim: A Synthesis of Research Findings. New York: John Wiley.
LaFree, G.D.
    1982   "Male power and female victimization: Toward a theory of interracial rape." Amer. J. of Sociology 88(2):311–328.
Laub, J.H.
    1983   "Urbanism, race, and crime." J. of Research in Crime and Delinquency 20 (2): 183–198.
LeBeau, J.L.
    1984   "Rape and race." J. of Offender Counseling Services and Rehabilitation 9 (1–2).
Lochwood, D.
    1980   Prison Sexual Violence. New York: Elsevier.
McCaghy, C.H.
    1980   Crime in American Society. New York: Macmillan.
Nettler, G.
    1984   Explaining Crime. New York: McGraw-Hill.
Parisi, N.
    1982   "Exploring female crime patterns: Problems and perspectives," pp. 462–470 in N.H. Rafter & E.A. Stanko (eds.) Judge Lawyer Victim Thief: Women, Gender Roles and Criminal Justice. Boston: Northeastern Univ. Press.
Pittman, D.J. and W. Handy
    1964   "Patterns in criminal aggravated assault." J. of Criminal Law, Crime and Political Science 55:462–470.

Reid, S.T.
　1976　Crime and Criminology. Hinsdale, IL: Dryden.
Sagarin, E.
　1977　"Forcible rape and the problem of the rights of the accused," pp. 142–160 in
　　　　D. Chappell et al. (eds.) Forcible Rape: The Crime, the Victim, and the Offender.
　　　　New York: Columbia Univ. Press.
Sanders, W.B.
　1983　Criminology. New York: Addison-Wesley.
Siegel, L.J.
　1983　Criminology. New York: West.
Sutherland, E.H. and D.R. Cressey
　1970　Criminology. Philadelphia: J.B. Lippincott.
Sykes, G.M.
　1978　Criminology. New York: Harcourt Brace Janovich.
U.S. Department of Justice, Bureau of Justice Statistics
　1981　Criminal Victimization in the United States, 1979. Washington, DC: U.S. Department
　　　　of Justice.
　1983　Criminal Victimization in the United States, 1981. Washington, DC: U.S. Department
　　　　of Justice.
Wilbanks, W.
　1984　Murder in Miami: An Analysis of Homicide Patterns and Trends in Dade County
　　　　(Miami) Florida, 1917–1983. Washington, DC: Univ. Press of America.
Wolfgang, M.
　1958　Patterns in Criminal Homicide. Philadelphia: Univ. of Pennsylvania Press.

8.　Women and the Commission of Crime: A Theoretical Approach

CAROL A. WHITEHURST

Because theories of deviant behavior have generally ignored women's crime, they have been considered theories less of deviant behavior than of male deviant behavior.[1] This oversight, which illustrates the larger problem of the invisibility of women in much of social science, underscores the need for a feminist analysis of crime not based on the white, middle-class male model (see Smith, 1974; Daniels, 1975; Millman and Kanter, 1975). Very few theorists have asked why women commit (or don't commit) crimes; those who have posed this question have often based their answers on biological or psychological assumptions, offering little or no evidence to support their contentions. An often-cited example is Otto Pollack's argument that women actually commit as much crime as men, but are addicted to crimes that are easily concealed and seldom reported (Pollack, 1950).

　　This paper will explore how sociological theories of deviance can help explain women's commission of crime in light of two important facts: (1) women's reported crime always has represented only a small proportion of men's reported crime, and (2) the proportion of total reported crimes committed by women has increased considerably since about 1960.

WOMEN'S CRIME AS A PROPORTION OF MEN'S CRIME

In 1980, men accounted for over 80 percent of all arrests for serious crimes.[2] However, for total violent crimes,[3] the proportions were 90 percent male, and 10 percent female. For property crimes,[4] the proportions were 78.5 percent male and 21.5 percent female. The crimes women were most likely to commit (other than prostitution) relative to men, were fraud, forgery and counterfeiting, larceny-theft, and embezzlement. Those crimes that women were least likely to commit (other than rape) relative to men, were burglary, weapons carrying and possession, robbery, sex offenses other than prostitution, vandalism, and motor vehicle theft.

THE INCREASE IN WOMEN'S CRIME SINCE 1960

Between 1960 and 1972, total female arrests increased far more than male. According to the F.B.I.'s *Uniform Crime Reports* (UCR), there was a 159.4 percent increase in male commission of robbery and a 277.2 percent increase for females; for larceny, there was an 82.3 percent increase for males and a 303.2 percent increase for females. Overall, male property crimes increased 71.9 percent while female rates increased 281.5 percent. However, because women start from a much smaller base, these statistics are misleading. It is more useful to examine the increase in the proportion of total arrests. Table 1 shows the increases from 1955 through 1980.

While total serious crimes increased, this was accounted for entirely by an increase in property rather than violent crimes, mostly occurring during the 1960s and early 1970s. Increases have been greater for juvenile girls than for adult women, and self-

Table 1. Women's Arrests as Percentages of All Crimes in Three Categories, 1955–1980

	Serious Crimes	Violent Crimes	Property Crimes
1955	9.12	12.03	8.36
1960	10.95	11.77	10.76
1965	14.37	11.41	14.99
1970	18.04	10.50	19.71
1980	19.10	10.00	21.50

Source: Adapted from *Uniform Crime Reports* (Washington D.C.: Federal Bureau of Investigation, U.S. Department of Justice, 1980), Table 27; and from Eileen B. Leonard, *Women, Crime and Society* (New York: Longman, 1982), p. 27.

report studies indicate that differences in crime commission for juveniles are smaller than arrest figures indicate (Cernkovich and Giordano, 1979; Hindelang, 1973).

ACCURACY OF FIGURES

The UCR figures represent only arrests, not actual commission of crime. Since actual crimes represent many times the number of arrests, these figures represent *reactions* to crime, not crime itself. The UCR figures are limited in a number of ways: data provided by law enforcement agencies are voluntary and therefore not necessarily representative (Chapman, 1980:58–59); many categories of crime, such as the majority of corporate crimes, are not included at all; figures are affected by demographic changes, such as the baby-boomers reaching the peak "at risk" years during the 1960s and 1970s, when crime rates rose the fastest; and figures are affected by changes in definitions and statutes in the criminal justice and police systems.

As examples of the last point, Chapman (1980) points out that arrest rates are affected by changed definitions of crime. Defining narcotics use as a crime and classifying female drug users as criminals contribute to a "female crime wave." After 1972 the $50 minimum for larceny was eliminated; this change contributed to much higher rates of larceny. Some crimes committed frequently by women, such as welfare fraud and shoplifting, have become more vigorously prosecuted (Chapman, 1980; Steffensmeier, 1980). Finally, as Feinman (1980) points out, the period of fastest increases in rates of crime for (primarily young) women was also the period when substantial numbers of "at risk" men were being sent to Vietnam. This factor increased the proportion of women offenders relative to men. As Chapman has said, trends in female criminality "may reflect greater changes in reporting, arrest, prosecution, and sentencing than in actual behavior" (1980:28).

It may be that female crime or arrest rates are more accurate now than in the past because of improved collection methods and a decline in "chivalry," or preferential treatment for women. The "chivalry" argument is that the perception of women as less aggressive and less likely to break the law has benefited women. Police didn't like to arrest women; judges, prosecutors, and juries didn't like to convict them; and women were less likely than men to be sent to prison if convicted (Simon, 1979). While there is some truth to this argument, actually only certain women have benefited from "chivalry" for some crimes. For crimes considered "unacceptable" for women (e.g., violent crimes and crimes of "sexual misconduct"), treatment has often been harsher for women (Chapman, 1980; Jones, 1980). In addition, it is only middle- and upper-class women, the least likely to come into contact with the criminal justice system, who have benefited from preferential treatment (Klein, 1976). As Feinman (1980) points out, the lower-class woman has never been accorded the "Madonna" aspect of the Madonna-whore duality.

Far more black and minority poor women than middle-class white women are arrested, and a majority of institutionalized women are from racial minorities, are poor, and are convicted of nonviolent crimes (Babcock, 1973). The typical American female criminal is young, black, and poor; has limited education and skills; is the head of a household and a mother; and is imprisoned most often for larceny or a drug offense (Chapman, 1980:60; Glick and Neto, 1977). Preferential treatment actually seems to be accorded more on the basis of class and race than on the basis of gender.

It may also be that chivalry is becoming a thing of the past. Most current studies tend to support the idea of a changing attitude within the criminal justice system, usually depending on the offense and the age of the offender. Crites's (1976) analysis of California data found evenhanded treatment for women and men in court, and Simon (1975) found similar proportions of women and men convicted in court. Kramer and Kempinen (1978) reported that the slight preferential treatment they found in 1970 had disappeared by 1975. They also found lighter sentences for women in 1970 and 1975, but smaller sex differences in 1975. The researchers felt that this was not necessarily because of a decline in chivalry, but was partly because of courts' increasing reluctance to prosecute on anything other than legal grounds or sentencing guidelines, which they attributed to the civil rights movement. Less frequent sentencing may also reflect lesser seriousness of the offenses.

Although arrest data are less clear, there are some indications that "Law enforcement agencies, responding to increased pressure from victims, are taking a more aggressive role in arresting women offenders" (Feinman, 1980:17; see also Steffensmeier, 1980). In another study, the decision of police to arrest was found to be influenced by demeanor and type of offense, not the sex of the offender (Moyer and White, 1979). Ward et al. (1980) found that 80 percent of women charged in robberies were accessories or partners, and more recent studies tend to reach similar conclusions (Klein and Kress, 1976; Simon, 1979). Studies conducted by the Federal Bureau of Prisons in 1973–1975 concluded that most women prisoners had been convicted for drug offenses, larceny-theft, and forgery — crimes that were, for the most part, fairly minor (Feinman, 1980:27).

Steffensmeier (1980) argues that women's crime rates have increased for a number of reasons, including greater likelihood that female suspects would be reported, greater suspicion and surveillance, increased pressure for equal application of the law, and a trend toward greater professionalism and universalistic standards among police. Steffensmeier also points out that crackdowns on welfare fraud and a trend toward computerized record-keeping and improved methods of detecting fraud recidivists would tend to increase female relative to male arrests for fraud.

Self-report data show smaller gaps between female and male crime than do official arrest records, which would tend to indicate some continuing tendency toward preferential treatment for some women for some crimes. However, the gap is smaller for juveniles, blacks, and lesser offenses (Cernkovich and Giordano, 1979; Hindelang, 1973; Shover et al., 1979; Smith, 1979; Smith and Visher, 1980). Thus, most studies would suggest that males continue to commit more crimes, especially serious ones, than do females; that the gap between females and males is smaller than is indicated by arrest rates; and that women's and girls' arrest rates are increasingly reflecting their actual commission of crime.

ETIOLOGY OF CRIME

Since the vast majority of women's reported crimes are property crimes, current researchers tend to conclude that women's crime is largely economically motivated. Rans (1975) found some general correlation between economic need and crime, and found that historically higher crime rates for women have been associated with inflation, unemployment, and greater family responsibilities. U.S. prison admissions for women peaked from 1931 to 1935 (during the depths of the Depression), from 1961 to 1963 (a period of economic recession), and during the 1970s (a period of instability in the economy with rising unemployment) (Chapman, 1980:63). Crime may be seen as an economic alternative for some poor women (Klein, 1976). Steffensmeier (1980) sees the large increases in arrests of women for larceny-theft as resulting from marketing consumption trends and the worsening economic position of many women in the United States; this author points out that women are increasingly required to support themselves and others and that poverty is increasingly a female problem. Feinman (1980:20) explains that women's economic situation has deteriorated since 1960—the gap in earnings has increased, more women are poor heads of households, and more women lost their jobs first in the recession of 1974–1975.

Widom and Stewart (1977) concluded that in cross-national comparisons, higher female arrest rates were associated with lower levels of economic differentiation by sex (e.g., equal pay laws), but lower female arrest rates were associated with female involvement in the labor force, college education, and having female legislators. Widom and Stewart concluded, "it is possible that [legal] equality without actual equality is related to high female crime rates, while a combination of legal and actual equality is related to lower female crime rates." Thus, if the increases in crime rates for women reflect actual changes in behavior, they indicate that more women are poor, single, and heads of households.

While it has been argued that women's expanding work opportunities would result in more white-collar crime because of greater opportunity to commit such crimes (Simon, 1975), there seems to be little support for this idea. The crimes that have increased substantially for women are larceny-theft, primarily shoplifting (Steffensmeier [1978] estimated that 70–80 percent of female larceny arrests were for shoplifting), and fraud/embezzlement, which reflects largely welfare[5] and credit-card fraud, the passing of bad checks, and lower-echelon embezzlement (Glick and Neto, 1977; Steffensmeier, 1978, 1980). It has been estimated that only about 1 percent of embezzlement cases are prosecuted in criminal courts, and these mainly are those at lower levels (Feinman, 1980:363). Feinman concluded that some of the increases in embezzlement during the 1960s and 1970s may have occurred because greater numbers of women were bank tellers, cashiers, payroll clerks, and so on. There is little evidence that lucrative white-collar crimes committed by females have increased. As Norland and Shover (1977) have observed, no clear-cut pattern of change in women's criminality is yet observable. (See also Bruck, 1975; Klein and Kress, 1976; Rans, 1975; Simon, 1979; Steffensmeier, 1978; Weis, 1976.)

It has also been argued that the increasing freedom of women and their increased aggressiveness would result in higher rates of violent crime (Adler, 1975). Adler attributed this not to the women's movement per se, but to the fact that women were smarter, were shrewder, and had bigger ideas. She argued that lessened restrictions and sex-role expectations for women, along with increased demands for assertiveness and more varied opportunities, would loosen social control and allow women's behavior to become like that of men. This argument assumes that women's roles, expectations, and socialization have been rapidly approaching equality with those of men, which is certainly debatable (see Baldwin, 1983; Leonard, 1982), and that female liberation equates with norm-violating, aggressive behavior. However, it is not violent crime that has increased for women relative to men. Walter Miller (1973) found little or no support for the claim that female criminality, in general or in connection with gang activity, was either more prevalent or more violent than in the past. Judges and attorneys interviewed by Rita Simon in 1975 reported that the women they were seeing were no different from those they had seen five to six years earlier (Simon, 1979).

Simon (1975) had suggested that women might actually commit less violent crime because of reduced frustration over their roles. She argued that as women's employment and educational opportunities expand, their feelings of being victimized and exploited decrease and their motivation to kill becomes muted (Simon, 1977). However, as Steffensmeier (1980) points out, female violence has neither declined relative to male violence, as Simon predicted, nor increased faster, as Adler predicted.

THE WOMEN'S MOVEMENT

There are several major difficulties in suggesting that the women's movement has led to an increase in female crime, in part because it is not a variable that can be operationalized (see Campbell, 1981:236). Secondly, if the women's movement were to blame, the greatest increases in female crime should have occurred in the past ten or twelve years (since about 1970), while actually the greatest changes occurred during the 1960s and have recently leveled off (Bartel, 1979; Gora, 1979; Steffensmeier and Steffensmeier, 1980). Specific aspects of the women's movement are not much more successful as explanations for the rise in female crime. Greater female participation in the labor force has mostly benefited white middle-class adult women, whereas the typical offender is poor, from a minority group, and young. Bartel (1979) found that increased labor force participation was negatively related to female crime.

The largest increases in the commission of crimes from 1960 to 1975 were among women under age eighteen who were mostly not in the labor force (Chapman, 1980:52). Opportunities have improved little for women, especially for women whose offenses are reflected in the statistics. If most women's crimes are committed out of economic need, greater opportunities could reduce rather than increase crime. On the other hand, if women's occupational opportunities at upper levels actually expand substantially, there could be an increase in this type of crime, although not necessarily, because of women's "vastly different historical, social, and economic experiences" (Leonard, 1982:182).

The "masculination" or increased aggressiveness of women because of the women's movement is not supported as a cause of crime because women's crimes are not violent but are still considered to be extensions of the traditional female role (Chapman, 1980; Crites, 1976; Klein and Kress, 1976; Smart, 1976; Steffensmeier, 1978; Weis, 1976). Further, there is little or no evidence that the women's movement has had any substantial effect on socialization practices (Baldwin, 1983). Finally, there is no support for the idea that feminist ideology or pro-feminist attitudes are related to female crime. Adler (1975) found many female offenders vocally opposed any association with the women's movement, and came from lower strata that traditionally recognize male domination and superiority. Widom (1979) found that female offenders were significantly less pro-feminist than non-offenders, and James and Thornton (1980) found that girls' positive attitudes toward feminism had little influence on their delinquent involvement; any effect at all was negative. Jones (1980:320) found that battered women who killed their husbands either ignored or opposed feminism. Giordano and Cernkovich (1979) found little or no association between liberated attitudes and self-reported delinquency in girls, and Bruck (1975) reported meeting no women offenders who felt any association with the women's movement or feminism at the time of their crimes.

Female college students reporting fewer nonviolent offenses were slightly more likely to subscribe to feminist ideology than those who reported more such offenses, and self-perceived "masculinity" in girls was moderately related to "fun crimes" (e.g., joyriding), but negatively related to feminism (Eve and Edmonds, 1978). Leventhal (1977) found that incarcerated women were more likely than female college students to support traditional female roles, and they had less positive attitudes toward the women's movement and feminism. Women's crime has risen in many countries where the women's movement has made no progress at all (Widom and Stewart, 1977). Steffensmeier (1980:1098) concluded, "The movement appears to have had a greater impact on changing the image of the female offender than [on] the types of criminal offenses that she is likely to commit." Available data indicate no connection between female crime and feminism, and any recognition of women's changed capacities or needs seems to have no political or ideological content (Adler, 1975).

It would seem to be more useful to argue that changes in female crime and the emergence of the women's movement both express larger social and economic changes. Datesman and Scarpitti (1980:3) argue that the women's movement cannot be seen as a direct cause of female crime, although it may have contributed to changes in how women are handled in the criminal justice system. These researchers also point out that women may now be more likely to adopt the "male" role as supporters of themselves and their children. However, the ideology of the women's movement itself is unrelated or negatively related to female crime. Until recently there has been little attempt to try systematically to explain women's deviance from the standpoint of established theories of deviant behavior. However, as others have recently pointed out (Crites, 1976; Leonard, 1982), some insights from these theories may help to develop a broader theoretical approach to male and female deviance.

THEORIES

Anomie theory, as developed by Merton (1938), seems to suggest that if goals are held out equally to men and women, then women should experience greater discrepancies and be more norm-violating (Harris, 1977). However, if we assume that women have not been socialized into the same goals of occupational and material success, then women may experience less means-ends discrepancy and thus less deviance (Campbell, 1981:69; Harry and Sengstock, 1977; Leonard, 1982; Steffensmeier, 1978). However, as women's goals shift from finding a husband and having children toward occupational and economic goals, crimes to achieve these should also increase, unless legal means for achieving them increase accordingly (Campbell, 1981:77–79; Datesman et al., 1975; Harry and Sengstock, 1977; Sandhu and Allen, 1969).

Subcultural, social role, social learning, socialization and differential association theories have in common the idea that females and males have fundamentally different subcultures and learn different values, expectations, aspirations and roles through a process of socialization in groups. Leonard (1982:137) suggests that violence, strength, and toughness are not avenues of status for girls, and Morris (1964) found that girls experienced a relative absence of subcultural supports for and more stringent disapproval of delinquency. Because of differential socialization, girls have been found to be more conformist (Bardwick and Douvan, 1971; Maccoby and Jacklin, 1980; Thomas and Weigart, 1971), to have fewer skills necessary for criminal activity (Hoffman-Bustamente, 1973), to be more obedient and nonaggressive (Block, 1978), and to receive an excess of definitions unfavorable to crime (Jensen, 1972). Girls also spend less time in groups and on the streets, and have fewer friends supportive of delinquent behavior (Campbell, 1981:64; Giordano, 1978; James and Thornton, 1980; Jensen and Eve, 1976; Simons et al., 1980). Thus, the low incidence of female crime and crimes typical of women can partly be seen as representing female subcultural values and role expectations (Crites, 1976; Heidensohn, 1968; Klein, 1976; Leonard, 1982; Morris, 1964; Rosenblum, 1975; Shover et al., 1979).

Social control or bonding theories suggest that parental supervision and control are negatively related to delinquency, and that girls tend to be more controlled and bonded than boys (Sutherland and Cressy, 1974:130; Thomas and Weigart, 1971). Girls who are less bonded to parents or who perceive little benefit from adherence to conventional norms are somewhat more likely to violate norms (Andrew, 1976; Campbell, 1981:80; James and Thornton, 1980; Jensen and Eve, 1976; McCord, 1979; Shover et al., 1979; Simons et al., 1980; Smith, 1979).

Labeling or societal reaction theory suggests that those most likely to be labeled are those with the least power to resist. This viewpoint overlooks the effects of positive labeling, which has benefited non poor white women, thus modifying rather than amplifying female deviance (Campbell, 1981:81; Heidensohn, 1968; Thorsell and Klemke, 1979). However, societal reaction to women can change with a change in women's image, and this new attitude toward women's potential for crime and violence can further be reflected in higher female crime rates (Jones, 1980; Leonard, 1982:85).

Conflict theories and radical criminology have been criticized for their failure to deal adequately with the position of women (Klein and Kress, 1976), but Campbell (1981:73) describes how radical criminologists have analyzed delinquency among youth subcultures in terms of the fads and fashions of their social strata. Girls preoccupied with appearance are particularly susceptible to the demands for consumption, which may lead to the typical female crime of shoplifting. Conflict approaches could develop a structural context in which the interaction of class, race, and sex roles could be analyzed to understand crime.

Although theories of deviant behavior have not generally been applied to women, they can be useful in understanding both the traditional patterns and recent changes in women's crime. Crime is best seen as an expression of structural changes in the economy, opportunities, societal values, and changing roles and relationships. These theories can be useful in understanding both women's and men's crimes.

Notes

1. Simons, Miller, and Aigner (1980) found that all the theories they tested (labeling, control, anomie, and differential association), with the possible exception of anomie theory, applied equally well to girls and boys.

2. Serious crimes include murder and non-negligent manslaughter, aggravated assault, rape, robbery, burglary, larceny-theft, motor-vehicle theft, and arson (Crime Index Total).

3. Violent crimes include murder and non-negligent manslaughter, aggravated assault, rape, and robbery.

4. Property crimes include burglary, larceny-theft, motor-vehicle theft, and arson.

5. Feinman (1980:17) reports that, according to the (October 5, 1978) ACLU *News*, welfare fraud accounted for 34 percent of all women arrested for fraud in 1976.

References

Adler, Freda. *Sisters in Crime* (New York: McGraw-Hill, 1975).

Alder, Freda, and Rita Simon. *The Criminology of Deviant Women* (Boston: Houghton Mifflin, 1979).

Andrew, J.M. "Delinquency, Sex, and Family Variables." *Social Biology*, 23 (1976):168–171.

Babcock, Barbara Allen. "Introduction: Women and the Criminal Law." *American Criminal Law Review*, 11 (Winter 1973):291–294.

Baldwin, Janice I. "The Effects of Women's Liberation and Socialization on Delinquency and Crime." *Humboldt Journal of Social Relations*, 10 (Spring 1983).

Bardwick, Judith, and Elizabeth Douvan. "Ambivalence: The Socialization of Women." In Vivian Gornick and Barbara K. Moran, *Women in Sexist Society* (New York: Basic Books, 1971), pp. 225–241.

Bartel, Ann P. "Women and Crime: An Economic Analysis." *Economic Inquiry*, 17 (January 1979):29–51.

Block, Jeanne H. "Another Look at Sex Differences in the Socialization Behavior of Mothers and Fathers." In Julia Sherman and Florence L. Denmark, eds., *Psychology of Women: Future Directions of Research* (New York: Psychological Dimensions, 1978).

Bruck, Connie. "Women Against the Law." *Human Behavior* (December 1975):24–33.

Campbell, Anne. *Girl Delinquents* (New York: St. Martin's Press, 1981).

Cernkovich, Stephen, and Peggy Giordano. "A Comparative Analysis of Male and Female Delinquency." *Sociological Quarterly*, 20 (Winter 1979):131–145.

Chapman, Jane Roberts. *Economic Realities and the Female Offender* (Lexington, Mass.: Lexington Books, 1980).

Crites, Laura. "Women Offenders: Myth Vs. Reality," in Crites, *The Female Offender* (Lexington, Mass.: Lexington Books, 1976), pp. 33–44.

Daniels, Arlene Kaplan. "Feminist Perspectives in Sociological Research," In Marcia Millman and Rosabeth Moss Kanter, *Another Voice: Perspectives on Social Life and Social Science* (New York: Anchor Books, 1975), pp. 340–380.

Datesman, Susan, and Frank Scarpitti. "The Extent and Nature of Female Crime." In Susan Datesman and Frank Scarpitti, *Women, Crime and Justice* (New York: Oxford University Press, 1980), pp. 3–64.

Datesman, Susan, Frank Scarpitti, and Richard Stephenson. "Female Delinquency: An Application of Self and Opportunity Theories." *Journal of Research in Crime and Delinquency*, 12 (July 1975):107–123.

Eve, Raymond A., and Kreelene R. Edmonds. "Women's Liberation and Female Criminality, or 'Sister, Will You Give Me Back My Dime?'" Paper presented at meeting of the National Society of Social Problems, San Francisco, Calif., September 1978.

Feinman, Clarice. *Women in the Criminal Justice System* (New York: Praeger, 1980).

Giordano, Peggy. "Girls, Guys and Gangs: The Changing Social Context of Female Delinquency." *Journal of Criminal Law and Criminology*, 69 (Spring 1978):126–132.

Giordano, Peggy, and Stephen A. Cernkovich. "On Complicating the Relationship Between Liberation and Delinquency." *Social Problems*, 26 (April 1979):467–481.

Glick, Ruth, and Virginia Neto. *National Study of Women's Correctional Programs* (Washington, D.C.: National Institute of Law Enforcement and Criminal Justice, 1977).

Gora, J.G. "A Cohort Analysis of Trends in Crime Seriousness, 1929–1976." Paper presented at meeting of the American Society of Criminology, Philadelphia, Pa., November 1979.

Harris, Anthony R. "Sex and Theories of Deviance: Toward a Functional Theory of Deviant Type-Scripts," *American Sociological Review*, 42 (February 1977):3–15.

Harry, Joseph, and Mary C. Sengstock. Comment on Harris's (*American Sociological Review*, February 1977) "Attribution, Goals and Deviance." *American Sociological Review*, 43 (April 1977):278–280.

Heidensohn, Frances. "The Deviance of Women: A Critique and an Inquiry." *The British Journal of Sociology*, 19 (June 1968):160–175.

Hindelang, Michael J. "Causes of Delinquency: A Partial Replication and Extension." *Social Problems*, 20 (1973):271–287.

Hoffman-Bustamente, Dale. "The Nature of Female Criminality." *Issues in Criminology*, 8 (Fall 1973):117–136.

James, Jennifer, and William Thornton. "Women's Liberation and the Female Delinquent." *Journal of Research in Crime and Delinquency*, 17 (1980):230–244.

Jensen, Gary F. "Parents, Peers, and Delinquent Action: A Test of the Differential Association Perspective." *American Journal of Sociology*, 78 (November 1972):562–575.

Jensen, Gary F., and Raymond Eve. "Sex Differences in Delinquency: An Examination of Popular Sociological Explanations." *Criminology*, 13 (February 1976):427–448.

Jones, Ann. *Women Who Kill* (New York: Holt, Rinehart and Winston, 1980).

Klein, Dorie. "The Etiology of Female Crime: A Review of the Literature." In Laura Crites, *The Female Offender* (Lexington, Mass.: Lexington Books, 1976), pp. 5–31.

Klein, Dorie, and June Kress. "Any Woman's Blues: A Critical Overview of Women, Crime and the Criminal Justice System." *Crime and Social Justice*, 1 (1976):34–49.

Kramer, John H., and Cynthia Kempinen, "Erosion of Chivalry? Changes in the Handling of Male and Female Defendants from 1970 to 1975." Paper presented at convention of the Society for the Study of Social Problems, San Francisco, Calif., September 1978.

Leonard, Eileen B. *Women, Crime and Society: A Critique of Theoretical Criminology* (New York: Longman, 1982).

Leventhal, Gloria. "Female Criminality: Is 'Women's Lib' to Blame?" *Psychological Reports*, 41 (December 1977):1179–1182.

Maccoby, Eleanor, and Carol Nagy Jacklin. "Sex Differences in Aggression: A Rejoinder and Reprise." *Child Development*, 51 (December 1980):964–980.

McCord, Joan. "Some Child-Rearing Antecedents of Criminal Behavior in Adult Men." *Journal of Personality and Social Psychology*, 37 (September 1979):1477–1486.

Merton, Robert K. "Social Structure and Anomie." *American Sociological Review*, 3 (October 1938):672–682.

Miller, Walter B. "The Molls." *Society*, 11 (November–December 1973). Reprinted in Susan Datesman and Frank Scarpitti, *Women, Crime and Justice* (New York: Oxford University Press, 1980), pp. 238–248.

Millman, Marcia, and Rosabeth Moss Kanter (eds.). *Another Voice: Feminist Perspectives on Social Life and Social Science* (New York: Anchor Books, 1975).

Morris, Ruth. "Female Delinquency and Relational Problems." *Social Forces*, 43 (October 1964):82–89.

Moyer, Imogene, and Garland F. White. "Police Processing of Female Offenders." Paper presented at annual meeting of the Academy of Criminal Justice Sciences, 1979.

Norland, Stephen, and Neal Shover. "Gender Roles and Female Criminality: Some Critical Comments." *Criminology*, 15 (May 1977):87–104.

Pollack, Otto. *The Criminality of Women* (Philadelphia: University of Pennsylvania Press, 1950).

Rans, Laurel. "Women's Arrest Statistics." *Woman Offender Report* (March–April 1975).

Rosenblum, Karen. "Female Deviance and the Female Sex Role: A Preliminary Investigation." *British Journal of Sociology*, 26 (June 1975):169–185.

Sandhu, H.S., and D.E. Allen. "Female Delinquency, Goal Obstruction and Anomie." *Canadian Review of Sociology and Anthropology*, 6 (1969):107–110.

Shover, Neal, Stephen Norland, Jennifer James, and William E. Thornton, "Gender Roles and Delinquency," *Social Forces*, 58 (September 1979):162–175.

Simon, Rita James. "A Look to the Future." In Freda Adler and Rita Simon, *The Criminology of Deviant Women* (Boston: Houghton Mifflin, 1979), pp. 6–9.

Simon, Rita James. *Women and Crime* (Lexington, Mass.: D.C. Heath, 1975).

Simon, Rita James. "Women and Crime In Israel" In Simha Landau and Leslie Sibba, *Criminology in Perspective* (Lexington, Mass: D.C. Heath, 1977), Chap. 7.

Simons, Ronald L., Martin G. Miller, and Stephen M. Aigner, "Contemporary Theories of Deviance and Female Delinquency: An Empirical Test." *Journal of Research in Crime and Delinquency*, 17 (January 1980):42–53.

Smart, Carol. *Women, Crime and Criminology: A Feminist Critique* (London: Routledge and Kegan Paul, 1976).

Smith, Dorothy E. "Women's Perspective as Radical Critique of Sociology." *Sociological Inquiry*, 44 (1974):7–13.

Smith, Douglas A. "Sex and Deviance: An Assessment of Major Sociological Variables." *Sociological Quarterly*, 20 (Spring 1979):183–196.

Smith, Douglas, and Christy A. Visher, "Sex and Involvement in Deviance/Crime: A Quantitive Review of the Empirical Literature." *American Sociological Review*, 45 (August 1980): 691–701.

Steffensmeier, Darrell J., "Crime and the Contemporary Woman: An Analysis of Changing Levels of Female Property Crime, 1960–1975." *Social Forces*, 57 (December 1978): 566–584.

Steffensmeier, Darrell J. "Sex Differences in Patterns of Adult Crime, 1965–77: A Review and Assessment." *Social Forces*, 58 (June 1980):1080–1108.

Steffensmeier, Darrell J., and Renee Steffensmeier, "Trends in Female Delinquency." *Criminology*, 18 (1980):62–185.

Sutherland, Edwin H., and Donald R. Cressey. *Criminology* (New York: J.B. Lippincott, 1974).

Thomas, Darwin L., and Andrew J. Weigart. "Socialization and Adolescent Conformity to Significant Others: A Cross-National Analysis." *American Sociological Review*, 36 (October 1971):835–847.

Thorsell, Bernard, and Lloyd W. Klemke, "The Labeling Process: Reinforcement and Deterrent?" In Delos H. Kelly, ed., *Deviant Behavior: Readings in the Sociology of Deviance* (New York: St. Martin's Press, 1979), pp. 654–664.

Ward, David, Maurice Jackson, and Renee Ward. "Crimes and Violence by Women." In Susan Datesman and Frank Scarpitti, *Women, Crime and Justice* (New York: Oxford University Press, 1980), pp. 171–191.

Weis, Joseph G. "Liberation and Crime: The Invention of the New Female Criminal." *Crime and Social Justice*, 6 (Fall–Winter 1976):17–27.

Widom, Cathy Spatz. "Female Offenders: Three Assumptions About Self-Esteem, Sex-Role Identity, and Feminism." *Criminal Justice and Behavior*, 6 (1979):365–382.

Widom, Cathy Spatz, and Abigail Stewart. "Female Criminality and the Changing Status of Women." Paper presented at annual meeting of the American Society of Criminology, Atlanta, Ga., November 1977.

9. Societal Change and Change in Family Violence from 1975 to 1985 as Revealed by Two National Surveys[*]

MURRAY A. STRAUS AND RICHARD J. GELLES

CHILD ABUSE AND WIFE BEATING IN PREVIOUS HISTORICAL PERIODS

Although the purpose of this article is to compare the rates for physical violence against children and spouses in 1985 with the rates found in a 1975 study, we begin with a brief historical overview because that information is helpful for evaluating the results to be reported for 1975–85.

Wife Beating

The subordinate status of women in American society, and in most of the world's societies, is well documented (Blumberg, 1978; Chafetz, 1984). Since physical force is the ultimate recourse to keep subordinate groups in their place, women in the history of Euro-American society have often been the victims of physical assault (Straus, 1976).

Blackstone's codification of the common law in 1768 asserted that a husband had the right to "physically chastise" an errant wife, provided the stick was no bigger than his thumb. As recently as 1867 this rule was upheld by an appellate court in North Carolina. It would be bad enough if the violence against women had been limited to this "rule of thumb." However, more severe beatings were common. In the Middle Ages women were burned alive "for threatening their husbands, for talking back to or refusing a priest, for stealing, for prostitution, for adultery, for bearing a child out of wedlock, for permitting sodomy (even though the priest or husband who committed it was forgiven), for masturbating, for Lesbianism, for child neglect, for scolding and nagging, and for miscarrying, even though the miscarriage was caused by a kick or a blow from the husband" (Davis, 1971).

Burning at the stake is now part of the dim historical past. The *right* to physically chastise has long since disappeared from the common law. However, what actually takes place in American marriages is a different matter. In 1975–76 we carried out a study of a nationally representative sample of 2,143 American couples. That study revealed that at least one violent incident occurred in 16% of American families during the year of the study (1975–76). If the referent period is since the marriage began, the figure is 28% (Straus, Gelles, and Steinmetz, 1980). Although about two-thirds of the violent incidents were minor assaults such as slapping and throwing things, the other third of the incidents were serious assaults such as punching, biting, kicking, hitting with an object, beating up, or assaults with a knife or gun.

Child Abuse

The history of Western society reveals that children have also been subject to unspeakable cruelties, including the abandonment of infants to die of exposure (Radbill, 1980). Although every American state now seeks to protect children through child abuse laws, the task which remains is huge. Even prisoners in jail cannot legally be hit or verbally abused, but physical punishment of children is legal in every state. Anyone who spends an afternoon in a supermarket or shopping mall is likely to observe instances of children being hit or verbally abused. And that is but the tip of the iceberg. Most of the physical and mental cruelty that children experience every day goes on behind the closed doors of millions of American homes.

The rate of physical child abuse revealed by the 1975 study is astounding. Interviews with parents indicate that 36 out of every thousand American children from 3 through 17 years old (i.e., almost 4%) experienced an assault that is serious enough to be included in our "Very Severe Violence Index." A rate of 36 per thousand means that of the 46 million children of this age group in the United States who were living with both parents in 1975, approximately 1.7 million were "abused" that year.[1]

It may be that these data overstated the amount of child abuse because a family is included if even one isolated incident of abusive violence occurred during the year. This was not the case. We found that if one assault occurred, several were likely. In fact, in only 6% of the child abuse cases was there a single incident. The mean number of assaults per year was 10.5 and the median 4.5.

IS THERE AN EPIDEMIC OF CHILD ABUSE AND SPOUSE ABUSE?

Child Abuse

Given the fact that millions of American children were physically abused by their parents in 1975 and that the number of cases of child abuse reported to social service agencies has been rising at a rate of about 10% per year since the mid-seventies

(American Humane Association, 1983), one is tempted to take this as evidence that child abuse is rapidly escalating. Certainly, the statistics gathered by the American Humane Association show a rising trend. However, neither the high incidence rate nor the increase in the officially reported rate necessarily mean that child abuse is increasing. In fact, those concerned with America's children might be pleased that each year's "official statistics" on child abuse tops the previous year's figures. This is because the figures might indicate something quite different from a real increase in the rate of child abuse. The true incidence of child abuse may actually be *declining*, even though the number of cases is increasing. What then do the reports from the 50 states indicate? There are at least two factors that might produce an increase in cases reported, even though the actual rate is declining.

The first factor is that all states now have compulsory child abuse reporting laws. As a result, a larger and larger proportion of the millions of previously unreported cases come to the attention of child welfare services. A dramatic example of this occurred in Florida. The year before the introduction of a statewide "hot-line" for reporting suspected cases of child abuse, only a few hundred cases of child abuse were known to state authorities. However, in the year following the introduction of the hot-line, several thousand cases were reported (Nagi, 1976).

The second factor is much more fundamental. Without it, the reporting system would not work even to the extent that it now operates. This is the fact that new standards are evolving in respect to how much violence parents can use in childrearing. American society is now undergoing a "moral passage" (Gusfield, 1963) in which the definition of child abuse is being gradually enlarged to include acts that were not previously thought of as child abuse. This can create the misleading impression of an epidemic of child abuse. Changed standards are also the real force behind the child abuse reporting laws. Were it not for these changing standards, the reporting laws would not have been enacted; or if enacted, they would tend to be ignored.

Wife Beating

Until recently, there were no statistics on wife-beating cases known to the police or social service agencies (Lerman, 1981). Consequently, even the data for the three states that now record such cases cannot tell us about trends. However, the number of cases reported in newspapers and the number of magazine articles and television documentaries on wife beating increased dramatically during the 1970s and '80s. Although most of these articles described an "epidemic" of wife beating, the apparent increase may reflect a growing awareness and recognition of an already existing high incidence of wife beating, combined with an inability or unwillingness to believe that this much violence could previously have been characteristic of an institution as sacred as the family.

Marital violence may, in fact, be increasing; or it may be declining. An earlier paper argued that both wife beating and child abuse are probably decreasing (Straus, 1981b), but no empirical evidence was presented at that time. The purpose of this paper is to report the results of a 1985 replication of the 1975–76 study. This replication enables the first comparison of rates of family violence from surveys at two time points.

DEFINITION AND MEASUREMENT OF VIOLENCE AND ABUSE

The term *abuse* is a source of considerable difficulty and confusion because it covers many types of abuse, not just acts of physical violence, and because there is no consensus on the severity of violence required for an act to be considered "abuse." Since there is no standard definition of abuse, and no consensus on severity, the best that can be done is to make clear the way the terms *violence* and *abuse* are used in this article.

Violence is defined as an act carried out with the intention, or perceived intention, of causing physical pain or injury to another person. See Gelles and Straus (1979) for an explication of this definition and an analysis of alternative definitions.[2]

The term *abuse* is restricted to *physical* abuse because we chose to concentrate the limited interview time with each family on this phenomenon. This decision was entirely a matter of research strategy. It does not imply that we think physical abuse is more important or more damaging than other types of abuse, such as psychological abuse and sexual abuse.

Child abuse was measured by the Very Severe Violence Index of the Conflict Tactics Scale (Straus, 1979, 1981a). From a scientific perspective it would be preferable to avoid the term *abuse* because of the definitional problems just mentioned and because it is a political and administrative term as well as a scientific term. Despite this, we will use *abuse* for two reasons. First, it is less awkward than "Very Severe Violence Index." Second, the term is so widely used that avoiding it creates communication difficulties.

Operationalizing Violence and Abuse

Violence was measured by the Conflict Tactics Scales (Straus, 1979, 1981a). This instrument has been used and refined in numerous studies of family violence (e.g., Allen and Straus, 1980; Cate, Henton, Koval, Christopher, and Lloyd, 1982; Henton, Cate, Koval, Lloyd, and Christopher, 1983; Giles-Sims, 1983; Hornung, McCullough, and Sugimoto, 1981; Jorgensen, 1977; Straus, 1974; Steinmetz, 1977).[3] Three different studies have established that the Conflict Tactics Scales (CTS) measure three factorially separate variables (Jorgensen, 1977; Schumm, Bollman, Jurich, and Martin, 1982; Straus, 1979): reasoning, verbal aggression, and violence or physical aggression. The violence index and the subindexes used as the measures of child abuse and spouse abuse are described below.

Format of the CTS. The introduction to the Conflict Tactics Scales asks respondents to think of situations in the past year when they had a disagreement or were angry with a specified family member and to indicate how often they engaged in each of the acts included in the CTS. The 1975 version of the CTS consisted of 19 items, 8 of which were acts of violence.

Violent Acts. The violent acts in the version of the CTS we used for this study are: threw something at the other; pushed, grabbed, or shoved; slapped or spanked; kicked, bit, or hit with a fist; hit or tried to hit with something; beat up the other; threatened with knife or gun; used a knife or gun.[4]

Violence Indexes. The violent acts included in the CTS can be combined to form a number of different violence indexes. The following measures are used in this study:

1. *Overall violence.* This measure indicates the percentage of parents or spouses who used *any* of the violent acts included in the CTS during the year covered by the study.

2. *Severe violence.* For purposes of this study, *severe violence* was defined as acts that have a relatively high probability of causing an injury. Thus, kicking is classified as severe violence because kicking a child or a spouse has a much greater potential for producing an injury than an act of "minor violence" such as spanking or slapping.[5] The acts making up the severe violence index are: kicked, bit, punched, hit with an object, beat up, threatened with a knife or gun, and used a knife or gun (see note 4).

3. *Child abuse.* What constitutes abuse is, to a considerable extent, a matter of social norms. Acts such as spanking or slapping a child, or even hitting a child with an object such as a stick, hair brush, or belt, are not abuse according to either the legal or informal norms of American society, although they are in Sweden and several other countries (Haeuser, 1985). Our operationalization of child abuse attempts to take such normative factors into consideration. In the present context, child abuse is the use by a parent of any of the acts of violence in the Severe Violence Index (see list above), except that, to be consistent with current legal and informal norms, hitting or trying to hit with an object such as a stick or belt is *not* included.

4. *Spouse violence and wife beating.* The problem of terminology and norms is even greater for violence between spouses than for violence by parents. Although slapping a child occasionally is not usually considered abuse (or even violence), our perception is that the same act is often considered to be violence if done to a spouse. Thus, in the case of violence between spouses, the "overall violence" rate is more important than is overall violence by parents.

In addition, because of the greater average size and strength of men, the acts in the Severe Violence list are likely to be more damaging when the assailant is the husband. Consequently, to facilitate focusing on the rate of severe violence by husbands, the term *wife beating* will be used to refer to that rate.

THE TWO NATIONAL SURVEYS

Sample and Administration of the 1975 Study

A national probability sample of 2,143 currently married or cohabiting persons was interviewed by Response Analysis Corporation with the use of an interview schedule designed by the authors. If the household included a child or children between the ages of 3 and 17 years, a "referent child" was selected by a random procedure. The restriction to children from 3 to 17 years old was made because one aim of the study was to obtain meaningful data on sibling violence, and we did not feel that the data on children aged 1 and 2 would be meaningful for this purpose. A random half of the respondents were women and the other half men. Interviews lasted approximately one hour. The completion rate of the entire sample was 65%. More detailed information on the methodology of the study is given in Straus, Gelles, and Steinmetz (1980).

The 1985 National Family Violence Re-Survey[6]

Data on a national probability sample of 6,002 households were obtained by telephone interviews conducted by Louis Harris and Associates. To be eligible for inclusion, a household had to include two adults, a male and female 18 years of age or older, who were (a) presently married, or (b) presently living as a male-female couple; or a household might include one adult 18 years of age or older who was either (c) divorced or separated within the last two years, or (d) a single parent living with a child under the age of 18. When more than one eligible adult was in the household, a random procedure was used to select the gender and marital status of the respondent. When more than one child under the age of 18 was in the household, a random procedure was used to select the "referent child" as the focus of the parent-to-child violence questions.

The sample was made up of four parts. The part analyzed for this article is a national probability sample of 4,032 households that were selected in proportion to the distribution of households in the 50 states. The spouse abuse data are based on the 3,520 households containing a currently married or cohabiting couple; households with a single parent or a recently terminated marriage are excluded. The child abuse data are based on the 1,428 of these households with a child aged 3 through 17 and with two caretakers present.[7]

Interviews lasted an average of 35 minutes. The response rate, calculated as "completed as a proportion of eligibles" was 84%. A detailed report on the methodology of the study is available from the authors, and the implications of the differences in methods between the two studies are discussed later in this article.

VIOLENCE AGAINST CHILDREN IN 1975 AND 1985[8]

Table 1 enables one to compare the 1975 and 1985 rates per thousand children for each violent act as well as three summary indexes of violence.[9] The data in Parts A and B show that, with the exception of the most unusual and severe forms of violence (Items 7 and 8: threatening and using guns and knives), *the occurrence of each form of violence toward children declined in the last 10 years.* However, only two of these differences are statistically significant. The more important and reliable results are those for the summary indexes shown in Part C and discussed below.

Overall Violence Rate

The Overall Violence row of Part C indicates whether a parent used *any* of the eight forms of violence at least once during the 12-month period covered by the survey. It shows that there was essentially no change in the rate of violence between 1975 and 1985. The decrease from 630 per thousand children in 1975 to 620 per thousand children in 1985 is equivalent to saying that in 1975 almost two-thirds of the parents in the sample (63%) reported hitting the "referent child" (the child selected as the focus of the interview) during the survey year, and that in 1985 the figure was 62%. However, these high rates are somewhat misleading because they do not take into

Table 1. Parent-to-Child Violence: Comparison of Rates in 1975 and 1985

	Rate per 1,000 Children Aged 3 through 17[a]		
Type of Violence	1975 $n = 1,146^b$	1985 $n = 1,428^c$	t for 1975–1985 Difference
A. Minor Violence Acts			
1. Threw something	54	27	3.41***
2. Pushed/grabbed/shoved	318	307	0.54
3. Slapped or spanked	582	549	1.68
B. Severe Violence Acts			
4. Kicked/bit/hit with fist	32	13	3.17**
5. Hit, tried to hit with something	134	97	1.41
6. Beat up	13	6	0.26
7. Threatened with gun or knife	1	2	0.69
8. Used gun or knife	1	2	0.69
C. Violence Indexes			
Overall Violence (1–8)	630	620	0.52
Severe Violence (4–8)	140	107	2.56**
Very Severe Violence (4, 6, 8) ("child abuse" for this article)	36	19	4.25***

[a] For two-caretaker households with at least one child 3 to 17 years of age at home.

[b] A few respondents were omitted because of missing data on some items, but the n is never less than 1,140.

[c] A few respondents were omitted because of missing data on some items, but the n is never less than 1,418.

*$p < .05$; **$p < .01$; ***$p < .001$ (two-tailed tests).

account the age of the child. For 3-year-olds, the 1975 figure was much higher: 97%. For children aged 15 and over, the rate was much lower: "only" about a third of 15-to-17-year-olds were hit by a parent during the year of the study.

Severe Violence

The second row of Table 1, Part C, shows that the rate of Severe Violence (kicking, biting, punching, hitting or trying to hit with an object, beating, threatening with a gun or knife, or using a gun or knife) declined from 140 per thousand children in 1975 to 107 in 1985.

Child Abuse Rate

The difficulty with the Severe Violence Index as a measure of physical child abuse is that many parents do not consider Item 5 (hitting with an object such as stick, hair brush, or belt) to be abuse. Consequently, as explained earlier, we used the Very Severe Violence Index, shown in the third row of Part C, as the measure of child abuse

Table 2.   Marital Violence Indexes: Comparison of 1975 and 1985

| | Rate per 1,000 Couples | | t for 1975–1985 |
Violence Index	1975	1985	Difference
A. Husband-to-Wife			
Overall Violence (1–6)	121	113	0.91
Severe Violence (4–8)	38	30	1.60
("wife beating")			
B. Wife-to-Husband			
Overall Violence (1–6)	116	121	0.57
Severe Violence (4–8)	46	44	0.35
C. Couple			
Overall Violence (1–6)	160	158	0.20
Severe Violence (4–8)	61	58	0.46
Number of cases[a]	2,143	3,520	

[a] A few respondents were omitted because of missing data on some items, but the n is never decreased by more than 10.

for this paper. This is the same as the Severe Violence Index, except that it omits hitting with an object and is therefore the index that comes closest to the public conception of child abuse. The rate of such indubitably abusive violence declined from 36 per thousand children to 19. This is *a decline of 47% in the rate of physical child abuse since 1975.*

VIOLENCE BETWEEN SPOUSES IN 1975 AND 1985[10]

Table 2 summarizes the findings on violence between married or cohabiting couples in the form of three indexes (data on each violent act separately is presented in Table 3). These indexes differentiate between "minor violence" (pushing, slapping, and throwing things) and "severe violence" (kicking, biting, punching, etc.). All but one of the nine comparisons in Table 2 show that the rate of violence was lower in 1985 than in 1975. However, as compared to the changes in parental violence, the decreases from 1975 to 1985 are much smaller.

Husband-to-Wife Violence

The first row of Table 2, Part A, shows that the Overall Violence rate of violence by husbands declined from 121 to 113. Thus, the husband-to-wife violence rate declined by 6.6%, which is not statistically significant.

The second row of Part A reports the rate of Severe Violence by husbands—our measure of "wife beating." It shows that the rate declined from 38 per thousand couples to 30 per thousand couples in 1985. A decrease of 8 per thousand may not

Table 3.   Marital Violence: Comparison of Specific Acts, 1975–1985

	Husband-to-Wife		Wife-to-Husband	
Type of Violence	1975	1985	1975	1985
A. Minor Violence Acts				
1. Threw something	28	28	52	43
2. Pushed/grabbed/shoved	107	93	83	89
3. Slapped	51	29**	46	41
B. Severe Violence Acts				
4. Kicked/bit/hit with fist	24	15*	31	24
5. Hit, tried to hit with something	22	17	30	30
6. Beat up	11	8	6	4
7. Threatened with gun or knife	4	4	6	6
8. Used gun or knife	3	2	2	2
Number of cases[a]	2,143	3,520	2,143	3,520

[a] A few respondents were omitted because of missing data on some items, but the n is never decreased by more than 10.
*$p < .05$; **$p < .01$ (two-tailed t tests for 1975–85 differences).

seem large, and it is not statistically significant ($p < .10$). However, it is worth interpreting because, relative to the 1975 rate, it represents a 26.6% decrease in the rate of wife beating, and the difference comes close to being significant. In addition, a decrease of 8 per thousand in the rate of wife beating is worth noting because, if correct, it represents a large number of couples. Specifically, if the 1975 rate for husband-to-wife severe violence had remained in effect, the application of this rate to the 54 million couples in the U.S. in 1985 results in an estimate of at least 2,052,000 severely assaulted wives each year. However, if there has been a 27% decrease in the rate, that translates to 1,620,000 beaten wives, which is 432,000 fewer than would have been the case if the 1975 rate prevailed. That would be an extremely important reduction. On the other hand, the 1985 estimate of 1.6 million beaten wives is hardly an indicator of domestic tranquility.[11]

Wife-to-Husband Violence

Although the trend for husband-to-wife violence is encouraging, the situation for wife-to-husband violence is at best mixed. Part B of Table 2 shows that the Overall Violence rate actually increased slightly. The rate for Severe Violence against a husband decreased, but only slightly. Neither of these changes is statistically significant.

In addition to the trends, the violence rates in Part B reveal an important and distressing finding about violence in American families – that, in marked contrast to the behavior of women outside the family, women are about as violent within the family as men. This highly controversial finding of the 1975 study is confirmed by the 1985 study and also by findings on other samples and by other investigators (Brutz and Ingoldsby, 1984; Gelles, 1974; Giles-Sims, 1983; Laner and Thompson, 1982; Lane and Gwartney-Gibbs, 1985; Jouriles and O'Leary, 1985; Makepeace, 1983; Sack, Keller and Howard, 1982; Saunders, 1986; Scanzoni, 1978; Steinmetz, 1977, 1977–78; Szinovacz, 1983).

Although the two national surveys and the ten studies just cited leave little doubt about the high frequency of wife-to-husband violence, the meaning and consequences of that violence are easily misunderstood. For one thing, as pointed out elsewhere (Straus, 1977; Straus, Gelles, and Steinmetz, 1980: 43), the greater average size and strength of men, and their greater aggressiveness (Maccoby and Jacklin, 1974; Tavris and Offir, 1977), mean that the same act (for example, a punch) is likely to be very different in the amount of pain or injury inflicted (see also Greenblat, 1983). Even more important, a great deal of violence by women against their husbands is retaliation or self-defense (Straus, 1980; Saunders, 1986). One of the most fundamental reasons why some women are violent within the family, but not outside the family, is that the risk of assault for a typical American woman is greatest in her own home (Straus, Gelles, and Steinmetz, 1980: chapters 1 and 2). Nonetheless, violence by women against their husbands is not something to be dismissed because of the even greater violence by husbands.

On the other hand, the cost of drawing attention to violence by wives is that the information will be used to defend male violence. Our 1975 data, for example, have been used against battered women in court cases, and also to minimize the need for shelters for battered women. However, in the long run, the results of the present study suggest that the cost of denial and suppression is even greater. Rather than attempting to deny the existence of such violence (see Pleck, Pleck, Grossman, and Bart, 1977, for an example and the reply by Steinmetz, 1978), a more productive solution is to confront the issue and attempt to eliminate violence by women. This is beginning to happen. Almost all shelters for battered women now have policies designed to deal with the high rate of child abuse, and some are also facing up to the problem of wife-to-husband violence.

Couple Violence and Specific Violent Acts

Couple Violence. Part C of Table 2 combines the data on violence by husbands and wives. The first row shows that in 1975, a violent act occurred in 160 out of every thousand families, and that the 1985 rate was almost as high. Similarly, the second row reveals only a small decrease in the rate of *severe* assaults on a spouse — from 61 to 58 per thousand couples. This is a 5% reduction, which is not statistically significant.

Specific Violent Acts. Table 3 presents the rates for each of the violent acts making up the 1975 and 1985 versions of the CTS. These rates are presented for the record and to show what went into the summary indexes discussed above.

PREVENTION AND TREATMENT PROGRAMS AND CHANGE IN FAMILY VIOLENCE

This section considers the extent to which change in different forms of intrafamily violence parallels the extent of the intensity of prevention and treatment programs.

Child Abuse

This form of physical violence entered the public agenda as a major social problem with the classic paper by Kempe, Silverman, Steele, Droegemueller, and Silver (1962). Since 1971, every state has adopted compulsory reporting laws, and an extensive educational effort has developed across the country. In comparison to other forms of domestic violence, the largest share of financial resources has been allocated to child abuse. There are now thousands of social workers assigned to child abuse work who were not available a decade or more ago. The fact that we found a larger decrease for child abuse than for any other aspect of family violence may reflect the fact that it has been the object of the longest and most intensive campaign.

Wife Beating

The campaign against wife beating, by contrast, began a decade or more later and has been less intensive, and far fewer resources have been invested. Providing shelters has mostly been a private endeavor of the women's movement. Even the feeble effort of the federal government in the form of an information clearinghouse was abolished early in the Reagan administration. Many bills to provide funds for shelters have been introduced and defeated. When a bill appropriating a modest sum was finally passed in 1985, the administration refused to spend the funds. Nevertheless, by 1985 the women's movement succeeded in creating a national consciousness and in establishing hundreds of shelters for battered women (Back, Blum, Nakhnikian, and Stark, 1980; Warrior, 1982); and by 1985 our study found a substantial reduction in the rate of wife beating.

Violence by Wives

Violence by wives has not been an object of public concern. There has been no publicity, and no funds have been invested in ameliorating this problem because it has not been defined as a problem. In fact, our 1975 study was criticized for presenting statistics on violence by wives.[12] Our 1985 finding of little change in the rate of assaults by women on their male partners is consistent with the absence of ameliorative programs.

Physical Punishment of Children

Not only has physical punishment of children not been a focus of a public effort, but most Americans consider it morally correct to hit a child who misbehaves (Straus, Gelles, and Steinmetz, 1980). Consistent with this, we found only small and nonsignificant differences between 1975 and 1985 in the overall rate of parent-to-child violence.

Overall, the findings of this study are consistent with the idea that the longer an aspect of violence has been the object of public condemnation, and the more resources that are put into the effort to change that aspect of violence, the greater the reduction in the objectionable behavior.

ALTERNATIVE INTERPRETATIONS OF THE FINDINGS

We have presented some startling and controversial findings. When the *Christian Science Monitor* interviewed criminologist Richard Berk concerning the results of this study ("2 researchers say," 18 November 1985, pp. 3–4), he commented, "Given all we know about the pattern of crime statistics, a 47% drop is so unprecedented as to be unbelievable. Never before has there been a drop of that magnitude, that rapidly." But, contrary to Berk's assertion, other crime rates *have* changed that much and that fast. The homicide rate, for example, increased by over 100% between 1963 and 1973; and in the four years from 1980 to 1984 homicide dropped by 29%–a rate which, if continued for another 6 years, will produce a 10-year decrease that is greater than the 47% decrease we found for child abuse (Straus, 1986).

The homicide statistics indicate that there is a precedent for changes in crime rates of the magnitude we found for physical child abuse and wife beating. In fact, our statistics on the decrease in child abuse and wife beating parallel the recent decreases in homicide, including intrafamily homicide (Straus, in press). Nevertheless, it is important to regard these results with caution because, with the data available, one can only speculate about the processes that produced the decreases. We will discuss three possible explanations for the findings.

Methodological Differences between the Two Surveys

Data for the 1975 survey were collected by in-person interview, while the 1985 survey was conducted over the telephone. Research on differences between telephone and in-person interviews has shown no major differences in results (Groves and Kahn, 1979; Marcus and Crane, 1986; Smith, in press), and telephone interviewing is now the most widely used method of conducting surveys, including the National Crime Survey. To the extent that there is a difference, we believe, the anonymity offered by the telephone leads to more truthfulness and, therefore, increased reporting of violence. The difference in interview method should have produced *higher*, not lower, rates of reported violence in 1985.

However, a characteristic of telephone surveys that is usually an advantage – the higher rate of completed interviews – might have affected the difference between the 1975 and 1985 rates. The 1985 survey had an 85% completion rate, versus 65% for the 1975–76 survey. Assuming that a higher completion rate means a more representative sample, the question is whether this makes for a lower or a higher rate of reported violence. That depends on whether those who refused to participate are more or less likely to be violent. If those who refused are less likely to be violent, then the fact that there were fewer refusals in 1985 would tend to reduce the violence rate. However, we think it more likely that the violence rate is higher among those who refuse to participate. If so, a reduction in refusals would tend to produce a higher rate of violence, whereas we found a lower rate of violence in 1985 despite the much lower number of refusals.

Another methodological difference is that, in the 1975–76 survey, respondents were handed a card listing the response categories for the Conflict Tactics Scales. All possible answers, including "never," were on the card. For the 1985 telephone survey, interviewers read the response categories, beginning with "once" and continuing to "more than 20 times." Respondents had to volunteer "never" or "don't know" responses. Experience has shown that rates of reported sensitive or deviant behavior are higher if the subject has to volunteer the "no" or "never" response (see, for example, Kinsey, Pomeroy, and Martin, 1948).

These differences in methodology between the two studies should have led to higher, not lower, rates of reported violence. Since the rates of child abuse and wife beating decreased, it seems unlikely that the change is due to the different methods of data collection.

Reluctance to Report

A second plausible explanation for the decline in the rate of child abuse and wife beating is that respondents may have been more reluctant to report severe violence in 1985 than in 1975. As indicated above, the last 10 years have seen a tremendous increase in public attention to the problem of child abuse and wife beating. National media campaigns, new child abuse and neglect laws, hot-lines, and almost daily media attention have transformed behaviors that were ignored for centuries into major social problems. The decrease in child abuse and wife beating may reflect a "moral passage" (Gusfield, 1963), as family violence becomes less acceptable and consequently fewer parents and fewer husbands are willing to admit to participating in violence. The implications of such a change in American culture are discussed at the conclusion of this article.

Change in Behavior

The third explanation is that there has indeed been a decline in child abuse and wife beating. This explanation is consistent with changes in the family and other developments during the last 10 years that might have served to reduce the rate of family violence. These fall into five broad categories: changes in the family and the economy that are associated with less violence, more alternatives for abused women, treatment programs, and deterrence.

Change in Family Structure.   There have been changes in a number of aspects of the family that are associated with violence, including: a rise in the average age at first marriage, an increase in the average age for having a first child, a decline in the number of children per family, and therefore, a corresponding decrease in the number of unwanted children (Statistical Abstract, 1985: Tables 120, 92, 63, 97). Parents in 1985 are among the first generation to be able to choose a full range of planned parenthood options (including abortion) to plan family size. All these factors are related to lower rates of child abuse and may have an indirect effect on spouse abuse by lowering the level of stress.[13] In addition, later marriage and the greater acceptability of divorce tend to equalize the balance of power between husband and wife.

The fact that, bit by bit, American marriages are becoming more equalitarian (Thornton, Alwin, and Camburn, 1983) has important implications for family violence because previous research shows that male-dominant marriages have the highest, and equalitarian marriages the lowest, rate of violence (Coleman and Straus, 1986; Straus, 1973; Straus, Gelles, and Steinmetz, 1980). There are many reasons for the increasing equality between husbands and wives in addition to the two mentioned above. For the decade in question, two of the most important factors are the diffusion of feminist ideology to a broader population base, and the increase in the percentage of women with paid jobs. Moreover, we found that full-time housewives experience a higher rate of wife beating (Straus, Gelles, and Steinmetz, 1980); thus the rapid increase in paid employment (Statistical Abstract, 1985: Tables 669–672) might also be associated with a lower rate of wife beating.

Economic Change.   Both child abuse and wife beating are associated with unemployment and economic stress. The economic climate of the country is better in 1985 than in 1975 (at least for the population we are examining—intact families). The rate of employment and inflation is down compared to 10 years ago (Statistical Abstract, 1985: Table 777). The one-year referent period used for the 1985 survey coincided with one of the more prosperous years in the past decade. Thus, the lower level of economic stress in 1985 may have contributed to the decline in severe violence.

Alternatives for Battered Women.   As noted earlier, there were only a handful of "safe houses" or "shelters" for battered women in 1975, as contrasted with about 700 in 1985 (Back et al., 1980; Warrior, 1982). The existence of shelters provides an alternative that did not exist in 1975. In addition, the fact that shelters provide an alternative may have emboldened more women to tell their partner that his violence is unacceptable, and to make this more than an idle threat. Similarly, the tremendous growth in paid employment of married women in the 1975–85 period not only helped rectify the imbalance of power between spouses, but also provided the economic resources that enable more women to terminate a violent marriage (Kalmuss and Straus, 1982). Finally, the increased acceptance of divorce probably also helped more women to terminate violent marriages.

Treatment Programs.   New and innovative prevention and treatment programs for child abuse and wife beating proliferated during or immediately before the 1975–85 decade. All 50 states enacted compulsory reporting laws for child abuse and neglect, and public and private social services have been developed to treat and prevent child abuse. Despite the underfunding and understaffing of these programs, the presence of thousands of new workers in child protective services is likely to have had an impact.[14] Only a small percentage of the cases they deal with are the gory (and difficult to treat) cases that make the newspaper headlines. Most are parents at their wits' end who can and do benefit from the help and the additional resources that state social service departments provide.

In respect to wife beating, whereas no treatment programs for men who assault their wives existed in the early 1970s, many such programs were available by 1985 (Pirog-Good and Stets-Kelly, 1985), including a number of court-mandated programs; and there is some evidence of their effectiveness (Lerman, 1981). Finally, family therapy of all types has grown tremendously. It was probably the fastest-growing human service profession in the 1975–85 decade.[15] The increased use of family counseling and the increasing proportion of therapists who directly raise the issue of violence may have had a part in reducing intrafamily violence.

Deterrence.   Deterrence of a crime depends on the perception of potential offenders that the act is wrong and that there is a high probability of being apprehended and punished (Williams and Hawkins, in press). The decade in question has been characterized by activities that were intended to change both internalized norms and objective sanctions about family violence. Extensive efforts have been made to alert the public to the problem of child abuse and wife beating. In addition, shelters for battered women may have an indirect effect. The process of publicizing the availability of a shelter can contribute to a husband's redefining "I just slapped her a few times" to "I was violent." Each of these activities probably contributed to a changed perception of the legitimacy of violence against children and wives and therefore plays a preventative or deterrent role. Public opinion poll data suggest that those programs seem to have been effective. A 1976 study found that only about 10% of Americans considered child abuse a serious problem (Magnuson, 1983), whereas a 1982 poll conducted by Louis Harris and Associates found that 90% felt that child abuse was a serious national problem. This is a huge increase in public awareness. The problem of wife beating, although emphasized less than child abuse, has also received a major amount of publicity. It is not implausible to suggest that the advertising campaigns and media attention have had some effect in making parents more cautious about assaulting children and husbands more cautious about severely assaulting wives.

Another important change affects the certainty and severity of legal sanctions for wife beating. The police are gradually changing methods of dealing with wife beating. At the time of the 1975 study, the training manual for police officers prepared by the International Association of Chiefs of Police recommended separating the warring parties and leaving the scene of the marital violence. That manual now recommends dealing with all assaults on the same bases, irrespective of whether they are in the home or elsewhere (International Association of Chiefs of Police, 1976). A growing number of police departments are doing that. To the extent that this change in police policy was known to potential offenders, it is not implausible to think that it has had an effect. Indeed, a study comparing three different methods used by the police to deal with domestic violence suggests that there is a lower recidivism rate when wife beating is treated as a criminal act rather than a private problem (Sherman and Berk, 1984).

SUMMARY AND CONCLUSIONS

This article compares the rates of physical violence against children and spouses from a 1975–76 survey with the rates from a 1985 study that used the same instrument to measure violence. The most important findings are as follows: (a) Physical child abuse (as measured by the number of children who were kicked, punched, bitten, beaten up, or attacked with a knife or gun) decreased by 47% from 1975 to 1985. (b) Wife beating (measured by the occurrence of these same acts, plus hitting with an object) decreased by 27%, but similarly severe assaults by wives on husbands decreased only 4.3%. (c) Even with these reductions, the rates of child abuse and wife beating remain extremely high.

Factors Underlying the Findings

The lower rates of severe violence in the 1985 study could have been produced by a number of factors, including: (a) differences in the methodology used in the two surveys, (b) a greater reluctance on the part of the respondents to report violence, or (c) a decrease in the amount of child abuse and wife beating. Our interpretation is that the decrease is probably not due to differences in the methods used in the two surveys because those differences would tend to increase rather than decrease the 1985 rate. This leaves two plausible explanations—the decrease could reflect a change in reporting behavior or a change in violent behavior.

From the perspective of the welfare of children and families, the most desirable interpretation is that the differences between 1975 and 1985 represent fewer physically abused children and fewer beaten wives. However, even if the reduction is entirely due to a greater reluctance to report violence, that is also important. It suggests that the effort to change public attitudes and standards concerning family violence have achieved a certain measure of success. In view of the fact that this decrease refers to changes in a relatively short period of 10 years, perhaps it could even be considered a remarkable degree of success. Moreover, a change in attitudes and cultural norms is an important part of the process leading to change in overt behavior. If all that has been accomplished in the last 10 years is to instill new standards for parents and husbands about the inappropriateness of violence, that is a key element in the process of reducing the actual rate of child abuse and wife beating.

Most likely the findings represent a combination of changed attitudes and norms along with changes in overt behavior. This interpretation is based on a number of changes in American society that took place during or immediately before the decade of this study, including: changes in the family, in the economy, in the social acceptability of family violence, in alternatives available to women, in social control processes, and in the availability of treatment and prevention services.

Policy Implications

If nationwide availability of child abuse treatment programs is one of the factors bringing about a decline in the child abuse rate, it helps explain the seeming contradictions between the decrease reported in this article and the even greater *increase* in cases known to child protective services (American Humane Association, 1983). To understand this, it is necessary to abandon the terminology used earlier in this article, which identifies the cases known to protective service workers as the "official" or "reported" rate, and the rate from our survey as the "real" rate of child abuse. Both are reported rates and both are real rates. The difference is not that one is right and the other wrong, but that they measure different phenomena. The rate based on cases known to child protective services in the various states can be thought of as a measure of services provided, or as a *treatment* rate, whereas the rate produced by our surveys is closer to an *incidence* rate.[16] The increase in the former (which is a proxy for the number of cases treated) is one of the factors that made possible the decrease in the number of child abuse incidents reported in this article.

The interpretations of the findings presented here have important policy implications that contrast sharply with the interpretation given in *Child Protection Report* under the headline "Gelles Study Strikes Discordant Note" (22 November 1985, p. 3), which reports that child protection advocates were angered at our findings because they fear the sharp decrease in rates of child abuse might undercut support for child abuse programs. But what if we had found no change? Critics could then argue that 10 years and millions of dollars of public and private funds had been wasted. We believe that the findings should be regarded in the same way as the findings on the sharp decrease in smoking by men, and the parallel finding that lung cancer rates for white males have turned down (*New York Times*, "Lung cancer," 3 December 1985, p. A1). Those findings supported rather than hindered increased efforts to reduce smoking.

As in the case of research on smoking, our findings provide a basis for believing that when a national effort is made about some aspect of intrafamily violence, a national accomplishment can be achieved. Moreover, the findings also show that an intensified effort is needed. Even if all the reductions from 1975 to 1985 were in actual assaults (i.e., none of it a reduction in reporting of assaults), and even disregarding the underestimate resulting from the omission of the "high risk" categories of single-parent families and children under three, a reduction in child abuse of 47% still leaves a minimum estimate of over a million abused children aged 3 through 17 in two-parent households. Similarly, a reduction of 27% in wife beating still leaves over a million and a half beaten wives each year in the United States.

Notes

*This paper was presented at the 1985 meeting of the American Society of Criminology. The study reported here is a product of the Family Violence Research Program, University of New Hampshire, Durham, NH 03824. Reprints and a bibliography listing other papers available for distribution will be provided upon request. We are indebted to John Harrop for coding to compute many complicated indexes and for getting a large, complicated data set to run; to members of the 1985–86 Family Violence Research Program Seminar (Angela Browne, Jean Ellison, David Finkelhor, Gerry King, Christine Smith, Jill Suitor, and Barbara Wauchope); and to Suzanne K. Steinmetz for comments and suggestions on an earlier draft. The research was carried out with funds provided by the National Institute of Mental Health, grant MH40027. It is also a pleasure to acknowledge sources of support for the larger research program of which this project is a part. These include the National Center on Child Abuse and Neglect, the National Institute of Justice, the Graduate School of the University of New Hampshire, and a "training grant" (T32 MH15161) from the National Institute of Mental Health.

1. See the section on definition and measurement for definitions of the terms *abuse* and *violence* as they are used in this report.

2. As pointed out in a previous theoretical article (Gelles and Straus, 1979), the fact of a physical assault having taken place is not sufficient for understanding violence. Several other dimensions also needed to be considered. However, it is also important that each of these other dimensions be measured separately so that their causes and consequences and joint effects can be investigated. Among the other dimensions are the seriousness of the assault (which can range from a slap to stabbing and shooting); whether a physical injury was produced (which can range from none to death); the motivation (which might range from a concern for a person's safety, as when a child is spanked for going into the street, to hostility so intense that the death of the person is desired); and whether the act of violence is normatively legitimate (as in the case of slapping a child) or illegitimate (as in the case of slapping a spouse), and which set of norms are applicable (legal, ethnic, or class norms, couple norms, etc.).

3. The reliability and validity of the Conflict Tactics Scales have been assessed in several studies over the 15-year period of their development. See Straus (1979) for evidence of internal consistency, reliability, concurrent validity, and construct validity. Other investigators have confirmed some of these findings. See, for example, Jouriles and O'Leary (1985), Jorgensen (1977), and Schumm et al. (1982).

4. The 1985 version contains an additional item for parent-child violence (scalding or burning) and an additional item for husband-wife violence (choking). These items are excluded from comparisons of 1975 rates with 1985 rates but will be presented in a later paper (Straus and Gelles, 1986). In addition, the 1985 CTS was supplemented by questions intended to assess the consequences or outcomes of acts of violence. We added a series of questions that asked whether an act of violence produced an injury that required medical attention—either seeing a doctor or overnight hospitalization—and also questions on depression and other possible mental health effects. These data will also be reported in a later paper.

5. It should be recognized that in most instances, being kicked, although painful, does *not* result in an injury. However, the absence of injury does not make it less abusive an act. Our distinction between minor and severe violence parallels the legal distinction between a "simple assault" and an "aggravated assault." An aggravated assault is an attack that is likely to cause grave bodily harm, such as an attack with a knife or gun, irrespective of whether the object of the attack was actually injured.

6. The 1985 survey differs from the 1975–76 study in a number of important ways. It includes several groups that were omitted from the first survey, such as single parents, and it includes additions to the CTS Violence Index. However, the instrumentation was designed to permit the comparable questions to be selected, and the sample was chosen in a way that permits selection of a comparable part of the 1985 sample to be used for the 1975-to-1985 change analysis. Unless otherwise indicated, the material reported in this article is restricted to the comparable parts of the 1985 sample and the comparable parts of the instrumentation. See also note 4.

7. The other three parts consisted of oversamples for specific purposes. First, certain states were oversampled because one objective of the second national survey was to collect data that could be aggregated by state for analysis of state-level trends and relationships. The oversample consisted of 958 households in 25 states. This was done to assure that there would be 36 states with at least 100 completed interviews per state. Finally, two additional oversamples were drawn—508 black and 516 Hispanic households. Future analyses that include these oversamples will be weighted to take into account the state, black, and Hispanic oversamples.

8. This section is relatively brief because violence against children is covered in detail in a companion paper focused entirely on that aspect of family violence (Gelles and Straus, 1985).

9. Previous reports on the 1975 study expressed the violence rate as a *percentage* of husbands, wives, or children, whereas, starting with this article, we use a rate per thousand couples

or children. There are three reasons for this. (a) *Rate per thousand is comparable with other crime and child abuse rates*. The National Crime Survey (U.S. Department of Justice, 1985), which has become the de facto standard for survey research on the incidence of crime and victimization, and the annual rates of child abuse cases reported to child protective services in the United States both use rate per thousand. Adopting that standard facilitates comparison of rates from this survey with the rates for reported cases of child abuse and with National Crime Survey rates for assault and other crimes. Another alternative is the Uniform Crime Reports system of rates per hundred thousand. However, such a rate is not appropriate, because our survey samples were in the thousands, not hundred thousands. (b) *Results are presented as integers*. It is customary in demography, criminology, and medical sociology to use a rate that enables the data to be presented in integers. For example, the 1981 cancer death rate is given in the *Visual Statistics* as 184 per 100,000 population rather than 0.00184 per capita or 0.184% because most people find it easier to conceptualize integers. Thus, the difference between the cancer rate and the suicide rate is more easily perceived when presented as 184 versus 12 per 100,000 rather than as 0.184% versus 0.012%. (c) *Rate per thousand avoids confusion with percentage change*. In the context of this article, using "X per thousand" instead of "X%" avoids confusion with "X% change" or the awkwardness in spelling out the latter as "X% change in the percentage violent."

10. For convenience and economy of wording, terms such as *marital, spouse, wife*, and *husband* are used to refer to couples, irrespective of whether they are married or nonmarried cohabiting persons. For an analysis of differences and similarities between married and cohabiting couples in the 1975–76 study, see Yllö (1978); Yllö and Straus (1981).

11. In addition, the 1985 rate presented in this article is restricted to the comparable part of the sample and the comparable list of violent acts. The figures to be presented in a later paper using all couples and the enlarged CTS list of violent acts yields a somewhat higher rate.

12. For a few years, the advocacy of karate on the part of some in the women's movement put women on record as favoring violence as a means of ending violence. The futility of such an approach is indicated by the fact that the willingness of men to use force does not protect them from assault. Three times as many men are murdered as women (Riedel and Zahn, 1985: Table 3-2), and three times as many men are victims of assault (Bureau of Justice Statistics, 1985: Table 3). Readiness to use force, in our opinion, is no more likely to provide security for women than it does for men.

13. Although this section focuses on changes in the family that are associated with a reduction in violence, there have also been changes in aspects of the family that are plausibly associated with an increase in violence (see Straus 1981b, for a listing and discussion).

14. Calls to several federal and private organizations concerned with child abuse revealed that no national statistics are available on the number of child protective service (CPS) workers. However, some indication of the magnitude of the change can be gleaned from data on the New England states. I am grateful to the directors or associate directors of the relevant departments for providing the following statistics in response to my telephone requests: *Connecticut*: The number of case workers assigned to children's services increased from 244.5 full-time equivalent workers in 1976 to 308 in 1985, an increase of 63.5, or 26%. *Maine*: The number of CPS workers increased from 163 in 1977 to 238 in 1985, an increase of 75, or 46%. *Massachusetts*: The budget for child protective services increased from $120 million in 1980 (the earliest date for which comparable figures are available) to $293 million in 1985, a 144% increase in the last five years of the 1975–85 decade. *New Hampshire*: Separate figures are not kept on CPS workers. The number of state-employed social workers increased from 95 in 1972 to 136 in 1985, an increase of 41, or a 43% increase. *Rhode Island*: The number of CPS workers increased from 12 in 1974 to 125 in 1985, a 792% increase. *Vermont*: Separate figures were not kept for CPS. The total number of state-employed social workers was essentially unchanged from 1975 to 1985 (from 105 to 110). However, a larger proportion of this staff was probably engaged in CPS work in 1985 than in 1975. Allowing for a few states such as Vermont, it is not unreasonable to assume that even small states added at least 50 CPS workers during the decade under review, and larger states many more. If each state added an average of only 50 CPS workers

during this decade, that would result in 2,500 CPS workers providing services in 1985 who were not engaged in child abuse intervention in the early 1970s.

15. For example, membership in the American Association of Marriage and Family Therapists tripled from 3,373 in 1975 to 12,302 in 1985 (information provided by telephone to Straus, 11 March 1986).

16. Of course, both rates are confounded with other factors. The rate of cases known to protective services is confounded with the resources available to conduct investigations and provide treatment. Consequently, it is much higher than the number of families actually receiving assistance. Similarly, the survey rate is confounded with willingness to self-report violence and is therefore much lower than the "true" incidence rate. Nevertheless, we regard the former as a reasonable indicator of trends in treatment and the latter as a reasonable indicator of trends in incidence.

References

Allen, Craig, and Murray A. Straus. 1980. "Resources, power, and husband-wife violence." Chapter 12 in Murray A. Straus and Gerald T. Hotaling (eds.), The Social Causes of Husband-Wife Violence. Minneapolis: University of Minnesota Press.

American Humane Association. 1983. Highlights of Official Child Neglect and Abuse Reporting. Denver, CO: American Humane Association.

Back, Susan M., Judith Blum, Ellen Nakhnikian, and Susan Stark. 1980. Spouse Abuse Yellow Pages. Denver, CO: Denver Research Institute, University of Denver.

Blumberg, Rae Lesser. 1978. Stratification: Socioeconomic and Sexual Inequality. Dubuque, IA: Wm. C. Brown.

Brutz, Judith, and Bron B. Ingoldsby. 1984. "Conflict resolution in Quaker families." Journal of Marriage and the Family 46:21–26.

Bureau of Justice Statistics. 1985. Criminal Victimization in the United States, 1985. Washington, DC: U.S. Department of Justice.

Cate, Rodney M., June M. Henton, James Koval, F. Scott Christopher, and Sally Lloyd. 1982. "Premarital abuse: A social psychological perspective." Journal of Family Issues 3:79–90.

Chafetz, Janet Saltzman. 1984. Sex and Advantage: A Comparative Macro-Structural Theory of Sex Stratification. Totowa, NJ: Rowman and Allanheld.

Coleman, Diane H., and Murray A. Straus. 1986. "Marital power, conflict, and violence." Violence and Victims 1:139–153.

Davis, Elizabeth Gould. 1971. The First Sex. New York: Putnam.

Gelles, Richard J. 1974. The Violent Home: A Study of Physical Aggression between Husbands and Wives. Beverly Hills, CA: Sage.

Gelles, Richard J., and Murray A. Straus. 1979. "Determinants of violence in the family: Towards a theoretical integration." Chapter 21 in Wesley R. Burr, Reuben Hill, F. Ivan Nye, and Ira L. Reiss (eds.), Contemporary Theories about the Family (Vol. 1). New York: Free Press.

Gelles, Richard J., and Murray A. Straus. 1985. "Is violence toward children increasing? A comparison of 1975 and 1985 national survey rates." Paper presented at the Seventh National Conference on Child Abuse and Neglect, Chicago.

Gelles study strikes discordant note. 1985. Child Protection Report, 22 November, p. 3.

Giles-Sims, Jean. 1983. Wife Battering: A Systems Theory Approach. New York: Guilford Press.

Greenblat, Cathy. 1983. "Physical force by any other name . . .: Quantitative data, qualitative data, and the politics of family violence research." In David Finkelhor, Richard J. Gelles, Gerald T. Hotaling, and Murray A. Straus (eds.), The Dark Side of Families: Current Family Violence Research. Beverly Hills, CA: Sage.

Groves, R. M., and R. L. Kahn. 1979. Surveys by Telephone: A National Comparison with Personal Interviews. New York: Academic Press.

Gusfield, J. 1963. Symbolic Crusade: Status Politics and the American Temperance Movement. Urbana, IL: University of Illinois Press.

Haeuser, Adrienne A. 1985. "Social control over parents' use of physical punishment: Issues for cross-national child abuse research." Paper presented at the United States–Sweden Joint Seminary on Physical and Sexual Abuse of Children, Satra Bruck, Sweden (June).

Henton, June, Rodney Cate, James Koval, Sally Lloyd, and Scott Christopher. 1983. "Romance and violence in dating relationships." Journal of Family Issues 4:467–482.

Hornung, Carlton A., B. Claire McCullough, and Taichi Sugimoto. 1981. "Status relationships in marriage: Risk factors in spouse abuse." Journal of Marriage and the Family 43: 675–692.

International Association of Chiefs of Police. 1976. Wife Beating. Training Key 245. Gaithersburg, MD.

Jorgensen, Stephen R. 1977. "Societal class heterogamy, status striving, and perception of marital conflict: A partial replication and revision of Pearlin's contingency hypothesis." Journal of Marriage and the Family 39:653–689.

Jouriles, E. N., and K. D. O'Leary. 1985. "Interspousal reliability of reports of marital violence." Journal of Consulting and Clinical Psychology 53:419–421.

Kalmuss, Debra S., and Murray A. Straus. 1982. "Wives' marital dependency and wife abuse." Journal of Marriage and the Family 44:277–286. Also reprinted in Bert N. Adams and John L. Campbell (eds.), Framing the Family: Contemporary Portraits. Prospect Heights, IL: Waveland Press, 1985.

Kempe, C. Henry, Frederic Silverman, Brandt Steele, William Droegemueller, and Henry Silver. 1962. "The battered child syndrome." Journal of the American Medical Association 181:17–24.

Kinsey, Alfred C., Wardell B. Pomeroy, and Clyde E. Martin. 1948. Sexual Behavior in the Human Male. Philadelphia: W. B. Saunders.

Lane, Katherine E., and Patricia A. Gwartney-Gibbs. 1985. "Violence in the context of dating and sex." Journal of Family Issues 6:45–59.

Laner, Mary Riege, and Jeanine Thompson. 1982. "Abuse and aggression in courting couples." Deviant Behavior: An Interdisciplinary Journal 3:229–244.

Lerman, Lisa G. 1981. Prosecution of Spouse Abuse: Innovations in Criminal Justice Response. Washington, DC: Center for Women Policy Studies.

Lung cancer in white men declines in U.S. 1985. New York Times, 3 December, p. A1.

Maccoby, Eleanor Emmons, and Carol Nagy Jacklin. 1974. The Psychology of Sex Differences. Stanford, CA: Stanford University Press.

Magnuson, E. 1983. "Child abuse: The ultimate betrayal." Time, 5 September, 122:20–22.

Makepeace, James M. 1983. "Life events stress and courtship violence." Family Relations 32:101–109.

Marcus, Alfred C., and Lori A. Crane. 1986. "Telephone surveys in public health research." Medical Care 24:97–112.

Nagi, Saad Z. 1976. Child Maltreatment in the United States: A Challenge to Social Institutions. New York: Columbia University Press.

Pirog-Good, Maureen, and Jan Stets-Kealey. 1985. "Domestic violence victimization: A multiyear perspective." Paper presented at the 1985 annual meeting of the American Society of Criminology, San Diego.

Pleck, Elizabeth, Joseph H. Pleck, Marlyn Grossman, and Pauline B. Bart. 1977. "The battered data syndrome: A comment on Steinmetz' article." Victimology: An International Journal 2:680–683.

Radbill, Samuel X. 1980. "Children in a world of violence: A history of child abuse." Chapter 1 in C. Henry Kempe and Ray E. Helfer (eds.), The Battered Child (3rd ed.). Chicago: University of Chicago Press.

Reidel, Mark, and Margaret A. Zahn. 1985. The Nature and Pattern of American Homicide. Washington, DC: National Institute of Justice.

Sack, Alan R., James F. Keller, and Richard D. Howard. 1982. "Conflict tactics and violence in dating situations." International Journal of Sociology of the Family 12:89–100.

Saunders, Daniel G. 1986. "When battered women use violence: Husband-abuse or self-defense?" Violence and Victims 1:47–60.

Scanzoni, John. 1978. Sex Roles, Women's Work, and Marital Conflict. Lexington, MA: Lexington Books.

Schumm, Walter R., Stephan R. Bollman, Anthony P. Jurich, and Michael J. Martin. 1982. "Adolescent perspectives on family violence." Journal of Social Psychology 117:153–154.

Sherman, Laurence, and Richard A. Berk. 1984. "The specific deterrent effects of arrest for domestic assault." American Sociological Review 49:261–272.

Smith, Michael D. 1985. "Woman abuse: The case for surveys by telephone." Paper presented at the 1985 meeting of the American Society of Criminology, San Diego.

Statistical Abstract of the United States (105th ed.). 1985. Washington, DC: U.S. Government Printing Office.

Steinmetz, Suzanne K. 1977. The Cycle of Violence: Assertive, Aggressive, and Abusive Family Interaction. New York: Praeger.

Steinmetz, Suzanne K. 1977–78. "The battered husband syndrome." Victimology: An International Journal 2:499–509.

Steinmetz, Suzanne K. 1978. "Services to battered women: Our greatest need. A reply to Field and Kirchner." Victimology: An International Journal 3:222–226.

Straus, Murray A. 1973. "A general systems theory approach to a theory of violence between family members." Social Science Information 13:105–125.

Straus, Murray A. 1974. "Leveling, civility, and violence in the family." Journal of Marriage and the Family 36:13–29.

Straus, Murray A. 1976. "Sexual inequality, cultural norms, and wife-beating." Victimology 1:54–76.

Straus, Murray A. 1977. "Wife-beating: How common, and why?" Victimology 2:443–458.

Straus, Murray A. 1979. "Measuring intrafamily conflict and violence: The Conflict Tactics (CT) Scales." Journal of Marriage and the Family 41:75–88.

Straus, Murray A. 1980. "Victims and aggressors in marital violence." American Behavioral Scientist 23:681–704.

Straus, Murray A. 1981a. "Re-evaluation of the Conflict Tactics Scale." Paper presented at the National Conference for Family Violence Researchers, University of New Hampshire (July).

Straus, Murray A. 1981b. "Societal change and change in family violence." Paper presented at the National Conference for Family Violence Researchers, University of New Hampshire (July).

Straus, Murray A. 1983. "Ordinary violence, child abuse, and wife beating: What do they have in common?" In David Finkelhor, Richard J. Gelles, Gerald T. Hotaling, and Murray A. Straus (eds.), The Dark Side of Families: Current Family Violence Research. Beverly Hills, CA: Sage.

Straus, Murray A. In press. "Domestic violence and homicide antecedents." Bulletin of the New York Academy of Medicine.

Straus, Murray A., and Richard J. Gelles. 1986. "How violent are American families: Estimates based on two national surveys and other studies." Paper in progress.

Straus, Murray A., Richard J. Gelles, and Suzanne K. Steinmetz. 1980. Behind Closed Doors: Violence in the American Family. Garden City, NY: Doubleday, Anchor Press.

Szinovacz, Maximiliane E. 1983. "Using couple data as a methodological tool: The case of marital violence." Journal of Marriage and the Family: 633–644.

Tavris, Carol, and Carole Offir. 1977. The Longest War: Sex Differences in Perspective. New York: Harcourt Brace Jovanovich.

Thorton, Arland, Duane F. Alwin, and Donald Camburn. 1983. "Causes and consequences of sex-role attitudes and attitude change." American Sociology Review 48:211–227.

"2 researchers say violence has plunged in the last 10 years, but . . . " 1985. Christian Science Monitor, 18 November, pp. 3–4.

U.S. Department of Justice. 1985. "Criminal victimization in the U.S., 1983." National Crime Survey Report NCJ-96459. Washington, DC: Government Printing Office.

Warrior, Betsy. 1982. Battered Women's Directory (8th ed.). Cambridge, MA: Author, 46 Pleasant Street, Cambridge, MA 02139.

Williams, Kirk R., and Richard Hawkins. In press. "Perceptual research on general deterrence: A critical review." Law and Society Review.

Yllö, Kersti. 1978. "Nonmarital cohabitation: Beyond the college campus." Alternative Lifestyles 1:37–54.

Yllö, Kersti, and Murray A. Straus. 1981. "Interpersonal violence among married and cohabiting couples." Family Relations 30:339–345.

10. School Crime and Individual Responsibility: The Perpetuation of a Myth?

DELOS H. KELLY AND WILLIAM T. PINK

Elsewhere (Kelly, 1979; Pink and Sweeney, 1978), we have introduced and detailed what can be termed the *interactional* and *organizational* paradigms. Both of these analytical tools, we have argued, can be used to obtain a more adequate understanding of the way in which various types of interpersonal *interactions* (e.g., teacher-student, psychiatrist-client, police-citizen) may give rise to certain outcomes that generate negative consequences both in the short and long term (e.g., the labeling of a student as a "misfit," a client as mentally disturbed, and a citizen as a criminal). We have also pointed out that a critical component in this labeling or typing ceremony is the observer's or the audience's reaction to the event. If, for example, and depending upon the specific *interactional context*, a student does not live up to a teacher's expectation of appropriate academic performance or behavior, then that student may be tagged with some type of negative label (e.g., "academic failure" or "behavior problem"). Similarly, in the psychiatric setting or out in the field, actors who violate selected expectations often become more vulnerable to some type of social and/or legal processing. Moreover, interactional exchanges such as these can serve as important precursors to the beginning stages of a variety of delinquent, criminal, and deviant careers. Hence, our concern in this paper with the concept of *evolving adolescent careers*.

Several researchers have noted that these critical diagnostic and labeling processes occur rather routinely in a range of different interactional settings and oftentimes without much forethought by the labelers (Becker, 1963; Kelly, 1976; Pink and Noblit, 1977; Rist, 1978; Rutter, 1979; Ryan, 1972; Schur, 1971). What emerges from a close reading of this research is that actions having in many cases rather long-term negative consequences are frequently justified because they are (1) taken "in the best interests" of youth and (2) supported by the operational logic of the school or agency. That is to say, the public labeling and subsequent differential processing of groups identified as "slow learners," the "mentally ill," and "criminals" is seen by both the major actors and the public at large as an integral and indeed necessary action of the school, psychiatric, and criminal justice systems, respectively. Regretfully, little interdisciplinary research has yet to focus on (1) the negative short- and long-term effects of such stigmatizing labels and (2) how the negative consequences of the labeling process in one area (e.g., the school) interface with similarly functioning labeling processes in other areas (e.g., the juvenile justice system and the occupational arena). Consequently, in this paper we shall detail how school labels originate and how such labels have negative consequences for adolescent behavior. We shall also offer a larger and more theoretically integrated view of the relationship between these commonplace labeling processes and school-based crimes.

THE TYPING CEREMONY AND DIAGNOSTIC STEREOTYPES

In terms of actually making sense out of any typing ceremony or the evolution of a broad category of deviant careers, it is critically important to analyze the role of *diagnostic stereotypes* (Scheff, 1965). As we have argued elsewhere (Kelly, 1979; Pink and Sweeney, 1978), diagnostic stereotypes play a central role in the initial *identifying* of clients for processing. If, for example, teachers believe that browns and blacks lack academic ability or are likely to be behavior problems, then such students will be singled out for special processing, treatment, or scrutiny (de Lone, 1979; Ogbu, 1974; Rist, 1978, 1979). Similarly, if certain police or juvenile probation officers are convinced that selected categories of people (e.g., the blacks and browns) constitute the "real" criminals or delinquents, then such individuals become more susceptible to some type of legal handling (Schafer and Polk, 1967; Schur, 1969; Skolnick, 1966). One significant outcome of this increased attention to specific groups is that any statistics generated by subsequent police activity will, of necessity, exhibit an overrepresentation of the targeted populations. Thus, one rather predictable outcome of this process is that the resulting data will be used as a rationale for keeping selected groups under surveillance. In short, more surveillance yields higher arrest rates, which in turn yield greater surveillance. Perhaps an even more subtle result centers around the fact that these data are subsequently utilized, both directly and indirectly, to perpetuate certain myths or misunderstandings about the nature and extent of delinquent, criminal, or deviant activity. We use the term myth or misunderstanding because little real analysis is attempted beyond the initial finding of differential involvement by race and class in the justice system. The net result of such poor analysis is not only a misinformed understanding of the origins of juvenile and adult crime, but also a clearly wrongheaded approach to treatment or rehabilitation.

If, by way of illustration, race, class, or ethnicity emerge as important factors in the police or court statistics, then any attempt at understanding or explanation must be predicated upon the importance of these variables. And, traditionally, this is what has occurred. To be more specific, most of the influential theories in the area of delinquency, crime, and deviance look to social class for their explanatory or independent factor. A typical representation would be an argument to the effect that being situated in the *lower* socioeconomic strata breeds a sense of frustration and failure as measured against the middle-class yardstick, which is then resolved by participation in aberrant or nonconforming behavior. Even though, intuitively, a statement of this order often appears most eloquent and plausible, there are several dangers or pitfalls associated with it.

Specifically, what seems to happen in more cases than not is that people operate as if a particular theory or statement is actually true without testing it out. Thus, the net result of class-based beliefs about crime is differential treatment, which can lead to changes in such factors as behavior and self-esteem. Moreover, such theoretical declarations frequently seem to operate as conceptual blinders in that only a limited set of variables is considered or examined empirically. Research appears to stop when a satisfactory or comfortable explanation for the data has been found. In terms of our example, one might ask: What about middle- and upper-class actors? Do they commit crimes? Further, if such individuals violate the law, do they do so because of personal frustration or failure, or are their violations a function of other factors? What about female, black, brown, yellow, and red crime? While additional questions of this type could be introduced, it must be recognized that whether a specific theory can explain the facts or not is really a matter determined through testing. Currently, not only do many of our statements lack theoretical sophistication, but those that do exist have not been tested adequately. This applies most appropriately to those explanations that have tried to make sense out of school crime. Consequently, while other unanswered questions are important, we want to focus this paper on an understanding of the involvement of young people in school crime.

DIAGNOSTIC STEREOTYPES AND SCHOOL CRIME

One statement we can make without fear of contradiction is that there is little agreement as to what constitutes school crime. This confusion arises primarily as a result of the differing authority structures existent between the school and the community. In short, what one school defines as a crime another defines as misbehavior. Each school with a different definition utilizes a different response. One reports all crimes to the police, while another uses an internal system of punishments (Greenberg, 1969; Senate Subcommittee, 1975; Rubel, 1977; NIE, 1978). While this problem with a definition for school crime exists, there is little disagreement concerning the range of student acts, including vandalism and violence both to persons and property, which constitutes a disruption to the schooling enterprise. Consequently, for our purposes in this paper, our definition of school crime shall be broad. We shall include all student acts which are disruptive to schools: acts from (1) showing disrespect to teachers and administrators, through (2) theft of school property and from persons, and (3) vandalism towards school property, to (4) riots and physical assaults of students and staff.

Frequently, attempts at explaining school crime have focused on the low-income child. Cohen (1955), for example, has argued that lower-class males are not equipped to function successfully in the middle-class oriented school environment, and thus they fail, both academically and otherwise. Dropping out of school offers one mechanism for coping with the resultant failure. Becoming involved in delinquency or the gang provide other outlets. In effect, then, Cohen's argument is structured in the following manner: low social class → school failure → dropout, delinquency, crime, and gang involvement (Phillips and Kelly, 1979). Interestingly, even though Cohen's interpretation continues to enjoy rather widespread acceptance and to form the theoretical basis for programs aimed at reducing delinquency and crime, it should be noted that the results of several other empirical investigations have been less than kind to his theory (Hargreaves, 1967; Kelly, 1978a; Kelly and Pink, 1973; Pink, 1978; Polk, 1969; Schafer and Polk, 1967; Rutter et al., 1979; Willis, 1977). More specifically, what the bulk of this evidence indicates is that school failure, independent of social class, is linked significantly to dropout, delinquency, and a host of other attitudinal and behavioral outcomes. Another way of saying this is that pupils, regardless of their class backgrounds, respond rather characteristically to failure. The available evidence also provides a basis upon which Cohen's argument can be expanded by the incorporation of race and ethnicity variables. Thus, we find that students in general respond most similarly to school failure. This finding may not appear especially startling to some, but the significance of the observation must be viewed within the traditional context that continues to permeate the study of delinquency, crime, and deviance.

Specifically, as we have noted briefly above, the class variable has frequently been invoked to explain a range of student or juvenile misconduct. Yet recent tests of the statements by Cohen and others do not generally support the primacy of social class as an explanatory variable. Rather, the bulk of this research supports the significance of such school factors as failure, tracking, and ability grouping. This distinction is important because a class-based theorist describes the causes of delinquency and crime in very different terms from the organizational theorist. One major difference is that the content of the diagnostic stereotypes generated by the two contrasting theories would be significantly different.

A social-class interpretation would direct us to an examination of what it is about an individual's class position and associated socialization experiences that would seem to be productive of aberrant behavior, while a school-factors interpretation would direct us to an investigation of what it is about the experience of failing in school that is productive of these same nonconformist behaviors. To date, it is the class-based position that has received the most attention and thus formed the interpretive foundation for the majority of teachers and administrators. This has remained the case even when research has demonstrated that lower-class youth can achieve in school and that levels of school disruption are highly related to the performance of the students in that building (Brookover et al., 1978; Edmonds, 1979; NIE, 1978). This widespread and strong belief in social class as a major explanatory factor in school crime is due to a number of interrelated factors that need examination.

SCHOOL CRIME: IS IT THE INDIVIDUAL OR SOCIETY?

Perhaps foremost is the fact that it is rather easy to examine an individual's social-class background and then make inferences about why, for example, there is a measured relationship between class, delinquency, and school crime. Thus, we are presented with a host of interpretive statements to the effect that lower-class individuals experience blockage, which is thereafter resolved by involvement in delinquency and crime (Cohen, 1955; Hirschi, 1969; Merton, 1968). In fact, it is worth noting that many of the recent efforts to reduce crime are predicated on the manipulation of those conditions thought to be responsible for producing blockage. Low-income and minority students are thus provided with early childhood intervention programs, tuition grants, tutors, and the like; while out in the public sphere, sporadic attempts are made to enhance job opportunities – efforts that have been notably unsuccessful, at least on a large scale (Pearl, 1972; Pink et al., 1979). The persistently high rate of unemployment and the extremely high dropout rate for blacks and browns more than amply attests to the general failure of such intervention to change this perceived experience blockage. Unfortunately, this lack of success in the area of opportunity manipulation seems not to have generated a search for new interpretive meanings for persistent school and societal failure but rather to have given rise to yet another set of class-based diagnostic stereotypes.

Perhaps of most significance in the failure of intervention programs to change outcomes is the fact that many subsequently argue that it is the individual, and not society, who is lacking (Ryan, 1972; Wyers, 1978). Placing "blame" with the victim fits nicely into the cultural ethos that every person can succeed given ambition and hard work. Moreover, failure viewed as a personal shortcoming removes each individual from feelings of responsibility or guilt for others' lack of success. Such a claim for individual pathology can then be used as the rationale for the implementation of a wide range of "people changing" programs. For example, there are currently urgent demands in the field of criminal justice for tougher laws and sentences, as well as for the restoration of capital punishment – demands that seem to be based additionally on the conclusion that attempts at correcting and rehabilitating the actor have been, in general, miserable failures. However, we must note that even though the recidivism rates are not encouraging, they should not be taken as conclusive evidence that failure is, necessarily, *individualistic* in nature. Such misplaced logic currently exists in special education programming. While there is a general cry for ever earlier and more refined diagnosis of learning problems, all based of course on the notion of various different individual failings, there seems to be little concern for the mounting evidence indicating that the diagnostic tools currently in vogue are themselves less than valid, and that the misappropriate use of them may have serious negative consequences for students incorrectly diagnosed and processed (Coles, 1978). We also have accumulating research which indicates that students from lower-class backgrounds and varying racial groups can succeed academically if the learning environment is positive and challenging. There are data which demonstrate that such students can overcome the perceived handicap of individual inadequacies and limitations (Brookover et al., 1978; Edmonds, 1979; Lezotte and Passalacqua, 1978; Madaus et al., 1978; Rutter et al., 1979).

What such data should fuel is a systematic and in-depth analysis of the relationship between class, race, achievement, and crime – this would include a thorough examination of those societal-structural conditions that appear to be related to high rates of delinquency and crime (e.g., racism, classism, ageism, and inequality). Failure to make such a commitment, in our estimation, will guarantee (1) the continued production of delinquency and crime and (2) the perpetuation of the (untested) myth that such deviance is a direct function of individual pathology. In short, we urge that future research should focus on testing the largely unsubstantiated but widely held beliefs about the class- and race-based nature of school crime, which currently serve to perpetuate a number of biased notions and negative stereotypes.

SCHOOL CRIME AND THE PERPETUATION OF A MYTH

We have suggested earlier that the school-factors evidence indicates that school failure, independent of status origins, is predictive of a host of attitudinal and behavioral outcomes. We have also suggested that if class, race, and ethnicity are not linked directly to school crime and other institutionally perceived deviant outcomes, new antecedent elements will have to be invoked as explanatory factors. Thus far, this search has not been accomplished with either rigor or regularity. The majority of educators still believe (1) that failure is an individual problem and not an educational or institutional problem, and (2) that low-income students, blacks, browns, and other disadvantaged students fail or drop out because of some specific individual deficiency or problem. What a posture of this sort means is that any responsibility for failure is deflected away from the school, and moreover, that the responsibility for improving performance or behavior lies squarely with the individual student and his/her family.

Predictably, with an individual pathology as a working ideology, schools continue to operate in much the same fashion as they have historically (e.g., perpetuating the timeworn stereotypes about the limited abilities of blacks and browns). Regretfully, too little in the experience of teachers and administrators suggests that serious consideration be given to the way in which education is dispensed or allocated to selected categories of students. Clearly, the current organizational logic of the school does not encourage or promote the observation that phenomena such as apathy, truancy, dropout, and school crime have *structural* origins or roots. To really begin to understand why, for example, blacks and browns have high rates of dropout and school crime, it is important to analyze how a specific *school career* arises and is perpetuated by school personnel and others. This analysis requires a basic examination of the way in which individual traits mesh with key organizational components and processes to produce certain outcomes, perhaps promoting the career of the "academic misfit" (Hargreaves, 1967; Kelly, 1978a; Pink and Sweeney, 1978; Polk and Pink, 1971; Schafer and Olexa, 1971; Willis, 1977).

SCHOOL CRIME AND THE EVOLUTION OF DEVIANT CAREERS: ABILITY GROUPING

Initially, it needs to be recognized that the educational system is organizationally geared to produce both success and failure. That is to say, there is a general belief, which then guides practice, that not all students will do well in school and that one of the major purposes of schooling is to select out those who have ability from those who do not. Thus, schools must "suffer" a proportion of students who are less than bright academically. This belief system can be substantiated easily, and particularly so if we understand that the organizational structure of most schools can be characterized by a readily visible set of deviant and nondeviant career lines (Hargreaves, 1967; Pink, 1975; Willis, 1977). At the lower grade levels, the best example of this would be ability grouping—a rather widely used system of student stratification in which students are divided into work or learning groups within the regular classroom setting. It is here that we find the "Bluebirds" and the "Blackbirds" or some other system of denoting different levels of academic performance and ability (Jackson, 1964; Ogbu, 1974; Pink and Sweeney, 1978; Rist, 1979). Students considered "bright" or likely to learn quickly are placed in fast-paced groups (e.g., Bluebirds), while students perceived as "dull" or slow are placed in slower-paced learning groups (e.g., Blackbirds). To many, including both educators and parents, this way of distinguishing among students appears rather innocuous. After all, they reason, the students in the lower or less prestigious groups (e.g., Blackbirds) will actually receive more help from the teacher and thus do better in the long haul. This may actually be the case for some students. However, there is accumulating evidence which suggests that assignment to low ability groups oftentimes signals decreased teacher interaction and increased problems with poor behavior and self-esteem. Clearly, the effects of ability grouping, or any system of differential student stratification for that matter, run deep.

Basically, being treated as different from the majority, by being situated at the lower end of stratification systems in general, is associated with a certain amount of enduring *stigma* (Goffman, 1963). Teachers, peers, and others soon learn what it means to be situated at the bottom end of the academic heap and act accordingly (Hargreaves, 1967). Unfortunately, so do the low-status students assigned to ability groups from which little is expected—a realization that can impact rather dramatically upon their subsequent school performance, as well as contribute to the rise of selected types of behavior problems. Such perceptions of differential status assignments are not found exclusively within the school. Parents, also, rarely question the academic decisions that have been rendered on behalf of their children. Consequently, whether they realize it or not, by virtue of their very inaction and failure to examine or question the educational decision-making process, parents are contributing to the perpetuation of those processes that frequently give rise to the dropout, school vandal, and the like.

Given the fact that the school is geared for both success and failure, it follows that the school must have ways of identifying the winners from the losers; hence, the student stratification systems that permeate our educational institutions. However, there is considerable evidence which indicates that decision-makers are not always using mandated, academic standards as a basis for placement decisions (Hargreaves, 1967; Kelly, 1976; Rist, 1979; Schafer and Olexa, 1971). Schafer and Olexa (1971), for example, noted that even when IQ and previous ability factors were controlled, blacks and low-income students were still more apt to be found in the basic- or low-ability tracks. Similarly, Hargreaves (1967) reports that lower-class students were overrepresented in the bottom streams (tracks) of the school he studied. It cannot be emphasized too strongly that this initial educational placement is critical, particularly as the notion of career is applied to the academic setting (Kelly and Grove, 1981).

Once an academic decision has been made, this sets into motion processes that operate in such a manner as to virtually guarantee that the affected student will comply with the decision. The schooling enterprise "works," for example, on the assumption that (1) students have different ability levels, (2) that it is the job of the staff to identify these different levels, and (3) that subsequently, the staff must tailor a variety of differing programs to meet these identified student needs. Thus, the school can be seen to be organized around the need to facilitate this assumption about differential abilities. Also, as we have noted earlier, in the vast majority of cases, teachers, peers, and family members buy into both the logic and the meaning of the label that has been bestowed upon the student. A process of this magnitude is not without its effects, especially if one understands the dynamics of the *self-fulfilling prophecy* (Rosenthal and Jacobson, 1968). More specifically, associated with any academic career decision (e.g., the placement of a student into a "fast" or "slow" learning group) is a set of expectations and corresponding labels. Thus, the low-ability group student is frequently viewed by educators and others as being less capable academically and/or a potential behavior problem, while the high-ability group pupil is often perceived as being academically gifted or talented and certainly not a behavior problem. Labels, such as "bright," "college material," and "gifted," are often routinely used to characterize these latter students. Teachers, peers, parents, and others come to "expect" less from the low-ability group student, and, not surprisingly, they most often get their wish. By contrast, more is expected of those in the high-ability group, and these expectations are also often realized (Rist, 1979). Further, if the low-ability group student engages in school misconduct, this is certainly understandable, especially since the potential for misbehavior forms a part of the expectational frame of reference that exists for such individuals. Similarly, if the low-ability group student fails, this, too, is understandable, as he or she is doing nothing more than living up to the expectations associated with his or her status (Hargreaves, 1967; Kelly, 1976; Pink and Sweeney, 1978; Willis, 1977). The impact of processes such as these also has a rather direct effect upon a student's (1) *personal identity* (i.e., how the individual views self), (2) *public identity* (i.e., how others view the individual), and (3) *self-image* (i.e., how the individual evaluates self, usually from a positive or negative frame of reference relative to others, along dimensions such as academic ability or general intelligence).

Specifically, the evidence suggests that being typed and processed as lacking in academic ability, or as a behavior problem, can produce an erosion of a student's academic self-image (Kelly, 1975; Schafer and Olexa, 1971). This is due primarily to the fact that the pupil's immediate and significant others are responding as if he or she is, in fact, incapable academically (Rist, 1978). Reactions such as these can also affect the pupil's personal identity. The affected student, for example, may come to view self as being mediocre or lacking the needed academic abilities and skills—traits which, if possessed, would probably insure some semblance of academic success within the educational domain (Ogbu, 1974). Thus, when such a student engages in school crime, he or she is probably not only living up to teacher, peer, parental, and self expectations, but he or she may also be striving to obtain some measure of success and well-being. Unfortunately, at least from the student's perspective, manifestations such as these are usually taken by the academic decision makers as conclusive evidence that the student is, in fact, a behavior problem. Thus, by using a somewhat circular form of argumentation, the misbehavior serves to confirm the initial diagnosis and labeling as a potential troublemaker.

We must never lose sight of the fact that the school arena is perhaps of most importance to the student. Both personal identity and self-esteem are fashioned within the day-to-day activities of the school. Thus, the classifications used by schools to identify and process students (e.g., "bright," "dull," "troublemaker," "college material") also carry great valency in the out-of-school world – again, these classifications tend to shape friendship choices, as well as personal identity and career options (Hargreaves, 1967; Kelly 1978a; Pink and Sweeney, 1978). Inasmuch as these school classifications carry over to the out-of-school world (e.g., are known and used), students carrying negative labels find it next to impossible to escape the stigma associated with such typing. Moreover, analysis of the cumulative nature of such processes reveals that original diagnoses and placements are infrequently changed. Thus, students diagnosed as "dull," or "lacking in academic potential," usually remain in low-status/slow-moving classes throughout their school days.

The move from school to school brings no relief from this pattern of diagnosis, labeling, and differential treatment. As students graduate from grade schools through college, their records will follow. The result is that others will quickly become aware of any stigmatizing labels or other negative and potentially damaging information – potentially discrediting material that can and usually is used as a basis for subsequent placement. In short, all school based decisions concerning such factors as ability, educability, behavior, character, and personality, decisions oftentimes made without the benefit of valid instrumentation, become a permanent part of each student's record or biography. Thus, inasmuch as (1) such information is cumulative, and (2) low status placements lead to lowered self-esteem and poor performance, which are in turn highly related to subsequent poor performance and involvement in school crime, (3) it becomes easy to understand how students placed in low-status groups find it next to impossible to reverse the school's uniformly low opinion of their general ability and worth and (4) break out of the deviant career lines they presently occupy.

SCHOOL CRIME, THE EVOLUTION OF DEVIANT CAREERS, ABILITY GROUPING, AND TRACKING: MAKING THE CONNECTION

It should be noted that to date, there have been no studies that have systematically addressed the manner in which academic careers evolve, are perpetuated, and perhaps transformed. However, bits of evidence, when pieced together, can offer some insight into how, for example, stigmatizing information acquired during the early stages of a student's academic career can be used to help crystallize and eventually structure the career of the "academic misfit." This is most apparent if we analyze the ways in which institutions, in general, interact with their clients (Kelly, 1978b, 1979, 1980). Probably some of the best insights into this process can be found in the area of tracking – another system of student stratification that exists in many junior and senior high schools. It should be noted initially that there are some important differences between ability grouping and tracking, the major difference being that tracking is schoolwide rather than within a single class and is therefore a much more rigid and closed system. Unlike ability grouping, where a student may be placed in a "fast" group for math, and an "intermediate" or "slow" group for reading, complete curriculums are structured by track position both within and across grade levels. Thus, if a student has been diagnosed initially as being "college material," he or she will be placed in the college-prep track. Thereafter, with minor exceptions, the students will then follow a prescribed course of study until graduation. A college-prep curriculum would include college-prep math, English, history, science, and a language. In addition, the best teachers would be rewarded with an assignment to teach these high-status students (Pink and Sweeney, 1978; Willis, 1977). By contrast, the noncollege-prep student would, throughout his or her school career, generally pursue a less academically oriented curriculum not designed for placing students into institutions of higher learning (e.g., noncollege-prep math, English, history, mechanical drawing, shop, home economics). Furthermore, such students do not usually receive instruction from the best teachers in the school. Upon graduation, the majority of these noncollege-prep students will enter the world of work, and will thereafter be unlikely to attend any kind of college (Kelly and Pink, 1971).

A second important feature of the track system is the observation that once a student has been assigned to a specific track he or she can expect to remain there. Thus, this seemingly innocent placement gains in importance given the recognition that different tracks systematically prepare students for different kinds of occupations. Schafer and Olexa (1971), in their three-year study of two American high schools, noted little movement either up or down between tracks. This led them to the conclusion that the track system operates much like a caste system, the track assignment serving to separate students in friendship choices, academic preparation, interests, behaviors, and subsequent career options. It is in this sense, then, that initial career-placement decisions, leading as they do to largely irreversible and qualitatively different patterns of treatment, must be viewed as critical. Perhaps most critical is the relationship between track assignment and subsequent involvements in school crime and later deviant activities.

Implicit in our discussion of some of the major features of track systems, as opposed to ability grouping, is the notion that discrediting or stigmatizing information is essential as far as placement in a school's low-status track or deviant career lines. Also implicit is the observation that the effects of negative school labels (e.g., school failure, delinquent, or low tracker) become accumulative over time. Thus, if a student fails academically, this often means that he or she is probably destined to fail again, and over time, the repeated instances of failure can help to produce the career of the "misfit," "delinquent," or "dropout." Similarly, if a student has been designated as lacking ability and treated accordingly, then the probability is also high that, over time, his or her performance level will be below grade level. It is our contention, moreover, that given the enduring and stigmatizing nature of deviant labels in general, the impact of school labels will become most noticeable when they mesh and interact with a highly stratified and formal track system. To say this, however, is not to overlook the fact that even where track systems are lacking, other criteria (e.g., grade point averages or English mark) will still be used by school personnel, students, and parents as a basis for differentiating students according to their presumed academic talents. The point is that public proclamations appear to be associated with rather pronounced effects, and most particularly when a set of rigid molds, as exemplified by the track systems, exists. Probably one of the better general discussions of the way in which the molds, track systems, or deviant career lines can evolve, as well as how they are used to process students, is contained in the work by Cicourel and Kitsuse (1963, 1968).

In particular, Cicourel and Kitsuse (1968, pp. 125-135) argue that any school can be characterized in terms of its deviant and nondeviant career lines, and as proof of this, they list and describe the three lines they uncovered during their investigation of a high school: (1) the academic, (2) the clinical, and (3) the delinquent. Somewhat predictably, in student selection for placement in the differentiated career lines, those who exhibited psychological or behavioral problems landed in the emotional and delinquent career lines, while the academically successful students ended up in the academic. What a study of this nature suggests very clearly is that educators and counselors, in particular, are looking for, or become highly sensitized to, specific bits of biographical information about students upon which to base their decisions. Much of this information, they report, has little to do with academic performance or potential. Also, and even more fundamentally, we must not lose sight of the fact that if a specific career line forms an integral part of the underlying organizational structure of the school, then students will be selected out for placement in it. This placement of people in existing structures is an inescapable fact—one that characterizes *people processing* (e.g., the schools) and *people changing* (e.g., correctional facilities) in general. Although Cicourel and Kitsuse do not deal specifically with the effects of social class, race, and ethnicity per se, it becomes a rather simple matter to expand their discussion by incorporating a concern for these and other critical variables. Schafer and Olexa (1971) observed the way in which class and race affected the track-assignment process. Specifically, they noted that even with key ability factors controlled (i.e., IQ and previous achievement), low-income pupils and blacks were more likely to be situated in the basic or noncollege-prep track. Such a finding certainly attests to the fact that nonacademic criteria, i.e., in this case, social class and race, were being applied in the processing of students. It also becomes a simple exercise to speculate that those students who have a record or history, either formal or informal, of some type of stigmatizing experience in the elementary or lower grades (e.g., placement in low-ability groups, being designating as having emotional problems, etc.) become prime candidates for the deviant career lines or lower tracks found in most secondary schools. In fact, several recent studies by Kelly (1976, 1978a; Kelly and Grove, 1981) support this observation. For example, Kelly's investigation of the way in which students were nominated for remedial reading (Kelly, 1976) found that even though they did not qualify academically for such placement, students who exhibited some type of previous contact with a stigmatizing program (e.g., remedial reading) were more apt to be nominated by their teachers than students with similar academic credentials but no previous contact with such stigmatizing programs.

What accumulating information such as this suggests is that (1) as students move through the schools, they acquire a reputation in the eyes of their teachers, counselors, and peers, and (2) that this reputation, once structured, becomes a rather permanent fixture of a student's very being or existence within that domain. In a sense, too, this "rep" can be viewed as constituting something akin to what Becker (1963) has termed a *master status* (i.e., a trait or status that assumes a certain priority and overrides other status considerations). As an example, Becker initially cites the case of the black physician and, thereafter, argues that probably in most cases, people will respond to the individual in terms of racial stereotypes and not according to the occupation. In this instance, race would be viewed as constituting a master status, while occupation would be conceptualized as being a *subordinate status*. Becker expands this discussion by pointing out that *deviant labels* can very easily be viewed as master statuses in the eyes of others, as well as in the eyes of the actor. He also stresses another extremely important feature of labels, namely that, instead of assuming that a person may be deviant in one respect, people tend to generalize or make imputations about the *total* person. Clearly, because of the size and bureaucratic nature of schools, these same types of processes are operative within this domain. Thus, if students are tagged as lacking in ability, as having behavior problems, as predelinquents, or as "misfits," such labels can become effectively viewed as their master status. People will, thereafter, regardless of the behavior exhibited, respond to the label and not to the person.

Thus far, we have sketched a brief outline of those interactional-organizational factors and conditions that seem critically important as far as moving students into and along various differentiated career routes. We have also, by incorporating the notion of career or, more specifically, career flows, illustrated how stigmatizing school labels may be passed on from one educational level to another, and, thus, actually may enhance the probability that the affected students will become more deeply mired in a deviant school career—a career that may be characterized by such phenomena as school misconduct and crime, apathy, truancy, or dropout. Understanding how this can come about requires further analysis of what it means, both organizationally and individually, to be situated in a deviant or low school status.

SCHOOL CRIME: AN INDICTMENT OF THE SYSTEM?

It may be recalled that during our earlier discussion of the origins of school crime and the evolution of deviant careers, we argued that instead of looking exclusively to particularistic personal characteristics of individuals to explain motivations or the reasons why deviant careers may evolve, it might be more productive to direct our attention to how the schools are actually structured and how that structure shapes student behavior. In this respect, we pointed out (1) that schools are actually geared to produce failures and (2) that via a complex of negative self, teacher, peer, and parental expectations, schools also manufacture various forms of school misconduct and crime. What this line of argumentation suggests is that the "system" actually demands and promotes nonconformity. Our discussion of tracking can be expanded to provide additional substance to this interpretation. We can achieve this by focusing on the *content* of the value systems that impact on students located in the various tracks (Hargreaves, 1967; Havighurst et al., 1962; Hollingshead, 1949; Kelly, 1974; Ogbu, 1974; Pink and Sweeney, 1978; Rist, 1979; Schafer and Olexa, 1971; Willis, 1977). Unfortunately, while all too little large scale and systematic research exists on this complex topic, some leads can be developed if attention is given to bits of existing data.

In his extended study of streaming (or tracking) in an English secondary school, Hargreaves (1967) locates and maps out the value systems that characterized the low and high streams. What he found was that the school operated on the basis of two distinct value systems: the *academic* and the *delinquescent*. Upon further observation and analysis, it became clear that not only were the systems significantly different, but that they also exerted a most direct, yet qualitatively different, influence upon pupil behavior. Thus, the low-stream (track) boys often received positive reinforcement from their peers for engaging in school misconduct or, more generally, antiacademic pursuits. The high-stream (track) boys, by contrast, were rewarded by their teachers and peers for promoting the academic values traditionally characteristic of their high-status academically oriented stream. Interestingly, and of great significance vis-a-vis the organizational perpetuation of negative stereotypes and deviant career lines, even the teachers seemed to accept and, thereby, condone the antiacademic orientation and subsequent low academic and behavioral performance on the part of the low-stream boys. Hargreaves's interviews with teachers support this observation, especially statements to the effect that the low streamers lack ability and are more interested in "messing." Also corroborative was the observation that a significantly greater number of low-stream boys had experienced official contact with the juvenile justice system. Quite clearly, teachers, peers, and the affected students (low streamers) are living up to the dictates of the label.

Similarly, in their study of the relationship between track assignment and student behavior and attitudes in two American high schools, Schafer and Olexa (1971) found that students consigned to low-status nonacademic tracks not only felt ashamed of their assignment, but also tried to conceal their books from their peers for fear of being considered dumb. They also found that students engaging in school crimes were concentrated in the nonacademic low-status tracks. This relationship remained significant even after IQ, previous academic performance, and social class were controlled in their data. They reasoned that low track assignment and the subsequent differential treatment associated with such placement serve to manufacture deviant behavior. Using both a different methodological strategy and setting, Willis (1977) reached remarkably similar findings. Willis conducted a long-term ethnographic investigation of the adaption of academically failing working-class boys to the culture of a secondary school in England. He reveals, in considerable detail, how the school streaming (tracking) process contributed to producing and maintaining low levels of achievement and aspiration among working-class students. Here is a setting in which both teachers and students understand and project the meaning of nonacademic placement and labels: a placement that signals graduation to low-status blue-collar jobs with little opportunity for advancement. Willis analyzes how, over time, failing students become progressively more alienated from the school, and how they systematically develop an antischool culture that is based upon (1) adult, rather than student, behavior (e.g., drinking, smoking, swearing) and (2) the flaunting of school rules (e.g., truancy, disrespect for teachers and school property). Again, he depicts a situation where poor to no performance and "messing" are the expectations of both teacher and student, a situation where the organizational logic of the school both requires and accommodates such a tragic and wasteful scenario.

What the studies indicate about the way in which identities are structured and maintained is that once a student has been tagged with a deviant label, this becomes an enduring fact of his or her biography. This will often mean that others will respond to the label and not to the person. The individual will also tend to react to the tag. There may occur a point in time where the labeled student not only *accepts* the label, but may begin to *act* in accordance with it. At this juncture, we can speak of the career or *secondary* deviant (Lemert, 1959). Another way of saying this is that if the pupil accepts the *public* identity imputed to him or her (e.g., the designation as an "academic misfit") and thereafter exhibits behavior and mannerisms commensurate with the newly chosen identity (e.g., creates problems, will not work, or exhibits a lack of respect), we are dealing with an individual who will become rather firmly entrenched in a career of school crime. In this instance, too, the student's personal identity meshes with the public identity. The individual is also acting in terms of the expectations associated with his or her low school status, both in the eyes of others and self.

REDUCING SCHOOL CRIME: A SUMMARY STATEMENT

The preceding analysis has indicated that the potential for school crime is an inherent feature of the underlying organizational structure of the school. More specifically, that as long as stratification systems, as commonly represented by ability grouping and tracking, comprise an integral component of the educational system, then society will continue to witness high rates of activities such as school crime, dropout, apathy, truancy, and delinquency among students inflicted with low school status. A very important implication of this process centers around the fact that any program or strategy that promotes the notion of individual pathology or failure, without recognizing the significance of school value systems (e.g., the delinquescent versus the academic), is doomed to failure. Correlatively, any proposed model for change that does not recognize how diagnostic stereotypes originate (e.g., notions about social class and race), are applied to students, and are perpetuated (e.g., passed on from one grade level to another) is also doomed to failure.

We would suggest that instead of looking rather exclusively within the individual to explain pathology, the search must be broadened to include an investigation of the structural origins of school crime. It is clear that, while beefing up the artillery may help (e.g., using more guards, monitors, or alarm devices), such a "solution" is only temporary at best, primarily because the "problem" has structural roots. Again, then, we urge a closer and more systematic examination of the short and long term consequences of commonplace educational practices that are (1) producing deviant career identities and (2) maintaining high rates of school crime.

References

Becker, H.S. *The outsiders*. New York: The Free Press, 1963.

Brookover, W.B., et al. Elementary school climate and school achievement, *American Educational Research Journal*, 1978, *15*, 301–318.

Cicourel, A.V., and Kitsuse, J.I. *The educational decision-makers*. Indianapolis: Bobbs-Merrill, 1963.

Cicourel, A.V., and Kitsuse, J.I. The social organization of the high school and deviant adolescent careers. In E. Rubington and M.S. Weinberg (Eds.), *Deviance: the interactionist perspective*, New York: Macmillan, 1968.

Cohen, A.K. *Delinquent boys: the culture of the gang.* New York: The Free Press, 1955.

Coles, G.S. The learning disabilities test battery: empirical and social issues, *Harvard Educational Review*, 1978, *48*, 313–340.

de Lone, R.H. *Small futures.* New York: Harcourt Brace Jovanovich, 1979.

Edmonds, R. Effective schools for the urban poor, *Educational Leadership*, 1979, *37*, 15–24.

Goffman, E. *Stigma: notes on the management of spoiled identity.* Englewood Cliffs: Prentice-Hall, 1963.

Greenberg, B. *School vandalism: a national dilemma.* Menlo Park, Calif.: Stanford Research Institute, 1969.

Hargreaves, D. *Social relations in a secondary school.* New York: Humanities Press, 1967.

Havighurst, R.J., et al. *Growing up in River City.* New York: John Wiley & Sons, 1962.

Hirschi, T. *Causes of delinquency.* Los Angeles: University of California Press, 1969.

Hollingshead, A.B. *Elmtown's youth.* New York: John Wiley & Sons, 1949.

Jackson, B. *Streaming: an educational system in miniature.* London: Routledge and Kegan Paul, 1964.

Kelly, D.H. Student perceptions, self-concept, and curriculum assignment. *Urban Education*, 1974, *9*, 257–269.

Kelly, D.H. Tracking and its impact upon self-esteem: a neglected dimension, *Education*, 1975, *96*, 2–9.

Kelly, D.H. The role of teachers' nomination in the perpetuation of deviant adolescent careers, *Education*, 1976, *96*, 209–217.

Kelly, D.H. The effects of legal processing upon a delinquent's personal and public identity: an analytical and empirical critique, *Education*, 1977, *97*, 280–289.

Kelly, D.H. *How the school manufactures "misfits."* South Pasadena: Newcal Publications, 1978(a).

Kelly, D.H. *Delinquent behavior: interactional and motivational aspects.* Belmont: Dickenson-Wadsworth, 1978(b).

Kelly, D.H. *Deviant behavior.* New York: St. Martin's, 1979.

Kelly, D.H. *Criminal behavior.* New York: St. Martin's, 1980.

Kelly, D.H., and Grove, W.D. Teachers' nominations and the production of academic "misfits." *Education*, 1981, *101*, 246–263.

Kelly, D.H., and Pink, W.T. School commitment and student career flows. *Youth and Society*, 1971, *3*, 225–236.

Kelly, D.H., and Pink, W.T. Social origins, school status, and the learning experience. *Pacific Sociological Review*, 1973, *16*, 121–134.

Lemert, E.M. *Social pathology.* New York: McGraw-Hill, 1959.

Lezotte, L.W., and Passalacqua, J. Individual school buildings: accounting for differences in measured school performance, *Urban Education*, 1978, *13*, 283–293.

Madaus, G.F., et al. The sensitivity of measures of school effectiveness, *Harvard Educational Review*, 1978, *49*, 207–230.

Merton, R.K. *Social theory and social structure.* New York: The Free Press, 1968.

National Institute of Education, *Violent schools—safe schools.* Washington, D.C.: U.S. Government Printing Office, 1978.

Ogbu, J. *The next generation.* New York: Academic Press, 1974.

Pearl, A. *The atrocity of education.* St. Louis: New Critics Press, 1972.

Phillips, J.C., and Kelly, D.H. School failure and delinquency: which causes which? *Criminology*, 1979, *17*, 194–207.

Pink, W.T. Rebellion and success in the high school, *Contemporary Education*, 1978, *49*, 78–84.

Pink, W.T., and Noblit, G.W. The consequences of labeling for early adult careers, *Education*, 1977, *98*, 32–40.

Pink, W.T., and Sweeney, M.E. Teacher nomination, deviant career lines and the management of stigma in the junior high school. *Urban Education*, 1978, *13*, 361–380.

Pink, W.T., et al. A resocialization strategy for black Vietnam veterans: a re-examination of a successful program, *Journal of Negro Education*, 1979, *48*, 500–512.

Polk, K. Class strain and rebellion among adolescents, *Social Problems*, 1969, *17*, 214–223.

Polk, K., and Pink, W.T. Youth culture and the school: a replication, *British Journal of Sociology*, 1971, *22*, 160–171.

Rist, R.C. Social class and teacher expectations: the self-fulfilling prophecy in ghetto education, *Harvard Educational Review*, 1979, *40*, 411–451.

Rist, R.C. *The invisible children.* Cambridge: Harvard University Press, 1978.

Rosenthal, R., and Jacobson, L. *Pygmalion in the classroom.* New York: Holt, Rinehart and Winston, 1968.

Rubel, R.J. *The unruly school: disorders, disruptions, and crimes.* Lexington: D.C. Heath, 1977.

Rutter, M., et al. *Fifteen thousand hours.* Cambridge: Harvard University Press, 1979.

Ryan, W. *Blaming the victim.* New York: Pantheon, 1972.

Schafer, W.E., and Olexa, C. *Tracking and opportunity: the locking-out process and beyond.* Scranton: Chandler, 1971.

Schafer, W.E., and Polk, K. Delinquency and the schools. In *Task force report: juvenile delinquency and youth crime.* Washington, D.C.: U.S. Government Printing Office, 1967, pp. 222–277.

Scheff, T.J. Typification in the diagnostic practices of rehabilitation agencies, In M.B. Sussman (Ed.), *Sociology and rehabilitation.* Washington, D.C.: American Sociological Association, 1965.

Schur, E.M. *Our criminal society.* Englewood Cliffs: Prentice-Hall, 1969.

Schur, E.M. *Labeling deviant behavior.* New York: Harper & Row, 1971.

Senate Subcommittee to Investigate Juvenile Delinquency. *Our nation's schools—a report card: "A" in school violence and vandalism.* Washington, D.C.: U.S. Government Printing Office, 1975.

Skolnick, J.H. *Justice without trial.* New York: John Wiley & Sons, 1966.

Willis, P.E. *Learning to labour.* Farnborough, England: Saxon House, 1977.

Wyers, N.L. Attitudes of income maintenance personnel: old paradigms revisited. *California Sociologist*, 1978, *1*, 151–167.

PART 3

EXPLAINING CRIME

In Parts 1 and 2, selections were presented on how laws may evolve and change over time and how crime is measured and assessed. This part deals with the question of *why* crime may exist in a social system, as well as *why* people may elect to violate the law—committing violations that may bring about the initial stages of the labeling or typing ceremony. Efforts at explaining the motivations for crime have taken many forms.

Biologists, psychologists, and psychiatrists tend to favor an individualistic or *clinical* perspective. Such a model of crime attempts to identify and locate the pathological or crime-producing factors *within* the individual, such as genetic aberration or arrested personality adjustment. Sociologists, in their use of a *structural* model, are more apt to look at societal conditions to explain crime. A typical explanation might be predicated on the importance of such factors as poverty, inequality, racism, urbanization, and the like. Still others (e.g., social psychologists) analyze how individual and structural elements interact with each other to produce pressures for crime. Regardless of the approach taken, however, it is generally recognized that various conditions must be satisfied before "criminal" behavior can occur. Selected factors or combinations of factors may stand out in the backgrounds of people labeled as criminals.

In this part, an initial overview of various levels and types of statements on crime is presented; this is followed by some of the better-known sociological and social-psychological explanations. They can, for our purposes, be grouped roughly into six major categories: (1) the functionalist perspective, (2) radical-conflict theory, (3) control theory, (4) cultural transmission theory, (5) cultural conflict theory, and (6) anomie or opportunity theory. While each approach focuses on certain basic assumptions and processes, there frequently exists a degree of overlap between or among the statements; this will become especially evident in the comparison of Merton, Cloward and Ohlin, and Cohen.

LEVELS AND TYPES OF EXPLANATIONS

Even though major attention is being given today to sociological and social-psychological viewpoints, other types of explanations continue to receive serious consideration. The lead article, by C. Ronald Huff, "Historical Explanations of Crime: From

Demons to Politics," underscores this point. Huff presents a chronology of the major explanations of crime. Many of the schools of thought reviewed, such as the supernatural, the physical-biological, and the psychopathological, are clinical, that is, they look to individual traits for an understanding of crime. In his discussion of sociological explanations, the author provides an excellent outline of Sutherland and Cressey's "differential association theory," a statement often invoked to explain how individuals learn criminal values and traditions. Central to their thesis is the notion that as we learn to become conformists, so too must we learn to become criminals. The learning itself occurs in interaction with others through a process of communication in small, intimate groups. A portion of this socialization entails not only picking up the techniques for committing a crime, as well as the accompanying "motives, drives, rationalizations, and attitudes," but also becoming familiar with definitions of the legal codes, both from a favorable and unfavorable light. Presumably, then, a person becomes delinquent or criminal "because of an excess of definitions favorable to violation of law over definitions unfavorable to violation of law." Huff concludes his review with a brief introduction to the labeling, conflict, and radical perspectives; these developing views, Huff maintains, have shifted the focus from an examination of the individual criminal to more of an analysis of social and political systems.

THE FUNCTIONALIST PERSPECTIVE

Criminologists who pursue a functionalist model contend that crime is a normal and integral part of a healthy society and such behavior satisfies some important societal need. As an example, when a violation occurs, attempts may be made by a sanctioning body to bring the criminal's or deviator's behavior back into line with acceptable community standards; this concern for demarcating boundaries, as well as their maintenance, is elaborated on by Emile Durkheim in "The Normal and the Pathological." Not only is crime present in all societies, but each society is confronted with the problem of criminality. Even though acts viewed as crime are not the same in all societies, there are those who offend the collective sentiments of the community and, hence, feel the brunt of penal sanctions or repression. He makes the important point that it is not the intrinsic quality of an act that designates it as a crime but, rather, such a characterization flows from the definition attached to it by the collective conscience of the community. Durkheim goes on to describe how crime can also serve as an important and useful precursor to change. Here he draws upon the example of Socrates who, in violating Athenian law relative to freedom of thought, was labeled a criminal; this crime, nonetheless, served as a prelude to subsequent reforms in this area.

RADICAL-CONFLICT THEORY

Proponents who align themselves with a radical-conflict theory of crime causation argue that it is the powerful, and frequently the state, who decide which behaviors are criminal and how individuals, once designated as criminals, are to be processed and treated. Raymond J. Michalowski, in "A Critical Model for the Study of Crime," presents an excellent, contemporary account of this view. He initially offers a model of crime that is comprised of four main elements: the mode of production, state law, individual characteristics, and individual behavior. He then uses these components to weave together his approach to the study of crime. The critical assumption underpinning his theory is that if one is to approach an understanding of the definition of cime and the parameters of crime control, focus must be given to a society's mode of production. Not only will the mode of production affect the definitions of property developed, as well as the laws created to protect it, but the laws themselves allow for the continued maintenance and protection of the existing social order. Michalowski goes on to describe the law-making institutions and the types of laws they create (i.e., substructural, superstructural, and order maintenance laws). He then discusses the range of individual characteristics that can shape human behavior and behavior itself (e.g., one's biological makeup and acquired skills). He concludes by outlining the variety of forms human behavior may take (e.g., acts of rebellion against the social order).

CONTROL THEORY

In "A Control Theory of Delinquency," Travis Hirschi outlines some of the basic tenets underlying control theory. A major assumption of control theorists is that when an individual's *bond* to society is weak or broken, criminal or delinquent acts are likely to result. Hirschi discusses various elements of the bond to society. For example, the "commitment" element refers to the fact that many people invest a great deal of time and energy in certain pursuits, such as obtaining an education or a job. Thus, when criminal activity is considered, they must assess the risks they run of losing their investment. Many of the elements of the bond to society can provide further insight into various selections in Part 4, particularly those that describe evolving criminal careers.

CULTURAL TRANSMISSION THEORY

As evident from selected statements examined thus far, much of what is viewed or labeled as criminal behavior is learned, and it is acquired through interaction with a range of others. It may also be recalled from Huff's discussion of Sutherland and Cressey that a portion of the learning involves picking up the techniques for committing a crime, as well as the associated rationalizations. Gresham M. Sykes and David Matza, in "Techniques of Neutralization: A Theory of Delinquency," provide further content to this notion. They are concerned specifically with how delinquents learn to justify the deviance of their acts and thus avoid self-blame and the blame of others. For example, they may deny responsibility for the act, claiming that bad companions, unloving parents, or slum conditions are at fault. Sykes and Matza note that rationalizations are operative before, during, and after the act has been committed. The authors thus place their focus on the actor, and it is he or she who must weigh the relative costs and advantages associated with committing a crime. Obviously, if one can legitimate or neutralize one's action, then the probability of succumbing to crime-producing stimuli would appear to be much greater. The career criminal, it can be noted, frequently possesses a rather sophisticated system of rationalizations or neutralizations.

CULTURAL CONFLICT THEORY

A basic assumption underpinning cultural conflict theory is the idea that, because of differing socializing experiences, influences, and cultural contexts, social actors may find themselves confronted with conflicting demands. Further, if they act in line with their own set of values, they may run the risk of being defined as criminal or deviant by those who are operating from a different frame of reference or set of values. In "Lower Class Culture as a Generating Milieu of Gang Delinquency," Walter B. Miller provides an account of how cultural clashes can, in fact, give rise to law-violating behavior that can be tagged as delinquent or criminal by others. Lower-class males, by aligning themselves with and acting in accordance with what Miller terms "focal concerns" (e.g., the emphasis on trouble, toughness, and excitement), automatically violate middle-class rules, regulations, and laws. Youth crime thus emerges as a by-product of the males' adherence to their cultural tradition. A central part of Miller's argument also revolves around the belief that growing up in a female-based household can create some serious identity problems for adolescent males; however, participation in single-sex peer groups can help to alleviate or assuage these difficulties. Not only are role models present, but by acting in terms of the dictates of the focal concerns, males can commit acts that reflect favorably upon the masculine identity they are perhaps trying to structure.

ANOMIE OR OPPORTUNITY THEORY

Those who subscribe to anomie or opportunity theory are concerned with those societal or structural conditions that may produce a strain toward deviation or crime. Robert K. Merton, in "Social Structure and Anomie," offers what many consider to be the classic statement in this vein. Rejecting explanations founded rather firmly on the importance of biological drives and states, Merton argues initially that a society can be characterized in terms of the relationship that exists between its goals and means. An integrated society, he reasons, exhibits a balance between these two elements and, accordingly, if actors desire to achieve selected states, ends, or goals, they will use the existing institutionalized and legitimate means for doing so. Other societies, however, do not maintain or exhibit this type of balance and associated affect, with the result being that people will often use whatever means necessary to achieve goals. American society can be characterized in this fashion. Not only is a heavy emphasis placed on obtaining societal ends (e.g., financial and material wealth), but many do not possess the means for realizing their goals. Hence, blockage is experienced (i.e., a gap develops between what they are taught to *aspire* to and what they can *expect* to achieve). Those frustrated or blocked the most are drawn from the lower classes.

These individuals, like all others, have been imbued with the success motif, yet when attempts are made to achieve goals, they will find themselves lacking the needed resources. If, however, they retain an allegiance to what Merton has termed the "common success goals," then goals can only be obtained via the illegitimate route; this may mean that the affected will become "innovators." Such individuals, because they lack the necessary legitimate means for goal achievement, will substitute illegitimate means in the pursuit of societal goals. This condition of the social structure (i.e., a disjunction between ends and means) may lead to cultural chaos or *anomie*.

Rather implicit in Merton's conceptualization is the notion that if failure is experienced in the attempts to use legitimate means, then one is guaranteed a measure of success if the illegitimate route is taken. Richard A. Cloward and Lloyd E. Ohlin, in "Differential Opportunity and Delinquent Subcultures," argue that this is not necessarily the case. Just as there are differentials in access to legitimate channels, so too are there differentials in access to illegitimate means. Not everyone, for example, can become a successful con artist, street hustler, or dope dealer. Furthermore, some are unable to succeed in either the legitimate or the illegitimate world. Cloward and Ohlin thus initially extend Merton's statement by emphasizing the notion of the *relative availability* of illegitimate opportunity structures. They then proceed to unite Merton's theory with Sutherland and Cressey's "differential association theory," which, it may be recalled, stresses the fact that criminal behavior, like most any behavior, is learned in interaction with others. Cloward and Ohlin elaborate on this view by describing how status-deprived, lower-class males may, depending on the availability of "criminal-learning environments," be recruited for subsequent training in crime. The authors stress the point that, even though many may be called, recruited, and trained, only a few will be allowed to join the adult criminal professions because of a lack of positions. They conclude by describing how various subcultures (i.e., the criminal, conflict, and retreatist) evolve. The type of subculture that emerges is actually a function of how a community is organized, particularly in terms of the relative availability of legitimate and illegitimate opportunity structures. In a neighborhood that has a high degree of interplay or integration between these structures, the criminal subculture is more apt to evolve. Such a subculture offers the status-deprived a source of material gain and provides them with a context in which they can learn and perform the required subcultural tasks. It should be noted that not only do Cloward and Ohlin provide a valuable account on subcultural formation, but their statements also help to highlight the linkages that may exist among such elements as the recruitment and training of juveniles, entry routes into crime, and adult criminal careers and professions.

The last selection in this part offers another variant of the anomie tradition, and it is also presented to illustrate, as well as underscore, the need for evaluating a theoretical statement in terms of its explanatory power. Whether or not a theory can make sense out of the phenomenon it was set up to explain holds certain important ramifications for the theorist, researcher, and practitioner. As an illustration, if, according to Merton, blocked opportunity actually emerges, empirically, as a major, intervening factor behind the production of criminal behavior within the lower classes, then a measure of corroboration has been provided for Merton's formulation. Moreover, such research, if replicated on various fronts, can serve as a basis for designing treatment and prevention programs aimed specifically at opening up opportunity structures for the lower classes. If, on the other hand, tests of the Mertonian framework are not especially supportive or kind, reformulations and subsequent testings are probably in order. Hence, a healthy respect must be maintained for the ongoing interplay among theory, research, and practice. In "Social Origins and School Failure: A Reexamination of Cohen's Theory of Working-Class Delinquency," Robert W. Balch and I provide an actual test of a theory. We begin by outlining several of the basic assumptions underlying Cohen's theory and then proceed to an examination of how his ideas stand up under empirical scrutiny. Cohen argues specifically that lower-class males will experience a most difficult time in the school. The school is a middle-class institution, and all comers are evaluated in terms of what he calls the "middle-class measuring rod" – a yardstick that emphasizes such values as the importance of hard work, individual responsibility, respect for property, and the like. Unfortunately, working-class males are poorly equipped to compete against such standards, and hence they fail, both academically and socially. Such failure produces a painful dilemma for them. They have bought into the goals but find themselves frustrated in their attempts to achieve them. Given that success is not available in the school, many of these status-deprived males collectively reject the middle-class way of life, turn its standards upside down, and institute a new or alternative status system of their own. This subculture can be characterized by a set of values that is anti-middle-class, and it offers a setting in which males can, if they align their attitudes and behaviors in accordance with the existing values and associated norms, achieve a measure of the success, esteem, and prestige that was denied to them in the school. Cohen also discusses how a negative school experience may produce an erosion of self-esteem, little involvement in school activities, school avoidance, and delinquency. Our data are not strongly supportive of Cohen's notions of how the social-class variable should operate. Although working-class males are more likely to have poor grades and low self-evaluations, dislike school, and be uninvolved, the relationships are weak, and the magnitude of association between our measures of delinquency and social class is slight. Our school variables, by contrast, are uniformly and in most cases strongly related to our dependent variables (i.e., truancy, dropout, smoking, drinking, cruising, and delinquency). Grade point average emerges as the strongest correlate of school avoidance and delinquency.

We conclude by discussing the theoretical and practical implications of our findings. Most significantly, it is our view that Cohen's emphasis on the need for examining the nature of the school experience – particularly in terms of how the class variable may articulate with existing organizational structures (e.g., the middle-class value structure of the school) – ought to be given greater scrutiny. And, I might add, a subsequent body of research since this (see, for example, the works cited in the Kelly-Pink article in Part 2) has produced additional evidence in support of this contention. Thus, Cohen's thesis has proven invaluable in terms of pointing researchers in the direction of potentially fruitful lines of inquiry within a critical domain (i.e., the school). Additionally, the basic ideas underpinning his theory, I believe, could be expanded to include a consideration of how, in terms of career flows, other selection factors (e.g., race, gender, ethnicity, etc.) interact with an existing range of in-school (e.g., ability groups and track systems) and out-school (e.g., neighborhood gangs) organizational structures. Such analyses would be in keeping with my view (Part 2) that attention should be given to how selection factors are actually mediated through organizational structures and components.

11. Historical Explanations of Crime: From Demons to Politics

C. RONALD HUFF

Man's historical concern with the existence of crime has been reflected in his diverse attempts to explain how and why crime occurs. Long before there was a scientific approach to the crime problem, there were speculative "explanations" of criminal behavior. Some of these earlier views concerning the nature of crime may seem absurd according to contemporary standards, but they must be viewed as symbolic expressions of the prevailing ideas and concerns of their own era. Similarly, it would be surprising if our currently fashionable theories of crime are not viewed as naive and unsophisticated in the next century.

Before discussing the major historical explanations of crime, it seems appropriate to ask what, if any, relevance such a discussion can have for students of criminology and criminal justice. While intellectual inquiry is justifiable for its own sake, the current discussion has contemporary relevance in at least two ways: (1) It presents an overview of the development of criminological theory, which should permit a greater understanding of contemporary explanations and their place in the continuity of thought on the subject of crime. (2) Since society's responses to crime depend, to a large extent, on its theories and its assumptions about the nature of crime, an understanding of those views is useful in attempting to analyze the numerous attempts to "prevent," "control," "deter," "cure," or otherwise contain criminal behavior. The operations of the various components of the criminal justice system (such as the police, the courts, and the prisons) can perhaps best be viewed by understanding the various assumptions which underlie their policies and procedures. Every major theory, explanation, or assumption about the nature and causes of crime may be viewed as having important implications for the strategies of social control which society elects to implement. The following discussion examines the existence of such connections between theory and practice.

SUPERNATURAL EXPLANATIONS

Primitive man's basic explanation of "criminal" behavior was that of diabolical possession. Criminal behavior was viewed as evidence that the culprit was under the control of evil spirits, or demons.[1] This view of deviant behavior was simply an extension of the prevailing view of nature—i.e., that every object or being was controlled by spiritual forces.[2] Obviously, such an explanation requires *belief* or *faith*, since it does not lend itself to scientific verification. Nevertheless, demonology had important implications for man's responses to crime.

Given such an explanation of crime, the only sensible solution was to try to exorcise the demons which were responsible for the behavior or, failing that, to do away with the criminal, either by exile or by execution. In a society where the gods were perceived as omnipotent and omnipresent, it was clearly a matter of the highest priority to appease them, no matter what the costs. Thus, the fate of the criminal was less related to the protection of society than to compliance with the will of the gods. The failure of the group to punish the wrongdoer was believed to leave the tribe open to the wrath and vengeance of the gods.

One who violated the norms dealing with endogamy, witchcraft, or treason was likely to receive the harshest punishment in primitive society. The offender might be hacked to pieces, exiled, or even eaten. All three of these sanctions accomplished the same goal—the removal of the offender from the group. Offenses of a private, rather than public, nature were generally dealt with by the victim's clan through the process known as "blood feud." Essentially, it was the duty of each member of a clan to avenge a fellow clan member. The principle which guided this pursuit of retaliation was the well-known *lex talionis*[3] ("an eye for an eye and a tooth for a tooth"). The idea of *lex talionis*, roughly, was that the punishment should fit the crime. Primitive obsession with making the retaliation exact was in some cases so fanatical that inanimate objects which had been instrumental in accidental deaths were actually "punished."[4]

There was very little use of any form of incarceration in primitive society, except for periods of detention while awaiting disposition and the incarceration related to cannibalistic practices. The only other major type of punishment did not appear until the late stages of primitive society. It was a form of compensation or restitution. This practice developed in response to the failure of blood feud as a method of criminal justice. Blood feuds all too often resulted in prolonged vendettas which exacted heavy tolls on both sides. The practice of paying a fixed monetary penalty therefore evolved as an alternative to the potentially genocidal blood feuds. Later, in the feudal period, the extended families or clans established a system of "wergeld" (man-money) by which the victim's status determined the amount assessed against the offender. This concept was gradually broadened to include differences in degree of responsibility, the individualization of responsibility, and even a distinction between "intent" and "accident." Eventually a specified value was set for each *type* of offense, and the system of restitutive fines paid by the offender to the victim came to be preferred over the blood feud. With the subsequent development of an appeal procedure whereby either party could protest an injustice, the roots of the modern-day court system emerged in embryonic form. Finally, through the absolute authority which accompanied kingships, especially in early *historic* society and during feudalism, all crimes became "crimes against the king's peace"; in other words, crimes came to be regarded as offenses against the *public* welfare. At that point man had, in a sense, come "full circle" in his efforts to rationalize law and punishment:

> The heavy fines imposed on places and people became an important source of revenue to the crown and to the barons and the lords of manors. . . .
> The State was growing strong enough to take vengeance; the common man was no longer feared as had been the well-armed Saxon citizen of old, and to the "common" criminal was extended the ruthless severity once reserved for the slaves . . . and the idea of compensation began to wane before the revenge instinct now backed by power.[5]

RATIONALISM AND FREE WILL

Just as demonological explanations dominated the thinking of early man, the so-called "classical period" of criminology (roughly 1700–1800) was characterized by its own conceptions of the nature of man. Man was seen as being rational, having free will, and seeking that which would be most productive of pleasure or happiness. Such views, of course, represented a significant departure from the idea that man was under the control of supernatural forces and that criminal behavior was a function of demons. For an understanding of the magnitude of this shift in thinking during the eighteenth century, it is best to examine the ideas of the two most influential contributors to classical criminology—Cesare Beccaria and Jeremy Bentham.

Beccaria, who was influenced by French rationalism and humanitarianism, strongly attacked the arbitrary and inconsistent "criminal justice" practices of the mid-eighteenth century. In his major work,[6] Beccaria reacted against the secret accusations, inhumane punishments, and lack of concern for the defendant's rights that characterized criminal justice. He articulated the framework of what came to be known as the classical school of criminology, i.e.: (1) that the motivation underlying all social action must be the utilitarian value of that action (the greatest happiness for the greatest number); (2) that crime is an injury to *society* and can only be measured by assessing the extent of that injury (focus on the act and the extent of damage, not intent); (3) that the prevention of crime is more important than its punishment; (4) that secret accusations and torture should be eliminated, while the trial process ought to be speedy and the accused treated fairly and humanely throughout the process; (5) that the only valid purpose of punishment is deterrence, *not* social revenge; and (6) that incarceration should be utilized more widely, but, at the same time, conditions for those confined must be vastly upgraded and systems of classification developed to prevent haphazardly mixing all types of inmates.

Beccaria had enormous influence on the reformation of criminal justice. For example, he proposed that the courts should mete out punishments to the offender in direct proportion to the harm caused by his crime. To accomplish this, it was necessary that all crimes be classified according to some assessment of their social harm and, further, that the penal codes must prescribe for each crime exact penalties that would be useful deterrents to crime:

> A scale of crimes may be formed of which the first degree should consist of those which immediately tend to the dissolution of society; and the last, of the smallest possible injustice done to a private member of society. Between those extremes will be comprehended all actions contrary to the public good, which are called criminal. . . . Any action which is not comprehended in the above mentioned scale, will not be called a crime, or punished as such.[7]

One need only observe the deliberations of state legislatures today during the process of revising a state's criminal code to understand and appreciate the lasting effect which Beccaria has had on our criminal laws. The arguments and considerations of lawmakers today are, for the most part, still influenced by this concept of the criminal as a rational person who acts as a result of free will on a pleasure-seeking basis.

Contemporary punishments prescribed by the law are generally well-defined, even though they are administered in a very inexact manner. And the widespread belief that the enactment of laws is the best method of social control clearly has at least some of its intellectual roots in the work of Beccaria.

Several of Beccaria's other ideas have contemporary significance. Perhaps the most notable of these is his assertion that the speed and certainty of punishment, rather than its severity, are the most critical factors in deterrence. The modern criminal justice system, characterized by broad discretion on the part of the police, prosecutors, judges, guards, and parole boards; discrimination against the poor and minorities; court delays and months of pretrial detainment; and the use of plea-bargaining, offers neither swiftness nor certainty. Furthermore, Beccaria's advocacy of the humane treatment of incarcerated offenders has certainly never been fully realized. Indeed, many contemporary reformers claim that we have largely replaced corporal punishment with psychological and social persecution.[8]

Jeremy Bentham, a contemporary of Beccaria, was also a major figure in utilitarian social philosophy, and he proposed that all acts must be evaluated so that "the greatest happiness for the greatest number" results. To make such assessments, one would obviously need some method of calculation; Bentham happened to have just such a method. His "felicity calculus" was a superficial, quasi-mathematical attempt to quantify the utility of all conceivable acts. Humorous in retrospect, his attempt to catalogue the almost infinite varieties of behavior was nevertheless understandable, given the uncertainties of the criminal justice system he was attempting to reform.

Bentham's theory of human motivation—that man pursues pleasure and tries to avoid pain—led him to argue that criminal penalties should prescribe a degree of punishment (pain) just sufficient to offset the potential gains (pleasure) of criminal behavior, so that the net result (negative utility) would be deterrence. Bentham further believed that the punishment should "fit the crime," and generally seemed to favor restitution over physical punishment. Given Bentham's concept of deterrence, punishment in general was regarded as a necessary evil intended to prevent greater harm or evil.[9]

The social control philosophy which characterized classical criminology, then, was based on the assumption that the would-be criminal could be deterred by the threat of punishment if that punishment were swift, certain, appropriate for the offense, and sufficiently unpleasant to offset any potential gains to be realized by committing the act. These principles were advocated by classicists across the entire range of available punishments, whether they involved the loss of money, the loss of freedom, or the loss of life. The impact of classical criminology on the penal codes remains clear, even though in actual practice much of the vagueness and arbitrary abuse of discretion remains problematic.

Despite the anticipated ability to administer the principles of the classical school, the fact was that enforcement and implementation were quite problematic. Especially controversial was the classical position that individual differences and particular situations were irrelevant in assigning responsibility. The focus on the act committed, rather than on any characteristics or qualities of the person, came to be regarded as imprudent as did the practice of treating persons who clearly were incompetent, for various reasons, as competent solely because of commission of a given act. These principles were criticized strongly because they did not promote justice anywhere except on paper, in an abstract sort of way.

The idealized concept of justice held by the classicists, perhaps best symbolized by the familiar image of a blindfolded Lady Justice holding scales in her hands, was regarded by neo-classical revisionists (1800–1876) as too impersonal and rigid. The classical theorists, in their indignation over the inconsistencies and other inadequacies of the criminal justice system, had overreacted. They had designed a system which was so dispassionate and "objective" that it could not deliver justice to a society of human beings not identical to one another.

The neo-classicists were successful in introducing some modifications of the free will doctrine. Criminological thought was revised to re-admit some determinism—not the magical, supernatural determinism of demonology, but rather an awareness that certain factors could operate to impair one's reason and thereby mitigate personal responsibility to an extent. While retaining the essential positions articulated by the classicists, considerations involving individual differences began to appear during the neo-classical period. Age, mental status, physical condition, and other factors which could alter one's ability to discern right from wrong were acknowledged grounds for a decision of partial responsibility.

Far from regarding their views as a general theory of human behavior, the neo-classicists were actually focusing on what they viewed as a small minority of the population. There was no attempt to assert that all persons (not even all criminals) are partially shaped and controlled by deterministic forces. On the contrary, neo-classicists continued to view man as a rational, pleasure-seeking being who was personally responsible for his behavior except in abnormal circumstances or in the case of children who were not old enough to know right from wrong.

The neo-classical revisions outlined above meant that criminology had developed a dominant theoretical perspective which viewed man as essentially rational and behavior as volitional, but allowed for some mitigation of responsibility under certain circumstances. This theoretical framework provided the foundation for many legal systems, including that of the United States. The implications for sentencing and for the criminal justice system included the recognition that a particular sentence could have different effects on different offenders and an awareness that the prison environment could affect the *future* criminality of the offender. This allowed for much more flexibility than did the classical school in determining the appropriate punishment. Many recent "reforms" in penology, such as probation, parole, suspended sentences, and many programs designed for certain "types" of offenders, would be inconsistent with the classical emphases on uniformity and certainty of punishment.[10]

DETERMINISM

A book written in 1876 by an Italian psychiatrist was to provide the impetus necessary to shift the focus of criminology from the crime to the criminal. The book was called *The Criminal Man*[11] and its author was Cesare Lombroso; the result was the development of the "positive school" in criminology. Lacking the moralistic tones of the earliest positivist, August Comte,[12] Lombroso's approach was clearly Darwinian, focusing on biological determinism.

As the title of his classic book implies, Lombroso believed that there was indeed a criminal *type*, or "born criminal," who was discernibly different from non-criminals in physical ways. In short, he was convinced that criminals bore bodily stigmata which marked them as a separate class of people. Following Darwin's monumental work by less than two decades, Lombrosian theory postulated that criminals had not fully evolved but were, instead, inferior organisms reminiscent of apelike, pre-primitive man, incapable of adapting to modern civilization. Specifically, Lombroso described the criminal as "atavistic" (a concept used earlier by Darwin) in that he was physically characteristic of a lower phylogenetic level. From his extensive physical measurements, autopsy findings, and other observations, Lombroso concluded that criminals disproportionately possessed an asymmetrical cranium; prognathism (excessive jaw); eye defects; oversized ears; prominent cheekbones; abnormal palate; receding forehead; sparse beard; wooly hair; long arms; abnormal dentition; twisted nose; fleshy and swollen lips; and inverted sex organs. He also noted such non-physical anomalies as a lack of morality, excessive vanity, cruelty, and tatooing.[13]

It would be misleading to imply that Lombroso held firmly to the idea that his was the sole explanation for crime. While continuing to believe that his theory explained part of the difference between criminals and non-criminals, Lombroso ultimately accepted environmental and other factors as equally valid contributing causes of crime.

While positivism, since Lombroso's day, has taken in a lot of intellectual territory, there remains a unifying framework which is visible in the work of his successors. That general framework consists of the following:

1. A general rejection of metaphysical and speculative approaches.
2. Denial of the "free-will" conception of man and substitution of a "deterministic" model.
3. A clear distinction between science and law, on one hand, and morals, on the other.
4. The application, as far as practicable, of the scientific method.[14]

These principles of positivism have been applied to the study of the criminal from various and diverse theoretical perspectives. Although these perspectives differ in significant ways, they retain the essence of positivism as described above. The theories to be discussed range from purely individualistic approaches to more macrolevel sociological theories.

The "Italian School"

The origins of positivism in criminology have a decidedly Italian character. Besides Lombroso, the other Italian pioneers in this school of thought were Enrico Ferri and Raffaele Garofalo. Although emphasizing different points as critical in the study of the criminal, both Ferri and Garofalo were adamant in their espousal of, and adherence to, the positivist approach.

Enrico Ferri, a pupil of Lombroso, is perhaps best known for his classification of criminals as insane, born, occasional, habitual, and drawn to criminality as a result of passion.[15] This typology of offenders represented an attempt by Ferri to conceptualize in anthropological categories the continuum of criminality. He believed that the differences between categories were differences of degree and of the danger represented for society.

The third member of the "Italian school," Raffaele Garofalo, attempted to construct a universal definition of crime—one which would be based on the concept of "natural crime," or acts which offend the basic moral sentiments of pity (a revulsion against the voluntary infliction of suffering on others) and probity (respect for the property rights of others). Garofalo's approach to the crime problem was primarily psychological and legal. He perceived some criminals as psychological degenerates who were morally unfit. His background as a jurist led him to advocate reforms in the criminal justice system so that the criminal could be dealt with in a manner more in line with his theory. Garofalo believed that the criminal must be eliminated, citing Darwin's observations on the functions of biological adaptation as a rationale for this "remedy." Since, according to this bio-organismic analogy, the criminal was one who had not adapted to civilized life, Garofalo saw only three alternatives—all of which involved some type of elimination: (1) death, where there is a permanent psychological defect; (2) partial elimination for those suitable to live only in a more primitive environment, including long-term or life imprisonment, transportation, and relatively mild isolation; and (3) enforced reparation, for those whose crimes were committed as a result of the press of circumstances.[16]

Physical-Biological Theories

The prototype for all physical-biological theories of crime were the early (and non-positivist) craniologists-phrenologists, who believed that the "faculties of the mind" were revealed by the external shape of the skull.[17] This vastly oversimplified and pseudo-scientific approach nevertheless pre-dates all other theories of a physical-biological nature.

Such theories have grown increasingly sophisticated and scientific since those earliest attempts to explain man's function by analyzing his cranial structure. In addition to the "Italian school," there have been a number of other intellectual contributions to this physical-biological tradition.

Charles Goring has been widely credited with refuting Lombroso's contention that there is a criminal "physical type." However, Goring's critique was aimed at Lombroso's methodology, not necessarily his theory or his conclusions, for which Goring had a certain affinity.[18] In Goring's famous book, *The English Convict*,[19] he presented an analysis of 3,000 English convicts and, as a matter of fact, he did find what he regarded as a positive association between certain physical differences and the offender's crime and social class. As Mannheim noted:

In the controversy "heredity or environment" . . . he was on Lombroso's side, and perhaps even more than the latter he was inclined to underrate environmental influences: "Crime

is only to a trifling extent (if to any) the product of social inequalities, of adverse environment or of other manifestations of . . . the force of circumstances."[20]

Goring's general interpretation of the height and weight deficiencies of the criminal population he studied was that the criminal suffered from hereditary inferiority.
He also believed that criminals were most different from non-criminals with respect
to their intelligence, which he found to be defective. Finally, Goring added a third
category—that of moral defectiveness—to account for those whose criminality could
not be explained by either of the first two factors. But the main thrust of Goring's
theoretical position was a physiological one, thus placing him within this tradition
of thought.

Not everyone agreed that Goring's criticisms of Lombroso's methodology were valid.
The leading skeptic was Earnest Hooton, an anthropologist at Harvard University. In
The American Criminal,[21] Hooton presented data and interpretations based on a
twelve-year study of 13,873 criminals and 3,203 non-criminals. After analyzing 107
physical characteristics, Hooton concluded that criminals, when compared with the
control group, were "organically inferior." Describing their distinctive characteristics,
he included low foreheads, high pinched nasal roots, compressed faces, and narrow
jaws. These he cited as evidence for his assertion of organic inferiority, and he
attributed crime to "the impact of environment upon low grade human organisms."[22]

Hooton also constructed a typology of criminals based on physical constitution. He
argued that murderers and robbers tended to be tall and thin; tall heavy men were
most likely to be killers and to commit forgery and fraud as well; undersized men were
disposed to commit assault, rape, and other sex crimes; and men lacking any notable
physical characteristics had no criminal specialty. The primary problem with all of this
is that Hooton had considered only the offender's *current* crime, while in fact half or
more of Hooton's prisoners had previously been imprisoned for an offense *other than*
that noted by Hooton.[23]

Studies by Ernst Kretschmer[24] and William Sheldon[25] are typical of the work of
more recent proponents of the constitutional inferiority-body type theorists. Although
differing in the details of their approaches, both men advocated the idea that body
type and temperament are closely related. Both developed typologies relating body
types to certain forms of behavior, including crime.

Some investigators have focused specifically on the effects of heredity, especially
genetic deficiencies, in producing criminality. In this regard, the studies of "criminal
families" were quite interesting. Perhaps the most well-known efforts along these
genealogical lines were those of Richard Dugdale[26] and Henry Goddard,[27] both of
whom attempted to analyze the apparently excessive criminality of entire families by
relating it to feeble-mindedness. The term "mental testers" has often been applied to
this method of inquiry.

More recently, another line of inquiry has focused on the criminality of twins.
Lange,[28] Rosanoff,[29] Christiansen,[30] and others have studied twins in an attempt to
determine the effect of heredity in producing criminality. The basic idea has been that
if a greater percentage of monozygotic ("identical") twins than of dizygotic ("frater-
nal") twins are concordant in being criminal (both criminal), then the effect of

heredity would, theoretically at least, have to be given greater weight than other factors. Although the methodological criticisms aimed at Rosanoff have been less damaging than those directed at Lange, the fact remains that neither study can be regarded as conclusive in finding that identical twins are far more likely to be concordant in terms of criminality.

Finally, some of the most sophisticated research employing a physical-biological model has been focused on the neuroendocrine system. The essential proposition of these theories has been that criminal behavior is often due to emotional disturbances produced by glandular imbalance. Often utilizing the electroencephalogram (EEG) as a diagnostic aid, this biochemical approach to crime thus far offers more promise than clear-cut and unequivocal findings.[31]

Psychopathology

A number of positivist theories of crime have utilized the paradigm based on individual psychopathology. The father of this approach was, of course, Sigmund Freud. His work, along with that of his intellectual successors, has focused on man's unconscious. The explanation for criminal behavior which grew out of this approach was that such behavior is largely the result of drives which are uncontrolled because of a defective personality structure. There are a seemingly endless number of applications of psychoanalytic theory to crime. Conditions such as psychosis and neurosis have been related to criminal behavior by psychoanalysts, as have most forms of deviant behavior. The essential contention of the psychoanalytic approach is that *all* behavior is purposive and meaningful. Such behavior is viewed as the symbolic release of repressed mental conflict. From this perspective, the criminal is one who acts not out of free will, as the classicists believed, but as an expression of deterministic forces of a subconscious nature. Such a view, of course, leads to a theory of social control based upon a clinical model of therapeutic rehabilitation.

A derivation of the psychoanalytic approach and the "mental testers" has been the emphasis on personality deviation as an explanation for crime. Relying on theoretical constructs of the "healthy" personality and the "abnormal" personality, the personality deviation approach has become increasingly popular, though not well validated. Using psychological tests such as Rorschach, the Wechsler Adult Intelligence Scale, the Minnesota Multiphasic Personality Inventory, the Thematic Apperception Test, and many others, psychologists have led in this attempt to construct causal theory. Advocates of this approach generally attempt to diagnose the psychopathological features of one's personality and then focus on these "target areas" using a variety of interventions.

Economic Factors

The effects of economic inequality are undeniably instrumental in producing great variability in one's "life chances." The pervasive day-to-day realities of poverty limit the chances of millions of people in securing adequate health care, housing, education, jobs, and opportunities. The crippling effects of poverty can hardly be comprehended by those not confronted with them on a daily basis. For these and related reasons, some theorists have attempted to relate at least some crimes to economic inequality. Such a theoretical position has had a special attraction for Marxists.

Historically, the most extensive application of Marxist theory to criminology was provided by Willem Bonger.[32] The central argument Bonger made is that capitalism, more than any other system of economic exchange, is characterized by the control of the means of production by relatively few people, with the vast majority of the population totally deprived of these means. The economic subjugation of the masses, he argues, stifles men's "social instincts" and leads to unlimited egoism, insensitivity, and a spirit of domination on the part of the powerful, while the poor are subjected to all sorts of pathogenic conditions: bad housing, constant association with "undesirables," uncertain physical security, terrible poverty, frequent sickness, and unemployment. Bonger maintained that the historical condition of this class of people was severely damaged by these conditions of economic subjugation. He attempted to demonstrate connections between certain types of crime (e.g., prostitution, alcoholism, and theft) and economic inequality. This explanation of crime suggests that the socioeconomic system is causally related to crime and would have to be restructured in order to reduce crime.

Although Bonger did not deny the influence of hereditary traits, he attributed no causal power to them in the absence of criminogenic environmental conditions. Throughout most of his writings, he stressed a socioeconomic view of crime and attacked the views of Lombroso and others of a physical-biological persuasion. His deterministic approach, along with his application of quantitative methods and his rejection of metaphysical, speculative "explanations" for crime, place Bonger in the positivist school, even though his primary focus was on the social structure, rather than the individual. Bonger's theory, which illustrates the economic approach to criminal etiology, is quite near the sociological approach in many ways, especially in its macrolevel focus on the structure of society.

Sociological Explanations

The economic depression of the 1930s and the social problems which accompanied it helped further an interest in socioeconomic factors related to crime. Not only the economic condition of the nation but also the seemingly disorganized condition of many areas of major American cities were causes for great concern on the part of those seeking explanations for crime. The so-called "Chicago school" dominated criminological thought for a number of years, focusing on a social disorganization model. Specifically, this school of thought held that the interstitial areas of our major cities (heavily populated at the time by immigrants) reflected a high degree of sociocultural heterogeneity. This, they believed, resulted in a breakdown in social organization and norms, which made deviant behavior much more commonplace. Utilizing analogies based on plant ecology, the Chicago school believed that rapid social change in "natural areas" of the city was undermining the basic social controls of a stable cultural heritage.

The theoretical successor to the Chicago school and its social disorganization approach was the culture conflict perspective, best articulated by Thorsten Sellin.[33]

This theory was based on the asssertion that crime should be viewed as the result of conduct norms, which might occur in any of three ways:

1. when these codes clash on the border of contiguous culture areas;
2. when, as may be the case with legal norms, the law of one cultural group is extended to cover the territory of another; or
3. when members of one cultural group migrate to another.

The essential contention of culture conflict theory is that crime results from the absence of one clear-cut consensual model of normative behavior. The increasing conflict in norms which came with immigration and the rapid pluralization of our society provided the most fertile ground for culture conflict theory. Although still applicable in nations with significant levels of immigration (such as Israel), it has largely been replaced in the United States by other perspectives.

There have been several sociological theories of cultural transmission, each of which has stressed different dynamics. One, known generally as "subcultural theory," had its general intellectual origins in the work of Emile Durkheim, but was initially applied in the U.S. by Robert Merton. For Merton, the explanation for crime rested in the disjunction existing for many between culturally defined success goals and the institutionalized means available to meet those goals. For some, this discrepancy results in criminal behavior, according to Merton.[34]

Elaborations of this same general statement were made later by Albert Cohen,[35] who saw the subculture which developed from this disjunction as a negative one which attempted to invert society's success goals and create its own, more realistic goals; and by Richard Cloward and Lloyd Ohlin,[36] who added the idea that illegitimate, as well as legitimate, opportunity structures were differentially accessible to individuals and that one could become either a criminal or a respected citizen, depending on which means were available.

Walter Miller[37] offered an alternative view of the lower-class subculture. He saw it as essentially characterized by its own value system and goals, not perpetually seeking to emulate the higher strata in order to gain status. Crime, for Miller, was a function of the normal socialization occurring in the subculture.

Another type of cultural transmission theory is that of Edwin Sutherland. Known as "differential association theory," it is essentially a learning theory suggestive of the earlier work of Gabriel Tarde,[38] a French social psychologist. Differential association theory posits that criminal behavior occurs via the following processes:

1. Criminal behavior is learned.
2. Criminal behavior is learned in interaction with other persons in a process of communication.
3. The principal part of the learning of criminal behavior occurs within intimate personal groups.
4. When criminal behavior is learned, the learning includes (a) techniques of committing the crime, which are sometimes very simple; (b) the specific direction of motives, drives, rationalizations, and attitudes.
5. The specific direction of motives and drives is learned from definitions of the legal codes as favorable or unfavorable.

6. A person becomes delinquent because of an excess of definitions favorable to violation of law over definitions unfavorable to violation of law.

7. Differential associations may vary in frequency, duration, priority, and intensity.

8. The process of learning criminal behavior by association with criminal and anticriminal patterns involves all of the mechanisms that are involved in any other learning.

9. While criminal behavior is an expression of general needs and values, it is not explained by those general needs and values, since noncriminal behavior is an expression of the same needs and values.[39]

Sutherland's theory was later modified by Daniel Glaser to take into account the perceived effect of the mass media and other methods of transmitting culture. Glaser's "differential identification theory" substituted for Sutherland's required personal interaction the following definition of the dynamics:

> A person pursues criminal behavior to the extent that he identifies himself with real or imaginary persons from whose perspective his criminal behavior seems acceptable.[40]

The foregoing presentation of positivism has been intended to provide an overview of the various types of theories comprising this "school." No attempt has been made to be exhaustive, but merely illustrative. Numerous other theoretical and empirical contributions could have been discussed; however, the above provide a representative sampling of positivist thought. Unlike either the demonologists of the pre-classical period or the classical advocates of a free-will, rational view of man, the positivists' concepts of causation were deterministic and anti-metaphysical. Therefore, their theories of social control have also been vastly different. They have advocated change—change of the personality, of the economic system, of the social system. Each of the positivist perspectives on crime developed its own ideas of how to deal with the crime problem, and these "solutions" were, of course, of a physical-biological, psychiatric-psychological, or social-economic nature. Their effect on penal policy is perhaps best symbolized in the name changes of our prisons—from "penitentiaries" to "correctional institutions."

But positivism is not the final chapter of this story. More recent theoretical developments have tended to concentrate on crime as a phenomenon which is determined by factors such as societal reaction (labeling), a system of laws which disproportionately reflects the interests of the wealthy and the powerful, and/or a corrupt and corrupting political system which is itself viewed as producing crime and criminals.

THE NEW EMPHASIS: "THE SYSTEM"

If positivism shifted society's focus from the crime to the criminal, then clearly that focus has shifted again with the development of the labeling and conflict perspectives, and especially with the emergence of a "radical" criminology perspective in the U.S. While these theories differ substantially in their interpretation of crime, one central feature which they have in common is their emphasis on the social and political systems as factors which help to generate the crime problem. Frequently, "the system" is identified as the "cause" of crime because of its unequal distribution of social and political power. Increasingly, the criminal is viewed as a victim — a victim of class struggle, racial discrimination, and other manifestations of inequality.

While there is, to be certain, some continuity between these relatively recent theories and some earlier sociological and economic perspectives, the general thrust of these new explanations is quite different. Most importantly, there is a much more pervasive political emphasis in current theoretical perspectives.

Labeling, Conflict, and Radical Perspectives

The labeling or "social reaction" approach to crime is reflected in the works of Becker,[41] Lemert,[42] Erikson,[43] Kitsuse,[44] and Schur.[45] This approach represents a significant departure from the absolute determinism of the positivists. The essence of labeling theory is its assertion that crime is relative and is defined (and thus *created*) socially. The oft-quoted statement of Howard Becker perhaps best sums up the approach:

> [S]ocial groups create deviance by making the rules whose infraction constitutes deviance, and by applying those rules to particular people and labeling them as outsiders. From this point of view, deviance is *not* a quality of the act the person commits, but rather a consequence of the application by others of rules and sanctions to an "offender." The deviant is one to whom that label has successfully been applied; deviant behavior is behavior that people so label.[46]

The labeling approach clearly shifts the focus of inquiry from the individual being labeled and processed to the group and the system doing the labeling and processing.

Finally, recent contributions to what has been called "radical" or "critical" or "Marxist" criminology include Richard Quinney,[47] Ian Taylor, Paul Walton and Jock Young,[48] Anthony Platt,[49] Barry Krisberg,[50] and Herman and Julia Schwendinger.[51] While there are some theoretical differences among these writers, they occupy common intellectual ground within this overview of the development of criminology theory. Their analysis of crime and social control, essentially Marxist in nature, is to be distinguished from the applications of conflict theory to criminology made by Austin Turk[52] and other non-Marxian conflict theorists, as well as the positivist approach taken by the formal Marxist Willem Bonger.

The "radical Marxist" criminologists focus their analysis on the state as a political system controlled by the interests of the "ruling capitalist class," especially through the use of law as a tool to preserve existing inequalities. Much of the work of these theorists deals with the historical conditions of classes which they link, theoretically, with the development and differential enforcement of criminal law. They reject the traditional (functionalist) view that law reflects society's consensus on the norms and values which should control behavior; instead, they argue that law emerges from a conflict of competing interests and serves the interests of the elite "ruling class."

Turk, on the other hand, essentially continues the intellectual tradition of Ralf Dahrendorf[53] and other non-Marxist conflict theorists who have analyzed crime as a result of conflict concerning the distribution of power and authority within society.

Rather than isolating the economic system and the class structure related to it, this perspective takes a broader view of the structural factors which produce conflict.

The implications of these perspectives for a philosophy of social control and for the criminal justice system are dramatically different from those suggested by earlier theorists. Again, the centrality of the political dimension is inescapable, whether one is discussing labeling theory, conflict theory, or "radical Marxist" theory. The labeling perspective, which emphasizes the discrepancy between actual criminal behavior and officially detected crime, is a societal reaction theory. It is not the deviance itself that is so important, but the way in which society reacts. This perspective generally is interpreted as advocating *less* intervention and less labeling of people as "criminal."[54] The criminal justice system is viewed as one which exacerbates the problem of crime; therefore, that system should be reduced and made less powerful.

Conflict and radical Marxist theory also would suggest that there is a need for societal restructuring. However, from these perspectives the criminal justice system merely reflects broader structural arrangements (i.e., the economy, the class system, and/or the distribution of power and authority). Radical Marxists advocate the abolition of capitalism and the development of a socialist society. They tend to view anything less than that as piecemeal "liberal tinkering" with a fatally flawed system. The alternative conflict view would argue that the particular economic system (e.g., capitalism) is not the basic problem and that crime exists in noncapitalist states as well. Crime is viewed as a structural problem resulting from the distribution of power and authority and as a reflection of unstable relationships between legal authorities and subjects.

In conclusion, it should be apparent that while man's attempts to explain crime have covered a tremendous range of ideas, there are parallels among these ideas. The idea that crime is a result of demonic possession is perhaps not a great deal different than the "mental illness" explanation advanced at a much later point in history. Both are largely deterministic, even though one is "magical" and the other "scientific."

Similarly, the rationales cited by the state for the use of imprisonment have varied from "moral reform" to "deterrence" to "rehabilitation," "public protection," and "punishment." Meanwhile, the perceptions of those imprisoned by the state have also changed, from passive acceptance of society's reaction to the increasing tendency to view themselves as "political prisoners" of an unjust legal and political system. It is apparent, therefore, that the linkage between theories of crime and social control philosophies must be evaluated on two levels: (1) the connections between theoretical explanations and formal policies, and (2) the changing rationales for employing essentially similar social control practices (e.g., "punitive" imprisonment vs. "therapeutic" correctional rehabilitation).

Notes

1. This is not to suggest that such views of man's nature were confined to primitive times. There are numerous contemporary examples of similar beliefs. However, the intent here is to present a chronology of the major explanations of crime.

2. George B. Vold, *Theoretical Criminology.* New York: Oxford University Press, 1958, pp. 5–6.

3. Harry Elmer Barnes and Negley K. Teeters, *New Horizons in Criminology*. New York: Prentice-Hall, 1945 (revised edition), p. 399.

4. E. P. Evans, *The Criminal Prosecution and Capital Punishment of Animals*. London: Heinemann, 1906.

5. George Ives. *A History of Penal Methods* (1914). Montclair, N.J.: Patterson Smith, 1970 (reprinted), pp. 9–10.

6. Cesare Beccaria, *An Essay on Crimes and Punishments* (originally published as *Trattato dei delitti e delle pene*, 1764). Albany, N.Y.: W. C. Little, 1872.

7. Vold, *op. cit.*, p. 21.

8. See, for example, Thomas S. Szasz, "Crime, Punishment, and Psychiatry." Pp. 262–285 in Abraham S. Blumberg (Ed.), *Current Perspectives on Criminal Behavior*. New York: Alfred A. Knopf, 1974.

9. Gilbert Geis, "Jeremy Bentham." Pp. 51–68 in Hermann Mannheim (Ed.), *Pioneers in Criminology* (1955). Montclair, N.J.: Patterson Smith, 1972 (revised).

10. Leon Radzinowicz, *Ideology and Crime: A Study of Crime in Its Social and Historical Context*. New York: Columbia University Press, 1966, p. 123.

11. Cesare Lombroso, *L'Uomo Delinquente*. Milan, Italy: Hoepli, 1876.

12. Lewis A. Coser, "Auguste Comte," *Masters of Sociological Thought*. New York: Harcourt Brace Jovanovich, 1971, pp 2–41. Also see Norman Birnbaum, *Toward a Critical Sociology*. New York: Oxford University Press, 1971, p. 205.

13. Marvin E. Wolfgang, "Cesare Lombroso." Pp. 232–291 in Mannheim, *op. cit.*

14. Hermann Mannheim (Ed.), *Pioneers in Criminology* (1955). Montclair, N.J.: Patterson Smith, 1972 (revised), pp. 10–11.

15. See Enrico Ferri, *Criminal Sociology*. Boston: Little, Brown, 1917.

16. Vold, *op. cit.*, p. 38.

17. Barnes and Teeters, *op. cit.*, p. 160.

18. Edwin D. Driver, "Charles Buckman Goring." Pp. 429–442 in Mannheim, *op. cit.*

19. Charles Buckman Goring, *The English Convict*. London: Her Majesty's Stationery Office, 1913.

20. Hermann Mannheim (Ed.), *Comparative Criminology*. Boston: Houghton Mifflin, 1965, p. 22B.

21. Earnest A. Hooton, *The American Criminal: An Anthropological Study*. Cambridge, Mass.: Harvard University Press, 1939.

22. Stephen Schafer, *Theories in Criminology*. New York: Random House, 1969, p. 187.

23. Vold, *op. cit.*, pp. 62–63.

24. Ernst Kretschmer, *Physique and Character*, trans. W. J. H. Sprott. New York: Harcourt, Brace, 1926.

25. William H. Sheldon, *The Varieties of Human Physique: An Introduction to Constitutional Psychology*. New York: Harper and Row, 1940.

26. Richard Dugdale, *The Jukes*. New York: Putnam's, 1877.

27. Henry H. Goddard, *The Kallikaks*. New York: Macmillan, 1914.

28. Johannes Lange, *Crime as Destiny*, trans. Charlotte Haldane. New York: C. Boni, 1930.

29. Aron J. Rosanoff, Leva M. Handy, and Isabel Rosanoff, "Criminality and Delinquency in Twins," *Journal of Criminal Law and Criminology*, 24 (Jan.–Feb.), 1934, pp. 923–924.

30. Karl O. Christiansen, "Threshold of Tolerance in Various Population Groups Illustrated by Results from the Danish Criminologic Twin Study." In A. V. S. de Reuck and R. Porter (Eds.), *The Mentally Abnormal Offender*. Boston: Little, Brown, 1968.

31. For an excellent summary and assessment of this research, see Saleem A. Shah and Loren H. Roth, "Biological and Psychophysiological Factors in Criminality." Pp. 144–147 in Daniel Glaser (Ed.), *Handbook of Criminology*. Chicago: Rand McNally, 1974.

32. William Bonger, *Criminality and Economic Conditions*, trans. Henry P. Horton. Boston: Little, Brown, 1916.

33. Thorsten Sellin, *Culture Conflict and Crime*. New York: Social Science Research Council, 1938.

34. See, for example, Robert K. Merton, "Anomie, Anomia and Social Interaction." Pp. 213–242 in Marshall B. Clinard (Ed.), *Anomie and Deviant Behavior.* New York: Free Press, 1964.

35. Albert K. Cohen, *Delinquent Boys: The Culture of the Gang.* New York: Free Press, 1955.

36. Richard A. Cloward and Lloyd E. Ohlin, *Delinquency and Opportunity: A Theory of Delinquent Gangs.* New York: Free Press, 1960.

37. Walter B. Miller, "Lower-class Culture as a Generating Milieu of Gang Delinquency." Pp. 351–363 in Marvin E. Wolfgang, Leonard Savitz, and Norman Johnston (Eds.), *The Sociology of Crime and Delinquency.* New York: Wiley, 1970.

38. Gabriel Tarde, *Penal Philosophy.* Boston: Little, Brown, 1912.

39. Edwin H. Sutherland and Donald R. Cressey, *Criminology.* Philadelphia: J. B. Lippincott, 1974 (9th edit.), pp. 75–76.

40. Daniel Glaser, "Criminality Theories and Behavior Images," *American Journal of Sociology,* 61 (March), 1956, p. 440.

41. Howard S. Becker, *Outsiders: Studies in the Sociology of Deviance.* New York: Free Press, 1963.

42. Edwin M. Lemert, *Human Deviance, Social Problems and Social Control.* Englewood Cliffs, N.J.: Prentice-Hall, 1972 (2nd edit.).

43. Kai T. Erikson, "Notes on the Sociology of Deviance," *Social Problems,* 9 (Spring), 1962, pp. 307–314.

44. John I. Kitsuse, "Societal Reaction to Deviant Behavior: Problems of Theory and Method," *Social Problems,* 9 (Winter), 1962, pp. 847–856.

45. Edwin M. Schur, *Labeling Deviant Behavior: Its Sociological Implications.* New York: Harper and Row, 1971.

46. Becker, *op. cit.,* p. 9.

47. Richard Quinney, *Critique of Legal Order: Crime Control in Capitalist Society.* Boston: Little, Brown, 1974.

48. Ian Taylor, Paul Walton, and Jock Young, *The New Criminology: For a Social Theory of Deviance.* London: Routledge & Kegan Paul, 1973.

49. Anthony Platt, "Prospects for a Radical Criminology in the United States," *Crime and Social Justice: A Journal of Radical Criminology,* I (Spring-Summer), 1974, pp. 2–10.

50. Barry Krisberg, *Crime and Privilege: Toward a New Criminology.* Englewood Cliffs, N.J.: Prentice-Hall, 1975.

51. Herman Schwendinger and Julia Schwendinger, "Defenders of Order or Guardians of Human Rights?" *Issues in Criminology,* 5 (Summer), 1970, pp. 123–157.

52. Austin T. Turk, *Criminality and the Legal Order.* Chicago: Rand McNally, 1969; also "Conflict and Criminality," *American Sociological Review,* 31 (June), 1966, pp. 338–352.

53. Ralf Dahrendorf, *Class and Class Conflict in Industrial Society.* London: Routledge & Kegan Paul, 1959.

54. See, for example, Edwin Schur, *Radical Non-intervention: Rethinking the Delinquency Problem.* Englewood Cliffs, N.J.: Prentice-Hall, 1973.

12. The Normal and the Pathological

EMILE DURKHEIM

Crime is present not only in the majority of societies of one particular species but in all societies of all types. There is no society that is not confronted with the problem of criminality. Its form changes; the acts thus characterized are not the same everywhere; but, everywhere and always, there have been men who have behaved in such a way as to draw upon themselves penal repression. If, in proportion as societies pass from the lower to the higher types, the rate of criminality, i.e., the relation between the yearly number of crimes and the population, tended to decline, it might be believed that crime, while still normal, is tending to lose this character of normality. But we have no reason to believe that such a regression is substantiated. Many facts would seem rather to indicate a movement in the opposite direction. From the beginning of the [nineteenth] century, statistics enable us to follow the course of criminality. It has everywhere increased. In France the increase is nearly 300 percent. There is, then, no phenomenon that presents more indisputably all the symptoms of normality, since it appears closely connected with the conditions of all collective life. To make of crime a form of social morbidity would be to admit that morbidity is not something accidental, but, on the contrary, that in certain cases it grows out of the fundamental constitution of the living organism; it would result in wiping out all distinction between the physiological and the pathological. No doubt it is possible that crime itself will have abnormal forms, as, for example, when its rate is unusually high. This excess is, indeed, undoubtedly morbid in nature. What is normal, simply, is the existence of criminality, provided that it attains and does not exceed, for each social type, a certain level, which it is perhaps not impossible to fix in conformity with the preceding rules.[1]

Here we are, then, in the presence of a conclusion in appearance quite paradoxical. Let us make no mistake. To classify crime among the phenomena of normal sociology is not to say merely that it is an inevitable, although regrettable phenomenon, due to the incorrigible wickedness of men; it is to affirm that it is a factor in public health, an integral part of all healthy societies. This result is, at first glance, surprising enough to have puzzled even ourselves for a long time. Once this first surprise has been overcome, however, it is not difficult to find reasons explaining this normality and at the same time confirming it.

In the first place crime is normal because a society exempt from it is utterly impossible. Crime, we have shown elsewhere, consists of an act that offends certain very strong collective sentiments. In a society in which criminal acts are no longer committed, the sentiments they offend would have to be found without exception in all individual consciousnesses, and they must be found to exist with the same degree as sentiments contrary to them. Assuming that this condition could actually be realized, crime would not thereby disappear; it would only change its form, for the very cause which would thus dry up the sources of criminality would immediately open up new ones.

Indeed, for the collective sentiments which are protected by the penal law of a people at a specified moment of its history to take possession of the public conscience or for them to acquire a stronger hold where they have an insufficient grip, they must acquire an intensity greater than that which they had hitherto had. The community as a whole must experience them more vividly, for it can acquire from no other source the greater force necessary to control these individuals who formerly were the most refractory. For murderers to disappear, the horror of bloodshed must become greater in those social strata from which murderers are recruited; but, first it must become greater throughout the entire society. Moreover, the very absence of crime would directly contribute to produce this horror; because any sentiment seems much more respectable when it is always and uniformly respected.

One easily overlooks the consideration that these strong states of the common consciousness cannot be thus reinforced without reinforcing at the same time the more feeble states, whose violation previously gave birth to mere infraction of convention — since the weaker ones are only the prolongation, the attenuated form, of the stronger. Thus robbery and simple bad taste injure the same single altruistic sentiment, the respect for that which is another's. However, this same sentiment is less grievously offended by bad taste than by robbery; and since, in addition, the average consciousness has not sufficient intensity to react keenly to the bad taste, it is treated with greater tolerance. That is why the person guilty of bad taste is merely blamed, whereas the thief is punished. But, if this sentiment grows stronger, to the point of silencing in all consciousnesses the inclination which disposes man to steal, he will become more sensitive to the offenses which, until then, touched him but lightly. He will react against them, then, with more energy; they will be the object of greater opprobrium, which will transform certain of them from the simple moral faults that they were and give them the quality of crimes. For example, improper contracts, or contracts improperly executed, which only incur public blame or civil damages, will become offenses in law.

Imagine a society of saints, a perfect cloister of exemplary individuals. Crimes, properly so called, will there be unknown; but faults which appear venial to the layman will create there the same scandal that the ordinary offense does in ordinary consciousnesses. If, then, this society has the power to judge and punish, it will define these acts as criminal and will treat them as such. For the same reason, the perfect and upright man judges his smallest failings with a severity that the majority reserve for acts more truly in the nature of an offense. Formerly, acts of violence against persons were more frequent than they are today, because respect for individual dignity was less strong. As this has increased, these crimes have become more rare; and also, many acts violating this sentiment have been introduced into the penal law which were not included there in primitive times.[2]

In order to exhaust all the hypotheses logically possible, it will perhaps be asked why this unanimity does not extend to all collective sentiments without exception. Why should not even the most feeble sentiment gather enough energy to prevent all dissent? The moral consciousness of the society would be present in its entirety in all the individuals, with a vitality sufficient to prevent all acts offending it—the purely conventional faults as well as the crimes. But a uniformity so universal and absolute is utterly impossible; for the immediate physical milieu in which each one of us is placed, the hereditary antecedents, and the social influences vary from one individual to the next, and consequently diversify consciousnesses. It is impossible for all to be alike, if only because each one has his own organism and that these organisms occupy different areas in space. That is why, even among the lower peoples, where individual originality is very little developed, it nevertheless does exist.

Thus, since there cannot be a society in which the individuals do not differ more or less from the collective type, it is also inevitable that, among these divergences, there are some with a criminal character. What confers this character upon them is not the intrinsic quality of a given act but that definition which the collective conscience lends them. If the collective conscience is stronger, if it has enough authority practically to suppress these divergences, it will also be more sensitive, more exacting; and, reacting against the slightest deviations with the energy it otherwise displays only against more considerable infractions, it will attribute to them the same gravity as formerly to crimes. In other words, it will designate them as criminal.

Crime is, then, necessary; it is bound up with fundamental conditions of all social life, and by that very fact it is useful, because these conditions of which it is a part are themselves indispensable to the normal evolution of morality and law.

Indeed, it is no longer possible today to dispute the fact that law and morality vary from one social type to the next, nor that they change within the same type if the conditions of life are modified. But, in order that these transformations may be possible, the collective sentiments at the basis of morality must not be hostile to change, and consequently must have but moderate energy. If they were too strong, they would no longer be plastic. Every pattern is an obstacle to new patterns, to the extent that the first pattern is inflexible. The better a structure is articulated, the more it offers a healthy resistance to all modification; and this is equally true of functional, as of anatomical, organization. If there were no crimes, this condition could not have been fulfilled; for such a hypothesis presupposes that collective sentiments have arrived at a degree of intensity unexampled in history. Nothing is good indefinitely and to an unlimited extent. The authority which the moral conscience enjoys must not be excessive; otherwise no one would dare criticize it, and it would too easily congeal into an immutable form. To make progress, individual originality must be able to express itself. In order that the originality of the idealist whose dreams transcend his century may find expression, it is necessary that the originality of the criminal, who is below the level of his time, shall also be possible. One does not occur without the other.

Nor is this all. Aside from this indirect utility, it happens that crime itself plays a useful role in this evolution. Crime implies not only that the way remains open to necessary changes but that in certain cases it directly prepares these changes. Where crime exists, collective sentiments are sufficiently flexible to take on a new form, and crime sometimes helps to determine the form they will take. How many times, indeed, it is only an anticipation of future morality—a step toward what will be! According to Athenian law, Socrates was a criminal, and his condemnation was no more than just. However, his crime, namely, the independence of his thought, rendered a service not only to humanity but to his country. It served to prepare a new morality and faith which the Athenians needed, since the traditions by which they had lived until then were no longer in harmony with the current conditions of life. Nor is the case of Socrates unique; it is reproduced periodically in history. It would never have been possible to establish the freedom of thought we now enjoy if the regulations prohibiting it had not been violated before being solemnly abrogated. At that time, however, the violation was a crime, since it was an offense against sentiments still very keen in the average conscience. And yet this crime was useful as a prelude to reforms which daily became more necessary. Liberal philosophy had as its precursors the heretics of all kinds who were justly punished by secular authorities during the entire course of the Middle Ages and until the eve of modern times.

From this point of view the fundamental facts of criminality present themselves to us in an entirely new light. Contrary to current ideas, the criminal no longer seems a totally unsociable being, a sort of parasitic element, a strange and unassimilable body, introduced into the midst of society.[3] On the contrary, he plays a definite role in social life. Crime, for its part, must no longer be conceived as an evil that cannot be too much suppressed. There is no occasion for self-congratulation when the crime rate drops noticeably below the average level, for we may be certain that this apparent progress is associated with some social disorder. Thus, the number of assault cases never falls so low as in times of want.[4] With the drop in the crime rate, and as a reaction to it, comes a revision, or the need of a revision in the theory of punishment. If, indeed, crime is a disease, its punishment is its remedy and cannot be otherwise conceived; thus, all the discussions it arouses bear on the point of determining what the punishment must be in order to fulfill this role of remedy. If crime is not pathological at all, the object of punishment cannot be to cure it, and its true function must be sought elsewhere.

Notes

1. From the fact that crime is a phenomenon of normal sociology, it does not follow that the criminal is an individual normally constituted from the biological and psychological points of view. The two questions are independent of each other. This independence will be better understood when we have shown, later on, the difference between psychological and sociological facts.

2. Calumny, insults, slander, fraud, etc.

3. We have ourselves committed the error of speaking thus of the criminal, because of a failure to apply our rule (*Division du travail social*, pp. 395–96).

4. Although crime is a fact of normal sociology, it does not follow that we must not abhor it. Pain itself has nothing desirable about it; the individual dislikes it as society does crime, and yet it is a function of normal physiology. Not only is it necessarily derived from the very constitution of every living organism, but it plays a useful role in life, for which reason it cannot be replaced. It would, then, be a singular distortion of our thought to present it as an apology for crime. We would not even think of protesting against such an interpretation, did we not know to what strange accusations and misunderstandings one exposes oneself when one undertakes to study moral facts objectively and to speak of them in a different language from that of the layman.

13. A Critical Model for the Study of Crime

RAYMOND J. MICHALOWSKI

A MODEL FOR THE STUDY OF CRIME

Purpose of a Model

The purpose of conceptual models such as the one presented in this chapter is to organize in a useful way the significant factors related to a particular phenomenon or problem. This organization then serves as a guide to our thinking about the issue at hand. We must remember, however, that *conceptual models are not exact depictions of reality.* They are ways of representing a certain thing, not the thing itself. Thus the diagram of an atom, with its neutrons, protons, and orbiting electrons, is only a way of representing the various components believed to constitute an atom. It is not an exact picture of an atom; indeed, physicists are not in total agreement about the actual nature of atoms.[1] However, we can say that atoms behave *as if* they were constructed according to this model, and to this degree the model is a useful tool for thinking about atoms.

Models can be similarly useful when studying social life. Human social life is a continuous web of interactions and interrelations. However, it is difficult to think about a world where everything is connected to everything else. To facilitate our thinking about the social world we often draw lines on the undifferentiated fabric of life as guideposts to our thinking. This is the purpose of the model presented here: to provide a framework within which to think about the complex social phenomenon that we call crime.

The model presented here (see Figure 1) is divided into four segments labeled mode of production, state law, individual characteristics, and individual behavior. Each of these segments represents specific levels of inquiry with respect to the study of crime.

Mode of Production: The Basis for Social Order

Social order is a set of patterned and predictable social relations between people. The nature of these relations is shaped by the interaction of a variety of factors (see Figure 2) that together can be called the mode of production. Understanding the nature of a society's mode of production is fundamental to understanding its definition of crime and its problems of crime control. This is true for several reasons.

First, it is the mode of production that will determine the nature and definition of property, and it is property that has always been the basic focus of law. While a body

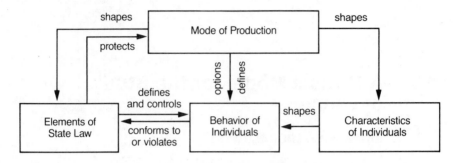

Figure 1. General Model for the Study of Crime

of material goods and resources exist in every society, "it is society and not the individual which creates the circumstances that make property out of it."[2] Second, the relations of production characteristic of any mode of production are *social relations*. That is, they are not merely abstract patterns of economic exchange but rather forms of social interaction that encompass a variety of patterned rules governing how people treat one another and how they feel toward one another. Third, the way people relate to one another with respect to the concept of property will fundamentally influence ideas about social life; that is, what is right and what is wrong.

The relations of property and the ideas about them vary with the economic organization of society. Among the traditional Eskimo, for example, hunting equipment not currently in use can be freely used by others. This pattern reflects the economic imperatives faced by nomadic hunters in a harsh environment where "it is necessary to keep all instruments of production in use as much of the time as possible." This externally imposed need for collective production also generates the cultural belief that "no man may own more capital goods than he himself can utilize."[3] This free exchange of the tools of production among the Eskimo and their beliefs about it differ radically from the kinds of relationships Americans have with one another concerning tools of production and items of value. In a capitalist society where nearly all things of material value are defined as the "property" of individuals, the acquisition or usage of someone else's property involves more complex relationships of exchange such as buying, selling, renting, leasing, and so forth. Thus the nature of possible conflict over property will be substantially different in these two societies.

A primary function of law is the maintenance of the mode of production in state societies. If the mode of production is feudal, for example, law is concerned primarily with issues of land tenure and inheritance. If it is capitalist, the bulk of law will emphasize the protection of private property in a more generalized sense. If the mode of production is socialist, law devotes considerably more attention to maintaining the desired relationships between individuals and the state as the organizer of productive activities. To understand the functions of law and the nature of crime necessitates an understanding of its mode of production.

Components of the Mode of Production. The mode of production in any society consists of three basic components: the elements of production, the relations of produc-

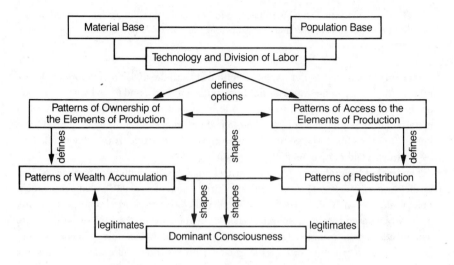

Figure 2. Components of the Mode of Production

tion, and the dominant consciousness. The elements of production and the relations of production each can be further subdivided.

Elements of Production. The *elements of production* consist of a society's material base, its population base, its technology, and its division of labor. Together these four elements determine the society's range of possibilities for producing the material required for social survival.

MATERIAL BASE   A society's material base is determined by the geographical area it encompasses and the resources for survival and economic development it contains. How a society responds to its material base depends upon a number of factors: population size, technology, division of labor, and so forth. The resources available to a society are of fundamental importance, for they limit the range of productive activities and the level of economic development possible without drawing on the resources of some other society.

POPULATION BASE   The population base of a society is determined by the size, distribution, and heterogeneity of the group that inhabits a given material base. Population size has some influence on the possibilities of technological advancement and material growth. Even if the natural resources are available, societies with relatively small populations cannot develop large-scale, diversified industrial economies unless they can expand the size of their labor force through increased birthrates, immigration, or conquest. For example, the rapid growth of the American industrial system from 1865 to 1928 was largely dependent upon successive waves of immigrants to meet the increasing need for factory and construction workers. As the political scientist and newspaper columnist Frederick J. Haskin wrote in 1913:

The "new immigrant," with his willingness to work in the dirt and the filth and the danger that are a concomitant, has made possible much of America's splendid industrial development. . . . [4]

TECHNOLOGY AND DIVISION OF LABOR Technology and the division of labor are closely related. Technology encompasses all those skills, methods, and tools by which a society produces its material existence. The level of technology determines the level of material development in a society. Simple technologies can generally only produce a limited amount of material goods from a given resource base; advanced technologies, by contrast, yield enormous amounts of such goods.

The level of technology in a society also shapes the distribution of work tasks, that is, the *division of labor*. The entire material production of a society with a simple technology may result from just a few different work tasks such as simple horticulture, gathering wild edibles, and making baskets or pottery, and each of these tasks are usually performed by large segments of the population. As technology becomes more advanced the production of material goods is broken down into an ever-increasing number of work tasks requiring highly specialized but often limited knowledge—limited, that is, in contrast to the total amount of knowledge in the society. Each individual experiences and often understands only a small part of how the society as a whole makes its living.

Relations of Production. While the resources and technology of a society constitute the basic elements of production, they are not sufficient for actual production. Human beings produce by working together and exchanging the products of this work. There has never been a human society where all individuals worked strictly by themselves for themselves, not sharing the fruits of their labor with others, even if only immediate kin. Production is a social act and requires that people enter into specific association with one another with respect to the elements or means of production (resources, tools, skills, etc.). These associations are what Karl Marx termed the relations of production.[5] The relations of production are shaped by the patterns of ownership of the means of production and the access to the means of production characteristic of a society.

Patterns of ownership and control regarding the elements of production are the most significant factors in determining the nature of productive relations within a given mode of production. Control over the elements of production means exclusive or near-exclusive right to determine *patterns of access*, that is, the right to use these things. In contemporary America, for example, managers of factories or other places of employment determine how many people and often which people will have access to the organization's resources in the form of jobs. By determining people's access to the elements of production, those in ownership and controlling positions play a large part in determining the *patterns of redistribution*, that is, who will get what share of the total amount of goods and services produced in the society. The greater the control some groups or individuals have over the access of others to the means of production, the larger will be the proportion of the total production received by those controlling access.[6]

Beyond a certain point, accumulated wealth can become the basis for acquiring additional shares of the redistributed production in societies with market economies, that is, societies where wealth can be bought, sold, or traded. In the United States, for instance, individuals with sufficient wealth to invest in stocks, securities, expansion of their businesses, or other income-producing activities can claim a proportion of the value produced through that investment independent of any other productive work. This can create a cycle of wealth accumulation and concentration that can have an important bearing on the likelihood that certain kinds of crimes and social injuries will be committed by the powerful within society.

Patterns of ownership and control over productive resources, tools, and technologies are the fundamental shapers of a society's mode of production. These patterns define who will have access to the elements of production, how they achieve this access, the methods and rules of redistribution, and how and to whom the wealth of the society will accrue.

The mode of production in any society will be shaped to some extent by the society's level of technology and its subsequent ability to utilize available resources. As technology becomes more complex both the resources and tools of production are transformed from freely available or easily produced commodities into ones that *potentially* can be claimed as the private property of certain individuals.

Ownership of property means the exclusive right to control the use and distribution of that property. Where the primary productive resources are such things as fish, game, wild edibles, and so forth, claims of individual ownership are meaningless since no individual can actually control these items. However, when productive resources become such things as land, minerals, domesticated animals, and the like, ownership claims become *possible*. Similarly, when basic productive tools are transformed from things that can be easily made by anyone (spears, arrows, fishnets, etc.) into items that are more complex and less readily made by any single individual (e.g., machines, factories, ships, etc.), it becomes possible for some individuals to claim ownership of these and to control the access of others to them.

Based on differences in patterns of ownership, access to the means of production, and redistribution of what is produced, we can identify five modes of production. These are egalitarian, slave, feudal, capitalist, and socialist modes of production.

Under an egalitarian mode of production, found only in the simplest human societies, individuals have nearly equal access to both the elements of production and the redistribution of the things produced. Under slave and feudal modes of production, both of which are based upon primarily agrarian technologies and the associated possibility of the ownership of land as a productive resource, the access of nonowners to both the means of production and the goods produced is determined by the owning class in very direct ways. Beyond its earliest phases, a capitalist mode of production is characterized by the industrial production of commodities and the division of society into a capitalist class consisting of those who own and/or manage the means of production on the one hand and a working class consisting of those seeking access to the means of production in the form of hourly-wage or salaried jobs on the other. Within this broad definition of capitalist and working class there exists a number of subgroups or class fragments: industrial wage workers and salaried public employees in the working class and small businessmen, financiers, and high-level corporate managers in the capitalist class.[7] Patterns of redistribution in capitalist economies arise from a combination of wealth accumulation through investment within the capitalist class and a complex wage hierarchy encompassing the working class.

A socialist mode of production defines the resources and tools of production as the collective property of all members of the society, and there is a greater emphasis upon equality of redistribution of production than in slave, feudal, or capitalist modes of production. However, because these societies tend to also be industrial, individuals do not have the same free access to the means of production found in egalitarian societies. Socialist societies generally subscribe to the view that all individuals have a right to work, and some, such as the Soviet Union, include the right to a job as a basic constitutional right.[8] In practice, though, this access is managed through various bureaucratic structures, and some (e.g., Jews in Russia, government critics in Czechoslovakia, union organizers in Poland) may find their access curtailed.

Consciousness. Human beings do more than engage in actions and enter into relationships. They *think about* what they do. This does not mean that we are always critically assessing our actions but rather that we have ideas and concepts that explain the meaning of our actions and those of others. When we go to the store and exchange paper for goods we say that we are "buying" something. When we "buy" something, we mentally recognize that it "belongs" to us. When we watch TV, play golf, go sailing, and so forth, we say we are "relaxing," and when we perform actions for which other people give us money we say we are "working." Each of these words imply a set of taken-for-granted social relationships. This taken-for-granted way of thinking about ourselves and the world around us is what is meant by the term "consciousness."

Societies are characterized by the existence of a *dominant consciousness*, that is, ways of thinking about the world that are taken for granted by most people in the society.[9] These accepted ways of thinking about the world provide people with explanations and justifications for their behavior and the behavior of others.

Consciousness is a product of experience; the kinds of relations people enter into will shape the way in which they think about the world. Hence, since the basic character of social relations in a society is largely determined by its mode of production, the dominant consciousness will reflect the mode of production. The meaning of the term "work" in American society, for example, is shaped by the fact that most Americans, to earn their subsistence, enter into relationships with others who own the means of production and who will return to workers, in the form of wages, a portion of the value workers produce by their labor. Because this is the way in which work is organized, the idea that one works for wages rather than an equal share of the value produced becomes part of the taken-for-granted way of understanding the nature of work.

The dominant consciousness of any society includes a number of abstract ideas concerning the nature of human relations. Regardless of how abstract, however, these ideas have their roots in the actual organization of the society. For example, ideas about human nature and human worth emerge from the actual nature of social relations in a society. If social organization is based upon competitive social relations, competitiveness will be viewed as a basic element of human nature, not because humans are in fact *inherently* competitive, but because competitive relations are predominant in the society. Similarly, in a society where *individuals* enter into com-

petitive social relations with one another, the concept of human rights will be understood as one of *individual* rights, since individuals rather than groups are seen as the
basic unit of action. Social organization shapes social behavior, and in doing so provides the raw material of experience from which abstract concepts about human
nature and society are constructed.

The development of human consciousness is a process of applying meaning to
events, experiences, and objects in our lives.[10] That is, humans *interpret* what they
experience and try to fit those interpretations into a general framework for understanding the world around them and their place in it. To the extent that a given group
or class of people derive special benefit from a particular mode of production they will
have an interest in creating and maintaining interpretations of the existing mode of
production that will contribute to its continuation. That is, they will have an interest in
the creation of an *ideology* that explains why the existing social order is natural,
appropriate, or inevitable. To the extent that they can establish this ideology as the
dominant way of thinking among *all segments* of the society they reduce the likelihood
of collective movements that seek to alter the social order from which they derive the
maximum benefit. During the era of American slavery, for example, proslavery forces
relied heavily upon ideas about the natural superiority of the white race and the God-
ordained mission to civilize and Christianize black Africans through the mechanism
of slavery to create an ideology that would minimize opposition to slavery among both
nonslave owners and slaves.[11] Similarly, the history of capitalism is characterized by
the development of ideologies that stress the "God-given" right of *individuals* to own
the elements of production, the "naturalness" of human competition to acquire
material advantage over others, and the appropriateness of broad disparities in wealth
as long as the wealthy achieved their position according to the rules of "fair play" as
established by liberal, democratic institutions of government. As part of the dominant
consciousness in a society, such ideologies serve both to legitimize and explain patterns of redistribution and patterns of wealth accumulation and to insulate those patterns from popular challenges.

The goal of dominant classes in any society is to achieve a position of *ideological
hegemony*, that is, to so dominate the everyday consciousness in the society as to make
unlikely the emergence of ways of interpreting everyday experiences that would
threaten their dominance.[12] While this hegemony is seldom ever total—there are
always individuals or groups who question the dominant way of thinking—it is often
sufficient to blunt or slow effective challenges. As Karl Marx observed:

> The ideas of the ruling class are, in every age, the ruling ideas: i.e., the class which is the
> dominant *material* force in society is at the same time the dominant *intellectual* force. The
> class which has the means of material production at its disposal, has control at the same
> time over the means of mental production. . . . The dominant ideas are nothing more than
> the ideal expression of dominant material relationships, the dominant material relation-
> ships grasped as ideas. . . . [13]

Individuals who achieve positions of dominance within a particular mode of
production tend to do so by adhering to the beliefs as well as the behaviors associated
with that mode of production. In modern capitalist societies, for example, the primary

route to economic and political power is through participation in and adherence to the beliefs and behaviors appropriate to capitalist relations of production. As a result, the majority of economically and/or politically powerful individuals tend to believe in the appropriateness, and often the inevitability, of competition, wealth accumulation, and *limited* forms of political democracy. While such individuals may disagree over the appropriate strategies to preserve and expand capitalism, they generally adhere to a belief in the appropriateness of its preservation. Because of their advantageous position within the economic order they are better able to present their world view to the rest of the society as the appropriate world view. This hegemony is achieved largely through financial inputs into major institutions of socialization such as education, the media, and religion. In the 1970s, for instance, the Business Roundtable—a group representing corporate interests—initiated a multimillion dollar "image-advertising" campaign to diffuse growing public opposition to such things as hazardous waste and low levels of corporate taxation. At the same time a number of American businesses pooled funds to establish 35 Chairs of Free Enterprise in universities, organize 150 Students in Free Enterprise Clubs, and launch an attack on media which carried "anti-business" news stories.[14] Proponents of ideologies—that is, ways of explaining the existing social order—that contradict the ideology of the economically and politically dominant classes generally lack equal money and opportunities to disseminate their world view to the population at large.

Law represents the institutionalization of abstract ideas about the appropriate form of human relations characteristic of the dominant consciousness in a state society. These abstract ideas generally reflect the ideology of the dominant class, whether this class consists of the owners and managers of the economy, as in America, or the bureaucratic elite in the USSR. When studying crime in America, it is important to identify the relationships that exist between abstract ideas expressed in the law (e.g., due process, legal equality, property rights, etc.) and the material and historical conditions that gave rise to the particular form of consciousness these concepts represent.

Institutions of Legal Order

The second component of the model consists of the political institutions of state law. Specifically, these are the institutions for making laws, the laws themselves, the institutions for enforcing laws and punishing offenders, and the institutions or mechanisms for resolving disputes and maintaining order. (See Figure 3.)

Law-Making Institutions. Legal order can be divided into several components, the first and most basic of which consists of institutions for making laws. These institutions constitute what we normally think of as the government of a society, though in its entirety government involves much more than the making of laws.

Law-making institutions can take a number of different, specific forms (e.g., a dictator and his counselors; a parliament, congress, or supreme soviet; etc.). However, they all share a common characteristic: They are based on the political power to make and enforce rules of conduct that are binding on other members of the society. This political power rests ultimately on force. It is the existence of and reliance upon centralized

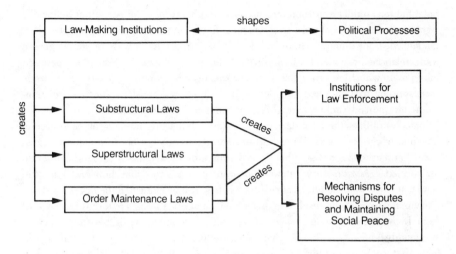

Figure 3.   Components of State Law

force in the form of political power that distinguishes state law from other forms of social control.

The existence of a political state—that is, a centralization of political power—depends upon the existence of one or more groups in the society possessing the power to dominate others. All state societies are class societies. While law-making institutions are based upon political power and the force it implies, in any particular state society the structure of political power, who wields it, who has access to it, and for what ends it will be used will be shaped by (1) basic characteristics of the society's mode of production and (2) limitations on state actions arising from beliefs inherent in the dominant consciousness (e.g., freedom of speech, equality under the law, due process, etc.) and embodied in the political organization of the state. These latter establish broad guidelines the violation of which can weaken or threaten state legitimacy.

The fundamental purpose of law is to protect social order. For this reason the law-making institutions of the United States, or any other nation, cannot be studied as abstract political processes. In an advanced capitalist society like America, the institutions of law making largely reflect the ideology and exigencies of modern capitalist society just as the law-making institutions of socialist states reflect the ideology and exigencies of socialist society. Laws and the institutions that make them must always be viewed in reference to the kind of social order they are designed to protect.

Legal Rules for Behavior.   State law consists of a body of legal rules for behavior backed by the political power of the state. This body of laws may consist of little more than the proclamation of a king or war lord, or it may encompass seemingly endless volumes of legislated law, judicial decisions, and governmental regulations. In general, the greater the number of competitive relations in a society, the greater will be its need for an extensive body of legal rules.[15] Competitive relations increase the potential for conflict and therefore increase the need for legal rules that define the rights and obligations of individuals so as to minimize this potential. In simple agrarian societies, for example, there is little need for an extensive body of laws to govern trade relationships since trade is relatively limited and usually takes place between individuals who have other ties such as kinship or community. However, as trade increases, so does the need for rules to govern trade relationships, for these relationships have considerable potential for misunderstanding and conflict.

State law defines the boundaries of acceptable behavior and also serves to predict how and when the state will respond to unacceptable behaviors or noncriminal disputes between citizens. Laws that specify what individual citizens can and cannot do are termed *substantive laws*. Laws whose purpose it is to define how and when the state will respond to violations of substantive law, or how and when the state's legal system can be used for the resolution of disputes between citizens, are termed *procedural laws*. Both substantive and procedural laws are important topics in the study of crime. While substantive laws define what behaviors constitute crimes, procedural laws in large part define the process whereby specific individuals are officially identified as criminals and specific disputes resolved.

As discussed in the preceding section, a primary function of law is to protect the basic social relations characteristic of society's mode of production. However, not all laws are specifically or directly concerned with this task. Instead, laws can be divided into three groups: substructural laws, superstructural laws, and public order laws. *Substructural laws* are those that serve to institutionalize, protect, or facilitate the basic relations of production in the society. For example, laws defining property rights and the rules for the exchange of property are substructural in focus. By defining what constitutes property and the rights of ownership (e.g., land law, patent law, laws governing water or mineral rights), legitimate patterns of redistribution (e.g., purchase vs. theft, "fair play" vs. fraud), legitimate forms of wealth accumulation (e.g., laws specifying the rights of investors and financiers), public versus private property (e.g., tax laws, laws of eminent domain) and the rights and obligations of individuals involved in specific economic relations (e.g., contract law, labor law), substructural laws institutionalize and protect a society's mode of production.

Superstructural laws are those that define and protect public and private institutional arrangements not directly involved in basic productive activities. They may involve such things as religion, politics, education, communication, charitable organizations, marriage, or any of the other patterned forms of activity found in a state society. The institutions governed by superstructural laws are not necessarily unrelated to basic relations of production. However, they are a secondary rather than a primary level of activity with respect to production. For example, in industrialized societies educational institutions play a central role in producing a labor force adequately trained to operate and expand the productive system. However, to the extent that schools and colleges are not operating factories, marketing commodities, or providing investment capital as a primary activity, they are institutionally one step removed from basic productive activities. Similarly, in the United States, Federal, state, and local governments are not primary investors, owners, or managers of actual productive facilities. Thus most of the laws defining the nature of governments are superstructural in character. This would not be the case, however, in countries where production is socialized and government managers become directly involved in production. In these states many of the laws concerning government and politics would be substructural.

Laws of public order are those that govern the behavior of individuals outside of the spheres of productive or institutionally arranged activities. These laws are primarily aimed at controlling behaviors that either tend to disrupt social peace (laws against assault or other forms of interpersonal violence, noise control laws, public nuisance laws) or that violate specific cultural values of the public in general or some segment of it (e.g., vice laws, laws against nude bathing, antiabortion laws, etc.). Like super-structural laws, laws of public order are not always unrelated to more basic relations of production. For example, it has been argued that laws in America prohibiting recreational drug use reflect an attempt to protect the values of hard work and rational-ity central to capitalist production in the United States. Yet while such laws may facili-tate certain aspects of productive relations as characterized by (in this case) a capitalist mode of production, primary proponents of these laws are often substantially removed from the direct benefits such laws might generate within the relations of production. Debates surrounding substructural laws such as tax laws, patent laws, and water rights laws are quite different, for here the various partisans are often specifically conscious of the economic benefits or liabilities that these laws will create.

Institutions of Law Enforcement.   The maintenance of legal order requires institutions that can enforce the legal rules created by the state. Only in the simplest state societies is law enforced by the same individuals who actually make the law. Beyond the level of tribal chiefdoms and small feudal societies, the task of law enforcement is carried out by specialized law workers using authority *delegated to them* by the law makers. In the United States these law workers are dispersed through a number of different institutions: police, courts, correctional agencies, tax collection agencies, numerous specialized regulatory agencies, and in some cases the military.

Law enforcement involves two interrelated tasks: securing compliance with the law and punishing those who violate it. The tasks of securing compliance and punishing criminals in the United States are performed by a variety of institutions. When con-sidering conventional crime, the most visible law enforcement institutions are the police, courts, and correctional agencies, along with their auxiliary personnel, which would include prosecutors and defense attorneys. Each of these institutions rests upon that portion of state power delegated to it by law-making institutions in the form of sub-stantive and procedural laws. Because law enforcement agencies have been delegated specialized functions (e.g., identifying and capturing suspected lawbreakers, assess-ing innocence or guilt and if guilty determining appropriate penalties, detaining con-victed offenders, etc.), they tend to develop specialized concerns and ways of understanding the law enforcement process. This specialization of concern can at times bring various law enforcement institutions into conflict. Police, for example, are delegated the authority to bring suspected offenders to justice. Courts, on the other hand, must assess not only whether the accused are guilty but also whether they were brought to justice in accordance with procedural law. Thus a court may refuse to prosecute a case based on what it defines as an illegal search, bringing it into direct conflict with the police, who view such "technicalities" as a serious impediment to the performance of their delegated function. Specialization increases conflict within law enforcement as well as in the society at large.

Dispute Resolution.   Disputes between individuals occur in every society. These may result from conflicting claims over property, insults, love triangles, unpaid debts, or any of the other ways in which human relations can go awry. In nonstate societies these disputes are usually resolved through face-to-face negotiation, negotiation through some chosen third party, and in extreme cases through self-help (e.g., simply taking what you think is owed to you) or resorting to witchcraft. As societies grow in size and complexity, important organizational relationships in the society become tied less to the bonds of kinship and community and more to comparatively impersonal market relations. Consequently, the possibilities for interpersonal disputes, particularly over property and money, increase while possibilities for face-to-face resolution decline.

An important function of the legal order in state society is to provide opportunities for the peaceful resolution of disputes between individuals. While some disputes are defined as crimes against the state and are prosecuted and punished by the state, others are not. However, many of these noncriminal disputes are seen as appropriate for resolution *within* the framework of the legal order. Such disputes may be submitted to a king or other leader for a resolution, or as in many modern, industrial states, argued in and resolved by a court of law.

In the United States the function of dispute resolution through law is performed primarily within civil courts. These courts adjudicate torts (noncriminal but legally recognized forms of harm), contract disputes, divorces, bankruptcy, patent claims, and a multiplicity of other cases, the bulk of which arise from disputes over property in some form.

Crime: Individual Characteristics

The third and fourth components of our model are focused on the individual characteristics that shape human behavior, and the behaviors themselves. It is the interaction between these two components which culminate in legal or illegal forms of behavior.

Where individual characteristics are concerned the model divides people into five separate components: biology, constitutionality, cognitive and emotional processes, acquired skills, and objective relations (see Figure 4). Yet human beings are not really mechanical assemblages of components. They are integrated organisms that perform a number of different functions such as growing, thinking, feeling, acting, and dying. None of the functions performed by the human organism is wholly disconnected from the others. What people think and believe influences what they will do, and what they do will have a bearing upon what they think and believe. Similarly, emotional and physical well-being cannot be seen as wholly distinct processes, for each can influence the other.

As with the previous two elements of the model (the mode of production and state law), the division of people into separate components is done for the sake of discussion and study. It must be remembered, however, that while these divisions provide a way *of talking about* human beings, what we are considering is actually a unified organism.

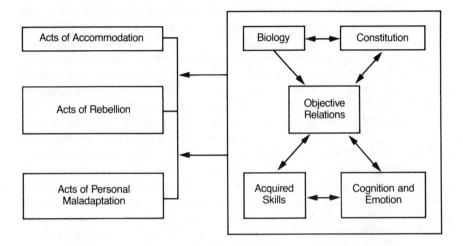

Figure 4. Individual Characteristics and Individual Behaviors

Biology. Human beings are biological organisms that have evolved through several million years of interaction with their physical environment and their own cultural creations. In recent years increased attention has been given to evolutionary biology and human genetics as a means of understanding human behavior. This increased attention is reflected in the writings of some criminologists, who see in human genetics possible explanations for criminality.[16]

This development has both positive and negative aspects. On the positive side, a more accurate understanding of the evolutionary processes by which humans achieved their present form can contribute to our overall understanding of the human organism. On the negative side in western science there is a longstanding history of overextending and misinterpreting the findings of evolutionary and genetic research in ways that are consistent with and supportive of the political and economic ideology of capitalist society.[17] In addition, some see in genetic theories of human behavior the attractive possibility of being able to identify and control *potential* as well as actual deviants.[18] At their worst, genetic theories of criminality and other forms of human behavior can advance politically expedient interpretations of crime under the authoritative banner of science.[19]

The study of crime should incorporate an appreciation of the fact that humans are biological organisms whose potentials for behavior are genetically determined. However, this appreciation must be tempered by the awareness that the process by which some of these potentials emerge as actual behavior is essentially social in nature. Furthermore, the *meaning* given these actual behaviors will be determined by fundamental economic, political, and social arrangements, not by a person's genetic makeup.

Constitutionality. The term "constitutionality" is used here to mean all those physical characteristics and conditions not strictly determined by a person's genetic makeup. Constitutionality includes such things as overall health, perceptual or motor defects, retardation (other than those forms caused by genetic abnormalities), and specific conditions caused by such things as dietary deficiencies and environmentally borne poisons.

The study of crime should not ignore or exclude the role of a person's constitutionality in the production of those behaviors defined as criminal. Like genetic makeup, however, constitutionality factors should not be thought of as *cause* of crime. For instance, lead poisoning in children is linked to high levels of aggressive behavior.[20] However, to say that this biological abnormality is the *cause* of aggressiveness is incorrect. Lead poisoning occurs most often among children of the poor who live in old, deteriorated housing where as toddlers they were exposed to flaking lead-based paints (in newer dwellings lead paints have not been used). Thus the *socially* derived system of inequality, which leads to some people living in deteriorating and inadequate housing, is as much a part of the aggressiveness in question as the lead poisoning itself.

Thus it is appropriate to include physical conditions as part of the study of crime. However, it is not appropriate to do so without examining the material, political, and social factors that influence the likelihood of those conditions and the definitions that will be applied to the behaviors to which they contribute.

Cognitive and Emotional Processes. The sociological and psychological study of crime has devoted considerable attention to the role of cognitive and emotional processes in the production of criminal behavior. People's attitudes, values, self-esteem, sense of alienation, feelings of powerlessness, need for social approval, and so forth have frequently been treated as key variables in the study of criminal behavior. Inquiries into beliefs, values, and emotional response patterns can be informative when trying to understand why some people engage more frequently in certain so-called criminal acts than others. However, when incorporating the study of cognitive and emotional processes into the study of crime, several cautions must be taken.

First, thoughts and feelings can only be inferred from what people say or do; they can never be directly observed. Thus, when criminologists study (for example) the relationship between self-concept and the willingness to participate in deviant or criminal activity, they must construct devices such as interview schedules or questionnaires that will serve as indicators of self-concept because the hypothesized operation of self-concept as an internal mental process cannot be directly observed.

Second, the relationship between thoughts and feelings on the one hand and behavior on the other is interactive. What people do will effect what they think and feel. Therefore, the kinds of thoughts and feelings expressed by people after they have committed crimes may not be the same as their thoughts and feelings before they ever broke the law. As a result, when criminological researchers find that lawbreakers respond to interview schedules, questionnaires, and other measures of hypothesized mental processes differently from noncriminals, it cannot be assumed that these differences are necessarily a cause of criminal behavior. They may be the result of having behaved criminally.

Third, what people think and feel is not the product of purely individual mental processes. Ways of thinking and feeling develop through experience with the very real social relations and other components of the external world. Criminologist Walter

Miller, for example, identified "fate"–a belief in luck–as one of the focal concerns supporting participation in deviant activity among lower-class youth.[21] However, we cannot treat an emphasis upon fate as the independent psychological invention of lower-class Americans. Individuals who as the result of poverty, oppression, and exploitation have little realistic opportunity to control their own life outcomes and who observe others around them meeting with failure more often than success are not likely to develop a strong sense that they are in charge of their own lives. Lacking the political awareness and the class consciousness to recognize the sociopolitical nature of their experiences, these individuals develop a generalized belief in fate as a means of adapting to the experiences of being a "lower-class" American.

Cognitive and emotional processes are part of the equation culminating in behaviors defined as crime by the state. However, they must be situated in their actual material, social, and political contexts and not treated as an abstract psychological creation.

Acquired Skills. The term "acquired skills" refers to learned abilities to perform specific behaviors. Nearly all human behaviors are learned through interaction with others. Our ability to speak, read, write, and perform life maintenance tasks (e.g., shopping, cooking, cleaning, etc.), work tasks (e.g., welding, accounting, carpentry, etc.), and all the other specific tasks that fill our days are learned through social interaction.

Learned behavioral skills define in part the boundaries of an individual's life chances. In industrial society, for example, individuals who are deficient in skill areas such as reading, writing, or mathematics will be unable to participate in certain kinds of occupations such as teaching, engineering, or management. Where there is a substantial difference in the income levels associated with various jobs, as in the United States, individuals deficient in these skills will find themselves limited to the lower-paying and less prestigious occupations. For some of these individuals, the reward from crime may seem a tempting alternative to the low reward from legitimate work.[22]

An individual's level of acquired occupational skills also determine his or her *options* for criminal behavior. Those who have acquired skills that qualify them for higher-paying and higher prestige jobs have options to participate in white-collar and corporate crimes unavailable to those in lower-paying jobs. Thus skill level influences a person's access both to legitimate and illegitimate sources of income.

Objective Relations. Every member of society is located within a set of specific material and social relations. These relations define the range of experiences various individuals are likely to have at any given time. In doing so they provide the raw material of experience to which each individual must respond, and for this reason they are an important part of understanding the production of specific human behaviors.

Many variables that criminologists have included in the study of crimes–poverty, social class membership, race, ethnicity, and education, for instance–are not static conditions or states. They are the manifestations of specific social and material relations. For instance, being black in America is not simply the condition of having darker skin. It is a set of social and material relations between black Americans and white Americans that extends back to the time the first black slaves were brought to the American colonies from Africa.

Being black in America means generally being less socially acceptable, and having on average less access to material and political resources *in comparison with whites.* Thus the meaning of being black in America is based on the material and social relations *between blacks and whites,* not on the quality of being black or being socialized into black culture.

Similarly, being poor means existing within and adapting to a set of material and social relations that provide others with greater access to wealth than oneself. Poverty in America is not simply a characteristic of the poor; it is the outcome of the particular material and social relations that characterize American capitalism.

Objective relations determine in large part the kinds of experiences to which an individual will have to adapt while at the same time contributing to the formation of the human self. To understand the "criminality" of any particular individual or group of individuals requires examining this process of experience, adaptation, and self-formation as it occurs within the context of specific material and social *relations,* rather than seeing individuals as being composed of some static set of qualities and characteristics such as age, race, sex, income, social class, or educational level.

Crime: One Variety of Human Behavior

Our model assumes three options for human behavior: behaviors that reflect conformist adaptations to the existing social order, behaviors that constitute acts of rebellion against the existing order, and acts of personal or interpersonal maladaptation, which while they may disrupt social harmony are not direct threats to more basic elements of the social order.

Acts of adaptation include all the varieties of everyday behavior that are commonly accepted as "normal," nondeviant, and law-abiding. They are termed acts of adaptation because they represent the various ways people conform to the requirements for getting along day by day. In America both getting a job and applying for welfare are conformist ways of adapting to the need to acquire some type of income. Not all acts of adaptation are, however, positive or neutral with respect to how they affect social life. Depending upon the dominant consciousness and the legal order arising in connection with a given mode of production, some very damaging behaviors can become legitimated as acceptable ways of adapting to everyday life. At one time in America, for example, owning slaves was an acceptable adaptation to the need to acquire income, just as at a later time employing child labor or exploiting workers in other extreme ways was also within the range of acceptable behavior. Thus the range of conformist adaptations is in a constant state of change as societies shift the line between acceptable and unacceptable forms of action and make, remake, or unmake laws.

Acts of rebellion are those varieties of nonconformist behavior that threaten the underlying bases for social order. In a capitalist society, for example, acquiring property in what is defined as an illegitimate manner such as theft or fraud would represent an act of rebellion. This does not mean that the individual engaging in such an act is necessarily undertaking some conscious or deliberate strategy to remake the social order. It means simply that the individual is rejecting the established, conformist routes for adapting to the demands of everyday life. The individual who decides to steal instead of, or in addition to, working for a living is rebelling against the constraints placed upon the acquisition of property as established by the society. Although most acts of rebellion are not undertaken with a view toward social change, genuine acts of revolution would also fall into this category.

Acts of personal or interpersonal maladaptation refer to those types of behaviors that have been defined by either law or popular belief as deviant but that do not threaten basic elements of social order. In America behaviors defined as insanity, drug abuse, illegal forms of domestic violence, or other acts that disrupt social peace in illegal or deviant ways would fall into the category of acts of maladaptation. Acts of maladaptation are most often misdirected attempts to deal with the problems and pressures of everyday life without recognizing their underlying sources. The person caught in a traffic jam who winds up in a fight with the driver who cut in front of him, for instance, is responding to the overall system of traffic flow by striking out at the nearest, but also most insignificant, source of his problem. Similarly, husbands who physically abuse their wives or parents who abuse their children are frequently using their victims as means of releasing frustrations generated by more complicated and distant forces affecting their lives and their level of frustration.

It is the political economy of a society in connection with its cultural history that determines the definition of what acts are adaptive, rebellious, or maladaptive in a society. In modern state societies it is the institutions of state law that have the additional task of controlling rebellious and maladaptive forms of behavior.

Notes

1. Gary Zukav, *The Dancing Wu Li Masters: Overview of the New Physics* (New York: William Morrow, 1979).

2. E. Adamson Hoebel, *The Law of Primitive Man* (New York: Atheneum, 1973), 58.

3. Ibid., 69.

4. Fredrick J. Haskins, *The Immigrant: An Asset and a Liability* (New York: Fleming H. Revell Co., 1913), 34.

5. Karl Marx, *Capital*, vol. 1 (Moscow: Progress Publishers, 1978), 80–81.

6. See Barry Indess and Paul Q. Hirst, *Pre-Capitalist Modes of Production* (London: Routledge and Kegan Paul, 1975).

7. This definition of capitalist class is similar to that utilized by Michael Useem, "The Inner Group of the American Capitalist Class," *Social Problems* 25 (February 1978): 225–240.

8. "Basic Principles of Civil Legislation in the USSR and Union Republics," cited in Chaldize, *Criminal Russia*, 189.

9. See Trent Schroyer, *The Critique of Domination* (Boston: Beacon Press, 1973), for a discussion of the role of consciousness in everyday life. Peter L. Berger and Thomas Luckman, *The Social Construction of Reality* (Garden City, N.Y.: Doubleday, 1966), also provide an excellent discussion of consciousness as "common-sense knowledge" from a non-Marxist perspective.

10. Herbert Blumer, *Symbolic Interactionism* (Englewood Cliffs, N.J.: Prentice-Hall, 1969), 2–3.

11. John Higham, "Toward Racism: The History of an Idea," in Norman R. Yetman and C. Hoy Steele, eds., *Majority and Minority* (Boston: Allyn and Bacon, 1975), 207–221.

12. Antonio Gramsci, *Prison Notebooks* (London: Lawrence and Wishart, 1971). See also Colin Sumner, *Reading Ideologies* (New York: Academic Press, 1979) for a detailed discussion of the various theories concerning the relationships between ideology, hegemony, and the law.

13. Karl Marx and Frederick Engels, "The German Ideology," in Marx and Engels, *Collected Works* (London, Lawrence and Wishart), vol. 5, 82–83.

14. Harry C. Boyte, *The Backyard Revolution* (Philadelphia: Temple University Press, 1980), 16; see also Liston Pope, *Millhands and Preachers* (New Haven, Conn.: Yale University Press, 1942) for a description of how education and religion can shape working-class consciousness in ways consistent with the interests of elites.

15. Some, such as Harold Pepinsky, *Crime and Conflict* (New York: Academic Press, 1976), argue that while increasing specificity in law is presumed to reduce potentialities for conflict, it actually leads to increases by creating ever more detailed points of contention.

16. See for example S. Mednick and K.D. Christiansen, *Biosocial Bases of Criminal Behavior* (New York: Gardener, 1977).

17. See Stephen Jay Gould, *The Mismeasure of Man* (New York: W.W. Norton, 1981) for a review of the ways in which scientific analysis has been misused and misinterpreted to support dominant ideologies about genetic and racial differences.

18. C. Ray Jeffery, "Criminology as an Interdisciplinary Behavior Science," *Criminology* 16, no. 2 (August 1978): 149–169.

19. See Ysabel Rennie, "Science and the Dangerous Offender," part II of *The Search for Criminal Man* (Boston: D.C. Heath, 1978), 57–96, for a description of "science" as a basis for politically advantageous definitions of who is the criminal.

20. J. Julian Chisholm, Jr., "Lead Poisoning," *Scientific American* 224 (February 1971): 3–11.

21. Walter Miller, "Lower Class Culture as a Generating Milieu of Gang Delinquency," *Journal of Social Issues* 14 (1958): 5–19.

22. Daryl A. Hellman, *The Economics of Crime* (New York: St. Martins Press, 1980), 38–42.

14. A Control Theory of Delinquency

TRAVIS HIRSCHI

Control theories assume that delinquent acts result when an individual's bond to society is weak or broken. Since these theories embrace two highly complex concepts, the *bond* of the individual to *society*, it is not surprising that they have at one time or another formed the basis of explanations of most forms of aberrant or unusual behavior. It is also not surprising that control theories have described the elements of the bond to society in many ways, and that they have focused on a variety of units as the point of control. . . .

ELEMENTS OF THE BOND

Attachment

In explaining conforming behavior, sociologists justly emphasize sensitivity to the opinion of others.[1] Unfortunately, . . . they tend to suggest that man *is* sensitive to the opinion of others and thus exclude sensitivity from their explanations of deviant behavior. In explaining deviant behavior, psychologists, in contrast, emphasize insensitivity to the opinion of others.[2] Unfortunately, they too tend to ignore variation, and, in addition, they tend to tie sensitivity inextricably to other variables, to make it part of a syndrome or "type," and thus seriously reduce its value as an explanatory concept. The psychopath is characterized only in part by "deficient attachment to or affection for others, a failure to respond to the ordinary motivations founded in respect or regard for one's fellows";[3] he is also characterized by such things as "excessive aggressiveness," "lack of superego control," and "an infantile level of response."[4] Unfortunately, too, the behavior that psychopathy is used to explain often becomes part of the *definition* of psychopathy. As a result, in Barbara Wootton's words: "[The psychopath] is . . . *par excellence*, and without shame or qualification, the model of the circular process by which mental abnormality is inferred from anti-social behavior while anti-social behavior is explained by mental abnormality."[5]

The problems of diagnosis, tautology, and name-calling are avoided if the dimensions of psychopathy are treated as causally and therefore problematically interrelated, rather than as logically and therefore necessarily bound to each other. In fact, it can be argued that all of the characteristics attributed to the psychopath follow from, are effects of, his lack of attachment to others. To say that to lack attachment to others is to be free from moral restraints is to use lack of attachment to explain the guiltlessness of the psychopath, the fact that he apparently has no conscience or superego. In this view, lack of attachment to others is not merely a symptom of psychopathy, it *is* psychopathy; lack of conscience is just another way of saying the same thing; and the violation of norms is (or may be) a consequence.

For that matter, given that man is an animal, "impulsivity" and "aggressiveness" can also be seen as natural consequences of freedom from moral restraints. However, since the view of man as endowed with natural propensities and capacities like other animals is peculiarly unpalatable to sociologists, we need not fall back on such a view to explain the amoral man's aggressiveness.[6] The process of becoming alienated from others often involves or is based on active interpersonal conflict. Such conflict could easily supply a reservoir of *socially derived* hostility sufficient to account for the aggressiveness of those whose attachments to others have been weakened.

Durkheim said it many years ago: "We are moral beings to the extent that we are social beings."[7] This may be interpreted to mean that we are moral beings to the extent that we have "internalized the norms" of society. But what does it mean to say that a person has internalized the norms of society? The norms of society are by definition shared by the members of society. To violate a norm is, therefore, to act contrary to the wishes and expectations of other people. If a person does not care about the wishes and expectations of other people – that is, if he is insensitive to the opinion of others – then he is to that extent not bound by the norms. He is free to deviate.

The essence of internalization of norms, conscience, or superego thus lies in the attachment of the individual to others.[8] This view has several advantages over the concept of internalization. For one, explanations of deviant behavior based on attachment do not beg the question, since the extent to which a person is attached to others can be measured independently of his deviant behavior. Furthermore, change or variation in behavior is explainable in a way that it is not when notions of internalization or superego are used. For example, the divorced man is more likely after divorce to commit a number of deviant acts, such as suicide or forgery. If we explain these acts by reference to the superego (or internal control), we are forced to say that the man "lost his conscience" when he got a divorce; and, of course, if he remarries, we have to conclude that he gets his conscience back.

This dimension of the bond to conventional society is encountered in most social control-oriented research and theory. F. Ivan Nye's "internal control" and "indirect control" refer to the same element, although we avoid the problem of explaining changes over time by locating the "conscience" in the bond to others rather than making it part of the personality.[9] Attachment to others is just one aspect of Albert J. Reiss's "personal controls"; we avoid his problems of tautological empirical *observations* by making the relationship between attachment and delinquency problematic rather than definitional.[10] Finally, Scott Briar and Irving Piliavin's "commitment" or "stake in conformity" subsumes attachment, as their discussion illustrates, although the terms they use are more closely associated with the next element to be discussed.[11]

Commitment

"Of all passions, that which inclineth men least to break the laws, is fear. Nay, excepting some generous natures, it is the only thing, when there is the appearance of profit or pleasure by breaking the laws, that makes men keep them."[12] Few would deny that men on occasion obey the rules simply from fear of the consequences. This rational component in conformity we label commitment. What does it mean to say that a person is committed to conformity? In Howard S. Becker's formulation it means the following:

> First, the individual is in a position in which his decision with regard to some particular line of action has consequences for other interests and activities not necessarily [directly] related to it. Second, he has placed himself in that position by his own prior actions. A third element is present though so obvious as not to be apparent: the committed person must be aware [of these other interests] and must recognize that his decision in this case will have ramifications beyond it.[13]

The idea, then, is that the person invests time, energy, himself, in a certain line of activity—say, getting an education, building up a business, acquiring a reputation for virtue. When or whenever he considers deviant behavior, he must consider the costs of this deviant behavior, the risk he runs of losing the investment he has made in conventional behavior.

If attachment to others is the sociological counterpart of the superego or conscience, commitment is the counterpart of the ego or common sense. To the person committed to conventional lines of action, risking one to ten years in prison for a ten-dollar holdup is stupidity, because to the committed person the costs and risks obviously exceed ten dollars in value. (To the psychoanalyst, such an act exhibits failure to be governed by the "reality-principle.") In the sociological control theory, it can be and is generally assumed that the decision to commit a criminal act may well be rationally determined—that the actor's decision was not irrational given the risks and costs he faces. Of course, as Becker points out, if the actor is capable of in some sense calculating the costs of a line of action, he is also capable of calculational errors; ignorance and error return, in the control theory, as possible explanations of deviant behavior.

The concept of commitment assumes that the organization of society is such that the interest of most persons would be endangered if they were to engage in criminal acts. Most people, simply by the process of living in an organized society, acquire goods, reputations, prospects that they do not want to risk losing. These accumulations are society's insurance that they will abide by the rules. Many hypotheses about the antecedents of delinquent behavior are based on this premise. For example, Arthur L. Stinchcombe's hypothesis that "high school rebellion . . . occurs when future status is not clearly related to present performance"[14] suggests that one is committed to conformity not only by what one has but also by what one hopes to obtain. Thus "ambition" and/or "aspiration" play an important role in producing conformity. The person becomes committed to a conventional line of action, and he is therefore committed to conformity.

Most lines of action in a society are of course conventional. The clearest examples are educational and occupational careers. Actions thought to jeopardize one's chances in these areas are presumably avoided. Interestingly enough, even nonconventional commitments may operate to produce conventional conformity. We are told, at least, that boys aspiring to careers in the rackets or professional thievery are judged by their "honesty" and "reliability"—traits traditionally in demand among seekers of office boys.[15]

Involvement

Many persons undoubtedly owe a life of virtue to a lack of opportunity to do otherwise. Time and energy are inherently limited: "Not that I would not, if I could, be both handsome and fat and well dressed, and a great athlete, and make a million a year, be a wit, a bon vivant, and a lady killer, as well as a philosopher, a philanthropist, a states-man, warrior, and African explorer, as well as a 'tone-poet' and saint. But the thing is simply impossible."[16] The things that William James here says he would like to be or do are all, I suppose, within the realm of conventionality, but if he were to include illicit actions he would still have to eliminate some of them as simply impossible.

Involvement or engrossment in conventional activities is thus often part of a control theory. The assumption, widely shared, is that a person may be simply too busy doing conventional things to find time to engage in deviant behavior. The person involved in conventional activities is tied to appointments, deadlines, working hours, plans, and the like, so the opportunity to commit deviant acts rarely arises. To the extent that he is engrossed in conventional activities, he cannot even think about deviant acts, let alone act out his inclinations.[17]

This line of reasoning is responsible for the stress placed on recreational facilities in many programs to reduce delinquency, for much of the concern with the high school dropout, and for the idea that boys should be drafted into the army to keep them out of trouble. So obvious and persuasive is the idea that involvement in conventional activi-ties is a major deterrent to delinquency that it was accepted even by Sutherland: "In the general area of juvenile delinquency it is probable that the most significant difference between juveniles who engage in delinquency and those who do not is that the latter are provided abundant opportunities of a conventional type for satisfying their recreational interests, while the former lack those opportunities or facilities."[18]

The view that "idle hands are the devil's workshop" has received more sophisticated treatment in recent sociological writings on delinquency. David Matza and Gresham M. Sykes, for example, suggest that delinquents have the values of a leisure class, the same values ascribed by Veblen to *the* leisure class: a search for kicks, disdain of work, a desire for the big score, and acceptance of aggressive toughness as proof of masculinity.[19] Matza and Sykes explain delinquency by reference to this system of values, they note that adolescents at all class levels are "to some extent" members of a leisure class, that they "move in a limbo between earlier parental domination and future integration with the social structure through the bonds of work and marriage."[20] In the end, then, the leisure of the adolescent produces a set of values, which, in turn, leads to delinquency.

Belief

Unlike the cultural deviance theory, the control theory assumes the existence of a common value system within the society or group whose norms are being violated. If the deviant is committed to a value system different from that of conventional society, there is, within the context of the theory, nothing to explain. The question is, "Why does a man violate the rules in which he believes?" It is not, "Why do men differ in their beliefs about what constitutes good and desirable conduct?" The person is assumed to have been socialized (perhaps imperfectly) into the group whose rules he is violating; deviance is not a question of one group imposing its rules on the members of another group. In other words, we not only assume the deviant *has* believed the rules, we assume he believes the rules even as he violates them.

How can a person believe it is wrong to steal at the same time he is stealing? In the strain theory, this is not a difficult problem. (In fact, . . . the strain theory was devised specifically to deal with this question.) The motivation to deviance adduced by the strain theorist is so strong that we can well understand the deviant act even assuming the deviator believes strongly that it is wrong.[21] However, given the control theory's assumptions about motivation, if both the deviant and the nondeviant believe the deviant act is wrong, how do we account for the fact that one commits it and the other does not?

Control theories have taken two approaches to this problem. In one approach, beliefs are treated as mere words that mean little or nothing if the other forms of control are missing. "Semantic dementia," the dissociation between rational faculties and emotional control which is said to be characteristic of the psychopath, illustrates this way of handling the problem.[22] In short, beliefs, at least insofar as they are expressed in words, drop out of the picture; since they do not differentiate between deviants and nondeviants, they are in the same class as "language" or any other characteristic common to all members of the group. Since they represent no real obstacle to the commission of delinquent acts, nothing need be said about how they are handled by those committing such acts. The control theories that do not mention beliefs (or values), and many do not, may be assumed to take this approach to the problem.

The second approach argues that the deviant rationalizes his behavior so that he can at once violate the rule and maintain his belief in it. Donald R. Cressey has advanced this argument with respect to embezzlement,[23] and Sykes and Matza have advanced it with respect to delinquency.[24] In both Cressey's and Sykes and Matza's treatments, these rationalizations (Cressey calls them "verbalizations," Sykes and Matza term them "techniques of neutralization") occur prior to the commission of the deviant act. If the neutralization is successful, the person is free to commit the act(s) in question. Both in Cressey and in Sykes and Matza, the strain that prompts the effort at neutralization also provides the motive force that results in the subsequent deviant act. Their theories are thus, in this sense, strain theories. Neutralization is difficult to handle within the context of a theory that adheres closely to control theory assumptions, because in the control theory there is no special motivational force to account for the neutralization. This difficulty is especially noticeable in Matza's later treatment of this topic, where the motivational component, the "will to delinquency," appears *after* the moral vacuum has been created by the techniques of neutralization.[25] The question thus becomes: Why neutralize?

In attempting to solve a strain-theory problem with control-theory tools, the control theorist is thus led into a trap. He cannot answer the crucial question. The concept of neutralization assumes the existence of moral obstacles to the commission of deviant acts. In order plausibly to account for a deviant act, it is necessary to generate motivation to deviance that is at least equivalent in force to the resistance provided by these moral obstacles. However, if the moral obstacles are removed, neutralization and special motivation are no longer required. We therefore follow the implicit logic of control theory and remove these moral obstacles by hypothesis. Many persons do not have an attitude of respect toward the rules of society; many persons feel no moral obligation to conform regardless of personal advantage. Insofar as the values and beliefs of these persons are consistent with their feelings, and there should be a tendency toward consistency, neutralization is unnecessary; it has already occurred.

Does this merely push the question back a step and at the same time produce conflict with the assumption of a common value system? I think not. In the first place, we do not assume, as does Cressey, that neutralization occurs in order to make a specific criminal act possible.[26] We do not assume, as do Sykes and Matza, that neutralization occurs to make many delinquent acts possible. We do not assume, in other words, that the person constructs a system of rationalizations in order to justify commission of acts he *wants* to commit. We assume, in contrast, that the beliefs that free a man to commit deviant acts are *unmotivated* in the sense that he does not construct or adopt them in order to facilitate the attainment of illicit ends. In the second place, we do not assume, as does Matza, that "delinquents concur in the conventional assessment of delinquency."[27] We assume, in contrast, that there is *variation* in the extent to which people believe they should obey the rules of society, and, furthermore, that the less a person believes he should obey the rules, the more likely he is to violate them.[28]

In chronological order, then, a person's beliefs in the moral validity of norms are, for no teleological reason, weakened. The probability that he will commit delinquent acts is therefore increased. When and if he commits a delinquent act, we may justifiably use the weakness of his beliefs in explaining it, but no special motivation is required to explain either the weakness of his beliefs or, perhaps, his delinquent act.

The keystone of this argument is of course the assumption that there is variation in belief in the moral validity of social rules. This assumption is amenable to direct empirical test and can thus survive at least until its first confrontation with data. For the present, we must return to the idea of a common value system with which this section was begun.

The idea of a common (or, perhaps better, a single) value system is consistent with the fact, or presumption, of variation in the strength of moral beliefs. We have not suggested that delinquency is based on beliefs counter to conventional morality; we have not suggested that delinquents do not believe delinquent acts are wrong. They may well believe these acts are wrong, but the meaning and efficacy of such beliefs are contingent upon other beliefs and, indeed, on the strength of other ties to the conventional order.[29]

Notes

1. Books have been written on the increasing importance of interpersonal sensitivity in modern life. According to this view, controls from within have become less important than controls from without in *producing* conformity. Whether or not this observation is true as a description of historical trends, it is true that interpersonal sensitivity has become more important in *explaining* conformity. Although logically it should also have become more important in explaining nonconformity, the opposite has been the case, once again showing that Cohen's observation that an explanation of conformity should be an explanation of deviance cannot be translated as "an explanation of conformity has to be an explanation of deviance." For the view that interpersonal sensitivity currently plays a greater role than formerly in producing con-

formity, see William J. Goode, "Norm Commitment and Conformity to Role-Status Obligations," *American Journal of Sociology*, LXVI (1960), 246–258. And, of course, also see David Riesman, Nathan Glazer, and Reuel Denney, *The Lonely Crowd* (Garden City, New York: Doubleday, 1950), especially Part I.

2. The literature on psychopathy is voluminous. See William McCord and Joan McCord, *The Psychopath* (Princeton: D. Van Nostrand, 1964).

3. John M. Martin and Joseph P. Fitzpatrick, *Delinquent Behavior* (New York: Random House, 1964), p. 130.

4. *Ibid.* For additional properties of the psychopath, see McCord and McCord, *The Psychopath*, pp. 1–22.

5. Barbara Wootton, *Social Science and Social Pathology* (New York: Macmillan, 1959), p. 250.

6. "The logical untenability [of the position that there are forces in man 'resistant to socialization'] was ably demonstrated by Parsons over 30 years ago, and it is widely recognized that the position is empirically unsound because it assumes [!] some universal biological drive system distinctly separate from socialization and social context—a basic and intransigent human nature" (Judith Blake and Kingsley Davis, "Norms, Values, and Sanctions," *Handbook of Modern Sociology*, ed. Robert E.L. Faris [Chicago: Rand McNally, 1964], p. 471).

7. Emile Durkheim, *Moral Education*, trans. Everett K. Wilson and Herman Schnurer (New York: The Free Press, 1961), p. 64.

8. Although attachment alone does not exhaust the meaning of internalization, attachments and beliefs combined would appear to leave only a small residue of "internal control" not susceptible in principle to direct measurement.

9. F. Ivan Nye, *Family Relationships and Delinquent Behavior* (New York: Wiley, 1958), pp. 5–7.

10. Albert J. Reiss, Jr., "Delinquency as the Failure of Personal and Social Controls," *American Sociological Review*, XVI (1951), 196–207. For example, "Our observations show . . . that delinquent recidivists are less often persons with mature ego ideals or nondelinquent social roles" (p. 204).

11. Scott Briar and Irving Piliavin, "Delinquency, Situational Inducements, and Commitment to Conformity," *Social Problems*, XIII (1965), 41–42. The concept "stake in conformity" was introduced by Jackson Toby in his "Social Disorganization and Stake in Conformity: Complementary Factors in the Predatory Behavior of Hoodlums," *Journal of Criminal Law, Criminology and Police Science*, XLVIII (1957), 12–17. See also his "Hoodlum or Business Man: An American Dilemma," *The Jews*, ed. Marshall Sklare (New York: The Free Press, 1958), pp. 542–550. Throughout the text, I occasionally use "stake in conformity" in speaking in general of the strength of the bond to conventional society. So used, the concept is somewhat broader than is true for either Toby or Briar and Piliavin, where the concept is roughly equivalent to what is here called "commitment."

12. Thomas Hobbes, *Leviathan* (Oxford: Basil Blackwell, 1957), p. 195.

13. Howard S. Becker, "Notes on the Concept of Commitment," *American Journal of Sociology*, LXVI (1960), 35–36.

14. Arthur L. Stinchcombe, *Rebellion in a High School* (Chicago: Quadrangle, 1964), p. 5.

15. Richard A. Cloward and Lloyd E. Ohlin, *Delinquency and Opportunity* (New York: The Free Press, 1960), p. 147, quoting Edwin H. Sutherland, ed., *The Professional Thief* (Chicago: University of Chicago Press, 1937), pp. 211–213.

16. William James, *Psychology* (Cleveland: World Publishing Co., 1948), p. 186.

17. Few activities appear to be so engrossing that they rule out contemplation of alternative lines of behavior, at least if estimates of the amount of time men spend plotting sexual deviations have any validity.

18. *The Sutherland Papers*, ed. Albert K. Cohen et al. (Bloomington: Indiana University Press, 1956), p. 37.

19. David Matza and Gresham M. Sykes, "Juvenile Delinquency and Subterranean Values," *American Sociological Review*, XXVI (1961), 712–719.

20. *Ibid.*, p. 718.

21. The starving man stealing the loaf of bread is the image evoked by most strain theories. In this image, the starving man's belief in the wrongness of his act is clearly not something that must be explained away. It can be assumed to be present without causing embarrassment to the explanation.

22. McCord and McCord, *The Psychopath*, pp. 12–15.

23. Donald R. Cressey, *Other People's Money* (New York: The Free Press, 1953).

24. Gresham M. Sykes and David Matza, "Techniques of Neutralization: A Theory of Delinquency," *American Sociologial Review*, XXII (1957), 664–670.

25. David Matza, *Delinquency and Drift* (New York: Wiley, 1964), pp. 181–191.

26. In asserting that Cressey's assumption is invalid with respect to delinquency, I do not wish to suggest that it is invalid for the question of embezzlement, where the problem faced by the deviator is fairly specific and he can reasonably be assumed to be an upstanding citizen. (Although even here the fact that the embezzler's nonshareable financial problem often results from some sort of hanky-panky suggests that "verbalizations" may be less necessary than might otherwise be assumed.)

27. *Delinquency and Drift*, p. 43.

28. This assumption is not, I think, contradicted by the evidence presented by Matza against the existence of a delinquent subculture. In comparing the attitudes and actions of delinquents with the picture painted by delinquent subculture theorists, Matza emphasizes – and perhaps exaggerates – the extent to which delinquents are tied to the conventional order. In implicitly comparing delinquents with a supermoral man, I emphasize – and perhaps exaggerate – the extent to which they are not tied to the conventional order.

29. The position taken here is therefore somewhere between the "semantic dementia" and the "neutralization" positions. Assuming variation, the delinquent is, at the extremes, freer than the neutralization argument assumes. Although the possibility of wide discrepancy between what the delinquent professes and what he practices still exists, it is presumably much rarer than is suggested by studies of articulate "psychopaths."

15. Techniques of Neutralization: A Theory of Delinquency

GRESHAM M. SYKES AND DAVID MATZA

As Morris Cohen once said, one of the most fascinating problems about human behavior is why men violate the laws in which they believe. This is the problem that confronts us when we attempt to explain why delinquency occurs despite a greater or lesser commitment to the usages of conformity. A basic clue is offered by the fact that social rules or norms calling for valued behavior seldom if ever take the form of categorical imperatives. Rather, values or norms appear as *qualified* guides for action, limited in their applicability in terms of time, place, persons, and social circumstances. The moral injunction against killing, for example, does not apply to the enemy during combat in time of war, although a captured enemy comes once again under the prohibition. Similarly, the taking and distributing of scarce goods in a time of acute social need is felt by many to be right, although under other circumstances private property is held inviolable. The normative system of a society, then, is marked by what Williams has termed *flexibility*; it does not consist of a body of rules held to be binding under all conditions.[1]

This flexibility is, in fact, an integral part of the criminal law in that measures for "defenses to crimes" are provided in pleas such as nonage, necessity, insanity, drunkenness, compulsion, self-defense, and so on. The individual can avoid moral culpability for his criminal action — and thus avoid the negative sanctions of society — if he can prove that criminal intent was lacking. *It is our argument that much delinquency is based on what is essentially an unrecognized extension of defenses to crimes, in the form of justifications for deviance that are seen as valid by the delinquent but not by the legal system or society at large.*

These justifications are commonly described as rationalizations. They are viewed as following deviant behavior and as protecting the individual from self-blame and the blame of others after the act. But there is also reason to believe that they precede deviant behavior and make deviant behavior possible. It is this possibility that Sutherland mentioned only in passing and that other writers have failed to exploit from the viewpoint of sociological theory. Disapproval flowing from internalized norms and conforming others in the social environment is neutralized, turned back, or deflected in advance. Social controls that serve to check or inhibit deviant motivational patterns are rendered inoperative, and the individual is freed to engage in delinquency without serious damage to his self-image. In this sense, the delinquent both has his cake and eats it too, for he remains committed to the dominant normative system and yet so qualifies its imperatives that violations are "acceptable" if not "right." Thus the delinquent represents not a radical opposition to law-abiding society but something more like an apologetic failure, often more sinned against than sinning in his own eyes. We call these justifications of deviant behavior techniques of neutralization, and we believe these techniques make up a crucial component of Sutherland's "definitions favorable to the violation of law." It is by learning these techniques that the juvenile becomes delinquent, rather than by learning moral imperatives, values, or attitudes standing in direct contradiction to those of the dominant society. In analyzing these techniques, we have found it convenient to divide them into five major types.

THE DENIAL OF RESPONSIBILITY

Insofar as the delinquent can define himself as lacking responsibility for his deviant actions, the disapproval of self or others is sharply reduced in effectiveness as a restraining influence. As Justice Holmes has said, even a dog distinguishes between being stumbled over and being kicked, and modern society is no less careful to draw a line between injuries that are unintentional, i.e., where responsibility is lacking, and those that are intentional. As a technique of neutralization, however, the denial of responsibility extends much further than the claim that deviant acts are an "accident" or some similar negation of personal accountability. It may also be asserted that delinquent acts are due to forces outside of the individual and beyond his control such as unloving parents, bad companions, or a slum neighborhood. In effect, the delinquent approaches a "billiard ball" conception of himself in which he sees himself as help-lessly propelled into new situations. From a psychodynamic viewpoint, this orientation toward one's own actions may represent a profound alienation from self, but it is important to stress the fact that interpretations of responsibility are cultural constructs and not merely idiosyncratic beliefs. The similarity between this mode of justifying illegal behavior assumed by the delinquent and the implications of a "sociological" frame of reference or a "humane" jurisprudence is readily apparent.[2] It is not the validity of this orientation that concerns us here, but its function of deflecting blame attached to violations of social norms and its relative independence of a particular personality structure.[3] By learning to view himself as more acted upon than acting, the delinquent prepares the way for deviance from the dominant normative system without the necessity of a frontal assault on the norms themselves.

THE DENIAL OF INJURY

A second major technique of neutralization centers on the injury or harm involved in the delinquent act. The criminal law has long made a distinction between crimes which are *mala in se* and *mala prohibita*—that is, between acts that are wrong in themselves and acts that are illegal but not immoral—and the delinquent can make the same kind of distinction in evaluating the wrongfulness of his behavior. For the delinquent, however, wrongfulness may turn on the question of whether or not anyone has clearly been hurt by his deviance, and this matter is open to a variety of interpretations. Vandalism, for example, may be defined by the delinquent simply as "mischief"—after all, it may be claimed, the persons whose property has been destroyed can well afford it. Similarly, auto theft may be viewed as "borrowing," and gang fighting may be seen as a private quarrel, an agreed-upon duel between two willing parties, and thus of no concern to the community at large. We are not suggesting that this technique of neutralization, labeled the denial of injury, involves an explicit dialectic. Rather, we are arguing that the delinquent frequently, and in a hazy fashion, feels that his behavior does not really cause any great harm despite the fact that it runs counter to law. Just as the link between the individual and his acts may be broken by the denial of responsibility, so may the link between acts and their consequences be broken by the denial of injury. Since society sometimes agrees with the delinquent, e.g., in matters such as truancy, "pranks," and so on, it merely reaffirms the idea that the delinquent's neutralization of social controls by means of qualifying the norms is an extension of common practice rather than a gesture of complete opposition.

THE DENIAL OF THE VICTIM

Even if the delinquent accepts the responsibility for his deviant actions and is willing to admit that his deviant actions involve an injury or hurt, the moral indignation of self and others may be neutralized by an insistence that the injury is not wrong in light of the circumstances. The injury, it may be claimed, is not really an injury; rather, it is a form of rightful retaliation or punishment. By a subtle alchemy the delinquent moves himself into the position of an avenger and the victim is transformed into a wrong-doer. Assaults on homosexuals or suspected homosexuals, attacks on members of minority groups who are said to have gotten "out of place," vandalism as revenge on an unfair teacher or school official, thefts from a "crooked" store owner—all may be hurts inflicted on a transgressor, in the eyes of the delinquent. As Orwell has pointed out, the type of criminal admired by the general public has probably changed over the course of years and Raffles no longer serves as a hero;[4] but Robin Hood, and his latter-day derivatives, such as the tough detective seeking justice outside the law, still capture the popular imagination, and the delinquent may view his acts as part of a similar role.

To deny the existence of the victim, then, by transforming him into a person deserving injury is an extreme form of a phenomenon we have mentioned before, namely, the delinquent's recognition of appropriate and inappropriate targets for his delinquent acts. In addition, however, the existence of the victim may be denied for the delinquent, in a somewhat different sense, by the circumstances of the delinquent act itself. Insofar as the victim is physically absent, unknown, or a vague abstraction (as is often the case in delinquent acts committed against property), the awareness of the victim's existence is weakened. Internalized norms and anticipations of the reactions of others must somehow be activated if they are to serve as guides for behavior; and it is possible that a diminished awareness of the victim plays an important part in determining whether or not this process is set in motion.

THE CONDEMNATION OF THE CONDEMNERS

A fourth technique of neutralization would appear to involve a condemnation of the condemners or, as McCorkle and Korn have phrased it, a rejection of the rejectors.[5] The delinquent shifts the focus of attention from his own deviant acts to the motives and behavior of those who disapprove of his violations. His condemners, he may claim, are hypocrites, deviants in disguise, or impelled by personal spite. This orientation toward the conforming world may be of particular importance when it hardens into a bitter cynicism directed against those assigned the task of enforcing or expressing the norms of the dominant society. Police, it may be said, are corrupt, stupid, and brutal. Teachers always show favoritism, and parents always "take it out" on their children. By a slight extension, the rewards of conformity—such as material success—become a matter of pull or luck, thus decreasing still further the stature of those who stand on the side of the law-abiding. The validity of this jaundiced viewpoint is not so important as its function in turning back or deflecting the negative sanctions attached to violations of the norms. The delinquent, in effect, has changed the subject of the conversation in the dialogue between his own deviant impulses and the reactions of others; and by attacking others, the wrongfulness of his own behavior is more easily repressed or lost to view.

THE APPEAL TO HIGHER LOYALTIES

Fifth, and last, internal and external social controls may be neutralized by sacrificing the demands of the larger society for the demands of the smaller social groups to which the delinquent belongs, such as the sibling pair, the gang, or the friendship clique. It is important to note that the delinquent does not necessarily repudiate the imperatives of the dominant normative system, despite his failure to follow them. Rather, the delinquent may see himself as caught up in a dilemma that must be resolved, unfortunately, at the cost of violating the law. One aspect of this situation has been studied by Stouffer and Toby in their research on the conflict between particularistic and universalistic demands, between the claims of friendship and general social obligations, and their results suggest that "it is possible to classify people according to a predisposition to select one or the other horn of a dilemma in role conflict."[6] For our purposes, however, the most important point is that deviation from certain norms may occur not because the norms are rejected but because other norms, held to be more pressing or involving a higher loyalty, are accorded precedence. Indeed, it is the fact that both sets of norms are believed in that gives meaning to our concepts of dilemma and role conflict.

The conflict between the claims of friendship and the claims of law, or a similar dilemma, has of course long been recognized by the social scientist (and the novelist) as a common human problem. If the juvenile delinquent frequently resolves his dilemma by insisting that he must "always help a buddy" or "never squeal on a friend," even when it throws him into serious difficulties with the dominant social order, his choice remains familiar to the supposedly law-abiding. The delinquent is unusual, perhaps, in the extent to which he is able to see the fact that he acts in behalf of the smaller social groups to which he belongs as a justification for violations of society's norms, but it is a matter of degree rather than of kind.

"I didn't mean it." "I didn't really hurt anybody." "They had it coming to them." "Everybody's picking on me." "I didn't do it for myself." These slogans or their variants, we hypothesize, prepare the juvenile for delinquent acts. These "definitions of the situation" represent tangential or glancing blows at the dominant normative system rather than the creation of an opposing ideology; and they are extensions of patterns of thought prevalent in society rather than something created *de novo*.

Techniques of neutralization may not be powerful enough to fully shield the individual from the force of his own internalized values and the reactions of conforming others, for as we have pointed out, juvenile delinquents often appear to suffer from feelings of guilt and shame when called into account for their deviant behavior. And some delinquents may be so isolated from the world of conformity that techniques of neutralization need not be called into play. Nonetheless, we would argue that techniques of neutralization are critical in lessening the effectiveness of social controls and that they lie behind a large share of delinquent behavior. Empirical research in this area is scattered and fragmentary at the present time, but the work of Redl,[7] Cressey,[8] and others has supplied a body of significant data that has done much to clarify the theoretical issues and enlarge the fund of supporting evidence. Two lines of investigation seem to be critical at this stage. First, there is need for more knowledge concerning the differential distribution of techniques of neutralization, as operative patterns of thought, by age, sex, social class, ethnic group, etc. On a priori grounds it might be assumed that these justifications for deviance will be more readily seized by segments of society for whom a discrepancy between common social ideals and social practice is most apparent. It is also possible, however, that the habit of "bending" the dominant normative system — if not "breaking" it — cuts across our cruder social categories and is to be traced primarily to patterns of social interaction within the familial circle. Second, there is need for a greater understanding of the internal structure of techniques of neutralization, as a system of beliefs and attitudes, and its relationship to various types of delinquent behavior. Certain techniques of neutralization would appear to be better adapted to particular deviant acts than to others, as we have suggested, for example, in the case of offenses against property and the denial of the victim. But the issue remains far from clear and stands in need of more information.

In any case, techniques of neutralization appear to offer a promising line of research in enlarging and systematizing the theoretical grasp of juvenile delinquency. As more information is uncovered concerning techniques of neutralization, their origins, and their consequences, both juvenile delinquency in particular and deviation from normative systems in general may be illuminated.

Notes

1. Cf. Robin Williams, Jr., *American Society*, New York: Knopf, 1951, p. 28.

2. A number of observers have wryly noted that many delinquents seem to show a surprising awareness of sociological and psychological explanations for their behavior and are quick to point out the causal role of their poor environment.

3. It is possible, of course, that certain personality structures can accept some techniques of neutralization more readily than others, but this question remains largely unexplored.

4. George Orwell, *Dickens, Dali, and Others*, New York: Reynal, 1946.

5. Lloyd W. McCorkle and Richard Korn, "Resocialization within Walls," *The Annals of the American Academy of Political and Social Science*, 293 (May, 1954), pp. 88–98.

6. See Samuel A. Stouffer and Jackson Toby, "Role Conflict and Personality," in *Toward a General Theory of Action*, edited by Talcott Parsons and Edward A. Shils, Cambridge, Mass.: Harvard University Press, 1951, p. 494.

7. See Fritz Redl and David Wineman, *Children Who Hate*, Glencoe, Ill.: The Free Press, 1956.

8. See D.R. Cressey, *Other People's Money*, Glencoe, Ill.: The Free Press, 1953.

16. Lower Class Culture as a Generating Milieu of Gang Delinquency

WALTER B. MILLER

The etiology of delinquency has long been a controversial issue and is particularly so at present. As new frames of reference for explaining human behavior have been added to traditional theories, some authors have adopted the practice of citing the major postulates of each school of thought as they pertain to delinquency, and of going on to state that causality must be conceived in terms of the dynamic interaction of a complex combination of variables on many levels. The major sets of etiological factors currently adduced to explain delinquency are, in simplified terms, the physiological (delinquency results from organic pathology), the psycho-dynamic (delinquency is a "behavioral disorder" resulting primarily from emotional disturbance generated by a defective mother-child relationship), and the environmental (delinquency is the product of disruptive forces, "disorganization," in the actor's physical or social environment).

This paper selects one particular kind of "delinquency"[1] — law-violating acts committed by members of adolescent street-corner groups in lower class communities — and attempts to show that the dominant component of motivation underlying these acts consists in a directed attempt by the actor to adhere to forms of behavior, and to achieve standards of value, as they are defined within that community. It takes as a premise that the motivation of behavior in this situation can be approached most productively by attempting to understand the nature of cultural forces impinging on the acting individual as they are perceived *by the actor himself* — although by no means only that segment of these forces of which the actor is consciously aware — rather than as they are perceived and evaluated from the reference position of another cultural system. In the case of "gang" delinquency, the cultural system which exerts the most direct influence on behavior is that of the lower class community itself — a long-established, distinctively patterned tradition with an integrity of its own — rather than a so-called "delinquent subculture" which has arisen through conflict with middle class culture and is oriented to the deliberate violation of middle class norms.

The bulk of the substantive data on which the following material is based was collected in connection with a service-research project in the control of gang delinquency. During the service aspect of the project, which lasted for three years, seven trained social workers maintained contact with twenty-one corner-group units in a "slum" district of a large eastern city for periods of time ranging from ten to thirty months. Groups were Negro and white, male and female, and in early, middle, and late adolescence. Over eight thousand pages of direct observational data on behavior patterns of group members and other community residents were collected; almost daily contact was maintained for a total time period of about thirteen worker years. Data

Chart 1. Focal Concerns of Lower Class Culture

Area	Perceived Alternatives (state, quality, condition)	
1. Trouble:	law-abiding behavior	law-violating behavior
2. Toughness:	physical prowess, skill;	weakness, ineptitude;
	"masculinity";	effeminacy;
	fearlessness, bravery, daring	timidity, cowardice, caution
3. Smartness:	ability to outsmart, dupe, "con";	gullibility, "con-ability";
	gaining money by "wits";	gaining money by hard work;
	shrewdness, adroitness in repartee	slowness, dull-wittedness, verbal maladroitness
4. Excitement:	thrill;	boredom;
	risk, danger;	"deadness," safeness;
	change, activity	sameness, passivity
5. Fate:	favored by fortune, being "lucky"	ill-omened, being "unlucky"
6. Autonomy:	freedom from external constraint;	presence of external constraint;
	freedom from superordinate authority;	presence of strong authority;
	independence	dependency, being "cared for"

include workers' contact reports, participant observation reports by the writer—a cultural anthropologist—and direct tape recordings of group activities and discussions.[2]

FOCAL CONCERNS OF LOWER CLASS CULTURE

There is a substantial segment of present-day American society whose way of life, values, and characteristic patterns of behavior are the product of a distinctive cultural system which may be termed "lower class." Evidence indicates that this cultural system is becoming increasingly distinctive, and that the size of the group which shares this tradition is increasing.[3] The lower class way of life, in common with that of all distinctive cultural groups, is characterized by a set of focal concerns—areas or issues which command widespread and persistent attention and a high degree of emotional involvement. The specific concerns cited here, while by no means confined to the American lower classes, constitute a distinctive *patterning* of concerns which differs significantly, both in rank order and weighting, from that of American middle class culture. Chart 1 presents a highly schematic and simplified listing of six of the major concerns of lower class culture. Each is conceived as a "dimension" within which a fairly wide and varied range of alternative behavior patterns may be followed by different individuals under different situations. They are listed roughly in order of the degree of *explicit* attention accorded each and, in this sense, represent a weighted ranking of concerns. The "perceived alternatives" represent polar positions which define certain parameters within each dimension. As will be explained in more detail, it is necessary in relating the influence of these "concerns" to the motivation of delinquent behavior to specify *which* of its aspects is oriented to, whether orientation is *overt* or *covert, positive* (conforming to or seeking the aspect) or *negative* (rejecting or seeking to avoid the aspect).

The concept "focal concern" is used here in preference to the concept "value" for several interrelated reasons: (1) It is more readily derivable from direct field observation. (2) It is descriptively neutral—permitting independent consideration of positive and negative valences as varying under different conditions, whereas "value" carries a built-in positive valence. (3) It makes possible more refined analysis of subcultural differences, since it reflects actual behavior, whereas "value" tends to wash out intracultural differences since it is colored by notions of the "official" ideal.

Trouble

Concern over "trouble" is a dominant feature of lower class culture. The concept has various shades of meaning; "trouble" in one of its aspects represents a situation or a kind of behavior which results in unwelcome or complicating involvement with official authorities or agencies of middle class society. "Getting into trouble" and "staying out of trouble" represent major issues for male and female, adults and children. For men, "trouble" frequently involves fighting or sexual adventures while drinking; for women, sexual involvement with disadvantageous consequences. Expressed desire to avoid behavior which violates moral or legal norms is often based less on an explicit commitment to "official" moral or legal standards than on a desire to avoid "getting into trouble," e.g., the complicating consequences of the action.

The dominant concern over "trouble" involves a distinction of critical importance for the lower class community—that between "law-abiding" and "non-law-abiding" behavior. There is a high degree of sensitivity as to where each person stands in relation to these two classes of activity. Whereas in the middle class community a major dimension for evaluating a person's status is "achievement" and its external symbols, in the lower class personal status is very frequently gauged along the law-abiding–non-law-abiding dimension. A mother will evaluate the suitability of her daughter's boyfriend less on the basis of his achievement potential than on the basis of his innate "trouble" potential. This sensitive awareness of the opposition of "trouble-producing" and "non-trouble-producing" behavior represents both a major basis for deriving status distinctions and an internalized conflict potential for the individual.

As in the case of other focal concerns, which of two perceived alternatives—"law-abiding" or "non-law-abiding"—is valued varies according to the individual and the circumstances; in many instances there is an overt commitment to the "law-abiding" alternative, but a covert commitment to the "non-law-abiding." In certain situations, "getting into trouble" is overtly recognized as prestige-conferring; for example, membership in certain adult and adolescent primary groupings ("gangs") is contingent on having demonstrated an explicit commitment to the law-violating alternative. It is most important to note that the choice between "law-abiding" and "non-law-abiding" behavior is still a choice *within* lower class culture; the distinction between the policeman and the criminal, the outlaw and the sheriff, involves primarily this one dimension; in other respects they have a high community of interests. Not infrequently brothers raised in an identical cultural milieu will become police and criminals respectively.

For a substantial segment of the lower class population "getting into trouble" is not in itself overtly defined as prestige-conferring, but is implicitly recognized as a means to other valued ends, e.g., the covertly valued desire to be "cared for" and subject to external constraint, or the overtly valued state of excitement or risk. Very frequently "getting into trouble" is multifunctional and achieves several sets of valued ends.

Toughness

The concept of "toughness" in lower class culture represents a compound combination of qualities or states. Among its most important components are physical prowess, evidenced both by demonstrated possession of strength and endurance and by athletic skill; "masculinity," symbolized by a distinctive complex of acts and avoidances (bodily tattooing, absence of sentimentality, nonconcern with "art" or "literature," conceptualization of women as conquest objects, etc.); and bravery in the face of physical threat. The model for the "tough guy"—hard, fearless, undemonstrative, skilled in physical combat—is represented by the movie gangster of the thirties, the "private eye," and the movie cowboy.

The genesis of the intense concern over "toughness" in lower class culture is probably related to the fact that a significant proportion of lower class males are reared in a predominantly female household and lack a consistently present male figure with whom to identify and from whom to learn essential components of a "male" role. Since women serve as a primary object of identification during preadolescent years, the almost obsessive lower class concern with "masculinity" probably resembles a type of compulsive reaction-formation. A concern over homosexuality runs like a persistent thread through lower class culture. This is manifested by the institutionalized practice of baiting "queers," often accompanied by violent physical attacks, an expressed contempt for "softness" or frills, and the use of the local term for "homosexual" as a generalized pejorative epithet (e.g., higher class individuals or upwardly mobile peers are frequently characterized as "fags" or "queers"). The distinction between "overt" and "covert" orientation to aspects of an area of concern is especially important in regard to "toughness." A positive overt evaluation of behavior defined as "effeminate" would be out of the question for a lower class male; however, built into lower class culture is a range of devices which permit men to adopt behaviors and concerns which in other cultural milieux fall within the province of women, and at the same time to be defined as "tough" and manly. For example, lower class men can be professional short-order cooks in a diner and still be regarded as "tough." The highly intimate circumstances of the street-corner gang involve the recurrent expression of strongly affectionate feelings towards other men. Such expressions, however, are disguised as their opposite, taking the form of ostensibly aggressive verbal and physical interaction (kidding, "ranking," roughhousing, etc.).

Smartness

"Smartness," as conceptualized in lower class culture, involves the capacity to outsmart, outfox, outwit, dupe, "take," "con" another or others and the concomitant capacity to avoid being outwitted, "taken," or duped oneself. In its essence, smartness involves the capacity to achieve a valued entity—material goods, personal status—through a maximum use of mental agility and a minimum use of physical effort. This capacity has an extremely long tradition in lower class culture and is highly valued.

Lower class culture can be characterized as "non-intellectual" only if intellectualism is defined specifically in terms of control over a particular body of formally learned knowledge involving "culture" (art, literature, "good" music, etc.), a generalized perspective on the past and present conditions of our own and other societies, and other areas of knowledge imparted by formal educational institutions. This particular type of mental attainment is, in general, overtly disvalued and frequently associated with effeminacy; "smartness" in the lower class sense, however, is highly valued.

The lower class child learns and practices the use of this skill in the street-corner situation. Individuals continually practice duping and outwitting one another through recurrent card games and other forms of gambling, mutual exchanges of insults, and "testing" for mutual "con-ability." Those who demonstrate competence in this skill are accorded considerable prestige. Leadership roles in the corner group are frequently allocated according to demonstrated capacity in the two areas of "smartness" and "toughness"; the ideal leader combines both, but the "smart" leader is often accorded more prestige than the "tough" one—reflecting a general lower class respect for "brains" in the "smartness" sense.[4]

The model of the "smart" person is represented in popular media by the card shark, the professional gambler, the "con" artist, the promoter. A conceptual distinction is made between two kinds of people: "suckers," easy marks, "lushes," dupes, who work for their money and are legitimate targets of exploitation; and sharp operators, the "brainy" ones, who live by their wits and "getting" from the suckers by mental adroitness.

Involved in the syndrome of capacities related to "smartness" is a dominant emphasis in lower class culture on ingenious, aggressive repartee. This skill, learned and practiced in the context of the corner group, ranges in form from the widely prevalent semi-ritualized teasing, kidding, razzing, "ranking," so characteristic of male peer group interaction, to the highly ritualized type of mutual insult interchange known as "the dirty dozens," "the dozens," "playing house," and other terms. This highly patterned cultural form is practiced on its most advanced level in adult male Negro society, but less polished variants are found throughout lower class culture—practiced, for example, by white children, male and female, as young as four or five. In essence, "doin' the dozens" involves two antagonists who vie with each other in the exchange of increasingly inflammatory insults, with incestuous and perverted sexual relations with the mother a dominant theme. In this form of insult interchange, as well as on other less ritualized occasions for joking, semi-serious, and serious mutual invective, a very high premium is placed on ingenuity, hair-trigger responsiveness, inventiveness, and the acute exercise of mental faculties.

Excitement

For many lower class individuals the rhythm of life fluctuates between periods of relatively routine or repetitive activity and sought situations of great emotional stimulation. Many of the most characteristic features of lower class life are related to the search for excitement or "thrill." Involved here are the highly prevalent use of alcohol by both sexes and the widespread use of gambling of all kinds—playing the numbers, betting on horse races, dice, cards. The quest for excitement finds what is perhaps its most vivid expression in the highly patterned practice of the recurrent "night on the town." This practice, designated by various terms in different areas ("honky-tonkin' "; "goin' out on the town"; "bar hoppin' "), involves a patterned set of activities in which alcohol, music, and sexual adventuring are major components. A group or individual sets out to "make the rounds" of various bars or night clubs. Drinking continues progressively throughout the evening. Men seek to "pick up" women, and women play the risky game of entertaining sexual advances. Fights between men involving women, gambling, and claims of physical prowess, in various combinations, are frequent consequences of a night of making the rounds. The explosive potential of this type of adventuring with sex and aggression, frequently leading to "trouble," is semi-explicitly sought by the individual. Since there is always a good likelihood that being out on the town will eventuate in fights, etc., the practice involves elements of sought risk and desired danger.

Counterbalancing the "flirting with danger" aspect of the "excitement" concern is the prevalence in lower class culture of other well-established patterns of activity which involve long periods of relative inaction or passivity. The term "hanging out" in lower class culture refers to extended periods of standing around, often with peer mates, doing what is defined as "nothing," "shooting the breeze," etc. A definite periodicity exists in the pattern of activity relating to the two aspects of the "excitement" dimension. For many lower class individuals the venture into the high-risk world of alcohol, sex, and fighting occurs regularly once a week, with interim periods devoted to accommodating possible consequences of these periods, along with recurrent resolves not to become so involved again.

Fate

Related to the quest for excitement is the concern with fate, fortune, or luck. Here also a distinction is made between two states—being "lucky" or "in luck" and being unlucky or jinxed. Many lower class individuals feel that their lives are subject to a set of forces over which they have relatively little control. These are not directly equated with the supernatural forces of formally organized religion, but relate more to a concept of "destiny," or man as a pawn of magical powers. Not infrequently this often implicit world view is associated with a conception of the ultimate futility of directed effort towards a goal: if the cards are right, or the dice good to you, or if your lucky number comes up, things will go your way; if luck is against you, it's not worth trying. The concept of performing semi-magical rituals so that one's "luck will change" is prevalent; one hopes as a result to move from the state of being "unlucky" to that of being "lucky." The element of fantasy plays an important part in this area. Related to and complementing the notion that "only suckers work" (Smartness) is the idea that once things start going your way, relatively independent of your own effort, all good things will come to you. Achieving great material rewards (big cars, big houses, a roll of cash to flash in a fancy night club), valued in lower class as well as in other parts of American culture, is a recurrent theme in lower class fantasy and folk lore; the cocaine dreams of Willie the Weeper or Minnie the Moocher present the components of this fantasy in vivid detail.

The prevalence in the lower class community of many forms of gambling, mentioned in connection with the "excitement" dimension, is also relevant here. Through cards and pool which involve skill, and thus both "toughness" and "smartness"; or through race horse betting, involving "smartness"; or through playing the numbers, involving predominantly "luck," one may make a big killing with a minimum of directed and persistent effort within conventional occupational channels. Gambling in its many forms illustrates the fact that many of the persistent features of lower class culture are multifunctional—serving a range of desired ends at the same time. Describing some of the incentives behind gambling has involved mention of all of the focal concerns cited so far—Toughness, Smartness, and Excitement, in addition to Fate.

Autonomy

The extent and nature of control over the behavior of the individual—an important concern in most cultures—has a special significance and is distinctively patterned in lower class culture. The discrepancy between what is overtly valued and what is covertly sought is particularly striking in this area. On the overt level there is a strong and frequently expressed resentment of the idea of external controls, restrictions on behavior, and unjust or coercive authority. "No one's gonna push *me* around," or "I'm gonna tell him he can take the job and shove it . . ." are commonly expressed sentiments. Similar explicit attitudes are maintained to systems of behavior-restricting rules, insofar as these are perceived as representing the injunctions and bearing the sanctions of superordinate authority. In addition, in lower class culture a close conceptual connection is made between "authority" and "nurturance." To be restrictively or firmly controlled is to be cared for. Thus the overtly negative evaluation of superordinate authority frequently extends as well to nurturance, care, or protection. The desire for personal independence is often expressed in such terms as "I don't need *nobody* to take care of me. I can take care of myself!" Actual patterns of behavior, however, reveal a marked discrepancy between expressed sentiment and what is covertly valued. Many lower class people appear to seek out highly restrictive social environments wherein stringent external controls are maintained over their behavior. Such institutions as the armed forces, the mental hospital, the disciplinary school, the prison or correctional institution provide environments which incorporate a strict and detailed set of rules, defining and limiting behavior and enforced by an authority system which controls and applies coercive sanctions for deviance from these rules. While under the jurisdiction of such systems, the lower class person generally expresses to his peers continual resentment of the coercive, unjust, and arbitrary exercise of authority. Having been released, or having escaped from these milieux, however, he will often act in such a way as to insure recommitment, or choose recommitment voluntarily after a temporary period of "freedom."

Lower class patients in mental hospitals will exercise considerable ingenuity to insure continued commitment while voicing the desire to get out; delinquent boys will frequently "run" from a correctional institution to activate efforts to return them; to be caught and returned means that one is cared for. Since "being controlled" is equated with "being cared for," attempts are frequently made to "test" the severity or strictness of superordinate authority to see if it remains firm. If intended or executed rebellion produces swift and firm punitive sanctions, the individual is reassured, at the same time that he is complaining bitterly at the injustice of being caught and punished. Some environmental milieux, having been tested in this fashion for the "firmness" of their coercive sanctions, are rejected, ostensibly for being too strict, actually for not being strict enough. This is frequently so in the case of "problematic" behavior by lower class youngsters in the public schools, which generally cannot command the coercive controls implicitly sought by the individual.

A similar discrepancy between what is overtly and covertly desired is found in the area of dependence-independence. The pose of tough rebellious independence often assumed by the lower class person frequently conceals powerful dependency cravings. These are manifested primarily by obliquely expressed resentment when "care" is not forthcoming rather than by expressed satisfaction when it is. The concern over autonomy-dependency is related both to "trouble" and "fate." Insofar as the lower class individual feels that his behavior is controlled by forces which often propel him into "trouble" in the face of an explicit determination to avoid it, there is an implied appeal to "save me from myself." A solution appears to lie in arranging things so that his behavior will be coercively restricted by an externally imposed set of controls strong enough to forcibly restrain his inexplicable inclination to get into trouble. The periodicity observed in connection with the "excitement" dimension is also relevant here; after involvement in trouble-producing behavior (assault, sexual adventure, a "drunk"), the individual will actively seek a locus of imposed control (his wife, prison, a restrictive job); after a given period of subjection to this control, resentment against it mounts, leading to a "break away" and a search for involvement in further "trouble."

FOCAL CONCERNS OF THE LOWER CLASS ADOLESCENT STREET-CORNER GROUP

The one-sex peer group is a highly prevalent and significant structural form in the lower class community. There is a strong probability that the prevalence and stability of this type of unit is directly related to the prevalence of a stabilized type of lower class child-rearing unit—the "female-based" household. This is a nuclear kin unit in which a male parent is either absent from the household, present only sporadically, or, when present, only minimally or inconsistently involved in the support and rearing of children. This unit usually consists of one or more females of childbearing age and their offspring. The females are frequently related to one another by blood or marriage ties, and the unit often includes two or more generations of women, e.g., the mother and/or aunt of the principal childbearing female.

The nature of social groupings in the lower class community may be clarified if we make the assumption that it is the *one-sex peer unit* rather than the two-parent family unit which represents the most significant relational unit for both sexes in lower class communities. Lower class society may be pictured as comprising a set of age-graded one-sex groups which constitute the major psychic focus and reference group for those over twelve or thirteen. Men and women of mating age leave these groups periodically to form temporary marital alliances, but these lack stability, and after varying periods of "trying out" the two-sex family arrangement, they gravitate back to the more "comfortable" one-sex grouping, whose members exert strong pressure on the individual *not* to disrupt the group by adopting a two-sex household pattern of life.[5] Membership in a stable and solidary peer unit is vital to the lower class individual precisely to the extent to which a range of essential functions—psychological, educational, and others—are not provided by the "family" unit.

The adolescent street-corner group represents the adolescent variant of this lower class structural form. What has been called the "delinquent gang" is one subtype of this form, defined on the basis of frequency of participation in law-violating activity; this subtype should not be considered a legitimate unit of study per se, but rather as one particular variant of the adolescent street-corner group. The "hanging" peer group is a unit of particular importance for the adolescent male. In many cases it is the most stable and solidary primary group he has ever belonged to; for boys reared in female-based households the corner group provides the first real opportunity to learn essential aspects of the male role in the context of peers facing similar problems of sex-role identification.

The form and functions of the adolescent corner group operate as a selective mechanism in recruiting members. The activity patterns of the group require a high level of intragroup solidarity; individual members must possess a good capacity for subordinating individual desires to general group interests as well as the capacity for intimate and persisting interaction. Thus highly "disturbed" individuals, or those who cannot tolerate consistently imposed sanctions on "deviant" behavior cannot remain accepted members; the group itself will extrude those whose behavior exceeds limits defined as "normal." This selective process produces a type of group whose members possess, to an unusually high degree, both the *capacity* and *motivation* to conform to perceived cultural norms, so that the nature of the system of norms and values oriented to is a particularly influential component of motivation.

Focal concerns of the male adolescent corner group are those of the general cultural milieu in which it functions. As would be expected, the relative weighting and importance of these concerns pattern somewhat differently for adolescents than for adults. The nature of this patterning centers around two additional "concerns" of particular importance to this group—concern with "belonging," and with "status." These may be conceptualized as being on a higher level of abstraction than concerns previously cited, since "status" and "belonging" are achieved *via* cited concern areas of Toughness, etc.

Belonging

Since the corner group fulfills essential functions for the individual, being a member in good standing of the group is of vital importance for its members. A continuing concern over who is "in" and who is not involves the citation and detailed discussion of highly refined criteria for "in-group" membership. The phrase "he hangs with us" means "he is accepted as a member in good standing by current consensus";

conversely, "he don't hang with us" means he is not so accepted. One achieves "belonging" primarily by demonstrating knowledge of and determination to adhere to the system of standards and valued qualities defined by the group. One maintains membership by acting in conformity with valued aspects of Toughness, Smartness, Autonomy, etc. In those instances where conforming to norms of this reference group at the same time violates norms of other reference groups (e.g., middle class adults, institutional "officials"), immediate reference group norms are much more compelling since violation risks invoking the group's most powerful sanction: exclusion.

Status

In common with most adolescents in American society, the lower class corner group manifests a dominant concern with "status." What differentiates this type of group from others, however, is the particular set of criteria and weighting thereof by which "status" is defined. In general, status is achieved and maintained by demonstrated possession of the valued qualities of lower class culture—Toughness, Smartness, expressed resistance to authority, daring, etc. It is important to stress once more that the individual orients to these concerns *as they are defined within lower class society*; e.g., the status-conferring potential of "smartness" in the sense of scholastic achievement generally ranges from negligible to negative.

The concern with "status" is manifested in a variety of ways. Intragroup status is a continued concern and is derived and tested constantly by means of a set of status-ranking activities; the intragroup "pecking order" is constantly at issue. One gains status within the group by demonstrated superiority in Toughness (physical prowess, bravery, skill in athletics and games such as pool and cards), Smartness (skill in repartee, capacity to "dupe" fellow group members), and the like. The term "ranking," used to refer to the pattern of intragroup aggressive repartee, indicates awareness of the fact that this is one device for establishing the intragroup status hierarchy.

The concern over status in the adolescent corner group involves in particular the component of "adultness," the intense desire to be seen as "grown up," and a corresponding aversion to "kid stuff." "Adult" status is defined less in terms of the assumption of "adult" responsibility than in terms of certain external symbols of adult status—a car, ready cash, and, in particular, a perceived "freedom" to drink, smoke, and gamble as one wishes and to come and go without external restrictions. The desire to be seen as "adult" is often a more significant component of much involvement in illegal drinking, gambling, and automobile driving than the explicit enjoyment of these acts as such.

The intensity of the corner group member's desire to be seen as "adult" is sufficiently great that he feels called upon to demonstrate qualities associated with adultness (Toughness, Smartness, Autonomy) to a much greater degree than a lower class adult. This means that he will seek out and utilize those avenues to these qualities which he perceives as available with greater intensity than an adult and less regard for their "legitimacy." In this sense the adolescent variant of lower class culture represents a maximization or an intensified manifestation of many of its most characteristic features.

Concern over status is also manifested in reference to other street-corner groups. The term "rep" used in this regard is especially significant and has broad connotations. In its most frequent and explicit connotation, "rep" refers to the "toughness" of the corner group as a whole relative to that of other groups; a "pecking order" also exists among the several corner groups in a given interactional area, and there is a common perception that the safety or security of the group and all its members depends on maintaining a solid "rep" for toughness vis-a-vis other groups. This motive is most frequently advanced as a reason for involvement in gang fights: "We *can't* chicken out on this fight; our rep would be shot!"; this implies that the group would be relegated to the bottom of the status ladder and become a helpless and recurrent target of external attack.

On the other hand, there is implicit in the concept of "rep" the recognition that "rep" has or may have a dual basis—corresponding to the two aspects of the "trouble" dimension. It is recognized that group as well as individual status can be based on both "law-abiding" and "law-violating" behavior. The situational resolution of the persisting conflict between the "law-abiding" and "law-violating" bases of status comprises a vital set of dynamics in determining whether a "delinquent" mode of behavior will be adopted by a group, under what circumstances, and how persistently. The determinants of this choice are evidently highly complex and fluid, and rest on a range of factors including the presence and perceptual immediacy of different community reference-group loci (e.g., professional criminals, police, clergy, teachers, settlement house workers), the personality structures and "needs" of group members, the presence in the community of social work, recreation, or educational programs which can facilitate utilization of the "law-abiding" basis of status, and so on.

What remains constant is the critical importance of "status" both for the members of the group as individuals and for the group as a whole insofar as members perceive their individual destinies as linked to the destiny of the group, and the fact that action geared to attain status is much more acutely oriented to the fact of status itself than to the legality or illegality, morality or immorality of the means used to achieve it.

LOWER CLASS CULTURE AND THE MOTIVATION OF DELINQUENT BEHAVIOR

The customary set of activities of the adolescent street-corner group includes activities which are in violation of laws and ordinances of the legal code. Most of these center around assault and theft of various types (the gang fight; auto theft; assault on an individual; petty pilfering and shoplifting; "mugging"; pocketbook theft). Members of street-corner gangs are well aware of the law-violating nature of these acts; they are not psychopaths, or physically or mentally "defective"; in fact, since the corner group supports and enforces a rigorous set of standards which demand a high degree of fitness and personal competence, it tends to recruit from the most "able" members of the community.

Why, then, is the commission of crimes a customary feature of gang activity? The most general answer is that the commission of crimes by members of adolescent street-corner groups is motivated primarily by the attempt to achieve ends, states, or conditions which are valued and to avoid those that are disvalued within their most meaningful cultural milieu, through those culturally available avenues which appear as the most feasible means of attaining those ends.

The operation of these influences is well illustrated by the gang fight—a prevalent and characteristic type of corner group delinquency. This type of activity comprises a highly stylized and culturally patterned set of sequences. Although details vary under different circumstances, the following events are generally included. A member or several members of group A "trespass" on the claimed territory of group B. While there they commit an act or acts which group B defines as a violation of their rightful privileges, an affront to their honor, or a challenge to their "rep." Frequently this act involves advances to a girl associated with group B; it may occur at a dance or party; sometimes the mere act of "trespass" is seen as deliberate provocation. Members of group B then assault members of group A, if they are caught while still in B's territory. Assaulted members of group A return to their "home" territory and recount to members of their group details of the incident, stressing the insufficient nature of the provocation ("I just *looked* at her! Hardly even said anything!"), and the unfair circumstances of the assault ("About *twenty* guys jumped just the *two* of us!"). The highly colored account is acutely inflammatory; group A, perceiving its honor violated and its "rep" threatened, feels obligated to retaliate in force. Sessions of detailed planning now occur; allies are recruited if the size of group A and its potential allies appears to necessitate larger numbers; strategy is plotted, and messengers dispatched. Since the prospect of a gang fight is frightening to even the "toughest" group members, a constant rehearsal of the provocative incident or incidents and declamations of the essentially evil nature of the opponents accompany the planning process to bolster possibly weakening motivation to fight. The excursion into "enemy" territory sometimes results in a full-scale fight; more often group B cannot be found, or the police appear and stop the fight, "tipped off" by an anonymous informant. When this occurs, group members express disgust and disappointment; secretly there is much relief; their honor has been avenged without incurring injury; often the anonymous tipster is a member of one of the involved groups.

The basic elements of this type of delinquency are sufficiently stabilized and recurrent as to constitute an essentially ritualized pattern, resembling both in structure and expressed motives for action classic forms such as the European "duel," the American Indian tribal war, and the Celtic clan feud. Although the arousing and "acting out" of individual aggressive emotions are inevitably involved in the gang fight, neither its form nor motivational dynamics can be adequately handled within a predominantly personality-focused frame of reference.

It would be possible to develop in considerable detail the processes by which the commission of a range of illegal acts is either explicitly supported by, implicitly demanded by, or not materially inhibited by factors relating to the focal concerns of lower class culture. In place of such a development, the following three statements condense in general terms the operation of these processes:

1. Following cultural practices which comprise essential elements of the total life pattern of lower class culture automatically violates certain legal norms.

2. In instances where alternate avenues to similar objectives are available, the non-law-abiding avenue frequently provides a relatively greater and more immediate return for a relatively smaller investment of energy.

3. The "demanded" response to certain situations recurrently engendered within lower class culture involves the commission of illegal acts.

The primary thesis of this paper is that the dominant component of the motivation of "delinquent" behavior engaged in by members of lower class corner groups involves a positive effort to achieve states, conditions, or qualities valued within the actor's most significant cultural milieu. If "conformity to immediate reference group values" is the major component of motivation of "delinquent" behavior by gang members, why is such behavior frequently referred to as negativistic, malicious, or rebellious? Albert Cohen, for example, in *Delinquent Boys* (Glencoe, Ill.: Free Press, 1955) describes behavior which violates school rules as comprising elements of "active spite and malice, contempt and ridicule, challenge and defiance." He ascribes to the gang "keen delight in terrorizing 'good' children, and in general making themselves obnoxious to the virtuous." A recent national conference on social work with "hard-to-reach" groups characterized lower class corner groups as "youth groups in conflict with the culture of their [sic] communities." Such characterizations are obviously the result of taking the middle class community and its institutions as an implicit point of reference.

A large body of systematically interrelated attitudes, practices, behaviors, and values characteristic of lower class culture are designed to support and maintain the basic features of the lower class way of life. In areas where these differ from features of middle class culture, action oriented to the achievement and maintenance of the lower class system may violate norms of middle class culture and be perceived as deliberately nonconforming or malicious by an observer strongly cathected to middle class norms. This does not mean, however, that violation of the middle class norm is the dominant component of motivation; it is a by-product of action primarily oriented to the lower class system. The standards of lower class culture cannot be seen merely as a reverse function of middle class culture—as middle class standards "turned upside down"; lower class culture is a distinctive tradition many centuries old with an integrity of its own.

From the viewpoint of the acting individual, functioning within a field of well-structured cultural forces, the relative impact of "conforming" and "rejective" elements in the motivation of gang delinquency is weighted preponderantly on the conforming side. Rejective or rebellious elements are inevitably involved, but their influence during the actual commission of delinquent acts is relatively small compared to the influence of pressures to achieve what is valued by the actor's most immediate reference groups. Expressed awareness by the actor of the element of rebellion often represents only that aspect of motivation of which he is explicitly conscious; the deepest and most compelling components of motivation—adherence to highly meaningful group standards of Toughness, Smartness, Excitement, etc.—are often unconsciously patterned. No cultural pattern as well established as the practice of illegal acts by members of lower class corner groups could persist if buttressed primarily by negative, hostile, or rejective motives; its principal motivational support, as in the case of any persisting cultural tradition, derives from a positive effort to achieve what is valued within that tradition, and to conform to its explicit and implicit norms.

Notes

1. The complex issues involved in deriving a definition of "delinquency" cannot be discussed here. The term "delinquent" is used in this paper to characterize behavior or acts committed by individuals within specified age limits which if known to official authorities could result in legal action. The concept of a "delinquent" individual has little or no utility in the approach used here; rather, specified types of *acts* which may be committed rarely or frequently by few or many individuals are characterized as "delinquent."

2. A three-year research project is being financed under National Institutes of Health Grant M-1414 and administered through the Boston University School of Social Work. The primary research effort has subjected all collected material to a uniform data-coding process. All information bearing on some seventy areas of behavior (behavior in reference to school, police, theft, assault, sex, collective athletics, etc.) is extracted from the records, recorded on coded data cards, and filed under relevant categories. Analysis of these data aims to ascertain the actual nature of customary behavior in these areas and the extent to which the social-work effort was able to effect behavioral changes.

3. Between 40 and 60 percent of all Americans are directly influenced by lower class culture, with about 15 percent, or twenty-five million, comprising the "hard core" lower class group—defined primarily by its use of the "female-based" household as the basic form of child-rearing unit and of the "serial monogamy" mating pattern as the primary form of marriage. The term "lower class culture" as used here refers most specifically to the way of life of the "hard core" group; systematic research in this area would probably reveal at least four to six major subtypes of lower class culture, for some of which the "concerns" presented here would be differently weighted, especially for those subtypes in which "law-abiding" behavior has a high overt valuation. It is impossible within the compass of this short paper to make the finer intracultural distinctions which a more accurate presentation would require.

4. The "brains-brawn" set of capacities are often paired in lower class folk lore or accounts of lower class life, e.g., "Brer Fox" and "Brer Bear" in the Uncle Remus stories, or George and Lennie in "Of Mice and Men."

5. Further data on the female-based household unit (estimated as comprising about 15 percent of all American "families") and the role of one-sex groupings in lower class culture are contained in Walter B. Miller, Implications of Urban Lower Class Culture for Social Work. *Social Service Review*, 1959, 33, No. 3.

17. Social Structure and Anomie

ROBERT K. MERTON

There persists a notable tendency in sociological theory to attribute the malfunctioning of social structure primarily to those of man's imperious biological drives which are not adequately restrained by social control. In this view, the social order is solely a device for "impulse management" and the "social processing" of tensions. These impulses which break through social control, be it noted, are held to be biologically derived. Nonconformity is assumed to be rooted in original nature.[1] Conformity is by implication the result of a utilitarian calculus or unreasoned conditioning. This point of view, whatever its other deficiencies, clearly begs one question. It provides no basis for determining the nonbiological conditions which induce deviations from prescribed patterns of conduct. In this paper, it will be suggested that certain phases of social structure generate the circumstances in which infringement of social codes constitutes a "normal" response.[2]

The conceptual scheme to be outlined is designed to provide a coherent, systematic approach to the study of socio-cultural sources of deviate behavior. Our primary aim lies in discovering how some social structures *exert a definite pressure* upon certain persons in the society to engage in nonconformist rather than conformist conduct. The many ramifications of the scheme cannot all be discussed; the problems mentioned outnumber those explicitly treated.

Among the elements of social and cultural structure, two are important for our purposes. These are analytically separable although they merge imperceptibly in concrete situations. The first consists of culturally defined goals, purposes, and interests. It comprises a frame of aspirational reference. These goals are more or less integrated and involve varying degrees of prestige and sentiment. They constitute a basic, but not the exclusive, component of what Linton aptly has called "designs for group living." Some of these cultural aspirations are related to the original drives of man, but they are not determined by them. The second phase of the social structure defines, regulates, and controls the acceptable modes of achieving these goals. Every social group invariably couples its scale of desired ends with moral or institutional regulation of permissible and required procedures for attaining these ends. These regulatory norms and moral imperatives do not necessarily coincide with technical or efficiency norms. Many procedures which form the standpoint of *particular individuals* would be most efficient in securing desired values, e.g., illicit oil-stock schemes, theft, fraud, are ruled out of the institutional area of permitted conduct. The choice of expedients is limited by the institutional norms.

To say that these two elements, culture goals and institutional norms, operate jointly

227

is not to say that the ranges of alternative behaviors and aims bear some constant relation to one another. The emphasis upon certain goals may vary independently of the degree of emphasis upon institutional means. There may develop a disproportionate, at times, a virtually exclusive, stress upon the value of specific goals, involving relatively slight concern with the institutionally appropriate modes of attaining these goals. The limiting case in this direction is reached when the range of alternative procedures is limited only by technical rather than institutional considerations. Any and all devices which promise attainment of the all-important goal would be permitted in this hypothetical polar case.[3] This constitutes one type of cultural malintegration. A second polar type is found in groups where activities originally conceived as instrumental are transmuted into ends in themselves. The original purposes are forgotten, and ritualistic adherence to institutionally prescribed conduct becomes virtually obsessive.[4] Stability is largely ensured while change is flouted. The range of alternative behaviors is severely limited. There develops a tradition-bound, sacred society characterized by neophobia. The occupational psychosis of the bureaucrat may be cited as a case in point. Finally, there are the intermediate types of groups where a balance between culture goals and institutional means is maintained. These are the significantly integrated and relatively stable, though changing, groups.

An effective equilibrium between the two phases of the social structure is maintained as long as satisfactions accrue to individuals who conform to both constraints, viz., satisfactions from the achievement of the goals and satisfactions emerging directly from the institutionally canalized modes of striving to attain these ends. Success, in such equilibrated cases, is twofold. Success is reckoned in terms of the product and in terms of the process, in terms of the outcome and in terms of activities. Continuing satisfactions must derive from sheer *participation* in a competitive order as well as from eclipsing one's competitors if the order itself is to be sustained. The occasional sacrifices involved in institutionalized conduct must be compensated by socialized rewards. The distribution of statuses and roles through competition must be so organized that positive incentives for conformity to roles and adherence to status obligations are provided *for every position* within the distributive order. Aberrant conduct, therefore, may be viewed as a symptom of dissociation between culturally defined aspirations and socially structured means.

Of the types of groups which result from the independent variation of the two phases of the social structure, we shall be primarily concerned with the first, namely, that involving a disproportionate accent on goals. This statement must be recast in a proper perspective. In no group is there an absence of regulatory codes governing conduct, yet groups do vary in the degree to which these folkways, mores, and institutional controls are effectively integrated with the more diffuse goals which are part of the culture matrix. Emotional convictions may cluster about the complex of socially acclaimed ends, meanwhile shifting their support from the culturally defined implementation of these ends. As we shall see, certain aspects of the social structure may generate countermores and antisocial behavior precisely because of differential emphases on goals and regulations. In the extreme case, the latter may be so vitiated by the goal-emphasis that the range of behavior is limited only by considerations of technical expediency. The sole significant question then becomes, which available means is most efficient in netting the socially approved value?[5] The technically most feasible procedure, whether legitimate or not, is preferred to the institutionally prescribed conduct. As this process continues, the integration of the society becomes tenuous and anomie ensues.

Thus, in competitive athletics, when the aim of victory is shorn of its institutional trappings and success in contests becomes construed as "winning the game" rather than "winning through circumscribed modes of activity," a premium is implicitly set upon the use of illegitimate but technically efficient means. The star of the opposing football team is surreptitiously slugged; the wrestler furtively incapacitates his opponent through ingenious but illicit techniques; university alumni covertly subsidize "students" whose talents are largely confined to the athletic field. The emphasis on the goal has so attenuated the satisfactions deriving from sheer participation in the competitive activity that these satisfactions are virtually confined to a successful outcome. Through the same process, tension generated by the desire to win in a poker game is relieved by successfully dealing oneself four aces, or, when the cult of success has become completely dominant, by sagaciously shuffling the cards in a game of solitaire. The faint twinge of uneasiness in the last instance and the surreptitious nature of public delicts indicate clearly that the institutional rules of the game are *known* to those who evade them, but that the emotional supports of these rules are largely vitiated by cultural exaggeration of the success-goal.[6] They are microcosmic images of the social macrocosm.

Of course, this process is not restricted to the realm of sport. The process whereby exaltation of the end generates a *literal demoralization*, i.e., a deinstitutionalization, of the means is one which characterizes many[7] groups in which the two phases of the social structure are not highly integrated. The extreme emphasis upon the accumulation of wealth as a symbol of success[8] in our own society militates against the completely effective control of institutionally regulated modes of acquiring a fortune.[9] Fraud, corruption, vice, crime, in short, the entire catalogue of proscribed behavior, becomes increasingly common when the emphasis on the *culturally induced* success-goal becomes divorced from a coordinated institutional emphasis. This observation is of crucial theoretical importance in examining the doctrine that antisocial behavior most frequently derives from biological drives breaking through the restraints imposed by society. The difference is one between a strictly utilitarian interpretation which conceives man's ends as random and an analysis which finds these ends deriving from the basic values of the culture.[10]

Our analysis can scarcely stop at this juncture. We must turn to other aspects of the social structure if we are to deal with the social genesis of the varying rates and types of deviate behavior characteristic of different societies. Thus far, we have sketched three ideal types of social order constituted by distinctive patterns of relations between culture ends and means. Turning from these types of *culture patterning*, we find five logically possible, alternative modes of adjustment or adaptation *by individuals* within the culture-bearing society or group.[11] These are schematically presented in the following table, where (+) signifies "acceptance," (−) signifies "elimination," and (±) signifies "rejection and substitution of new goals and standards."

	Culture Goals	Institutionalized Means
I. Conformity	+	+
II. Innovation	+	−
III. Ritualism	−	+
IV. Retreatism	−	−
V. Rebellion[12]	±	±

Our discussion of the relation between these alternative responses and other phases of the social structure must be prefaced by the observation that persons may shift from one alternative to another as they engage in different social activities. These categories refer to role adjustments in specific situations, not to personality *in toto*. To treat the development of this process in various spheres of conduct would introduce a complexity unmanageable within the confines of this paper. For this reason, we shall be concerned primarily with economic activity in the broad sense, "the production, exchange, distribution, and consumption of goods and services" in our competitive society, wherein wealth has taken on a highly symbolic cast. Our task is to search out some of the factors which exert pressure upon individuals to engage in certain of these logically possible alternative responses. This choice, as we shall see, is far from random.

In every society, Adaptation I (conformity to both culture goals and means) is the most common and widely diffused. Were this not so, the stability and continuity of the society could not be maintained. The mesh of expectancies which constitutes every social order is sustained by the modal behavior of its members falling within the first category. Conventional role behavior oriented toward the basic values of the group is the rule rather than the exception. It is this fact alone which permits us to speak of a human aggregate as comprising a group or society.

Conversely, Adaptation IV (rejection of goals and means) is the least common. Persons who "adjust" (or maladjust) in this fashion are, strictly speaking, *in* the society but not *of* it. Sociologically, these constitute the true "aliens." Not sharing the common frame of orientation, they can be included within the societal population merely in a fictional sense. In this category are *some* of the activities of psychotics, psychoneurotics, chronic autists, pariahs, outcasts, vagrants, vagabonds, tramps, chronic drunkards, and drug addicts.[13] These have relinquished, in certain spheres of activity, the culturally defined goals, involving complete aim-inhibition in the polar case, and their adjustments are not in accord with institutional norms. This is not to say that in some cases the source of their behavioral adjustments is not in part the very social structure which they have in effect repudiated nor that their very existence within a social area does not constitute a problem for the socialized population.

This mode of "adjustment" occurs, as far as structural sources are concerned, when both the culture goals and institutionalized procedures have been assimilated thoroughly by the individual and imbued with affect and high positive value, but where those institutionalized procedures which promise a measure of successful attainment of the goals are not available to the individual. In such instances, there results a twofold mental conflict insofar as the moral obligation for adopting institutional means conflicts with the pressure to resort to illegitimate means (which may attain the goal) and inasmuch as the individual is shut off from means which are both legitimate *and* effective. The competitive order is maintained, but the frustrated and handicapped individual who cannot cope with this order drops out. Defeatism, quietism, and resignation are manifested in escape mechanisms which ultimately lead the individual to "escape" from the requirements of the society. It is an expedient which arises from continued failure to attain the goal by legitimate measures and from an inability to adopt the illegitimate route because of internalized prohibitions and institutionalized compulsives, *during which process the supreme value of the success-goal has as yet not been renounced.* The conflict is resolved by eliminating *both* precipitating elements, the goals and means. The escape is complete, the conflict is eliminated, and the individual is associated.

Be it noted that where frustration derives from the inaccessibility of effective institutional means for attaining economic or any other type of highly valued "success," that Adaptations II, III, and V (innovation, ritualism, and rebellion) are also possible. The result will be determined by the particular personality, and thus the *particular* cultural background, involved. Inadequate socialization will result in the innovation response whereby the conflict and frustration are eliminated by relinquishing the institutional means and retaining the success-aspiration; an extreme assimilation of institutional demands will lead to ritualism wherein the goal is dropped as beyond one's reach but conformity to the mores persists; and rebellion occurs when emancipation from the reigning standards, due to frustration or to marginalist perspectives, leads to the attempt to introduce a "new social order."

Our major concern is with the illegitimacy adjustment. This involves the use of conventionally proscribed but frequently effective means of attaining at least the simulacrum of culturally defined success—wealth, power, and the like. As we have seen, this adjustment occurs when the individual has assimilated the cultural emphasis on success without equally internalizing the morally prescribed norms governing means for its attainment. The question arises, Which phases of our social structure predispose toward this mode of adjustment? We may examine a concrete instance, effectively analyzed by Lohman,[14] which provides a clue to the answer. Lohman has shown that specialized areas of vice in the near north side of Chicago constitute a "normal" response to a situation where the cultural emphasis upon pecuniary success has been absorbed, but where there is little access to conventional and legitimate means for attaining such success. The conventional occupational opportunities of persons in this area are almost completely limited to manual labor. Given our cultural stigmatization of manual labor, and its correlate, the prestige of white-collar work, it is clear that the result is a strain toward innovational practices. The limitation of opportunity to unskilled labor and the resultant low income cannot compete *in terms of conventional standards of achievement* with the high income from organized vice.

For our purposes, this situation involves two important features. First, such antisocial behavior is in a sense "called forth" by certain conventional values of the culture *and* by the class structure involving differential access to the approved opportunities for legitimate, prestige-bearing pursuit of the culture goals. The lack of high integration between the means-and-end elements of the cultural pattern and the particular class structure combine to favor a heightened frequency of antisocial conduct in such groups. The second consideration is of equal significance. Recourse to the first of the alternative responses, legitimate effort, is limited by the fact that actual advance toward desired success-symbols through conventional channels is, despite our persisting open-class ideology,[15] relatively rare and difficult for those handicapped by little formal education and few economic resources. The dominant pressure of group standards of success is, therefore, on the gradual attenuation of legitimate, but by and large ineffective, strivings and the increasing use of illegitimate, but more or less effective, expedients of vice and crime. The cultural demands made on persons in this situation are incompatible. On the one hand, they are asked to orient their conduct toward the prospect of accumulating wealth and on the other, they are largely denied effective opportunities to do so institutionally. The consequences of such structural inconsistency are psychopathological personality, and/or antisocial conduct, and/or revolutionary activities. The equilibrium between culturally designated means and ends becomes highly unstable with the progressive emphasis on attaining the prestige-laden ends by any means whatsoever. Within this context, Capone represents the triumph of amoral intelligence over morally prescribed "failure," when the channels of vertical mobility are closed or narrowed[16] *in a society which places a high premium on economic affluence and social ascent for* all *its members.*[17]

This last qualification is of primary importance. It suggests that other phases of the social structure besides the extreme emphasis on pecuniary success must be considered if we are to understand the social sources of antisocial behavior. A high frequency of deviate behavior is not generated simply by "lack of opportunity" or by this exaggerated pecuniary emphasis. A comparatively rigidified class structure, a feudalistic or caste order, may limit such opportunities far beyond the point which obtains in our society today. It is only when a system of cultural values extols, virtually above all else, certain *common* symbols of success *for the population at large* while its social structure rigorously restricts or completely eliminates access to approved modes of acquiring these symbols *for a considerable part of the same population* that antisocial behavior ensues on a considerable scale. In other words, our egalitarian ideology denies by implication the existence of noncompeting groups and individuals in the pursuit of pecuniary success. The same body of success-symbols is held to be desirable for all. These goals are held to *transcend class lines*, not to be bounded by them, yet the actual social organization is such that there exist class differentials in the accessibility of these *common* success-symbols. Frustration and thwarted aspiration lead to the search for avenues of escape from a culturally induced intolerable situation; or unrelieved ambition may eventuate in illicit attempts to acquire the dominant values.[18] The American stress on pecuniary success and ambitiousness for all thus invites exaggerated anxieties, hostilities, neuroses, and antisocial behavior.

This theoretical analysis may go far toward explaining the varying correlations between crime and poverty.[19] Poverty is not an isolated variable. It is one in a complex of interdependent social and cultural variables. When viewed in such a context, it represents quite different states of affairs. Poverty as such, and consequent limitation of opportunity, are not sufficient to induce a conspicuously high rate of criminal behavior. Even the often mentioned "poverty in the midst of plenty" will not necessarily lead to this result. Only insofar as poverty and associated disadvantages in competition for the culture values approved for *all* members of the society are linked with the assimilation of a cultural emphasis on monetary accumulation as a symbol of success is antisocial conduct a "normal" outcome. Thus, poverty is less highly correlated with crime in southeastern Europe than in the United States. The possibilities of vertical mobility in these European areas would seem to be fewer than in this country, so that neither poverty *per se* nor its association with limited opportunity is sufficient to account for the varying correlations. It is only when the full configuration is considered, poverty, limited opportunity, and a commonly shared system of success-symbols, that we can explain the higher association between poverty and crime in our society than in others where rigidified class structure is coupled with *differential class symbols of achievement.*

In societies such as our own, then, the pressure of prestige-bearing success tends to eliminate the effective social constraint over means employed to this end. "The-end-justifies-the-means" doctrine becomes a guiding tenet for action when the cultural structure unduly exalts the end and the social organization unduly limits possible recourse to approved means. Otherwise put, this notion and associated behavior reflect a lack of cultural coordination. In international relations, the effects of this lack of integration are notoriously apparent. An emphasis upon national power is not readily coordinated with an inept organization of legitimate, i.e., internationally defined and accepted, means for attaining this goal. The result is a tendency toward the abrogation of international law, treaties become scraps of paper, "undeclared warfare" serves as a technical evasion, the bombing of civilian populations is rationalized,[20] just as the same societal situation induces the same sway of illegitimacy among individuals.

The social order we have described necessarily produces this "strain toward dissolution." The pressure of such an order is upon outdoing one's competitors. The choice of means within the ambit of institutional control will persist as long as the sentiments supporting a competitive system, i.e., deriving from the possibility of outranking competitors and hence enjoying the favorable response of others, are distributed throughout the entire system of activities and are not confined merely to the final result. A stable social structure demands a balanced distribution of affect among its various segments. When there occurs a shift of emphasis from the satisfactions deriving from competition itself to almost exclusive concern with successful competition, the resultant stress leads to the breakdown of the regulatory structure.[21] With the resulting attenuation of the institutional imperatives, there occurs an approximation of the situation erroneously held by utilitarians to be typical of society generally wherein calculations of advantage and fear of punishment are the sole regulating agencies. In such situations, as Hobbes observed, force and fraud come to constitute the sole virtues in view of their relative efficiency in attaining goals—which were for him, of course, not culturally derived.

It should be apparent that the foregoing discussion is not pitched on a moralistic plane. Whatever the sentiments of the writer or reader concerning the ethical desirability of coordinating the means-and-goals phases of the social structure, one must agree that lack of such coordination leads to anomie. Insofar as one of the most general functions of social organization is to provide a basis for calculability and regularity of behavior, it is increasingly limited in effectiveness as these elements of the structure become dissociated. At the extreme, predictability virtually disappears and what may be properly termed cultural chaos or anomie intervenes.

This statement, being brief, is also incomplete. It has not included an exhaustive treatment of the various structural elements which predispose toward one rather than another of the alternative responses open to individuals; it has neglected, but not denied the relevance of, the factors determining the specific incidence of these responses; it has not enumerated the various concrete responses which are constituted by combinations of specific values of the analytical variables; it has omitted, or included only by implication, any consideration of the social functions performed by illicit responses; it has not tested the full explanatory power of the analytical scheme by examining a large number of group variations in the frequency of deviate and conformist behavior; it has not adequately dealt with rebellious conduct which seeks to refashion the social framework radically; it has not examined the relevance of cultural conflict for an analysis of culture-goal and institutional-means malintegration. It is suggested that these and related problems may be profitably analyzed by this scheme.

Notes

1. E.g., Ernest Jones, *Social Aspects of Psychoanalysis*, 28, London, 1924. If the Freudian notion is a variety of the "original sin" dogma, then the interpretation advanced in this paper may be called the doctrine of "socially derived sin."

2. "Normal" in the sense of a culturally oriented, if not approved, response. This statement does not deny the relevance of biological and personality differences which may be significantly involved in the *incidence* of deviate conduct. Our focus of interest is the social and cultural matrix; hence we abstract from other factors. It is in this sense, I take it, that James S. Plant speaks of the "normal reaction of normal people to abnormal conditions." See his *Personality and the Cultural Pattern*, 248, New York, 1937.

3. Contemporary American culture has been said to tend in this direction. See André Siegfried, *America Comes of Age*, 26–37, New York, 1927. The alleged extreme(?) emphasis on the goals of monetary success and material prosperity leads to dominant concern with technological and social instruments designed to produce the desired result, inasmuch as institutional controls become of secondary importance. In such a situation, innovation flourishes as the *range of means* employed is broadened. In a sense, then, there occurs the paradoxical emergence of "materialists" from an "idealistic" orientation. Cf. Durkheim's analysis of the cultural conditions which predispose toward crime and innovation, both of which are aimed toward efficiency, not moral norms. Durkheim was one of the first to see that "contrairement aux idées courantes le criminel n'apparait plus comme un être radicalement insociable, comme une sorte d'elément parasitaire, de corps étranger et inassimilable, introduit au sein de la société; c'est un agent régulier de la vie sociale." See *Les Règles de la Méthode Sociologique*, 86–89, Paris, 1927.

4. Such ritualism may be associated with a mythology which rationalizes these actions so that they appear to retain their status as means, but the dominant pressure is in the direction of strict ritualistic conformity, irrespective of such rationalizations. In this sense, ritual has proceeded farthest when such rationalizations are not even called forth.

5. In this connection, one may see the relevance of Elton Mayo's paraphrase of the title of Tawney's well-known book. "Actually the problem *is not that of the sickness of an acquisitive society; it is that of the acquisitiveness of a sick society.*" *Human Problems of an Industrial Civilization*, 153, New York, 1933. Mayo deals with the process through which wealth comes to be a symbol of social achievement. He sees this as arising from a state of anomie. We are considering the unintegrated monetary-success goal as an element in producing anomie. A complete analysis would involve both phases of this system of interdependent variables.

6. It is unlikely that interiorized norms are completely eliminated. Whatever residuum persists will induce personality tensions and conflict. The process involves a certain degree of ambivalence. A manifest rejection of the institutional norms is coupled with some latent

retention of their emotional correlates. "Guilt feelings," "sense of sin," "pangs of conscience" are obvious manifestations of this unrelieved tension; symbolic adherence to the nominally repudiated values or rationalizations constitute a more subtle variety of tensional release.

7. "Many," and not all, unintegrated groups, for the reason already mentioned. In groups where the primary emphasis shifts to institutional means, i.e., when the range of alternatives is very limited, the outcome is a type of ritualism rather than anomie.

8. Money has several peculiarities which render it particularly apt to become a symbol of prestige divorced from institutional controls. As Simmel emphasized, money is highly abstract and impersonal. However acquired, through fraud or institutionally, it can be used to purchase the same goods and services. The anonymity of metropolitan culture, in conjunction with this peculiarity of money, permits wealth, the sources of which may be unknown to the community in which the plutocrat lives, to serve as a symbol of status.

9. The emphasis upon wealth as a success-symbol is possibly reflected in the use of the term "fortune" to refer to a stock of accumulated wealth. This meaning becomes common in the late sixteenth century (Spenser and Shakespeare). A similar usage of the Latin *fortuna* comes into prominence during the first century B.C. Both these periods were marked by the rise to prestige and power of the "bourgeoisie."

10. See Kingsley Davis, "Mental Hygiene and the Class Structure," *Psychiatry*, 1928, 1: esp. 62–63; Talcott Parsons, *The Structure of Social Action*, 59–60, New York, 1937.

11. This is a level intermediate between the two planes distinguished by Edward Sapir; namely, culture patterns and personal habit systems. See his "Contribution of Psychiatry to an Understanding of Behavior in Society," *Amer. J. Sociol.*, 1937, 42:862–870.

12. This fifth alternative is on a plane clearly different from that of the others. It represents a *transitional* response which seeks to *institutionalize* new procedures oriented toward revamped cultural goals shared by the members of the society. It thus involves efforts to *change* the existing structure rather than to perform accommodative actions *within* this structure, and introduces additional problems with which we are not at the moment concerned.

13. Obviously, this is an elliptical statement. These individuals may maintain some orientation to the values of their particular differentiated groupings within the larger society or, in part, of the conventional society itself. Insofar as they do so, their conduct cannot be classified in the "passive rejection" category (IV). Nels Anderson's description of the behavior and attitudes of the bum, for example, can readily be recast in terms of our analytical scheme. See *The Hobo*, 93–98, *et passim*, Chicago, 1923.

14. Joseph D. Lohman, "The Participant Observer in Community Studies," *Amer. Sociol. Rev.*, 1937, 2:890–898.

15. The shifting historical role of this ideology is a profitable subject for exploration. The "office-boy-to-president" stereotype was once in approximate accord with the facts. Such vertical mobility was probably more common then than now, when the class structure is more rigid. (See the following note.) The ideology largely persists, however, possibly because it still performs a useful function for maintaining the *status quo*. For insofar as it is accepted by the "masses," it constitutes a useful sop for those who might rebel against the entire structure, were this consoling hope removed. This ideology now serves to lessen the probability of Adaptation V. In short, the role of this notion has changed from that of an approximately valid empirical theorem to that of an ideology, in Mannheim's sense.

16. There is a growing body of evidence, though none of it is clearly conclusive, to the effect that our class structure is becoming rigidified and that vertical mobility is declining. Taussig and Joslyn found that American business leaders are being *increasingly* recruited from the upper ranks of our society. The Lynds have also found a "diminished chance to get ahead" for the working classes in Middletown. Manifestly, these objective changes are not alone significant; the individual's subjective evaluation of the situation is a major determinant of the response. The extent to which this change in opportunity for social mobility has been recognized by the least advantaged classes is still conjectural, although the Lynds present some suggestive materials. The writer suggests that a case in point is the increasing frequency of cartoons which observe in a tragi-comic vein that "my old man says everybody can't be President. He says if ya can get three days a week steady on W.P.A. work ya ain't doin' so bad either." See F.W.

Taussig and C.S. Joslyn, *American Business Leaders*, New York, 1932; R.S. and H.M. Lynd, *Middletown in Transition*, 67 ff., chap. 12, New York, 1937.

17. The role of the Negro in this respect is of considerable theoretical interest. Certain elements of the Negro population have assimilated the dominant caste's values of pecuniary success and social advancement, but they also recognize that social ascent is at present restricted to their own caste almost exclusively. The pressures upon the Negro which would otherwise derive from the structural inconsistencies we have noticed are hence not identical with those upon lower class whites. See Kingsley Davis, *op. cit.*, 63; John Dollard, *Caste and Class in a Southern Town*, 66 ff., New Haven, 1936; Donald Young, *American Minority Peoples*, 581, New York, 1932.

18. The physical coordinates of these processes have been partly established by the experimental evidence concerning *Anspruchsniveaus* and levels of performance. See Kurt Lewin, *Vorsatz, Willie and Bedurfnis*, Berlin, 1926; N.F. Hoppe, "Erfolg und Misserfolg," *Psychol. Forschung*, 1930, 14:1–63; Jerome D. Frank, "Individual Differences in Certain Aspects of the Level of Aspiration," *Amer. J. Psychol.*, 1935, 47:119–128.

19. Standard criminology texts summarize the data in this field. Our scheme of analysis may serve to resolve some of the theoretical contradictions which P.A. Sorokin indicates. For example, "not everywhere nor always do the poor show a greater proportion of crime . . . many poorer countries have had less crime than the richer countries. . . . The [economic] improvement in the second half of the nineteenth century, and the beginning of the twentieth, has not been followed by a decrease of crime." See his *Contemporary Sociological Theories*, 560–561, New York, 1928. The crucial point is, however, that poverty has varying social significance in different social structures, as we shall see. Hence, one would not expect a linear correlation between crime and poverty.

20. See M.W. Royse, *Aerial Bombardment and the International Regulation of War*, New York, 1928.

21. Since our primary concern is with the socio-cultural aspects of this problem, the psychological correlates have been only implicitly considered. See Karen Horney, *The Neurotic Personality of Our Time*, New York, 1937, for a psychological discussion of this process.

18. Differential Opportunity and Delinquent Subcultures

RICHARD A. CLOWARD AND LLOYD E. OHLIN

THE AVAILABILITY OF ILLEGITIMATE MEANS

Social norms are two-sided. A prescription implies the existence of a prohibition, and *vice versa*. To advocate honesty is to demarcate and condemn a set of actions which are dishonest. In other words, norms that define legitimate practices also implicitly define illegitimate practices. One purpose of norms, in fact, is to delineate the boundary between legitimate and illegitimate practices. In setting this boundary, in segregating and classifying various types of behavior, they make us aware not only of behavior that is regarded as right and proper but also of behavior that is said to be wrong and improper. Thus the criminal who engages in theft or fraud does not invent a new way of life; the possibility of employing alternative means is acknowledged, tacitly at least, by the norms of the culture.

This tendency for proscribed alternatives to be implicit in every prescription, and *vice versa*, although widely recognized, is nevertheless a reef upon which many a theory of delinquency has foundered. Much of the criminological literature assumes, for example, that one may explain a criminal act simply by accounting for the individual's readiness to employ illegal alternatives of which his culture, through its norms, has already made him generally aware. Such explanations are quite unsatisfactory, however, for they ignore a host of questions regarding the *relative availability* of illegal alternatives to various potential criminals. The aspiration to be a physician is hardly enough to explain the fact of becoming a physician; there is much that transpires between the aspiration and the achievement. This is no less true of the person who wants to be a successful criminal. Having decided that he "can't make it legitimately," he cannot simply choose among an array of illegitimate means, all equally available to him. . . . it is assumed in the theory of anomie that access to conventional means is differentially distributed, that some individuals, because of their social class, enjoy certain advantages that are denied to those elsewhere in the class structure. For example, there are variations in the degree to which members of various classes are fully exposed to and thus acquire the values, knowledge, and skills that facilitate upward mobility. It should not be startling, therefore, to suggest that there are socially structured variations in the availability of illegitimate means as well. In connection with delinquent subcultures, we shall be concerned principally with differentials in access to illegitimate means within the lower class.

Many sociologists have alluded to differentials in access to illegitimate means without explicitly incorporating this variable into a theory of deviant behavior. This is particularly true of scholars in the "Chicago tradition" of criminology. Two closely related theoretical perspectives emerged from this school. The theory of "cultural transmission," advanced by Clifford R. Shaw and Henry D. McKay, focuses on the development in some urban neighborhoods of a criminal tradition that persists from one generation to another despite constant changes in population.[1] In the theory of "differential association," Edwin H. Sutherland described the processes by which criminal values are taken over by the individual.[2] He asserted that criminal behavior is learned, and that it is learned in interaction with others who have already incorporated criminal values. Thus the first theory stresses the value systems of different areas; the second, the systems of social relationships that facilitate or impede the acquisition of these values.

Scholars in the Chicago tradition, who emphasized the processes involved in learning to be criminal, were actually pointing to differentials in the availability of illegal means—although they did not explicitly recognize this variable in their analysis. This can perhaps best be seen by examining Sutherland's classic work, *The Professional Thief*. "An inclination to steal," according to Sutherland, "is not a sufficient explanation of the genesis of the professional thief."[3] The "self-made" thief, lacking knowledge of the ways of securing immunity from prosecution and similar techniques of defense, "would quickly land in prison; . . . a person can be a professional thief only if he is recognized and received as such by other professional thieves." But recognition is not freely accorded: "Selection and tutelage are the two necessary elements in the process of acquiring recognition as a professional thief. . . . A person cannot acquire recognition as a professional thief until he has had tutelage in professional theft, *and tutelage is given only to a few persons selected from the total population.*" For one thing, "the person must be appreciated by the professional thieves. He must be appraised as having an adequate equipment of wits, front, talking-ability, honesty, reliability, nerve and determination." Furthermore, the aspirant is judged by high standards of performance, for only "a very small percentage of those who start on this process ever reach the stage of professional thief. . . ." Thus motivation and pressures toward deviance do not fully account for deviant behavior any more than motivation and pressures toward conformity account for conforming behavior. The individual must have access to a learning environment and, once having been trained, must be allowed to perform his role. Roles, whether conforming or deviant in content, are not necessarily freely available; access to them depends upon a variety of factors, such as one's socioeconomic position, age, sex, ethnic affiliation, personality characteristics, and the like. The potential thief, like the potential physician, finds that access to his goal is governed by many criteria other than merit and motivation.

What we are asserting is that access to illegitimate roles is not freely available to all, as is commonly assumed. Only those neighborhoods in which crime flourishes as a stable, indigenous institution are fertile criminal learning environments for the young. Because these environments afford integration of different age-levels of offender, selected young people are exposed to "differential association" through which tutelage is provided and criminal values and skills are acquired. To be prepared for the role may not, however, ensure that the individual will ever discharge it. One important limitation is that more youngsters are recruited into these patterns of differential associations than the adult criminal structure can possibly absorb. Since there is a surplus of contenders for these elite positions, criteria and mechanisms of selection must be evolved. Hence a certain proportion of those who aspire may not be permitted to engage in the behavior for which they have prepared themselves.

Thus we conclude that access to illegitimate roles, no less than access to legitimate roles, is limited by both social and psychological factors. We shall here be concerned primarily with socially structured differentials in illegitimate opportunities. Such differentials, we contend, have much to do with the type of delinquent subculture that develops.

LEARNING AND PERFORMANCE STRUCTURES

Our use of the term "opportunities," legitimate or illegitimate, implies access to both learning and performance structures. That is, the individual must have access to appropriate environments for the acquisition of the values and skills associated with the performance of a particular role, and he must be supported in the performance of the role once he has learned it.

Tannenbaum, several decades ago, vividly expressed the point that criminal role performance, no less than conventional role performance, presupposes a patterned set of relationships through which the requisite values and skills are transmitted by established practitioners to aspiring youth:

> It takes a long time to make a good criminal, many years of specialized training and much preparation. But training is something that is given to people. People learn in a community where the materials and the knowledge are to be had. A craft needs an atmosphere saturated with purpose and promise. The community provides the attitudes, the point of view, the philosophy of life, the example, the motive, the contacts, the friendships, the incentives. No child brings those into the world. He finds them here and available for use and elaboration. The community gives the criminal his materials and habits, just as it gives the doctor, the lawyer, the teacher, and the candlestick-maker theirs.[4]

Sutherland systematized this general point of view, asserting that opportunity consists, at least in part, of learning structures. Thus "criminal behavior is learned" and, furthermore, it is learned "in interaction with other persons in a process of communication." However, he conceded that the differential-association theory does not constitute a full explanation of criminal behavior. In a paper circulated in 1944, he noted that "criminal behavior is partially a function of opportunities to commit [i.e., to perform] specific classes of crime, such as embezzlement, bank burglary, or illicit heterosexual intercourse." Therefore, "while opportunity may be partially a function of association with criminal patterns and of the specialized techniques thus acquired, it is not determined entirely in that manner, and consequently differential association is not the sufficient cause of criminal behavior."[5]

To Sutherland, then, illegitimate opportunity included conditions favorable to the performance of a criminal role as well as conditions favorable to the learning of such a role (differential associations). These conditions, we suggest, depend upon certain features of the social structure of the community in which delinquency arises.

We believe that each individual occupies a position in both legitimate and illegitimate opportunity structures. This is a new way of defining the situation. The theory of anomie views the individual primarily in terms of the legitimate opportunity structure. It poses questions regarding differentials in access to legitimate routes to success-goals; at the same time it assumes either that illegitimate avenues to success-goals are freely available or that differentials in their availability are of little significance. This tendency may be seen in the following statement by Merton:

> Several researchers have shown that specialized areas of vice and crime constitute a "normal" response to a situation where the cultural emphasis upon pecuniary success has been absorbed, but where there is little access to conventional and legitimate means for becoming successful. The occupational opportunities of people in these areas are largely confined to manual labor and the lesser white-collar jobs. Given the American stigmatization of manual labor *which has been found to hold rather uniformly for all social classes*, and the absence of realistic opportunities for advancement beyond this level, the result is a marked tendency toward deviant behavior. The status of unskilled labor and the consequent low income cannot readily compete *in terms of established standards of worth* with the promises of power and high income from organized vice, rackets and crime. . . . [Such a situation] leads toward the gradual attenuation of legitimate, but by and large ineffectual, strivings and the increasing use of illegitimate, but more or less effective, expedients.[6]

The cultural-transmission and differential-association tradition, on the other hand, assumes that access to illegitimate means is variable, but it does not recognize the significance of comparable differentials in access to legitimate means. Sutherland's "ninth proposition" in the theory of differential association states:

> *Though criminal behavior is an expression of general needs and values, it is not explained by those general needs and values since non-criminal behavior is an expression of the same needs and values.* Thieves generally steal in order to secure money, but likewise honest laborers work in order to secure money. The attempts by many scholars to explain criminal behavior by general drives and values, such as the happiness principle, striving for social status, the money motive, or frustration, have been and must continue to be futile since they explain lawful behavior as completely as they explain criminal behavior.[7]

In this statement, Sutherland appears to assume that people have equal and free access to legitimate means regardless of their social position. At the very least, he does not treat access to legitimate means as variable. It is, of course, perfectly true that "striving for social status," "the money motive," and other socially approved drives do not fully account for either deviant or conforming behavior. But if goal-oriented behavior occurs under conditions in which there are socially structured obstacles to the satisfaction of these drives by legitimate means, the resulting pressures, we contend, might lead to deviance.

The concept of differential opportunity structures permits us to unite the theory of anomie, which recognizes the concept of differentials in access to legitimate means, and the "Chicago tradition," in which the concept of differentials in access to illegitimate means is implicit. We can now look at the individual, not simply in relation to one or the other system of means, but in relation to both legitimate and illegitimate systems. This approach permits us to ask, for example, how the relative availability of illegitimate opportunities affects the resolution of adjustment problems leading to deviant behavior. We believe that the way in which these problems are resolved may depend upon the kind of support for one or another type of illegitimate activity that is given at different points in the social structure. If, in a given social location, illegal or criminal means are not readily available, then we should not expect a criminal subculture to develop among adolescents. By the same logic, we should expect the manipulation of violence to become a primary avenue to higher status only in areas where the means of violence are not denied to the young. To give a third example, drug addiction and participation in subcultures organized around the consumption of drugs presuppose that persons can secure access to drugs and knowledge about how to use them. In some parts of the social structure, this would be very difficult; in others, very easy. In short, there are marked differences from one part of the social structure to another in the types of illegitimate adaptation that are available to persons in search of solutions to problems of adjustment arising from the restricted availability of legitimate means.[8] In this sense, then, we can think of individuals as being located in two opportunity structures—one legitimate, the other illegitimate. Given limited access to success-goals by legitimate means, the nature of the delinquent response that may result will vary according to the availability of various illegitimate means.[9]

VARIETIES OF DELINQUENT SUBCULTURE

As we have noted, there appear to be three major types of delinquent subculture typically encountered among adolescent males in lower-class areas of large urban centers. One is based principally upon criminal values; its members are organized primarily for the pursuit of material gain by such illegal means as extortion, fraud, and theft. In the second, violence is the keynote; its members pursue status ("rep") through the manipulation of force or threat of force. These are the "warrior" groups that attract so much attention in the press. Finally, there are subcultures which emphasize the consumption of drugs. The participants in these drug subcultures have become alienated from conventional roles, such as those required in the family or the occupational world. They have withdrawn into a restricted world in which the ultimate value consists in the "kick." We call these three subcultural forms "criminal," "conflict," and "retreatist," respectively.[10]

These shorthand terms simply denote the *principal* orientation of each form of adaptation from the perspective of the dominant social order; although one can find many examples of subcultures that fit accurately into one of these three categories, subcultures frequently appear in somewhat mixed form. Thus members of a predominantly conflict subculture may also on occasion engage in systematic theft; members of a criminal subculture may sometimes do combat in the streets with rival gangs. But this should not obscure the fact that these subcultures tend to exhibit essentially different orientations.

The extent to which the delinquent subculture organizes and controls a participant's allegiance varies from one member to another. Some members of the gang are almost totally immersed in all the perspectives of the subculture and bring them into play in all their contacts; others segregate this aspect of their lives and maintain other roles in the family, school, and church. The chances are relatively slight, however, that an adolescent can successfully segregate delinquent and conforming roles for a long period of time. Pressures emanate from the subculture leading its members to adopt unfavorable attitudes toward parents, school teachers, policemen, and other adults in the conventional world. When he is apprehended for delinquent acts, the possibility of the delinquent's maintaining distinctly separate role involvements breaks down, and he is confronted with the necessity of choosing between law-abiding and delinquent styles of life. Since family, welfare, religious, educational, law-enforcement, and correctional institutions are arrayed against the appeal of his delinquent associates, the decision is a difficult one, frequently requiring either complete acceptance or complete rejection of one or the other system of obligations.[11]

At any one point in time, however, the extent to which the norms of the delinquent subculture control behavior will vary from one member to another. Accordingly, descriptions of these subcultures must be stated in terms of the fully indoctrinated member rather than the average member. Only in this way can the distinctiveness of delinquent styles of life be made clear. It is with this understanding that we offer the following brief empirical characterizations of the three main types of delinquent subculture.

The Criminal Pattern

The most extensive documentation in the sociological literature of delinquent behavior patterns in lower-class culture describes a tradition which integrates youthful delinquency with adult criminality.[12] In the central value orientation of youths participating in this tradition, delinquent and criminal behavior is accepted as a means of achieving success-goals. The dominant criteria of in-group evaluation stress achievement, the use of skill and knowledge to get results. In this culture, prestige is allocated to those who achieve material gain and power through avenues defined as illegitimate by the larger society. From the very young to the very old, the successful "haul"—which quickly transforms the penniless into a man of means—is an ever-present vision of the possible and desirable. Although one may also achieve material success through the routine practice of theft or fraud, the "big score" remains the symbolic image of quick success.

The means by which a member of a criminal subculture achieves success are clearly defined for the aspirant. At a young age, he learns to admire and respect older criminals and to adopt the "right guy" as his role-model. Delinquent episodes help him to acquire mastery of the techniques and orientation of the criminal world and to learn how to cooperate successfully with others in criminal enterprises. He exhibits hostility and distrust toward representatives of the larger society. He regards members of the conventional world as "suckers," his natural victims, to be exploited when possible. He sees successful people in the conventional world as having a "racket"—e.g., big businessmen have huge expense accounts, politicians get graft, etc. This attitude successfully neutralizes the controlling effect of conventional norms. Toward the in-group the "right guy" maintains relationships of loyalty, honesty, and trustworthiness. He must prove himself reliable and dependable in his contacts with his criminal associates although he has no such obligations toward the out-group of noncriminals.

One of the best ways of assuring success in the criminal world is to cultivate appropriate "connections." As a youngster, this means running with a clique composed of other "right guys" and promoting an apprenticeship or some other favored relationship with older and successful offenders. Close and dependable ties with income-producing outlets for stolen goods, such as the wagon peddler, the junkman, and the fence, are especially useful. Furthermore, these intermediaries encourage and protect the young delinquent in a criminal way of life by giving him a jaundiced perspective on the private morality of many functionaries in conventional society. As he matures, the young delinquent becomes acquainted with a new world made up of predatory bondsmen, shady lawyers, crooked policemen, grafting politicians, dishonest businessmen, and corrupt jailers. Through "connections" with occupants of these half-legitimate, half-illegitimate roles and with "big shots" in the underworld, the aspiring criminal validates and assures his freedom of movement in a world made safe for crime.

The Conflict Pattern[13]

The role-model in the conflict pattern of lower-class cultures is the "bopper" who swaggers with his gang, fights with weapons to win a wary respect from other gangs, and compels a fearful deference from the conventional adult world by his unpredictable and destructive assaults on persons and property. To other gang members, however, the key qualities of the bopper are those of the successful warrior. His performance must reveal a willingness to defend his personal integrity and the honor of the gang. He must do this with great courage and displays of fearlessness in the face of personal danger.

The immediate aim in the world of fighting gangs is to acquire a reputation for toughness and destructive violence. A "rep" assures not only respectful behavior from peers and threatened adults but also admiration for the physical strength and masculinity which it symbolizes. It represents a way of securing access to the scarce resources for adolescent pleasure and opportunity in underprivileged areas.

Above all things, the bopper is valued for his "heart." He does not "chicken out," even when confronted by superior force. He never defaults in the face of a personal insult or a challenge to the integrity of his gang. The code of the bopper is that of the warrior who places great stress on courage, the defense of his group, and the maintenance of honor.

Relationships between bopping gang members and the adult world are severely attenuated. The term that the bopper uses most frequently to characterize his relationships with adults is "weak." He is unable to find appropriate role-models that can designate for him a structure of opportunities leading to adult success. He views himself as isolated and the adult world as indifferent. The commitments of adults are to their own interests and not to his. Their explanations of why he should behave differently are "weak," as are their efforts to help him.

Confronted by the apparent indifference and insincerity of the adult world, the ideal bopper seeks to win by coercion the attention and opportunities he lacks and cannot otherwise attract. In recent years the street-gang worker who deals with the fighting gang on its own "turf" has come to symbolize not only a recognition by conventional adult society of the gang's toughness but also a concession of opportunities formerly denied. Through the alchemy of competition between gangs, this gesture of attention by the adult world to the "worst" gangs is transformed into a mark of prestige. Thus does the manipulation of violence convert indifference into accommodation and attention into status.

The Retreatist Pattern

Retreatism may include a variety of expressive, sensual, or consummatory experiences, alone or in a group. In this analysis, we are interested only in those experiences that involve the use of drugs and that are supported by a subculture. We have adopted these limitations in order to maintain our focus on subcultural formations which are clearly recognized as delinquent, as drug use by adolescents is. The retreatist preoccupation with expressive experiences creates many varieties of "hipster" cult among lower-class adolescents which foster patterns of deviant but not necessarily delinquent conduct.

Subcultural drug-users in lower-class areas perceive themselves as culturally and socially detached from the life-style and everyday preoccupations of members of the conventional world. The following characterization of the "cat" culture, observed by Finestone in a lower-class Negro area in Chicago, describes drug use in the more general context of "hipsterism."[14] Thus it should not be assumed that this description in every respect fits drug cultures found elsewhere. We have drawn heavily on Finestone's observations, however, because they provide the best descriptions available of the social world in which lower-class adolescent drug cultures typically arise.

The dominant feature of the retreatist subculture of the "cat" lies in the continuous pursuit of the "kick." Every cat has a kick—alcohol, marijuana, addicting drugs, unusual sexual experiences, hot jazz, cool jazz, or any combination of these. Whatever its content, the kick is a search for ecstatic experiences. The retreatist strives for an intense awareness of living and a sense of pleasure that is "out of this world." In extreme form, he seeks an almost spiritual and mystical knowledge that is experienced when one comes to know "it" at the height of one's kick. The past and the future recede in the time perspective of the cat, since complete awareness in present experience is the essence of the kick.

The successful cat has a lucrative "hustle" which contrasts sharply with the routine and discipline required in the ordinary occupational tasks of conventional society. The many varieties of the hustle are characterized by a rejection of violence or force and a preference for manipulating, persuading, outwitting, or "conning" others to obtain resources for experiencing the kick. The cat begs, borrows, steals, or engages in some petty con-game. He caters to the illegitimate cravings of others by peddling drugs or working as a pimp. A highly exploitative attitude toward women permits the cat to view pimping as a prestigeful source of income. Through the labor of "chicks" engaged in prostitution or shoplifting, he can live in idleness and concentrate his entire attention on organizing, scheduling, and experiencing the esthetic pleasure of the kick. The hustle of the cat is secondary to his interest in the kick. In this respect the cat differs from his fellow delinquents in the criminal subculture, for whom income-producing activity is a primary concern.

The ideal cat's appearance, demeanor, and taste can best be characterized as "cool." The cat seeks to exhibit a highly developed and sophisticated taste for clothes. In his demeanor, he struggles to reveal a self-assured and unruffled manner, thereby emphasizing his aloofness and "superiority" to the "squares." He develops a colorful, discriminating vocabulary and ritualized gestures which express his sense of difference from the conventional world and his solidarity with the retreatist subculture.

The word "cool" also best describes the sense of apartness and detachment which the retreatist experiences in his relationships with the conventional world. His reference group is the "society of cats," an "elite" group in which he becomes isolated from conventional society. Within this group, a new order of goals and criteria of achievement is created. The cat does not seek to impose this system of values on the world of the squares. Instead, he strives for status and deference within the society of cats by cultivating the kick and the hustle. Thus the retreatist subculture provides avenues to success-goals, to the social admiration and the sense of well-being or oneness with the world which the members feel are otherwise beyond their reach.

Notes

1. See esp. C.R. Shaw, *The Jack-Roller* (Chicago: University of Chicago Press, 1930); Shaw, *The Natural History of a Delinquent Career* (Chicago: University of Chicago Press, 1931); Shaw et al., *Delinquency Areas* (Chicago: University of Chicago, 1940); and Shaw and H.D. McKay, *Juvenile Delinquency and Urban Areas* (Chicago: University of Chicago Press, 1942).

2. E.H. Sutherland, ed., *The Professional Thief* (Chicago: University of Chicago Press, 1937); and Sutherland, *Principles of Criminology*, 4th Ed. (Philadelphia: Lippincott, 1947).

3. All quotations on this page are from *The Professional Thief*, pp. 211–13. Emphasis added.

4. Frank Tannenbaum, "The Professional Criminal," *The Century*, Vol. 110 (May–Oct. 1925), p. 577.

5. See A.K. Cohen, Alfred Lindesmith, and Kark Schuessler, eds., *The Sutherland Papers* (Bloomington, Ind.: Indiana University Press, 1956), pp. 31–35.

6. R.K. Merton, *Social Theory and Social Structure*, Rev. and Enl. Ed. (Glencoe, Ill.: Free Press, 1957), pp. 145–46.

7. *Principles of Criminology, op. cit.*, pp. 7–8.

8. For an example of restrictions on access to illegitimate roles, note the impact of racial definitions in the following case: "I was greeted by two prisoners who were to be my cell buddies. Ernest was a first offender, charged with being a 'hold-up' man. Bill, the other buddy, was an older offender, going through the machinery of becoming a habitual criminal, in and out of jail. . . . The first thing they asked me was, 'What are you in for?' I said, 'Jack-rolling.' The hardened one (Bill) looked at me with a superior air and said, 'A hoodlum, eh? An ordinary sneak thief. Not willing to leave jack-rolling to the niggers, eh? That's all they're good for. Kid, jack-rolling's not a white man's job.' I could see that he was disgusted with me, and I was too scared to say anything" (Shaw, *The Jack-Roller, op. cit.*, p. 101).

9. For a discussion of the way in which the availability of illegitimate means influences the adaptations of inmates to prison life, see R.A. Cloward, "Social Control in the Prison," *Theoretical Studies of the Social Organization of the Prison*, Bulletin No. 15 (New York: Social Science Research Council, March 1960), pp. 20–48.

10. It should be understood that these terms characterize these delinquent modes of adaptation from the reference position of conventional society; they do not necessarily reflect the attitudes of members of the subcultures. Thus the term "retreatist" does not necessarily reflect the attitude of the "cat." Far from thinking of himself as being in retreat, he defines himself as among the elect.

11. Tannenbaum summarizes the community's role in this process of alienation by the phrase "dramatization of evil" (Frank Tannenbaum, *Crime and the Community* [New York: Columbia University Press, 1938], pp. 19–21). For a more detailed account of this process, see Chap. 5, *infra*.

12. See esp. C.R. Shaw, *The Jack-Roller* (Chicago: University of Chicago Press, 1930); Shaw, *The Natural History of a Delinquent Career* (Chicago: University of Chicago Press, 1940); Shaw and H.D. McKay, *Juvenile Delinquency and Urban Areas* (Chicago: University of Chicago Press, 1942); E.H. Sutherland, ed., *The Professional Thief* (Chicago: University of Chicago Press, 1937); Sutherland, *Principles of Criminology*, 4th ed. (Philadelphia: J.P. Lippincott Co., 1947); and Sutherland, *White Collar Crime* (New York: Dryden Press, 1949).

13. For descriptions of conflict groups, see Harrison Salisbury, *The Shook-up Generation* (New York: Harper & Bros., 1958); *Reaching the Unreached*, a Publication of the New York City Youth Board, 1952; C.K. Myers, *Light the Dark Streets* (Greenwich, Conn.: Seabury Press, 1957); Walter Bernstein, "The Cherubs are Rumbling," *The New Yorker*, Sept. 21, 1957; Sam Glane, "Juvenile Gangs in East Side Los Angeles," *Focus*, Vol. 29 (Sept. 1959), pp. 136–41; Dale Kramer and Madeline Karr, *Teen-Age Gangs* (New York: Henry Holt, 1953); S.V. Jones,

"The Cougars—Life with a Brooklyn Gang," *Harper's*, Vol. 209 (Nov. 1954), pp. 35–43; P.C. Crawford, D.I. Malamud, and J.R. Dumpson, *Working with Teen-Age Gangs* (New York Welfare Council, 1950); Dan Wakefield, "The Gang That Went Good," *Harper's*, Vol. 216 (June 1958), pp. 36–43.

14. Harold Finestone, "Cats, Kicks and Color," *Social Problems*, Vol. 5 (July 1957), pp. 3–13.

19. Social Origins and School Failure: A Reexamination of Cohen's Theory of Working-Class Delinquency

DELOS H. KELLY AND ROBERT W. BALCH

It is widely assumed that the incidence of juvenile delinquency is inversely related to social class, and many popular theories of delinquent behavior are predicated on this assumption. One of the most influential of these theories was formulated by Albert Cohen (1955). According to Cohen, middle-class success goals permeate our society. No one is immune to them, including school boys from working-class homes. Unfortunately, working-class boys are sorely ill-equipped to compete for success in a middle-class world. In Cohen's (1955: 97) words, the working-class person "is less likely to possess, to value or to cultivate the polish, the sophistication, the fluency, the 'good appearance' and the 'personality' so useful in 'selling oneself' and manipulating others in the middle-class world." These liabilities become painfully evident in the classroom. Schools are thoroughly middle-class institutions, and, according to Cohen, students are inevitably evaluated in terms of a "middle-class measuring rod." This yardstick emphasizes ambition, worldly asceticism, respect for property, and so on (Cohen, 1955: 88–93). Because working-class boys are so poorly equipped to compete against middle-class standards, they ultimately fail—academically and socially. Theirs is a painful dilemma. They have internalized middle-class goals, but are unable to achieve them. Cohen contends that many of these boys resolve their dilemmas by collectively rejecting the middle-class way of life and turning its standards upside down, instituting a status system of their own. This is the delinquent solution which occupies Cohen's attention. It is the working-class boy's answer to status frustration (Cohen, 1955: ch. 5).

There have been surprisingly few explicit attempts to test Cohen's theory. In one well-known study, Reiss and Rhodes (1963) examined the relationship between "status deprivation" and delinquency. As a measure of relative deprivation, they used responses to the question, "Would you say that most of the students in your school have better clothes and a better house to live in than you have?" (Reiss and Rhodes,

1963: 137). Contrary to what Cohen might have predicted, they found only a slight relationship between social class and perceived deprivation, and virtually no relationship between deprivation and delinquency. However, their study cannot be considered a fair test of Cohen's theory.

Their measure of status deprivation does not tap the process so critical to the theory. According to Cohen, working-class boys are frustrated because they are unable to compete for rewards in a middle-class environment, particularly the school. One may be thoroughly deprived according to the Reiss and Rhodes criterion, yet still possess the intellectual and social skills necessary to win approval and respect from middle-class adults.

In addition, Cohen says that delinquency is a *solution* for status deprivation. Delinquent boys reject the middle-class values they cannot obtain. However, their solution is far from perfect. In fact, "lingering ambivalence" toward middle-class values is responsible for the reaction formation which Cohen (1955: 132, 133) proposes to explain the malicious content of the delinquent subculture. If Cohen's reaction formation thesis is true, then delinquent boys should vigorously *deny* that they are deprived. Reiss and Rhodes used questionnaires to assess status deprivation, but depth interviews may be required to reveal feelings of deprivation which boys are not even willing to admit to themselves. On the other hand, if delinquent boys are not as ambivalent as Cohen says—if they really *do* reject middle-class values—they have no reason to feel deprived. In that case, delinquency and status deprivation would not be strongly related in a cross-sectional study like that of Reiss and Rhodes, even with depth interviews. Status deprivation, therefore, is an elusive variable which is difficult to handle empirically.

The authors also deal with only three variables in Cohen's system—social class, status deprivation, and delinquency. While these are Cohen's most important variables, exclusive attention to them has obscured the intervening processes by which they are related. Specifically, Cohen discusses several unfortunate consequences of growing up in a working-class family which lead to juvenile misbehavior.

Because working-class boys are intellectually, emotionally, and behaviorally unable to succeed in school, they fail more often than their middle-class peers. Cohen says (1955: 115), "both in terms of 'conduct' and in terms of academic achievement, the failures in the classroom are drawn disproportionately from the lower social class levels." Working-class boys hold themselves in low regard, especially when they compare themselves intellectually to higher-class boys. Their low self-esteem emerges from the constant negative appraisal they presumably receive from their teachers. "It seems reasonable to assume that out of all this there arise feelings of inferiority and perhaps resentment and hostility" (Cohen, 1955: 112). "The failure of our own behavior to conform to our own expectations is an elementary and commonplace fact which gives rise to the tremendously important consequences of guilt, self-recrimination, anxiety and self-hatred" (Cohen, 1955: 126). Finally, Cohen says (1955: 119) working-class boys are likely to be under-involved in school activities. "Working-class children are less likely to participate, and if they participate are less likely to achieve prominence, in extracurricular activities, which are an important arena for the competition for status in the eyes of the students themselves." They are uninvolved partly by choice, defensively avoiding an unpleasant situation, and partly because they are excluded by middle-class students (Cohen, 1955: 118, 119).

There are two ways these boys can cope with their failure. The one which occupies most of Cohen's (1955: ch. 5) attention is, of course, delinquency. Another way of coping with failure is to physically withdraw from school, by either cutting classes or dropping out (Cohen, 1955: 129). According to Cohen, the second solution characterizes nondelinquent "corner boys" as well as delinquents.

Thus Cohen says it is not social class per se that causes delinquent and conforming behavior. Rather, the effect of class background on delinquency depends on the working-class boy's experience in school. Cohen's *independent variable* is social class. His *dependent variables* are school avoidance and delinquency. Academic performance, self-evaluation, and school involvement are all *intervening variables*. If Cohen's theory is correct, the following pattern of relationships should exist:

1. Social class will be directly related to academic performance, self-evaluation, and school involvement.

2. Social class will be inversely related to school avoidance and delinquency.

3. Academic performance, self-evaluation, and school involvement will be inversely related to school avoidance and delinquency.

4. When the intervening school variables are held constant, the relationships between social class and the dependent variables will disappear or be substantially reduced.

Since social class is temporally prior to all other variables in the system, this pattern of relationships would clearly indicate that the school variables are intervening rather than antecedent. See Rosenberg (1968: ch. 2) for a discussion of intervening and antecedent variables.

You will notice that our hypotheses pertain to the working-class boy's attempt to cope with his *school experience*. As Cohen (1955: 112) points out, "one of the situations in which children of all social levels come together and compete for status in terms of the same set of middle-class criteria and in which working-class children are most likely to be found wanting is in the school." Although Cohen apparently believes the school is only one of many such situations, so much of his discussion revolves around the school that we consider it essential to his theory.

We have also completely ignored the concept of status deprivation, for two reasons. First, as we suggested above, the concept is extremely difficult to handle, at least within the context of Cohen's theory. Second, social class is really Cohen's most important independent variable. He apparently believes the relationship between working-class origins and status deprivation is so strong that middle-class delinquency calls for a completely different explanation (Cohen, 1955: 157–169). Exclusive attention to status deprivation would ignore the main thrust of Cohen's theory because, conceivably, status deprivation may be independent of social class. Indeed, Reiss and Rhodes (1963) found evidence of status deprivation at all class levels, and Elliott (1962) and Stinchcombe (1964) found that their measures of status frustration were related to both middle- and working-class delinquency.

PROCEDURES

Data for the present study were drawn from an ongoing investigation of adolescent boys in western Oregon. In 1964, a questionnaire containing a wide variety of demographic, school, family, work, and peer variables was administered to all male sophomores (1,227) enrolled in the high schools of a medium-sized county (1960 population of 120,888). Data were also drawn from school transcripts and juvenile court records.

Using the Hollingshead Index of Social Position, together with an Oregon supplement, we classified our subjects as middle or working class according to their father's occupation. Middle-class occupations included executive, professional, sales, and clerical positions. Skilled, semiskilled, and unskilled jobs made up the working-class category.[1] Of our initial population of 1,227, 1,011 boys could be classified. Forty-eight percent of these were placed in the working-class category. The remaining 216 subjects who could not be classified were concentrated in unspecified farming and logging occupations.

We used four indicators to operationalize our intervening variables. Academic performance was determined by one's accumulated grade point average at the beginning of his sophomore year. Grades were divided into "high" (2.00–4.00) and "low" (0.0–1.99) categories.[2] In order to ascertain academic self-evaluation, responses to four highly intercorrelated questionnaire items were combined in a four-factor index. Our respondents were asked to compare themselves with other sophomore boys on four school-related dimensions: spelling ability, language usage, grades, and general intelligence. Each time a boy rated himself average or above on one of the four dimensions, he received a score of one. If he rated himself below average, he received a score of zero. All those with total scores of two or less were regarded as having a low opinion of their academic capabilities. We used two indicators to tap the dimension of school involvement. Positive and negative affect toward school were determined by responses to a Likert-type item: "School is dull and boring." Boys who agreed with this statement were considered to have negative feelings toward school. Another aspect of school involvement is participation in extracurricular activities. We asked, "How many in-school clubs, organizations and athletic groups do you belong to?" Boys who said they did not belong to any groups were classified as uninvolved in school activities.

Eight items make up our dependent variables. We classified all boys with four or more absences during their freshman year as truants. (The median for the sample was 2.5.) Boys who eventually dropped out of school before graduation were classified as dropouts. Delinquency was determined in three different ways: (1) boys who had appeared in court at least once were classified as delinquent; (2) boys who had appeared in court more than once were classified as frequent delinquents; and (3) those who had been apprehended for committing felonies were classified as serious offenders.[3] Finally, three additional items were included as indicators of youthful rebellion which is not specifically delinquent: "Do you smoke?" "Do you drink beer?" and a Likert-type item, "I really enjoy 'cruising around' at night just to see what is going on."

Table 1. Academic Performance, Academic Self-Evaluation, School Involvement, and School Avoidance and Deviant Behavior, by Social Origins (in percentages)[a]

	Social Origins	
	MIDDLE CLASS	WORKING CLASS
Academic Performance		
Failing grade point average	21	32
Academic Self-Evaluation		
Low self-evaluation	39	60
School Involvement		
Negative affect toward school	27	37
Uninvolved in activities	27	37
School Avoidance and Deviant Behavior		
Truancy	30	34
Dropout	8	15
Smoking	17	25
Drinking	16	23
Cruising	56	70
Delinquency (juvenile court contact)	24	26
(1) Frequent delinquency (more than one contact)	10	11
(2) Serious delinquency (felony count)	12	16

[a] Percentages rounded to nearest whole percent.

Before proceeding, some general comments on our sample, and indicators are in order. First, one could argue that Cohen was concerned with urban slum delinquency, and therefore our sample cannot legitimately be used to test hypotheses derived from his theory. However, the only references to urban slum delinquency in *Delinquent Boys* are in the second chapter, where Cohen (1955: 32,33,43) briefly alludes to the prevalence of delinquency in disorganized "interstitial" areas. Otherwise there is nothing in the book which would restrict his theory to the urban scene. Presumably working-class boys encounter the same middle-class barriers in small communities as they do in big cities.

Second, we have been severely handicapped because our data were originally collected for reasons unrelated to the purposes of this study. For example, we have not derived any hypotheses about the delinquent *subculture* because there were simply no items in the questionnaire which dealt with this aspect of Cohen's theory. For the rest of our hypotheses we have had to pick and choose to find appropriate indicators, sometimes with less than satisfying results. Hopefully the weaknesses of any single indicator are overcome by the consistent pattern of results which emerges in our analysis.

FINDINGS

Table 1 shows the relationships between the independent and each of our intervening (school) and dependent variables. Although the relationships are small, they are all in the predicted direction. Working-class boys are more likely to get poor grades, have low self-evaluations, dislike school, and be uninvolved in extracurricular activities.

Table 2. School Avoidance and Deviant Behavior, by Academic Performance, Academic Self-Evaluation, Affect toward School, and Involvement in School Activities (in percentages)

	Grade Point Average		Academic Self-Evaluation Index		Affect toward School		Involvement in School Activities	
	HIGH	LOW	HIGH	LOW	POSITIVE	NEGATIVE	INVOLVED	UNINVOLVED
Truancy	27	50	29	38	31	35	27	38
Dropout	3	33	5	20	7	20	6	18
Smoking	15	39	15	28	15	35	14	27
Drinking	17	30	17	25	15	33	15	25
Cruising	57	80	54	73	57	75	61	66
Delinquency	20	36	21	28	21	32	21	27
(1) Frequent	7	21	9	13	8	16	8	13
(2) Serious	3	9	12	16	12	18	12	15

The relationships with respect to school avoidance and deviant behavior are even smaller. As we predicted, working-class boys are more likely to cut classes, drop out of school, smoke, drink, and go cruising with their friends. However, the relationship between delinquency and social class is slight to nonexistent. The differences between middle- and working-class boys on our three indicators of delinquency are only two, one, and four percent.[4] The mean percentage difference for the entire table is only six percent—considerably less than we expected.

Table 2 shows the relationships between our intervening and dependent variables. The relationships between grade point average and each of the dependent variables are fairly strong and consistently in the predicted direction. The lower a boy's grade point average, the more likely he is to cut classes, drop out, smoke, drink, and go cruising. There is also an inverse relationship between grades and each indicator of delinquent behavior.

The remaining data in Table 2 exhibit a similar pattern. Self-evaluation, affect toward school, and involvement in school activities are all inversely related to our dependent variables. Although none of them is as strongly related to the dependent variables as grade point average, the relationships are consistently in the predicted direction.

So far the pattern of results is only partly consistent with Cohen's theory. Our school variables are consistently related to the independent and dependent variables in the way we predicted. However, not all of our dependent variables are related to social class, and even then the relationships are smaller than we expected. Delinquency, our most important dependent variable, is not related to social origins, even when measured in three different ways. Nevertheless, before we can draw any conclusions from the data, we must examine the relationships between social class and each of the dependent variables while holding the intervening variables constant. If academic performance, self-evaluation, and school involvement really are intervening variables, then the observed relationships between social origins and the dependent variables should disappear when the school variables are controlled.

Table 3. School Avoidance and Deviant Behavior, by Social Origins and Academic Performance (in percentages)

| | Grade Point Average | | | |
| | HIGH | | LOW | |
	MC[a]	WC	MC	WC
Truancy	27	26	47	51
Dropout	2	4	28	34
Smoking	11	18	38	41
Drinking	14	19	29	31
Cruising	51	62	78	82
Delinquency	19	22	44	35
(1) Frequent	6	7	26	20
(2) Serious	9	13	24	22

[a] MC—middle class; WC—working class.

In Table 3, we examine the relationship between social origins and each of the dependent variables while controlling academic performance. For most of the dependent variables, the observed class differences persist. Grades also have a strong independent effect on each dependent variable, and there is a tendency for the effects of class and grades to combine in an additive fashion. There are four exceptions to the general pattern. For boys with high grades, class differences in truancy—which were slight to begin with—disappear. For those with low grades, middle-class boys are somewhat more likely to be delinquent on each of the three indicators. We are not sure what significance to attach to the latter finding. According to Stinchcombe (1964: ch. 6) middle-class failures in school are more likely to be rebellious than are working-class boys who fail. He believed that failure is more frustrating for middle-class boys because they have higher aspirations. However, if this explanation were valid, middle-class boys with low grades should also have higher rates of truancy, dropout, smoking, drinking, and cruising. Moreover, Stinchcombe (1964; chs. 1 and 2) was not con-

Table 4. School Avoidance and Deviant Behavior, by Social Origins and Academic Self-Evaluation (in percentages)

| | Academic Self-Evaluation Index | | | |
| | HIGH | | LOW | |
	MC[a]	WC	MC	WC
Truancy	27	28	36	37
Dropout	4	6	14	20
Smoking	11	19	26	30
Drinking	13	19	21	26
Cruising	47	60	72	76
Delinquency	19	26	31	26
(1) Frequent	8	9	14	13
(2) Serious	11	15	15	16

Table 5.   School Avoidance and Deviant Behavior, by Social Origins and Affect toward School (in percentages)

| | Affect toward School | | | |
| | POSITIVE | | NEGATIVE | |
	MC	WC	MC	WC
Truancy	29	29	31	37
Dropout	5	7	12	23
Smoking	12	16	27	40
Drinking	11	16	30	34
Cruising	50	64	68	77
Delinquency	20	21	34	33
(1) Frequent	8	7	15	17
(2) Serious	11	12	16	21

cerned with delinquency, but with "rebellion" and "expressive alienation" which are conceptually very similar to our nondelinquent dependent variable. In order to invoke Stinchcombe's theory to explain our curious class differences in delinquency, we would have to find similar—perhaps even stronger—differences in the rest of our dependent variables. At any rate, none of these results could have been predicted from Cohen's theory.

There is a very similar pattern in Table 4. Class differences do not disappear as predicted, and self-evaluation is related to each of the dependent variables even when class is controlled. Among those with low self-evaluations, middle-class boys are a bit more likely to have at least one juvenile court contact, but for all practical purposes there are no class differences in the frequency or seriousness of delinquency.

In Tables 5 and 6, the pattern is even more consistent. Social origins and the control variables continue to have independent, additive effects on the dependent variables. Generally speaking, class differences remain small and are negligible for delinquency.

Table 6.   School Avoidance and Deviant Behavior, by Social Origins and Involvement in School Activities (in percentages)

| | Involvement in School Activities | | | |
| | INVOLVED | | UNINVOLVED | |
	MC	WC	MC	WC
Truancy	25	26	37	37
Dropout	6	7	10	20
Smoking	12	16	22	30
Drinking	13	17	19	26
Cruising	57	67	56	70
Delinquency	22	21	26	29
(1) Frequent	8	8	13	14
(2) Serious	11	13	13	17

DISCUSSION

Our results clearly do not support Cohen's theory. For all practical purposes, there is no relationship between delinquency and social class. There is a slight relationship between class and the rest of the dependent variables, but it does not disappear when academic performance, self-evaluation, or school involvement are controlled. In other words, the relationship between social class and our dependent variables does not depend on school experience as Cohen implies. Cohen assumed that academic performance, self-evaluation, and school involvement are intervening variables. Instead, social class and the school variables are independently related to the dependent variables. Furthermore, the effect of social class is weak and inconsistent, while the four school variables are uniformly and in many cases strongly related to the dependent variables. Of all the variables, academic performance is most strongly related to each of the dependent variables.

In part, our small class differences could be a function of geography. Our data were collected in a relatively young western county. In the East, where class lines are more rigid, social class may be a more influential variable. Nevertheless, our results are similar to those reported in a recent study of Tennessee high school students by Rhodes and Reiss (1969). They found that English grades were strongly related to apathy, truancy, juvenile court contacts, and serious delinquency, even when social class was held constant. English mark was also much more strongly related to their dependent variables than was social class.

Our findings may have some additional theoretical and practical implications. They lend support to a "school status" theory of delinquency. Although school status advocates vary in emphasis, they seem to agree that one's location in the reward structure of the school is a far more important determinant of nonconforming behavior than one's social-class background (Schafer and Polk, 1967).

In his study of an English secondary school, Hargreaves (1967) found that boys in the school's lowest "streams" (tracks) were treated as if they were incapable of assuming responsibility. Their teachers treated them with disdain and regarded their classroom duties as more custodial than academic. On the other hand, boys in the top stream received considerable recognition and encouragement from their teachers. They were carefully groomed for their grammar-school qualifying examination and maintained close ties with the faculty. Each stream also had its own teachers and its own activities. Not surprisingly, interaction and friendship choices were largely stream-bound. Unlike their upper-stream counterparts, boys in the lowest streams received poor grades, lacked commitment to school, and were more involved in troublesome activities. Hargreaves believed that differences between the streams were caused by the streaming process itself; but his data are inconclusive because he failed to control background factors like social class.

Fortunately, a study by Schafer et al. (1970) is more definitive. Their data showed that even when social class, IQ, and past performance were held constant, there were still significant differences between upper and lower tracks in two midwestern high schools. Students in the lower track were more apt to receive low grades, drop out of school, and become delinquent.

Academic failure may have similar negative consequences, regardless of track position. Gold (1963) found that delinquents had lower grades and more negative attitudes toward school than nondelinquents *before* their first police contact. Stinchcombe (1964) believed that failure leads to alienation and rebellion because it severely restricts one's chances of achieving his occupational goals. As we mentioned in the previous section, Stinchcombe contends that failure is especially damaging for middle-class boys because they have high aspirations. If middle-class boys fail, they will be headed for working-class occupations. But if lower-class boys fail, they will simply retain their present socioeconomic status.

However, Polk (1969) was unable to support the hypothesis that downwardly mobile white-collar boys are more rebellious than their blue-collar counterparts. Instead, school failure had a strong independent effect on rebellion. Regardless of their social class, boys who were failing in school were more likely to be delinquent than boys who were doing well. Polk concluded that Stinchcombe may have given too much weight to the implications of school experience for one's future status in life. Rather, the immediate effects of failure might be more damaging. For example, Vinter and Sarri (1965: 9) found that poor students were denied

> a wide variety of privileges and opportunities within the school. They lost esteem among their classmates, they were seldom chosen for minor but prestigeful classroom or school assignments, and they were excluded from participation in certain extra-curricular activities. This process, in turn, often subjected such students to negative parental responses, representing a third penalty.

Exclusion from school activities may be critical. Polk and Halferty (1966) have described involvement in extracurricular activities as a series of "side-bets" that keep students interested in school and out of trouble. Even students having no academic interests whatsoever have an interest in conformity if they are highly involved in school activities. At any rate, whether we follow Stinchcombe or Polk in our interpretation of school failure, the school-status model is still more versatile then Cohen's theory because it can explain both middle- and working-class delinquency.

While our data are consistent with the school-status approach, they do not permit us to choose between competing hypotheses. Assignment to a lower track apparently increases the probability of failure as well as delinquency, but many writers have treated failure as an *independent* variable. Although we are speculating, we believe that failure probably has an effect on youthful deviance that is independent of track position. Boys in the lowest track who are also failing should be the most delinquent of all.

We have assumed, of course, that failure causes delinquency, but the causal arrow could point the other way. In fact, it probably points in both directions, but there is good reason for treating school experience as an independent variable. Gold's (1963) study clearly shows that failure *preceded* delinquency. Similarly, Elliott (1966) found that the delinquency rates of future dropouts *declined* after they left school. In fact, their out-of-school rates were lower than the delinquency rates of those boys who stayed in school and eventually graduated.

What, then, are the practical implications of this study? Although the weak relationships between social class and our dependent variables may be disappointing to some, they should be heartening to those who want to *do* something about delinquency. We cannot change a boy's social class, but we can do something about his school. If we can make the classroom, and school activities generally, more rewarding and more engrossing for students, perhaps we can reduce the amount of juvenile delinquency. Like so many glib recommendations, this is more easily said than done, but no one can deny that it is easier to modify a school than to change the social backgrounds of its students.

Notes

1. In our analysis of the class variable we have found no indication that dichotomization of the occupational scale alters our results.
2. 4.00 perfect.
3. Many writers have objected to the use of official statistics as an indicator of delinquent behavior. Unfortunately, our data did not include self-reported delinquency. However, there is some evidence that the most *serious* delinquent acts do come to the attention of the court. The trivial offenses most often go undetected (Chilton, 1967; Gibbons, 1970: 24–27; Gold, 1966). Hopefully, we have overcome some of the weaknesses of the official statistics by taking seriousness into consideration.
4. Even when we examine the percentage of delinquents by social status without dichotomizing the occupational scale, there is still virtually no relationship.

References

Chilton, Roland J., 1967, "Middle-Class Delinquency and Specific Offense Analysis." Pp. 91–101 in E.W. Vaz (ed.) Middle-Class Juvenile Delinquency. New York: Harper & Row.

Cohen, Albert K., 1955, *Delinquent Boys: The Culture of the Gang.* New York: Free Press.

Elliott, Delbert S., 1962, "Delinquency and Perceived Opportunity." Soc. Inquiry 32 (Spring): 216–227.

Elliott, Delbert S., 1966, "Delinquency, School Attendance and Dropout." Social Problems 13 (Winter): 307–314.

Gibbons, Don C., 1970, *Delinquent Behavior.* Englewood Cliffs: Prentice-Hall.

Gold, Martin, 1963, Status Forces in Delinquent Boys. Ann Arbor: Univ. of Michigan Press.

Gold, Martin, 1966, "Undetected Delinquent Behavior." J. of Research in Crime and Delinquency 3 (January): 27–46.

Hargreaves, David, 1967, *Social Relations in a Secondary School.* New York: Humanities Press.

Polk, Kenneth, 1969, "Class, Strain and Rebellion among Adolescents." Social Problems 17 (Fall): 214–224.

Polk, Kenneth and David S. Halferty, 1966, "Adolescence, Commitment, and Delinquency." J. of Research in Crime and Delinquency 3 (July): 82–96.

Reiss, Albert J., Jr., and A. Lewis Rhodes, 1963, "Status Deprivation and Delinquent Behavior." Soc. Q. 4 (Spring): 135–149.

Rhodes, A. Lewis and Albert J. Reiss, Jr., 1969, "Apathy, Truancy and Delinquency as Adaptations to School Failure." Social Forces 48 (September): 12–22.

Rosenberg, Morris, 1968, *The Logic of Survey Analysis.* New York: Basic Books.

Schafer, Walter E. and Kenneth Polk, 1967, "Delinquency and the Schools." Pp. 222–227 in Task Force Report: Juvenile Delinquency and Youth Crime. Washington, D.C.: Government Printing Office.

Schafer, Walter E., Carol Olexa, and Kenneth Polk, 1970, "Programmed for Social Class: Tracking in High School." Trans-Action 7 (October): 39–46, 63.

Stinchcombe, Arthur, 1964, *Rebellion in a High School.* Chicago: Quadrangle.

Vinter, Robert D. and Rosemary C. Sarri, 1965, "Malperformance in the Public School: A Group Work Approach." Social Work 10 (January): 3–13.

PART 4

BECOMING CRIMINAL

While selections in this part touch upon existing laws (Part 1) and the reasons why individuals violate them (Part 3), the focus is on how people, through various types of associations and contacts, learn criminal activities, values, and traditions. The readings range from an introduction to the basic learning processes that occur in the early stages of criminal careers, to descriptions of selected types of crimes, to an assessment of the impact that involvement in crime may have on an individual's personal and public identity.

LEARNING CRIME

The statement by Frank Tannenbaum, in "Definition and the Dramatization of Evil," presents what many would consider to be a classic account of how social actors may be selected out for special processing and treatment by the community. Tannenbaum also provides an excellent overview of the "labeling" or "societal reactions" perspective—a viewpoint that emphasizes, in part, the processes underlying the labeling ceremony and the social products that may flow from it (e.g., the criminalization of acts and the labeling of actors as criminals). He contends initially that two opposing definitions of an event may arise. And behavior viewed as play or fun by a young person may be perceived as a form of "evil" by community agents. These differing perceptions may, over time, produce a shift "from a definition of the specific acts as evil to a definition of the individual as evil." In a sense, the individual becomes viewed by the community as an evil person; this type of treatment produces feelings of injustice, and the affected actor begins to realize that he is different from others in the neighborhood, school, and community. Tannenbaum suggests that the individual may not only exhibit changes in self (e.g., he may begin to view himself as a criminal or delinquent), but the child's isolation may also force him into association with "other children similarly defined and the gang becomes his means of escape, his security." Tannenbaum continues by offering some valuable comments that have direct relevance for any program aimed at change. He argues that a direct attack on the individual will probably fail; this is due primarily to the fact that by the time one becomes a criminal, a person's behavior and attitudes have become firmly shaped. The attack thus must be on the whole group, for only by changing those stimuli that impact on the individual (e.g., attitudes, habits, and values) can we expect the individual to change. He also notes that his explanation behind the rise of criminal behavior is more appropriate to those who pursue the criminal career. As such, it would not seem to account for the accidental criminal, or for one who commits a crime of passion.

Implicit in Tannenbaum's analysis is the idea that not only must one gain exposure and entry into some type of criminal endeavor, but once situated, the novice must begin the socialization process. This concern for "learning the ropes" is given more specific focus by John Rosecrance ("The Stooper: A Professional Thief in the Sutherland Manner") in his 18-month study of a group of professional thieves known as *stoopers*. These are individuals who frequent racetracks and rummage through the litter in search of winning tickets that have been mistakenly discarded. Stooping is often in violation of local pandering laws, and those caught are subject to criminal prosecution and banishment from the track. In his data analysis, Rosecrance, in following Sutherland's model of professional crime, examines five main elements of the stooping profession: (1) technical skills, (2) status, (3) consensus, (4) differential association, and (5) organization. For example, the stooper must learn how to remain unobtrusive while looking for the discarded ticket. In fact, learning how to blend in with the crowd is considered to be the most basic skill. They must also learn how to redeem large payoffs. Rosecrance observes that there is a definite status system among the stoopers, with the professionals viewing the "amateurs" with a great deal of distaste and scorn. He notes that, in terms of social organization, the stooping profession is informally organized and is not part of any criminal underworld. Rather, they view themselves as a special type of thief, and they work together to enhance their financial opportunities. Most have, with respect to tutelage, learned their trade from an older, more skilled stooper. Several stoopers comment on the ready supply of potential recruits that could serve as apprentices.

As shown by the preceding materials, criminal activities, careers, and patterns may vary. This is evident in Rosecrance's discussion of those factors that produce a professional thief. Obviously, and as several of the works in Part 3 illustrated (e.g., Cloward and Ohlin's theory), not all who aspire to a lucrative or successful career in crime will succeed—there are frequently identity and structural barriers to overcome. The readings in the next section offer additional insight into how criminal careers and identities may be launched. They also describe other types of crime. Throughout, one can see how individual attributes may interact with organizational components and events to produce a criminal act. David F. Luckenbill, for example, analyzes the role that *situational determinants* play in the production of criminal behavior.

SITUATIONAL-PERSONAL CRIME

In "Criminal Homicide as a Situated Transaction," Luckenbill contends that though criminal homicide is often thought of as a one-sided event with the victim taking a passive role, this is frequently not the case. Rather, such acts of violence are often the result of situational factors and conditions. To support this claim, Luckenbill reconstructs actual incidents of homicide that occurred over a 10-year period, using police and witness reports, offender interviews, and the like. He concludes that murder is "the outcome of a dynamic interchange between an offender, victim, and, in many cases, bystanders" and that certain patterns seem to hold relatively independent of age, sex, race, time and place, use of alcohol, and proffered motive.

In "Rape in Marriage: A Sociological View," David Finkelhor and Kersti Yllo offer some data and observations on the nature and extent of another personal and often violent crime, marital rape. Their initial assumption is that rape in marriage is not a rare crime, but rather, it is a persistent problem for many marriages. They cite evidence in support of this and then present some data they gathered through in-depth interviews with 50 women. The question posed to the subjects was: "Has your current partner (or previous partner) ever used force or threat of force to try to have sex with you?" Three types of forced sex experiences were uncovered (battering rapes, nonbattering rapes, and obsessive rapes). The researchers provide case materials and proceed to analyze the amount of force employed by the men, as well as the amount of resistance offered by the victims. For example, some women felt that if they resisted, they would be punched, bruised, or beaten; this type of response was especially characteristic of those who had been battered or beaten before. Finkelhor and Yllo conclude by offering a discussion of such topics as the trauma involved with marital rape, the relationship between forced marital sex and the law, and public attitudes about marital rape.

Evan Stark and Anne H. Flitcraft, in "Women and Children at Risk: A Feminist Perspective on Child Abuse," continue the look at personal crime by examining the connection between battering and child abuse. A basic assumption is that these problems arise because of clashes between gender identity and male authority, with males exercising their authority through the violent control of women and children. The authors contend that the available clinical knowledge also contributes to the problems by perpetuating distorted images of women and children. They set about exploring a number of the questions and concerns that frequently characterize the study of battering and abuse (e.g., the attributes of the typical abuser, the typical context within which abuse occurs, and how protective services respond to battered women with abused children) and then present some data obtained on 116 mothers whose children have been referred to a special investigative committee in the hospital under study. Some interesting findings emerge. For example, 45 percent of the women in the study population had been battered. In examining what the researchers term the "mother's battering risk group," as well as looking at the identity of the abuser, 50 percent of the referred children of women situated in the "at-risk" category had been abused by a male batterer; this compares to 35 percent who had been abused by the mother. The remainder had been abused by "both" or others. They observe that when a control for danger to the child is introduced, battered women, as opposed to nonbattered, are more apt to lose their children; this prompts the authors to conclude that the responses on the part of the child abuse system "are ineffective at best and punitive at worst."

STREET CRIME

"Street," or "ordinary," crimes generally refer to such illegal activities as hustling, mugging, pimping, purse snatching, auto theft, drug dealing, and the like. In "Drugs-Crime Connections: Elaborations from the Life Histories of Hard-Core Heroin

Addicts," Charles E. Faupel and Carl B. Klockars examine the nature and extent of the relationship between heroin use and crime. They note that two competing hypotheses surround the drugs-crime controversy: (1) "drugs cause crimes," and (2) "crimes cause drugs." The researchers, in their efforts to unravel the temporal sequence to drug use and crime, draw upon life-history interviews with 32 hard-core heroin addicts. Their data indicate that all of the addicts reported some type of criminal involvement prior to their use of heroin. They note, however, that most of the respondents felt that their criminal and addict careers emerged independently of each other, even though the careers ultimately became interconnected. Two major factors shape and influence the drug and crime careers that evolve: the *availability* of heroin and *life structure* (i.e., "the regularly occurring patterns of daily, domestic, occupational, recreational, or criminal activity"). Faupel and Klockars use these two dimensions to develop a typology of heroin-use career phases; this produces four addict types: (1) the stabilized junkie, (2) the free-wheeling junkie, (3) the occasional user, and (4) the street junkie. The researchers, in their analysis of each addict type, also describe how addicts may shift from one type to another. The street junkie conforms most closely to the stereotypes people hold of heroin addicts. Such individuals have difficulty maintaining a steady supply of heroin, and they have trouble trying to establish a stable life structure. Hence, they find it necessary to resort to short-term crimes, jobs, opportunities, and hustles. The authors note that because street crimes pay so little and must be repeated, the street addict runs a very high risk of being arrested. Faupel and Klockars conclude by discussing the various research and policy implications suggested by their research. They point to the need for more longitudinal studies (i.e., examining the behavior of individuals over time) of the drugs-crime connection, particularly research that examines drug use and criminal behavior on a more regular basis (e.g., on a weekly or daily interval). The "addict career" must also be given more focus—this in view of the observation that heroin use and crime are not necessarily stable patterns throughout an addict's career. Addicts may, as a result of existing structural conditions (i.e., the availability of heroin and the nature of one's life structure), shift from one career-addict phase to another.

ORGANIZED CRIME

Although public and scholarly attention have traditionally focused on crimes of individuals, these cannot begin to compete with organized or corporate crime in terms of the sums of money involved. There are many reasons why the crimes of organizations have received less notice. One is the difficulty of gaining access to organizations and their records. Another is that even if indictments are levied against a corporation or underworld figure, the indicted party can usually afford to retain the very best legal counsel; this often means that court cases, as the result of the appeal procedure, may drag on for years.

In "Casinos and Banking: Organized Crime in the Bahamas," Alan A. Block and Frank R. Scarpitti describe the ways in which criminal interests may use offshore banks and businesses to launder money and evade taxes. They note initially that, although there are many tax-haven countries, those in the Caribbean have grown the fastest in recent years; this is due primarily to the fact that these countries are close to the United States and serve as important stops for drug trafficking enterprises. The authors focus specifically on the Bahamas, where strict rules of bank secrecy not only apply but where disclosure of an account holder's name or finances is punished. This code of secrecy also applies to the ownership of corporations. The context thus exists in which taxpayers and others hide money so they can avoid taxes or misrepresent their financial transactions or situation. Racketeers and drug dealers can also hide their "dirty" money while it is being cleaned or laundered for subsequent use. Block and Scarpitti go on to outline how, historically, organized crime, through its use of gambling and banking interests, gained a solid foothold on many Bahamian offshore banks and gambling casinos. The role of Meyer Lansky, a noted underworld gambling czar, is particularly enlightening.

CORPORATE CRIME

Assessing the nature and extent of business crime is hampered by a lack of access to records and operations. In addition, people seem to be more accepting of corporate or white-collar crime; many people view such crimes as illegal but not criminal. The tendency toward tolerance or leniency also carries over into the courts. Thus corporate crime is viewed from a different frame of reference, even though it often exacts greater personal and financial tolls, such as through exposure to nuclear radiation or unsafe products and increased cost of products as a result of monopolies or price fixing.

Raymond J. Michalowski and Ronald C. Kramer, in "The Space between Laws: The Problem of Corporate Crime in a Transnational Context," examine the topic of corporate crime from an expanded, international perspective. Of particular focus is an examination of how transnational corporations (TNCs) operating in developing countries have engaged in injurious corporate activities that, although legal in the host country, would be viewed as violations of laws, codes, and regulations in the home country. This lack of definitional congruence among nations creates difficulties for those interested in studying corporate crime. Researchers must, therefore, develop their own definitions of what constitutes the appropriate subject matter for inquiry. Michalowski and Kramer propose to do so. They focus specifically on the sociopolitical construction of laws and political labels relative to injurious corporate acts. The analysis of the *corporate criminalization process* has been studied primarily at the level of the state. However, the spread of TNCs requires an expanded focus—one that not only analyzes the processes behind the construction of political labels, but one that also incorporates a concern for the impact of what they term "analogous social injuries." The authors go on to analyze how TNCs have expanded over the last quarter, with the most significant pattern being their location in Third World or developing nations. The growth of these TNCs has been associated with a range of corporate hazards and deviance. Given the lack of legal controls over the workplace, the environment, and industrial hazards, the potential for corporations to engage in socially injurious acts is great. The authors conclude by discussing how the "space between laws" can be dealt with (e.g., using international codes as guidelines, or using the United Nations as a body for creating new laws and regulations).

GOVERNMENT CRIME

The Watergate scandal helped to sensitize people to the fact that, like corporations and their executives, governments and their representatives also commit crimes. The crimes attributed to governmental agents have ranged from illegal break-ins and wiretaps, smear campaigns against individuals, and opening up mail, to conducting experiments on naive subjects and political assassinations.

In "The State and Organizing Crime," William J. Chambliss analyzes the connection among organized crime, drug smuggling, and the CIA. He begins by noting that the smuggling of arms and drugs on the national and international levels involves a mammoth enterprise that not only amounts to hundreds of billions of dollars annually but that also impacts on millions of lives, international relations, other governments, and war. Chambliss elaborates on this by initially describing the role that opium and its derivatives (morphine and heroin) have played in this process. He notes that even though the Harrison Act of 1914 made the sale or possession of heroin and its derivatives illegal, there existed a large population of opium-addicted individuals who demanded drugs. Hence, the smuggling of illegal drugs flourished, and in the thirties, with the labeling of marijuana and cocaine as illegal drugs, Chambliss notes that smuggling became an international enterprise. He continues by describing the role that Meyer Lansky, a well-known smuggler of alcoholic beverages, played in setting up lucrative and efficient smuggling routes. The established patterns of drug smuggling changed dramatically, however, after the United States entered the Vietnam War and inherited the dependence on opium. To meet this need, the CIA and military personnel began to organize smuggling routes out of Southeast Asia. Chambliss' description of the CIA's role in this process, as well as other involved parties, is particularly insightful. For example, the CIA's airline, Air America, would transport opium out of the Golden Triangle to heroin laboratories in Saigon, Hong Kong, and Bangkok. Some interesting case materials are offered in support of these observations. Chambliss proceeds to document other ways in which the CIA and its operatives became involved in the smuggling of drugs and arms, money laundering, and other criminal activities. He concludes by trying to explain the reasons why such agencies as the CIA, the National Security Council, the Defense Department, and the State Department became involved in illegal enterprises. His answer is predicated on the various structural contradictions that exist within the U.S. The military-intelligence establishment, for example, is committed to fighting the spread of "communism," yet the support of Congress and the president may be lacking; this often means that programs become undermined by a lack of resources, or even hindered by the passage of new laws. Such threats to existing programs, as well as the very mission of the CIA, prompted the search for alternative sources of revenue. The existing international networks for drug smuggling, arms smuggling, money laundering, and the like provided ready-made sources.

EFFECTS OF INVOLVEMENT

As noted previously, involvement in activities viewed or defined as criminal is frequently not without its personal and social costs. The sex offender and the street hustler, for example, are committing crimes that, if detected, can lead to institutional processing and sentencing. Thus criminals must manage their behavior and mannerisms so as to avoid detection by social control agents. They must also try to protect their self-image. The last selection in Part 4 deals with this problem.

Carl B. Klockars, in "The Fence and Society: Vincent's *Apologia Pro Vita Sua*," not only introduces another type of criminal—the professional fence—but focuses on the "techniques of neutralization" (Sykes and Matza, Part 3) that are used by Vincent (a fence) to rationalize his involvement in illegal activities. Klockars stresses that many of the rationalizations are nothing more than extensions of statements used by all of us. "If I don't buy it, somebody else will" and "Sure, I've done some bad things in my life, who hasn't?" are examples.

20. Definition and the Dramatization of Evil

FRANK TANNENBAUM

In the conflict between the young delinquent and the community there develop two opposing definitions of the situation. In the beginning, the definition of the situation by the young delinquent may be in the form of play, adventure, excitement, interest, mischief, fun. Breaking windows, annoying people, running around porches, climbing over roofs, stealing from pushcarts, playing truant—all are items of play, adventure, excitement. To the community, however, these activities may and often do take on the form of a nuisance, evil, delinquency, with the demand for control, admonition, chastisement, punishment, police court, truant school. This conflict over the situation is one that arises out of a divergence of values. As the problem develops, the situation gradually becomes redefined. The attitude of the community hardens definitely into a demand for suppression. There is a gradual shift from the definition of the specific acts as evil to a definition of the individual as evil, so that all his acts come to be looked upon with suspicion. In the process of identification his companions, hang-outs, play, speech, income, all his conduct, the personality itself, become subject to scrutiny and question. From the community's point of view, the individual who used to do bad and mischievous things has now become a bad and unredeemable human being. From the individual's point of view there has taken place a similar change. He has gone slowly from a sense of grievance and injustice, of being unduly mistreated and punished, to a recognition that the definition of him as a human being is different from that of other boys in his neighborhood, his school, street, community. This recognition on his part becomes a process of self-identification and integration with the group which shares his activities. It becomes, in part, a process of rationalization; in part, a simple response to a specialized type of stimulus. The young delinquent becomes bad because he is defined as bad and because he is not believed if he is good. There is a persistent demand for consistency in character. The community cannot deal with people whom it cannot define. Reputation is this sort of public definition. Once it is established, then unconsciously all agencies combine to maintain this definition even when they apparently and consciously attempt to deny their own implicit judgment.

Early in his career, then, the incipient professional criminal develops an attitude of antagonism to the regulated orderly life that he is required to lead. This attitude is hardened and crystallized by opposition. The conflict becomes a clash of wills. And experience too often has proved that threats, punishments, beatings, commitments to institutions, abuse and defamation of one sort or another, are of no avail. Punishment breaks down against the child's stubbornness. What has happened is that the child has been defined as an "incorrigible" both by his contacts and by himself, and an attempt at a direct breaking down of will generally fails.

The child meets the situation in the only way he can, by defiance and escape — physical escape if possible, or emotional escape by derision, anger, contempt, hatred, disgust, tantrums, destructiveness, and physical violence. The response of the child is just as intelligent and intelligible as that of the schools, of the authorities. They have taken a simple problem, the lack of fitness of an institution to a particular child's needs, and have made a moral issue out of it with values outside the child's ken. It takes on the form of war between two wills, and the longer the war lasts, the more certainly does the child become incorrigible. The child will not yield because he cannot yield — his nature requires other channels for pleasant growth; the school system or society will not yield because it does not see the issues involved as between the incompatibility of an institution and a child's needs, sometimes physical needs, and will instead attempt to twist the child's nature to the institution with that consequent distortion of the child which makes an unsocial career inevitable. The verbalization of the conflict in terms of evil, delinquency, incorrigibility, badness, arrest, force, punishment, stupidity, lack of intelligence, truancy, criminality, gives the innocent divergence of the child from the straight road a meaning that it did not have in the beginning and makes its continuance in these same terms by so much the more inevitable.

The only important fact, when the issue arises of the boy's inability to acquire the specific habits which organized institutions attempt to impose upon him, is that this conflict becomes the occasion for him to acquire another series of habits, interests, and attitudes as a substitute. These habits become as effective in motivating and guiding conduct as would have been those which the orderly routine social institutions attempted to impose had they been acquired.

This conflict gives the gang its hold, because the gang provides escape, security, pleasure, and peace. The gang also gives room for the motor activity which plays a large role in a child's life. The attempt to break up the gang by force merely strengthens it. The arrest of the children has consequences undreamed-of, for several reasons.

First, only some of the children are caught though all may be equally guilty. There is a great deal more delinquency practiced and committed by the young groups than comes to the attention of the police. The boy arrested, therefore, is singled out in specialized treatment. This boy, no more guilty than the other members of his group, discovers a world of which he knew little. His arrest suddenly precipitates a series of institutions, attitudes, and experiences which the other children do not share. For this boy there suddenly appear the police, the patrol wagon, the police station, the other delinquents and criminals found in the police lock-ups, the court with all its agencies such as bailiffs, clerks, bondsmen, lawyers, probation officers. There are bars, cells, handcuffs, criminals. He is questioned, examined, tested, investigated. His history is gone into, his family is brought into court. Witnesses make their appearance. The boy, no different from the rest of his gang, suddenly becomes the center of a major drama in which all sorts of unexpected characters play important roles. And what is it all about? about the accustomed things his gang has done and has been doing for a long time. In this entirely new world he is made conscious of himself as a different human being than he was before his arrest. He becomes classified as a thief, perhaps, and the entire world about him has suddenly become a different place for him and will remain different for the rest of his life. . . .

The first dramatization of the "evil" which separates the child out of his group for specialized treatment plays a greater role in making the criminal than perhaps any other experience. It cannot be too often emphasized that for the child the whole situation has become different. He now lives in a different world. He has been tagged. A new and hitherto nonexistent environment has been precipitated out for him.

The process of making the criminal, therefore, is a process of tagging, defining, identifying, segregating, describing, emphasizing, making conscious and self-conscious; it becomes a way of stimulating, suggesting, emphasizing, and evoking the very traits that are complained of. If the theory of relation of response to stimulus has any meaning, the entire process of dealing with the young delinquent is mischievous in so far as it identifies him to himself or to the environment as a delinquent person.

The person becomes the thing he is described as being. Nor does it seem to matter whether the valuation is made by those who would punish or by those who would reform. In either case the emphasis is upon the conduct that is disapproved of. The parents or the policeman, the older brother or the court, the probation officer or the juvenile institution, insofar as they rest upon the thing complained of, rest upon a false ground. Their very enthusiasm defeats their aim. The harder they work to reform the evil, the greater the evil grows under their hands. The persistent suggestion, with whatever good intentions, works mischief, because it leads to bringing out the bad behavior that it would suppress. The way out is through a refusal to dramatize the evil. The less said about it the better. The more said about something else, still better.

> The hard-drinker who keeps thinking of not drinking is doing what he can to initiate the acts which lead to drinking. He is starting with the stimulus to his habit. To succeed he must find some positive interest or line of action which will inhibit the drinking series and which by instituting another course of action will bring him to his desired end.[1]

The dramatization of the evil therefore tends to precipitate the conflict situation which was first created through some innocent maladjustment. The child's isolation forces him into companionship with other children similarly defined, and the gang becomes his means of escape, his security. The life of the gang gives it special mores, and the attack by the community upon these mores merely overemphasizes the conflict already in existence, and makes it the source of a new series of experiences that lead directly to a criminal career.

In dealing with the delinquent, the criminal, therefore, the important thing to remember is that we are dealing with a human being who is responding normally to the demands, stimuli, approval, expectancy, of the group with whom he is associated. We are dealing not with an individual but with a group.

> In a study of 6,000 instances of stealing, with reference to the number of boys involved, it was found that in 90.4 percent of the cases two or more boys were known to have been involved in the act and were consequently brought to court. Only 9.6 percent of all the cases were acts of single individuals. Since this study was based upon the number of boys brought to court, and since in many cases not all of the boys involved were caught and brought to court, it is certain that the percentage of group stealing is therefore even greater

than 90.4 percent. It cannot be doubted that delinquency, particularly stealing, almost invariably involves two or more persons.[2]

That group may be a small gang, a gang of children just growing up, a gang of young "toughs" of nineteen or twenty, or a gang of older criminals of thirty. If we are not dealing with a gang we may be dealing with a family. And if we are not dealing with either of these especially we may be dealing with a community. In practice all these factors—the family, the gang, and the community—may be important in the development and the maintenance of that attitude towards the world which makes a criminal career a normal, accepted and approved way of life.

Direct attack upon the individual in these circumstances is a dubious undertaking. By the time the individual has become a criminal his habits have been so shaped that we have a fairly integrated character whose whole career is in tune with the peculiar bit of the environment for which he has developed the behavior and habits that cause him to be apprehended. In theory isolation from that group ought to provide occasion for change in the individual's habit structure. It might, if the individual were transplanted to a group whose values and activities had the approval of the wider community, and in which the newcomer might hope to gain full acceptance eventually. But until now isolation has meant the grouping in close confinement of persons whose strongest common bond has been their socially disapproved delinquent conduct. Thus the attack cannot be made without reference to group life.

The attack must be on the whole group; for only by changing its attitudes and ideals, interests and habits, can the stimuli which it exerts upon the individual be changed. Punishment as retribution has failed to reform, that is, to change character. If the individual can be made aware of a different set of values for which he may receive approval, then we may be on the road to a change in his character. But such a change of values involves a change in stimuli, which means that the criminal's social world must be changed before he can be changed.

The point of view here developed rejects all assumptions that would impute crime to the individual in the sense that a personal shortcoming of the offender is the cause of the unsocial behavior. The assumption that crime is caused by any sort of inferiority, physiological or psychological, is here completely and unequivocally repudiated.

This of course does not mean that morphological or psychological techniques do not have value in dealing with the individual. It merely means that they have no greater value in the study of criminology than they would have in the study of any profession. If a poor IQ is a bad beginning for a career in medicine, it is also a poor beginning for a career in crime. If the psychiatrist can testify that a psychopath will make an irritable doctor he can prove the same for the criminal. But he can prove no more. The criminal differs from the rest of his fellows only in the sense that he has learned to respond to the stimuli of a very small and specialized group; but that group must exist or the criminal could not exist. In that, he is like the mass of men, living a certain kind of life with the kind of companions that make that life possible.

This explanation of criminal behavior is meant to apply to those who more or less consistently pursue the criminal career. It does not necessarily presume to describe the accidental criminal or the man who commits a crime of passion. Here perhaps the

theories that would seek the cause of crime in the individual may have greater application than in attempting to deal with those who follow a life of crime. But even in the
accidental criminal there is a strong presumption that the accident is the outcome of
a habit situation. Any habit tends to have a background of social conditioning.

> A man with the habit of giving way to anger may show his habit by a murderous attack upon
> someone who has offended. His act is nonetheless due to habit because it occurs only once
> in his life. The essence of habit is an acquired predisposition to *ways* or modes of response,
> not to particular acts except as, under special conditions, these express a way of behaving.
> Habit means special sensitiveness or accessibility to certain classes of stimuli, standing
> predilections and aversions, rather than bare recurrence of specific acts. It means will.[3]

In other words, perhaps the accidental criminal also is to be explained in terms such
as we use in discussing the professional criminal.

Notes

1. John Dewey, *Human Nature and Conduct*, p. 35. New York, 1922.
2. Clifford R. Shaw and Earl D. Myers, "The Juvenile Delinquent," *The Illinois Crime Survey*,
pp. 662–663. Chicago, 1929.
3. Dewey, op. cit., p. 42.

21.   The Stooper: A Professional Thief in the Sutherland Manner

JOHN ROSECRANCE

The professional criminal is traditionally defined as one who obtains a major portion
of his or her income from illegal activity (Blumberg, 1981: 46). Professional crime
generally refers to nonviolent patterns of criminal behavior undertaken with skill and
planning, the execution of which minimizes the possibility of apprehension (Inciardi,
1975: 5). Sutherland was the seminal source of a systematic analysis of professional
crime. In 1937, he advanced the concept of a behavior system to explain the existence
of this form of criminal activity. Typically, members of such a system shared a distinct
argot, an ideology of legitimation, normative expectations, a specialized activity, and
a degree of technical expertise (Sutherland, 1937: 197–216). Sutherland's model
gained acceptance by many criminologists and police officials as an accurate representation of professional crime.

Since his pioneering work, there have been various criticisms of Sutherland's concept of professional crime. Criticisms have coalesced around three issues: (1) the existence of an established professional criminal organization, (2) the specialized

character of professional crime, and (3) the contention that Sutherland's model is either too narrow or outdated. Lemert (1958) and Einstadter (1969), after investigating check forgers and armed robbers, respectively, concluded that these offenders, who otherwise met the criteria of professional criminals, worked alone, were not part of a criminal system, and had not been tutored by other criminals. After conducting studies for a president's commission on crime, researchers (Gould, Bittner, Messinger, Powledge, and Chaneles, 1966) contended that professional thieves were not specialists but instead were generalists—that is, "hustlers" who sought available opportunities for illegal gain. Other criminologists (Shover, 1973; Klein, 1974; Inciardi, 1974, 1975) have indicated that professional criminals are not reproducing themselves and their behavior systems are dying out: "Professional theft will continue to atrophy until its unique qualities become only references within the history of crime" (Inciardi, 1975: 82). Walker (1981: 171) has argued that Sutherland's model is unnecessarily narrow and can be applied accurately only to highly successful professionals who represent a criminal elite (for example, class cannons or jewel thieves).

The research discussed here considers a group of contemporary thieves whose behavior patterns closely resemble the Sutherland model of professional crime. Following an analysis of this striking resemblance, the conclusion reached is that Sutherland's concept of professional crime is still applicable and can serve as a useful guide in depicting a modern criminal behavior system. The criminal group studied is that of racetrack stoopers. A stooper has been defined as "someone who looks through the litter of discarded [racetrack] tickets for a winner mistakenly thrown away" (Martinez, 1983: 222). Although this group has been acknowledged by prior researchers (Scott, 1968; Maurer, 1974; Surface, 1976), their criminal activities have apparently never been delineated.

Those who frequent racetracks for the purpose of stooping are in violation of pandering laws. Stoopers are subject to both criminal prosecution and administrative banishment by track officials. They fit the general criteria of a sneak thief as one "who does not, at the outset of his crime, proclaim his intentions by some work or act; he is a thief who has the ability to remain unnoticed, blending with his environment while stealing in the proximity of his awake and active victims" (Inciardi, 1974: 306).

This paper describes the activities of professional stoopers and demonstrates how their behavior closely parallels the original Sutherland model of professional crime. This will demonstrate that in this case, the major criticisms of Sutherland's concept have not lessened its applicability to a contemporary criminal behavior system. The accumulated data reveal that this group is reproducing itself, a finding that belies the contention that Sutherland's professional thief should be considered merely a historical reference. This research is in general accord with that of Chambliss (1972: 168):

> the overwhelming evidence is that professional theft is no more dead today than it has ever been. There have always been a small cadre of devotees who consider themselves professional thieves; who plan their capers carefully; who develop their craft through apprenticeship and with planning.

Chambliss's finding is extended by applying Sutherland's concept of professional crime to a heretofore unresearched criminal system.

METHODOLOGY

It is always difficult to collect data about professional criminals (Clinard and Quinney, 1967: 429; Cressey, 1967: 102; Letkemann, 1973: 165–166; Abadinsky, 1983: 4). By design, professional thieves are secretive and take elaborate steps to remain unobtrusive. This was certainly the case with the group under investigation. Stoopers attempt to mingle with other race-goers in a chameleon-like deception. Professional stoopers have achieved virtual anonymity and conduct their business unnoticed by even long-time racing fans. The author began his investigation of stoopers by first interviewing racetrack officials and security personnel. After learning how to identify stoopers, he observed their actions at racetracks in California, Louisiana, Maryland, and West Virginia. Because most stoopers refuse to discuss their activities, he was unable to interview any of them until he located a stooper in California who agreed to be an informant. This stooper introduced him to others and he was able to conduct interviews with eight stoopers in California. In Louisiana the author developed a relationship with another informant and was able to interview five stoopers in that area. The stoopers who consented to be interviewed were all male, ranged in age from 25 to 55, and generally had minor criminal records. The author did not use a structured questionnaire, but asked such questions as the following:

1. How did you get into stooping?
2. Why do you remain a stooper?
3. Can you support yourself by stooping?
4. Do you follow the horses from track to track?
5. Have you done time in jail?
6. Do you know other stoopers?
7. Do you work with other stoopers?
8. What steps do you take to avoid detection?
9. What do your family or friends think of your stooping?

During the study the author was guided by the principles of grounded theory (Glaser and Strauss, 1967) and sought to develop analyses that were generated directly from the data gathered from the interviews with stoopers, racetrack officials, and personnel.

FINDINGS

An analysis of the research data revealed that, in most respects, the behavior system of racetrack stoopers corresponds to that described by Sutherland in his classic work, *The Professional Thief.* This finding will be clarified by describing their demonstrated behavior in terms of the five characteristics of professional crime outlined by Sutherland (1937: 198): (1) technical skill, (2) status, (3) consensus, (4) differential association, and (5) organization.

Technical Skills

In 1984 at California racetracks, over three million dollars worth of winning tickets were not cashed.[1] At one track alone (Belmont Park, New York) during a single racing season, tickets worth more than one and a half million dollars were not redeemed (Surface, 1976: 183). In most states these unclaimed winnings subsequently revert to state treasuries. Racing patrons, who for various reasons lose their winning mutuel tickets, create a source of illegal income for stoopers. In the racing argot, live tickets (those that can be cashed) are there for the taking. However, actually finding and retrieving discarded winning tickets involves the application of skillful techniques.

The development and implementation of technical skills among stoopers closely resembles Sutherland's conceptualizations. According to Sutherland (1937: 197), "the professional thief has a complex of abilities and skills, just as do physicians, lawyers, or bricklayers." He indicated that these abilities were based upon cleverness and stealth, not upon strength or physical dexterity. Sutherland conceived of professionals as specialists who concentrated their talents in a particular form of criminal activity.

Professional stoopers are definitely specialists. They devote their efforts to finding winning tickets and rarely participate in other illegal endeavors. The time, commitment, and specialization involved in becoming a successful stooper precludes active participation in other illegal activities. The comment of a veteran stooper reflects this situation:

> I have to work so hard at stooping I just don't have time for other capers. Some guys I know are into stealing and fencing. I suppose I could get in on their action. But with busting my ass six days a week at the track I gotta pass. Besides, even though I know how to make it at the track, I don't know diddly shit about heavy-duty thieving.

The skills involved in stooping are not related to unusual physical abilities; moderate eyesight and normal mobility comprise the basic physical requirements.

The process of stooping is divided into four stages: (1) blending, (2) hunting, (3) identifying, and (4) cashing. During each of these stages the use of skillful techniques is required. Remaining unobtrusive while also looking for discarded tickets is the stooper's most basic skill. Stoopers often talk of the necessity of blending.

> You become part of the crowd—just like any other guy at the track. Security won't hassle you as long as you don't call attention to yourself. You're OK if you just act natural. First, last, and always you have to blend.

Stoopers are careful to dress like other racing fans. Those who "work" the grandstand where blue-collar patrons congregate, dress in jeans or work clothes. Appropriately, stoopers who situate themselves in the clubhouse, where middle-class patrons are in the majority, wear jackets, dress slacks, and polished shoes. Most stoopers are not active gamblers. A stooper explained: "I haven't got the time to look at a Racing Form—too busy hustling tickets. Half the time I don't even know who's running." However, in order to blend they occasionally wager on races. "I throw away a few bucks every day just to look the part. I never saw a racing man who didn't bet some." Professional stoopers refrain from drinking or arguing while on the job to avoid "sticking out."

While remaining unnoticed is essential, the stooper must also develop an aptitude for finding discarded winning tickets. "Hunting" is a commonly used term to describe this search. Although stoopers maintain a continuing vigil, they usually do not begin a serious search until the middle of the racing day when a significant number of discarded tickets has accumulated. A stooper described this practice, "I can't bear down and go all out after each race. I'd get bummed out. I usually don't get serious until after the fifth race when the losers start to go home."

Certain kinds of race results and betting situations dictate an extensive search. Just after a disqualification (when the actual order of finish is changed) is considered by many stoopers to be an excellent time for locating cashable tickets. Although gamblers are always cautioned by the track announcer to "hold all tickets until the race is declared official," they often disregard this warning and throw their tickets away before the official winners are posted. Frequently, when bettors discover that a disqualification has made their seemingly worthless tickets winning ones, they are unable to locate the discarded ticket. Often the tickets have been picked up by an alert stooper who has blended into the crowd. Other situations that are conducive to mistakenly throwing away winning tickets occur when, for betting purposes, more than one horse is combined to form an entry (horses trained by the same person) or a field (more than 12 horses are entered in a single race). When such situations arise, stoopers must redouble their efforts in order to take advantage of a potential windfall.

If stoopers are to be successful, they must identify those mutuel tickets that can eventually be cashed. This must be accomplished quickly to avoid being noticed. A veteran stooper related, "Instant recall is required in this business. You can't linger over a ticket trying to remember whether it's live." Such identification necessitates that stoopers be able to recall a multitude of winning ticket numbers. They must remember numbers of the win, place, and show horses in each of nine races plus daily double, exacta, and quinella combinations. This form of mental acuity is often facilitated by development of a memory system. One stooper related that he used the childhood nursery rhyme "One-two, buckle my shoe; three-four, shut the door" to remember the winning numbers. Others have used color combinations or personally significant codes such as their age, social security number, and birthdate as recall keys.

Patience and persistence are important during the hunting and identification phases. Some days stoopers "come up empty," while other days tickets they locate result in payoffs between $2 and $20. On occasion, tickets worth over $100 or even $1,000 have been found. One of the informants indicated, "I find a lot of two-buck show tickets but every once in awhile I make a big score. Those big ones are out there for the taking—keeps me coming back."

Once a live ticket has been retrieved, it must be redeemed at one of the cashier windows. Stoopers employ skillful techniques to achieve this end. Tickets with a low monetary value can be routinely cashed by presenting them at varied cashier locations. However, tickets that will result in large payoffs must be handled more circumspectly. Stoopers are aware that most security personnel and track officials know them on sight. Collecting a large payoff could attract unwanted attention and might cause the security department to more closely monitor their activities. In order to avoid notoriety, stoopers hire beards or accomplices to cash large-value tickets. These beards are usually "straight types" who are not regular track patrons. To the track cashier the beard appears as a solid citizen and is able to receive large payouts without incident.

Status

Accomplished stoopers, in common with Sutherland's professional thieves, have achieved status. This status is drawn from the attitudes of racetrack authorities, especially security personnel and other track insiders. Stoopers, like other professional thieves, are "contemptuous of amateur thieves and have many epithets which they apply to amateurs" (Sutherland, 1937: 200).

Security personnel and local police assigned to the track expressed a grudging admiration for successful stoopers. Such respect works to the advantage of stoopers. The observation of a security chief reflects this situation.

> The pros are really something else. They don't even bend over until they spot a live ticket. Once they stoop you can bet they will come up with something good. These guys don't cause anyone any trouble and they go out of their way to avoid a hassle. They are real pros. I could bust 'em, but what's the point? As long as they keep out of everybody's way we don't bother them.

Others who work at the racetrack—for example, trainers, jockeys, grooms, and ticket sellers—also acknowledge the professional status of stoopers. A long-time horse trainer commented, "I don't know how those boys do it, but they sure can find live tickets. I guess it's because they're real professional about what they do."

At every racetrack there are people who attempt to find live tickets. Most of these searchers are not professional in their manner or technique and are considered amateurs by track insiders. A popular method used by nonprofessional stoopers involves picking up all the tickets they can find and then openly culling through them. Some amateurs send their children around the grandstand area to scoop lost tickets into a bag. Children who engage in obvious ticket collection are less likely to arouse the ire of security forces than are adults. Other track bustouts will steal tickets from pockets, wallets, and purses, or take them directly from a winning bettor. One technique is grabbing and running with tickets taken from bar patrons who have waved them about while happily proclaiming, "I've got a winner." Security personnel report that many of these "snatch and grab" (Sutherland, 1937: 201) thieves have tried stooping but did not have the skill or patience to be successful and instead have turned to more visible or violent criminal activities.

Professional stoopers heap scorn and ridicule upon amateurs "who give stooping a bad name" and disdain methods deemed "unprofessional." Such perspectives can be illustrated by the statement of an accomplished stooper.

> Those assholes who run around the track with shopping bags while grabbing tickets off the floor are pathetic. They never find anything and security runs 'em off quick. The jokers who roll drunks or grab purses are just thugs and deserve to be put in the slammer. If I ever resort to those tactics I hope someone locks me up.

By most standards, stoopers are not financially successful. Because earnings fluctuate drastically, it is difficult to estimate their annual incomes. However, estimates among ten of the stoopers interviewed ranged from \$6,000 to \$20,000 per year. But most were quick to point out "it's all tax free." An important source of status among stoopers is their independence and ability to operate outside the system. They frequently talked of the "uptight assholes" who lead a routine, structured life. Stoopers pride themselves on their ability to function without bureaucratic support.

> It's a heady feeling living without a safety net. There's no Blue Cross, dental plan, company retirement plan, sick days, or paid vacations to fall back on. On the other hand, there's no forms to fill out, supervisors to suck up to, or time clocks to punch. I don't work for wages. I can come and go as I want. I live by my wits alone. Sure beats being a scared little pencil-pusher.

Consensus

As a group, stoopers because of their common endeavor have developed similar attitudes and values. Shared feelings include rationalizations for their type of criminal activity as well as perspectives concerning their victims. Consensus among stoopers has fostered an informal but extant "code of helpfulness" (Sutherland, 1937: 203).

Professional stoopers are able to rationalize much of their criminal activity by adhering to a prevailing societal attitude subsumed within the popular expression, "finders, keepers; losers, weepers." Such an attitude holds that careless persons should not expect to have their property returned by good samaritans. The responsibility to adequately safeguard one's personal property is a basic American tenet. Stoopers contend that by thoughtlessly throwing away winning tickets, racing patrons have forfeited their right to those tickets. They maintain that "If the sucker is not sufficiently smart enough to protect himself, his rights are gone" (Sutherland, 1937: 173). Security personnel, while acknowledging that stooping is theft, also feel little sympathy for the victim. A security guard expressed that view: "Any jerk who throws away a live ticket gets what's coming to him—a lost ticket." Stoopers do not conceive of their activities as victimless crimes. They all have seen the frantic look of desperation on the faces of those searching for the discarded winning tickets that are already in the stooper's possession. Notwithstanding the victim's understandable anguish, there is a consensus among professionals that the victim's carelessness absolves the stooper of moral responsibility.

There is an implicit code among stoopers which stipulates that other professional stoopers should be treated with respect, protected from being apprehended, and given financial aid when needed. Adherence to this code, while not always absolute, does add to the consensual relationship among group members. Stoopers relate to one another in a generally friendly manner and are careful not to openly criticize each other. If stoopers are apprehended or detained, they do not attempt to curry favor from the authorities by "ratting on a buddy." Stoopers, in common with other racetrack types (Rosecrance, 1985: 138), frequently lend each other money to mitigate their fluctuating financial fortunes. Stoopers are constrained to follow their code since their numbers are few and their professional reputations are at stake. An informant succinctly described this phenomenon: "I wouldn't screw other stoopers. It wouldn't be professional. Besides, I might need their help later on. The track's a small world."

Differential Association

Stoopers are separated from larger society both by the racetrack milieu in which they operate and by their own specialized illegal activity. This pattern of differential association tends to form social barriers which further accentuate the differences between them and nongroup members. They are often reluctant to discuss their stooping with those outside their social world, even with family members and close friends. Stoopers believe that "outsiders would never understand what we do." Frequently they tell their significant others that they are working at the track as cashiers, trainers, or even security workers. The stoopers' behavior system fits Sutherland's (1937: 207) characterization that the "group defines its own membership." Only accomplished stoopers who act professionally are fully accepted into the inner world of this group. Those considered amateurs or part-timers must function on their own, without assistance from professional stoopers. Once accepted by other professionals, social contacts are generally contained within this group.

Although separated by differential association, stoopers are not totally isolated from the larger society. During their stooping efforts they must mingle and associate with the general population, even while planning to fleece them. Occasionally they need the assistance of those in conventional society—for example, beards, lawyers, and bail bondsmen. Stoopers, while engaged in an illegal endeavor, share many of society's basic values. They tend to be conservative, to strongly favor a capitalistic system, and to believe that hard work will ultimately be rewarded.

Social Organization

Even though stoopers are informally organized to help one another, they are not part of a larger criminal underworld. They do not have ties with either organized crime or large mobs, and typically do not associate or hang out with the general body of criminals. Consequently, they have little contact with traditional criminal organizations. In this respect, the stoopers' behavior patterns do not fit precisely the Sutherland model.

Stoopers prefer instead to consider themselves as a special breed of thief. Among themselves they cooperate and work together to increase their financial opportunities. The supply of discarded winning tickets is not inexhaustible, and most tracks cannot support more than four to six full-time stoopers. Professional stoopers divide the racetrack into work areas and then do not infringe on one another's territory.

The stoopers' pattern of tutelage closely resembles that described by Sutherland (1937: 211–213). In most cases, stoopers have learned the business from an older and more accomplished professional. As tyros, they were introduced to the complex of skills that make up professional stooping by an already established thief. "In the course of this process a person who is not a professional may first become a neophyte and then a recognized professional thief" (Sutherland, 1937: 212). Older, more established stoopers indicated that there was no shortage of potential recruits, and they could choose carefully their apprentices. One such professional said, "I don't know where these young guys come from, but every few months one comes around and wants to learn the business. Most of them I can't help but every once in awhile I take a liking to a guy and show him the ropes."

SUMMARY AND CONCLUSIONS

This paper has described and analyzed the criminal system of a little-known group of professional thieves. Accomplished racetrack stoopers are few in number, and their illegal activity does not represent a serious threat to society. For the most part, police officials are unaware of their existence, and knowledgeable security personnel have shown little interest in apprehending or prosecuting them. The victims, careless bettors, and the state treasuries that are entitled to the uncashed winnings have not demanded that action be taken to halt their loss. While stoopers are involved in illegal activity and their victims do incur financial loss, their interest to the criminology community rests upon the theoretical implications of the stoopers' empirically demonstrated behavior patterns, not the scope of their criminal activity.

Sutherland's (1937) original conceptualization of professional crime has been hailed as "an unforgettable moment for the disciplines of criminology, police science, and correctional administration," and has been said to have "made manifest the nature and complexity of a criminal career" (Inciardi, 1975: 5). However, in the intervening years there has been a host of criticisms of Sutherland's definition of professional crime (Lemert, 1958; Gould et al., 1966; Einstadter, 1969; Jackson, 1969; Klein, 1974; Walker, 1981). Researchers have also contended that a rapidly changing, modern technology has rendered the Sutherland model obsolete (Shover, 1973; Inciardi, 1974, 1975; Wickman and Whitten, 1980). Sutherland's perspective of professional crime has been labeled traditional (Staats, 1977), and there is a suggestion that the professional thief may be "more the creation of journalism, romanticism, and commercialism than an empirically demonstrable social type" (Turk, 1969: 15).

The research findings here demonstrate that the Sutherland model is still viable and that it has relevance to contemporary criminal activity. These findings lend support to Chambliss's (1972: 168) contention that "professional theft is not about to become extinct." The ongoing behavior system of racetrack stoopers manifests the major characteristics of professional crime as delineated by Sutherland. A consideration of these characteristics has demonstrated that, with respect to this group, the major criticisms of Sutherland's concept of professional crime (enumerated in the introduction) have not detracted from its applicability.

Professional stoopers employ a specialized complex of skills to perpetrate a unique form of criminal behavior. Although not financially successful by most standards, stoopers derive status from their professional manner, and in turn are contemptuous of amateur practitioners. Due to a common endeavor and the specialized nature of their activity, stoopers have developed a consensus which includes shared rationalization, attitudes toward victims, and an informal code of behavior. Through a process of differential association, stoopers are separated but not isolated from traditional society. While not belonging to a larger criminal network, stoopers are informally organized and tutelage is necessary to become part of that organization.

Professional crime as described by Sutherland should not be relegated to the status of a romanticized footnote. While modern technology may have drastically altered some forms of professional crime, in the case of racetrack stoopers it has not radically changed their behavior system. Contemporary stoopers go on plying their trade in much the same manner as their earlier counterparts. There is no evidence of a diminution of skills or that modern-day stoopers ignore the tenets of their code. Novice stoopers are being tutored, and there are many indications that stooping will provide a regular source of income for a determined cadre of skilled thieves. Racetrack patrons show no signs of becoming more careful, and a continuing supply of discarded live tickets seems assured. In this instance, a group of professional criminals continues to behave in the Sutherland manner.

Note

1. The figure of three million dollars was given to the author by John Regan of the California Horse Racing Board during a phone conversation of August 14, 1985.

References

Abadinsky, Howard
    1983   The Criminal Elite. Westport, CT: Greenwood.
Blumberg, Abraham S.
    1981   Typologies of criminal behavior. In Abraham Blumberg (ed.), Current Perspectives on Criminal Behavior. New York: Knopf.
Chambliss, William
    1972   Box Man: A Professional Thief's Journal. New York: Harper Torchbooks.
Clinard, Marshall B. and Richard Quinney
    1967   Criminal Behavior Systems: A Typology. New York: Holt, Rinehart, and Winston.
Cressey, Donald
    1967   Methodological problems in the study of organized crime as a social problem. Annals of American Academy of Political and Social Sciences 374:98–120.
Einstadter, Werner J.
    1969   The social organization of armed robbery. Social Problems 17:64–83.
Glaser, Barney and Anselm L. Strauss
    1967   The Discovery of Grounded Theory. Chicago: Aldine.
Gould, Leroy C., Egon Bittner, Sheldon Messinger, Fred Powledge, and Sol Chaneles
    1966   Crime as a Profession. Washington, D.C.: U.S. Government Printing Office.
Inciardi, James
    1974   Vocational crime. In Daniel Glaser (ed.), Handbook of Criminology. Chicago: Rand McNally.
    1975   Careers in Crime. Chicago: Rand McNally.
Jackson, Bruce
    1969   A Thief's Primer. Englewood Cliffs, NJ: Prentice-Hall.
Klein, John F.
    1974   Professional theft: The utility of a concept. Canadian Journal of Criminology and Corrections 16:133–144.
Lemert, Edwin
    1958   The behavior of the systematic check forger. Social Problems 6:141–148.
Letkemann, Peter
    1973   Crime as Work. Englewood Cliffs, NJ: Prentice-Hall.
Martinez, Tomas
    1983   The Gambling Scene. Springfield, IL: Thomas.
Maurer, David W.
    1974   The American Confidence Man. Springfield, IL: Thomas.
Rosecrance, John D.
    1985   The Degenerates of Lake Tahoe: A Study of Persistence in the Social World of Horse Race Gambling. New York: Lang.

Scott, Marvin B.
1968   The Racing Game. Chicago: Aldine.
Shover, Neal
1973   The social organization of burglary. Social Problems 20:499–514.
Staats, Gregory R.
1977   Changing conceptualization of professional criminals. Criminology 15:49–65.
Surface, Bill
1976   The Track. New York: MacMillan.
Sutherland, Edwin H.
1937   The Professional Thief. Chicago: University of Chicago Press.
Turk, Austin
1969   Criminality and the Legal Order. Chicago: Rand McNally.
Walker, Andrew
1981   Sociology and professional crime. In Abraham Blumberg (ed.), Current Perspectives on Criminal Behavior. New York: Knopf.
Wickman, Peter and Phillip Whitten
1980   Criminology: Perspectives on Crime and Criminality. Lexington, MA: Heath.

22. Criminal Homicide as a Situated Transaction

DAVID F. LUCKENBILL

By definition, criminal homicide is a collective transaction. An offender, victim, and possibly an audience engage in an interchange which leaves the victim dead. Furthermore, these transactions are typically situated, for participants interact in a common physical territory (Wolfgang, 1958: 203–205; Wallace, 1965). As with other situated transactions, it is expected that the participants develop particular roles, each shaped by the others and instrumental in some way to the fatal outcome (cf. Shibutani, 1961: 32–37, 64–93; Blumer, 1969: 16–18). However, research, with few exceptions, has failed critically to examine the situated transaction eventuating in murder (Banitt et al., 1970; Shoham et al., 1973). At most, studies have shown that many victims either directly precipitate their destruction, by throwing the first punch or firing the first shot, or contribute to the escalation of some conflict which concludes in their demise (Wolfgang, 1958: 245–265; Schafer, 1968: 79–83; Goode, 1969: 965; Toch, 1969; Moran, 1972). But how transactions of murder are organized and how they develop remain puzzles. What are the typical roles developed by the offender, victim, and possible bystanders? In what ways do these roles intersect to produce the fatal outcome? Are there certain regularities of interaction which characterize all transactions of murder, or do patterns of interaction vary among transactions in a haphazard fashion? Making the situated transaction the unit of investigation, this paper will address these questions by examining the character of the transaction in full.

METHOD

Criminal homicide is presently defined as the unlawful taking of a person's life, with the expressed intention of killing or rendering bodily injury resulting in death, and not in the course of some other criminal activity. This conceptualization excludes such forms of unnatural death as negligent homicide and vehicular manslaughter. This investigation will examine all forms of criminal homicide but felony murder, where death occurs in the commission of other felony crimes, and contract murder, where the offender conspires with another to kill in his behalf for payment.

The present data were drawn from all cases of criminal homicide over a ten-year period, 1963–1972, in one medium-sized (350,000) California county. Sampling was of a multistage nature. Because criminal homicide may be mitigated through charging or plea negotiation to various types of manslaughter, it was necessary to gather all cases, for the years 1963–1972, found in the four charge categories of first and second degree murder, voluntary and involuntary manslaughter. In this way, ninety-four cases were gathered. Taking all cases of unnatural death except suicide documented in coroner's reports, those twenty-three cases not fitting the present conception of criminal homicide were eliminated. These consisted of fourteen vehicular manslaughters, eight felony murders, and one negligent homicide. The remainder, seventy-one deaths or seventy transactions (one double murder), were examined.

All official documents pertaining to these cases were secured. The character of the larger occasion as well as the organization and development of the fateful transaction were reconstructed from the content analysis of police, probation, psychiatric, and witness reports, offender interviews, victim statements, and grand jury and court testimony. These materials included information on the major and minor participants; who said and did what to whom; the chronology of dialogue and action; and the physical comportment of the participants. Material relating to matters of law and legal processing were not examined.

In reconstructing the transaction, I first scrutinized each individual document for material relating only to the step-by-step development of the transaction. I then used the information to prepare separate accounts of the transaction. When all the individual documents for each case were exhausted, one summary account was constructed, using the individual accounts as resources. In the process of case reconstruction, I found that the various parties to the transaction often related somewhat different accounts of the event. Discrepancies centered, in large part, in their accounts of the specific dialogue of the participants. Their accounts were usually consistent with respect to the basic structure and development of the event.[1] In managing discrepancies, I relied on interparticipant consistency in accounts.

This methodological strategy should provide a fairly strong measure of reliability in case reconstruction. By using several independent resources bearing on the same focal point, particular biases could be reasonably controlled. In other words, possible biases in singular archival documents could be corrected by relying on a multitude of independently produced reports bearing on the transaction. For example, the offender's account could be compared with witnesses' accounts and with reports on physical evidence.

THE SOCIAL OCCASION OF CRIMINAL HOMICIDE

Criminal homicide is the culmination of an intense interchange between an offender and victim. Transactions resulting in murder involved the joint contribution of the offender and victim to the escalation of a "character contest," a confrontation in which at least one, but usually both, attempt to establish or save face at the other's expense by standing steady in the face of adversity (Goffman, 1967: 218–219, 238–257). Such transactions additionally involved a consensus among participants that violence was a suitable if not required means for settling the contest.

Before examining the dynamics of these transactions, it is useful to consider the larger context in which they were embedded. A "situated transaction" refers to a chain of interaction between two or more individuals that lasts the time they find themselves in one another's immediate physical presence (Goffman, 1963: 167). A "social occasion," in contrast, refers to a wider social affair within which many situated transactions may form, dissolve, and re-form (Goffman, 1963: 18). And, as Goffman aptly demonstrates, social occasions carry boundaries of sorts which establish what kinds of transactions are appropriate and inappropriate.

Social occasions which encompassed transactions ending in murder shared several features. First, all such transactions occurred in occasions of non-work or leisure-time (cf. Bullock, 1955; Wolfgang, 1958: 121–128; Wallace, 1965). The majority of murders occurred between the leisure hours of six P.M. and two A.M. and especially on weekends. More important, they were always found in leisure settings: almost half the cases occurred while members engaged in leisure activities at home; 15 percent occurred while members frequented a favorite tavern; another 15 percent occurred while members habituated a street corner or "turf"; little over 12 percent occurred while the offender and victim drove or "cruised" about the city, highway, or country roads; the few remaining cases occurred while members engaged in activities in some other public place such as a hotel room.

Second, occasions of murders were "loose" informal affairs permitting a wide range of activities definable by members as appropriate (cf. Goffman, 1963: 198–215). In contrast to work and such tighter occasions of leisure as weddings and funerals, where members are bound by rather strict sets of expectations, occasions of murder were permissive environs allowing the performance of various respectable and non-respectable activities. An "evening at home," the most prominent occasion in the cases, finds people engaging in many activities deemed suitable under the aegis of the private residence yet judged inappropriate for more formal affairs (cf. Cavan, 1963). Similarly, "an evening at the corner tavern," "hanging out on street corner," or "cruising about town" have long been recognized as permissive settings providing access and opportunity to drink, take drugs, sell and purchase sex, or gamble without fear of censure by colleagues.

In the sample, members engaged in a variety of activities within such loosely structured occasions. In about 75 percent of the cases, the offender and victim were engaged in pleasurable pursuits. They sought to drop serious or work roles and pursue such enjoyable activities as drinking alcoholic beverages, dancing, partying, watching television, or cruising main street. In the remainder of the cases, members were engaged in reasonably serious concerns. Here, conversations of marital or relational futures, sexual prowess, beauty, trustworthiness, and integrity were central themes about which members organized.

A third feature of such occasions was their population by intimates. In over 60 percent of the cases, the offender and victim were related by marriage, kinship, or friendship. In the remaining cases, while the offender and victim were enemies, mere acquaintances, or complete strangers, at least one but often both were in the company of their family, friends, lovers, or co-workers.

DYNAMICS OF THE SITUATED PERFORMANCE

These are the occasions in which situated transactions resulted in violent death. But examination of the development of these situated interchanges is not to argue that such transactions have no historical roots. In almost half the cases there had previously occurred what might be termed rehearsals between the offender and victim. These involved transactions which included the escalation of hostilities and, sometimes, physical violence. In 26 percent of these cases, the offender and, sometimes, victim entered the present occasion on the assumption that another hostile confrontation would transpire.

Whether or not murderous episodes had such rehearsals, an examination of all cases brings to light a conception of the transaction resembling what Lyman and Scott (1970: 37–43) term a "face game." The offender and victim, at times with the assistance of bystanders, make "moves" on the basis of the other's moves and the position of their audience (cf. Goffman, 1967: 239–258; 1969: 107–812). While these moves are not always of the same precise content or degree, it was possible to derive a set of time-ordered stages of which each shares certain basic properties. Let me first say that the "offender" and "victim" are heuristic labels for the statuses that either emerge in the transaction or are an artifact of the battle. In 71 percent of the cases, the statuses of offender and victim are determined by one's statement of intent to kill or injure the other. Hence, in 63 percent of the cases, the victim initiates the transaction, the offender states his intention to kill or injure the victim, and the offender follows through by killing him. In 8 percent of the cases, the offender initiates the transaction, later states his intention to kill or injure the victim, and follows through by killing him. But in 29 percent of the cases, the statuses of offender and victim are determined by the results of the battle. Here, the initially cast victim initiates the transaction while the initially cast offender states his intention to kill or injure the victim. Due to strength or resources, the initially cast victim kills the initially cast offender in the course of battle. In discussing the first five stages, the labels of offender and victim will be used to refer to the statuses that emerge in the course of interaction and not the statuses resulting from the battle. Furthermore, the labels will be employed in a manner consistent with the pattern characteristic of the majority of the cases. Consequently, in 36 percent of the cases (those where the initially cast victim kills the initially cast offender and those where the offender initiates the transaction, later states his intention to kill or injure, and follows through), the adversary labeled "victim" kills while the adversary labeled "offender" is killed. In the discussion of the sixth stage the labels of offender and victim will be used to refer to the statuses resulting from the battle.

Stage I

The opening move in the transaction was an event performed by the victim and subsequently defined by the offender as an offense to "face," that image of self a person claims during a particular occasion or social contact (Goffman, 1967: 5). What constitutes the real or actual beginning of this or any other type of transaction is often quite problematic for the researcher.[2] The victim's activity, however, appeared as a pivotal event which separated the previous occasioned activity of the offender and victim from their subsequent violent confrontation. Such a disparaging and interactionally disrupting event constitutes the initial move.

While the form and content of the victim's move varied, three basic types of events cover all cases. In the first, found in over 41 percent of the cases, the victim made some direct verbal expression which the offender subsequently interpreted as offensive. This class of events was obviously quite broad. Included were everything from insults levied at some particular attribute of the offender's self, family, or friends to verbal tirades which disparaged the overall character of the offender:

> *Case 34* The offender, victim, and two friends were driving toward the country where they could consume their wine. En route, the victim turned to the offender, both of whom were located in the back seat, and stated: "You know, you really got some good parents. You know, you're really a son-of-a-bitch. You're a leech. The whole time you were out of a job, you were living with them, and weren't even paying. The car you have should be your father's. He's the one who made the payments. Any time your dad goes to the store, you're the first in line to sponge off him. Why don't you grow up and stop being a leech?" The offender swore at him, and told him to shut up. But the victim continued, "Someone ought to come along and really fuck you up."

A second type, found in 34 percent of the cases, involved the victim's refusal to cooperate or comply with the requests of the offender. The offender subsequently interpreted the victim's action as a denial of his ability or right to command obedience. This was illustrated in transactions where parents murdered their children. When the parent's request that the child eat dinner, stop screaming, or take a bath went unheeded, the parent subsequently interpreted the child's activity as a challenge to rightful authority. In other cases, the violent escalation came about after the victim refused to conciliate a failing or dead relationship. In yet other cases, the victim failed to heed the offender's demand that he not enter some "off limits" territory, such as the "turf" of a juvenile gang.

The third type of event, found in 25 percent of the cases, involved some physical or nonverbal gesture which the offender subsequently defined as personally offensive. Often this gesture entailed an insult to the offender's sexual prowess, and took the form of affairs or flirtation:

> *Case 10* When the victim finally came home, the offender told her to sit down; they had to talk. He asked her if she was "fooling around" with other men. She stated that she had, and her boyfriends pleased her more than the offender. The offender later stated that "this was like a hot iron in my gut." He ripped her clothes off and examined her body, finding scars and bruises. She said that her boyfriends liked to beat her. His anger magnified.

Of course, the victim's activity was not always performed on the murderous occasion. In 15 percent of the cases, the event was performed on some previous occasion when the offender was not present. Nevertheless, it was on the murderous occasion that the event was made known to the offender by the victim or bystanders and so was symbolically reenacted.

Although the content and the initial production of these events varied, each served to disrupt the social order of the occasion. Each marked the opening of a transformation process in which pre-homicide transactions of pleasurable, or serious yet tranquil, order came to be transactions involving an argumentative "character contest."

Stage II

In all cases ending in murder the offender interpreted the victim's previous move as personally offensive. In some cases the victim was intentionally offensive. But it is plausible that in other cases the victim was unwitting. In case 43, for instance, the victim, a five-week-old boy, started crying early in the morning. The offender, the boy's father, ordered the victim to stop crying. The victim's crying, however, only heightened in intensity. The victim was too young to understand the offender's verbal order, and persistent crying may have been oriented not toward challenging his father's authority, but toward acquiring food or a change of diapers. Whatever the motive for crying, the child's father defined it as purposive and offensive. What the victim intends may be inconsequential. What the offender interprets as intentional, however, may have consequences for the organization of subsequent activity.

In 60 percent of the cases, the offender learned the meaning of the victim's move from inquiries made of the victim or audience. In reply, the offender received statements suggesting the victim's action was insulting and intentional. In 39 percent of the cases, the offender ascertained the meaning of the impropriety directly from the victim:

> *Case 28* As the offender entered the back door of the house his wife said to her lover, the victim, "There's ___." The victim jumped to his feet and started dressing hurriedly. The offender, having called to his wife without avail, entered the bedroom. He found his wife nude and the victim clad in underwear. The startled offender asked the victim, "Why?" The victim replied, "Haven't you ever been in love? We love each other." The offender later stated, "If they were drunk or something, I could see it. I mean, I've done it myself. But when he said they loved each other, well that did it."

In another 21 percent of the cases, however, the offender made his assessment from statements of interested bystanders:

> *Case 20* The offender and his friend were sitting in a booth at a tavern drinking beer. The offender's friend told him that the offender's girlfriend was "playing" with another man (victim) at the other end of the bar. The offender looked at them and asked his friend if he thought something was going on. The friend responded, "I wouldn't let that guy fool around with [her] if she was mine." The offender agreed, and suggested to his friend that his girlfriend and the victim be shot for their actions. His friend said that only the victim should be shot, not the girlfriend.

In the remaining 40 percent of the cases the offender imputed meaning to the event on the basis of rehearsals in which the victim had engaged a similar role. The incessant screaming of the infant, the unremitting aggressions of a drunken spouse, and the never-ending flirtation by the lover or spouse were activities which offenders had previously encountered and assessed as pointed and deliberate aspersions:

> *Case 35* During a family quarrel the victim had broken the stereo and several other household goods. At one point, the victim cut her husband, the offender, on the arm. He demanded that she sit down and watch television so that he could attend to his wound in peace. On returning from the bathroom he sat down and watched television. Shortly after, the victim rose from her chair, grabbed an ashtray, and shouted, "You bastard, I'm going to kill you." As she came toward him, the offender reached into the drawer of the end table, secured a pistol, and shot her. On arrest, the offender told police officers, "You know how she gets when she's drunk? I had to stop her, or she would have killed me. She's tried it before, that's how I got all these scars," pointing to several areas on his back.

Such previous activities and their consequences served the offender as an interpretive scheme for immediately making sense of the present event.

Stage III

The apparent affront could have evoked different responses. The offender could have excused the violation because the victim was judged to be drunk, crazy, or joking. He could have fled the scene and avoided further interaction with the victim by moving into interaction with other occasioned participants or dealt with the impropriety through a retaliatory move aimed at restoring face and demonstrating strong character. The latter move was utilized in all cases.

In countering the impropriety, the offender attempted to restore the occasioned order and reaffirm face by standing his or her ground. To have used another alternative was to confirm questions of face and self raised by the victim. The offender's plight, then, was "problematic" and "consequential" (Goffman, 1967: 214–239). He could have chosen from several options, each of which had important consequences both to the face he situationally claimed and to his general reputation. Thus, the offender was faced with a dilemma: either deal with the impropriety by demonstrating strength of character, or verify questions of face by demonstrating weakness (Goffman, 1969: 168–169).

In retaliating, the offender issued an expression of anger and contempt which signified his opinion of the victim as an unworthy person. Two basic patterns of retaliation were found. In 86 percent of the cases, the offender issued a verbal or physical challenge to the victim. In the remaining cases, the offender physically retaliated, killing the victim.

For the latter pattern, this third move marked the battle ending the victim's life:

> *Case 12*   The offender, victim, and group of bystanders were observing a fight between a barroom bouncer and a drunk patron on the street outside the tavern. The offender was cheering for the bouncer, and the victim was cheering for the patron, who was losing the battle. The victim, angered by the offender's disposition toward the fight, turned to the offender and said, "You'd really like to see the little guy have the shit kicked out of him, wouldn't you, big man?" The offender turned toward the victim and asked, "What did you say? You want the same thing, punk?" The victim moved toward the offender and reared back. The offender responded, "OK, buddy." He struck the victim with a single right cross. The victim crashed to the pavement, and died a week later.

Such cases seem to suggest that the event is a one-sided affair, with the unwitting victim engaging a passive, noncontributory role. But in these cases the third stage was preceded by the victim's impropriety, the offender's inquiry of the victim or audience, and a response affirming the victim's intent to be censorious. On assessing the event as one of insult and challenge, the offender elicited a statement indicating to participants, including himself, his intended line of action, secured a weapon, positioned it, and dropped the victim in a single motion.

While ten cases witness the victim's demise during this stage, the typical case consists of various verbal and physically nonlethal moves. The most common type of retaliation was a verbal challenge, occurring in 43 percent of the cases. These took the form of an ultimatum: either apologize, flee the situation, or discontinue the inappropriate conduct, or face physical harm or death:

> *Case 54*   The offender, victim, and two neighbors were sitting in the living room drinking wine. The victim started calling the offender, his wife, abusive names. The offender told him to "shut up." Nevertheless, he continued. Finally, she shouted, "I said shut up. If you don't shut up and stop it, I'm going to kill you and I mean it."

In about 22 percent of the cases, the offender's retaliation took the form of physical violence short of real damage or incapacitation.

> *Case 4*   The offender, victim, and three friends were driving in the country drinking beer and wine. At one point, the victim started laughing at the offender's car which he, the victim, scratched a week earlier. The offender asked the victim why he was laughing. The victim responded that the offender's car looked like junk. The offender stopped the car and all got out. The offender asked the victim to repeat his statement. When the victim reiterated his characterization of the car, the offender struck the victim, knocking him to the ground.

In another 10 percent, retaliation came by way of countering the victim's impropriety with similar insults or degrading gestures. The response entailed a name-calling, action-matching set of expressions resembling that which would be found between boys in the midst of a playground argument or "playing the dozens" (cf. Berdie, 1947).

The remaining cases, some 11 percent of the sample, were evenly divided. On the one hand, offenders issued specific commands, tinged with hostility and backed with an aggressive posture, calling for their victims to back down. On the other hand, offenders "called out" or invited their victims to fight physically.

This third stage is the offender's opening move in salvaging face and honor. In retaliating by verbal and physically nonlethal means, the offender appeared to suggest to the victim a definition of the situation as one in which violence was suitable in settling questions of face and reputation.

Stage IV

Except for cases in which the victim has been eliminated, the offender's preceding move placed the victim in a problematic and consequential position: either stand up to the challenge and demonstrate strength of character, or apologize, discontinue the inappropriate conduct, or flee the situation and thus withdraw questions of the offender's face while placing one's own in jeopardy. Just as the offender could have dismissed the impropriety, fled the scene, or avoided further contact with the victim, so too did the victim have similar alternatives. Rather than break the escalation in a manner demonstrating weakness, all victims in the remaining sample came into a "working" agreement with the proffered definition of the situation as one suited for violence. In the majority of cases, the victim's move appeared as an agreement that violence was suitable to the transaction. In some cases, though, the offender interpreted, sometimes incorrectly, the victim's move as implicit agreement to violence. A working agreement was struck in several ways.

The most prominent response, found in 41 percent of the cases, involved noncompliance with the offender's challenge or command, and the continued performance of activities deemed offensive:

> *Case 54*   The victim continued ridiculing the offender before friends. The offender finally shouted, "I said shut up. If you don't shut up and stop it, I'm going to kill you and I mean it." The victim continued his abusive line of conduct. The offender proceeded to the kitchen, secured a knife, and returned to the living room. She repeated her warning. The victim rose from his chair, swore at the offender's stupidity, and continued laughing at her. She thrust the knife deep into his chest.

Similarly, a spouse or lover's refusal, under the threat of violence, to conciliate a failing marriage or relationship served as tacit acceptance that violence was suitable to the present transaction.

Whether the victim's noncompliance was intentional or not, the offender *interpreted* the move as intentional. Take, for example, the killing of children at the hands of parents. In an earlier illustration, the first move found the parent demanding obedience and backed by a hostile, combative stance. In several of these cases, the child was too young to understand what the parent demanded and the specific consequences for noncompliance. Nevertheless, the child's failure to eat dinner or stop screaming was interpreted by the parent as a voluntary protest, an intentional challenge to authority. Consequently, the unwitting activities of victims may contribute to what offenders define as very real character contests demanding very real lines of opposition.

A second response, occurring in 30 percent of the cases, found victims physically retaliating against their offenders by hitting, kicking, and pushing—responses short of mortal injury:

> *Case 42*   The offender and a friend were passing by a local tavern and noticed the victim, a co-worker at a food-processing plant, sitting at the bar. The offender entered the tavern and asked the victim to repay a loan. The victim was angered by the request and refused to pay. The offender then pushed the victim from his stool. Before the victim could react, the bartender asked them to take their fight outside. The victim followed the offender out the door and, from behind, hit the offender with a brick he grabbed from a trash can immediately outside the door. The offender turned and warned the victim that he would beat the victim if he wouldn't pay up and continued his aggressions. The victim then struck the offender in the mouth, knocking out a tooth.

In the remaining cases, victims issued counter-challenges, moves made when offenders' previous moves involved threats and challenges. In some cases, this move came in the form of calling the offender's bluff. In other cases, the counter came in the form of a direct challenge or threat to the offender, a move no different from the ultimatum given victims by offenders.

Unlike simple noncompliance, physical retaliation against offenders and issuance of counter-challenges signify an explicit acceptance of violence as a suitable means for demonstrating character and maintaining or salvaging face.

Just as the victim contributed to the escalation toward violence, so too did the audience to the transaction. Seventy percent of all cases were performed before an audience. In these cases, onlookers generally engaged one or two roles. In 57 of these cases, interested members of the audience intervened in the transaction, and actively encouraged the use of violence by means of indicating to opponents the initial improprieties, cheering them toward violent action, blocking the encounter from outside interference, or providing lethal weapons:

> *Case 23*   The offender's wife moved toward the victim, and hit him in the back of the head with an empty beer bottle stating, "That'll teach you to [molest] my boy. I ought to cut your balls off, you motherfucker." She went over to the bar to get another bottle. The victim pushed himself from the table and rose. He then reached into his pocket to secure something which some bystanders thought was a weapon. One of the bystanders gave the offender an axe handle and suggested that he stop the victim before the victim attacked his wife. The offender moved toward the victim.

In the remaining cases, onlookers were neutral. They were neither encouraging nor discouraging. While neutrality may have been due to fear, civil inattention, or whatever reason, the point is that inaction within a strategic interchange can be interpreted by the opponents as a move favoring the use of violence (cf. Goffman, 1967: 115).[3] Consider the statement of the offender in the following case:

> *Case 48*   Police Officer: Don't you think it was wrong to beat [your daughter] when her hands were tied behind her back? [Her hands and feet were bound to keep her from scratching.]
>   Offender: Well, I guess so. But I really didn't think so then, or [my wife] would have said something to stop me.

Stage V

On forging a working agreement, the offender and, in many cases, victim appeared committed to battle. They contributed to and invested in the development of a fateful transaction, one which was problematic and consequential to their face and wider reputation. They placed their character on the line, and alternative methods for assessing character focused on a working agreement that violence was appropriate. Because opponents appeared to fear displaying weakness in character and consequent loss of face, and because resolution of the contest was situationally bound, demanding an immediacy of response, they appeared committed to following through with expressed or implied intentions.

Commitment to battle was additionally enhanced by the availability of weapons to support verbal threats and challenges. Prior to victory, the offender often sought out and secured weapons capable of overcoming the victim. In about 36 percent of the cases, offenders carried hand guns or knives into the setting. In only 13 percent of these cases did offenders bring hand guns or knives into the situation on the assumption that they might be needed if the victims were confronted. In the remainder of these cases such weapons were brought in as a matter of everyday routine. In either event, to inflict the fatal blow required the mere mobilization of the weapon for action. In 64 percent of the cases, the offender either left the situation temporarily to secure a hand gun, rifle, or knife, or transformed the status of some existing situational prop, such as a pillow, telephone cord, kitchen knife, beer mug, or baseball bat into a lethal weapon. The possession of weapons makes battle possible and, in situations defined as calling for violence, probable.

The particular dynamics of the physical interchange are quite varied. In many cases, the battle was brief and precise. In approximately 54 percent of the cases, the offender secured the weapon and dropped the victim in a single shot, stab, or rally of blows. In the remaining cases, the battle was two-sided. One or both secured a weapon and exchanged a series of blows, with one falling in defeat.

Stage VI

Once the victim had fallen, the offender made one of three moves which marked the termination of the transaction. In over 58 percent of the cases, the offender fled the scene. In about 32 percent of the cases, the offender voluntarily remained on the scene for the police. In the remaining cases, the offender was involuntarily held for the police by members of the audience.

These alternatives seemed prompted by two lines of influence: the relationship of the offender and victim and the position of the audience vis-à-vis the offense. When there is no audience, the offender appeared to act on the basis of his relationship to the victim. When the offender and victim were intimately related, the offender typically remained on the scene and notified the police. Sometimes these offenders waited for minutes or hours before reporting the event, stating they needed time to think, check the victim's condition, and make arrangements on financial matters, the children, and work before arrest. In contrast, when victims were acquaintances or enemies, offenders typically fled the scene. Moreover, these offenders often attempted to dispose of their victims and incriminating evidence.

Seventy percent of the cases, however, occurred before an audience, and offenders' moves seemed related to audience reactions to the offense. Bystanders seemed to replace the victim as the primary interactant, serving the offender as the pivotal reference for his exiting orientations. The audience assumed one of three roles: hostile, neutral, or supportive. In the hostile role, accounting for nearly 35 percent of the cases, bystanders moved to apprehend the offender, assist the victim, and immediately notify police. Such audiences were generally comprised of persons who either supported the victim or were neutral during the pre-battle escalation. In several of these cases, bystanders suggested, without use of force, that the offender assist the victim, call the police, and so forth. These audiences were comprised of the offender's intimates, and he followed their advice without question. In either case, hostile bystanders forced or suggested the offender's compliance in remaining at the scene for police.

In almost 17 percent of the cases, the audience was neutral. These people appeared as shocked bystanders. Having witnessed the killing, they stood numb as the offender escaped and the victim expired.

In the remainder of the cases, the audience was supportive of the offender. These audiences were usually comprised of persons who encouraged the offender during the pre-battle stages. Supportive bystanders rendered assistance to the offender in his escape, destroyed incriminating evidence, and maintained ignorance of the event when questioned by the police, breaking down only in later stages of interrogation. Thus, while a hostile audience directs the offender to remain at the scene, the supportive audience permits or directs his flight.

CONCLUSION

On the basis of this research, criminal homicide does not appear as a one-sided event with an unwitting victim assuming a passive, noncontributory role. Rather, murder is the outcome of a dynamic interchange between an offender, victim, and, in many cases, bystanders. The offender and victim develop lines of action shaped in part by the actions of the other and focused toward saving or maintaining face and reputation and demonstrating character. Participants develop a working agreement, sometimes implicit, often explicit, that violence is a useful tool for resolving questions of face and character. In some settings where very small children are murdered, the extent of their participation cannot be great. But generally these patterns characterized all cases irrespective of such variables as age, sex, race, time and place, use of alcohol, and proffered motive.

Notes

1. Whenever detectives encountered discrepancies in accounts of the structure and development of the transaction, they would routinely attend to such discrepancies and repair them through their subsequent investigation.

2. The offender's location of the pivotal event may be self-serving. That is, the offender may select as an event leading to his violence one which places the brunt of responsibility for the murder on the victim. Whether or not the offender's location of the pivotal event is accurate is moot, for the victim may not be able to report his opinion. In this discussion I accept the offender's contention that a particular activity performed by the victim was pivotal to the organization of his action.

3. When the audience voices its dissatisfaction over the escalation of a character contest, it typically deteriorates. Of the thirty-two rehearsals found in the histories of the cases, about half did not result in death because of the intervention of a dissenting bystander. Discouragement usually took the form of redefining the victim's impropriety as unintentional, or suggesting that backing down at the outset of the escalation is appropriate given the occasion as one for fun and pleasure. While bystanders can be either encouraging or neutral in situations of murder, Wallace (1965) found that in 20 percent of the cases with an audience, some bystanders sought to discourage a violent confrontation, and would themselves often end [up] in the hospital or city morgue. It cannot be determined if my findings are inconsistent with Wallace. He does not specify at what point in the development of the transaction discouraging bystanders intervene. While I found that bystanders were not discouraging in the escalation toward battle, I did find that several cases involved bystanders trying to discourage violence once opponents were committed to or initiated it. It was common in these cases for the bystander to suffer physical injury.

References

Banitt, Rivka, Shoshana Katznelson, and Shlomit Streit. 1970. "The situational aspects of violence: A research model." Pp. 241–258 in Israel Studies in Criminology, edited by Shlomo Shoham. Tel-Aviv: Gomeh.

Berdie, Ralph. 1947. "Playing the dozens." Journal of Abnormal and Social Psychology 42 (January): 102–121.

Blumer, Herbert. 1969. Symbolic Interactionism: Perspective and Method. Englewood Cliffs, N.J.: Prentice-Hall.

Bullock, Henry A. 1955. "Urban homicide in theory and fact." Journal of Criminal Law, Criminology and Police Science 45 (January–February): 565–575.

Cavan, Sherri. 1963. "Interaction in home territories." Berkeley Journal of Sociology 8: 17–32.

Goffman, Erving. 1963. Behavior in Public Places: Notes on the Social Organization of Gatherings. Glencoe: Free Press; 1967. Interaction Ritual: Essays on Face-to-Face Behavior. Garden City, N.Y.: Doubleday; 1969. Strategic Interaction. New York: Ballantine.

Goode, William J. 1969. "Violence among intimates." Pp. 941–977 in Crimes of Violence, prepared by Donald J. Mulvihill and Melvin M. Tumin. Washington: U.S. Government Printing Office.

Lyman, Sanford M. and Marvin B. Scott. 1970. A Sociology of the Absurd. New York: Meredith.

Moran, Alvin. 1971. "Criminal homicide: External restraint and subculture of violence." Criminology 8 (February): 357–374.

Shibutani, Tamotsu. 1961. Society and Personality: An Interactionist Approach to Social Psychology. Englewood Cliffs, N.J.: Prentice-Hall.

Shoham, Shlomo, Sara Ben-David, Rivka Vadmani, Joseph Atar, and Suzanne Fleming. 1973. "The cycles of interaction in violence." Pp. 69–87 in Israel Studies in Criminology, edited by Shlomo Shoham. Jerusalem: Jerusalem Academic Press.

Schafer, Stephan. 1968. The Victim and His Criminal. New York: Random House.

Toch, Hans. 1969. Violent Men: An Inquiry into the Psychology of Violence. Chicago: Aldine.

Wallace, Samuel E. 1965. "Patterns of violence in San Juan." Pp. 43–48 in Interdisciplinary Problems in Criminology: Papers of the American Society of Criminology, 1964, edited by Walter C. Reckless and Charles L. Newman. Columbus: Ohio State University Press.

Wolfgang, Marvin E. 1958. Patterns of Criminal Homicide. Philadelphia: University of Pennsylvania Press.

23. Rape in Marriage: A Sociological View

DAVID FINKELHOR AND KERSTI YLLO

The subject of marital rape is cropping up with increasing frequency in the media in recent years. Yet, attention has focused almost entirely on court cases—such as those of John Rideout in Oregon and James Chretien in Massachusetts and on state legislatures, where efforts have been made to criminalize this form of sexual assault (Celarier, 1979: Croft, 1979; Laura X, 1980).

While lawyers and legislators debate the issue, those in positions best suited to understanding this form of abuse and to offering help to victims have generally remained silent. Surprisingly little attention has been paid to the problem of marital rape by researchers, counselors, therapists, and doctors. Even feminist recognition of marital rape is coming well after other types of violence against women became national concerns.

Nonetheless, public and professional awareness that marital rape exists is growing. The slowly accumulating evidence suggests that rape in marriage is not a rare crime that may blossom into a headline-grabbing trial, but that it is a persistent problem in a large number of marriages.

PREVALENCE OF MARITAL RAPE

Evidence about violence against wives in general leads to a suspicion that forced sex in marriage is fairly commonplace. For a long time, wife abuse also was considered a rather unusual crime, but results of recent large-scale surveys have reversed this notion. Straus, Gelles, and Steinmetz (1980) found that 16 percent of all American couples admitted to a violent episode in the course of the previous year, and for 4 percent the violence was severe enough to qualify as wife-battering.

Testimony from battered women confirms their high vulnerability to marital rape. Spektor (1980) surveyed 304 battered women in 10 shelters in the state of Minnesota and found that 36 percent said they had been raped by their husband or cohabitating partner. Giles-Sims (1979) found a similar proportion of women in shelters reporting a forced sex experience, and Pagelow (1980) reported a figure of 37 percent based on a sample of 119 women in California. Forced sex is clearly a common element in the battering situation.

Diana Russell (1980) has gathered some of the first direct evidence about the prevalence of marital rape experiences in the population at large. Russell surveyed a random sample of 930 women residents of San Francisco, 18 years and older, about any incident of sexual assault they had had at any time throughout their lives. Fourteen percent of the 644 married women in the sample reported a sexual assault by a husband. Twelve percent had been forced to have intercourse, and two percent experienced other types of forced sex. *Sexual assaults by husbands were the most common kinds of sexual assault reported, occurring over twice as often as sexual assault by a stranger.*

It is important in evaluating Russell's finding to realize that she did not ask any of her respondents whether they had been "raped," a stigmatizing term that many women are reluctant to use to describe sexual assault experiences. Instead, she asked women to describe any kind of unwanted sexual experience with a husband or ex-husband, and then only included in her tally those women who described encounters that met the legal definition of rape: "forced intercourse, or intercourse obtained by physical threat(s) or intercourse completed when the woman was drugged, unconscious, asleep, or otherwise totally helpless and hence unable to consent."

Russell's finding that marital rape is the most common kind of rape cannot thus be ascribed to semantics. She used the same definition of sexual assault in tabulating the experiences with husbands as she did with strangers.

The findings from Russell's study are bolstered by results from a survey we recently completed in Boston. In a study on the related subject of childhood sexual abuse, we also asked a representative sample of 326 women whether a spouse or person they were living with as a couple had ever used physical force or threat to try to have sex with them. *Ten percent* of the women who had been married (or coupled) answered "yes." These women, too, reported more sexual assaults by husbands than assaults by strangers (10% versus 3%). Forced sex in marriage is a frequent—perhaps the most frequent—type of sexual assault.

WIVES AVOID RAPE LABEL

Few women whose husbands have forced them to have sex define themselves as having been raped (Gelles, 1979). Most women see rape as something that primarily happens between strangers. They too share the cultural and legal assumption that there is no such thing as rape between husband and wife. Violent and unpleasant as a husband's assault might have been, most wives would resist calling it rape. No doubt raped wives, like battered wives, use many self-deceptions to avoid facing the realities of an intolerable marriage because the alternatives—loneliness, loss of financial security, admission of failure—are so frightening (Gelles, 1979).

For these reasons, asking women whether they have been raped by their husbands is an unpromising course. To use a term that more victims could identify with, we used the term "forced sex" rather than "marital rape" throughout our research.

VARIETIES OF COERCION

Another definitional problem concerns the question of when sex is forced. It has been argued that given the power inequality in the institution of marriage, *all* marital sex is coerced (Brogger, 1976). It may be that when sex is not explicitly desired it should be considered forced. Obviously, many different sanctions and pressures are brought to bear by husbands to gain sexual access. Although all these sanctions have elements of coercion, some important distinctions can be made among them.

Four basic types of coercion can be identified. Some women submit to sex in the absence of desire because of social pressure—because they believe it is their wifely duty. This can be considered *social coercion*. Other wives comply because they fear their husbands will leave them if they do not, or because their husbands have threatened to cut off their source of money or humiliate them in some way. In these cases husbands use their resource and power advantage to force their wives. This second type of coercion, *interpersonal coercion*, refers to threats by husbands that are not violent in nature. The third type involves the *threat of physical force*. Threatened force can range from an implied threat that a woman could get hurt if she doesn't give in to an explicit threat she will be killed if she doesn't comply. For many women, the memory of previous beatings is enough to ensure cooperation.

The fourth kind of coercion, *physical coercion*, requires little explanation. Instances of physical coercion range from physically holding a woman down to striking her, choking her, tying her up, or knocking her out to force sex on her.

FOCUS ON PHYSICAL FORCE

The varieties of sexual coercion in marriage would be the subject of an intriguing study; however, it is beyond the scope of this research. We have limited our study to physical force for two main reasons. First, such force is most life- and health-threatening and in that sense most extreme. Second, the presence or absence of physical threats and actual violent coercion is somewhat easier to determine empirically than is the presence or absence of other, more subtle forms of coercion. This is not meant to imply that other forms of coercion cannot be brutal or that "marital rape" can occur only when physical force is involved.

IN-DEPTH INTERVIEWS

The following sections represent an overview of our exploratory study of marital rape from the victim's perspective. Our findings are based on 50 in-depth interviews with women whose husband or partner had used force or threat of force to try to have sex with them. Our interviewees were recruited from a number of sources. The majority (56%) were clients of Family Planning agencies in northern New England. These clinics routinely take a limited sexual history from each client. For the purposes of this study an additional question was added to the form: "Has your current partner (or a previous partner) ever used force or threat of force to try to have sex with you?" If the answer indicated that the client had had such an experience with a spouse or cohabitant, she was asked to participate in an additional interview for research purposes, for which she would be paid ten dollars.

Other interviewees (16%) were recruited through area battered-wives shelters. When it was determined that a woman's violent experiences included forced sex, she was asked to participate in the research, if shelter staff felt that she was up to an interview. Additional interviewees (28%) were self-referrals. These women heard of our research in the media or through our public speaking and contacted us, offering to discuss their experiences. Finally, a few interviews (10%) were arranged as a result of an ad placed in *Ms.* magazine requesting interviews.

Although the sample is not a representative one, we do not regard this as a serious drawback because of the nature of this research. Our goal in this exploratory study was not to determine incidence rates or demographic data (our Boston survey provides such information). Rather, our purpose was to talk at length with women who were willing to discuss their forced sex experiences so that we could gain a qualitative understanding of marital rape and begin to outline issues for further research. The clinics and shelters were sites where these intimate subjects could be raised fairly easily and where intervention services could be made available to women needing them.

THREE TYPES UNCOVERED

The forced sex experiences of the women we interviewed can be divided roughly into three types. One group can be described as typically "battered women." These women were subject to extensive physical and verbal abuse, much of which was unrelated to sex. Their husbands were frequently angry and belligerent to them and often had alcohol and drug problems. The sexual violence in these relationships appeared to be just another aspect of the general abuse. Along with the other kinds of anger and physical pain which these men heaped on their wives, they also used violent sex.

Let us quote briefly from a case study of one of these *"battering rapes"*:

> The interviewee was a 24-year-old woman from an affluent background. Her husband was a big man, over six feet tall, compared to her 5′ 2″. He drank heavily and often attacked her physically. The most frequent beatings occurred at night after they had had a fight and she had gone to bed. She would awaken to find him physically abusing her. Such attacks, at their worst, occurred every couple of weeks. After one incident her face was so bruised that she could not attend class for a full week.
>
> Their sexual activities had violent aspects, too. Although they shared the initiative for sex and had no disagreements about its timing or frequency, she often felt that he was brutal in his love-making. She said, "I would often end up crying during intercourse, but it never seemed to bother him. He probably enjoyed my pain in some way."
>
> The most violent sexual episode occurred at the very end of their relationship. Things had been getting worse between them for some time. They hadn't talked to each other in two weeks. One afternoon she came home from school, changed into a housecoat and started toward the bathroom. He got up from the couch where he had been lying, grabbed her, and pushed her down on the floor. With her face pressed into a pillow and his hand clamped over her mouth, he proceeded to have anal intercourse with her. She screamed and struggled to no avail. Afterward she was hateful and furious. "It was very violent . . .," she said, ". . . if I had had a gun there, I would have killed him."
>
> Her injuries were painful and extensive. She had a torn muscle in her rectum so that for three months she had to go to the bathroom standing up. The assault left her with hemorrhoids and a susceptibility to aneurysms that took five years to heal.

The second group of women have somewhat different relationships. These relationships are by no means conflict-free, but on the whole, there is little physical violence. In this group, the forced sex grew out of more specifically sexual conflicts. There were long-standing disagreements over some sexual issue, such as how often to have sex or what were appropriate sexual activities. The following is an excerpt from a case study of a *"nonbattering rape"*:

> The interviewee was a 33-year-old woman with a young son. Both she and her husband of ten years are college graduates and professionals. She is a teacher and he is a guidance counselor. Their marriage, from her report, seems to be of a modern sort in most respects. There have been one or two violent episodes in their relationship, but in those instances, the violence appears to have been mutual.
>
> There is a long-standing tension in the relationship about sex. She prefers sex about three times a week, but feels under considerable pressure to have more. She says that she is afraid that if she refuses him that he will leave her or that he will force her.

He did force her about two years ago. Their love-making on this occasion started out pleasantly enough, but he tried to get her to have anal intercourse with him. She refused. He persisted. She kicked and pushed him away. Still, he persisted. They ended up having vaginal intercourse. The force he used was mostly that of his weight on top of her. At 220 pounds, he weighs twice as much as she.

"It was horrible," she said. She was sick to her stomach afterward. She cried and felt angry and disgusted. He showed little guilt. "He felt like he'd won something."

In addition to the sexual assaults we classified as battering and nonbattering, there were a handful that defied such categorization. These rapes were sometimes connected to battering and sometimes not. All, however, involved bizarre sexual obsessions in the husbands that were not evident in the other cases. Husbands who made up this group were heavily involved in pornography. They tried to get their wives to participate in making or imitating it. They sometimes had a history of sexual problems, such as difficulty in getting aroused, or guilt about earlier homosexual experiences. Sometimes these men needed force or highly structured rituals of sexual behavior in order to become aroused. A case study of one of these *obsessive rapes* is illustrative:

> The interviewee was a 31-year-old marketing analyst for a large corporation. She met her husband in high school and was attracted to his intelligence. They were married right after graduation because she was pregnant.
>
> After the baby was born, he grew more and more demanding sexually. "I was really just his masturbating machine," she recalls. He was very rough sexually and would hold a pillow over her face to stifle her screams. He would also tie her up and insert objects into her vagina and take pictures which he shared with his friends.
>
> There were also brutal "blitz" attacks. One night, for example, they were in bed having sex when they heard a commotion outside. They went out in their bathrobes to investigate to discover it was just a cat fight. She began to head back to the house when her husband stopped her and told her to wait. She was standing in the darkness wondering what he was up to when, suddenly, he attacked her from behind. "He grabbed my arms behind me and tied them together. He pushed me over the log pile and raped me," she said. As in similar previous assaults, he penetrated her anally.
>
> The interviewee later discovered a file card in her husband's desk which sickened her. On the card, he had written a list of dates, dates that corresponded to the forced sex episodes of the past months. Next to each date was a complicated coding system which seemed to indicate the type of sex act and a ranking of how much he enjoyed it.

FORCE AND RESISTANCE

The incidents uncovered in our study so far varied both in the amount of force used by the men and the amount of resistance offered by the women. In some cases the man applied massive force, dragging the woman somewhere, tearing off her clothes, and physically beating her. In other situations, particularly where the couple was already in bed, the force was more moderate. In several cases the women mentioned the men's weight and their persistent attempts to penetrate them as the main elements of force.

Many women said they did not put up much of a fight, however. They felt that it was no use or wasn't worth it. This is an important point to understand better, because so many victims of sexual force have been ridiculed for not meeting the masculine stereotype of how vigorously a threatened person should resist. Lack of violent resistance is often interpreted as a sign that the victims really "wanted" sex on some level or that it wasn't so traumatic.

There appear to be three main factors that inhibited the women's attempts to ward off sexual aggression from their partners. First, many of the women felt they could not ward off their partners' aggression no matter how hard they tried. They perceived their partners to be very strong. Indeed, we were struck by the large size disparity between our subjects and their partners. Women who are much smaller than their husbands may be a particularly vulnerable group, not only because they *are* weak in comparison but because they *feel* weak as well.

Second, many of the women feared that if they resisted they would be hurt even worse, especially the women who had been beaten before. They expected that if they resisted they would be punched, bruised, and manhandled and that the sexual act itself would be more painful and damaging.

Third, many of the women believed that they themselves were in the wrong. In several cases, their husbands had convinced them that they were frigid. They believed that they were at fault for whatever marital dispute was in process, and felt responsible for their husband's mood or frustration. Although they did not want the sexual act, they were not armed with the conviction that they were *justified* in not wanting it. This made it difficult for them to put up a fight.

In general, it seemed that certain kinds of ultimate resistance tactics seemed out of the question for these women. Most did not run out of the house or physically resist by gouging at the partner's eyes or kicking him in the groin. No doubt they were hampered by their socialization not even to consider such actions. Moreover, unless they were prepared to leave, they knew that they would have to face this man later on, in the morning or the next day. Since most were not prepared to make it on their own, a central goal was "keeping the peace." They were not willing to bring out the ultimate weapons, because they had to continue living with this person. And they wanted to make things more tolerable for themselves. So appeasement rather than massive resistance appeared to be the preferable approach from their immediate point of view.

TRAUMA OF MARITAL RAPE

Many people fail to get alarmed about the problem of marital rape because they think it is a rather less traumatic form of rape. Being jumped by a stranger in the street, they imagine, must be so much more damaging than having sex with someone you have had sex with several times before.

This misconception is based on a failure to understand the real violation involved in rape. Those who see rape primarily in sexual terms think the degradation comes from the woman having been robbed of her reputation. Although this element can be present, what is most salient for rape victims is most often the violence, the loss of control, and the betrayal of trust.

Women raped by strangers often go through a long period of being afraid, especially about their physical safety. They become very cautious about being alone, where they go, and whom they go with (Burgess and Holmstrom, 1974). Women raped by husbands, however, are often traumatized at an even more basic level: in their ability to trust. The kind of violation they have experienced is much harder to guard against, short of a refusal to trust any man. It touches a woman's basic confidence in forming relationships and trusting intimates. It can leave a woman feeling much more powerless and isolated than if she were raped by a stranger.

Moreover, a woman raped by her husband has to live with her rapist, not just a frightening memory of a stranger's attack. Being trapped in an abusive marriage leaves many women vulnerable to repeated sexual assaults by their husbands. Most of the women we interviewed were raped on multiple occasions. These women do not have the option of obtaining police protection (as do other rape victims) because these rapes are legal in most states.

The research bears out the traumatic impact of marital rape. Russell found that the marital rape victims in her study rated their experiences as having a more serious impact on their lives than did the victims of stranger rape (Russell, 1980). Other studies, too, have shown that rape by intimates in general is more, not less, traumatic than rape by strangers (Bart, 1975).

FORCED MARITAL SEX AND THE LAW

While research cited earlier has highlighted the high prevalence of forced marital sex, and this research has documented some of its human cost, the criminal justice system is locked in anachronistic view of the subject. As of January 1982, approximately 36 of the 50 states and the District of Columbia exempt a husband from prosecution for the rape of a wife with whom he is currently living. (An excellent review of the laws on a state-by-state basis is available from the National Center on Women and Family Law; see Schulman, 1980.) Most states have a so-called spousal exemption in their rape laws, and 13 states extend this exemption not just to husbands but also to cohabiting lovers (Schulman, 1980). Such laws effectively deny the possibility of charging a husband with rape, no matter how brutal or violent he may have been in the pursuit of sex. They also contain the implicit assumption that upon marrying, a woman gives permanent and irrevocable (short of divorce) consent to any and all sexual approaches a husband wishes to make.

Changing such laws has been vehemently opposed in some quarters on the grounds that it will result in a rash of fabricated complaints or that such behavior is already adequately prohibited under existing assault laws. However, evidence from countries and states where marital rape is a crime shows that few frivolous complaints are brought (Geis, 1978). Moreover, as this and other research on rape shows, sexual assault is a crime different from other assaults, with particular motives and particularly humiliating effects on its victims. Marital rape, just like other rape, deserves special classification within the legal system (*New York University Law Review*, 1977).

PUBLIC ATTITUDES ABOUT MARITAL RAPE

However, it would be naive to think that the simple removal of the spousal exemption will dramatically reduce the occurrence of marital rape. Evidence suggests that even where such laws exist, they are infrequently used (Geis, 1978). Even the minority of women who may recognize that their husbands have committed a crime against them, for various reasons—loyalty, fear, unwillingness to go through a grueling public exposure—are still extremely reluctant to press charges. The lesson of spouse abuse is that laws alone have relatively little effect (Field and Field, 1973). Physical spouse abuse is a crime and has been for many years; yet in spite of such laws, all evidence suggests that such abuse is epidemic.

The spousal exemption is merely one manifestation of a complex of social attitudes surrounding the physical and sexual abuse of wives. Until these attitudes also change, the problem will remain critical with or without a law. These social attitudes portray marital rape as acceptable behavior, at least under some circumstances, and even if sometimes objectionable, at least not very seriously so.

For insight on these attitudes, we asked groups of undergraduate students for their opinions about marital rape, and some of their replies are revealing.

Some denied entirely that the phenomenon could occur: "No. When you get married, you are supposedly in love and you shouldn't even think of love-making as rape under any circumstances."

Others expressed the view that implicit in the marriage contract is an acceptance of the use of force. "Sexual relations are a part of marriage and both members realize this before they make a commitment," said one in explaining why there was no such thing as marital rape.

A number of students believed that forced sex was a reasonable solution to marital conflict. "If the wife did not want to have sex . . . after many months the husband may go crazy. [Rape] would be an alternative to seeking sexual pleasure with someone else."

"If she doesn't want sex for a long amount of time, and has no reason for it—Let the old man go for it!"

Besides expressing the opinion that force is an acceptable way of trying to salvage a marriage, such statements reveal other attitudes which work to justify marital rape: for example, the belief in a man's overpowering need for sex and the belief that women withhold sex from their husbands for no good reason. Note also the myth, discussed earlier, that forced sex is primarily a response to a woman who is denying satisfaction to her husband.

The refusal on the part of politicians and the public to see marital rape as a crime is also based on the belief that it is not a very serious offense. Peter Rossi presented a random sample of people living in Baltimore with descriptions of 140 offenses ranging from the planned killing of a policeman to being drunk in a public place. While the respondents ranked "forcible rape after breaking into a home" as the fourth most serious of all 140 offenses, just *above* the "impulsive killing of a policeman," they ranked "forcible rape of a former spouse" sixty-second, just above "driving while drunk" (Rossi, Waite, Bose, and Berk, 1974).

So while people consider some rape a serious offense, rape of a former spouse is not seen as very serious. Imagine how low the ranking would have been had Rossi asked about rape of a "current" rather than a "former" spouse. This corresponds with what we know about attitudes toward violence: The more intimate the victim, the less serious the assault is considered to be.

This can be read as rather sobering evidence that the "marriage license is a raping license." Not only is it true that by marrying, a man gains immunity (a form of license) to the charge of rape, but it also appears true that people are much less likely to disapprove of sexually violent behavior if he directs it against a woman to whom he is married rather than some other woman.

If people do not think that spousal rape is a serious offense, it certainly contributes to a climate where husbands feel they can do it with impunity. The climate also affects the victims who conclude from such social attitudes that they are wrong to be so upset and that few people will sympathize with them, so why bring it up.

Although changing the spousal exemption law is unlikely to bring many offenders to court for their offenses, it may have some effect on the general climate of acceptance of marital rape. For one thing, the political debate should alert the community, the criminal justice system, and mental health professionals about the existence of this problem. The change in the law may also put on notice some potential husband rapists that their behavior is not generally acceptable and in fact is a crime. Finally, the change may give vulnerable women a potential tool in protecting themselves.

The deterrent effect of changing the law was illustrated in the case of one woman we interviewed. Her recently separated husband kept returning and trying to have sex with her, and he was becoming more and more aggressive in his attempts. When she told some friends about the problem, they counseled her to tell him that if he tried it again she would have him prosecuted for marital rape. Apparently the husband was familiar with the recent publicity around the marital rape trials, because after she made her threat he relented and did not molest her again. This is an encouraging incident and shows that legal changes and the public discussions they stir need not be measured merely by the number of new arrests and convictions they produce.

CONCLUSION

This review of current information about marital rape and our findings regarding wives' forced sex experiences are a first step toward a full understanding of this social problem. Our research shows that "marital rape" is not a contradiction in terms, but rather a form of violence against wives which is not rare, just rarely discussed.

The case studies and typologies developed here are intended to encourage the generation of hypotheses and further analysis of forced sex in marriage, its antecedents, consequences, and implications. As a whole, our research is intended to add to the groundswell of concern about violence against women and to signal that the time has arrived for concerted investigation and discussion of the problem of rape in marriage and for action in political, legal, academic, and clinical arenas.

Note

Funds from NIMII grants MI115161, MI130930, and MI134109, as well as from the research office of the University of New Hampshire, helped make this research possible. Ruth Miller assisted in the preparation of this manuscript. Portions of this chapter were presented to the Society for the Scientific Study of Sex in Dallas, November 1980, and to the American Orthopsychiatric Association in New York, April 1981.

References

Bart, P. (1975). Rape doesn't end with a kiss. *Viva*, 40–42, 101–107.

Brogger, S. (1976). *Deliver us from love.* New York: Delacorte.

Burgess, A., and Holstrom, L. (1974). *Rape: Victims of crisis.* Bowie, MD: Brady.

Celarier, M. (1979, January). I kept thinking maybe I could help him. *In These Times*, 10–16.

Croft, G. (1979, September 15). Three years in rape of wife. *Boston Globe.*

Doron, J. (1980). *Conflict and violence in intimate relationships: Focus on marital rape.* Paper presented at the annual meetings of the American Sociological Association, New York.

Field, M., and Field, H. (1973). Marital violence and the criminal process: Neither justice nor peace. *Social Service Review, 47* (2), 221–240.

Geis, G. (1978). Rape-in-marriage: Law and law reform in England, the U.S. and Sweden. *Adelaide Law Review, 6,* 284–302.

Gelles, R.J. (1979). *Family violence.* Beverly Hills, CA: Sage.

Giles-Sims, J. (1979). *Stability and change in patterns of wife-beating: A systems theory approach.* Unpublished Ph.D. dissertation, University of New Hampshire.

Hunt, M. (1974). *Sexual behavior in the 1970's.* Chicago: Playboy Press.

Marital rape exemption. (1977). *New York University Law Review, 52,* 306–323.

Pagelow, M.D. (1980). *Does the law help battered wives? Some research notes.* Madison, WI: Law and Society Association.

Rossi, P., Waite, E., Bose, C., and Berk, R. (1974). The seriousness of crimes: Normative structures and individual differences. *American Sociological Review, 39,* 224–237.

Russell, D. (1980). *The prevalence and impact of marital rape in San Francisco.* Paper presented at the annual meetings of the American Sociological Association, New York.

Schulman, J. (1980a). The marital rape exemption. *National Center on Women and Family Law Newsletter, 1* (1), 6–8.

Schulman, J. (1980b). Expansion of the marital rape exemption. *National Center on Women and Family Law Newsletter, 1* (2), 3–4.

Spektor, P. (1980, February 29). Testimony delivered to the Law Enforcement Subcommittee of the Minnesota House of Representatives.

Straus, M.A., Gelles, R.J., and Steinmetz, S.K. (1980). *Behind closed doors: Violence in the American family.* Garden City, NY: Doubleday.

Wolfe, L. (1980). The sexual profile of the Cosmopolitan girl. *Cosmopolitan, 189* (3), 254–257, 263–265.

X, Laura. (nd). *The Rideout trial.* Women's History Research Center, mimeo.

24. Women and Children at Risk: A Feminist Perspective on Child Abuse

EVAN STARK AND ANNE H. FLITCRAFT

Introduction

In this article we examine the link between woman battering and child abuse from a feminist perspective. Viewing child abuse through the prism of woman battering reveals that both problems originate in conflicts over gender identity and male authority. Male authority is directly expressed in violent control over women and children. But just as important are the construction and use of clinical knowledge that distorts how women are perceived and subordinates their needs.

While a feminist approach to woman battering has gained some currency in mainstream thinking, feminists have had comparatively little impact on how child abuse is understood or managed. In part, this is because the view is widely shared that child abuse results from some combination of maternal pathology/inadequacy and "environmental stress." Where child abuse occurs against a background of "family violence," the presumption is that the violence is transmitted intergenerationally. A man who was beaten as a child now beats his wife. Then, unable to cope, she uses the child as scapegoat. Politics — including the politics of family life — play no role in this analysis.

In marked contrast to this emphasis, Gertrude Williams (1) suggests that sexism and pronatalism have taught these women that motherhood is the only fulfilling activity. Breines and Gordon (2) note a number of other gender-related issues, including the fact that women are primary parents, the lack of well-paid work alternatives to mothering, and the inadequacy of sex education (as well as contraceptive methods) leading to a large number of unwanted pregnancies.

Neither the conventional wisdom nor the nascent feminist analysis resolves these key questions:

1. Are men or women primarily responsible for child abuse?
2. What is the typical control for child abuse? Part of the answer to this question involves the link to battering and part lies in establishing whether the behavior of abusing parent, regardless of gender, reflects some combination of pathology and stress (the dominant view) or a political struggle for control.
3. How do child protective services respond to battered women whose children are abused? The issue here is how women are "known" in clinical settings as well as how they are treated.
4. How do clinical interventions affect the dynamics in abusive relationship?
5. How can the current approach be improved?

The data examined in the first part of this article bear on the first three questions. We then sketch a theoretical framework that may account for the evidence and explain the effects of current interventions, and conclude with an examination of current and proposed policy in child abuse.

The Argument

Interestingly, even work that considers gender accepts the claim that child abuse is primarily a female crime. To the contrary, we argue, surveys and hospital and medical examiner's records indicate that men may be the typical child abusers, particularly when serious injury is involved (3–6). Similarly unfounded is the belief that battered mothers or mothers of abused children are "sick." In fact, while a significant minority have multi-problem backgrounds, the typical context for child abuse is a battering relationship for which the woman bears little responsibility. Widespread beliefs that women are responsible for child abuse and that child abuse results from environmental stress or family pathology justify interventions—such as therapy for mothers—that exacerbate the gender inequities from which battering and child abuse stem in the first place. Holding women responsible for child abuse and targeting their inadequacies as parents as the cause can deepen a woman's resentment toward her child and constrain her to behave in gender-stereotyped ways that seriously increase her risk in a battering relationship.

The problem goes beyond faulty assumptions and misguided policies and treatment strategies. In fact, law, social service practice, and psychological theory hold women "responsible" for child abuse even when a male assailant is clearly identified and is also battering the mother. This singular emphasis on women and their traditional roles converges with battering in the home. One result is that women experience gender identity as a vehicle for male domination, what we term "patriarchal mothering," and their consequent resentment can often become violent.

CHILD ABUSE: GENDER POLITICS OR FEMALE PATHOLOGY?

Mothers or Fathers?

A classic vignette of the physically abused child has been that of an undernourished infant with multiple musculoskeletal trauma inflicted at different times by his or her depressed mother. Child abuse has been variously traced to maternal violence or neglect in the family of origin (7), current psychological dynamics such as role reversal (8), a lack of parenting skills (9), poverty or other environmental deprivations (6), the absence of needed institutional supports (10), or some combination of provocation, psychological predisposition, and environmental "trigger" events (11). But whether female psychology or a malfunctioning family system is emphasized, whether "destructive, disturbed mothers" are perceived or merely "sad, deprived, needy human beings," the fact that abuse results from breakdown in appropriate mother-child bonding is taken as self-evident. The normative character of female domesticity and mothering is an unquestioned presumption in child psychology, pediatric medicine, and children's services. Thus, the social consequences of adapting these images in problem solving remain unexamined.

But are most child abusers women? Representative sample surveys indicate that fathers may be as likely as or more likely than mothers to abuse children. Gil (6) estimates that 40 percent of the children in a national survey were abused by fathers, and an American Humane Society survey concluded that males were the assailants in 55 percent of reported cases of child abuse (3). Smaller surveys have produced somewhat different results, estimates of abuse by fathers running as low as 25 percent (12). Even this is remarkable given the division of child-care responsibilities and the proportion of children raised by single women.

While the percentage of abusing males is disputed, there is little doubt that, if a man is present, he is many more times likely to abuse the child than is the mother. For example, national survey data indicate that men were responsible for two-thirds of reported incidents in which men were present (6), probably an underestimate of male responsibility. Surveys measure single acts without taking their consequences into account and cannot distinguish documented from alleged abuse or identify abuse resulting in severe injury or death. Of equal importance, punitive welfare regulations and fear of violence lead many women to conceal relationships with men.

A recent study of hospital and medical examiner's records indicates that men, not women, are primarily responsible for serious child abuse. In comparing the records of child abuse cases for two time periods, 1971–73 and 1981–83, Bergman, Larsen and Mueller (4) report that while the incidence of hospitalized cases has not changed, the proportion of severe injuries has increased dramatically. Also increasing is the proportion of known male perpetrators reported, rising from 38 percent to 49 percent for all cases, and from 30 percent to 64 percent for the severe cases. Meanwhile, for all cases the proportion of female perpetrators has decreased from 32 percent to 20 percent, and for severe cases from 20 percent to 6 percent. Fully 80 percent of the fatal cases in the most recent group are attributed to men, and 20 percent are "unknown." None are attributed to women. Finally, if a male perpetrator is identified, there is a 70 percent chance that the child's injury is severe, up from 25 percent a decade earlier. The authors (4) wisely suggest that the apparent increase in severe abuse by men—and a corresponding decline in cases categorized as "unknown"—reflects a growing willingness to report "male friends," not an actual shift in violence.

Battering and Male Control

Earlier work shows that child abuse occurs disproportionately in battering relationships, although it may be a relatively rare event overall (13–16). But how central is battering in child abuse? Is it merely one of many background factors? Or does its frequency as an etiological factor point to a common cause? And, in the latter case, is this cause inherited violence or current deficits? Or is female independence the root issue, as feminist theory suggests, whether it is the batterer or the abused woman who assaults the child?

Evidence is strong that male control over women, not female pathology, environmental "stress," or family history, leads to battering (17). Battered women experience a disproportionate risk of mental illness, alcoholism, and other problems only *after* the onset of abuse and frustrated help-seeking (16, 18), indicating that violence breeds psychopathology, not the reverse. Differences in battering by social class, race, and employment status are small (17). By contrast, "fights" typically center on gender issues (such as sex, housework, child care, and women's right to money and wage work) (19); rates of male violence against women who are single, separated, or divorced are actually higher than against married women (17); and the nature and pattern of assaultive injury strongly suggest the violence is directed at a woman's gender indentity (including her sexual identity) and is neither impulsive nor random (13, 18, 20).

Have batterers "learned" their behavior from their own abuse as children? Although this belief is widely shared, its empirical support comes mainly from secondhand or anecdotal reports, psychiatric studies of unrepresentative or deviant populations (such as presidential assassins), and vague notions of childhood abuse. Thus a leading psychiatric authority on intergenerational transmission defines "abuse" and "neglect" as a "lack of empathetic mothering" (7) or "a variety of less than ideal responses of the caretaker (usually the mother) to the infant," which leads to "a lack of confidence or trust" in the child as an adult (21). The single random survey tracing abuse in the family-of-origin to current male violence finds "a clear trend for violence in childhood to produce violence in adult life" (22). But the actual data show the reverse. While boys experiencing violence as children are disproportionately violent as adults, 90 percent of all children from violent homes and even 80 percent from homes described as "most violent" do not abuse their wives. Conversely, a current batterer is more than twice as likely to have had a "nonviolent" than a violent childhood (7, p. 3) and seven times more likely to have had a nonviolent than a "most violent" childhood. Reviewing studies in this genre, Kaufman and Zigler (23) conclude that no more than 30 percent of those who experienced or witnessed violence as children are currently abusive, an estimate we believe is too high.

Medicine and Battering

Violence is only one dimension of the male control that entraps women in battering relationships. The other dimension is the response when abused women seek help. Although woman abuse is second only to male-male assault as a source of serious injury to adults (and is a major cause of death among younger black females), clinicians rarely identify the problem, minimize its significance, inappropriately medicate and label abused women, provide them with perfunctory or punitive care, refer them for secondary psychosocial problems but not for protection from violence, and emphasize family maintenance and compliance with traditional role expectations rather than personal safety (13–16, 24). Battering—the ongoing entrapment of women—is broken down into its medical symptoms (e.g., injuries, complaints, and psychosocial reactions to stress) and then the symptoms are reinterpreted so that the violence appears to result from rather than cause a woman's multiple problems. Within the health care system, women are increasingly isolated by inappropriate medication (such as tranquilizers), labels, psychiatric maintenance, and punitive interventions. And this process supports their being locked ever more tightly into relationships in which ongoing abuse is virtually inevitable.

In effect, clinical interventions manage the efforts of battered women to resist and escape domination, not domination itself. The political dimensions of battering are concealed behind a picture of "chaotic" families that need help "coping." "Restored functioning" is typically equated with getting the woman to better manage family conflict, usually by suppressing her own need for autonomy and development and by resuming traditional domestic responsibilities. As battering progresses through a range of increasingly severe psychosocial problems, abused women may come to know themselves as they are known. Thus, like their clinicians and their assailants, battered women in psychiatric facilities deny their problem, minimize its importance, or blame themselves (25).

Child Abuse: Responsible Mothers and Invisible Men

Can child abuse be understood as an extension of this entrapment process, as a problem rooted in the politics of gender inequality, occasioned by male violence and aggravated by the institutional response?

In contrast to battering, where sexist interpretations and practices confront a grassroots political movement, in the child abuse field, stereotypic and patronizing imagery of women goes unchallenged. One result is that men are invisible. Another is that "mothers" are held responsible for child abuse, even when the mother and child are being battered by an identifiable man.

Despite the evidence that men are a significant subset of abusive parents, there are few articles in the child abuse literature specifically on men. In a recent literature review, for instance, Martin (26) could identify only two individual case reports about men. Even in the minority of studies that consider both parents, women are the only source of direct information, no attempt is made to control for gender or to differentiate parental behavior and/or motivation by sex, and "abusing parent" is often a euphemism for mother.

Men are equally invisible in programs for abusing parents. Starting with images of appropriate gender behavior such as mother-child bonding, interventions proceed as if noncompliance with these norms reflects a character deficit that puts mother and child at risk. Varying combinations of parent education, counseling, peer pressure, and sanctions are used to instill appropriate maternal behavior, presumably so that the mother will adequately care for and protect the developing child.

Broad moral conceptions of women's "responsibility" for violence are incorporated in state regulations that define the mother's battering as a failure of her protective function. In New York State, for instance, an abusing parent includes one who "allows to be created a substantial risk of physical injury to the child," and this is frequently interpreted to mean allowing a child to witness violence against the mother. In Connecticut as well as many other states, women are interviewed by child protective services in determining foster placements, but not men, a practice undoubtedly linked to high rates of child abuse in foster homes.

Two decades of experience and thousands of monographs and programs offer no convincing evidence that child abuse has been reduced, let alone prevented, by this broad approach to mothering. But if child abuse is primarily a male crime and is rooted in subordinating women in gender-stereotyped roles, then the current emphasis on mothering may actually aggravate the problem it is designed to solve.

If violence is evoked by struggles around traditional sex roles, the practical result of re-enforcing these roles may be to restrict a woman's perceived options, increase her vulnerability to violence, decrease her capacity to protect her children from violence, exacerbate her own frustration and anger, and increase the probability that she will be destructive to self and others, including her children. This is what feminist theory leads us to expect. In this case, the best way to prevent child abuse is to protect women's physical integrity and support their empowerment. At a minimum, this implies close collaboration between child protective services and community-based shelters and a shift in child protection away from parenting education, therapy, and the removal of children. The question of whether the child-protection establishment would be receptive to this approach is examined later ("Conclusions").

BATTERING AND CHILD ABUSE: A STUDY

The disproportionate association of child abuse with battering is well established. Our earlier work (14, 17) indicates that battered women in a medical population are six times more likely than nonbattered women to have a report of child abuse (or "fear of child abuse") listed on their medical records (6 percent versus 1 percent). In their national survey of domestic violence, meanwhile, Straus and associates (22) found that abused women were 150 percent more likely to use severe violence with their children than were nonabused women. And after questioning women in a British shelter, Gayford (27) reported that 54 percent of abusive husbands and 37 percent of abused wives had also abused their children. From the vantage of its effect on children, exposure to parental violence may itself be counted as a form of "abuse."[1] Hilberman and Munson (13) report that one-third of 209 children exposed to marital violence exhibited somatic, psychological, and behavioral dysfunctions. Meanwhile, in his local medical practice, Levine (29) found that difficulty coping with children was a common presentation of women battering. He suggests that the child's reaction depends on how violence is experienced. If the batterer's relation to the children is nonviolent, their response is limited to psychiatric problems. But in instances where children attempt to intervene and are, in turn, used as scapegoats and beaten by the batterer, they become more aggressive in their other relations.

It is possible that although children are at risk for abuse in battering relationships, battering is a relatively minor etiological factor in child abuse. This study identifies the importance of battering in the etiology of child abuse, examines whether the identity of the assailant and the parent held responsible are the same, assesses the role of disposition, and asks whether battered mothers have a distinctive psychiatric profile.

Study Population

At Yale–New Haven Hospital, the medical records of children suspected of being abused or neglected are specially marked or "darted" and the children are referred for investigation and disposition to a special hospital "Dart Committee." The *study population* includes the mothers of all children referred to the hospital Dart Committee for suspicion of abuse and/or neglect between July 1977 and June 1978, 116 mothers in all. Dart Committee reports on children were matched to the medical records of their mothers, and the mothers were then classified as battered or nonbattered based on their adult trauma history and the risk classification described below. The analysis of medical records was supplemented by data from family background notes in Dart Committee reports.

Methodology

The trauma screen employed in the study was designed to identify abuse in a population that had not been explicitly identified as battered and to generate sufficiently large groups of abused and nonabused women to permit statistical analysis and comparison. Each adult hospital visit prompted by trauma after the age of 16 was reviewed, and women were assigned to a "battering risk group" according to the following criteria:

• *Positive:* At least one episode in the woman's trauma history was attributed to assault by a male family member or male intimate.
• *Probable:* At least one episode in the trauma history was an assault (kicked, beaten, stabbed, etc.) but no personal etiology was indicated. (Note that muggings and anonymous assaults were *not* included in category.)
• *Suggestive:* At least one episode in the trauma history was not well explained by the recorded alleged etiology.
• *Negative:* All episodes in the trauma history were well explained by the recorded injury, including those sustained in muggings, anonymous assaults, etc.

Data were gathered on (*a*) the significance of battering in families experiencing child abuse, (*b*) the identity of perpetrators, (*c*) whether mothers who are battered come disproportionately from problem homes (as some research suggests), and (*d*) whether current dispositions respond appropriately to the family situation.

Findings

Prevalence and frequency of battering. Of the 116 women, 52 (45 percent) had a trauma history that indicated battering and another 6 (5 percent) had a history of "marital conflict," though it was impossible to tell from their trauma history or other medical information whether they had been abused. Twenty-nine women (25 percent) presented "positive" episodes, an additional 18 (16 percent) were "probables," and five (4 percent) were "suggestive." Fifty-eight women (50 percent) had no documented trauma history indicating abuse and no record of "marital conflict." This frequency of at-risk women (45 percent) is 2.4 times greater than the frequency of battering among women presenting injuries to the surgical service (19 percent) and twice as great as the frequency of battering in the prenatal clinic (21 percent), making this the highest at-risk population yet identified. This information is summarized in Table 1.

The 52 abused women presented a total of 217 injury episodes during their adult histories, for a mean of 4.2 trauma presentations per woman. Women in the positive

Table 1. Number of Trauma Episodes among Battered and Nonbattered Mothers of Abused Children

Mother's Battering Risk Group[a]	N	No. of Episodes in Risk Group	Mean No. of Trauma Episodes per Woman
Positive	29	143	4.9
Probable	18	61	3.4
Suggestive	5	13	2.6
Total at-risk	52	217	4.2
Marital conflict	6	11	1.8
Negative	58	64	1.1

[a] See text for details of risk groups.

group averaged 4.9 episodes each, while those in the probable and suggestive groups each averaged 3.4 episodes. By contrast, women in the negative group averaged only 1.1 injury episodes, as one would expect in a "normal" population. Interestingly, the 1.8 trauma episodes averaged by the six mothers with a history of "marital conflict" fell somewhere between the suggestive and negative groups (Table 1). Conceivably this group constitutes a battering risk category outside the purview of an identification method based solely on the trauma history. At any rate, for battered mothers as for battered women generally, abusive assault is an ongoing process, not an isolated incident.

Family History

A frequent claim is that the link between battering and child abuse reflects a multi-problem family history that includes violence or other serious problems. This was explored by drawing information on alcoholism, violence, "chaos" or "disorganization," suicide attempts, and incest, common indicators of a high-risk family history, from social services notes in the medical record and from Dart Committee files. To strengthen the conservative bias, women with a history of "marital conflict" were included with "negatives."

As shown in Table 2, a significant subpopulation of these 116 mothers came from high-risk families of origin. It is evident, however, that abused mothers do not typically

Table 2. Problems in the Family Histories of Mothers of Abused Children

Problem	No. among Mothers in the At-Risk[a] Groups, N = 52	No. among Mothers in the Negative and Marital Conflict Risk Groups, N = 64
Alcoholism	6 (12%)	12 (19%)
Violence	9 (17%)	10 (16%)
Suicide attempts	5 (10%)	7 (11%)
Incest	1 (2%)	4 (6%)
Chaotic family	12 (23%)	12 (19%)

[a] Includes the positive, probable, and suggestive battering risk groups.

Table 3.   Reasons for "Dart"[a]

Mother's Battering Risk Group	N	Mother Needs Support	Neglect and/or Suspicious Injury	Abuse
Positive	29	15 (50%)	5 (18%)	9 (32%)
Probable	18	6 (33%)	8 (44%)	4 (22%)
Suggestive	5	2 (40%)	2 (40%)	1 (20%)
Total at-risk	52	23 (44%)	15 (29%)	14 (27%)
Marital conflict and negative	64	29 (46%)	23 (35%)	12 (19%)

[a] See text for explanation of this term.

come from multi-problem backgrounds, are far less likely to come from a background that includes incest and/or alcoholism, and, perhaps most important, are no more likely to have a family background that includes violence. In sum, battered mothers of abused children cannot be distinguished by a background of family disorganization and, if anything, are even less likely than nonbattered mothers in this group to have such a background.

Reason for "Dart"

Most children are "darted" because a clinician believes that they are "at risk" of abuse, neglected, or injured under "suspicious circumstances," or because the mother needs "support" to help her cope. As indicated in Table 3, only a minority are darted because of documented physical abuse. However, children whose mothers have a positive history of being battered are twice as likely as the children of nonbattered mothers to be darted for actual abuse. Interestingly, they are also more likely to be darted because "mother needs support." At best, this represents a tacit recognition of the battered woman's predicament since in almost no instance is "abuse" or "battering" actually noted.

The mothers in this study were selected because their children were darted in 1977–78. Thus it is not surprising that virtually all their trauma visits preceded the child's referral. The fact that battering is the context within which child abuse develops for these women cannot be generalized to other populations of women. Conceivably, mothers currently classified as nonbattered will be abused in the future. However, since a longer history of assault is associated with "positive" women whose children are also most likely to be physically abused, child abuse seems to appear after a pattern of battering is established, an issue taken up in the Discussion.

Identity of the Abuser

Dart Committee reports give the identity of the parent allegedly responsible for abusing the child. For families in which the mother is battered, the father or father substitute is more than three times more likely to be the child's abuser than in families of nonbattered mothers. Approximately 50 percent of darted children of at-risk women are abused by the male batterer, 35 percent are abused by the mother who is also being battered, and the rest are abused by others or by "both."

Removal of the Child

Of children darted for all reasons, almost one-third are removed from homes where mothers are being battered. This is significantly higher than the percentage of children removed for all reasons from families with nonbattered mothers. Does this simply reflect the greater likelihood, documented above, that children of battered mothers will be physically abused? To control for this possibility, we compared the disposition only for cases in which the children have been allegedly neglected or in which the mothers needed support. Here too, if the mother was battered, the child was far more likely to be removed from her home than if she was not. Whatever the rationale for disproportionately removing children from battered mothers, the effect is obviously punitive.

DISCUSSION

The findings support an analysis of child abuse as a component of female subordination. Even a highly conservative definition of battering requiring that at least one abusive injury be serious enough for hospital treatment reveals that 45 percent of these young mothers are battered and another 5 percent are experiencing "marital conflict." The documented prevalence of battering in this population is greater than in any other group yet identified, including emergency surgical patients, female alcoholics, drug abusers, women who attempt suicide, rape victims, mental patients, women filing for divorce, or women using emergency psychiatric or obstetrical services (15, 17). These women have already presented an average of four injury episodes to the hospital, only slightly fewer than the far older emergency-room sample, corroborating our suspicion that child abuse in these relationships represents the extension of ongoing violence and is an intermediary point in an unfolding history of battering. Not only are the children of battered mothers significantly more likely to be physically abused than neglected, for instance, but the batterer also appears to be the typical source of child abuse, not a mother "overwhelmed with problems." The data shed little light on the dynamics of child abuse in battering homes. Again, however, the battering clearly predates the child abuse and, even when the battered mother is the abusive parent, she is less likely to have had a violent or "disorganized" family-of-origin, both facts suggesting that "transmission" involves the extension of the same unresolved conflict that elicits battering. The mothers divide into women with a problematic family history whose children are suspected of "neglect," and battered women whose background appears comparatively nonproblematic. In either case, the popular stereotype of the mother "predisposed by her history" to be battered and to abuse her child is a convenient fiction with little relation to documented cases.

To those familiar with the literature on child abuse, the clinical response to families in which mothers are battered will come as no surprise. As is the literature, the records of battered mothers are silent about physical abuse and the children's records rarely mention the man's violence. Instead, the mother's failure to fulfill her feminine role is emphasized ("mother needs support coping"). Here too, as in the clinical response to battering or in the literature on child abuse, women are held responsible when things go wrong. Even when we control for danger to the child, battered mothers are more likely to lose their children than nonbattered mothers.

Behind the ultimate threat—that a woman will lose her child—providers require periodic displays of nurturance and homemaker efficiency as prerequisites for basic family supports. In many cases, the mother does not report the abusing male and the caseworker lists the source of violence as "unknown" or "other." This may be because the woman defines the worker as her adversary, is afraid of the batterer's retaliation, or fears the withdrawal of welfare benefits if her relation with an unrelated man is discovered.

Ironically, since there are no therapeutic modalities to deal with men, foster placement—a punitive intervention as far as the mother is concerned—is more likely when a man is battering the mother and child. Not only are the mothers who pose least danger to their children most likely to lose them, but they may also lose access to whatever meager resources resulted from agency concern. With foster placement, the therapeutic focus shifts from the natural parents onto the child and his or her new milieu, while the underlying problems—including any violence toward the mother— are ignored (30).

In summary, and contrary to the prevalent view in the field, men are primarily responsible for child abuse, *not women;* battering is the typical context for child abuse, *not maternal deficits;* battered mothers whose children are abused are not distinguished by a family background of violence or psychopathology; and the response of the child abuse system—including neglect of the violence, support for mothering, and removal of the child to foster care—are ineffective at best and punitive at worst. . . .

Note

1. *But* Rosenbaum and O'Leary (28) found no differences for male children among violent, discordant, and satisfactorily married couples on the Behavior Problem Checklist. Interestingly, while they found no more behavioral problems in abused children than in those who had not been abused, 70 percent of the children whose mothers had been victims of spouse abuse were above the mean for a normative sample, suggesting that the psychological consequences of spouse abuse may be more serious for children than those of child abuse.

References

1. Williams, G. Toward the eradication of child abuse and neglect at home. In *Traumatic Abuse and the Neglect of Children at Home,* edited by G. Williams and J. Money, pp. 588–605. Johns Hopkins University Press, Baltimore, 1980.

2. Breines, W., and Gordon, L. The new scholarship on family violence. *Signs: Journal of Women and Culture in Society* 8(3): 490–531, 1983.

3. American Humane Society. *National Analysis of Official Child Neglect and Abuse Reporting.* AHS, Denver, 1978.

4. Bergman, A., Larsen, R. M., and Mueller, B. Changing spectrum of serious child abuse. *Pediatrics* 77(1): 113–116, 1986.

5. Stark, E., and Flitcraft, A. Woman-battering, child abuse and social heredity: What is the relationship? In *Marital Violence,* edited by N. K. Johnson, pp. 147–171. *Sociological Review Monograph,* No. 31. Routledge and Kegan Paul, London, 1985.

6. Gil, D. *Violence Against Children: Physical Child Abuse in the United States.* Harvard University Press, Cambridge, Mass., 1973.

7. Steele, B., and Pollack, C. A psychiatric study of parents who abuse infants and small children. In *The Battered Child,* edited by R. Helfer and C. Henry Kempe, pp. 103–147. University of Chicago Press, Chicago, 1976.

8. Kempe, R., and Kempe, C. H. Assessing family pathology. In *Child Abuse and Neglect: The Family and the Community,* edited by R. Helfer and C. H. Kempe, Ballinger, Cambridge, Mass., 1976.

9. Newberger, C. B., and Newberger, E. The etiology of child abuse. In *Child Abuse: A Medical Reference,* edited by N. F. Ellerstein, pp. 11–20. John Wiley and Sons, New York, 1981.

10. Newberger, E., and Bourne, R. E. The medicalization and legalization of child abuse. *Am. J. Orthopsychiatry* 48(4): 593–606, 1978.

11. Helfer, R. F. Basic issues concerning prediction. In *Child Abuse and Neglect: The Family and the Community,* edited by R. E. Helfer and C. H. Kempe, Ballinger, Cambridge, Mass., 1976.

12. Baher, E., et al. *At Risk: An Account of the Work of the Battered Child Research Department,* National Society for Prevention of Cruelty to Children. Routledge and Kegan Paul, Boston, 1976.

13. Hilberman, E., and Munson, K. Sixty battered women. *Victimology: An International Journal* 2(3–4): 460–470, 1977/78.

14. Stark, E., and Flitcraft, A. Personal power and institutional victimization: Treating the dual trauma of woman battering. In *Post-Traumatic Therapy,* edited by F. Ochberg. Bruner and Mazel, New York, 1987.

15. Stark, E. The Battering Syndrome: Social Knowledge, Social Therapy and the Abuse of Women, Doctoral dissertation, Department of Sociology, State University of New York, Binghamton, 1984.

16. Stark, E., Flitcraft, A., and Frazier, W. Medicine and patriarchal violence: The social construction of a "private" event. *Int. J. Health Serv.* 9(3): 461–493, 1979.

17. Stark, E., and Flitcraft, A. Violence among intimates: An epidemiological review. In *Handbook of Family Violence,* edited by V. N. Hasselt et al. Plenum Press, New York, 1987.

18. Stark, E., et al. *Wife Abuse in the Medical Setting: An Introduction for Health Personnel,* Monograph No. 7. Washington, D.C., Office of Domestic Violence, 1981.

19. Dobash, R. E., and Dobash, R. *Violence Against Wives.* Free Press, New York, 1979.

20. Rosenberg, M., Stark, E., and Zahn, M. A. Interpersonal violence: Homicide and spouse abuse. In *Maxcy-Rosenau: Public Health and Preventive Medicine,* Ed. 12, edited by J. M. Last, pp. 1399–1426. Appleton-Century-Crofts, New York, 1985.

21. Steele, B. F. Violence within the family. In *Child Abuse and Neglect: The Family and the Community,* edited by R. E. Helfer and C. H. Kempe, Ballinger, Cambridge, Mass., 1976.

22. Straus, M., Gelles, R., and Steinmetz, S. K. *Behind Closed Doors: A Survey of Family Violence in America.* Doubleday, New York, 1980.

23. Kaufman, J., and Zigler, E. Do abused children become abusive parents? *Am J. Orthopsychiatry* 57(2): 186–193, 1987.

24. Kurz, D., and Stark, E. Health education and feminist strategy: The case of woman abuse. In *Feminist Perspectives on Wife Abuse,* edited by M. Bograd and K. Yllo. Sage, Beverly Hills, Calif., 1987.

25. Carmen, E. H., Rieker, P. P., and Mills, T. Victims of violence and psychiatric illness. In *The Gender Gap in Psychotherapy, Social Realities and Psychological Processes,* edited by P. P. Rieker and E. H. Carmen, pp. 199–213. Plenum Press, New York, 1984.

26. Martin, J. Maternal and paternal abuse of children: Theoretical and research perspectives. In *The Dark Side of Families: Current Family Violence Research,* edited by D. Finkelhor et al., pp. 293–305. Sage, Beverly Hills, Calif., 1983.

27. Gayford, J. J. Wife battering: A preliminary survey of 100 cases. *Br. Med. J.* 25: 194–197, 1975.

28. Rosenbaum, A., and O'Leary, D. Children: The unintended victims of marital violence. *Am. J. Orthopsychiatry* 51(4): 692–699, 1981.

29. Levine, M. Interparental violence and its effect on the children: A study of 50 families in general practice. *Med. Sci. Law* 15(3): 172–183, 1975.

30. Green, A. Societal neglect and child abusing parents. *Victimology: An International Journal* 11(2): 285–293, 1977.

31. Baker-Miller, J. *Toward a New Psychology of Women.* Beacon Press, Boston, 1976.

32. Chodorow, N. J. Gender, relation and difference in psychoanalytic perspective. In *The Future of Difference,* edited by H. Eisenstein and A. Jardine, pp. 3–20. Rutgers University Press, New Brunswick, N.J., 1985.

33. Flax, J. Mother-daughter relationships: Psychodynamics, politics and philosophy. In *The Future of Difference,* edited by H. Eisenstein and A. Jardine, pp. 20–41. Rutgers University Press, New Brunswick, N.J., 1985.

34. Bernardez, T. Women and Anger, Cultural Prohibitions and the Feminine Ideal. Paper presented at Learning from Women: Theory and Practice, Boston, April 1987.

35. Brown, G. W., and Harris, T. *Social Origins of Depression—A Study of Psychiatric Disorder in Women.* Tavistock, London, 1978.

36. Weissman, M. The depressed mother and her rebellious adolescent. In *Children of Depressed Parents: Risk, Identification and Intervention,* edited by H. Morrison, Grune and Stratton, New York, 1983.

37. Henriques, J., et al. *Changing the Subject: Psychology, Social Regulation and Subjectivity.* Methuen, London, 1984.

38. Howell, M. C. Pediatricians and mothers. In *The Cultural Crisis of Modern Medicine,* edited by J. Ehrenreich, Monthly Review Press, New York, 1979.

39. Ehrenreich, B., and English, D. *For Her Own Good.* Anchor Books, New York, 1979.

40. Caplan, P., and Hall-McCorguodale, I. The scapegoating of mothers: A call for change. *Am. J. Orthopsychiatry* 55(4): 610–613, 1985.

41. Caplan, P. Mother blaming in major clinical journals. *Am. J. Orthopsychiatry* 55(5): 345–353, 1985.

42. Garbarino, J., and Sherman, D. High risk neighborhoods and high risk families: The human ecology of child maltreatment. *Child Dev.* 51(1), 1980.

43. Robertson, B. A., and Juritz, J. M. Characteristics of the families of abused children. *Child Abuse and Neglect* 3: 861, 1979.

44. Kott-Washburne, C. A feminist analysis of child abuse and neglect. In *The Dark Side of Families,* edited by D. Finkelhor et al., pp. 289–293. Sage, Beverly Hills, Calif., 1984.

45. Rosen, B. Self-concept disturbance among mothers who abuse their children. *Psychol. Rep.* 43: 323–326, 1978.

46. Nelson, B. *Making an Issue of Child Abuse: Political Agenda Setting for Social Problems.* University of Chicago Press, Chicago, 1984.

47. National Center on Child Abuse and Neglect. *Child Abuse and Family Violence.* U.S. Children's Bureau, Washington, D.C., 1978.

48. Besharov, D. J. Right versus rights: The dilemma of child protection. *Public Welfare* 43(2): 19–46, 1985.

49. Newberger, E. Child abuse. In *Source Book: Surgeon General's Workshop, Violence and Public Health.* Leesberg, Va., 1985.

50. Herman, J. Sexual Violence. Paper presented at Learning from Women: Theory and Practice, Boston, April 1987.

51. Rhodes, R. M., and Zelman, A. B. An ongoing multifamily group in a women's shelter. *Am. J. Orthopsychiatry* 56(1): 120–131, 1986.

52. Alessi, J. J., and Hearn, K. Group treatment of children in shelters for battered women. In *Battered Women and Their Families: Intervention Strategies and Treatment Programs,* edited by A. R. Roberts, Springer, New York, 1978.

25. Drugs-Crime Connections: Elaborations from the Life Histories of Hard-Core Heroin Addicts

CHARLES E. FAUPEL AND CARL B. KLOCKARS

The debate over the nature and extent of the relationship between heroin use and criminal activity is a long-standing one which has generated a voluminous literature. A 1980 survey (Gandossey et al., 1980) lists over 450 citations to books, articles, and research reports which directly or indirectly bear upon the heroin-crime relationship. Since 1980 the study of this relationship has continued, and several large-scale quantitative studies (Anglin and Speckart, 1984; Ball et al., 1981, 1983; Collins et al., 1984, 1985; Johnson et al., 1985) generally support the thesis that an increase in criminality commonly occurs in conjunction with increased heroin use in the United States. These studies, together with a host of others preceding them (e.g., Ball and Snarr, 1969; Chein et al., 1964; Inciardi, 1979; McGlothlin et al., 1978; Nash, 1973; Weissman et al., 1974), have moved the focus of the debate from the empirical question of whether or not there is a heroin-crime connection to empirical and theoretical questions about the dynamics of that connection.

In particular, two hypotheses, neither of which is new, currently occupy center stage in the drugs-crime controversy. The first, stated by Tappan a quarter of a century ago, maintains that the "addict of lower socio-economic class is a criminal primarily because illicit narcotics are costly and because he can secure his daily requirements only by committing crimes that will pay for them" (1960:65–66). This hypothesis maintains that heroin addict criminality is a consequence of addiction, albeit an indirect one. As physical dependence upon and tolerance for heroin increase, and the cost of progressively larger dosages of heroin increase proportionally, the addict is driven to criminal means to satisfy his or her habit. Empirically, this hypothesis predicts a linear increase in heroin consumption and a corresponding increase in criminal activity necessary to support it. In contrast, a second hypothesis maintains that the "principal explanation for the association between drug abuse and crime . . . is likely to be found in the subcultural attachment" (Goldman, 1981:162) comprised of the criminal associations, identifications, and activities of those persons who eventually become addicted. The basis for this hypothesis can only be understood in the context of the contemporary socio-legal milieu in which narcotics use takes place. Since the criminalization of heroin in 1914, the social world of narcotics has become increasingly intertwined with the broader criminal subculture (Musto, 1973). Consequently, would-be narcotics users inevitably associate with other criminals in the highly criminal copping areas of inner cities, and, indeed, are often recruited from delinquent and criminal networks. Through these criminal associations, therefore, the individual is introduced to heroin, and both crime and heroin use are facilitated and maintained. Empirically, this second hypothesis predicts increases in heroin use following or coinciding with periods of criminal association and activity.

A shorthand title for the first hypothesis is "Drugs cause crimes"; for the second, "Crimes cause drugs." Each, as we shall see below, is subject to a number of qualifications and reservations; but each, as we shall also see below, continues to mark a rather different approach to understanding the drugs-crime connection. Furthermore, each hypothesis has quite different policy implications associated with it.

METHODOLOGY

Our contribution to understanding the dynamics of the drugs-crime connection is based upon life-history interviews with 32 hard-core heroin addicts in the Wilmington, Delaware area. We purposely selected the respondents on the basis of their extensive involvement in the heroin subculture. All of the respondents had extensive contact with the criminal justice system. At the time of interview, 24 of the 32 respondents were incarcerated or under some form of correctional authority supervision (e.g., supervised custody, work release, parole, or probation). While this places certain limits on the generalizations that can be made from these data, the focus of this study is the dynamics of addiction among heavily involved street addicts. For example, controlled users or "chippers" will not have experienced many of the dynamics reported here. Similarly, physicians, nurses, and middle-class "prescription abusers" are not typically subject to many of the constraints experienced by lower-class street users. Hence, it is important to emphasize that the findings we report here are intended to describe "hard-core" urban heroin addicts.

Women are slightly overrepresented, constituting 14 of the 32 respondents. Ethnically, the sample consists of 23 blacks and nine whites; Hispanics are not represented because there is not a sizable Hispanic drug-using population in the Wilmington area.

Respondents were paid five dollars per hour for their interview time, which undoubtedly contributed to the 100 percent response rate. The interviews ranged from 10 to 25 hours in length, with each interview session averaging between three and four hours. With a single exception, all of the interviews were tape recorded and transcribed. Respondents were promised confidentiality and, without exception, they spoke openly of their drug, crime, and life-history experience.

The incarcerated respondents and most of the street respondents were selected with the aid of treatment personnel who were carefully instructed regarding the goals of the research and selection criteria. This strategy proved invaluable for two reasons. First, by utilizing treatment personnel in the screening process, we were able to avoid the time-consuming task of establishing the "appropriateness" of respondents for the purposes of this research; the treatment personnel were already intimately familiar with the drug-using and criminal histories of the respondents. Second, the treatment personnel had an unusually positive relationship with Wilmington-area drug users. The treatment counselor in the prison system was regarded as an ally in the quest for better living conditions, appeals for early release, etc., and was regarded as highly trustworthy in the prison subculture. His frequent confrontations with prison authorities over prisoner rights and privileges enhanced his reputation among the inmates. Similarly, the treatment counselor who aided in the selection of street respondents was carefully selected on the basis of his positive involvement with street addicts. His relationship with area addicts is a long-standing and multifaceted one. His reputation among street addicts was firmly established when he successfully negotiated much needed reforms in one of the local treatment agencies. Because of the long-standing positive relationship they had with area addicts, this initial contact by treatment personnel greatly facilitated our establishing necessary rapport.

After a few initial interviews were completed, several broad focal areas emerged which formed the basis for future questioning. Respondents were interviewed regarding: (1) childhood and early adolescent experiences which may have served as *predisposing factors* for eventual drugs/criminal involvement; (2) *initial encounters* with various types of drugs and criminality; (3) the *evolution* of their drug and criminal careers; (4) their patterns of activity during *peak periods* of drug use and criminality, including descriptions of *typical days* during these periods; (5) their *preferences* for types of crimes and drugs; (6) the *structure of understanding* guiding drug use and criminal activity; and (7) their perceptions of the nature and effectiveness of *drug treatment*. Structuring the life-history interviews in this way insured that most relevant career phases were covered while at the same time it permitted the respondents a great deal of flexibility in interpreting their experiences.

DRUGS CAUSE CRIMES VERSUS CRIMES CAUSE DRUGS

One of the earliest strategies for testing the Drugs-cause-crimes versus Crimes-cause-drugs hypotheses involved trying to establish a temporal sequence to drug use and criminal behavior. If it can be established that a pattern of regular or extensive criminal behavior typically precedes heroin addiction, that finding would tend to support the Crimes-cause-drugs hypothesis. Conversely, if a pattern of regular or extensive criminality tends to develop after the onset of heroin addiction, that finding would tend to support the Drugs-cause-crimes hypothesis. Previous research on this question is mixed, but mixed in a systematic way. Most of the early studies found little criminality before the onset of opiate addiction (Pescor, 1943; Terry and Pellens, 1928). Later studies, by contrast, have shown a high probability of criminality preceding heroin addiction (Ball and Chambers, 1970; Chambers, 1974; Jacoby et al., 1973; Inciardi, 1979; O'Donnell, 1966; Robins and Murphy, 1967).

Our life-history interviews are consistent with the findings of the recent studies. All of our respondents reported some criminal activity prior to their first use of heroin. However, for nearly all of our respondents, both their criminal careers and their heroin-using careers began slowly. For the respondents in our study, a median of 3.5 years elapsed between their first serious criminal offense and subsequent involvement in criminal activity on a regular basis. Likewise, all of our respondents reported at least occasional use of other illicit drugs prior to their first experience with heroin. Moreover, many of our respondents indicated that they spent substantial periods of time — months and even years — using heroin on an occasional basis ("chipping" or "chippying"), either inhaling the powder ("sniffing" or "snorting"), injecting the prepared ("cooked") mixture subcutaneously ("skinpopping"), or receiving occasional intravenous injections from other users before becoming regular users themselves. Perhaps most importantly, virtually all of our respondents reported that they believed that their criminal and drug careers began independently of one another, although both careers became intimately interconnected as each evolved. In the earliest phases of their drug and crime careers, the decision to commit crimes and the decision to use drugs were choices which our respondents believe they freely chose to make and which they believe they could have discontinued before either choice became a way of life (also see Fields and Walters, 1985; Morris, 1985).

DRUG AND CRIME CAREER PATTERNS

From our interviews it appears that two very general factors shape and influence the drug and crime careers of our respondents, not only during the early stages of each career but as each career evolves through different stages. The first of these factors is the *availability* of heroin rather than the level of physical tolerance the user has developed. "The more you had the more you did," explains "Mona" a thirty-year-old female. "And if all you had was $10 then that's all you did. . . . But if you had $200 then you did that much." Addicts are able to adjust to periods of sharply decreased availability (e.g., "panic" periods when supplies of street heroin disappear) by reducing consumption or by using alternative drugs (e.g., methadone). They are also able to manipulate availability, increasing or decreasing it in ways and for reasons we discuss below.

As we use the term, availability also means something more than access to sellers of heroin who have quantities of the drug to sell. By availability we also mean the resources and opportunities to buy heroin or obtain it in other ways as well as the skills necessary to use it. In short, availability is understood to include considerations of all of those opportunities and obstacles which may influence a heroin user's success in introducing a quantity of the drug into his or her bloodstream.

The second general factor shaping the drugs and crime careers of our life-history interviewees is *life structure*. By "life structure" we mean regularly occurring patterns of daily domestic, occupational, recreational, or criminal activity. Recent ethnographic accounts of heroin-using careers in several major cities reveal that, like their "straight" counterparts, most addicts maintain reasonably predictable daily routines (Beschner and Brower, 1985; Walters, 1985). Throughout their lives our respondents fulfilled, to one degree or another, conventional as well as criminal and other subcultural roles. In fact, during most periods of their crime and drug careers, our interviewees spent far more time engaged in conventional role activities than in criminal or deviant ones. Many worked conventional jobs. Women with children performed routine housekeeping and child-rearing duties. Many leisure-time activities did not differ from those of non-addicts. These hard-core addicts spent time grocery shopping, tinkering with cars, visiting relatives, talking with friends, listening to records, and watching television in totally unremarkable fashion.

Life structure in the hard-core criminal addict's life can be also provided by some rather stable forms of criminal activity. Burglars spend time staking out business establishments. Shoplifters typically establish "runs," more or less stable sequences of

Availability	Life Structure	
	High	Low
High	The Stabilized Junkie	The Free-Wheeling Junkie
Low	The Occasional User	The Street Junkie

Figure 1. A Typology of Heroin Use Career Phases

targeted stores from which to "boost" during late morning, noon, and early afternoon hours, saving the later afternoon for fencing what they have stolen. Prostitutes typically keep a regular evening and night-time schedule, which runs from 7 P.M. to 3 A.M. Mornings are usually spent sleeping and afternoons are usually occupied with conventional duties.

It is within this structure of conventional and criminal roles that buying ("copping"), selling ("dealing"), and using ("shooting") heroin take place. For example, shoplifters typically structure their runs to allow times and places for all three activities. Likewise, prostitutes seek to manage their drug use so that neither withdrawal symptoms ("joneses") nor periods of heroin-induced drowsiness will interfere with their work. In order to meet the demands of criminal or conventional roles, addicts in our sample often used other drugs (e.g., marijuana, barbituates, alcohol, amphetamines, methadone) to alter their moods and motivations, saving heroin as a reward for successfully completing a job or meeting other obligations.

A Typology of Career Patterns

These two dimensions—*availability* and *life structure*—are critical to understanding the dynamics of addict careers. According to our respondents, differences in the way addicts manage these functions and variations in these two dimensions that are beyond the control of addicts combine to produce fairly distinct patterns, periods, or stages in their careers. The interaction of availability and life structure may be understood to describe addict career phases that are familiar to participants or observers of the heroin scene.

In Figure 1, we identify four such familiar career phases, each of which is marked by a different interaction of heroin availability and life structure. It is important to note that while each denotes an addict type, none of the "types" imply a single career pattern. That is, throughout their drug-crime careers, addicts typically move through periods in which they may at one time be described as one type and later as another. In our discussion of each type, we describe some of the ways in which transitions seem to occur.

The Occasional User—Low Availability/High Life Structure. Initiates into the heroin-using subculture typically begin as occasional users. For the beginning heroin user, a variety of factors typically serve to limit the availability of heroin. The initiate has usually not spent enough time in the heroin subculture to develop extensive drug connections. In addition, the beginner must be taught how and where to buy heroin, and also must learn how to use it. Moreover, the typical beginning heroin user is unlikely to have sufficient income to maintain any substantial level of heroin consumption, and is most unlikely to have either the connections or the knowledge necessary to increase availability through low-level dealing or through shrewd buying and reselling as experienced addicts sometimes do.

In addition to these factors which tend to limit the availability of heroin to the beginning user and hold him or her to an occasional user role, a variety of factors related to life structure also tend to oblige the beginning heroin user to play an occasional user role, or at least to do so until that life structure can be modified to accommodate a higher level of heroin use. In many cases beginning heroin users are young, dependent, involved in school, and bear family roles and obligations which are not easily changed. Likewise, adult role obligations, such as full-time employment, housekeeping, and child rearing, can be altered so as to be compatible with occasional patterns of heroin use, but not without considerable difficulty if those patterns include high or even moderately high levels of addiction.

One of our respondents, "Belle," explained how she and her husband, "Taps," maintained a very long period of occasional use, due largely to Taps' determination to keep his full-time job:

> I know of people that does half a bag generally. Do you understand what I'm saying? That they automatically live off of half a bag and got a jones. Like I said, Taps worked—and he would shoot no more than half a bag of dope at any time he took off and wouldn't do no wrong. He would not do no wrong. He worked each and every day. And this is what I told you before—I said I don't know how he had a jones and worked, but he worked every day.

Moreover, Belle went on to explain that when the life structure Taps provided for her lapsed—and availability increased—she did not remain an occasional user:

> Taps had me limited a long, long time. I mean a long time limited to nothing but a half a bag of drugs, until he completely stopped hisself. Then when he stopped, I went "Phwee!"—because I didn't have anybody to guide me. I didn't have to take half a bag and divide it in half for him. And I went from one bag to more.

"Ron," another addict in our sample, played the role of "occasional user" without interruption for nearly eight years. During this period he consumed an average of $10–$15 in street heroin per day, while holding down a full-time job and living with his mother, who refused to allow him to use drugs in her home. Toward the end of the eight-year period he became a "tester" for a local drug dealer, a role which increased the availability of heroin. At about the same time, he also lost his job and moved out of his mother's home. Having lost the support of the stable routine imposed by his job and living arrangements at the same time heroin became more readily available to him in his role of "tester," his drug use escalated dramatically within a very short time.

Interestingly, the low availability/high life structure pattern of occasional use, which typically marks the beginning addict's entrance into the drug-using world, is characteristic of many addicts' attempts to leave it. Many formal drug rehabilitation programs impose conditions of low (or no) heroin availability combined with high life structure upon addicts enrolled in their programs (Faupel, 1985). Likewise, as Biernacki (1986) and Waldorf (1983) have extensively demonstrated, addicts who attempt to quit on their own often seek to do so by limiting or eliminating altogether their contacts with addict friends, self-medicating with "street" methadone, and devoting themselves intensively to some highly demanding routine activity such as a full-time job or caring for young children.

The Stabilized Junkie—High Availability/High Life Structure. For the occasional user to become a stabilized junkie, heroin must become increasingly available in large and regular quantities, and his or her daily structure must be modified to accommodate regular heroin use. Making heroin regularly available in sufficiently large quantities is not only a matter of gaining access to reliable sources of supply of the drug; it also involves learning new and more sophisticated techniques for using and obtaining it as well as getting enough money to be able to buy it regularly.

During the time beginning addicts play occasional user roles, they typically learn the fundamentals of copping, cooking, cutting, and spiking. These are all drug-using skills that take time to learn. It was not uncommon for the addicts in our sample to report that a sharp increase in their level of heroin use followed their learning to shoot themselves. When an occasional user learns to self-inject and no longer requires the more knowledgeable drug-using friends to "get off," this new level of skill and independence, in effect, increases the availability of heroin.

Likewise, copping skills and contacts which might have been sufficient to support occasional use require upgrading to support the needs of the stabilized junkie. The would-be stabilized junkie who must rely solely on low-quality, "street" heroin, who gets "ripped" by paying high prices for "bad dope," or who is totally dependent on what quality or quantity of heroin a single supplier happens to have available must seek to stabilize both the quantity and quality of regularly available heroin. Doing so seems to require extending and developing contacts in the drug subculture. In the words of one of our respondents:

> . . . you got to start associating with different people. You got to be in touch with different people for the simple reason that not just one person has it all the time. You got to go from one person to the other, find out who's got the best bag and who hasn't. . . . You want to go where the best bag is for your money, and especially for the money *you're* spending. You got to mingle with so many different people.

Making, developing, and maintaining the contacts that are helpful if not absolutely necessary to stable heroin use seem to invite natural opportunities for the most common modification in the stabilized junkie's life structure: dealing. From the point of view of the would-be stabilized junkie, dealing has two major advantages over most other forms of routine daily activity. First, it can be carried on in the course of the stabilized junkie's search for his or her own supply of drugs and, second, it can be a source of money for the purchase of drugs or a source of drugs itself. Dealing can be rather easily accommodated to the needs of both availability and life structure.

All of our respondents reported that at some time in their drug-using careers they had played the role of dealer, if only occasionally. Becoming an occasional dealer is almost an inevitable consequence of becoming a competent, regular user. A stabilized junkie will not only be approached to "cop" for occasional users and addicts whose suppliers are temporarily out of stock, but the stabilized junkie will come to recognize occasions on which especially "good dope" can be purchased and resold at a profit to drug-using friends.

Because the work of dealing drugs on a small scale does not require much more time or effort than that which goes into buying drugs regularly for one's own use, dealing also has another advantage which makes it an attractive activity for the stabilized junkie. Namely, it can be carried on as a source of drugs or income without undue interference with whatever other "hustle," if any, constitutes the stabilized junkie's additional source of support. This is particularly true if, in the course of carrying on the hustle—be it theft, shoplifting, pimping, prostitution, bookmaking, or dealing in stolen property—the stabilized addict is likely to come into regular contact with other drug users.

The extent to which dealing can be carried on along with other hustles depends, of course, both on the nature of that hustle and on the extent of the dealing. The stabilized junkie will tend to divide his or her hustling efforts between dealing and other hustles with an eye toward which one delivers the highest profit. However, dividing those efforts will also involve other considerations such as the stabilized junkie's personal preference for one type of work, life style and community reputation considerations, opportunities to practice one type of hustle or another, and the physical demands each type of hustle tends to require. Among female heroin users, a rather common accommodation to the profits and opportunities of dealing and those of other hustles is a live-together arrangement with a male user. In this division of labor each tries to conduct their outside hustle during hours when the other can be at home to handle dealing transactions. An important feature of this arrangement is that, if necessary, it can be structured so as to permit the stabilized female junkie to be at home for housekeeping and child-rearing duties as well as dealing.

The Free-wheeling Junkie—High Availability/Low Life Structure. Although most heroin users spend some portion of their drug-using careers as stabilized junkies and many manage to live for years with high heroin availability and highly structured daily routines, at least two properties of the stabilized junkie's situation tend to work against the maintenance of stability. One is the pharmacological property of heroin. It is a drug to which users tend to develop a tolerance rather rapidly, although as Zinberg (1984) has demonstrated, such tolerance is neither necessary nor universal. Moreover, as we have pointed out earlier, numerous factors in the social setting of heroin use mitigate the destabilizing effect of the drug. Work routines, household duties, and even subcultural roles all serve to structure drug consumption. However, in the absence of external structures of constraint, or when such routines are temporarily disrupted, the pharmacological properties of heroin tend to destabilize the lifestyle of the addict further. In sum, contrary to popular belief, heroin use does not inevitably lead to a deterioration of lifestyle. Rather, the physiological dynamics of narcotics use tend to be most destabilizing under conditions where life structure is already weak and incapable of accommodating the physiological demands imposed by increased tolerance.

The other property of the stabilized junkie's life which tends to undermine stability is the hustle the junkie uses to finance his or her habit. According to our respondents, it is not hard times or difficulties in raising money through hustles which tend to destabilize the stabilized junkie's life. "You can adjust yourself to a certain amount of drugs a day," explained Belle, "that you don't have to have but just that much." In addition to reducing their drug consumption, stabilized junkies accommodate themselves to such lean periods by substituting other drugs for heroin, working longer and harder at their hustling, or changing the type of hustle they work.

On the contrary, it is the unusual success, the "big sting" or "big hit," that tends to destabilize the stabilized junkie's high degree of life structure. The "big sting" or "big hit" can come in many forms. One of our respondents—an armed robber who usually limited his robbing to street mugging, gas stations, and convenience stores—"hit" a bank, which to our respondent's surprise, produced a "take" of over $60,000. He increased his heroin consumption dramatically and, while doing so, abandoned virtually all the stabilizing routines which marked his life prior to his windfall take. In another instance, a relatively stable junkie dealer was "fronted" several thousand dollars of heroin on consignment. Instead of selling it as he had agreed to do, he absconded with it to another state, shot up most of it himself, and gave the rest away. In still another case, a relatively low-level burglar/thief came across $10,000 in cash in the course of one of his burglaries. He took the money to New York where he intended to cop a "big piece" that he could bring back to the city in which he lived and sell for a nice profit. However, instead of selling it, he kept it for his own use and his habit rapidly increased from a stable three bags per day to nearly a "bundle"—25 bags per day.

Although the "big hit" or "big sting" appears to be the most common precipitator of the transition from the status of stabilized or occasional heroin user to the status of free-wheeling junkie, many other variants of similar destabilizing patterns are common. The stabilized junkie may not be the one who makes the big sting. It may be his or her spouse, roommate, paramour, addict friend, or regular trick who receives a windfall of drugs or money and invites the stabilized junkie to share in the benefits of good fortune. "Goody," a part-time street prostitute, moved in with a big-time drug dealer who provided her with all the heroin she wanted in exchange for domestic services, sexual favors, and some modest help in cutting and packaging drugs. Although her supply of drugs was virtually limitless, she took her child-raising obligations and responsibilities very seriously and they kept her to a modest level of use. However, after a year of domestic living she began to miss the "street" life and the friends she had there and to resent her total ("bag bitch") dependence on her dealer boyfriend. She returned to the street and used the money she earned from "'hoing" and "ripping" her tricks to purchase drugs in addition to what she got at home for free. This behavior not only destabilized her drug use, but it also disrupted her home life to such an extent that she parted with her dealer and returned to the street full-time. Interestingly, this return to prostitution, theft, and robbery as her sole means of support forced her to develop a new life structure and abandon the free-wheeling pattern into which she had drifted when she had a dual source of supply.

Unless heroin addicts are disciplined by a life structure to which they are so committed and obligated that it effectively prevents them from doing so, they will expand their consumption of heroin to whatever level of use the availability of drugs or funds to buy them makes possible. What marks the career stage of the free-wheeling junkie is the almost total absence of structures of restraint. In the words of "Little Italy," who described a "free-wheeling" stage of his addict career:

> I can remember, I wouldn't be sick, I wouldn't need a shot. . . . And some of the guys might come around and get a few bags [and say] "Hey man, like I don't have enough money. Why don't you come down with me?". . . I'm saying [to myself], "Oh-oh, here I go!" and I would shoot drugs I didn't even need to shoot. So I let it get out of control.

The problem for the first free-wheeling junkie is that the binge cannot last forever and is typically fairly short-lived. After a month or two of free-wheeling heroin use — during which time the free-wheeling junkie may have no idea of how much heroin he or she is consuming daily — not only is a modest usage level unsatisfying but the life structure within which he or she might support it is likely to have been completely abandoned or at least be in severe disrepair.

The Street Junkie — Low Availability/Low Life Structure. At the point in a free-wheeling junkie's career when heroin availability drops precipitously and life structure does not provide the support necessary to stabilize heroin use, the free-wheeling junkie may manage to rebuild that life structure and accommodate to a new and lower level of availability. To the extent that this rebuilding and accommodation can be managed, the free-wheeling junkie may be able to return to the life of a stabilized junkie. However, if the rebuilding of life structure cannot be managed, the free-wheeling junkie may become a street junkie.

Street junkies most closely approximate the public stereotype of heroin addicts, if only because their way of life — both where and how they live — make them the most visible variety of heroin addict. Cut off from a stable source of quality heroin, not knowing from where his or her next "fix" or the money to pay for it will come, looking for any opportunity to make a buck, getting "sick" or "jonesing," being pathetically unkempt and unable to maintain even the most primitive routines of health or hygiene, the street junkie lives a very difficult, hand-to-mouth (or more precisely arm-to-arm) existence.

In terms of our typology, the street junkie's life may be understood as a continuous but typically unsuccessful effort to stabilize life structure and increase heroin availability. The two problems are intimately related in such a way that unless the street junkie can solve both problems at once, neither problem will be solved at all. That is, unless the street junkie can establish a stable life structure, he or she will be unlikely to increase the availability of heroin. Likewise, unless the street junkie is able to increase the availability of heroin, he or she will be unlikely to establish a stable life structure.

To illustrate how this relationship works in less abstract terms, it is helpful to begin with a description of what low life structure means in the life of the street. Goldstein (1981:69) captures the tenor of the street junkie's situation nicely when he observes that

> [if] any single word can describe the essence of how street opiate users "get over," that word is *opportunism*. Subjects were always alert to the smallest opportunity to earn a few dollars. The notion of opportunism is equally relevant to predatory criminality, nonpredatory criminality, employment, and miscellaneous hustling activities.

The cause of the street junkie's opportunism is his or her failure to establish a stable life structure which regularly produces enough income to support an addiction. Consequently, the street junkie's life is a series of short-term crimes, jobs, and hustles. Street junkies steal or rob when opportunities arise to do so. For a price or in exchange for heroin, they will "cop" for an out-of-towner, "taste" for a dealer, "tip" for a burglar, rent their "works" to another junkie, sell their "clinic meth" and food stamps, or share their "crib" (accommodations) with a junkie who needs a place to "get off" or a "'hoe" who needs a room to take her "tricks." They will do odd jobs, wash cars, paint apartments, deliver circulars, move furniture, carry baggage, or snitch to the police. The problem is not only that this opportunistic crime, hustling, or legitimate work pays very little, but that none of it is stable. While one or more of these activities may produce enough income today, none of them may be counted on to do so tomorrow. Moreover, because typical street addict crimes pay so little, because such crimes must be repeated frequently to produce any sizable income, and because they are so unpredictably opportunistic, the chance that the street addict will be arrested sooner or later is very, very high. This was the unfortunate experience of Little Italy who, after falling out with his supplier, was forced to discontinue drug sales as a major means of income and turned to armed robbery to support his use.

> I know today, I can say that if you don't have a plan you're gonna fuck up man. . . . Now those robberies weren't no plan. They didn't fit in nowhere . . . just by the spur of the moment, you know what I mean? I had to find something to take that place so that income would stand off properly, 'cause I didn't have a plan or didn't know anything about robbery . . .

As Little Italy's experience demonstrates, street junkies' lives are further complicated by the fact that "big dealers"–vendors of quantities of good quality heroin–often refuse to sell to them. The reasons they refuse are directly related to the instability of street junkies' lives. Because street junkies can never be certain when and for how much they will "get over," they are frequently unable to afford to buy enough drugs to satisfy their "jones." In the face of such a shortage they will commonly beg drugs from anyone they know who might have them or have access to them, try to "cop short" (buy at less than the going rate), attempt to strike a deal to get drugs loaned or "fronted" (given on consignment) to them on a short-term basis, or, if necessary, engage in opportunistic hustling. Also, because street junkies are the type of addict most vulnerable to arrest they are also the most likely category of addict to be "flipped" by police into the role of an informant. Usually street junkies will be promised immunity from prosecution on the charge for which they were arrested if they "give up" somebody "big." Given the frequency with which street addicts "come up short," the relatively small amount of profit to be made in each individual transaction with them, and the higher than normal risk of police involvement, few "big dealers" are willing to put up with all of the attendant hassles and hustles that dealing with street junkies typically involves.

While there are exceptions—the most common being big dealers who are relatives of street junkies or their friends of long standing—street addicts are mainly limited to "street dope," heroin that has been repeatedly "stepped on" (diluted) as it is passed from the highest level of dealer to the lowest. In fact, some studies (Leveson and Weiss, 1976:119) have shown that as much as 7 percent of street dope may have no heroin in it at all, while other studies (Smith, 1973) show a heroin concentration of from 3 to 10 percent in street dope as compared with an average concentration of nearly 30 percent in bags seized from "big dealers." The irony in this situation is that, as a consumer of "street dope," the street addict pays a higher per-unit price for heroin than any other person in the distribution chain. Furthermore, this very low and often unpredictable quality of heroin available to the street junkie serves to destabilize his or her life structure further.

RESEARCH AND POLICY IMPLICATIONS

The life-history data presented here have some important research and policy implications which merit brief consideration. Particularly relevant are the implications for: (1) the nature of the drugs-crime connection itself; (2) drug law enforcement; and (3) treatment policy.

The Drugs-Crime Connection

As we have pointed out above, early studies examining the relationship between drug use and crime have utilized the strategy of establishing the temporal priority of the onset of drug use versus criminality. While the earliest of these studies tended to find that drug use preceded the onset of criminal behavior, virtually all of the studies conducted since 1950 have found a reverse pattern, thus posing once again the perplexing question of the theoretical nature of the relationship between drug use and criminal behavior. Because the methodologies employed in these "sequence" studies are incapable of examining the dynamic nature of this relationship over time, they have succeeded in raising theoretical questions which continue to beg for explanation. More recent studies — particularly those of Ball et al. (1981, 1983) and Johnson et al. (1985) — have moved beyond the sequence issued by examining drug-using and criminal behavior on a daily or weekly basis over a period of time. These longitudinal methodologies represent a major breakthrough toward establishing the dynamic nature of the drugs-crime relationship.

This study further contributes to the emerging "post-sequence" literature by examining the drugs-crime nexus in the broader context of addict careers. Perhaps the most significant finding to emerge from our data is that the relationship between heroin use and crime is not necessarily consistent throughout the career of the addict. During the "occasional user" phase, for example, the issue is a moot one for many addicts; their limited level of drug use is quite affordable with a legitimate income, and any criminal activity that does take place is often quite spurious to drug use. During the "stabilized junkie" and "free-wheeling junkie" periods, the level of drug use seems to be largely a function of availability, typically enhanced through criminal income. Rather than *drug use causing crime*, however, it seems more accurate to suggest that *crime facilitates drug use* during these periods. Quite the reverse is the case during the "street junkie" phase, where availability through normal channels is lacking but the addict lacks the necessary structure to regulate his or her drug needs. Under these conditions the drug habit does indeed appear to "cause" crime in the manner commonly depicted.

Moreover, the life history data reveal that the relationship between drugs and crime is more dynamic than phrasing the issue in terms of "cause" typically suggests. In addition to providing necessary income for the purchase of heroin, criminal activity also serves to *structure* the drug using behavior of the addict. Crime thus provides the addict with a daily routine which for many addicts actually serves to limit or at least regulate their drug use.

In short, the respondents in this study have revealed that the relationship between drug use and criminal behavior is far more complex and dynamic than previous research has suggested. While in any given instance, it may be possible to specify a causal sequence, our data suggest that any generalizations suggesting a simple cause-effect scheme fail to capture the complexity of the drugs-crime connection throughout an addict's career.

Drug Law Enforcement

Since the passage of the Harrison Act in 1914, drug law enforcement in the United States has been dominated by the "criminal model" of drug use (Inciardi, 1974). While variously articulated, this model understands drug use as primarily a *criminal* issue which should be addressed by imposing criminal sanctions on both users and dealers, and by taking steps to prevent the import and distribution of heroin. Insofar as there is a relationship between drug use and other criminal behavior, the narcotics user is understood to be a criminal, first and foremost, whose drug using behavior is an important and contributing component in an extensive pattern of related criminal behavior.

Not surprisingly, the criminalization of heroin has profoundly affected the dynamics of the drugs-crime nexus. Virtually all of the post-1950 studies have found that criminal histories preceded expensive drug-using histories of the respondents in their samples as suggested by the subculturally based "Crimes cause drugs" model. Our life-history data support and qualify the implications for the criminal model suggested by these studies. While our respondents do report criminal involvement prior to their first exposure to heroin, the drug-using histories began quite independently of their criminal involvement. Throughout their early "occasional use" phase, most of these individuals were supporting their drug use without relying on a stable income from systematic criminal activity. As their careers progressed, however, they cultivated criminal skills and associations which played an important role in facilitating a greatly expanded level of heroin use.

However, our research suggests that even if such enforcement efforts rightly characterize the drugs-crime connection, enforcement approaches may not have their intended effects of controlling or suppressing drug use or the crimes related to it. We find no reason to conclude that enforcement efforts may have an effect on very early periods in addict careers. During the period of occasional use, addicts can easily adjust to dramatic variations in the level of supply of heroin and our respondents report little need to support such occasional use through systematic criminal activity. Even in those periods of the hard-core addict's life history which we have described as characterized by a "stabilized junkie" model, our respondents report being able to adjust to periods in which heroin supplies are sharply reduced, only to return to previous levels of use when their channels of supply are restored. Moreover, our respondents report that during stabilized junkie periods in their life histories they cultivated a variety of sources of supply. Given this variety, not only could they choose vendors who appeared to offer the best quality product, but they could adjust relatively easily to the temporary or permanent loss of a supplier. Unless enforcement efforts managed a simultaneous elimination of virtually all of these sources of supply, we would not anticipate that they would have much effect on the stabilized junkie's pattern of stable use, nor on the criminal activity which the stabilized junkie typically pursues to support it. Likewise, enforcement efforts may not be expected to have much impact on hard-core addicts during "free-wheeling" phases in their life histories. Particularly insofar as these periods are precipitated by "big scores" or "big hits" and marked by short-term, unlimited availability of drugs or the money to purchase them, enforcement is already too late.

The street junkie, by contrast, faced with the lack of ready availability of adequate supplies of heroin and without the necessary life structure to constrain his or her felt need for drugs, is most vulnerable to law enforcement activity. Indeed, our data would suggest that the effectiveness of current law enforcement efforts is largely limited to this career phase. The addict is this situation is often confronted with the alternative of arrest or informing on other addicts. Either alternative almost inevitably imposes a criminal transition in the career of the addict. Arrest typically culminates either in treatment or incarceration, both of which impose a disengagement from street routine. Even if the addict subsequently returns to the street, the conditions of availability and life structure will be profoundly altered. While informing on other addicts may buy more time on the street, this alternative will only further alienate the street junkie from the subculture. While such a strategy of "flipping" informants may be helpful in locating "big dealers," its overall impact in limiting the availability of drugs to non-street junkies appears negligible unless, as we have suggested, all major dealers are "hit" simultaneously. Unless our drug policies give balanced weight to educational and treatment efforts, law enforcement effectiveness appears relegated to the already vulnerable "street junkie."

Treatment Policy

Narcotics treatment in the United States has also been characterized by an overriding concern with the anti-social behavior associated with heroin use. Methadone maintenance is currently the dominant model of treatment, and has generated a voluminous literature addressing its effectiveness as a deterrent to crime (see, for example, Dole et al., 1968, 1969; Gearing, 1974; Judson et al., 1980; Lukoff and Quatrone, 1973; Nash, 1973; Newman and Gates, 1973). These and other studies have reported widely varying effects of methadone treatment upon criminality ranging from a 99.9 percent reduction (Gearing, 1974) to an actual *increase* in crime following admission to treatment (Lukoff and Quatrone, 1973). Unfortunately, our understanding of the effect of methadone maintenance on criminality is severely limited because of the many methodological difficulties associated with these studies (Faupel, 1981).

However, our data suggest that to the extent that a long-term reduction in criminality is a central goal of drug treatment, treatment policy must attend to more than simply the physiological demand for heroin. Drug-free residential programs, in particular, attempt to reduce availability by imposing abstinence for a substantial period of time. Beyond simply curtailing access to heroin, however, successful treatment will require provision for an alternative life structure which facilitates and rewards conventional behavior, thus reducing demand as well. We would argue that such an agenda not only requires renunciation of past routines but also the facilitation of long-term alternative behavior patterns through a concerted effort at community reintegration (see Dembo et al., 1982; Faupel, 1985; Goldbart, 1982; Hawkins, 1979). Involvement in conventional employment, voluntary associations, and even organized leisure-time activities should tightly structure the addicts' daily routine. Just as importantly, since access to drugs is largely a function of social networks, renunciation of "street" relationships and subsequent integration into supportive conventional social networks should serve to reduce availability and demand simultaneously.

Note

This research was supported in part by DHEW Grant No. 1 RO1 DA 01827 from the Division of Research, National Institute of Drug Abuse. Correspondence to Faupel: Department of Sociology, Anthropology, and Social Work, Auburn University, Auburn, AL 36849-3501.

References

Anglin, M. Douglas and George Speckart
    1984 Narcotics Use and Crime: A Confirmatory Analysis. Unpublished Report, University of California, Los Angeles.
Ball, John C. and Carl D. Chambers
    1970 The Epidemiology of Heroin Use in the United States. Springfield, IL: Charles C. Thomas.
Ball, John C., Lawrence Rosen, John A. Flueck and David Nurco
    1981 "The criminality of heroin addicts when addicted and when off opiates." Pp 39–65 in James A. Inciardi (ed.), The Drugs-Crime Connection. Beverly Hills, CA: Sage Publications.
Ball, John C., John W. Shaffer and David Nurco
    1983 "The day to day criminality of heroin addicts in Baltimore: a study of the continuity of offense rates." Drug and Alcohol Dependence 12:119–42.
Ball, John C. and Richard W. Snarr
    1969 "A test of the maturation hypothesis with respect to opiate addiction." Bulletin of Narcotics 21:9–13.
Beschner, George M. and William Brower
    1985 "The scene." Pp. 19–29 in Bill Hanson, George Beschner, James M. Walters and Elliot Bovelle (eds.), Life with Heroin: Voice from the Inner City. Lexington, MA: Lexington Books.

Biernacki, Patrick
    1986   Pathways from Heroin Addiction: Recovery without Treatment. Philadelphia: Temple University Press.
Chambers, Carl D.
    1974   "Narcotic addiction and crime: an empirical overview." Pp. 125–42 in James A. Inciardi and Carl D. Chambers (eds.), Drugs and the Criminal Justice System. Beverly Hills, CA: Sage Publications.
Chein, Isidor, Donald L. Gerard, Robert S. Lee and Eva Rosenfeld
    1964   The Road to H: Narcotics, Juvenile Delinquency, and Social Policy. New York: Basic Books.
Collins, James J., Robert L. Hubbard, and J. Valley Rachal
    1984   Heroin and Cocaine Use and Illegal Income. Center for Social Research and Policy Analysis. Research Triangle Park, NC: Research Triangle Institute.
    1985   "Expensive drug use and illegal income: a test of explanatory hypotheses." Criminology 23:743–64.
Dembo, Richard, James A. Ciarlo and Robert W. Taylor
    1983   "A model for assessing and improving drug abuse treatment resource use in inner city areas." The International Journal of Addictions 18:921–36.
Dole, Vincent P., Marie E. Nyswander and Alan Warner
    1968   "Successful treatment of 750 criminal addicts." Journal of the American Medical Association 206:2708–11.
Dole, Vincent P., J. Waymond Robinson, John Orraca, Edward Towns, Paul Searcy and Eric Caine
    1969   "Methadone treatment of randomly selected criminal addicts." New England Journal of Medicine 280:1372–75.
Faupel, Charles E.
    1981   "Drug treatment and criminality: methodological and theoretical considerations." Pp. 183–206 in James A. Inciardi (ed.), The Drugs-Crime Connection. Beverly Hills, CA: Sage Publications.
    1985   "A theoretical model for a socially oriented drug treatment policy." Journal of Drug Education 15:189–203.
Fields, Allen and James M. Walters
    1985   "Hustling: supporting a heroin habit." Pp. 49–73 in Bill Hanson, George Beschner, James M. Walters and Elliot Bovelle (eds.), Life with Heroin: Voices from the Inner City. Lexington, MA: Lexington Books.
Gandossy, Robert P., Jay R. Williams, Jo Cohen and Hendrick J. Harwood
    1980   Drugs and Crime: A Survey and Analysis of the Literature. National Institute of Justice. Washington, DC: U.S. Government Printing Office.
Gearing, Frances R.
    1974   "Methadone maintenance treatment five years later—where are they now?" American Journal of Public Health 64:44–50.
Goldbart, Stephen
    1982   "Systematic barriers to addict aftercare program implementation." Journal of Drug Issues 12:415–30.
Goldman, Fred
    1976   "Drug markets and addict consumption behavior." Pp. 273–96 in Drug Use and Crime: Report of the Panel on Drug Use and Criminal Behavior. National Technical Information Service publication number PB-259 167. Springfield, VA: U.S. Dept. of Commerce.
    1981   "Drug abuse, crime and economics: the dismal limits of social choice." Pp. 155–81 in James A. Inciardi (ed.), The Drugs-Crime Connection. Beverly Hills, CA: Sage Publications.
Goldstein, Paul
    1981   "Getting over: economic alternatives to predatory crime among street drug users."

Pp. 67–84 in James A. Inciardi (ed.), The Drugs-Crime Connection. Beverly Hills, CA: Sage Publications.

Hanson, Bill, George Beschner, James M. Walters and Elliot Bovelle.
1985   Life with Heroin: Voices from the Inner City. Lexington, MA: Lexington Books.

Hawkins, J. David
1979   "Reintegrating street drug abusers: community roles in continuing care." Pp. 25–79 in Barry S. Brown (ed.), Addicts and Aftercare. Beverly Hills, CA: Sage Publications.

Inciardi, James A.
1974   "The vilification of euphoria: some perspectives on an elusive issue." Addictive Diseases 1:241–67.
1979   "Heroin use and street crime." Crime and Delinquency 25:335–46.

Jacoby, Joseph E., Neil A. Weiner, Terence P. Thornberry and Marvin E. Wolfgang
1973   "Drug use in a birth cohort." Pp. 300–43 in National Commission on Marijuana and Drug Abuse, Drug Use in America: Problem in Perspective, Appendix I. Washington, DC: U.S. Government Printing Office.

Johnson, Bruce D., Paul J. Goldstein, Edward Preble, James Schmeidler, Douglas S. Lipton, Barry Spunt and Thomas Miller
1985   Taking Care of Business: The Economics of Crime by Heroin Abusers. Lexington, MA: Lexington Books.

Judson, Barbara, Serapio Ortiz, Linda Crouse, Thomas Carney and Avram Goldstein
1980   "A follow-up study of heroin addicts five years after admission to a methadone treatment program." Drug and Alcohol Dependence 6:295–313.

Leveson, Irving and Jeffrey H. Weiss
1976   Analysis of Urban Health Problems. New York: Spectrum.

Lukoff, Irving and Debra Quatrone
1973   "Heroin use and crime in a methadone maintenance program: a two year follow-up of the Addiction and Research Corporation Program: a preliminary report." Pp. 63–112 in Gil J. Hayim, Irving Lukoff and Debra Quatrone (eds.), Heroin Use in a Methadone Maintenance Program. Washington, DC: U.S. Department of Justice, National Institute of Law Enforcement and Criminal Justice.

McGlothlin, William H., M. Douglas Anglin and Bruce D. Wilson
1978   "Narcotic addiction and crime." Criminology 16:293–315.

Morris, Richard W.
1985   "Not the cause, nor the cure: self-image and control among inner city black male heroin users." Pp. 135–53 in Bill Hanson, George Beschner, James M. Walters and Elliot Bovelle (eds.), Life with Heroin: Voices from the Inner City. Lexington, MA: Lexington Books.

Musto, David
1973   The American Disease: Origins of Narcotic Control. New Haven, CT: Yale University Press.

Nash, George
1973   "The impact of drug abuse treatment upon criminality: a look at 19 programs." Upper Montclair, NJ: Montclair State College.

Newman, Robert G., Sylvia Bashkow and Margot Gates
1973   "Arrest histories before and after admission to a methadone maintenance treatment program." Contemporary Drug Problems 2:417–24.

O'Donnell, John A.
1966   "Narcotic addiction and crime." Social Problems 13:374–85.

Pescor, Michael J.
1943   "A statistical analysis of the clinical records of hospitalized drug addicts." Public Health Reports Supplement, 143.

Robins, Lee N. and George E. Murphy
1967   "Drug use in a normal population of young Negro men." American Journal of Public Health 570:1580–96.

Smith, Jean Paul
    1973   "Substances in illicit drugs." Pp. 13–30 in Richard H. Blum and Associates (eds.), Drug Dealers–Taking Action. San Francisco: Jossey Bass.

Tappan, Paul
    1960   Crime, Justice and Correction. New York: McGraw-Hill.

Terry, Charles E. and Mildred Pellens
    1928   The Opium Problem. New York: The Haddon Craftsman.

Waldorf, Dan
    1983   "Natural recovery from opiate addiction: some social-psychological processes of untreated recovery." Journal of Drug Issues 13:237–80.

Walters, James M.
    1985   "'Taking care of business' updated: a fresh look at the daily routine of the heroin user." Pp. 31–48 in Bill Hanson, George Beschner, James M. Walters and Elliot Bovelle (eds.), Life with Heroin: Voices from the Inner City. Lexington, MA: Lexington Books.

Weissman, James C., Paul L. Katsampes and Thomas A. Giacienti
    1974   "Opiate use and criminality among a jail population." Addictive Diseases 1:269–81.

Zinberg, Norman E.
    1984   Drug Set and Setting: The Basis for Controlled Intoxicant Use. New Haven, CT: Yale University Press.

26. Casinos and Banking: Organized Crime in the Bahamas

ALAN A. BLOCK AND FRANK R. SCARPITTI

Within the past few years, both the President's Commission on Organized Crime and the U.S. Senate's Permanent Subcommittee on Investigations have reported on the extensive use of offshore banks and businesses by American criminal interests to launder money and evade taxes (Permanent Subcommittee on Investigations, 1983; President's Commission on Organized Crime, 1984). A recent government report "concludes that the use of so-called 'secret' offshore facilities has become so pervasive that it challenges basic assumptions regarding the ability of federal and state authorities to enforce the laws" (Permanent Subcommittee on Investigations, 1983:1). Such enterprises are established in tax-haven countries around the world, but for a number of reasons, those in the Caribbean have grown fastest in recent years and now appear to control billions of dollars of illegally gained and untaxed money. Although the Caribbean's proximity to the United States makes it especially attractive to Americans wanting to hide money, its development as an important stop in the South American drug traffic and the fact that some countries have stringent bank secrecy laws also contribute to its contemporary popularity. In fact, a few Caribbean nations have been so corrupted by illegal foreign dollars that they have virtually offered themselves as crime havens (Permanent Subcommittee on Investigations, 1983:49–95).

Among the Caribbean nations active in hosting offshore enterprises owned by Americans have been the Bahamas. Like all tax havens, the Bahamas are characterized by the essential elements of strict rules of bank secrecy and little or no taxes. Since 1965 bank secrecy has been based on legislation which prohibits and punishes the disclosure by a bank employee of an account holder's name or financial situation (the 1965 legislation increased the severity of the crime of disclosure). The strict secrecy associated with banks also applies to the activities and ownership of corporations. In addition, there are no income, profit, capital gains, gift, inheritance, estate or withholding taxes in the Bahamas. Although the nation does tax imports and some real property, this has little effect on those who own or use its many banks and corporations. Hence, for a small initial cost and annual fee, one may own a bank or company that can receive and disburse large sums of money in complete secrecy and without the threat of taxation. These advantages, of course, are available to bank depositors as well.

Even though offshore tax havens may provide legitimate investment opportunities for American citizens wishing to avoid taxes, a practice recognized as lawful by U.S. courts, it is the evasion of taxes by using tax-haven services that now concerns law enforcement authorities. "Tax evasion . . . involves acts intended to misrepresent or to conceal facts in an effort to escape lawful tax liability" (Workman, 1982:667). Tax havens may be used to hide income or to misrepresent the nature of transactions in order to put the taxpayer in a more favorable tax position. A corollary problem concerns the "laundering" of illegal money gained from strictly criminal activity. This "is the process by which one conceals the existence, illegal source, or illegal application of income, and then disguises that income to make it appear legitimate" (President's Commission on Organized Crime, 1984:1). Offshore tax havens, with their strict secrecy laws, dependence on foreign deposits, and disregard for the sources of overseas cash, provide ideal vehicles for assorted racketeers, drug dealers and financial manipulators to hide "dirty" money while it is being cleaned for further use. For both the tax evader and money launderer, the offshore haven guarantees that any paper trail will be blocked.

The popularity of the Bahamas as an offshore tax haven may be seen in the amount of corporate and bank activity which it hosts. This small island nation of just over 200,000 inhabitants has some 15,000 active companies and 330 chartered banks, or one bank for every 600 residents (Lernoux, 1984:85). The vast majority of these banks are shells of "brass plate" operations consisting of little more than a shared office and an address (Lernoux, 1984:85). Nevertheless, Bahamian banks held over $95 billion of foreign assets in 1978 (Workman, 1982:680), and a 1979 Ford Foundation study estimated that the flow of U.S. criminal and tax-evasion money into the Bahamas was $20 billion per year (Blum and Kaplan, 1979). Even though the accuracy of these figures may be questioned, due largely to the Bahamian government's and banking industry's reluctance to provide reliable data, it seems obvious that the American contribution to these questionable assets constitutes a considerable resource for the Bahamas and a substantial loss in taxes for the United States.

The Bahamas evolved into an offshore haven for tax evaders and money launderers in a very short period of time. The process included receptive public officials, international entrepreneurs and American racketeers entering into formal and informal relationships designed to serve their respective financial positions. A partial examination of the history of the Bahamas reveals the extent of the collusion among political, business and criminal interests to serve their illicit purposes.

This history also demonstrates the important relationship between offshore banks and gambling casinos. In fact, key Bahamian offshore banks were formed by or for individuals deeply involved in Nevada casinos and who subsequently played big roles in developing the first large-scale, modern casinos in the Bahamas. Most likely, the relationship between the casinos and banks emerged in order to hide the casinos' "skim," that portion of casino profits unreported to taxing authorities. The historical material which follows discussed those individuals whose mutual interests embraced both casino gambling and haven banking and who were instrumental in providing organized criminal elements with both an economic bonanza and sanctuary.

THE MAKING OF FREEPORT

The process started on Grand Bahama Island located about 60 miles from the Florida coast. The prime mover on Grand Bahama was an American named Wallace Groves who first came to the Bahamas in the 1930s. Groves' background had been in investment trusts administered through a firm called Equity Corporation which he sold for $750,000. Following this, he became affiliated with a company known as the General Investment Corporation. After these deals were in place, Groves sailed to the Bahamas, started two Bahamian companies (Nassau Securities Ltd. and North American Ltd.), and purchased an island, Little Whale Cay, about 35 miles from Nassau, the capital of the country. During this first, eventful trip, Groves met Stafford Sands, a member of the local political elite known as the Bay Street Boys. This elite was composed of certain merchants and attorneys who met on a regular basis after work in a club located on Bay and Charlotte Streets in Nassau. They were invariably white and, by the standards of the Bahamas, wealthy and influential. The Bay Street Boys controlled Bahamian development, both the licit and illicit, until 1967 when the first black Prime Minister was elected (United Kingdom, 1971).

Unfortunately for Groves, in the late fall of 1938 he was indicted on numerous counts of mail fraud and looting the General Investment Corporation of almost one million dollars. Eventually, Groves was convicted and sentenced to two years in prison. He was released in 1944 and returned to the Bahamas. During Groves' time of troubles, his associate, Stafford Sands, was busy arranging a way for casinos to operate legally. Sands successfully sponsored a bill in the Assembly which allowed casinos under certain circumstances. By securing a Certificate of Exemption from the local government, a gambling casino could operate with what amounted to a government license. The bill passed in 1939 and certificates of exemption were granted to two small casinos which had been operating illegally for years.[1]

It was in the 1950s that Groves, Sands, and others to be discussed shortly put their talents together on Grand Bahama Island. They created a new city, Freeport, which soon had a casino and several significant "haven" banks. Stafford Sands, who had become Chairman of the Bahamas Development Board (equivalent to Minister of Tourism) in the 1950s, crafted legislation "to establish a port and an industrial complex" on Grand Bahama Island (United Kingdom, 1971:6). The Hawksbill Creek Act, as the legislation was entitled, was signed on August 4, 1955. The deal called for Groves to "organize a company, to be called the Grand Bahama Port Authority Limited, which would undertake to dredge and construct a deep water harbour and turning basin at Hawksbill Creek as a preliminary and an aid for factories and other industrial undertakings to be set up there" (United Kingdom, 1971:6). In return, the government made available thousands of acres of Crown Land to the Port Authority for one pound per acre (equivalent then to around $2.80 an acre). In fact, by 1960 Groves' company had acquired a total of 138,296 acres which were officially "designated as a town (Freeport) in Grand Bahama" (United Kingdom, 1971:6).

The terms of the initial Hawksbill Creek Act allowed "that the whole of Freeport was to be the private property of the Port Authority in whom was vested the supreme right to its administration and control" (United Kingdom, 1971:16). An analysis of the legislation by a Royal Commission in 1971 commented on this extraordinary transfer of authority noting that the company had "exclusive responsibility" for traditional governmental services such as education, health, communications, energy "and all other public utilities and services and the performance of all aviation activities." The Commission also wrote that no one was allowed to interfere with the Port Authority's decisions, especially in awarding licenses or otherwise controlling firms doing business in Freeport.

The major shareholders of the Grand Bahama Port Authority in 1959 included Wallace Groves and his wife, Georgette, who individually held a small amount of shares but whose company, Abaco Lumber, held almost one million. Other significant owners were Variant Industries, which represented the interests of Charles W. Hayward, an English entrepreneur, and held just over one half million shares; Charles Allen, whose family's financial interests in New York and Hollywood (especially motion-picture companies) were very extensive and who held over a quarter million shares; Arthur Rubloff, a Chicago real-estate agent, who had over 70,000 shares; and Charles C. Goldsmith, who owned about 100,000 shares and listed his affiliation in 1959 as the New York Cosmos Bank. Wallace Groves was the company's Director and Charles Hayward and his son, Jack, were other important officers (Grand Bahama Port Authority, 1959). Although Allen and Goldsmith appeared to play no managerial role in the company, they "were well aware that the major partner in the enterprise . . . was . . . a convicted stock manipulator who had served time in federal prison for mail fraud and conspiracy" (McClintick, 1982:89).

Even with his new financiers, Groves' project was barely limping along in 1960. Because the industrial development of Freeport was extremely far off, perhaps farfetched, Groves and others decided that Freeport could best be developed around tourism. Hence, an amendment to the original Hawksbill Creek Act was enacted which, among other things, allowed the Port Authority to build a "first-class deluxe resort hotel" (United Kingdom, 1971:7). By the time the hotel was completed in 1963, it had the added attraction of a casino, and the Bahamas had become the new Caribbean headquarters of Meyer Lansky's underworld gambling enterprise.

Lansky had operated in the Caribbean for quite some time, of course, running casinos in Cuba with the full cooperation of that country's government. With the overthrow of Batista, however, American organized crime figures and their gambling operations were no longer welcomed and were soon thrown out of the country by Fidel Castro. Even before that actually happened, Lansky was looking around for another site in the Caribbean, a place where tourists from the United States would come for the sun and the gambling, where local officials would be cooperative, and where he could establish a worldwide gambling empire (Messick, 1971:225). The Bahamas appeared to be the ideal spot.

According to Lansky biographer, Hank Messick, the gambling czar moved quickly once he decided to seek additional fortunes in the Bahamas. Early in 1960 he dispatched an associate, Louis Chesler, to the islands to meet with Groves and Sands, presumably to discuss plans by which the Port Authority would be salvaged and gambling established in Freeport (Messick, 1971:228). In order to accomplish the first part of the plan, the Port Authority formed a company called Grand Bahama Development Corporation (known as DEVCO). DEVCO immediately placed Chesler on its Board of Directors, giving him an official position in the Bahamas from which he could supervise the development of casino gambling. Another Lansky associate, Max Orovitz, was also placed on the DEVCO board (Grand Bahama Development Corporation, 1964). But it was Chesler who would protect Lansky's interests and serve as a dominant force in the early development of Bahamian gambling.

Chesler's earliest known contacts with organized crime began in 1942 when he had as partners in several businesses John Pullman and Pullman's brother-in-law, A. C. Cowan (McClintick, 1982:87–93). Pullman, an important associate of Meyer Lansky for a number of decades, had served a prison term for bootlegging in the early 1930s. By the mid-1950s, Pullman had moved to Canada and been granted Canadian citizenship (Charbonneau, 1976). Chesler, also Canadian, had a series of dealings with Lansky and Lansky's associates prior to the formation of DEVCO which are revealing. He hired, for instance, a key Lansky operative, Mike McLaney, as the manager of a Miami Beach dinner club which Chesler owned.

In 1958, Chesler's association with Lansky became more visible through the financial machinations of Maxwell Golhar, another of his partners. Golhar became Chairman of the Board of an enterprise called New Mylamaque Explorations Ltd. A well-known Lansky associate, Sam Garfield, purchased 100,000 shares of New Mylamaque which he divided in the following manner: Edward Levinson, 50,000 shares; Moe Dalitz, former Cleveland racketeer, 25,000; and Allard Roen, 25,000. Roen's shares were then divided further with Ben Siegelbaum receiving 15,000 and Meyer Lansky 10,000. Finally, 50,000 more shares of New Mylamaque were parcelled out, with 10,000 going to Dalitz, 15,000 to Siegelbaum, and 25,000 to Lansky. This same group of investors also provided capital for Miami's new international airport hotel in 1958. Other investors in the hotel (brought in by Lansky and Chesler) were Bryant B. Burton, connected to the Sands and Freemont Hotels in Las Vegas, and Jack Cooper, who owned a highly successful dog track in Miami (New York State Senate, n.d. a).

With the formation of DEVCO there was only one hurdle left to transform Freeport into a center for casino gambling run by organized crime. That hurdle was acquiring the necessary Certificate of Exemption. The second Certificate ever granted in the Bahamas was offered on March 27, 1963, to a new company called Bahamas Amusement Ltd., which had been formed only the previous week. The Certificate allowed Bahamas Amusement to operate a casino at the Lucayan Beach Hotel in Freeport. In order to secure the Certificate a considerable amount of money had been passed to key members of the government by DEVCO. Stafford Sands acted as the financial intermediary between DEVCO and Sands' political cronies who were hired as "consultants" and paid very handsome fees (United Kingdom, 1967). The original directors of Bahamas Amusement included Chesler, Georgette Groves, and a member of the Hayward family.

Less than a week after the Certificate was granted there were meetings attended by Meyer Lansky and his brother Jake, Lou Chesler, Max Orovitz, and others to discuss issues concerning both the hotel and the casino, called the Monte Carlo. A number of important Lansky racketeers were hired to work in the casino, including Dino Cellini, George Saldo, Charles Brudner, Max Courtney, and Frank Ritter. Other subjects discussed at this time included the purchase of casino equipment from Las Vegas and probably the Beverly Hills Club in Newport, Kentucky, and the establishing of a casino training school in London, England (United Kingdom, 1967; Messick, 1971; Block and Klausner, 1985–86). About ten months after the Certificate was granted, the hotel and casino formally opened with the Lansky men firmly entrenched in casino management as well as overseers of all credit arrangements.

BAHAMIAN BANKS

Let us now turn to those banks formed by or for individuals with multi-million dollar investments in Nevada casinos and deeply involved in the Freeport development. John Pullman, mentioned above as a Chesler associate since 1942 and, in effect, an important member of Meyer Lansky's organized crime syndicate, was responsible for putting the banks and casinos together. Pullman, recently identified as a "Canadian organized crime figure" (Pennsylvania Crime Commission, 1980:195), was instrumental in forming two banks (with subsequent numerous off-shoots) created to handle the skim from the Monte Carlo and most likely the Sands and Frontier casinos in Nevada (New York State Senate, n.d. a).

The bank connected to the Monte Carlo was the International Credit Bank (ICB) which was formed by John Pullman in partnership with a Dr. Tibor Rosenbaum (New York State Senate, n.d. c). The bank was located in Geneva, Switzerland, with branches in the Bahamas. The major shareholder was a trust (International Credit Trust) resident in Vaduz, Lichtenstein. At least part of the Monte Carlo skim undoubtedly travelled from the casino to the Bahamian branch of Pullman's ICB, then to Switzerland, and ultimately to the obscurity of Lichtenstein. Other more direct but clumsy avenues for the skim no doubt existed. For instance, a Royal Commission reported that "large quantities of cash up to $60,000, and in one case $120,000, were being dispatched by the Amusements Company to the Marine Midland Grace Trust Co., of New York. They were being parcelled up in Pauli Girl beer cartons" (United Kingdom, 1967:19).

Although formed as a conduit for unreported casino profits, the ICB quickly developed additional interests. One of the early major clients for ICB Geneva, for example, was Investor Overseas Services, the infamous mutual fund operation run by Bernard Cornfeld and later looted by Robert Vesco. The relationship between the fund and the bank became exceptionally close when ICB people were used to smuggle money out of various countries into Switzerland on behalf of mutual fund clients. One of the principal ICB money couriers, Sylvain Ferdman, was identified as an organized crime money mover by Life magazine in 1967. Ferdman performed the same function for another Bahamian bank called Atlas Bank. Actually, Ferdman and Dr. Rosenbaum were two of the directors of Atlas. A close scrutiny of both Atlas and ICB indicates they were virtually identical in ownership, management and function. Furthermore, there is some evidence to suggest that ICB and Atlas, which both had several branches or permutations, were also linked to another bank located in Beirut, Lebanon, which, in turn, appeared to own a major Lebanese casino (Fortune, 1966:93).

The ICB and Atlas banks are two primary examples of the links between organized crime gamblers and the offshore banking industry put together in the Bahamas. Another major example involving much the same cast was the Bank of World Commerce, formed on September 21, 1961, most likely to launder the skim from Nevada casinos (New York State Senate, n.d. c; Wall Street Journal, 1976). John Pullman was the president and director, while the former Lieutenant Governor of Nevada, Clifford A. Jones, was one of the larger shareholders, holding about 8 percent of the total. The other directors included Alvin I. Malnik and Philip J. Matthews who owned about 32 percent of the shares.

Malnik was believed to have been one of Meyer Lansky's closest associates and, when Lansky died in 1982, some speculated that Malnik may have inherited much of Lansky's action (New York State Senate, n.d. a). In 1980, the Pennsylvania Crime Commission detailed a series of shady transactions involving Caesars World, Inc., which owned casinos in Las Vegas and Atlantic City, and "Alvin I. Malnik and Samuel Cohen, who have ties to Meyer Lansky, a major financial advisor to organized criminals" (Pennsylvania Crime Commission, 1980:252). The Crime Commission also stated that "Vincent Teresa, a former Cosa Nostra capo, said that, in the underworld, dealing with Malnik is the same as dealing with Lansky and that the purpose of Malnik's association with Lansky is to launder illegal cash by investing it in real estate" (Pennsylvania Crime Commission, 1980:252). Other reports cited by the Crime Commission had Malnik with Lansky and members of the Carlo Gambino crime syndicate discussing "the construction and/or ownership of two or three casinos in Florida if a gambling referendum passed. Some $20 million to $25 million was to be invested in the casinos and profits were to be skimmed off the top and channeled back to the investors" (Pennsylvania Crime Commission, 1980:255).

The relationships among Malnik, Pullman, and Matthews (the largest single shareholder in the bank) preceded the formation of the Bank of World Commerce (New York State Senate, n.d. c). Several years earlier, Malnik and Matthews had been involved with two closely connected firms, including one called Allied Empire, Inc. When the Bank of World Commerce started, Allied Empire showed up as a shareholder and then as the recipient of a large loan from the new bank. Furthermore, Malnik, Matthews and a former racketeer associate of Louis Buchalter (executed by the State of New York in 1944 for murder) had worked together long before the founding of the Bank of World Commerce to purchase a small, "brass plate," Bahamian bank from one of Lou Chesler's associates.

Chesler, Pullman, Lansky, Malnik, Matthews, and other gamblers and racketeers from New York, Miami, Newport, Kentucky, Montreal, Toronto, Las Vegas, and Los Angeles formed both gambling casinos and offshore Bahamian banks, the latter to solve the problem of "washing" the money generated by the former. Stock manipulators like Wallace Groves, allied with well-known financiers from the United States and the United Kingdom, organized crime figures, and, of course, important local politicians, turned Grand Bahama Island into an experimental station for money gathering and laundering. To help the scheme along, the Bahamian government actually relinquished part of its sovereign territory to this mixed group.

SOME CONSEQUENCES

The impact the developers had on the original inhabitants of Grand Bahama Island was hardly beneficial. Prior to the Bahamian government's enacting the Hawksbill Creek Agreement, the island was described by a Royal Commission as nothing more than "a pine barren with less than 5,000 inhabitants" (United Kingdom, 1971:5). After the Agreement and the building of Freeport, most of the island remained a pine barren with the exception of the area around Freeport which the Royal Commission found to be "predominantly non-Bahamian" (United Kingdom, 1971:31). Bahamians made up only 34 percent of the population of Freeport in 1968, as compared with about 84 percent on New Providence Island where the capital, Nassau, is situated. And although some held DEVCO's many construction projects to be a benefactor for Bahamian labor, in fact DEVCO turned to Haiti for a supply of cheap labor whenever it could. Through 1968, the percentage of Haitians in Freeport was over four times that of New Providence Island (United Kingdom, 1971:31). The Port Authority, of course, contributed to the pattern of exploitation engaged in by its creation, DEVCO. About 30 percent of the licenses granted by the Port Authority to people wishing to do business in its part of Grand Bahama went to non-Bahamians (United Kingdom, 1971:33).

The combination of Certificates of Exemption, bank secrecy laws, and the Hawksbill Creek Agreement set more than Freeport into motion. It stamped the Bahamas as a center for organized crime activities. Indeed, as we noted earlier, the Bahamas has been recognized as one of the principal trans-shipment points for drug traffickers moving cocaine and marijuana from South America to the U.S. and Canada (Royal Canadian Mounted Police, 1983:42–46). In one recent narcotics case, the defendants were charged with buying and using "the Darby Islands, a group of five islands in the Bahamas, as a trans-shipment point," and using Bahamian companies including banks and a major Bahamian Trust Company to launder their money (U.S. District Court, 1981). In another case, an officer of the Columbus Trust Company, Nassau, has been charged with using the trust company, a Bahamian corporation named Dundee Securities, Barclays Bank International (The Bahamas), and the Southeast First National Bank of Miami in a complicated scheme to wash millions of dollars for a drug syndicate (U.S. District Court, 1980).

The symbiotic relationships among casinos, offshore banks and professional criminals are complex, to say the least. In numerous contemporary cases, professional criminals utilize both casinos and banks to launder money. An IRS Special Agent reporting on a major drug and tax case gave an example of this as he detailed how a financial services corporation served drug racketeers. The "laundering" method included (1) exchanging the smugglers' initial small denomination cash (mostly tens and twenties) for $100 bills in a Las Vegas casino; (2) moving the new "casino" money from the U.S. to offshore banks and depositing it in secret accounts; (3) returning the money to the U.S. "disguised as offshore loans"; and (4) investing the phony loans in businesses through blind trusts and fictitious corporate fronts (U.S. District Court, n.d.).

Even without the use of offshore banks, casinos themselves perform many clandestine banking services for professional criminals. Drug Enforcement Administrator, Gary D. Liming, testified that casinos "exchange small bills for large bills, travellers' checks or money orders; wire transfer money overseas to associate casinos; provide safety deposit boxes; and make loans . . . without being required to report the transactions to the Department of the Treasury" (Judiciary Committee, 1984:8–9). Casinos, therefore, are acting like offshore banks providing anonymity for depositors (players) and various "laundering" options. Consequently, there are enforcement agents who are convinced that certain casinos have been built solely to launder the proceeds of drug transactions.[2]

However, long before the full potential of casinos working either alone or with offshore banks and other shady financial institutions was realized by drug traffickers, developers in the Bahamas had started the process of bringing casinos and banks together. Within less than a decade, the groundwork for organized crime's penetration of the Bahamas was established. Networks of banks, trust companies, holding companies, casinos, hotels, marinas, mutual funds, and so on representing illicit interests all across the U.S. and many other countries were, and most importantly remain, paramount.

Notes

1. The two illegal casinos included one opened by American Frank Reid for private membership in 1920. By 1923, Reid's club was joined by another called the Bahamian Club, run by a gambler known as Honest John Kelly. Over the course of the Prohibition Era, the Bahamian Club was managed first by Kelly, then Herbert McGuire, and then purchased by Willard McKenzie and Frank Dineen. Like all Bahamian tourist-supported establishments, it was only open during the three winter months when the wealthy arrived to escape the seasonal rigors. At least one other casino was opened during Prohibition. On a privately owned island close by the Bahamian fishing resort of Bimini, New Yorker Louis Wasey opened a private membership casino called the Cat Cay Club. (Authors' interviews conducted in the Bahamas, 1984.)

2. Authors' interview with Special Agent, Department of Labor, June 1985.

References

Block, Alan A. and Patricia Klausner
1985– "Masters of Paradise Island, part 1: Organized crime, neo-colonialism and the
1986 Bahamas." Dialectical Anthropology. Winter.
Blum, Richard and John Kaplan
1979 "Offshore banking: Issues with respect to criminal use." Report submitted to the Ford Foundation.
Charbonneau, Jean-Pierre
1976 The Canadian Connection. Montreal: Optimum Publishing Company.
Fortune
1966 "Business around the globe." 77:93–99.
Grand Bahama Development Corporation
1964 Letter to the Registrar in the Bahama Registry.
Grand Bahama Port Authority
1959 "Annual report." Bahamas Registry.
Judiciary Committee
1984 U.S. House of Representatives. "Statement of Gary D. Liming on casino money laundering." Washington, D.C.: Government Printing Office.
Lernoux, Penny
1984 In Banks We Trust. New York: Anchor/Doubleday.
McClintick, David
1982 Indecent Exposure: A True Story of Hollywood and Wall Street. New York: Dell.
Messick, Hank
1971 Lansky. New York: Putnam.
New York State Senate
n.d. a Select Committee on Crime. Bahamian File: Lansky Folder.
n.d. b Select Committee on Crime. Bahamian File: ICB Folder.
n.d. c Select Committee on Crime. Bahamian File: Bank of World Commerce Folder.

Pennsylvania Crime Commission
1980   A Decade of Organized Crime: 1980 Report. Commonwealth of Pennsylvania.
Permanent Subcommittee on Investigation
1983   Committee on Government Affairs, U.S. Senate. Crime and Secrecy: The Use of Offshore Banks and Companies. Washington, D.C.: Government Printing Office.
President's Commission on Organized Crime
1984   The Cash Connection: Organized Crime, Financial Institutions, and Money Laundering. Interim Report to the President and the Attorney General.
Royal Canadian Mounted Police
1983   National Drug Intelligence Estimate, 1982. Ottawa: Minister of Supply and Services.
U.S. District Court
1980   Western District of Pennsylvania. Indictment, U.S. versus Thomas E. Long, et al.
1981   Northern District of Georgia. Indictment, U.S. versus Tilton Lamar Chester, Jr., et al.
n.d.   Southern District of Mississippi. Affidavit for Search Warrant, U.S. versus Offices and Premises of Red Carpet Inns International, Biloxi, Mississippi.
United Kingdom
1967   Commission of Inquiry into the Operation of the Business of Casinos in Freeport and in Nassau. Report published in the Nassau Guardian.
1971   Royal Commission Appointed on the Recommendation of the Bahamas Government to Review the Hawksbill Creek Agreement. Report, Volume 1. Her Majesty's Stationery Office.
Wall Street Journal
1976   "Empire builder." December 15.
Workman, Douglas J.
1982   "The use of offshore tax havens for the purpose of criminally evading income taxes." The Journal of Criminal Law and Criminology 73:675–706.

27. The Space between Laws: The Problem of Corporate Crime in a Transnational Context*

RAYMOND J. MICHALOWSKI AND RONALD C. KRAMER

Transnational corporations (TNCs)[1] engage in a wide variety of socially injurious actions (Barnet and Muller, 1974; Simon and Eitzen, 1986). These harmful corporate acts raise a number of important sociological questions. One central set of questions concerns the conceptualization of these corporate harms for purposes of criminological research. Some have argued that the concept of crime only refers to criminal convictions and violations of criminal law (Shapiro, 1983; Tappan, 1947). Others have proposed that the traditional definition of crime be expanded to include violations of civil and regulatory law, as well as violations of specific criminal statutes (Blum-West and Carter, 1983; Clinard and Yeager, 1980; Schrager and Short, 1978; Sutherland, 1940, 1949). Still others claim that state definitions are too restrictive and unduly influenced by corporate power, and therefore, should be abandoned in favor of broader social definitions of crime based on concepts such as human rights (Schwendinger and Schwendinger, 1970; Tift and Sullivan, 1980).

The increasing global reach of modern transnational corporations aggravates the difficulties of arriving at a satisfactory conception of corporate crime. TNCs at times engage in practices which, while they would be illegal in their home nations, are legal in a number of host nations. The ability of TNCs to have a significant influence on the legal climate in host countries further renders the particular laws of these nations an inadequate basis for the study of corporate crime.

The purpose of this paper is to contribute to the resolution of this conceptual dilemma. The first step, following Blum-West and Carter (1983), is to separate the study of the organization and causation of socially injurious corporate actions from a consideration of the socio-political definition of these acts. This distinction creates two "research domains" (Blum-West and Carter, 1983:552) or "paradigms" (Kramer, 1985:472). In the first paradigm, the objective is to explain (and eventually control) the harmful corporate actions of TNCs. Corporate crime researchers operating within this paradigm need to develop their own behavioral definitions to delimit the subject matter and identify cases for study. We will offer such a definition in this paper.

The definitional paradigm is concerned with the socio-political construction of legal definitions of corporate acts that cause social injury. The goal of this paradigm is to understand the historical origins and development of laws and political labels concerning harmful corporate behavior. This corporate criminalization process has been studied almost exclusively at the level of the nation state. However, we intend to show that the spread of TNCs requires that we broaden this focus in two ways: by examining the social construction of political labels in the international arena as exemplified by the development of United Nations codes of conduct for TNCs, and by incorporating what we term *analogous social injuries* within the scope of corporate crime research.

TRANSNATIONAL CORPORATIONS AND THE RELOCATION OF CORPORATE HAZARDS

Over the last quarter century, foreign investment by TNCs has expanded dramatically (United Nations, 1978:36). In the 20 years from 1960 to 1980, the revenues of TNCs grew tenfold—from 199 billion dollars to 2,155 billion dollars—with U.S. based corporations accounting for 50 percent of this growth (Cavanaugh and Clairmonte, 1983:17). By 1983, the worldwide profits of TNCs had reached a record high of 130 billion dollars (*Multinational Monitor*, 1984:11). This internationalization of corporate activity necessitates an expansion of corporate crime research beyond its dominant focus on offenses by corporations in their home countries.[2]

While, on a dollar basis, foreign investment in developed nations exceeds that in developing nations (Hamilton, 1983:3; United Nations, 1978:40; U.S. Department of Commerce, 1984:8), it is transnational investments *in developing nations* that pose the greatest likelihood of injurious corporate activity, and which raise the most perplexing problems for the definition and study of corporate crime. There are several reasons for this.

First, the most significant change in patterns of foreign investment since the Second World War has been the increased location of TNC industrial facilities in developing nations (United Nations, 1978:40–41). Three-fourths of all U.S. companies with sales over 100 million dollars had manufacturing facilities in other countries by 1975 (United Nations, 1978:222). By 1977, developing nations had surpassed developed ones in dollar value as locations for manufacturing by U.S. industries (U.S. Department of Commerce, 1981:159). Reimportation of overseas assembly by U.S. companies increased five-fold between 1969 and 1983, and in the textiles and electronics industries more than half of all current sales by U.S. corporations are now assembled abroad (Grunwald and Flamm, 1985:12–13). As TNCs export their industrial operations to developing nations, many of the hazards of industrial production and the associated possibilities for corporate crime are relocated from developed to developing countries. Moreover, as the fatal poisoning of over 2,000 residents of Bhopal, India, dramatized (Hazarka, 1984:1), the settlement patterns, population density, and limited disaster preparedness of developing nations means that, when problems do occur, the human and environmental costs are likely to be greater than those resulting from similar incidents in developed countries.

Second, the growth in consumer exports to the Third World, as well as the increased local production of consumer goods by TNCs in developing nations, has generated significant consumer safety issues. Differences in marketing practices of TNCs in home versus host nations, variations in the provision of information by TNCs regarding product hazards, and variations in cultural practices regarding product usage has led to unnecessary injury, illness, and death for Third World consumers of TNC products (Mattelart, 1983).

Finally, in comparison to developed nations, developing nations frequently have fewer legal controls over workplace, environmental, and consumer hazards of industrial production (Braithwaite, 1984; Castleman, 1975; Dewar, 1978; Vieira, 1985). Therefore, the potential for corporations to behave in socially injurious ways in developing nations is greater. For these reasons the growing internationalization of business points to developing nations as a significant emerging arena for injurious corporate activity.

TRANSNATIONAL CORPORATIONS AND CORPORATE DEVIANCE IN THE THIRD WORLD

In recent years corporate injuries to workers, physical environments, and consumers in developing nations have revealed significant problems with respect to the control of corporate activity in these countries. We will explore each of these arenas, with particular attention to injurious actions that arise in the space between legal systems—actions which were prohibited in home nations, but permissible in the host countries where they occurred.

Working Conditions

According to the International Labor Organization (1985:55), industrial workers in TNCs in developing nations "suffer from more safety and health problems than similar workers in the developed countries." While in some cases TNC manufacturing operations provide better working conditions than locally owned factories (Blake, 1980; International Labor Organization, 1985:44), it is the comparison between TNC operations in home and host countries, rather than between TNCs and local conditions, that raises the most perplexing questions for the study of injurious corporate activities.

In a number of instances, occupational safety and other working conditions in TNC operations have been found to fall below those mandated by law in more developed countries. The exposure of workers in electronics assembly plants to levels of carcinogens and other toxic materials beyond those allowed in the United States, for instance, has been one of the consequences of the exportation of this "clean" industry (LaDou, 1984). In the more obviously "dirty" industries such as asbestos and chemical production, foreign workers in U.S. subsidiaries have been knowingly exposed to toxic levels that were illegal in the United States. In 1972 for instance, Amatax, a Pennsylvania asbestos yarn mill, moved its entire production facility to Mexico to take advantage of the fact that Mexico had no laws regulating exposure of workers to asbestos fibers. Similarly, in 1974 Raybestos-Manhattan acquired 47 percent of the stock in a Venezuelan asbestos plant in order to take advantage of Venezuelan law which allows higher levels of airborn asbestos fibers than does the Occupational Safety and Health Administration (OSHA) in the United States (Castleman, 1979). In a similar case, Arasco, the only U.S. producer of arsenic, moved its entire operation to Mexico when OSHA lowered the U.S. limit for exposure to airborne arsenic from 500 to 4 micrograms per cubic meter of air (Mattelart, 1983:102). In the electronics industry, Third World workers in U.S. subsidiaries have been found to suffer eye strain and eye failure due to constant peering into microscopes without the benefit of rest breaks on company time required by law in the United States (Fuentes and Ehrenreich, 1983:6).

Industrial operations by some TNCs in developing host countries have used wage and employment practices prohibited in their more developed home nations. In some cases, work is contracted out to home workers at piece rates which require a level of effort comparable to nineteenth-century garment sweatshops. These contract workers enjoy no benefits in terms of holidays, health insurance, sick leave or pensions—all of which are legally protected worker rights in more developed nations (Fernandez-Kelly, 1983: 118). Likewise, the practice of using extended "probationary" periods during which workers (often women) are paid a lower wage rate and then "laid off" just prior to completing this period would be illegal under U.S. labor law (Fuentes and Ehrenreich, 1983:9–10). As Fernandez-Kelly (1983:114) found in the "maquiladoras" factories of the Mexican border, a variation on this theme is to bring prospective workers in for a "test" during which they spend a day or more sewing garments for no pay in the hopes of possible employment. Ong (1983:431) suggested that employers also deliberately keep workers on "temporary status" for prolonged periods to minimize the risks of unionization. This strategy makes it easy to fire workers who organize or join unions.

Environmental Pollution

In some instances TNCs have located and/or relocated high-pollution industries in less-developed countries in order to escape the pollution control costs imposed by environmental protection laws in their home nation. Blake and Walters (1976:159) have suggested that TNCs "will be very sensitive to disparities among various [national] pollution control standards which affect production costs and competitiveness in international trade" as a means of expanding or protecting profit margins. This sensitivity reflects the fact that pollution control costs in the United States are higher than in most other countries (Pearson and Pryor, 1978:170). Robert Strauss (1978:451), President Carter's chief trade negotiator, warned in 1978 of a developing "pattern of flight" as U.S. companies are drawn to developing nations with less costly pollution control laws. Castleman (1978:3) similarly noted that "hazard export is emerging as a driving force in new plant investment in many hazardous and polluting industries." In some cases entire industries involving highly toxic substances such as asbestos, arsenic, mercury, and benzidene dyes have been exported to rapidly developing nations such as Korea, Mexico, Brazil, India, and Ireland (Leonard and Duerksen, 1981:55). Even computer and electronics assembly, once thought to be "clean" industries, often expose the environments of developing nations to a wide range of toxic substances that are more closely regulated in the United States (*Cultural Survival*, 1981; *Dollars and Sense*, 1984:6).

There has been some disagreement over whether pollution control costs actually play a significant role in location decisions (Flamm, 1985:77–78; Randall, 1977:v). However, the debate over the relative importance of pollution regulations for location decisions speaks only to the question of corporate motivation, not the consequences of corporate behavior. Even if they are not actively seeking "pollution havens," in many developing nations TNCs remain legally free to expose the water, air, soil, and bodies of workers to hazardous substances at rates higher than those allowed in their home countries (Vieira, 1985).

In addition to the problem of pollutants produced by TNCs operating in host countries, hazardous waste produced *in developed countries* has begun to find its way into developing nations. Some TNCs have sought to avoid the costs of mandated controls on hazardous waste storage in their home nation by transporting wastes to countries which have few or no legal controls on hazardous waste disposal (Centre on Transnational Corporations, 1985:59–60). In these cases, the TNCs involved are clearly acting to circumvent laws in their home nations rather than simply being passive beneficiaries of the difference in laws between home and host nations.

Consumer Safety

According to the U.N. Centre on Transnational Corporations (1985:58) "the one issue that has generated the greatest emotion and controversy in the 1980s regarding transnational corporations . . . is the exportation of products deemed to be harmful to health and the environment." Several cases in recent years have dramatized the kinds of hazards consumers in developing nations face when TNCs circumvent product regulations in their home nations.

The export of children's sleepwear treated with the carcinogenic flame retardant Tris, after the sale of such sleepwear was banned in the United States, was one of the first cases of knowingly exported consumer hazards to receive widespread attention (*New York Times*, 1978:26). In the late 1970s, A.A. Robbins Company arranged (with the help of United States Agency for International Development) for the distribution of the Dalkon Shield intrauterine device in a number of developing countries. This overseas market was sought after Robbins already knew that the Shield was responsible for 20,000 cases of serious uterine infection, that it had resulted in several thousand hysterectomies among its users in the United States, and that the product would soon be banned at home (Dowie and Johnston, 1976; Mintz, 1985). In another case, Parke-Davis, a U.S. pharmaceutical company, successfully promoted the drug chloramphenicol on a non-prescription basis in 39 nations but provided no information concerning its dangerous and sometimes fatal side effects – even though the drug was banned in the United States and Japan (Mattelart, 1983:100–101).

In addition to the hazards posed by consumer goods, it is estimated that annually 375,000 people in the developing world are poisoned – 10,000 of them fatally – through the misuse of industrial and agricultural chemicals exported from developed nations. There is evidence that much of this poisoning results from the failure of TNCs to provide adequate information on the hazards of their chemical exports, and from their active attempts to find markets for chemicals banned at home (Bull, 1982; Weir and Schapiro, 1981). In one such instance, paraquat was successfully promoted for use as a marijuana defoliant in Latin America after it was banned for that purpose in the United States (del Olmo, 1986).

Most of the injurious corporate actions described above were not prosecutable as crimes or regulatory violations in the nations where they occurred. Yet to omit them from the study of corporate crime on this basis does little to help us understand either the organization and causation of injurious actions by TNCs, or the definitional process by which these actions have been rendered legal in host nations. Moreover, as we argue in the next section, the ability of TNCs to influence regulatory climates in host nations may play a crucial role in keeping injurious actions by TNCs from being defined and prosecuted as crimes.

TRANSNATIONAL CORPORATIONS AND REGULATORY CLIMATES

TNCs can influence the regulatory climates of developing host nations in indirect and direct ways. The logic of development in the free-market world necessitates that developing nations create hospitable environments for foreign investment. Simply by holding the economic keys to development, TNCs indirectly limit the political willingness of developing nations to establish strict controls over potential or actual corporate harms. At times, TNCs have also exerted pressure in more direct ways to forestall legislation contrary to their interests, and in some cases to subvert political movements or leaders deemed inhospitable to these interests. We now examine this relationship between TNCs and regulatory climates in closer detail, with a particular focus on labor policies.

Indirect Influences

Free-market nations that have followed a capitalist model of development based on foreign investment find their potentials for economic growth closely linked to their ability to attract TNCs. Domestic elites in developing nations frequently find that general economic improvement and political stability in their countries, as well as their own economic and political success, depend upon creating hospitable environments for investment by foreign TNCs. The deepening need for inflows of foreign investment in developing nations, and the pressures this places on domestic policy, have been extensively examined by a number of dependency theorists.[3] The specific regulatory adaptations that have been made to attract TNCs have been examined in less detail. However, there is some evidence that the existence of a profitable double-standard which allows TNCs in host countries to do what they are prohibited from doing in their home nations is related to the desire of host nations to attract foreign investment by creating regulatory climates hospitable to the interests of TNCs.

Controls over the rights of workers to organize for improved wage and working conditions is a good example of how TNCs become the passive beneficiaries of policies designed to attract them. Labor costs represent one of the most significant factors in the location of manufacturing plants (Burns, 1984). For instance, assembly line workers in the United States often earn per hour what assembly workers in developing nations earn per day (Fuentes and Ehrenreich, 1983:5). The desire to take advantage of significant differentials in national wage rates has been the primary stimulus for the location of TNC production facilities in developing nations (Grunwald and Flamm, 1985:3–9). Leaders in some developing nations have used limitations on worker rights as a strategy to convince foreign companies that, if they do invest, they will enjoy continued benefits from lower labor costs. The belief that this will attract foreign investment has received a degree of confirmation from investment practices of TNCs.[4] For instance, investment in Thailand by the U.S. semiconductor industry did not reach significant levels until 1977, the year following the installment of a military junta that ended a period of democratic government characterized by strikes and other movements for increased popular control over the economy. Similarly, foreign direct investment in semiconductor assembly in the Philippines entered a period of significant growth beginning in 1972, the year Marcos declared martial law (Grunwald and Flamm, 1985:77). In 1982, Marcos continued his efforts to create a profitable climate for these TNCs by issuing a decree banning all strikes in the semiconductor industry as being against the "national interest" (O'Connor and Wong, 1983).

Another strategy used in developing nations to attract foreign investment at the expense of labor rights protected by law in developed nations is the creation of *economic free zones* (EFZs). In some cases these zones are little more than labor camps "where trade unions, strikes and freedom of movement are severely limited, if not forbidden" (Fuentes and Ehrenrich, 1983:5). For example, advertisements for Caribbean Assemblies, a set of EFZs in Haiti and the Dominican Republic, promise foreign companies a "large, urbanized, low-cost labour pool" and "strict anti-strike and labour regulation laws" (Matellart, 1983:106). A promotional document by the South Korea government offers this description of its EFZ:

> The zone has the characteristics of a reserved territory in which the application of laws or relevant regulations is partially or totally suppressed or attenuated. . . . It is an industrial territory in which a series of fiscal and legal privileges are offered to firms of foreign capital (Medawar, 1979:62).

Promotional materials such as these make it abundantly clear that limitations on the rights of workers are part of the bait that EFZs offer to foreign companies in some developing nations.

Lim (1983:14) has argued that locating TNC industrial facilities in developing countries is beneficial to workers in nations where unemployment and poverty are widespread, even if the rights of these workers are minimal. This perspective is manifest in the June 6, 1980, issue of *Fortune* magazine which asks, "Even though the people working on Castle and Cooke's banana plantations in Central America earn far less than the U.S. minimum wage, would they be better off if the company decided to move elsewhere?" However, the economic conditions that TNCs "improve" cannot be analyzed in isolation from the economic domination by foreign business interests that characterizes the history of many developing host nations. Moreover, while the factory work provided by TNCs may improve the incomes of some workers, the dependent development it represents generally results in a distorted economy, a split labor market, and exploitation of women who are the primary laborers in these factories (Amin, 1974; Frank, 1975; Nash, 1979; Wallerstein, 1979).

Direct Influences

In addition to benefiting indirectly from restrictive labor climates, TNCs have at times actively used their economic power in developing nations to limit the rights of workers to organize into unions to protect and promote their interests. In some cases, TNCs have used the threat of the runaway shop to discipline workers. For instance, when the Malaysian government indicated in 1983 that it might permit the formation of a union for electronics workers, U.S. electronics firms in Malaysia indicated that, should this happen, they would consider moving their plants elsewhere. Subsequently, the Malaysian government shelved its plans for the union. In a similar case, Control Data Corporation closed a Korean production facility in response to attempts by workers to unionize (O'Connor and Wong, 1983). Such threats or actual incidents of capital flight can have a chilling effect on both labor activism and governmental support for labor rights in nations dependent on foreign investment.

Besides attempts to influence specific policies, some TNCs have used their economic and political power to alter the flow of broader political developments in host nations. In some cases, TNCs have contributed to the elimination of progressive or socialist governments in favor of conservative ones. Activities of this sort are often based on clandestine contacts between TNCs and governments in home or host nations. As a result, relatively little is known about their scope or frequency. However, cases such as ITT's contributions to the overthrow of Allende in Chile, the participation of United Fruit, International Railways of Central America, and Electric Bond and Share in bringing about the downfall of the progressive leader, Jacobs Arbenz, in Guatemala in 1954, and the more recent financial support provided by some U.S. corporations to the Nicaraguan *contras* in their efforts to overthrow the socialist government there, indicate that TNCs are not above using their power to alter the flow of political events in developing nations (Bonner, 1983; Jensen, 1973; Kenworthy, 1973; LaFeber, 1984; Langley, 1985:142–43).

Overall, the combined effects of economic pressures to create a favorable climate for foreign investment, and support by transnational corporate capital for governments or political parties hospitable to their interests, can create a set of structural/legal conditions which allow TNCs in host countries to do what would be illegal in their country of origin. We are not suggesting that all TNCs have taken full advantage of these favorable structural/legal climates, or that all actively engage in efforts to create these climates. We are suggesting that researchers must always be sensitive to the political influences of TNCs on the political climates and legal frameworks of host countries. Accordingly, the laws governing corporate behavior in these nations are a poor starting place for setting the scope of inquiry into corporate offenses in a transnational context. In the following sections, we consider an alternative definitional framework for research on injurious actions by TNCs: the U.N. codes of corporate conduct.

THE U.N. CODE AS INTERNATIONAL POLITICS

Multinational business is now international politics. Multinational companies are increasingly being forced to operate in a framework not just determined by the laws of supply and demand . . . but also by a proliferating set of inter-governmental arrangements specifically targeted at them (Robinson, 1983:3).

Recognizing that the political power of TNCs is truly transnational and hegemonic, and that independent national action is limited, many developing countries have come to believe that the only way they can confront and control TNCs is through the creation of international standards. The two most far-reaching attempts to establish worldwide standards for TNCs have been undertaken by the United Nations with the Draft Codes of Conduct on Transnational Corporations and the Guidelines for Consumer Protection. The development of these codes is a unique and highly relevant empirical case for a theoretical examination of the political definition of harmful corporate actions.

The definitional process that created the U.N. codes supports Robinson's (1983) assertion that multinational business is now international politics. The code development process has brought into sharp focus the fundamental differences of perspectives and interests between developed and developing nations, and between free-market and centrally planned economies. Charles Lindblom (1977:ix) succinctly characterized these differences when he wrote: "Aside from the difference between despotic and libertarian government, the greatest distinction between one government and another is in the degree to which market replaces government or government replaces market." The formation of the draft codes for consumer protection and transnational corporate behavior at the United Nations represents an attempt to replace markets with politics. That is, through the political mechanisms of the United Nations, non-aligned and less developed nations are seeking to implement a set of rules governing the market relations between TNCs, and the citizens and governments of the nations in which they operate. This process assumes the primacy of politics over markets, and in this way, transnational business has indeed become international politics.

Historical Background

The politicalization of international business, and the origins of the U.N. codes, have their roots in the "multinational debate" of the 1960s that reached its climax in the confrontation between developing and industrialized nations in the early 1970s (Robinson, 1983). The developing nations, many of them recently enfranchised, made claims concerning the harmful practices of TNCs and called for a New Economic Order and some form of binding control over TNCs. Throughout the 1970s, the United Nations led the crusade for a comprehensive, legally binding international code of conduct for TNCs. Within the United Nations, this crusade was led by the developing countries – grouped together as the so-called Group of 77 – international trade unions, and some small, developed nations, such as the Scandinavian states (Hamilton, 1983).

The U.N. code of conduct on TNCs has its direct roots in a 1972 decision of the United Nations Economic and Social Council (ECOSOC) to establish a group of "eminent persons" to make recommendations for international action on TNCs (Robinson, 1983). Their report, "The Impact of Multinational Corporations on Development and International Relations," was published in May 1974, and it provided the rationale for the subsequent development of the code. In December 1974, ECOSOC created a Commission and Centre on Transnational Corporations. The Commission was charged with the job of drawing up a set of recommendations which could become the basis for a Code of Conduct dealing with TNCs.

The Commission on Transnational Corporations met annually from 1975 into the 1980s. However, the economic downturn associated with the 1974 oil crisis and the corresponding increased need of the developing nations for foreign investment tempered the Commission's work (Robinson, 1983). The multinational issue was no longer a debate—it had become a negotiation. The principal forum for the negotiations was the "Intergovernmental Working Group on a Code of Conduct" which first met in January 1977, and its reports to the Commission on Transnational Corporations.

As the Intergovernmental Working Group began its task, several other international groups issued guidelines for TNCs. In 1976, the Organization for Economic Cooperation and Development (OECD) established its *Guidelines for Multinational Enterprises*, and one year later, the International Labor Organization (ILO) approved the *Declaration of Principles Concerning Multinational Enterprises and Social Policy*. In 1980, the United Nations Conference on Trade and Development (UNCTAD) promulgated the *Set of Multilaterally Agreed Equitable Principles and Rules for the Control of Restrictive Business Practices*, and the World Health Organization's (WHO) International Code of Marketing of Breast Milk Substitutes was passed by the General Assembly in May of 1981.

The ILO, UNCTAD and WHO guidelines are all sectoral codes for international business within the United Nations. They were developed to deal with specific problems that may arise from TNC activity and must be understood in the context of the more general negotiations occurring within the United Nations concerning TNCs. The OECD guidelines were a preemptive Western strike at the general U.N. codes. As Robinson (1983:7) points out:

> . . . the guidelines are a calculated compromise by Western governments between, on the one hand, the need to sensitize firms to their social, economic, and political responsibilities and, on the other, the need to make the rest of the world aware, and in particular the LDCs negotiating a UN code of conduct for transnational corporations, that the West is not prepared to see excessive constraints imposed on their major creators of wealth.

Despite the passage of these other international guidelines, the U.N. code of conduct remains in draft form. The Intergovernmental Working Group concluded its work on the code in May 1982 at its seventeenth session. However, at this time the code has not yet been adopted by the General Assembly. On the other hand, the Consumer Code promulgated by the Economic and Social Council was approved by the General Assembly in November 1984.

Key Actors and Issues in the Definitional Process

The primary impulse behind the U.N. codes was the desire of the developing countries—the Group of 77—to establish a "New Economic Order" and some mechanism for legal control over TNCs. Their manifesto for a U.N. code, produced in 1976, included a 21-point list of grievances and criticisms concerning the behavior of TNCs (Robinson, 1983). Their position, to use Lindblom's (1977:ix) terms, was that international politics must replace markets. The economic crisis of the mid-1970s mellowed the ideological tenor of the Group of 77 and they increasingly came to realize that to have any chance of success they would need to compromise with the developed countries. The major issue on which they compromised was the binding character of the code. They acknowledged that any code of conduct must be voluntary and not legally binding at this point in time.

The major ally of the developing countries was the international trade union move-ment centered in Western Europe. In fact, the unions and the TNCs were key interest group participants in the political struggle to shape the U.N. codes. As Robinson (1983:195) points out,

> . . . there is no doubt that the war of influence that has engaged the trade unions and mul-tinational business since the start of the TNC debate in the 1960s, has an often determin-ing impact on the measures being drawn up in . . . the UN and its specialized agencies.

The trade unions favor increased regulation of big business and are supportive of attempts to increase public control of the international economy. In addition, the European unions generally bring to the debate over the codes an overt anti-capitalist ideology which broadens the framework of discussion. Furthermore, Robinson (1983) points out that the trade unions have a streamlined and interlocking organiza-tion that allows them to significantly influence international policy.

The industrialized or developed countries, including the United States, West Ger-many, and the United Kingdom, have generally taken a much more conservative stance toward the whole idea of a code of conduct for TNCs. As the home countries of the majority of TNCs, these states have a much more positive assessment of TNC behavior. They have been concerned with making the codes voluntary arrangements that provide stable conditions for international investment. They have argued that the code of conduct must include a statement about the general treatment of TNCs by the countries in which they operate. They have also been concerned about the issues of nationalization and compensation.

Of course, the TNCs themselves are significantly involved in trying to shape the U.N. codes. At the beginning of the definitional process, the TNCs appeared to be resigned to the prospect of international codes of conduct and their strategy was to try to shape codes that they could at least live with. More recently though, big business and its lob-bies (the International Chamber of Commerce in particular) have stepped up the attack on the fundamental principles that lay behind the codes. The TNCs are more forcefully asserting the primacy of markets over politics in the debates on the code. The election of Ronald Reagan in 1980 may provide a partial explanation for the aggressive stance of the TNCs. The Reagan administration has been quite vociferous in its condemnation of the codes and its support of markets over politics. As Caplan and Malcomson (1986:108) note, ". . . it is clear that the international business community, alone and in partnership with the Reagan Administration, is engaged in an active and effective assault on U.N. initiatives that are perceived as threats to corporate profits."

Speaking before the American Enterprise Institute in December 1983, Jeane Kirk-patrick, then U.S. Ambassador to the United Nations, stated that the "proliferation of activities aimed at the regulation of international business [is] a very big problem" (Kirkpatrick, 1983). These regulatory efforts, she said, arise not from hazards posed by TNCs, but from "ideological distortions," such as the view of poor nations that they are victims of exploitation by TNCs. She went on to say that such regulation would result in "global paternalism" by the United Nations, a view similar to that expressed by the Reagan Administration in its opposition to the Infant Formula Code (Kirk-patrick, 1983). Echoing Kirkpatrick's concern, Murray Weidenbaum (1983:1), former chairman of President Reagan's Council of Economic Advisors, has accused the United Nations of trying to become a "global nanny," and warned that "the United Nations is in a growth phase in its attempts to control private enterprise" (1984:13).

Advertising Age, the trade paper of the advertising industry, worried that the consumer codes could limit the free choice of consumers in Third World countries as well as the freedom of merchants to promote their wares in the way they deem most effective (1984:58). *Chemical Week*, the trade organ of the U.S. chemical industry, expressed a similar concern (1981:15). In perhaps the most strident attack on the U.N. activities, the Heritage Foundation warned that "a new wave of extremist, anti–free enterprise consumer organizations" is using "distortions to undermine the multinational corporations and the private sector approach to development." This threat to free enterprise results, they say, from the fact that:

> Various consumer, union and church organizations have been banding together and refining and sharing their techniques. . . . They are developing international networks that allow them to draw attention to targeted issues . . . forcing multinational firms to pay closer attention to their corporate activities (Heritage Foundation, 1983).

Emerging Political Definitions and Their Significance

Out of the sharp political and ideological conflicts within the United Nations, and despite the opposition of the international business community, a Draft Code of Conduct on Transnational Corporations has been produced. This code, along with the consumer code, constitutes a set of international norms for the conduct of transnational business — a new set of political definitions concerning the behavior of TNCs. While space does not permit a full description of the code of conduct, the outline in Table 1 highlights the major areas and topics covered by the code. The specific standards formulated under the topic headings in the draft code have one key notion running through them — accountability. As Robinson (1983:224) notes:

> By accountability is meant the accountability of business to new constituencies — to governments, to the general public, and, above all, to the workforce. And being accountable to such new constituencies, the multinational company is forced into a new context of political and social responsibility.

Caplan and Malcomson (1986) offer another perspective on the code when they observe that it modestly seeks to universalize much of what we in the United States have already achieved in imperfect form — consumer protection, safeguards against exposure to hazardous products, control over national resources, corporate accountability, and economic sovereignty.

It is important not to overestimate the significance of the codes. The code of conduct on TNCs has not yet been adopted by the General Assembly. Neither code is legally binding or enforceable. The code of conduct also sets standards for the treatment of TNCs by the countries in which they operate. Some observers believe that the impact of the codes has already been eviscerated by the international business community (Caplan and Malcomson, 1986). Another observer warns that the codes may actually

Table 1. Activities of Transnational Corporations Covered by U.N. (Draft) Code of Conduct

A. General and Political
1. Respect for national sovereignty and observance of domestic laws, regulations and administrative practices
2. Adherence to economic goals and development objectives, policies and priorities
3. Adherence to socio-cultural objectives and values
4. Respect for human rights and fundamental freedom
5. Non-interference in internal political affairs
6. Non-interference in intergovernmental relations
7. Abstention from corrupt practices

B. Economic, Financial and Social
1. Ownership and control
2. Balance of payments and financing
3. Transfer pricing
4. Taxation
5. Competition and restrictive business practices
6. Transfer of technology
7. Consumer protection
8. Environmental protection

Source: *CTC Reporter*, 1982:3–4, 23–24

benefit TNCs by securing a stable international business framework and, by placing them on an equal footing with government, legitimize their activities in the eyes of their critics (Hamilton, 1983).

Whatever the truth of these observations, the real significance of the U.N. codes is that they create transnational standards for evaluating the behavior of TNCs. A worldwide set of general principles has emerged out of the political definitional process within the uniquely distinctive setting of the United Nations. Just as broader conceptions of human rights and corporate crime emerged in the United States through class struggle and the political mobilization of a wide range of interest groups (Coleman, 1983), the United Nations has provided a global arena for political struggles between developing and developed nations and between the trade union movement and the international business community over the dominance of politics or markets, and the appropriateness of specific actions by TNCs. Finally, even though we have noted the hegemonic process of legal definition in developing nations, the legitimacy of transnational standards in conjunction with the political power of the United Nations may allow the U.N. codes to serve as model legislation to be enacted within specific developing nations.

THE SEARCH FOR ALTERNATIVE FRAMEWORKS

The evolution of U.N. codes for the conduct of TNCs returns us to our central problematic – that the laws of nation-states represent theoretically inappropriate frameworks for the study of injurious actions by TNCs. The need for criminological researchers to derive behavioral standards independent of law is not a new concern for criminologists. Nearly a half-century ago Thorsten Sellin (1938:104–5) argued that criminologists should not limit their investigations to "categories set up by the criminal law," because these categories "do not arise intrinsically from the nature of the subject matter," but instead, reflect the "character and interests of those groups in the population which influence legislation." In recent years some criminologists have responded to this challenge by employing various concepts of "human rights" in constructing alternative definitions of crime (Schwendinger and Schwendinger, 1970; Tift and Sullivan, 1980). These "human rights" definitions of crime, in turn, have generated their own set of criticisms.

The central critique of "human rights" definitions of crime has been that researchers who utilize them simply substitute their personal moral concerns for those contained in law. Schapiro (1983:307) argues that corporate crime research that extends beyond the boundaries of what is illegal is inevitably flawed because it is suffused with the "moral agenda" of the observer. A more trenchant criticism is offered by John Braithwaite (1985:18) who suggests that:

> Those who choose to study violations of "politically defined human rights," or some other imaginative definition of deviance, will deserve to be ignored for indulging their personal moralities in a social science that has no relevance for those who do not share that morality.

The typical rejoinder to criticisms of this type is that relying upon law to define the boundaries of criminological inquiry is no less suffused with moral choice than is choosing definitions based on concepts of human rights. For instance, Schwendinger and Schwendinger (1970:142) argue that:

> No scholar involved in the controversy about the definitions of crime has been able to avoid direct or indirect use of moral standards in the solution to this problem. . . . In light of this, the claim that moral judgments have no place in the formulation of the definitions of crime is without foundation.

While the observation that law contains no less a moral and political agenda than any other definition of transgression may be correct, it provides no particular guidance regarding why we should choose one particular framework for defining the parameters of study over another. We suggest that the first step beyond this set of mutual accusations is to distinguish between the positivist concept of *lack of bias* and critical theory's concept of *reflexivity*. Within a positivist conception of social science *bias* is a preference for one set of social outcomes over another. This should be avoided in favor of a value-free science in which the researcher holds no brief with respect to the world in view.

The presumed attainability of a science without bias arises from the attempt in positivist epistemology to separate the powers of human reason from the inevitability of human commitment to the social world. This separation of reason from commitment, according to Habermas (1974:264), produces the goal of unbiased inquiry through which reason is applied to developing the technical means of control over environments and people, but from which the application of that same reason to inquiry regarding the purposes of that control is excluded. Within this framework, social scientists who reveal preferences for some social agendas over others are suspected of allowing ideology to distort science, that is, commitment is thought to compromise reason.

The positivist *commitment* to a world developed through technical application of scientific rationality, by contrast, is interpreted not as commitment but as reason:

> Efficiency and economy, which are the definitions of this [positivist] rationality cannot, in turn, be themselves conceived as values, and yet, within the framework of positivism's understanding of itself, they can only be justified as though they were values (Habermas, 1974:269).

The search for a social science devoid of bias is a misdirected and futile endeavor. As Karl Heilbroner (1974:23) observes:

> The position of the social researcher differs sharply from that of the observer of the natural world. The latter . . . is not morally imbedded in the field he scrutinizes. By contrast the social investigator is inextricably bound up with the objects of his scrutiny . . . bringing with him feelings of animus or defensiveness to the phenomenon he observes.

In contrast to positivist notions of unbiased science, critical reflexivity is a mode of analysis that recognizes the existence of moral preferences in ourselves and others, and demands of us that we analyze the nature and construction of those preferences so that they contribute to rather than detract from our ability to achieve the purposeful understanding we seek and the type of social world to which we are committed. Rather than following the path outlined by a positivist model of inquiry presumably shorn of moral commitments, the study of injurious actions by TNCs should be guided, we suggest, by principles of critical reflexivity. This perspective provides a theoretically grounded way to expand the scope of study beyond the limits of the law, and to incorporate a positive commitment to the reduction of social injuries by corporate actors within the framework of research concerns.

Critical reflexivity according to Habermas (1973:15) develops when we examine what he terms taken-for-granted "validity claims" and "redeem or dismiss them on the basis of arguments." Because of their taken-for-granted nature, however, validity claims are only revealed through discourses where "participants, themes and contributions are not restricted except with reference to the goal of testing the validity claims in question," and where "no force except that of the better argument is exercised" (Habermas, 1973:108).

Law is a socially and historically legitimated authority system. The validity claims implicit in laws — including the assumption that law is the final arbiter of transgressive action — have been established not through the type of discourses described above, but through the historical interplay of a variety of economic and political forces. If law is used to define the scope of corporate crime studies, the possibilities for a critical understanding of transgressive actions is negated by the consequently unanalyzed history of power — relations imbedded in law. Moreover, alternative discourses which perceive the validity claims of established laws as problematic are omitted from our inquiry, further narrowing our ability to analyze the transgressive actions of TNCs from a critically reflexive standpoint.

With respect to the study of corporate crime, critical reflexivity does not mean seeking out some set of definitions that are free of moral implications. We are never without preferences with respect to outcomes in the social world. However, we can begin to develop critical reflexivity by using and entering into less restricted discourses which question rather than accept those validity claims that either the law or other conceptions of human rights treat as non-problematic. The evolving U.N. codes for the conduct of TNCs represent this type of expanded discourse, and offer a broader framework for the study of injurious actions by TNCs than does limiting our inquiry to the laws of nation states.

CONCLUSION: TOWARD A DEFINITION OF CORPORATE TRANSGRESSIONS

Where injurious actions by TNCs violate existing national laws there is little conceptual difficulty in placing them within the purview of corporate crime studies. However, only by moving beyond national laws can we begin to study transgressions that arise in the space between national legal systems. The study of injurious actions by corporations that operate at the level of the world-system requires a conception of transgression developed through discourse at the same level, and which is capable of adapting to changing forms of injurious corporate action. With this in mind we offer the following expanded framework for the study of corporate wrongdoing:

Corporate transgressions by TNCs encompass any action in pursuit of corporate goals which violates national laws, or international standards such as codes of conduct for TNCs developed within the U.N., or which results in social injury analogous in severity and source to that caused by corporate violations of law or international standards.

We have substituted the term corporate *transgressions* for the more common phrase corporate *crime* for two reasons. First, the term transgressions avoids the semantic and theoretical problems that arise when corporate actions that are not specifically adjudicable under law are defined as *crime*. Second, the concept of *transgression* retains a sense of fundamental wrongfulness similar to that associated with "crime." This references *our* commitment to the reduction of avoidable, injurious actions committed against people by organizations in the pursuit of capital accumulation. We prefer the concept of corporate transgression to that of "corporate deviance," which can encompass any action that offends any organized constituency, whether it be consumers or stockholders (Ermann and Lundman, 1982:16–19). The term corporate transgressions is less relativistic and better conveys, we feel, the severity of harm that can arise from the actions of TNCs.

The general principles outlined in the U.N. codes, as well as the specific provisions under each, provide a conceptual framework which allows us to expand the scope of inquiry without the epistemological hazards of definitions derived from personal conceptions of human rights. The U.N. codes represent the current stage of political struggle to refine the concept of human rights, and rights of national sovereignty, *vis-a-vis* large, transnational, corporate institutions. As such they are the appropriate reference point for understanding what constitutes transgressions by these institutions.

In addition, definitions of corporate transgressions evolved at a world level through a process in which all members of the world community participate represents a type of expanded discourse. This expanded discourse offers greater possibilities for the development of critical reflexivity where injuries by TNCs are concerned than do the laws of individual nations. The U.N. codes are not products of Habermas' ideal form of discourse conducted in the absence of all force except the better argument. However, they represent concepts of transgression negotiated in a context *freer* of the political pressures and limitation on viewpoints that surround the more hegemonic processes of national legislation. The discourse surrounding the U.N. codes incorporates a broader range of voices, some of which are silent within individual nation-states. Representatives of the non-aligned developing nations, the developed free-market states, and the developed and developing planned-economy states have each had opportunities to articulate their conceptions of corporate transgression, and to negotiate for provisions consistent with their views (U.N. Chronicle, July, 1983:103). This interplay of perspectives provides a climate wherein the normally hidden validity claims of legal systems in different nations are revealed for critical assessment.

We recognize that truly equal input into the deviance-defining process is not easily or likely to be achieved in any political context, including the United Nations. However, the political process surrounding the development of the U.N. consumer and corporate codes brings together into a single communicative forum a wider range of participants and perspectives than national debates. Consequently, a broader range of validity claims regarding the control of corporate activities is revealed for examination than in national forums. For those whose interest is the definitional process underlying concepts of corporate deviance, the opportunity to examine the conflicting validity claims that arise within the context of international debate regarding the behavior of TNCs is invaluable.

The inclusion of injuries that are demonstrably analogous in severity and source to those which violate national laws or international standards – even if they do not violate these laws or standards – advances both the behavioral and the definitional research domains in the study of injurious corporate actions.[5] Corporate crime studies regarding the organization and causation of injurious corporate actions are primarily concerned with explaining and eventually controlling these injurious actions. As shown by cases such as Nestles' marketing of breast milk substitutes (Chetley, 1979), or the current spread of genetic engineering beyond the reach of existing national laws (Schneider, 1986a, 1986b), new forms of injurious corporate actions can emerge more swiftly than laws or standards aimed at controlling them. Excluding analogous forms of corporate injuries because they have not been politically defined as transgressive confounds the behavioral paradigm with inappropriate definitional criteria. It places the behavioral paradigm under the authority of political processes. Inclusion of analogous corporate injuries advances the behavioral paradigm within corporate crime studies in another way. It makes it possible to compare the organization and causation of injurious actions that are defined as transgressive with those that are not. Comparisons of this type will improve our understanding of the relationship between causation and control of corporate behavior.

Inclusion of analogous forms of corporate injury is essential for any real development within the definitional research domain. A necessary component of any mature inquiry into the application of meaning to corporate behavior is comparative analyses of the processes whereby some corporate injuries are selected for control while others are defined as acceptable or necessary consequences of economic practices. Excluding injurious activities from definitional studies because they have not been politically defined as transgressive closes off this crucial area of inquiry. The study of injurious actions by TNCs can make substantial contributions to the definitional paradigm in corporate crime studies—but only if our conceptualizations do not prohibit us from examining the processes by which some forms of corporate injury are defined as transgressive at either the national or international level and others are not. In general, we suggest that researchers interested in the study of corporate crime by TNCs maintain a clear distinction between behavioral and definitional research domains, recognize the limitations of legal criteria for setting the scope of study, and expand existing frameworks to include both violations of international standards of corporate conduct and all other analogous forms of corporate transgression.

Notes

*We would like to thank David Ermann, David Kowalewski, Martha Huggins, Marjorie Zatz, and several anonymous reviewers for helpful comments on an earlier draft of this paper. Correspondence to: Michalowski, Department of Sociology and Anthropology, University of North Carolina at Charlotte, Charlotte, NC 28223.

1. There is an ideological distinction and a political debate over whether the term "transnational corporation" or the designation "multinational corporation" should be used to name the modern world-company. The term *trans*/national implies an entity with an existence above and beyond the states in which it operates, while "multinational" suggests only a business with operations *in* more than one country. We use the term "transnational" here for two reasons. First, we agree with the theory that the corporations in question have an existence that *trans*/cends the nation state. Second, the designation "transnational corporations" or "TNCs" is consistent with the majority of the United Nations documents regarding business across borders.

2. For example see: Clinard (1946); Clinard and Yeager (1980); Conklin (1977); Denzin (1977); Edelhertz (1970); Farberman (1975); Geis (1967); Hartung (1950); Leonard and Weber (1970); Shapiro (1984); Shover (1980); Sutherland (1940, 1949); Vaughn (1983).

3. See in particular Amin (1974); Chase-Dunn (1978); Frank (1975); Sunkle (1973); and Wallerstein (1979).

4. From the point of view of TNCs there are limits to the attractiveness of strict controls over labor rights. Regimes that are so repressive as to lose legitimacy can incite significant popular unrest. If the regime is not able to control this opposition, the resulting political instability can negate the benefits of a strong anti-labor government (International Labour Organization, 1985:62–63). The 1986 ouster of Marcos, a strong anti-labor dictator, from the Philippines is a case in point.

5. For elaborated discussions of analogous social injury see Kramer (1985) and Michalowski (1985:314–18).

References

Advertising Age
  1984   "U.N. proposed regulations menacing to U.S. marketers." Advertising Age 55 (June):58.
Amin, Samir
  1974   Accumulation on a World Scale. New York: Monthly Review Press.

Barnet, Richard J. and Ronald E. Muller
1974   Global Reach: The Power of the Multinational Corporations. New York: Simon and Schuster.
Blake, David H. and Robert S. Walters
1976   The Politics of Global Economic Relations. Englewood Cliffs, NJ: Prentice Hall.
Blake, Michael
1980   A Case Study on Women in Industry. Bangkok: Asian and Pacific Centre for Women and Development.
Blum-West, Steve and Timothy J. Carter
1983   "Bringing white-collar crime back in: an examination of crimes and torts." Social Problems 30:545–54.
Bonner, Raymond
1983   "U.S. ties to anti-Sandinistas are reported to be extensive." New York Times, April 3:A1.
Braithwaite, John
1984   Corporate Crime in the Pharmaceutical Industry. London: Routledge and Kegan Paul.
1985   "White collar crime." Annual Review of Sociology 11:1–25.
Bull, David
1982   A Growing Problem: Pesticides and the Third World Poor. Oxford: Oxfam.
Burns, James J.
1984   "International siting priorities for a high technology firm." Industrial Development 153:11.
Caplan, Richard and Scott L. Malcomson
1986   "Giving the U.N. the business." The Nation 243 (August 16):108–12.
Castleman, Barry
1975   "The flight of hazardous industries to unregulating countries." Report issued by the Maryland Public Interest Group.
1978   "How we export dangerous industries." Business and Society Review 27:7–14.
1979   "The export of hazardous factories to developing nations." International Journal of Health Services 9:569–606.
Cavanagh, John and Fredrick F. Clairmonte
1983   "From corporations to conglomerates." Multinational Monitor 4 (January):16–20.
Centre on Transnational Corporations
1985   Environmental Aspects of the Activities of Transnational Corporations: A Survey. New York: Centre on Transnational Corporations.
Chase-Dunn, Christopher K.
1978   "Core-periphery relations: the effects of core competition." Pp. 159–76 In Barbara H. Kaplan (ed.), Social Change in the Capitalist World Economy. Beverly Hills, CA: Sage.
Chemical Week
1981   "Codes of conduct: worry over new restraints on multinationals." Chemical Week 129 (July 15):15.
Chetley, A.
1979   The Baby Killer Scandal. London: War on Want.
Clinard, Marshall B.
1946   "The black market." American Sociological Review 11:250–70.
Clinard, Marshall B. and Peter Yeager
1980   Corporate Crime. New York: Free Press.
Coleman, James W.
1983   The Criminal Elite: The Sociology of White Collar Crime. New York: St. Martin's.
Conklin, John
1977   Illegal But Not Criminal: Business Crime in America. Englewood Cliffs, NJ: Prentice Hall.

CTC Reporter
1982   "The United Nations Code of Conduct on Transnational Corporations." The CTC Reporter 12:3–4, 23–26.
Cultural Survival
1982   "Poisons in the Third World." Cultural Survival 6 (Winter): 3–10.
del Olmo, Rosa
1986   "Aerobiologia y drogas." Paper presented at the Fourth Annual Latin-American Conference of Critical Criminology, Havana.
Denzin, Norman K.
1977   "Notes on the criminogenic hypothesis: a case study of the liquor industry." American Sociological Review 42:905–20.
Dewar, Helen
1978   "Study cites firms flight to Third World to avoid safeguards." Washington Post, June 30:A2.
Dollars and Sense
1984   "High tech and health." Dollars and Sense 99 (September):6–7.
Dowie, Mark and Tracy Johnston
1976   "A case of corporate malpractice." Mother Jones 2 (November):36–50.
Edelhertz, Herbert
1970   The Nature, Impact and Prosecution of White Collar Crime. Washington, DC: National Institute of Law Enforcement and Criminal Justice.
Ermann, David M. and Richard J. Lundman
1982   Corporate Deviance. New York: CBS College Publishing.
Farberman, Harvey
1975   "A criminogenic market structure: the automobile industry." Sociological Quarterly 16:438–57.
Fernandez-Kelly, Maria
1983   For We Are Sold, I and My People. Albany: State University of New York Press.
Flamm, Kenneth
1985   "The semiconductor industry." Pp. 38–138 In Joseph Grunwald and Kenneth Flamm (eds.), The Global Factory. Washington, DC: The Brookings Institution.
Fortune
1980   "The corporation haters." Fortune 101 (June, 16):126–36.
Frank, Andre Gunder
1975   On Capitalist Underdevelopment. London: Oxford University Press.
Fuentes, Annette and Barbara Ehrenreich
1983   "The new factory girls." Multinational Monitor 4 (August):5–10.
Geis, Gilbert
1967   "The heavy electrical equipment antitrust cases of 1961." In Marshall B. Clinard and Richard Quinney (eds.), Criminal Behavior Systems. New York: Holt, Rinehart and Winston.
Grunwald, Joseph and Kenneth Flamm
1985   The Global Factory. Washington, DC: The Brookings Institution.
Habermas, Jürgen
1973   Legitimation Crisis. Boston: Beacon Press.
1974   Theory and Practice. London: Heinemann.
Hamilton, Geoffrey
1983   "International codes of conduct for multinationals." Multinational Business 12 (Summer):1–10.
Hartung, Frank E.
1950   "White collar offenses in the wholesale meat industry." American Journal of Sociology 56:22–34.
Hazarka, Sanjoy
1984   "Gas leak in India said to kill 410." New York Times, December 4:A1.

Heilbroner, Karl
1974   An Inquiry Into the Human Prospect. New York: Norton.
Heritage Foundation
1983   Multinationals: First Victim of the U.N. War on Free Enterprise. Washington, DC:
        Heritage Foundation.
International Labour Organization
1985   Women Workers in Multinational Enterprises in Developing Countries. Geneva:
        International Labour Office.
Jensen, Michael
1973   "Allende target of proposals." New York Times, June 22:A1.
Kenworthy, E.W.
1973   "Senate group finds ITT and U.S. at fault on Chile." New York Times, June 22:A1.
Kirkpatrick, Jeane
1983   "Kirkpatrick criticizes U.N. for 'class rule' ideology." Multinational Monitor 4 (Janu-
        ary):8.
Kramer, Ronald C.
1985   "Defining the concept of crime: a humanistic perspective." Journal of Sociology and
        Social Welfare 12:469–87.
LaDou, James
1984   "The not-so-clean business of making chips." Technology Review 87:23–36.
LaFeber, Walter
1984   Inevitable Revolutions: The United States in Central America. New York: Norton.
Langley, Lester P.
1985   Central America: The Real Stakes. New York: Crown.
Leonard, H. Jeffrey and Christopher J. Duerksen
1981   "Environmental regulation and the location of industry: an international perspec-
        tive." Columbia Journal of World Business 15:55–68.
Leonard, William N. and Marvin Weber
1970   "Automakers and dealers: a study of criminogenic market forces." Law and Society
        Review 4:407–24.
Lim, Linda
1983   "Are multinationals the problem? No." Multinational Monitor 4 (August):15.
Lindblom, Charles
1977   Politics and Markets. New York: Basic Books.
Mattelart, Armand
1983   Transnationals and the Third World. South Hadley, MA: Bergin and Garvey.
Medawar, Charles
1979   Insult or Injury. London: Social Audit.
Michalowski, Raymond
1985   Order, Law, and Crime. New York: Random House.
Mintz, Morton
1985   At Any Cost: Corporate Greed, Women and the Dalkon Shield. New York: Pan-
        theon.
Multinational Monitor
1984   "Profits climb; foreign investments fall." Multinational Monitor 5 (January):11.
Nash, June
1979   "Men, women and the international division of labor." Paper presented at the
        annual meetings of the Latin American Studies Association, Philadelphia.
New York Times
1978   "Safety panel votes to ban export of Tris sleepwear." New York Times, May 7:A26.
O'Connor, David and Chia Siew Wong
1983   "Are multinationals the problem? Yes." Multinational Monitor 4 (August):16.
Ong, A.
1983   "Global industries and Malay peasants in peninsular Malaysia." Pp. 426–39 in

June Nash and M.P. Fernandez-Kelly (eds.), Women, Men and the International Division of Labor. Albany, NY: State University of New York Press.

Pearson, Charles and Anthony Pryor
1978   Environment: North and South. New York: Wiley Interscience.

Randall, Kenneth
1977   "Forward." Pp. i–ix in James R. Basche Jr. (ed.), Production Costs, Trends and Outlook: A Study of International Business Experience. New York: Conference Board.

Robinson, John
1983   Multinationals and Political Control. New York: St. Martin's Press.

Schrager, Laura Shill and James F. Short, Jr.
1978   "Toward a sociology of organizational crime." Social Problems 25:407–19.

Schneider, Keith
1986a   "Argentina protests use of live vaccine by scientists of U.S." New York Times, November 11:A1.
1986b   "Second gene-altered vaccine tested outside the U.S." New York Times, November 13:A28.

Schwendinger, Herman and Julia Schwendinger
1970   "Defenders of order or guardians of human rights." Issues in Criminology 5:123–57.

Sellin, Thorsten
1938   Culture Conflict and Crime. New York: Social Science Research Council.

Shapiro, Susan
1983   "The new moral entrepreneurs: corporate crime crusaders." Contemporary Sociology 12:304–307.
1984   Wayward Capitalists. New Haven: Yale University Press.

Shover, Neal
1980   "The criminalization of corporate behavior: federal surface coal mining." Pp. 98–125 in Gilbert Geis and Ezra Stotland (eds.), White Collar Crime: Theory and Research. Beverly Hills, CA: Sage.

Simon, David R. and D. Stanley Eitzen
1986   Elite Deviance. Second Edition. Boston: Allyn and Bacon.

Strauss, Robert
1978   Interview. Environment Reporter 9 (July):451.

Sunkle, Oscar
1973   "Transnational capital and national disintegration in Latin America." Social and Economic Studies 22:132–71.

Sutherland, Edwin H.
1940   "White collar criminality." American Sociological Review 5:1–12.
[1949] White Collar Crime. New York: Holt, Rinehart and Winston.

Tappan, Paul.
1947   "Who is the criminal?" American Sociological Review 12:96–102.

Tift, Larry and Donald Sullivan
1980   The Struggle to be Human: Crime, Criminology, and Anarchism. Sanday, Orkney U.K.: Cinfuegos Press.

United Nations
1978   Transnational Corporations in World Development. New York: U.N. Commission on Transnational Corporations.

U.N. Chronicle
1983   "Despite further agreement on code work remains incomplete." U.N. Chronicle 20:102–104.

U.S. Department of Commerce
1981   U.S. Direct Investment Abroad. Washington, DC: U.S. Government Printing Office.
1984   U.S. Direct Investment Abroad. Washington, DC: U.S. Government Printing Office.

Vaughn, Diane
    1983   Controlling Unlawful Organizational Behavior. Chicago: University of Chicago Press.
Vieira, Anna Da Soledade
    1985   Environmental Information in Developing Nations: Politics and Policies. Westport, CT: Greenwood Press.
Wallerstein, Immanuel
    1979   The Capitalist World-Economy. New York: Cambridge.
Weidenbaum, Murray
    1983   "The U.N.'s bid to play consumer cop." New York Times, June 26:E1.
    1984   "U.N.'s regulatory riptide poses threat to international trade." Christian Science Monitor, January 5:B5.
Weir, David and Mark Schapiro
    1981   Circle of Poison: Pesticides and People in a Hungry World. San Francisco: Institute for Food and Development Policy.

28. The State and Organizing Crime

WILLIAM J. CHAMBLISS

In Seattle it was not obvious how the various rackets ranked in order of importance. Drugs, gambling, fraud, and stolen property were as intertwined as straw in a bale of hay. When I began investigating national and international crime networks, however, it became clear almost immediately that smuggling narcotics and military weapons was head and shoulders above other forms of organized criminality in importance, i.e., profits. This difference between local and national and international crime networks is of profound importance. Local networks handle the wholesale and retail traffic in drugs. The profits are substantially greater than those from bookmaking, poker games, stolen property, and other rackets, but the importance of drugs on the retail market in a city the size of Seattle does not overshadow the importance of other illegal enterprises.

On the national and international level, however, the smuggling of arms and drugs is the foundation on which rests a mammoth enterprise amounting to hundreds of billions of dollars annually. It is an enterprise which not only affects millions of lives directly, it affects international relations, governments, and war.

OPIUM: THE MAGIC PLANT

Historically, opium and its powerful commercial derivatives, morphine and heroin, are among the most important products smuggled internationally. While opium is grown in many parts of the world, the most important centers of production traditionally have been the Middle East (especially Turkey, Pakistan, and Afghanistan) and Southeast Asia (especially the Golden Triangle which covers parts of Laos, Burma and Thailand).

Opium grows abundantly and with little cultivation in the mountain chain that stretches from Turkey through Afghanistan, India, China, and into the Golden Triangle. In the eighth century Turkish traders carried opium to Asia and exchanged it for teas and spices. In the sixteenth century Portuguese ships cruising the oriental seas pirated opium from local traders and used it to trade for teas and spices. In the nineteenth century England went to war against China on two occasions to protect its merchants' profitable trade in opium. In the early 1900s a German pharmaceutical company, Bayer, developed a drug that could be chemically produced from the opium plant. Bayer's drug had the same euphoric and analgesic effect as opium but was more potent and had the advantage of being injectable. Bayer called their new product, which they claimed was nonaddictive, heroin.

Bayer lied. Not only was heroin even more addictive than raw opium, it was deadly dangerous if the dosage was not carefully controlled. In 1914 the sale or possession of opium and its derivatives, including heroin, was made illegal with the passage of the Harrison Act. By 1914, however, there was a large population of opium-addicted workers, housewives, and merchants, not to mention the Chinese immigrants who brought opium habits with them when they emigrated to the U.S.

It is an economic axiom that where there is a market, large profits, and an available supply of a commodity, people will find ways to supply the demand. The merchants who profited from opium and heroin when it was legal did not immediately cease their operations simply because of international agreements and statutes making their business illegal. Quite predictably they continued to trade in opium, although the illegal nature of the enterprise changed the character of the business considerably. Distribution practices had to change, police and customs officials had to be bribed, but the import business thrived in spite of the complications that accompanied the illegality of the enterprise.

As we saw in the last chapter, when prohibition ended in 1932, the specialists and organizations that had grown up to facilitate the smuggling of alcoholic beverages transferred their talents, contacts, and personnel to the smuggling of drugs. When, in the thirties, marijuana and cocaine were added to the list of illegal drugs, the business expanded and smuggling became an international enterprise of gigantic proportions.

The affluence in the U.S. that followed the end of World War II brought record sales to the manufacturers and industrialists. The affluence was equally kind to the purveyors of illegal commodities and services. Between 1945 and 1965 narcotics consumption in the United States and Europe grew by leaps and bounds. First the ghettoes then the middle and upper classes comprised the market, just as the mining towns and factories had been the mainstay of the market in the 1800s.

LANSKY TRAVELS TO EUROPE

In the 1950s the ever-watchful business eye of Meyer Lansky saw the potential. Lansky was in a good position to get into the narcotics business in a big way. His experience gained during prohibition in smuggling alcoholic beverages gave him the know-how and the international connections necessary for successful smuggling operations. He knew where to locate investors with "venture capital," was connected with banks, politicians, and law enforcement people nationally and internationally, and could take advantage of all these networks to maximize profits and minimize risks for himself and his investors.

Lansky took a trip to Marseilles, France in the late fifties. Following World War II this French port city became the international center for converting raw opium from the Middle East into the highly refined #4 heroin much in demand in America. Lansky carried with him a satchel containing six million dollars.[1] With this he contracted with Marseilles' heroin manufacturers to provide his network with a steady supply of high quality heroin. He also dispatched key members of his organization to Latin America, particularly to Paraguay and Cuba, where cooperative government officials joined the network to assure safe passage of heroin through their countries and into the United States.

The enterprise worked marvelously for a number of years despite the mostly symbolic efforts of drug enforcement agencies and international commissions to break up illegal drug shipments. Of course, adjustments had to be made from time to time: When Fidel Castro led a successful revolution against Lansky's close ally, Cuban dictator Batista, an alternative route for smuggling drugs through Latin America into the U.S. had to be found. Temporary disruptions occurred but the overall pattern of drug trafficking survived well into the 1960s. The pattern changed dramatically, however, after the United States became mired in a war in Southeast Asia.

OPIUM AND THE VIETNAM WAR

From the early days of colonialism in Indochina, the French depended on the profits from opium to finance the colonial government. In 1946 when the Vietnamese rebelled against the French, France's dependence on profits from the opium traffic increased.[2] The cost to the French of sustaining colonialism increased but more importantly, the French needed the military support of the warlords of the Golden Triangle who maintained their control of the hill tribes by serving as a conduit for the opium produced in the hills. France also depended on the support of the hill tribe warlords because of their proximity to the Chinese border and France's fear that China would enter the war on the side of the insurgents. That support, in turn, required that France cooperate with the production and distribution of opium.

When the United States entered the Vietnam War after France's ignominious defeat at Dien Bien Phu, the U.S. inherited the dependence on opium. The U.S. military and particularly the CIA set about organizing opium smuggling out of Southeast Asia to an unprecedented degree. The Central Intelligence Agency arranged to pick up and distribute the opium to the major cities of Southeast Asia where laboratories sprang up that converted the opium into morphine and heroin. For this purpose, the CIA established an airline called Air America: ". . . in 1965, the CIA's airline, Air America, began flying Meo opium out of the hills to Long Cheng and Vientiane."[3]

During these years Gen. Vang Pao, commander of a CIA-run secret army, operated a heroin factory at Long Cheng, headquarters for CIA operations in northern Laos.[4]

In 1974 I went to Thailand to find out how the opium from the Golden Triangle was getting out of Asia and into the United States. I lived in Chiang Mai, a northern city that is a center for the organization and coordination of opium traffic in Southeast Asia. During my four months in Chiang Mai, I interviewed CIA agents, drug enforcement agents, Thai officials, and opium smugglers and growers. My research in Thailand and the Golden Triangle in 1974 established beyond a doubt the connection between the CIA, U.S. politics, and international narcotics smuggling. Interviews with present and former CIA agents in Southeast Asia confirmed that the CIA was complicitous in the movement of opium out of the Golden Triangle to heroin laboratories in Saigon, Hong Kong, and Bangkok. Within ten days of arriving in Chiang Mai, I was able to interview several former CIA operatives. They all told the same story: the CIA and its airline, Air America, worked hand in glove with the warlords of the Golden Triangle to smuggle opium. A small Thai, Pok, who worked with the CIA from 1965 to 1974, was unequivocal: "The CIA is the biggest opium dealer in Asia. Their planes fly into the hills, pick up crates of opium, and deliver them to airports in Bangkok and

Hong Kong. I've been there when they land and watched the crates unloaded and stored in warehouses at the airport."

General Ouane Rattikone, former General of the Laotian Army, told me:

> I organized the hill tribes and provided protection for the shipment of the raw opium through the hills. It's very dangerous because there are many people willing to die to get their hands on opium. But we provide the military protection necessary. When we reach the flatland where planes can land Air America flies in and picks up the opium. It is hypocritical of America to criticize this. If we (Laos) did not have the profits from opium production our government would fall to the communists in twenty four hours. The Americans know this and they do the only thing they can.[5]

An American soldier who was an eyewitness to the opium trafficking in Laos reported:

> There is trouble in Long Cheng, the secret Central Intelligence Agency military base in north Laos. Meo guerilla leaders are demanding full operational control over the dozen or so aircraft that work daily from this 5,000-foot paved runway in the middle of nowhere. The Americans resist, knowing only too well what the implications of giving in would be. They hassle. Everybody, of course, knows the stakes in this little game. Everybody knows that the Meo have their own ideas as to how these flying machines can be put to efficient use. It's there for everybody to see: the neat, banana-leaf wrapped cubes of raw opium stacked neatly alongside the runway, not quite a hundred yards from the air-conditioned shack from which Agency officers command a clear view of the entire area. In the end, General Vang Pao, commander of the Meo army, has his way. The Americans who are supporting this army might regret the small loss of operational control. But the war must go on. Anyway, even if the Meo rack up all the planes, more can always be brought in. . . . It mattered not what ancillary problems were created by our presence. Not, that is, so long as the Meo leadership could keep their wards in the boondocks fighting and dying in the name of, for these unfortunates anyway, some nebulous cause. If for the Americans this meant, as it did, increasing the potential reward, or quite literally, payoffs, to the Meo leadership in the form of a carte blanche to exploit U.S.-supplied airplanes and communications gear to the end of greatly streamlining opium operations, well, that was the price to be paid.[6]

Time and again in interviews with people close to the opium traffic, the Laotian city of Long Cheng was mentioned as a major transfer point for opium out of the Golden Triangle. Several of my CIA informants, the American soldier quoted above as well as General Ouane Rattikone, told of the importance of Long Cheng. At the time I paid little attention to the names of the CIA operatives who I was told were running the operation at Long Cheng in the 1960s. It was only years later when their names resurfaced in connection with a bank in Sydney, Australia, that I came to see the significance of their work in Long Cheng. Among the dozens of names given to me as American CIA agents who were at Long Cheng in the 1960s were four men whose subsequent careers raise serious questions about the role of the CIA in international drug trafficking and arms smuggling after the end of the Vietnam War. I was told, and recent reports support the allegation, that Michael Hand worked at Long Cheng with Thomas Clines and Theodore Shackley.[7] To understand the importance of these relationships let us look in some detail at the career of the Green Beret, Vietnam veteran and Long Cheng CIA operative, Michael Hand.

MICHAEL HAND GOES TO AUSTRALIA

In 1969 Michael Hand left Vietnam and moved to Sydney, Australia. There is no evidence that he was still working for the CIA or the U.S. military. It must be remembered, however, that it is standard intelligence practice to supply undercover agents with phony papers that end their military or intelligence career while in fact they remain career military or intelligence officers.

On arriving in Australia Michael Hand entered into a business partnership with an Australian national, Frank Nugan. They formed an investment company and began several businesses. In 1976 Michael Hand and Frank Nugan established the Nugan Hand Bank, Sydney,[8] which began as a storefront operation with minimal capital investment but which almost immediately had deposits of over $25 million from large deposits of secret funds made by narcotics traffickers, arms smugglers, and the CIA.

In addition to the records from the bank that suggest the CIA was using the bank as a conduit for its funds, the bank's connection to the CIA and other U.S. intelligence agencies is evidenced by the people who formed the directors and principal officers of the bank, including:

• Admiral Earl F. Yates, president of the Nugan Hand Bank, was, during the Vietnam War, chief of staff for strategic planning of U.S. forces in Asia and the Pacific.
• General Edwin F. Black, president of Nugan Hand's Hawaii branch, was commander of U.S. troops in Thailand during the Vietnam War and, after the war, assistant army chief of staff for the Pacific.
• General Erle Cocke, Jr., head of the Nugan Hand Washington office.
• George Farris worked in the Nugan Hand Hong Kong and Washington, D.C., offices. He was a military intelligence specialist who worked in a special forces training base in the Pacific.
• Bernie Houghton was Nugan Hand's representative in Saudi Arabia. Houghton was also a U.S. naval intelligence undercover agent.
• Tom Clines, director of training in the CIA's Clandestine Service, London operative for Nugan Hand who helped the takeover of a London-based bank.
• Dale Holmgreen, former flight service manager in Vietnam for Civil Air Transport, which became Air America. He was on the board of directors of Nugan Hand and ran their Taiwan office.
• Walt McDonald, an economist and former deputy director of the CIA for economic research, specializing in petroleum. He became a consultant to Nugan Hand and served as head of its Annapolis, Maryland, branch.
• General Roy Manor ran the Nugan Hand Philippine office. He was a Vietnam veteran who helped coordinate the aborted attempt to rescue the Iranian hostages and was chief of staff for U.S. Pacific Command and the U.S. government's liaison officer to Philippine President Ferdinand Marcos.

On the board of directors of the parent company formed by Michael Hand that preceded the Nugan Hand Bank were Grant Walters, Robert Peterson, David M. Houton, and Spencer Smith, all of whom listed their address as c/o Air America, Army Post Office, San Francisco, California. Also working through the Nugan Hand Bank was Edwin F. Wilson, a CIA agent involved in smuggling arms to the Middle East and later sentenced to prison by a U.S. court for smuggling illegal arms to Libya. Edwin Wilson's associate in Mid-East arms shipments was Theodore S. Shackley, head of the Miami, Florida, CIA station. It was Shackley who, along with Rafael "Chi Chi" Quintero, a Cuban-American, forged the plot to assassinate Fidel Castro by using organized crime figures Santo Trafficante, Jr., John Roselli, and Sam Giancana.[9] In 1973, when William Colby was made director of the Central Intelligence Agency, Shackley replaced him as head of covert operations for the Far East.

In 1980 the Nugan Hand Bank began to unravel. Frank Nugan, Hand's Australian partner, was found dead in his Mercedes on a remote road. Nugan died of gunshot wounds. In his pants pocket was the business card of Nugan Hand's lawyer, William Colby. On the back of the card was Colby's itinerary for his upcoming trip to Australia. Next to the dead Frank Nugan was a Bible with a meat-pie wrapper marking a page. On the wrapper were the names of William Colby and Bob Wilson, the then California congressman who was the ranking Republican member of the House Armed Services Committee. The police determined the cause of death to be suicide.

Australian bank auditors called in to investigate the bank opened up a veritable Pandora's box of crime and intrigue. Millions of dollars were missing. The list of bank depositors revealed that many of the principal depositors of the bank were known to be connected with international narcotics trafficking in Asia and the Middle East. The U.S. Central Intelligence Agency was using Nugan Hand to finance gun smuggling and a vast array of other clandestine operations. Bank records also revealed that they spent millions of dollars on political campaigns throughout the world in an effort to secure the election of politicians to their liking. The CIA even used the bank to pay for a disinformation campaign designed to unseat the liberal Australian Prime Minister Gough Whitlam. This disinformation campaign falsely accused Whitlam of various immoral and illegal acts. Whitlam was forced out of office by the British government invoking powers to impeach Commonwealth officials.

Once auditors discovered millions of dollars were missing from the Nugan Hand Bank and the connection between the bank and the CIA was revealed, a CIA agent from Washington, D.C., flew to Sydney with a false passport for Michael Hand. He and Hand flew to the United States and Michael Hand disappeared.[10] Inquiries to Michael Hand's father were answered with denials of any information about him.

The CIA's intimate involvement in the Nugan Hand bank owned by one of its former (or perhaps continuing) operatives combined with the uncanny number of intelligence and military officers connected to the bank makes it untenable to suppose that the CIA was unaware of the bank's involvement in money laundering and the financing of international narcotics smuggling. A more plausible explanation is that the CIA did not stop its practice of supporting and cooperating with narcotics smugglers at the end of the Vietnam War but continued to promote these relationships as a way of paying for clandestine operations and continuing the support of drug traffickers they had come to depend upon.[11]

At least since the 1980s the CIA has been cooperating with narcotics smugglers in Latin America as a means of supporting the guerilla war against the Nicaraguan government. In her excellent study of the CIA, Leslie Cockburn quotes Ramon Milian-

Rodriguez who, until his indictment in 1983, laundered $200 million a month for clients such as Pablo Escobar and Jorge Ochoa who were in control of about 40 percent of the world's supply of cocaine:

> There seems to be a big to-do about the CIA having connections with drugs. It might be news now, but it's something that has been quite prevalent for quite some time. Outside of the United States, drug dealers are very powerful people. They have the ability to put governments in power or topple them, if they do it subtly. They have cash. The CIA deals primarily with items outside of the U.S. If they want to deal in foreign countries' policies and politics, they are going to run up against, or run with, the drug dealers. It can't be done any other way . . . if the end result is for the benefit of everyone, it usually works. You know, whether the players are the contras today or the Tupamaros or whatever, as far as I've been able to see, that's the way it's always been.[12]

An article in the *Washington Post* claims that independent counsel Lawrence E. Walsh was given a report detailing a connection between a Colombian cocaine trafficker and Southern Air Transport.[13] Southern Air Transport is a subsidiary of Air America and is the airline which flew a C123 that was shot down in Nicaragua on October 6, 1986, while delivering an illegal shipment of arms to the Contras. Southern Air Transport also was involved in illegally smuggling arms to Iran and to the Contras after Congress passed the Boland Amendment, which prohibited the shipment of military aid to the Contras.

Thus, the evidence is very persuasive that the CIA has become the world's most important smuggling operation dealing in narcotics and military weapons. As a consequence, there have been some fundamental changes in organized crime in the last twenty years. These changes help to explain the "unusual events" I observed in the late sixties. The underlying cause and the consequence of the changes can be summarized thus:

1. Political parties in the United States depend on acquiring vast sums of money for political campaigns. One source of political money that is unusually valuable to political parties is money from organized crime activities. This is so because the money can be easily hidden and can be used as either a source of personal profiteering or political campaign expenditures.

2. Organized crime activities such as gambling, fraud, smuggling, and usury depend on the cooperation of law enforcement officials, politicans, and legitimate business people for successful operation.

3. Therefore it follows that a symbiotic relationship serving shared interests will develop between people capable of providing illegal goods and services, legitimate business people, politicians, and law enforcement agencies.

4. When criminal networks were developing in the thirties and forties, the most successful entrepreneurs in these networks aligned themselves with Democrats. This resulted quite naturally from the fact that the Democrats during these years were the party of greatest power. For an understanding of organized crime in America, two important exceptions to this pattern are California and Florida, both of which since World War II have split their voting between the Republicans and the Democrats.

5. Meyer Lansky's established connections to the Democrats led Santo Trafficante, Jr., (and others such as Carlos Marcello of New Orleans) to forge political alliances with Republicans, which he did quite successfully both in Florida and nationally.

6. With Richard Nixon's election in 1968 (which dovetailed, incidentally, with the election of a Republican governor of Nevada), law enforcement agencies and policies were unleashed, which effectively, undermined some of Meyer Lansky's most important financial holdings. These efforts included (1) forcing him to sell his holdings in casinos in Nevada to Howard Hughes, a longtime supporter of Richard Nixon and the Nevada Republican Governor Paul Laxalt; (2) forcing him to sell his interests in Miami and Key West banks to a consortium of businessmen including Nixon's lifelong, closest friend, Bebe Rebozo; (3) obtaining indictments against him in Florida and Nevada and putting pressure on Turkey and France to conscientiously enforce the laws against the production of opium and heroin. Since Lansky's heroin trafficking empire depended on the "French Connection," this effort was a significant blow to Lansky's enterprises.

7. Lansky struck back by trying to influence elections on the state and national level of people who would intervene in his behalf. One of the places he offered financial backing was Seattle, Washington, which is why he offered to underwrite the campaign of a Democrat against a Republican.

8. Lansky's longtime competitor in Florida and Cuba (see below), Santo Trafficante, Jr., went to Southeast Asia and arranged for the shipment of heroin into the United States.

9. The U.S. government threatened to cut off military aid to Turkey if they did not make a concerted effort to curtail opium production. The Drug Enforcement Agency posted over a hundred agents in France to work with the French to eliminate heroin production in Marseilles.

10. In Southeast Asia the CIA cooperated with opium and heroin producers and the proportion of heroin coming into the United States that originated in Southeast Asia rose to almost 50 percent in the years between 1968 and 1972. The amount of heroin originating in the Middle East dropped proportionately.

11. On the municipal and state levels, U.S. attorneys were given the green light to investigate political and law enforcement corruption in cities with powerful Democratic Party machines. Particularly targeted were cities like Chicago and Seattle where the organized crime network was allied with Democratic politicians. Chicago was especially important because of the wealth and power controlled by Sam Giancana, who dominated one of Chicago's most powerful organized crime networks and supported the Democratic Party locally and nationally. Giancana was so powerful that he claimed to have been responsible for John F. Kennedy's election (and Nixon's defeat) in 1960.[14]

12. During these years, then, between 1968 and 1974, a sea change took place in the power structure of national organized crime networks and in international narcotics and arms smuggling. The CIA, in collaboration with established organized crime network leaders such as Santo Trafficante, Jr., entered into drug trafficking and money laundering through banks that they either owned or substantially controlled.

13. The relationship between the CIA and organized crime networks continued through the 1970s and 1980s and helped finance illegal arms smuggling to Iran and

to the Contras in Nicaragua. In fact, many of the *same* people were involved in the smuggling of arms to Iran and the Contras who played a part in the smuggling of opium in Vietnam. The complicity of the CIA in the illegal smuggling of drugs has apparently expanded out of Southeast Asia in recent years and includes the support of political leaders who control and operate drug smuggling networks in Latin America. Heading this list are military dictators such as Noriega in Panama and the military junta in Haiti.[15] WHY?

Why would the CIA, the National Security Council, the Defense Department, and the State Department become involved in smuggling arms and narcotics, money laundering, and other criminal activities? The answer lies in the structural contradictions that inhere in nation-states.[16]

The military-intelligence establishment in the United States is resolutely committed to fighting the spread of "communism" throughout the world. This mission is not new but has prevailed since the early 1900s. From the point of view of those who are committed to this goal, the sad reality is that the Congress and the presidency are not consistent in their support for the money and policies thought by the front-line warriors to be necessary to accomplish their lofty goals. As a result, programs under way are sometimes undermined by a lack of funding and even by laws that prohibit their continuation (such as the Congress' passage of laws prohibiting support for the Contras). Officials of government agencies adversely affected by political changes are thus placed squarely in a dilemma: if they comply with the new limitations on their activities, they sacrifice their mission. The dilemma is heightened by the fact that they can anticipate future policy changes which would reinstate their resources and their freedom. When that times comes, however, programs adversely affected will be difficult if not impossible to recreate.

A number of events that occurred between 1960 and 1980 left the military and the CIA with badly tarnished images. These events and political changes underscored their vulnerability.

The CIA lost considerable political clout with elected officials when its planned invasion of Cuba (the infamous Bay of Pigs Invasion) was a complete and utter disaster. Perhaps as never before in its history, the U.S. showed itself vulnerable to the resistance of a small nation. The CIA was blamed for this fiasco even though it was the president's decision to go ahead with the plans that he inherited from the previous administration. To add to the agency's problems, the complicity between it and ITT to invade Chile was yet another scar. Although this time successful in its goal to overthrow the government of Chile, it was nonetheless a very controversial enterprise which was made worse by the revelation that the CIA was at least indirectly involved in the assassination of General Renee Schneider, the Chilean army chief of staff. The involvement of the CIA in narcotics smuggling in Vietnam was yet another embarrassment to the agency.

These and other political realities led to a serious breach between Presidents Kennedy, Johnson, Nixon, and Carter and the CIA. During President Nixon's tenure in the White House, one of the CIA's top men, James Angleton, referred to Nixon's national security advisor, Henry Kissinger (who became secretary of state), as "objectively, a Soviet agent."[17] Another top agent of the CIA, James McCord (later implicated in the Watergate burglary), wrote a secret letter to his superior, General Paul Gaynor, in January 1973, in which McCord said:

> When the hundreds of dedicated fine men and women of CIA no longer write intelligence summaries and reports with integrity, without fear of political recrimination—when their fine Director (Richard Helms) is being summarily discharged in order to make way for a politician who will write or rewrite intelligence the way the politicians want them written, instead of the way truth and best judgment dictates, our nation is in the deepest of trouble and freedom itself was never so imperiled. Nazi Germany rose and fell under exactly the same philosophy of governmental operation.[18]

McCord spoke for many of the top military and intelligence officers in the United States when he wrote in his autobiography: "I believed that the whole future of the nation was at stake. If the Administration could get away with this massive crime of Watergate and its cover up, it would certainly stop at nothing thereafter. The precedent such would set for the nation would be beyond belief, beyond recovery, and a disaster beyond any possible reversal, if it were able to succeed in the cover up."[19]

These views show the depth of feeling toward the dangers of political "interference" with what is generally accepted in the military-intelligence establishment as their mission.[20]

When Jimmy Carter was elected president, he appointed Admiral Stansfield Turner as director of the Central Intelligence Agency. At the outset, Turner made it clear that he and the president did not share the agency's view that they were conducting their mission properly.[21] Turner centralized power in the director's office and took an active part in overseeing clandestine and covert operations. He met with a great deal of resistance. Against considerable opposition from within the agency, he reduced the size of the covert operation section from 1,200 to 400 agents. The agency people still refer to this as the "Halloween massacre."

Old hands at the CIA do not think their work is dispensable. They believe zealously, protectively, and one is tempted to say, with religious fervor, that the work they are doing is essential for the salvation of humankind. With threats from both Republican and Democratic administrations, it is not difficult to imagine that the old guard would seek an alternative source of revenue to carry out their mission. The alternative was already in place with the connections to the international narcotics traffic, arms smuggling, the existence of secret corporations incorporated in foreign countries that guaranteed secrecy (such as Panama), and the established links to banks for the laundering of money for covert operations.

While the CIA and its former or present agents were setting up dummy corporations and money-laundering banks throughout the world to facilitate their smuggling operations and to finance their clandestine operations including planned assassinations and the overthrow of governments, they inevitably got involved with international criminal networks whose expertise in smuggling, dummy corporations, money laundering, and clandestine relations with cooperative segments of foreign countries had been successfully cultivated for at least fifty years.

THE AFTERMATH

The CIA's involvement in narcotics and the sea changes taking place in the organization of criminal enterprises in the United States has a ripple effect on American politics and government as well. It was the beginning of the creation of a shadow government, and despite months of congressional hearings and the appointment of a special prosecutor to look into the criminality of government officials, the real nature of the operations and the sinister implications remain unexplored by the congressional committees that by design or from ignorance refuse to inquire into the connections between organized crime networks, narcotics smuggling, and the CIA.

The changes in international arms and drug smuggling are caused by the same structural contradictions that are the source of the creation, maintenance, and characteristics of crime networks that organize gambling, narcotics, prostitution, stolen property, and sundry other criminal activities in the United States.

Notes

1. Messick, *Lansky.*
2. McCoy, *The Politics of Heroin in Southeast Asia.*
3. Ibid., p. 52.
4. Ibid., pp. 247–49.
5. Interview with General Ouane Rattikone. Another side to the duplicity of the U.S. policies vis-à-vis opium trafficking in Southeast Asia was expressed by General Rattikone in an interview published in the *Bangkok Post* of November 27, 1973. See William J. Chambliss, "Markets, Profits, Labor and Smack," *Contemporary Crises* vol. 1, no. 1 (January 1977), pp. 53–77.
6. Ronald Rickenbach, "Eyewitness Testimony," *Harper's Magazine*, October 1972: 120–21.
7. *New York Times*, Sunday, March 8, 1987. See also Jonathan Kwitny, *The Crimes of Patriots: A True Tale of Dope, Dirty Money and the CIA* (New York: W.W. Norton and Co., 1987); Peter Dale Scott, "Shadow Networks," forthcoming, p. 13.
8. New South Wales Federal Parliament Report, 1982.
9. Pike Report, "CIA Involvement in Planned Assassinations" (New York, Spokesman Books, 1977).
10. *New York Times*, March 8, 1987. Information supplied by confidential informant.
11. New South Wales Federal Parliament Report, 1982; John Owen, *Sleight of Hand: The $25 Million Nugan Hand Bank Scandal* (Sydney: Calporteur Press, 1983). Jim Hougan, *Spooks: The Haunting of America—The Private Use of Secret Agents* (New York: Random House, 1978); idem, *Secret Agenda* (New York: Random House, 1984); Henrik Kruger, *The Great Heroin Coup* (Boston: South End Press, 1980).
12. Leslie Cockburn, *Out of Control* (New York: The Atlantic Monthly Press, 1987), p. 152.
13. *Washington Post*, January 20, 1987: 12.
14. Giancana was sent to prison as a result of the campaign to get him. On his release he was to testify before a congressional committee investigating the assassination of Kennedy. Before he could testify he was murdered in his kitchen early in the morning as he went to the refrigerator to get a glass of milk.

Giancana's closest ally in organized crime was John Roselli, who testified before the same commission, but before his testimony could be completed he disappeared and was later found floating in an oil drum in Biscayne Bay near Miami, Florida. A recent report in *People*

Magazine quotes Judith Exner, a former mistress of John F. Kennedy and Sam Giancana, as stating that she routinely took sealed envelopes back and forth between her two lovers. She confirms the fact that Giancana bragged that he was responsible for putting Kennedy in office in 1960. Kennedy won that election against Richard Nixon on the strength of votes from Chicago. There were at the time claims that the voting was rigged. See Kitty Kelley, "The Dark Side of Camelot," *People Weekly*, Feb. 29, 1988. pp. 106–14.

15. E. A. Wayne, "Drug Charges Hit Top Haitian Officer," *Christian Science Monitor*, Feb. 11, 1988; "Our Man in Panama," *The Nation*, February 20, 1988.

16. William J. Chambliss and Robert B. Seidman, *Law, Order and Power* (2nd ed.) (Reading, Mass.: Addison-Wesley, 1982); William J. Chambliss, *Exploring Criminology* (New York: Macmillan, 1988).

17. Hougan, 1985, p. 75.

18. Ibid., pp. 26–27.

19. James W. McCord, Jr., *A Piece of Tape* (Rockville, Md.: Washington Media Services, 1974, p. 60.

20. Joseph C. Goulden, *Death Merchant: The Brutal True Story of Edwin P. Wilson* (New York: Simon and Schuster, 1984).

21. Stansfield Turner, *Secrecy and Democracy: The CIA in Transition.* (New York: Houghton Mifflin, 1981); Goulden, *Death Merchant.*

29. The Fence and Society: Vincent's *Apologia Pro Vita Sua*

CARL B. KLOCKARS

DENIAL OF RESPONSIBILITY

> The way I look at it, I'm a businessman. Sure I buy hot stuff, but I never stole nothin' in my life. Some driver brings me a couple a cartons, though, I ain't gonna turn him away. If I don't buy it, somebody else will. So what's the difference? I might as well make money with him instead of somebody else.

In the above statement Vincent (1) denies that he ever stole anything in his life. He then asserts either directly or by implication (2) that there is an important distinction between stealing and receiving stolen goods; (3) that the criminal act of receiving would take place even if he were not the one to do it; and (4) that he does not cause the goods to be stolen. Let us consider each of these defenses separately.

He Never Stole Anything in His Life

In two rigorous senses Vincent has stolen. First, in a number of anecdotes about his childhood . . . Vincent has described his juvenile industry at theft. He dismisses those events as irrelevant to the above statement, explaining that although he says "never in my life," his childhood does not count. This is illogical in a strict sense of the words used. However, biographical claims are often intended more as moral advertisements than historical descriptions. When such is the intention, it is quite acceptable social form to exclude from public reflections on "true character" those moments of one's life when one was not in full control of one's self. Consider such statements as "All my life I've followed the Golden Rule." (From age two? seven? ten? twenty-one?) Or, "He really is a gentle man, but watch out when he's drunk."

Second, according to a strict legal interpretation of his adult behavior, Vincent does steal. He does, as the common-law definition of theft provides, "take the goods of another, without permission, with the intent to permanently deprive that person of his rightful property." However, the law makes distinctions between theft and receiving (often attaching a lower penalty to receiving), and I suspect that few readers are troubled by Vincent's simultaneous claim both that he has never stolen anything and that he does buy stolen property. It is, for most of us, an understandable social distinction. What Vincent means is that he is not a thief.

There Is an Important Distinction between
Stealing and Receiving

Vincent claims not to be a thief, and we understand what he means. For Vincent himself, there are differences not only between thieves and receivers, but also between thieves and drivers.

> See, Carl, what you gotta understand is when I say "driver" I don't mean "thief." I don't consider a driver a thief. To me, a thief is somebody who goes into a house an' takes a TV set and the wife's jewelry an' maybe ends up killin' somebody before he's through. An' for what? So some nothin' fence will steal the second-hand shit he takes? To me that kind a guy is the scum of the earth.
>
> Now a driver, he's different. A driver's a workin' man. He gets an overload now an' then or maybe he clips a carton or two. He brings it to me. He makes a few bucks so he can go out on a Friday night or maybe buy his wife a new coat. To me, a thief an' a driver is two entirely different things.

Those things which distinguish the driver and the thief in Vincent's estimation may point to distinctions that the larger society makes between receiving stolen goods and actually stealing them. The fence, like the driver, does not enter homes or stores to remove property; there is no danger of violence in his presence. A thief, on the other hand, could do anything; he may well be a drug addict, rapist, robber, burglar, or assaulter, or, if the situation arose, a murderer. Society has no clear expectations about the limits of criminality involved.

On the other hand, a fence, Vincent claims, is a businessman who buys and sells stolen property. Like the driver, the fence commits his crime in the course of behavior which differs only minutely from that of legitimate members of his trade. And like the driver, the fence has a relatively stable social identity: the driver will presumably be at work again tomorrow; Vincent is in his store every day of the week. Vincent buys and sells things, waits on customers, and walks public streets openly. Truck drivers perform public tasks as well. Thieves are shadowy figures, sneaking around behind the scenes and even hiding their right names behind aliases.[1]

In sum, when Vincent begins his apologia by saying "I never stole nothin' in my life," he magnifies a common distinction between a receiver and a thief. He means, first, that he does not actually take merchandise from its owners. But second, and more importantly, he means that the fear, disgust, and distaste which "thief" connotes to some people should not and do not properly apply to him. The law, his customers, his friends, and his neighbors know there are differences between thieves and receivers, and so does Vincent.

Receiving Would Take Place Even without Him

By saying "If I don't buy it, somebody else will," Vincent attempts to minimize his responsibility by pointing to the presumed consequences of his private refusal to buy.

They are, he asserts, nil; therefore his responsibility is nil. This is a patently attractive moral position, and one which is echoed frequently. Let us first examine the accuracy of the assertion before evaluating the moral position which Vincent derives from it.

Would someone else buy the merchandise if Vincent refused? I think they probably would. Although Vincent is able to dispose of some merchandise which other fences might have great difficulty selling (e.g., dental supplies), the vast majority of merchandise in which Vincent trades could be handled by many other fences. The related question, of course, is whether or not the particular thief or driver who approached Vincent with stolen property would be able to locate another fence to sell to if Vincent refused. This is problematic. In my estimation, many would find another outlet almost immediately, some would find one after a bit of looking and asking, and a very few might not be able to find another buyer. Depending on the character both of the merchandise and of his friends and neighbors, the thief or driver might well be able to sell stolen merchandise to them at a better price than he could get from Vincent.

If the accuracy of Vincent's statements is conceded, its moral implications remain to be considered. Certainly one can find examples of the same form of rationalization being offered in quite disparate social situations. The physician on trial for performing a criminal abortion claims that he performed the requested operation rather than have the woman find another, possibly less competent, conspirator. The arms manufacturer claims that he cannot be held responsible for a war because if he had not sold weapons to the participants they would have bought them elsewhere. Likewise, the conscripted soldier who opposes war but fights anyway may take comfort in the knowledge that his participation will not affect the waging of a given war or its outcome.

The moral position upon which such arguments rest is that a person's culpability for participation in an immoral or illegal act disappears or is mitigated if the act is likely to occur even if he does not participate in it. Such a position can be extended to cover situations even less pleasant than those listed above. For example, it removes responsibility in almost all incidents of mob violence. Is no one in a lynch mob responsible because others are also willing to string the victim up? Is looting at a riot scene excusable because others are looting too? Is vandalism blameless when it is a group affair? To push the position harder still, one could envision a small team of paid professional killers who always shoot their victims simultaneously so that no one gunman feels guilty. Even firing squads, so legend has it, reject such nonsense by actually loading one gun with blanks.

Responsibility for action is responsibility for action. Whether or not an act is likely to occur without one is simply irrelevant to the evaluation of one's own conduct. To surrender that elementary premise of simple moral philosophy is to abandon the responsibility to refuse to participate when one believes that others are doing wrong. Middle-class mothers everywhere, sensitive always to the seductions of the world, have correctly admonished their children who "went along with the crowd": "Just because everybody else jumps off a cliff doesn't mean you have to." It is an admonition of considerable rhetorical sophistication which has absolutely nothing to do with jumping off of cliffs, but gets instantly to the heart of patently attractive denials of responsibility like "If I don't buy it somebody else will."

He Does Not Cause the Goods to Be Stolen

With this statement Vincent suggests his relationship to drivers (and, by extension, thieves) who supply him with stolen merchandise. In Vincent's consideration he is merely a commercial respondent to theft whereas it is thieves and drivers who must bear responsibility for it.

For Vincent, the etiology of theft is a considerably less difficult problem than it is for criminologists: people steal because they want money. Why else should anyone steal? In general, why they want money is their own business, but Vincent, like most small businessmen, is close enough to those he works with to reflect on their motives. For most thieves, Vincent finds that drugs, gambling, and "high living" (Cadillacs for blacks is Vincent's most frequent example) are the main incentives for illegal earnings. Drivers, on the other hand, often use the proceeds from what they sell to add "a little extra" to the family income. To Vincent, it is preposterous to suggest that it is he, rather than the factors which thieves and drivers themselves cite, that is responsible for theft. . . .

DENIAL OF VICTIMS

The first line of defense in Vincent's apologia is his denial of responsibility for theft and his argument that for him to refrain from buying stolen goods would be inconsequential. His second line of argument is to deny that his activities have any meaningful victims or inflict any significant injury. To appreciate Vincent's second defense one must consider some of the experiences from which he reasons.

More than most people, Vincent witnesses extensive violations of the law against receiving. He sees respectable society, including police and judicial officials, coming to him for bargains that they know are suspect. Because of his reputation, he is often solicited by otherwise legitimate businessmen interested in buying something that they deal in should he come across it. He also encounters respectable types who find something romantic about his being a fence. For example:

> I got to know my doctor real good when I was in for my last operation. Somebody told him about me, I guess. Well, I started tellin' him about stuff, you know, buyin', sellin', thieves, boosters. He just couldn't get over it. He wanted me to get him some hot suits. You know, have him pick out the suits and send some boosters in to get 'em. He really wanted to do it. You shoulda seen how excited he was talkin' about swag. Imagine a guy like that, a big doctor an' all, gettin' so excited about hot stuff.

This widespread trafficking with him, and occasional fascination for his work, have consequences for the way Vincent sees his own behavior. First of all, he is conscious of a certain hypocrisy in society's attitude toward dealing in stolen property. He is aware of the legal prohibition against receiving, yet sees frequent evidence of willful, guilt-free violation of it by those who ought to know better. Vincent's recall of occasions when highly respectable citizens bought stolen goods or what they thought were stolen goods is extremely acute. Legitimate citizens of high status are truly "significant others" for Vincent.

Indeed, Vincent sees the patronage of such legitimate citizens as a reflection of his own worth. Their buying from him and maintaining friendly relations with him are considered by Vincent to constitute an important vindication of the possibly shady character of what he does. It is true that Vincent is an attractive and enjoyable person; but even if his friendly acquaintances seek him out only for this social aspect of his personality, Vincent finds it easy to perceive that they are not sufficiently offended by his receiving to limit their association with him.[2]

Given the highly supportive character of Vincent's immediate environment he is able to think of his victim and the injury he receives as someone or something "out there," removed from him physically and normatively, and separated by the intervening actions and responsibility of the thief or driver. Only very rarely does Vincent ever confront the victim of a theft. The latter is likely to direct his rage at the thief, his employee's carelessness, or his faulty security system rather than at the fence who eventually buys what was stolen from him.

From this detached perspective, Vincent contemplates the extent of his victims' losses:

> Did you see the paper yesterday? You figure it out. Last year I musta had $25,000 worth a merchandise from Sears. In this city last year they could'a called it Sears, Roebuck, and Swaggi. Just yesterday in the paper I read where Sears just had the biggest year in history, made more money than ever before. Now if I had that much of Sears's stuff can you imagine how much they musta lost all told? Millions, must be millions. And they still had their biggest year ever.

Vincent reads Sears's declaration of success as evidence of the inconsequential character of his receiving their stolen merchandise. Hence, he considers any possible claim on their part that he or hundreds of others like him are substantially harming business as at least greedy if not absurd. The logic of such an analysis is the same, on a larger scale, as the "Ma Bell can afford it" reasoning invoked by the pay-phone patron who receives a windfall from a malfunctioning unit. Vincent does not stop there in his consideration of Sears's success, however.

> You think they end up losing when they get clipped? Don't you believe it. They're no different from anybody else. If they don't get it back by takin' it off their taxes, they get it back from insurance. Who knows, maybe they do both.
>
> Carl, if I told you how many businessmen I know have a robbery every now an' then to cover expenses you wouldn't believe it. What does it take? You get some trusted employee, and you send him out with an empty truck. He parks it somewhere an' calls in an' says he was robbed. That's it. The insurance company's gotta pay up. The driver makes a couple a hundred bucks and it's an open-an'-shut case. You can't do it every year but once in a while it's a sure thing.
>
> Oh, there's millions a ways to do it. You come in in the mornin' an' break your window. Call the cops, mess some stuff up. Bang! You got a few thousand from the insurance company. I'm tellin' ya, it happens all the time.

Thus Vincent denies significant injury to Sears not only because of their net profits but because they can be seen as recovering most of their loss from insurance payments or through tax write-offs.[3] The reality for Vincent, in sum, is the comparatively trivial effect of theft on the insured victim. Inconvenient, perhaps, devastating, no! Hence: no real injury, no real victim.

The problem remaining is the general effect on pricing that theft produces. As a businessman, Vincent is in agreement with his counterparts that theft and shrinkage result in higher mark-ups and higher prices. But Vincent again falls back on the question of the ultimate consequences of his particular refusal to buy. Assuming his thieves and drivers could not find anyone else to sell to, the entire result of Vincent's private refusal to buy might amount to a penny a person for the entire year, if it were distributed over the total population of the city. And on the other side of the ledger, Vincent reckons that some of his other services to the general welfare of the community more than balance what he takes out.

The questions of the moral responsibility involved in buying stolen goods, and of the consequences of such an act for any putative victims, would be even less problematic for Vincent's customers than for Vincent were they to confront them. Given that a particular item is on Vincent's shelf and is known to be stolen, a particular purchase will not affect Vincent's survival as a fence. I do not believe that a rational economic argument can be made against an individual decision to buy stolen goods. The claim that theft costs everyone as reflected in high costs and insurance rates is inadequate. It costs everyone surely, but those who buy stolen goods manage to offset these higher costs and rates. In fact, were it simply a question of a personal economic strategy, one might argue that the only way to beat the consequences of the thieves' market is to patronize it. The only argument left seems to be to appeal to a responsibility to the general welfare of others.

To legalize receiving stolen goods would legitimize an institution which is intolerable. It would encourage theft and have a pernicious effect on society. Clearly it is an absurd suggestion. But the conflict is still real. The department-store sweater costs $15.99. Vincent is selling it for $10.00. In this particular case it is a question of saving $5.99 or making an economic gesture to the general welfare. All day long Vincent sees the general welfare lose out to bargains. . . .

THE METAPHOR OF THE LEDGER

> Sure I've done some bad things in my life. Who hasn't? Everybody's got a skeleton in his closet somewhere. But you gotta take into account all the good things I done too. You take all the things I done in my life and put 'em together, no doubt about it, I gotta come out on the good side.

As a businessman, Vincent is familiar with the use of a ledger for evaluating the success or failure of enterprise. He knows that there are different ways of setting up and managing accounts. Some entries are puffed a bit more than they deserve; other profits don't show up in the counting. Occasionally, one shows a loss so as to make things look normal or to prevent having to pay too much in the end. Business accounts, properly managed by able accountants, set things in order for the businessman and those who are interested in judging what he has accomplished. When all is said and done, the ledger tells whether or not one comes up in the red or in the black.

A metaphorical ledger is equally useful in evaluating life histories: good in the credit column is balanced against evil in the debit column. Thus, acts of charity and benevolence offset entries of greed or selfishness. It is an attractive metaphor. From the scales of justice to the Great Book of St. Peter, the notion of a balancing between good and evil has proven to be a persuasive one for the common comprehension and consideration of penance, indulgence, grace, judgment, atonement, salvation, and contrition.[4]

To Vincent, a businessman all his life, the metaphor of the ledger comes easily. In accounting for his conduct, Vincent considers his criminality and his exemplary behavior on the same balance sheet.

> When it comes to fences I consider myself in a class by myself. I don't consider your street-corner fences, buyin' an' sellin' secondhand stuff, to be anything like me at all. For one thing they're all no good. They're all cheap, greedy bastards who'd sell their mother if they had a chance. I figure I have a certain class, ya know, a certain way of doin' things. To me them guys are nothin'. They're stupid, ignorant people. I can't even stand bein' around 'em.

Thieves and Drivers

In reckoning credits for his self-evaluation, Vincent points to those good things he has done for people which his role did not require him to do. For example:

> Take what I done for Artie, for instance. Now there's a guy, he's been a thief for years, an' nothin' to show for it. That year alone I musta given him $25,000. One day I'd give 'em a hundred bucks, the next day he'd be back askin' for a loan. So I had a talk with him. I told him, "Look, you're makin' good money. Why don't you put it toward a house?" So we set up a little deal where I'd keep a little each time we had a deal; then when he had enough we'd put it toward a house.
>
> Well it took about three months an' he had bout $1,500 with me. So I got a real-estate agent I knew to get him a place, nothin' fancy but a pretty good neighborhood. It was colored but clean. Well, you know what happened? His wife came down with his kids an' she couldn't thank me enough. They had been livin' in one of those welfare high rises and she hated it. Every now an' then she comes by to tell me how things are goin'.
>
> Don't get me wrong. I made a lot of money off of Artie, but I set him straight too.

What places Vincent's efforts in Artie's behalf on the credit side of the ledger is the fact that Artie and his wife appreciated Vincent's assistance and that Vincent did not have to give it. Vincent has repeated similar anecdotes to me frequently.

> I am good to children. You know "Eyeball," right? All the trouble I had with him? His wife came in at Christmastime last year. When she left she had at least a hundred dollars worth of clothes and toys for her kids. I knew Eyeball was in jail an' she didn't have nothin'. Carl, if you knew how much stuff I gave to people, outright gifts, you wouldn't believe it.
>
> Would you believe it if I told you that I got a thief who calls me his "white father"? It's true. I been good to him. Posted bail for him a couple of times. He tells everybody, "Vincent Swaggi, he's my white father."

The matter of the posted bail in the second anecdote raises a number of complications in the matter of crediting Vincent's generosity. One could interpret Vincent's bailing out the thief as self-serving, since Vincent knew that once back on the street, the thief would resume bringing him merchandise. The extent to which such actions should be seen as impelled by generosity becomes even more problematic in those cases where Vincent benefits more than does the recipient. Many people turn to Vincent for "help" when they are in a jam and don't know what to do. Providing alibis, referrals to persuasive lawyers, loans at high interest, and the kind of encouragement a man occasionally needs to get back to his work are all well appreciated. Just a little bit of help sometimes pays off handsomely.

> I had this guy bringin' me radios. Nice little clock radios, sold for $34.95. He worked in the warehouse. Two a day he'd bring me, an' I'd give him fifteen for the both of 'em. Well, after a while he told me his boss was gettin' suspicious 'cause inventory showed a big shortage. So I asked him how he was gettin' the radios out. He says he puts 'em in his locker at lunch an' takes 'em to me after work. So I ask him if anybody else is takin' much stuff. He says a couple of guys do. I tell him to lay off for a while an' the next time he sees one of the other guys take somethin' to tip off the boss. They'll fire the guy an' clear up the shortage. Well he did it an' you know what happened? They made my man assistant shipper. Now once a month I get a carton delivered right to my store with my name on it. Clock radios, percolators, waffle irons, anything I want, fifty off wholesale.

Though Vincent is reluctant to place such profitable assistance in his credit column, one must consider the matter from the perspective of the new appointed shipper: Vincent advised him well. He saved him from his suspicious boss, cleared his reputation, got him promoted, probably with a raise, and made it possible for him not only to increase his earnings from theft but to steal with greater security as well. For Vincent, on the other hand, such an incident cancels itself out; it was good advice which paid off. Yet, although such events cannot, because they paid off so well, be offered individually as evidences of virtue, in the aggregate they enhance Vincent's professional self-conception. However, they leave a residual magnanimity which surfaces in statements such as the following:

> I treat the people I deal with right. If they're in a jam an' I can help 'em out, I'll do it. And I don't mean just your high-class types either. I mean thieves, drivers, police, customers, anybody. I'm known for helpin' people out when I can.
>
> You don't have to be a bastard to be in this business. You can treat people decent. Some guys, like my brother, never learn that. They think a black man comes into the store, you can push 'em around, call him "colored" or "boy"; you just can't do that no more. Times have changed.

Notes

1. The matter of "potential for deviance," by which I mean people's estimations of the probability that one type of deviance implies the capacity for other types, merits systematic criminological examination. As an example, our treatment of the insane by incarceration seems to presume that relatively mild violations of social propriety suggest a capacity for more serious and perhaps violent deviance. Similarly, before the time when long hair was co-opted by an economic establishment willing to capitalize on it, long hair seemed to be regarded by many as a certain sign of the willingness of the wearer to engage in other, non-tonsorial forms of deviance. Likewise, society may well assume that, all other things being equal, a thief has a greater "potential for deviance" than a fence.

2. The idea of *innocence by association* raises important questions for researchers in the sociology of deviance. Simply by associating with deviants the field researcher gives tacit reinforcement to them. My association with Vincent was interpreted by him as quite complimentary, and the vast majority of thieves I have interviewed have felt similarly flattered. My generally nonjudgmental attitude was uniformly construed as approval. Likewise, I find that a text like my own is easy to interpret as being supportive of deviant careers in spite of my protestations that it is primarily descriptive and analytical, in the way sociology must be. A similar case can be made regarding the degree of attention paid to militant blacks in the liberal press. (See Nathan Glazer and Daniel P. Moynihan. *Beyond the Melting Pot*, 2d ed., rev. [Cambridge: M.I.T. Press, 1970], p. lxxxvii).

3. Months after Vincent told me about his views on Sears's profits in spite of their losses from theft, I ran across the following obscure news item (John Manning, ed., "No Money Down" [Philadelphia: Publication of the Model Cities Consumer Protection Program, vol. 1, no. 3], p. 3). It is rather perverse to print it here but I cannot resist the irony.

> SEARS FASTBUCK: Second Income News relates how Richard W. Sears, founder of Sears, Roebuck, got started in business. Sears was a railroad telegrapher with a sideline business of selling watches. His gimmick was to buy watches at $2 apiece, affix $20 price-tags, and mail them to fictitious locations across the country. When the packages came back "undeliverable," Sears would open them in presence of fellow employees and palm the watches off as "bargains"– at $10 apiece.

4. Reference to a Book of Life wherein all of man's deeds are recorded is found throughout Scripture. For example, Rev. 20: 11–15 states:

> [11] Then I saw a great white throne and him who sat upon it; from his presence earth and sky fled away, and no place was found for them. [12] And I saw the dead, great and small, standing before the throne, and books were opened. Also another book was opened, which is the book of life. And the dead were judged by what was written in the books, by what they had done. [13] And the sea gave up the dead in it, Death and Hades gave up the dead in them, and all were judged by what they had done. [14] Then Death and Hades were thrown into the fire; [15] And if any one's name was not found written in the book of life, he was thrown into the lake of fire.

PART 5

CONTROLLING CRIME AND THE CRIMINAL

In Part 4 we looked at interactional processes and conditions that may lead to criminal activities and ultimately a criminal career. We also saw how involvement in crime affects an actor's view of self and carries with it the risk of criminal processing – and of being officially labeled as a criminal.

The selections in this part explore how social control agents attempt to regulate crime and the criminal. First, we examine methods used to identify clients for processing as criminals. Then the processing and sentencing procedures themselves are described. These readings provide insight not only into how the "organizational paradigm" (described in the General Introduction) operates but also into how social control agents – the police, the courts, and others – actually produce crime data. The part concludes by offering an assessment of how the accused person and the agents who deal with him or her perceive and respond to criminal processing.

FINDING CRIMINALS

As was pointed out in Part 2, little systematic attention has been given to how crime rates are arrived at, despite a consensus that they often present an inaccurate picture of crime and the criminal. If one is to make statements and generalizations about causation, distribution, prevention, and needed treatment and control strategies, one needs to analyze how crime data are organizationally generated; this requires, to begin with, an analysis of how institutional personnel go about identifying people for processing.

In "Patterns of Police Investigation of Urban Crimes," William B. Waegel examines how police detectives go about investigating citizen complaints of serious crimes. He notes initially that the organizational context that impacts on the detectives produces certain constraints on their activities. There are, for example, bureaucratic pressures to produce completed reports and the proper number of arrests within a specified time frame, and those who do not conform will be sanctioned or asked to leave the detective division. It is within this context that Waegel proceeds to describe how the detectives actually carry out their routines. The detectives rely very heavily on what he terms "case interpretive schemes," which enable them to make initial sense out of cases. These classificatory schemes provide links between the crime, available information about the crime, and classification of the crime as either routine or nonroutine, as well as the type of investigation required. Waegel presents a table in which he describes various types of "incident features and investigative patterns." He goes on to illustrate how these typical bureaucratic case-handling patterns are actually translated into action by the detectives. He focuses on five different types of crime: burglary, robbery, aggravated assault, rape, and homicide. For example, routine burglaries that are seen as warranting little effort may be suspended immediately, or suspended after a brief interview or investigation. He observes that when the victim is a low-status person, the investigators feel safe in suspending the case; however, when the victim is middle-class, or the burglary occurs in a "respectable" establishment or area, more effort is expended prior to suspending the case (e.g., the crime scene will be inspected, the victim interviewed, and witnesses contacted). The higher-status people may, the detectives believe, be more apt to question the progress of the case, or complain to superiors. Waegel's discussion of the *content* of the investigative report is equally revealing. Not only do organizational constraints affect the nature of the written report, but detectives may, in being mindful of the bureaucratic pressures placed on them, actually tailor the report in such a way as to impress superiors. In many cases, then, the effort expended is often a direct function of a victim's social status, the victim's attitude toward prosecution, whether evidence is available to link a suspect to the crime, and the area in which the crime was committed. Waegel thus provides an enlightening account of how bureaucratic structures and constraints can affect the approach to the solving of a range of crimes and, in this sense, his research helps to highlight further the need for examining how existing bureaucratic-organizational structures impact on the activities and routines of decision makers.

Michael L. Benson, William J. Maakestad, Francis T. Cullen, and Gilbert Geis, in "District Attorneys and Corporate Crime: Surveying the Prosecutorial Gatekeepers," provide additional insight into how alleged criminal cases may or may not be presented to the district attorney for possible prosecution; their focus is given to corporate offenders. They begin by noting that, traditionally, illegal corporate behavior has not consistently resulted in criminal prosecution. This lack of prosecution is ascribed to two main factors: the political and economic power corporations enjoy, and the difficulties involved in trying to apply criminal law to corporate violators. The authors elaborate on these views by outlining some of the actual legal, political, and economic factors that may influence whether an alleged case of corporate misconduct moves forward. The investigators also present some data on this process. Examination of the responses obtained from a survey of 45 California district attorneys produces some interesting findings. For example, insufficient resources and the availability of alternative remedies (e.g., deferring the case to federal prosecutors) emerge as the greatest obstacles to corporate crime prosecution. They also note that, in terms of the potential influence that *community context* may have on responses to corporate crime, small communities that are dependent on the corporation for its existence or livelihood may not be so inclined to prosecute corporate offenders. By contrast, successful prosecution of corporate violators may impress the voters and enhance a prosecutor's reputation. They conclude by describing how other factors (e.g., environmental) can affect the selection and processing of cases.

PROCESSING CRIMINALS

Once criminal cases have been identified, they may become subject to prosecution. The decision to prosecute, however, is not necessarily based on standardized criteria or procedures. In "The Impact of the Ethnicity and Gender of Defendants on the Decision to Reject or Dismiss Felony Charges," Cassia Spohn, John Gruhl, and Susan Welch examine the issue of racial and sexual discrimination within the criminal justice system, particularly as it relates to the decision to prosecute. The researchers use data obtained from some 33,000 cases filed with the Los Angeles County District Attorney's Office from 1977 to 1980. They initially examine the reasons given by the district attorney for rejecting or reducing a charge at the initial screening session. Their data indicate that evidence problems (e.g., insufficient evidence that a crime has occurred, or evidence that is inadmissible) constitute the main reason behind the rejection of a charge for the majority of the defendants in each group. This lack of variation by gender and ethnicity prompts the researchers to question whether such factors play a role in the decision-making process. An examination of *pretrial dispositions*, however, does exhibit a pattern of discrimination in terms of the prosecutor's decision to reject the charge. Specifically, females are more likely than males, and whites more likely than either blacks or browns, to have their charges reduced. As a further indicator of the preferential treatment accorded women and whites, females in each ethnic category are more likely than their male counterparts to experience a charge reduction. Also, the rejection rates are higher for both white men and women than for any other comparison group. Further analyses indicate that even though the prosecutor may file a charge against an individual, the judge may dismiss the charge after the preliminary hearing. These data indicate a pattern where gender, and not race, plays a role in the decision to dismiss the charge, with females in each racial group being more likely to have the charge dismissed. The researchers conclude by offering some possible reasons that may account for their findings. It is suggested, for example, that one reason why there are ethnic and gender differences in the district attorney's decision to reject, but only gender differences in the judge's decision to dismiss, is because of the nature of the setting and the visibility of the processing. As the case moves throughout the criminal justice system, the process becomes more visible and the norms against discrimination become more pronounced. Hence, it is reasoned that "there may be a greater acceptance of the idea that racial discrimination is wrong than of the notion that it is wrong to treat women more leniently." Such findings, the researchers note, underscore the need for closer examination of the pretrial stages of processing.

Barbara F. Reskin and Christy A. Visher, in "The Impacts of Evidence and Extralegal Factors in Jurors' Decisions," take the judicial decision-making process another step. They are concerned with examining how jurors use evidence, and they focus on the role that evidence, recall, and extralegal factors may play in a juror's judgment of guilt. They draw upon data obtained from observations of thirty-eight forcible sexual-assault trials, plus interviews with 331 jurors involved with the trials. The results exhibit some clear patterns. The initial analyses indicate that the evidence presented at the trial affects the jurors' perceptions of guilt. For example, the most influential variable, at the trial-level, was a recovered weapon. A weapon, it is reasoned, not only attests to the use of force — a legal element of rape — but it underscores the assault's seriousness. A similar pattern emerges in terms of jurors' perceptions of evidence, with a recovered weapon being the most influential factor and eyewitness testimony being the least. An examination of extralegal factors (e.g., a defendant's appearance and employment status, and a victim's moral character) indicates that selected characteristics of both defendant and accuser can affect a juror's decision. If defendants seemed attractive or were gainfully employed, they were less likely to be viewed as guilty. By contrast, if a woman was perceived as not exercising caution or being of questionable moral character, the defendant was more apt to be judged not guilty. The effects of extralegal factors, the researchers observe, must be examined in conjunction with the evidence factors, and when this is accomplished, the ability to explain predeliberation verdicts increases. The researchers conclude with an examination of how "strong" and "weak" cases may affect jurors' judgments. For weak cases (i.e., those that lacked hard evidence), the jurors tended to invoke extralegal factors; whereas for hard cases, the jurors relied more on the nature of the evidence presented and not on extralegal factors.

Once a jury returns a verdict, other components of the criminal justice system are set in motion. If found guilty, a decision must be made relative to the disposition of the case. Is, for example, the guilty party to be granted probation, fined, or incarcerated? It is at this stage in the criminal processing of clients that presentence investigations and reports assume a critical importance. J. William Spencer, in "Conducting Presentencing Investigations: From Discourse to Textual Summaries," analyzes how probation officers (POs) construct their presentence reports. Spencer focuses on the ways in which the officers elicit, interpret, and utilize data obtained from a variety of sources. Even though material is gathered from several sources (case files, arrest reports, and the like), the most critical information is obtained during the presentence interview with the defendant. Once the information is elicited, it must be interpreted by the POs in such a manner as to make sense out of it; this often means that the officers draw upon and use meaningful or familiar configurations. Finally, the POs utilize the information gleaned as a basis for making and justifying their recommendations. The recommendations, Spencer notes, often correspond with existing "informal and formal bureaucratic protocol." Spencer gives substance to this process by using data obtained during a nine-month study of a probation department. He describes, for example, how POs actually go about eliciting information from defendants. They are concerned, he notes, with gathering three major types of information: legal data (e.g., the nature of the offense), extralegal data (e.g., age and sex), and material on the defendant's subjective orientations or feelings toward the crime (e.g., attitude about the consequences of the offense, or about changing behavior). Once gathered, this information is used as a basis for classifying an individual in accordance with a threefold typology based upon a defendant's assessed risk (i.e., high-risk defendants, low-risk defendants, and indeterminate- or problematic-risk defendants). Spencer ends with a description of how the POs prepare the presentence report. Particularly insightful are the ways in which the officers match offender characteristics with existing categories and their associated recommendations. High-risk individuals, for example, are more apt to receive larger fines and longer sentences, and they have less chance for probation.

Jeffrey H. Reiman's work, "The Rich Get Richer and the Poor Get Prison: Sentencing," discusses the final outcome of court processing: the official adjudication of a person as guilty or innocent, and sentencing. His major contention is that the poor often lack the resources needed to post bail or retain legal counsel; as a result, many remain in prison until their trial and have public defenders assigned to their cases. These lawyers, according to Reiman, do not generally devote the time and resources necessary for the defense of their clients. Reiman concludes by giving examples of the relatively light sentences meted out to affluent defendants and the heavier ones given to the poor.

EFFECTS OF CRIMINAL PROCESSING

The effect of criminal processing on a suspect's self-image is described by Abraham S. Blumberg in "The Moral Career of an Accused Person." During the processing, the accused's public and private identity is subjected to attack by various institutions and their agents, who often perceive and respond to the person as a criminal. This, in turn, may mean that the accused is pressured into accepting a criminal status. Blumberg notes that although the poor and powerless are most likely to succumb to the pressures, even an individual with considerable personal and economic resources has great difficulty resisting them. A redefinition of self as guilty may alleviate an identity crisis for the accused; it also enables the police and the courts to process a case with the greatest possible dispatch.

30. Patterns of Police Investigation of Urban Crimes

WILLIAM B. WAEGEL

The response of police investigators to citizen complaints of serious crimes constitutes a neglected area in the sociological literature of the police. Yet these activities are crucial to an understanding of the operation of the criminal justice system, for in most jurisdictions it is the exclusive task of detectives to investigate serious crimes. An examination of the interaction between police investigators, crime victims, witnesses, and perpetrators can enhance our understanding of the administration of justice and the functioning of the social control system.

Studies of uniformed police through participant observation are central among the works which have contributed to an understanding of day-to-day police activities. Skolnick (1967), Bittner (1967), Reiss (1971), Rubinstein (1973), Lundman (1974, 1979), Sykes and Clark (1975), Van Maanen (1978), and Manning (1978) have produced field studies which have examined and clarified the social world of the police, police-citizen encounters, and routine police practices.

However, few participant observation studies have focused on the critical area of detective work. Skolnick (1967) does devote some attention to specialized divisions, such as vice and detective bureaus, but much of his attention centers around police relationships with informers. This article utilizes data obtained through participant observation to examine the patterned activities involved in police investigations of urban crimes.[1]

CASE HANDLING ORIENTATION

The organizational context in which detective work is carried out places significant constraints on investigative activities. In the department studies, the salient constraints are not rooted in supervisory surveillance, which generally is minimal, but rather in the bureaucratic requirements of producing completed investigative reports for each case within a rigid time frame while also producing an expected number and type of arrests.

For every case assigned, the detective must produce a completed investigative report within 14 days. In this report, there must be a description of the relevant information about the incident, the investigative activities undertaken, and a classification of the status of the investigation. Three classifications are available: (1) *closed*, which indicates that an arrest has been made and no further activity will be devoted to the case; (2) *suspended*, where the available information is such that further investigation is not warranted; and (3) *open*, which indicates that a continued investigation beyond the 14-day period holds some promise of resulting in an arrest. However, generally only "major cases" may remain classified as open, and special justification is always required. Supervisors seldom challenge the content of these reports, but compliance with time deadlines is closely monitored and used as a basis for evaluating individual performance. Detectives experience paperwork deadlines as a central source of pressure in their work, and view these deadlines as a fundamental constraint on how thoroughly any ordinary case can be investigated.

Detectives must also produce arrests, especially in burglary cases which comprise the majority of cases handled. While there is no formal arrest quota in the detective division, an informal understanding exists that one should produce at least two arrests per week if one desires to remain a detective and avoid transfer "back to the pit" (that is, back into uniform in the patrol division). Assignment to the detective division is the most prestigious position in the department, and it entails the additional benefit of rotating between only two, rather than three, work shifts. Although salary scales of patrol officers and detectives are the same for each rank, the latter have the luxury of wearing plain clothes and are free from the requirement of being available to handle radio calls. There is additionally the sense that detectives are engaged primarily in the "real police work" (that is, crime control as opposed to peace-keeping). The novitiate detective soon learns that he must produce an acceptable number and type of arrests, while at the same time comply with paperwork deadlines, if he is to remain a member of the detective division.

These features of the work setting generate an orientation to case handling which detectives refer to as "skimming." Skimming refers to selecting out for vigorous investigative effort those cases from one's workload which appear likely to result in an arrest, while summarily suspending or performing only a cursory investigation in the remainder of one's ordinary cases. Supervisors are certainly aware of this practice and of the fact that it ensures that the majority of ordinary cases will never receive a thorough investigation. However, supervisors themselves find their performance assessed in crude quantitative terms and are likely to be questioned by superiors if arrest levels drop from previous norms.

Within this context, understanding detective work thus requires an examination of the processes by which cases are attended to and assessed with regard to their likelihood of producing an arrest. Case-handling decisions are not guided by formal procedures for allocating time and effort to cases having different configurations of information. Rather, a set of informal interpretive schemes are used by detectives to manage the twin practical problems of paperwork deadlines and producing arrests. Through experience in working cases and through interaction with other members, detectives employ an instrumental shorthand for recognizing potentially productive cases which warrant vigorous investigative effort, and unproductive cases which are viewed as consuming time but having no tangible rewards. Because all the detectives experience similar problems in managing their caseloads, and because of the recognized utility of this case assessment shorthand, the interpretation and handling of cases by different detectives tend to be quite similar.

Burglary and robbery cases which are viewed as having little likelihood of producing an arrest are termed "routine cases" and receive minimal investigative effort. Assault, rape, and homicide cases generally receive a somewhat higher level of investigative effort. However, these latter offenses frequently involve acquainted parties,[2] and information is readily available to the investigator identifying the perpetrator. Such straightforward personal offense cases are also referred to as routine cases, for little effort is required to close the case. However, since no great investigative acumen is involved, less credit is accorded arrests in this type of case. Assault, rape and homicide cases involving nonacquainted parties ordinarily are designated major cases by supervisors, and methodical investigative work is called for. In general, the police are rather unsuccessful in solving this latter type of case.[3]

CASE INTERPRETATION SCHEMES

The preceding has suggested that detectives are constrained in their conception and handling of cases, not by the formal organization of their work or by supervisory surveillance, but rather by the bureaucratic pressure of writing reports and producing the proper number and quality of arrests. Given the case-working orientation previously described, an understanding of detective work requires an examination of the shorthand schemes which link typical case patterns with specific investigative activities.[4]

Observation of detective-victim interviews and examination of written case reports provide the data for specifying the content of the interpretive schemes used by detectives. In the victim interview, the kinds of questions asked and the pieces of information sought are revealing of the case patterns recognized as typical for different offenses. However, in attempting to make sense of the incident at hand, the detective attends to much more than is revealed in his explicit communication with the victim. His interpretation of the case is also based upon his understanding of the victim's lifestyle, racial or ethnic group, class position, and possible clout or connections, as these factors bear upon such concerns as the likelihood of the victim inquiring into the progress of the investigation, the victim's intentions regarding prosecution, and the victim's competence and quality as a source of information.

The interpretive schemes employed also receive partial expression in the written investigative reports which must be produced for each case. These reports contain a selective accounting of the meaning assigned to a case, the information and understandings upon which this interpretation is based, and the nature of the investigative activities undertaken.[5]

The following sections examine typical case patterns and associated investigative activities for the five offenses commonly dealt with by detectives: burglary, robbery, aggravated assault, rape, and homicide. Table 1 provides a summary of case-handling patterns.

"PORK CHOP" BURGLARIES

Routine burglary incidents which are seen as warranting only low-effort treatment are commonly referred to as "pork chop" burglaries. Where an instant case displays sufficient correspondence with this general category, detectives understand that appropriate ways of handling the case are to summarily suspend it, suspend it after a brief victim interview or perfunctory investigation, or reclassify it to a lesser offense.

Table 1. Incident Features and Investigative Patterns

Crime	Readily Available Information	Case Interpretation	Case Handling
Burglary	Identifies suspected perpetrator	Nonroutine	Vigorous effort; arrest anticipated
	No concrete identifying information	Routine, "pork chop" burglary	Case suspended; level of effort varies according to victim characteristics
Robbery	Potentially identifying	Nonroutine	Vigorous effect
	Does not identify	Routine robbery	Case suspended; level of effort varies according to victim characteristics and whether weapon used
Assault	Identifies perpetrator	Routine "Mom and Pop," "barroom" assault	Arrest made; minimal investigative effort
	Does not identify	Nonroutine	Level of effort varies depending on severity of injury and victim characteristics; may be major case
Rape	Acquaintance of victim identified as perpetrator and victim seen as having certain characteristics	"Suspect," "morning after" rape	Vigorous effort to test veracity of victim's account
	Unknown perpetrator	Nonroutine	Major case
Homicide	Identifies perpetrator acquainted with victim	"Killing"	Perfunctory investigation
	Does not identify perpetrator	"Murder"	Major case

Since burglary cases constitute roughly two-thirds of all cases handled, the interpretive schemes for these cases tend to be the most crystalized and nonproblematic. A burglary victim's ability or inability to provide information identifying the perpetrator or a probable perpetrator constitutes the single feature of burglary cases which is given greatest interpretive significance. In those few cases where the victim provides the name of a suspected perpetrator (often an ex-boyfriend, a relative, or a neighboring resident),[6] the case is a nonroutine one. When burglary cases are distributed at the beginning of each work shift, detectives quickly scan the original report prepared by a patrol officer and select out any cases having named suspects for immediate attention.

However, less than 10 percent of the patrol reports list a suspect by name. For the remaining cases, the initial inclination is to treat them as routine burglaries deserving of only minimal investigative effort.[7] In these cases, the social characteristics of the victim, particularly the victim's class position and race, have a decisive impact on the particular handling strategy adopted.

For example, where the victim is a low-status individual, detectives generally feel that it is safe and appropriate to summarily suspend the case or suspend it after briefly contacting the victim by telephone. A personal visit to the crime scene and a neighborhood canvass seldom are undertaken. Detectives assume that the patrol officer probably got all the information that was available from "the kind of people in that area."

When the victim is middle-class or when the burglary occurred in a "respectable" commercial establishment, detectives will commonly inspect the crime scene in person, interview the victim at some length, inquire of neighboring residents if they witnessed anything unusual, and, in general, sponsor the appearance of a reasonably thorough investigation. A more detailed investigative report is prepared explaining and justifying why the case has been suspended. This higher-effort handling strategy is employed largely because of a belief that this latter type of victim is more likely to inquire as to the progress of the investigation or complain to superiors about the detective's lack of success in solving the case. Detectives speak of cases "coming back on them" when they have not taken sufficient steps to impress victims that the case is being thoroughly investigated.

THE VICTIM INTERVIEW

The detective's fundamental concern upon receiving burglary cases centers around an effort to assess the typicality of the incident. This assessment is made on the basis of information contained in the original patrol report and/or information obtained during an interview with the victim.

Two contrasting types of victim interviews for routine burglary cases will be examined. In cases 1 and 2, the incidents are initially interpreted as routine and the detectives structure interviews with the victims accordingly. In case 3, the available information generates an understanding that appropriate handling of the case must include a rather lengthy victim interview and an attempt to sponsor the impression that the incident is being investigated thoroughly.

> *Case 1* A burglary had occurred at a disreputable bar located in a low-income area of the city. A few bottles of liquor were the only items taken. The fingerprint report from the evidence detection unit had not been received, so the detective introduced himself to the proprietor of the bar and asked to see the point of entry. He examined the area around the door which had been dusted for fingerprints and concluded that no useful prints had been obtained. Turning to the proprietor, the detective asked three questions: Do you have any idea who broke into your place? Do you think any of the neighbors around here might have seen anything when this occurred? Have you seen or heard about anyone suspicious hanging around here? After receiving negative replies to all three questions, the detective informed the proprietor that he would be contacted if anything came up and left the bar. Approximately 6 to 8 minutes were spent with the victim. As we got back into the car the detective told me he was suspending the case and remarked, "This (referring to the victim interview) is basically public relations work."

Case 2 A detective drove to the scene of a residential burglary in the same area of the city. The stolen items were noted, the victim stated that she had no idea who was responsible, and we left the victim's residence less than 4 minutes after we had arrived. "Kids," the detective remarked as he made some notes for future use in writing the investigative report. "I'll break it down to a criminal mischief." In the investigative report, the case was reclassified from burglary (a felony) to a misdemeanor and suspended. This handling strategy is encouraged by superiors, for it deletes both the incident and the fact that an arrest was never made from the Part 1 crime statistics and the felony clearance rate.

Some burglary cases, in spite of the fact that the detective has interpreted the incident pattern as routine and unproductive, nevertheless are seen as requiring a different kind of victim interview and handling strategy.

Case 3 A detective was assigned a residential burglary in a transitional area of the city. He stopped in front of the address, read the original patrol report, and mentioned that this was the only white family on the block and that the row houses on either side of the victim's were vacant. An evidence detection report showed that four cards of fingerprints had been obtained from the scene. The detective asked the victim to show him the point of entry, and we were led through comfortably furnished rooms to the basement, where a large hole had been made in the brick wall separating her basement from the basement of the vacant house next door. The victim, a middle-aged woman who had lived in the house for over 20 years, stated that the loss was substantial and consisted mostly of jewelry, coin collections, camera equipment, and cash.

After returning upstairs, the detective pulled out his notebook and explained that he wished to record as much information about the incident as the victim could provide. She replied that an older group of males had come into the area recently, and she thought they were an organized group of house burglars. "I see them every morning when I leave for work. There's one guy who stands on either corner, and they're the lookouts. Apparently, they work with whoever is doing these burglaries, and they sit there and watch to see who works during the day, what time they leave, and what time they come back. Then they have all day to break into a place and rob it blind." The detective asked if she knew the names, or even nicknames, of any of these persons. She replied that she didn't and that she would have trouble pointing out specific persons because the group was new in the area. The detective listened to her extended response to his original question, but did not record any of it.

A complete listing and description of all items taken in the burglary was then compiled. The detective took voluminous notes, paying particular attention to items with recorded serial numbers and to pieces of jewelry which had identifying engraving. He assured the victim that this information would be followed up, and that she would be contacted if any of the articles were recovered or there were any other developments. The interview lasted 1 hour and 40 minutes.

Once outside, I asked the detective what he thought of the case. He replied by asking whether I had noticed that the burglars ignored two color television sets which were sitting out in plain view. He remarked, "The guys who did this weren't kids. They knew what they were doing."[8]

The detective's superficial handling of this case differed considerably from the handling strategies employed in cases 1 and 2. However, the minor nature of the subsequent investigative activities undertaken by the detective indicates that his interpretation of the case was that it was routine and unproductive. He entered serial numbers and other identifying information regarding the stolen articles into the computerized stolen property file "to cover myself, just in case." Later in the week he asked another detective assigned to the same sector if he had heard anything from his informants about anyone involved in daytime burglaries in that particular area of the city. The other detective replied that he had not, and at the end of the second week the investigator suspended the case and concluded his investigative report by stating that "all avenues of investigation have been exhausted."

The above discussion has presented contrasting examples of the handling of routine burglary cases. Handling strategies for such cases range from essentially no investigative effort, where a detective simply contacts the victim and inquires if the person has any idea who committed the burglary, to a perfunctory investigation in which weak information or minimal leads are pursued in a casual manner. The latter handling strategy usually involves an effort to convince the victim that "something is being done" about the incident in question. These different methods of handling routine burglary cases stem largely from differences in the characteristics of, and assumptions made about, the victims.

THE INVESTIGATIVE REPORT

Further clarification of the relationship between typical case patterns and associated handling strategies may be gained by examining the content of the formal investigative reports produced by detectives. This section will also serve to highlight the general nature of the organizational constraints and demands which form the context in which case assessments are made.

The case reports presented here are reproduced verbatim.[9]

> *Case 4* CORRECT OFFENSE: Burglary. Total value stolen: $280.
>
> INVESTIGATIVE PROCEDURE: At [time, date] this investigator spoke with the victim in this complaint, at her residence. [She] gave this investigator the same basic information as is stated in the original report. Also, adding that she does not have any serial numbers on the stolen items, and that she has a few suspects from the neighborhood, some boys that live in the East 10th Street area, between Poplar and Wilson Streets. The victim does not know the names of these individuals, but stated that they frequent the area of the 900 block of Wilson Street.
>
> CONCLUSION: This complaint is to be SUSPENDED at this time, N.I.L.

N.I.L. is an acronym for "no investigative leads" that is often used regarding routine burglary cases. The detective suspended this case after simply contacting the victim by telephone. Less than 2 minutes were spent speaking with the victim, and another 3 to 4 minutes dictating the report.

> *Case 5* CORRECT OFFENSE: Burglary, 2nd degree. Total value stolen: $110.
>
> SUMMARY: This is a burglary that occurred between [date, time] at [address in a public housing project] where unknown person(s) entered that location by removing a board from the rear door, and once inside, removed the below described article.
>
> PROPERTY STOLEN: One (1) Sharp 19-inch portable color TV in a brown and black cabinet. The television had a dial broken from off the side. [Victim] said value was $100. Miscellaneous frozen meats at $10.
>
> PHYSICAL EVIDENCE: No physical evidence was obtained at this time.

VICTIM INTERVIEW: [Name], black female, [address]. On [date, time] this investigator spoke with the victim who informed me that between the above dates, some unknown person(s) entered her house by knocking a board from the rear door and once inside removed the above TV and frozen meats. [Victim] has no serial or model numbers on the TV and has no suspects in this investigation. The victim stated she did not wish any prosecution in this case. She is only concerned about recovering her TV.

On [date, time] the investigator made a canvass of the neighborhood for possible witnesses, but met with negative results.

A check of pawn sheets has been made with negative results.

CONCLUSION: Due to the fact that all avenues of investigation have been exhausted, and the victim does not want to prosecute, this case is SUSPENDED.

The detective who wrote the report fabricated both the neighborhood canvass and check of the pawn sheets to impress his supervisor that he had done as much as possible in a case where only meager information was available. For all practical purposes, the decision to suspend the case was made at the conclusion of the victim interview. The detective took for granted that in this neighborhood no one would volunteer that they witnessed the incident and that a search through the pawn sheets would be fruitless.

Cases 1 through 5 highlight the basic features of routine burglary cases and the associated patterns of investigative activity. The feature of burglary cases which is accorded primary interpretive significance is the availability of information which identifies a suspected perpetrator. Any case having an identified suspect is selected out for vigorous effort. Since there are no named suspects in the great majority of burglaries, most are interpreted and treated as routine. The amount of effort devoted to such cases is most directly linked to the victim's social status. Additional interpretive features include: (1) the victim's expressed or presumed attitude toward prosecution; (2) whether the offense was committed in such a way that physical evidence is available which could conclusively link a suspect to the crime; and (3) the area in which the incident occurred, particularly as this bears on the detective's beliefs about the inclinations of potential witnesses in that area.

The discussion of routine burglary cases and their handling illustrates the content of the shorthand schemes used by detectives in working burglary cases. Discussion of the remaining four types of routine offense patterns is based on the same kind of observation and documents, although space considerations will not permit the same volume of illustrative material to be presented.

Routine Robberies

The majority of persons who are apprehended for robbery are caught within 10 to 15 minutes after the commission of the crime. Those cases in which a suspect is not apprehended shortly after the incident are assigned to detectives for investigation. Detectives have less latitude in the handling strategies they may employ when a firearm is used in a robbery and the victim is a business establishment or a middle-class individual. Where a robbery incident has these features, the detective must conduct at least a perfunctory investigation and produce a very detailed investigative report. There is an assumption of offense repetition in armed robberies, and detectives anticipate that information in the report may have future value if a person is apprehended for a similar robbery incident.

Greater latitude exists in the handling of strong-arm robberies or muggings. Routine purse-snatching incidents usually receive either a perfunctory investigation or are suspended after an unproductive victim interview; the former strategy tends to be employed when the victim is middle-class and the latter when the victim is a poor person. When the victim of a strong-arm robbery is seen as a thoroughly "disreputable type" (such as a skid-row resident who has been "rolled"), the incident may be reclassified to a simple theft and suspended.

The feature accorded primary interpretive significance in assessing the routine or nonroutine nature of robbery incidents is the ability of the victim or witnesses to provide potentially identifying information regarding the perpetrator. Robbery occurs in a face-to-face setting, although masks are occasionally worn and perpetrators sometimes strike quickly from behind the victim. Victims and witnesses are often stunned by the speed and shock of the incident and, accordingly, the nature of the information they are able to provide varies widely. When this information takes the form of a simple clothing description, the incident is likely to be treated as a routine one. Regardless of the victim's characteristics, where potentially identifying information is provided which holds out the possibility of making an arrest, the case is defined as nonroutine, and a vigorous investigation is conducted. The crucial question asked during the victim or witness interview is, "Would you recognize the guy if you saw him again?" or "Would you recognize the guy if you saw a picture of him?"

The interpretation of robbery incidents is also based on the manner in which the offense was committed. The typical armed robbery is seen as involving one or two young males wearing nondistinctive clothing and masks who enter a small business establishment (generally a corner grocery store, liquor store, or convenience store) for less than 2 minutes and do not leave fingerprints or other physical evidence behind. The typical mugging incident is seen as involving a middle-aged or elderly female victim and one or more teenage males who approach the victim from behind and then quickly move to a place where they are out of view of searching police. Further, detectives take into consideration the area of the city in which the incident occurred and, as in burglary cases, make assumptions about residents with regard to their cooperation with the police and the likelihood of a neighborhood canvass.

Cases 6 and 7 are illustrative of the interpretation and handling of routine and nonroutine robbery incidents.

Case 6 A young cab driver who was new to the job had been robbed by two males who hailed the cab and then displayed a gun and ordered the driver to take them to a street bordering the city reservoir. They took the cash box and driver's wallet, pulled out the cab's microphone cord, and ordered the driver to lay down in the seat as they fled.

In the detective hall, the victim was questioned at length regarding a description of the two males. He could only provide a general clothing description since they had been in the back seat. It was noted that they had worn gloves during the incident. The driver was shown "hot" mugshots of persons recently involved in armed robberies, but none of these was identified as the perpetrator. Still visibly shaken by the incident, the driver was unclear about where he had picked the two up and the precise location where they had exited the cab. The driver stated that he thought he would be able to identify the male with the gun, and he was asked to come back the next day to look through additional mugbooks.

After the driver had left, and approximately 2½ hours after the robbery had occurred, the detective remarked: "That kid doesn't know what he is doing. And what kind of witness would he make. I'm ready to suspend the case right now."

Arrangements were never made for the victim to return to look through mugbooks because it was assumed that this would be fruitless (mugshots are very small (2″ × 3″) and are commonly several years old; identification through mugshots is rare). Nor was a neighborhood canvass for witnesses conducted, for it was assumed that residents in that area would be unlikely to volunteer information. The case was suspended 3 days later.

Robbery cases in which an arrest is not made shortly after the incidents are solved either through luck or gross incompetence on the part of the perpetrator, or through a major and time-consuming investigation involving informants and stakeouts. The latter situation occurs when an individual or group of persons is believed responsible for a series of robberies. The former situation is more common than one might suspect, as illustrated in the following case:

> *Case 7* An armed robbery had occurred at a small cleaning establishment when only one female clerk was present. Two males entered, placed a jacket on the counter, and asked to have it cleaned. As the clerk was filling out the slip, one male displayed a gun, ordered the clerk into a backroom, emptied the cash register and fled.
>
> Two detectives responded and one began questioning the clerk. As she was describing the incident, she pointed to the jacket on the counter which the perpetrators had not taken with them when they fled. The second detective casually picked up the jacket and began looking through the pockets. In a small inside pocket was a document from the public defender's office containing a person's name. The case was solved simply by obtaining a photograph of this person and showing it to the clerk.

In summary, case features which constitute the basic interpretive framework for robbery incidents include:

1. The availability of information potentially identifying a suspect from the victim or witnesses

2. The social characteristics of the victim and witnesses which, within the interpretive schemes employed by detectives, make different categories of people more or less consequential as victims and more or less reliable sources of information

3. The victim's actual or presumed attitude toward spending the time and effort necessary in prosecuting the case

4. Whether the incident was carried out in such a way that physical evidence is obtainable

5. The area in which the incident occurred and the perceived likelihood of obtaining useful information from residents of that area through such procedures as a neighborhood canvass.

ROUTINE ASSAULTS

The majority of aggravated assault incidents observed occurred between persons who knew one another. Detectives use the term "Mom and Pop assault" or "barroom assault" to refer to incidents which involve acquainted parties. Unlike burglary and robbery cases, in assault incidents the victim frequently is able to provide the name of the perpetrator to responding police. Therefore, routine assault cases—those which are dealt with by means of low-effort handling strategies—generally result in an arrest. Where the victim and assailant were not previously acquainted in an assault incident, the case generally is defined as a nonroutine one requiring vigorous investigative effort.

There are no formal guidelines for handling assault incidents having different statutorily defined degrees of severity. Thus, an attempted murder incident involving a husband and wife in which the victim tells police that she was shot by her spouse is commonly handled in a purely routine manner. The detective takes written statements from both parties and any witnesses, attempts to locate and confiscate the weapon if one was used, orders photographs taken of the crime scene, and collects any relevant physical evidence. However, these tasks are performed in a casual, almost mechanical way, for the detective does not feel that he is actively seeking information about what happened, but merely collecting information and evidence which is largely superfluous. This casual investigative approach is partly traceable to a belief among detectives that their investigative methods will seldom come under court scrutiny in routine assault cases because most cases of this type will be resolved through a negotiated plea of guilty.

Since the time lag between the occurrence of the offense and the police response is seen as critical, detectives usually respond directly to the scene of felony assaults. Thus, within a short period of time detectives are able to ask the questions and seek out the basic information enabling them to make sense of the event and assess its routine or nonroutine nature.

The feature of assault cases having primary interpretive significance is the existence and nature of a prior social relationship between the involved parties. Detectives obtain a sense of what happened and what needs to be done in an assault incident when they learn that it involved a man and woman who have been living together, acquaintances who got into an argument outside a bar, or strangers.

The following incident, although involving an assault with a deadly weapon, was understood by the detective as requiring essentially no investigative effort.

> *Case 8* During the early morning hours, a man had assaulted his common-law wife with a knife, inflicting a laceration which required hospital treatment. During the drive to the public housing project where the parties lived, the detective remarked, "The drunks over here are always fightin' and cuttin' one another." It was noted from the patrol report that uniformed officers had advised the woman to sign a warrant and she had done so. The detective found the man standing in front of his residence and called out, "C'mon John, come with me. I gotta lock you up." No questions were asked about the incident during the drive to the station or during the handling of the arrest paperwork. No attempt was made to obtain a statement from the man for use in prosecuting the case. I later expressed surprise that the man had been released on his own recognizance for a felony assault, but the

detective matter-of-factly replied, "Why not? She'll never show up in court and prosecute it anyhow. Why waste my time and everybody else's on it?"

No investigation was conducted. In assault cases of this type, detectives ordinarily write a brief report detailing the victim's account of the incident and "let the courts sort it out."

Detectives also attend to whether the precipitating circumstances were normal for the parties involved. Domestic assaults are seen as typically growing out of a heated, verbal argument over any number of personal issues. With regard to barroom-type assaults between males, one detective expressed the opinion that "money, booze, and women are the main reasons the natives go at it." If the precipitating circumstances are not seen as corresponding to such normal motives, but are found to lie in a dispute over stolen goods or a drug deal, a more vigorous investigation may be undertaken.

Detectives also base their interpretation on the lifestyles and social characteristics of the involved parties. A shared belief exists among detectives that physical violence is a normal aspect of the lifestyles of lower-class persons and especially members of minority groups. As one detective remarked during the early stage of my field work, "There's one thing you've got to understand. These people are savages, and we're here to keep peace among the savages." On the other hand, where physical confrontation is not seen as a normal aspect of the lifestyle of the parties involved, a detective is likely to interview the parties at greater length in an effort to determine why the assault occurred. Photographs of the victim's injuries may be ordered and an interview with the attending physician conducted, for parties having different social characteristics and lifestyles are seen as having different likelihoods of resolving the matter through plea bargaining or through formal judicial procedures.

Routine assault cases are constructed from the following elements. The existence and nature of a prior social relationship between the involved parties constitutes the feature of assault incidents which is accorded primary interpretive significance. The interpretation and handling of assault incidents is also contingent upon:

1. Understanding of the lifestyles and social characteristics of the parties involved
2. The victim's attitude toward prosecution, which may derive from explicit statements made by the victim or which may be assumed on the basis of understandings about the relationship between, and the lifestyle of, the involved parties
3. Whether the precipitating circumstances are seen as normal for the type of incident in question.

The seriousness of the injury to the victim has little bearing on the assessment of the incident as routine or nonroutine, but it has substantial impact on whether the case will be summarily suspended or whether some investigative activities will be performed.

"MORNING AFTER" RAPES

Rape generally is viewed as so serious an offense that it warrants an intensive investigation. If the victim is attacked by an unknown assailant, supervisors almost invariably impose a major case definition on the incident, assign several detectives to the case full time, and sometimes play an active role in the investigation themselves. Where the victim is a poor person or a member of a minority group, the police response is typically of a lesser magnitude, although initially one or two detectives are likely to be assigned to the case full time. In other words, rape complaints generally receive a vigorous investigative effort.

However, there is one commonly recognized pattern of features regarding rape complaints which elicits a qualitatively different police response. When this configuration of features exists in a specific allegation of rape, detectives refer to the incident as a "morning after" or "suspect" rape, their initial reaction to the complaint is one of suspicion. Initial police efforts are concerned with and concentrate on attempting to establish the legitimacy of the complainant's allegations. Among detectives, it is viewed as a mark of investigative competence and acumen to "see through" a suspect rape complaint. This status dimension is sustained by frequent recounting of past cases in which a female did in fact falsely allege rape, in combination with the oft-repeated caution that "rape is the only crime where a person's word can send a guy to jail for life."[10]

The following case displays typical features of incidents categorized as "morning after" rapes.

> *Case 9* Two detectives were assigned to investigate a rape complaint which had been reported at approximately 3:00 A.M. After notifying police, the victim was immediately taken to a hospital for a medical examination. The physician indicated that the test for ejaculate was negative, but the victim had noticeable bruises on her vulva and inner thighs. The complainant was returned to the detective hall and questioned for over 4 hours. She stated that she had been alone walking to her residence at about 11:30 P.M. when a car pulled up to the curb beside her. She recognized the driver as a person she had known in high school and, after some discussion, agreed to ride around with him as he attempted to buy some marijuana. Some time later, she indicated that she needed to use a bathroom and asked to be taken home. The driver replied that she could use the one in his apartment. The complainant stated that when she arrived, she was sexually assaulted by the driver and three other males already in the apartment. She had difficulty expressing exactly what had happened, stating simply that they had "attacked her." One detective remarked that the victim appeared to be mentally retarded.
>
> At 8:00 A.M., I asked a supervising detective what he thought of the case. He replied "It stinks. She keeps changing her story. She knows the guys who were supposed to have done it plus no sperm showed up in the test at the hospital. There is one guy locked up downstairs on a 2-hour detention, but it looks right now like there probably won't be any arrests made."

The case was eventually handled as an unfounded complaint, meaning that the investigators believed there was not sufficient evidence to warrant a criminal charge.

There is a shared belief among detectives that young, lower-class females are the most likely persons to falsely allege rape. Any indication of mental or emotional disturbance on the part of the victim heightens the detective's suspicion regarding the legitimacy of her allegation. Where a victim having these characteristics alleges that she has been raped by someone with whom she is acquainted, the initial orientation of detectives is to seek out information to categorize the event as a suspect or legitimate rape. It is standard procedure in rape investigations to transport the victim to a hospital immediately for a medical examination to test for the presence of ejaculate. Although there is an awareness that ejaculation within the victim does not occur in all rapes and that penetration and ejaculation are not statutorily required elements of the crime of rape, detectives nonetheless assign considerable interpretive significance to whether or not the rape has been "confirmed" by medical examination.

Additional information enabling detectives to categorize an incident as suspect or legitimate is sought out during the victim interview. Where the victim possesses social characteristics believed to be typically associated with false allegations of rape, the questioning tends to take on a predictable form. Do you know the guy? How long have you known him? Have you ever had sexual relations with him before? Did he use a weapon or other means of force? Did you report this to the police as soon as you were able to? How did you come in contact with him prior to the incident? Did you voluntarily get into his car or accompany him home? Did you resist?

Where the victim provides the name of her alleged assailant, this person is brought in for questioning. The primary issue of interest is whether or not he indicates that the victim consented. At this point, sufficient information has usually been obtained to categorize the incident as suspect or legitimate. Investigative strategies differ radically depending on this assessment. Suspect rape incidents typically are unfounded or reduced to a lesser charge such as sexual assault or sexual misconduct.

"Morning after" rape cases consist of some combination of the features presented below. The feature assigned primary interpretive significance is whether a victim having specific social characteristics believed to be typical of females who falsely allege rape knew her assailant prior to the incident. An interpretation of a rape complaint as suspect is likely to be made when this feature exists in combination with some or all of the following elements:

1. Certain conduct by the victim prior to and during the incident may be construed as cooperative or consenting behavior. Voluntarily accompanying the alleged perpetrator to the place where the incident occurred, or voluntarily entering his vehicle, may be taken as indications of willingness on the part of the victim. The victim's failure to fight back to attempt to resist the assault may be seen as an indication that "she really didn't mind." Consumption of alcohol or other drugs by the two parties together prior to the incident is seen as cooperative and contributing behavior on the part of the victim.

2. Any delay in reporting the incident to police is seen as entailing the possibility that the victim has some ulterior motive in making the complaint. Revenge against the person named by the victim is seen as the most common motive for false allegations of rape.

3. An emotional state and attitude displayed toward the incident by the victim which are viewed as inappropriate for a female who has just been sexually abused raises suspicion. After listening to a rape complainant calmly and matter-of-factly describe the details of an incident, one detective expressed doubt regarding the victim's account, noting, "She should be more upset than this." Another detective stormed out of an interview with a 15-year-old resident of a juvenile group home who

alleged that she had been raped by three other residents of the home and stated, "If she doesn't give a shit about what happened then why should I?"

4. Any contradictions or inconsistencies in the victim's account of the incident during extended questioning by different detectives are seen as indicative of a false complaint. One older, experienced detective expressed the opinion to the researcher that many investigators expect a clear, coherent, and consistent account of the incident in spite of the fact that the interview is being conducted within hours after the assault and in spite of the likelihood that many victims are embarrassed by, and are trying to forget, what has just happened to them. If the victim is asked to take a polygraph examination and declines for any reason, detectives are likely to conclude that a legitimate rape did not occur. If the victim consents to a polygraph examination and the results are termed "inconclusive" (a rather frequent outcome), the same inference is likely to be drawn.

5. A medical examination which does not confirm the presence of ejaculate within the victim is seen as reason for suspicion regarding the validity of the complaint.

6. The person named as the perpetrator provides an account of the incident in which the female consented to sexual relations.

KILLINGS

Detectives distinguish two types of homicides: killings and murders. In the former, the information and evidence available at the crime scene rather easily leads to the identification of the perpetrator. Commonly, such information is available from: (1) the perpetrator who remains at the scene of the crime when police arrive (such as the remorseful spouse); (2) persons who either witnessed the crime or have knowledge of a person who had threatened the victim, had been arguing with the victim, or had reason to assault the victim; or (3) a "dying declaration" provided by the victim.[11] Detectives recognize that most homicides occur between persons who know one another, and that often in such cases the perpetrator makes no serious attempt to conceal his or her deed. Where a particular case is seen as corresponding to the general category of routine killings, detectives view their task as a reasonably straightforward one involving apprehending the perpetrator, gathering any potential evidence, taking statements from any relevant parties, and writing a detailed report for use by the prosecutor.

In contrast, an incident is defined as a murder when available information does not readily identify the perpetrator. Different motives or precipitating circumstances are believed to be associated with this type of homicide, and methodical investigative work is deemed necessary.

The following case is typical of the interpretation and handling of routine killing incidents:

> *Case 10* Two detectives were assigned to a homicide case which had originally been handled by patrol officers as a routine assault case. The incident involved a lover's triangle between two males and a female who lived in the same block in one of the most deteriorated, skid-row type areas of the city. All three persons were described as long-term

alcoholics. Patrol officers originally responded to the scene following a report of an assault in progress. Apparently the younger of the two males had argued with the female about her relationship with the other male. The female had been struck on the forehead during this argument and had suffered a serious scalp laceration. The older male was found lying in his apartment with a head laceration and was taken to a hospital where he was treated and kept for observation. He informed patrol officers that he had been beaten by the younger man, but he was highly intoxicated during this interview. Patrol officers arrested the younger man for assault on the female, and he was released on an unsecured bond. Three days later the older man died in the hospital.

The case was assigned to two detectives the following morning as a possible homicide. The detectives discussed possible classification of the incident: death from natural causes, homicide, or self-defense. It was decided that nothing further would be done until the medical examiner's office classified the death in the afternoon. When it was learned that the cause of death was a fractured skull, the detectives cursed and discussed what would have to be done "to cover ourselves." They obtained the victim's blood-stained clothing as possible evidence. An attempt was made to locate the suspect in the immediate area of his residence, but he was not found. After a brief inspection of the room where the victim was found, photographs were taken, and it was decided that a slipcover and a chair showing what appeared to be blood should be tagged as evidence. Both detectives repeatedly expressed their revulsion over the condition of the residence and the tasks they were performing. It was decided to make no further attempt to locate the suspect that day, but rather to wait and see whether he would show up for a scheduled court appearance the next day pertaining to the assault charge. "I could care less about this case, I'd be just as happy if drunks like these were left to kill each other off."

The following morning the suspect came into the detective hall to turn himself in. He was advised of his rights and told that he had an opportunity to make a statement about what happened. He stated that he had been extremely intoxicated that night, had passed out, and doesn't remember anything that happened. No further attempt was made to interrogate the suspect, and the interview lasted less than 30 minutes.

Obtaining a formal statement from the female assault victim about the incident and preparing a four-page investigation report concluded the detectives' work on the case. The total time and effort devoted to this investigation was comparable to that for a minor burglary case having a named suspect.

In homicide cases, primary interpretive significance is accorded a combination of two case features: (1) whether information available at the scene or in initial interviews identifies and links a person to the crime, and (2) whether there was a prior relationship between that person and the victim. Where both of these features are present in an instant case, the event ordinarily is interpreted as a killing and handled routinely.

The assessment of the routine or nonroutine nature of homicide incidents is also based on the social characteristics and lifestyles of the parties involved. In part, this assignment of identities to the principals in the case is made on the basis of territorial knowledge which includes assumptions and understandings about the typical inhabitants of an area and their likely patterns of behavior.

Detectives also attend to whether the motive and the circumstances precipitating the incident were normal for the parties involved. If the apparent motive and precipitating circumstances in a case map onto a common and understandable pattern for domestic killings or barroom-type killings, the incident tends to be readily categorized and treated as routine. In domestic killings, a heated argument regarding one party's sexual fidelity is seen as an ordinary precipitating circumstance. Similarly, for barroom-type killings involving two males, a verbal argument or challenge concerning a woman, money, or a number of other normal bases for heated arguments are seen as ordinary motives and precipitating circumstances. Further investigative effort is seen as necessary when such a common and readily understandable pattern is not evident in a case.

SUMMARY AND CONCLUSIONS

Police handling of criminal investigations is guided by a set of interpretive schemes through which cases having different configurations of information are seen as warranting different levels and methods of investigation. Organizational demands and constraints generate a distinctive work orientation for the frequently handled crimes of burglary and robbery. Detectives select out for vigorous effort readily solvable cases while devoting only cursory effort to the remaining cases. Case stereotypes also function to provide standard recipes for the handling of assault, rape, and homicide incidents which display typical features.

Investigative work in the department studied was vigorous and methodical in only a small percentage of the cases handled. Indeed an image of detective work as involving a special arsenal of sophisticated techniques is substantially misleading for most ordinary criminal investigations. If the victim or witnesses are able to provide potentially identifying information in burglary and robbery incidents, the case will be vigorously pursued. In the great majority of cases, such information is not available, and minimal effort is devoted to the case. The work orientation referred to as "skimming" enhances our understanding of the low clearance rates for burglary and robbery. The relatively small portion of incidents categorized as major cases receive a higher level of investigative effort and a wider variety of investigative techniques are used.

Case-handling methods also vary according to the victim's social status. The differential treatment of crime victims flows in part from a set of stereotypic assumptions about criminal incidents which center around the detectives' concern with potential solvability. Thus, in certain neighborhoods methodical investigative procedures, such as an area canvass, seldom are undertaken because of a belief that they would prove fruitless. A work orientation emphasizing practicality and productivity serves to encourage this substitution of assumptions for information gathering.

Acknowledgment

This article draws on data collected during a larger research project on police information systems sponsored by The Twentieth Century Fund. An earlier version of this paper was presented at the Annual Meeting of the Society for the Study of Social Problems in Boston, August 1979.

1. The description and analysis presented here are based on 9 months of participant observation field work in a city police detective division. At the conclusion of the field work, the formulations contained in this article were discussed with various detectives in the context of "how the work is actually done." The patterned activities described here were recognized by experienced detectives as standard features of everyday practices. Further information about departmental characteristics, access problems, daily routines, and the field role adopted during the research is available from the author.

2. Statistics on the offender and victim relationship for personal offenses are broken down into categories for primary relationship, nonprimary (such as acquaintance, neighbor, sex rival, or enemy), stranger, other, and unknown. For homicide the respective figures are 33.7 percent, 28.1 percent, and 38.2 percent; for aggravated assault, 20.6 percent, 25.3 percent, and 55 percent; and for rape, 10.2 percent, 32.6 percent, and 57.2 percent (Dunn 1976:11).

3. This finding is also documented in survey research on police investigations. A recent study found that substantially more than half of all serious reported crimes receive no more than superficial attention from investigators. Further, if information identifying the perpetrator is not available at the time the crime is reported, the perpetrator generally will not be subsequently identified. See Greenwood et al. (1975).

4. A theoretical interpretation of the centrality of typificatory schemes in decision making by police and other legal agents is provided in Waegel (1981).

5. Garfinkel (1967:186–207) argues that organizational records are not to be treated as accurate or mirror reflections of the actual handling of a client or case by organizational members. However, these records can be employed to examine how members go about constructing a meaningful conception of a client or case and use it for their own practical purposes. Any valid sociological use of such records requires detailed knowledge on the part of the researcher regarding the context in which the records are produced, background understandings of members, and organizationally relevant purposes and routines.

6. Although "named suspects" (persons named in the original patrol report) are most commonly obtained from victims, other sources occasionally provide this information. A neighbor may come forward and volunteer that he or she witnessed the incident or has heard that a certain person or persons have been committing burglaries in the vicinity. Informants sometimes provide similar information.

7. There is a formal constraint on the detective's discretion regarding how much effort to devote to a burglary case. If the loss is in excess of $2,000, a lieutenant may impose a major case definition on the incident. The vast bulk of the city burglaries I observed involved much smaller losses.

8. There is a widespread misunderstanding concerning the utility of fingerprints obtained from a crime scene. Prior to my research, I had believed that a fingerprint obtained from a crime scene could automatically be used to identify the perpetrator. Unknown latent fingerprints from a crime scene cannot be identified from fingerprint files. The FBI fingerprint laboratory will only compare unknown latent prints with the file prints of identified suspects. Unknown prints from a crime scene and file prints of a suspect or suspects must be packaged together and sent to the FBI lab where technicians simply make comparisons. There are presently no automated procedures for comparing an unknown fingerprint against the millions of file prints.

9. The detectives dictate investigative reports through the desk telephones in the large detective room. The fact that this room is often crowded and noisy accounts for much of the fractured grammar in these reports. Identifying information has been deleted.

10. This statement means that rape cases are sometimes prosecuted successfully without corroboration of the victim's testimony and without direct evidence, such as fiber intermingling on clothing.

11. A surprising number of homicide victims do not expire immediately after receiving mortal injuries. Detectives immediately respond to any call involving a serious assault and, if the victim is conscious, ask two questions: Do you know who did this to you, and do you know why? If a dying declaration is obtained under the proper legal circumstances, the victim's statement will be admissible in court as an exception to the hearsay rule.

References

Bittner, Egon. 1967. The Police on skid row: A study of peace keeping. *Am. Sociol. Rev.* 32:699–715.

Dunn, Christopher S. 1976. *The patterns and distribution of assault incident characteristics.* Albany, NY: Criminal Justice Research Center.

Garfinkel, Harold. 1967. *Studies in ethnomethodology.* Englewood Cliffs: Prentice-Hall.

Greenwood, P., Chaiken, J., Petersilia, J., and Prusoff, L. 1975. *The criminal investigation process: Volume III.* Santa Monica, CA: Rand Corporation.

Lundman, Richard J. 1974. Routine arrest practices: A commonwealth perspective. *Social Problems* 22:127–141.

Lundman, Richard J. 1979. Organizational norms and police discretion: An observational study of police work with traffic law violators. *Criminology* 17:159–171.

Manning, Peter K. 1974. Police lying. *Urban Life* 3:283–306.

Reiss, Albert. 1971. *Police and the public.* New Haven: Yale Univ. Press.

Rubinstein, Jonathan. 1973. *City police.* New York: Ballantine.

Skolnick, Jerome. 1967. *Justice without trial.* New York: Wiley.

Sykes, Richard, and Clark, John P. 1975. A theory of deference exchange in police-civilian encounters. *Am. J. Sociol.* 81:584–600.

Van Maanen, John. 1978. The asshole. In *Policing: A view from the street*, edited by Peter K. Manning and John Van Maanen. Santa Monica, CA: Goodyear.

Waegel, William B. 1981. Case routinization in investigative police work. *Social Problems* 28:263–275.

31. District Attorneys and Corporate Crime: Surveying the Prosecutorial Gatekeepers

MICHAEL L. BENSON, WILLIAM J. MAAKESTAD, FRANCIS T. CULLEN, AND GILBERT GEIS

Business conduct is coming increasingly under the purview of law enforcement officials. Federal, state, and local governments appear to share a growing willingness to use criminal sanctions to deter corporate misconduct. White-collar cases accounted for only 8% of federal criminal prosecutions in 1970, but by 1984 they made up nearly 25% of such prosecutions (Marcotte, 1987). In 1972, the state attorneys general singled out one form of business crime, consumer fraud, as a major concern

(Skoler, 1982: 67). In the following year, the National District Attorneys' Association began an Economic Crime Project to enhance the capabilities of local prosecutors to deal with white-collar crimes (Edelhertz and Rogovin, 1982: ix–x). In addition, ample evidence exists that the public holds remarkably punitive attitudes toward corporate crimes (Braithwaite, 1985; Cullen et al., 1982, 1983; Schrager and Short, 1980). These developments suggest that a social movement against white-collar and corporate crime is now under way (Cullen et al., 1987; Katz, 1980).

The growing willingness of governments to apply the criminal law to corporations portends a potentially dramatic shift in the balance of power among the state, business elites, and private citizens. It suggests that the way in which society defines and responds to corporate misconduct is changing, and hence, the form of social control applied to that conduct is also changing. It becomes important, then, to learn how these developments are viewed by persons with the institutional responsibility for applying the law.

In recent years, social control responses to white-collar and corporate crime have been explored in a variety of settings. Some investigators have examined plea bargaining and sentencing of white-collar offenders in federal courts (Benson and Walker, 1988; Hagan et al., 1980; Katz, 1976b; Wheeler et al., 1982). Others have focused on decision making in federal regulatory agencies (Shapiro, 1984; Shover et al., 1986) and in the Antitrust Division of the Department of Justice (Weaver, 1977). Prosecutorial discretion in federal business fraud cases has also been examined (Rakoff, 1985). These studies have significantly enhanced our understanding of federal responses to white-collar and corporate crimes.

Investigators have paid less attention to local responses to corporate illegalities. Little is known about the experiences and views of district attorneys, the officials who make the decision to prosecute corporate criminal cases at the local level. The paucity of research on this topic led us to survey California district attorneys. The survey focused on three central issues: (1) How frequently do corporate crime cases come to the attention of district attorneys? (2) What factors limit the likelihood of their accepting these cases for prosecution? (3) Do district attorneys anticipate increasing their involvement in these cases in the future?

TWO VIEWS OF CORPORATE CRIME PROSECUTION

Sutherland's (1949) pioneering study of white-collar crime made clear that most illegal corporate conduct does not result in criminal prosecution (Clinard and Yeager, 1980). There are two views on why this is so. One view stresses the political and economic power of corporations, the other the practical difficulties of applying the criminal law to corporate offenders. These views represent recurrent themes in research on corporate crime. Although they are not mutually exclusive, different authors tend to emphasize one over the other.

Some have argued that corporate and other well-to-do offenders escape the criminal law because of their economic and political power (Reiman, 1979: 139). According to this view, corporations influence the administration of the criminal law so it is rarely applied to them. Most local district attorneys are elected officials; this politicization significantly influences prosecutorial decision making in corporate cases (Bequai, 1978: 147). Prosecutors are reluctant to offend potential supporters in the business community and their powerful political allies.

Additionally, depending on the importance of the business to the local economy, imposing criminal sanctions on a corporation can have significant negative consequences for the economic health of the community. The community may lose jobs and tax revenues, for example, if criminal prosecution causes a corporation to move to another locality where the legal climate is more favorable (Moore, 1987). In light of these political realities, local prosecutors may be reluctant to investigate and prosecute corporate criminal offenses.

In recent years, another view of the social control of corporate crime has gradually emerged. According to this view, corporate offenses pose special investigatory and prosecutorial difficulties that make the successful application of the criminal law problematic (Levi, 1987; Rakoff, 1985; Shapiro, 1984; Stone, 1975). The failure of prosecutors to apply the criminal law to corporate delicts results from insufficient resources, legal constraints, and the availability of alternative sanctions.

Unlike most ordinary offenders, corporate lawbreakers possess substantial resources with which to delay investigation and prosecution. Their attorneys often can raise time-consuming objections to legal proceedings; of more importance they are apt to try to control the investigator's and prosecutor's access to crucial information (Mann, 1985). Case studies of corporate crimes suggest that isolated local prosecutors lack the necessary organizational resources to overcome such obstacles (Cullen et al., 1987; Schudson et al., 1984; Vaughan, 1983).

Prosecutors also must contend with legal difficulties. Seldom is it possible for a prosecutor to offer dramatic "smoking-gun" proof of criminal knowledge or intent in a corporate context. Proof of such knowledge or intent is critical, for it is the element of *mens rea* that can turn what might have been a civil suit into a criminal proceeding. In today's complex and often labyrinthian corporate structures, it can be extremely difficult to pinpoint individual responsibility for specific decisions. In addition, large-scale organizations develop mechanisms for shielding their members from responsibility for corporate actions (Gross, 1978; Katz, 1977, 1979a). These problems in developing evidence seriously complicate a prosecutor's decision-making calculus.

A welter of federal and state regulatory agencies have jurisdiction over various aspects of corporate conduct. Prosecutors must depend on those agencies both for technical expertise and for the development of crucial evidence. Traditionally, regulatory agents have been more concerned with encouraging compliance than with punishing wrongdoing. They do not see themselves as law enforcers and often are reluctant to use the criminal law in response to corporate misconduct (Braithwaite, 1985: 10; Levi, 1987: 163). Given the difficulty of getting regulators to cooperate in criminal proceedings against corporations, prosecutors may opt for noncriminal rather than criminal sanctions.

In this study, we examine the importance of political and practical considerations for district attorneys as they decide whether to prosecute corporate criminal offenses.

PROCEDURES

In June 1987, we surveyed California district attorneys on their experiences with and general office policies toward prosecuting corporate crime. We mailed questionnaires to all 58 district attorneys. After a second mailing and follow-up phone calls by personnel from the California Bureau of Criminal Statistics, 45 questionnaires (78%) were returned.[1] All of the large urban districts responded to the survey.

The districts (i.e., counties) represented in this study vary dramatically in population size and in the district attorney's office budget and office staff. The district attorney for the smallest district serves fewer than 2,000 people, while the district attorney for the largest district serves over 8 million. The district with the smallest budget spends around $75,000 annually; the largest district spends over $65 million. In a few jurisdictions, one district attorney handles all legal matters, while in other jurisdictions assistant district attorneys number in the hundreds.

We defined corporate crime as "any violation of an existing criminal statute by corporate entities and/or by individual business executives that is committed on behalf and for the benefit of a corporation (or any other form of business association, such as a partnership)." Although we asked the district attorneys to complete the survey themselves, in some jurisdictions assistants filled out the questionnaires. Since our questions primarily concerned general office policies, the assistants' answers should also adequately address the central issues.

RESULTS

Complaints, Referrals, and Prosecutions

We asked the district attorneys to estimate the number of complaints from citizens and referrals from regulatory agencies alleging corporate misconduct they had received since January 1986. Of those responding to this question, a substantial majority received at least one complaint or referral. Three-quarters received complaints from citizens; three-fifths received referrals from regulatory agencies. Slightly over half of the districts reported 4 or more complaints by citizens, and nearly one-third reported receiving over 10 citizen complaints. We also asked the district attorneys how many of the complaints and referrals they had accepted for prosecution. Almost two-thirds had accepted at least one citizen complaint for prosecution, and about three-fifths had accepted at least one referral from a regulatory agency. The overall pattern of the responses suggests that district attorneys reject only a small number of allegations of corporate misconduct.

We asked the district attorneys to indicate whether it was within the proper jurisdiction of their office to prosecute each of the following categories of corporate crimes: financial, environmental, and workplace-related offenses. All indicated that financial and environmental crimes committed in the course of business were within their jurisdiction, and slightly over 80% had jurisdiction over workplace-related offenses.

Most of the prosecutions during the previous 5 years involved financial or environ-

Table 1. Percentage Distribution of Districts Reporting Corporate Crime Prosecutions during Previous Five Years

Prosecutions	Financial Offenses	Enviromental Offenses	Workplace Offenses
0	26.2%	32.6%	57.5%
	(11)	(14)	(23)
1	4.8	14.0	15.0
	(2)	(6)	(6)
2–3	19.0	14.0	17.5
	(8)	(6)	(7)
4–5	7.1	11.6	7.5
	(3)	(5)	(3)
6–10	4.8	9.3	0.0
	(2)	(4)	(0)
Over 10	38.1	18.6	2.5
	(16)	(8)	(1)
Total Responding	100%	100%	100%
	(42)	(43)	(40)

NOTE: District attorneys in office for less than 5 years were instructed to use their actual tenure in office as a reference point.

mental offenses (see Table 1). About three out of four districts prosecuted at least one financial offense by a corporation; two out of three prosecuted at least one environmental offense. By comparison, less than half the sample prosecuted corporations for workplace-related cases — still a significant figure considering that nearly 20% indicated that such prosecutions were outside the scope of their legal jurisdiction.[2]

The number of complaints and referrals received since January 1986 was approximately equal to the number of prosecutions reported for the previous 5 years. This suggests that the attrition rate for corporate cases is high.

LIMITING FACTORS

To assess the influence of political and practical considerations on the decision to prosecute, we asked the district attorneys to rank 15 items on a four-point scale. The response categories ranged from "would definitely limit" to "would definitely not limit" the prosecutor's likelihood of undertaking a corporate crime case. Two intermediate categories substituted "probably" for "definitely." We grouped the items into four categories: resources, alternative remedies, legal and technical difficulties, and political factors. (See the appendix for a list of the items.)

First, we analyzed the responses for the entire sample. From this analysis we found that insufficient resources and the availability of alternative remedies were the most important limiting factors. Over 90% of the districts responding indicated that the lack of adequate investigatory and prosecutorial staff would limit their willingness to proceed with criminal charges against a corporation. Just over half of the sample reported that budgetary problems might constrain their actions. The availability of alternative remedies also was an important reason why local prosecutors forgo corporate crime prosecutions; more than 83% of the district attorneys indicated that they would defer to pending federal prosecution, and 54% would defer to pending regulatory action.

In contrast, very few district attorneys regarded political factors as potentially limiting. One-quarter thought that the state of the local economy would influence their willingness to undertake a corporate prosecution. Fewer than one in ten were concerned about the resources corporations might have to defend themselves. Similarly small proportions indicated concern over lack of public support or the possibility that such prosecutions could adversely affect their careers.

Overall, the results for the sample suggest that problems of resource management strongly influence the decision to proceed in cases of corporate criminal misconduct. When federal prosecutors or regulatory agencies are involved, local prosecutors appear willing to forgo expending their own resources. Political factors receive less consideration.

To determine whether the concern over lack of resources is more prevalent in smaller districts, we split the sample according to the size of each district's population.[3] One-half of the district attorneys (n = 22) reported serving populations of less than 200,000, and the other half (n = 22) 200,000 or more. Table 2 shows the percentage of respondents indicating that an item would be a limiting factor for each subsample.

Except for three items, smaller districts were more likely to be limited by any given factor than larger districts. Lack of staff and deference to federal prosecutorial action ranked as the most important limiting concerns among both large and small districts. About one-half of the smaller districts reported being limited by the length of time a corporate case might take, but only about one-fifth of the larger districts shared this concern. Another notable difference between large and small districts was their respective concerns over the local economy. Over 40% of the smaller districts indicated this factor would limit their proceeding, but only 5% of the larger districts were concerned about the local economy. Surprisingly, attorneys from the larger districts were slightly more likely than those from smaller districts to say they would be limited by a lack of expertise in the technical issues involved in corporate prosecutions. They also were more concerned about the difficulties of establishing *mens rea* in corporate cases than their counterparts from small districts were.

As prosecutors gain experience with corporate cases, they may become more aware of the legal and technical difficulties raised by these cases. To explore this possibility, we divided the sample into two groups based on the number of corporate cases actually prosecuted in the previous 5 years: three and under versus four and over. We then compared the responses on the legal and technical items (see Table 3). Except for one item, less experienced district attorneys were more likely to be limited by legal and technical factors than their more experienced counterparts. Contrary to this pattern, over half of the more experienced prosecutors said that difficulties in establishing *mens rea* would limit the likelihood of their undertaking a corporate crime prosecution, and about one-third of the less experienced prosecutors felt this way.

Table 2. Percentage Responding that an Item Would Limit the Likelihood of Prosecution, by Population of District

	Probably or Definitely Would Limit	
	POPULATION	
Limiting Condition	Up to 200,000	Over 200,000
Resources		
Lack of Staff	95.5%	90.9%
Strain on Office Budget	59.1	40.9
Length of Time It Takes to Prosecute a Corporate Crime Case	50.0	18.2
Alternative Remedies		
Defer to Federal Prosecutors	84.2	81.8
Defer to Regulatory Action	66.7	40.9
Defer to Private Civil Suits	33.3	13.6
Legal and Technical Difficulties		
Investigatory Problems	72.7	50.0
Establishing *Mens Rea*	38.1	50.0
Inappropriateness of Criminal Statutes	38.1	31.8
Lack of Technical Expertise	40.9	50.0
Lack of Experience in Prosecuting Corporate Crimes	31.8	19.0
Political Factors		
State of Local Economy	42.9	4.5
Level of Resources a Corporation Might Have to Defend Itself	14.3	0.0
Lack of Public Support	9.1	4.5
Adverse Impact on Career Goals	0.0	9.1

NOTE: See appendix for the actual wording of each item.

Future Trends

Nearly 40% of the sample said that they anticipated allocating more resources to corporate crime in the future. More experienced district attorneys were more likely to report that they anticipated devoting increased resources to corporate crime in the future.

DISCUSSION AND IMPLICATIONS

Despite the considerable level of prosecutorial activity by district attorneys, California has by no means substituted "regulation by prosecution" for the more traditional sanctions and incentives favored by such agencies as the Environmental Protection Agency or the Occupational Safety and Health Administration. The number of corporate crime prosecutions still represents only a fraction of state prosecutors'

Table 3. Percentage Responding that a Legal or Technical Issue Would Limit Prosecution, by Number of Corporate Crimes Prosecuted in Previous Five Years

	Probably or Definitely Would Limit	
	NUMBER OF PROSECUTIONS	
Legal and Technical Difficulties	3 or Less	4 or More
Investigatory Problems	71.4	52.4
Establishing Mens Rea	35.0	52.4
Inappropriateness of Criminal Studies	38.1	28.6
Lack of Technical Expertise	52.4	19.0
Lack of Experience in Prosecuting Corporate Crimes	38.1	15.0

NOTE: See appendix for actual wording of each item.

caseloads. Nevertheless, the percentage of district attorneys who both claim jurisdiction over and actually prosecute corporate offenses demonstrates a broad acceptance of concepts of corporate criminal liability at the local level. That a sizable minority anticipates devoting more resources to corporate offenses in the future suggests that prosecutors see corporate crime as a problem of increasing importance and that their reactions to it are becoming more punitive.

The survey revealed a strong consensus among district attorneys that the greatest obstacle to corporate crime prosecutions is not political but practical: the level of resources available. Notably, such potential barriers as corporate defense resources, concurrent civil suits, lack of public support, and potentially adverse career consequences appear to have minimal impact on the decision to prosecute.

These findings must be interpreted with caution, however. Since our questions about allocational decisions referred to hypothetical situations, the responses may not reflect how district attorneys actually make decisions in corporate cases. Indeed, it is unlikely that prosecutors would frankly grant that they place their own career goals over enforcement of the law. Neither are prosecutors likely to admit that they are intimidated by the financial and political resources of powerful corporations. One could argue that the emphasis prosecutors place on resource problems in corporate cases is indicative of an underlying ideology in which the crimes of corporations are not viewed as seriously as the crimes of street offenders. Investigators who use other methodologies may find that political considerations are more influential in deterring prosecution in corporate cases than our survey indicates.

Nevertheless, we have confidence in the validity of our data for two reasons. First, case studies of corporate crime prosecutions clearly suggest that prosecutors feel morally and professionally obligated to apply the law equally to all wrongdoers. But, when confronted with corporate lawbreaking, they often lack the necessary resources to fulfill this obligation (Cullen et al., 1987; Schudson et al., 1984; Vaughan, 1983; Weaver, 1977).

Second, it is not clear how political considerations influence decision making in the justice system. According to some investigators, the political power of corporations enables them to corrupt enforcement efforts against corporate law violators (Coleman, 1985: 187–88; Conklin, 1970: 115). Contrary to this view, Katz (1980) argues that the professional and political aspirations of prosecutors may lead them to be more, rather than less, aggressive toward business criminals. He identified politically ambitious federal prosecutors as an important force in generating the social movement against white-collar crime.

The same may be true of local prosecutors. Successful prosecution of an offending corporation may be viewed as a way to impress voters and to make political capital. Political considerations, then, can cut both ways; in some situations, they may promote, rather then deter, corporate prosecutions.

District attorneys in less populous counties reported greater sensitivity to the potential impact of a corporate crime prosecution on the local economy than their counterparts in more populous areas. The influence of community context on social control responses to corporate crime may explain this finding. In more populous jurisdictions, where there are many major employers, prosecution of any single corporation would have less potential negative impact on the local economy than would a similar prosecution in a less populous jurisdiction. Accordingly, prosecutors in smaller communities may be less willing to prosecute corporate illegalities than prosecutors in metropolitan centers.

That community context influences social control responses to corporate misconduct has been noted in several recent investigations. In her study of the Securities and Exchange Commission (SEC), Shapiro (1984) found significant variation in the kinds of cases handled, enforcement priorities articulated, and investigative strategies developed by regional SEC offices. Shover et al. (1986) show that the Federal Office of Surface Mining adopted more stringent enforcement strategies in Appalachian states than in western states. Others have shown that environmental factors influence how regulatory agencies select and process cases (Bardach and Kagan, 1982; Feldman and Zeckhauser, 1978). Studies of the sentencing of white-collar offenders also reveal substantial variation in sentence severity among districts and over time (Benson and Walker, 1988; Hagan and Palloni, 1986; Hagan and Parker, 1985; Hagan et al., 1980; Wheeler et al., 1982). It appears that in response to local conditions, regulatory and criminal justice agencies develop different enforcement styles for white-collar and corporate crimes.

In conclusion, our results suggest that, in deciding whether to prosecute corporate crimes, the practical difficulties of applying the criminal law in a corporate context limit district attorneys more than the political and economic power of corporations. The relative importance of these factors is influenced, however, by the community context in which local prosecutors work. Social control responses to corporate lawbreaking appear to be more constrained in less populous jurisdictions than they are in metropolitan areas.

Notes

1. Some of the respondents did not answer all of the questions. As a result, the n's reported in some of the tables do not equal 45.

2. The actual prosecutions covered a broad range of offenses. District attorneys reported prosecuting corporations for financial crimes, such as grand theft, securities fraud, investment fraud, false advertising, and tax fraud. In the area of environmental offenses, they mentioned violations of air and water pollution laws and violation of the California Hazardous Waste Control Act. Among workplace-related offenses, they had prosecuted employers for involuntary manslaughter, failure to supply safety equipment, and maintaining substandard working conditions.

3. Although we have several measures of the resources available to district attorneys' offices, we believe population size is the most reliable and valid indicator. Some respondents reported only the portion of their budgets and staff devoted to criminal matters. Others combined criminal and civil budgets and staff. Hence, both budget and staff size may not be reliable measures of available resources. Population size correlates strongly with both of these measures ($r > .95$).

APPENDIX

Factors That Might Limit the Likelihood of a Prosecutor's Proceeding with a Prosecution of a Corporation

Resources

1. Lack of investigatory and prosecutorial staff.
2. The strain that a corporate criminal prosecution would place on my office's budget.
3. The length of time it takes to prosecute a corporate criminal case.

Alternative Remedies

4. Deference to actual or pending action taken by federal prosecutors in response to the alleged corporate crime committed in my jurisdiction.
5. Deference to actual or pending action taken by a regulatory agency in response to the alleged corporate crime committed in my jurisdiction.
6. Deference to a private civil suit for damages that have been filed in response to the alleged corporate crime committed in my jurisdiction.

Legal and Technical Difficulties

7. Difficulties in investigating and securing information for the development of a corporate criminal case.
8. Difficulties in establishing *mens rea* in a corporate criminal context.
9. Inappropriateness of present state criminal statutes as applied to corporations and/or individual business executives.
10. Lack of expertise in dealing with technical issues involved in corporate criminal cases.
11. Lack of experience in prosecuting corporate criminal cases.

Political Factors

12. The general state of the economy in my jurisdiction.
13. The level of resources that a corporation might have to defend itself.
14. Lack of public support for prosecuting corporate criminal cases.
15. The possibility that a corporate criminal prosecution could have an adverse impact on personal career goals.

References

Bardach, Eugene and Robert A. Kagan
   1982   Going by the Book. Philadelphia: Temple University Press.

Benson, Michael L. and Esteban Walker
1988   Sentencing the white-collar offender. American Sociological Review 33: 301–309.
Bequai, August
1978   White-Collar Crime: A 20th Century Crisis. Lexington, Mass.: Lexington Books.
Braithwaite, John
1985   White-Collar Crime. Annual Review of Sociology, Vol. 11. Palo Alto, Calif.: Annual Reviews, Inc.
Clinard, Marshall and Peter C. Yeager
1980   Corporate Crime. New York: The Free Press.
Coleman, James W.
1985   The Criminal Elite. New York: St. Martin's Press.
Conklin, John E.
1970   Illegal but not Criminal. Englewood Cliffs, N.J.: Prentice-Hall.
Cullen, Francis T., Bruce G. Link, and Craig W. Planzi
1982   The seriousness of crime revisited: Have attitudes toward white-collar crime changed? Criminology 20: 83–102.
Cullen, Francis T., William J. Maakestad, and Gray Cavender
1987   Corporate Crime Under Attack. Cincinnati, Ohio: Anderson.
Cullen, Francis T., Richard A. Mathers, Gregory A. Clark, and John B. Cullen
1983   Public support for punishing white-collar crime: Blaming the victim revisited? Journal of Criminal Justice 11: 481–493.
Edelhertz, Herbert and Charles H. Rogovin
1982   Implementing a national strategy. In Herbert Edelhertz and Charles Rogovin (eds.), A National Strategy for Containing White-Collar Crime. Lexington, Mass.: Lexington Books.
Feldman, Lenny H. and Richard J. Zeckhauser
1978   Some sober thoughts on health care regulation. In Chris Argyris (ed.), Regulating Business: The Search for an Optimum. San Francisco: ICS Press.
Gross, Edward
1978   Organizational crime: A theoretical perspective. In Norman Denzin (ed.), Studies in Symbolic Interaction. Vol. 1. Greenwood, Conn.: JAI Press.
Hagan, John, Ilene Nagel-Bernstein, and Celesta Albonetti
1980   The differential sentencing of white-collar offenders in ten federal district courts. American Sociological Review 45: 802–820.
Hagan, John and Alberto Palloni
1986   "Club fed" and the sentencing of white-collar offenders before and after Watergate. Criminology 24: 603–622.
Hagan, John and Patricia Parker
1985   White-collar crime and punishment: The class structure and legal sanctioning of securities violations. American Sociological Review 50: 302–316.
Katz, Jack
1977   Cover-up and collective integrity: On the natural antagonisms of authority internal and external to organizations. Social Problems 25: 3–17.
1979a   Concerted ignorance: The social construction of cover-up. Urban Life. 8: 295–316.
1979b   Legality and equality: Plea bargaining in the prosecution of white-collar and common crimes. Law and Society Review 13: 431–459.
1980   The social movement against white-collar crime. In Egon Bittner and Sheldon Messinger (eds.), Criminology Review Yearbook. Vol. 2. Beverly Hills, Calif.: Sage.
Levi, Michael
1987   Regulating Fraud. London: Tavistock.
Mann, Kenneth
1985   Defending White-Collar Crime. New Haven, Conn.: Yale University Press.

Marcotte, Paul
  1987   Corporations under the gun. ABA Journal 73: 32–33.
Moore, Charles A.
  1987   Taming the giant corporations? Some cautionary remarks on the deterrability of
            corporate crime. Crime & Delinquency 33: 379–402.
Rakoff, Jed S.
  1985   The exercise of prosecutorial discretion in federal business fraud prosecutions. In
            Brent Fisse and Peter A. French (eds.), Corrigible Corporations and Unruly Law.
            San Antonio, Tex.: Trinity University Press.
Reiman, Jeffrey
  1979   The Rich Get Richer and the Poor Get Prison. New York: John Wiley & Sons.
Schrager, Laura Shill and James F. Short
  1980   How serious a crime? Perceptions of common and organizational crimes. In Gilbert
            Geis and Ezra Stotland (eds.), White-Collar Crime. Beverly Hills, Calif.: Sage.
Schudson, Charles B., Ashton P. Onellion, and Ellen Hochstedler
  1984   Nailing an omelet to the wall: Prosecuting nursing home homicide. In Ellen
            Hochstedler (ed.), Corporations as Criminals. Beverly Hills, Calif.: Sage.
Shapiro, Susan P.
  1984   Wayward Capitalists. New Haven, Conn.: Yale University Press.
Shover, Neal, Donald A. Clelland, and John P. Lynxwiler
  1986   Enforcement or Negotiation. Albany, N.Y.: State University of New York Press.
Skoler, Daniel L.
  1982   White-collar crime and the criminal justice system: Problems and challenges. In
            Herbert Edelhertz and Charles Rogovin (eds.), A National Strategy for Containing
            White-Collar Crime. Lexington, Mass.: Lexington Books.
Stone, Christopher
  1975   Where the Law Ends. New York: Harper & Row.
Sutherland, Edwin S.
  1949   White-Collar Crime. New York: Holt, Rinehart & Winston.
Vaughan, Diane
  1983   Controlling Unlawful Organizational Behavior. Chicago: University of Chicago
            Press.
Weaver, Suzanne
  1977   Decision to Prosecute: Organization and Public Policy in the Antitrust Division.
            Cambridge, Mass.: The MIT Press.
Wheeler, Stanton, David Weisburd, and Nancy Bode
  1982   Sentencing the White-Collar Offender: Rhetoric and Reality. American Sociologi-
            cal Review 47: 641–659.

32. The Impact of the Ethnicity and Gender of Defendants on the Decision to Reject or Dismiss Felony Charges*

CASSIA SPOHN, JOHN GRUHL, AND SUSAN WELCH

Social scientists have long been interested in the issue of racial and sexual discrimination within the criminal justice system. The bulk of the research has centered on the effect of race on convicting and sentencing male defendants. Most recent studies have concluded that black men are no more likely than white men to be convicted but are significantly more likely than white men to be incarcerated (for reviews, see Hagan, 1974; Kleck, 1981; Spohn, Gruhl, and Welch, 1981–1982; Hagan and Bumiller, 1983). A few studies have compared the treatment of Anglo and Hispanic male defendants and have found few differences in conviction or incarceration rates or in sentence length (Unnever, 1981; Zatz, 1981, 1984; Welch, Gruhl, and Spohn, 1984, 1985).

The effect of the gender of defendants on their conviction and sentencing has received increasing attention over the past two decades. While some researchers have found few differences (compare Green, 1961; Simon, 1975; Katzenelson, 1976; Bishop and Frazier, 1984), most have found that adult female defendants are treated more leniently than male defendants. They are more likely to be released prior to trial (Nagel and Weitzman, 1971; Swigert and Farrell, 1977) [and less likely to be] sentenced severely (Engle, 1971; Pope, 1976b; Bernstein, Cardascia, and Ross, 1979) and incarcerated (Baab and Fergesun, 1967; Nagel and Weitzman, 1972; Simon, 1975; Sutton, 1978; Bernstein et al., 1979; Spohn, Welch, and Gruhl, 1985; Steffensmeier and Kramer, 1982; Gruhl, Welch, and Spohn, 1984).

Considered together, these studies provide evidence for the developing consensus that there is not as much racial discrimination in convicting and sentencing as would be predicted from the amount of racial inequality in society generally. They also substantiate the assertion that women receive more lenient treatment because of judicial paternalism on the part of prosecutors, juries, and judges.

But these conclusions are limited, for the most part, to the more formal and visible convicting and sentencing stages of the criminal justice process. They say nothing about possible discrimination in the police officer's decision to arrest, the prosecutor's decision to charge, or the parole board's decision to grant parole (compare Black, 1974).

Police, prosecutors, and parole officers have considerable amounts of discretion in deciding whether to arrest, charge, or grant parole. While there may be little or no racial discrimination in convicting and sentencing, a significant amount of racial bias

425

could exist at these other less formal and visible pre- and posttrial stages. Being less formal, these stages may not require decision makers to follow equally strict procedures. Being less visible, they are by definition less subject to scrutiny by outsiders. Thus, there is greater potential for discrimination at the pre- and posttrial stages than at the convicting and sentencing stages.

This paper examines the issue of pretrial discrimination by focusing on the prosecutor's (and, to a lesser extent, the judge's) decision to reject or dismiss charges against black, Anglo, and Hispanic male and female defendants. Using data on over 33,000 felony defendants in Los Angeles, the hypothesis is tested that there is both ethnic and gender discrimination in the decision to reject or dismiss charges.

PROSECUTORIAL DISCRETION—THE DECISION TO CHARGE OR NOT

It obviously is important to examine the decision to prosecute or not and to identify the role that ethnicity and gender play in the decision. As Justice Jackson noted in 1940, "the prosecutor has more control over life, liberty, and reputation than any other person in America" (Davis, 1969: 190). This power is reflected in the fact that in most states from one third to one half of all felony cases are dismissed by the prosecutor prior to a determination of guilt or innocence (Brosi, 1979; Vera Institute of Justice, 1981; Boland, 1983). Prosecutors can reject charges at the initial screening, either because they believe the suspect is innocent or, more frequently, because they believe the suspect is guilty but a conviction would be unlikely (Vera Institute of Justice, 1981). Prosecutors also can reject charges if they feel it would not be in the "interest of justice" to continue the case—perhaps because the crime is too trivial, because of a perception that the suspect has already been punished enough, or because the suspect will provide information in other, more serious, cases (Silberman, 1978: 271). Finally, prosecutors can reject charges as felonies but prosecute them as misdemeanors.

If a formal charge is filed by the prosecutor, it still can be dismissed by the court later. Typically, it is dismissed upon a recommendation by the prosecutor. Often witnesses disappear or indicate they will not cooperate (Vera Institute of Justice, 1981). Sometimes other problems weaken the cases. Judges can use similar reasons in initiating a dismissal. Also, judges may dismiss a charge in response to a defense motion to dismiss on the grounds that the government has failed to establish that the defendant committed the crime. Unlike the prosecutor's decision to reject the charge, the decision to dismiss a charge already filed requires official court action.

Silberman (1978) and Brosi (1979) have noted that rejection and dismissal rates vary from jurisdiction to jurisdiction, depending in large part upon the extent to which the prosecutor screens cases before the preliminary hearing or grand jury investigation. In some counties the prosecutor initially rejects one half or more of all felony cases, while in others the prosecutor files charges in a majority of the cases, shifting the screening function to a later stage in the process.

For example, Los Angeles County, where the data used for this study were obtained, has a system of early and careful screening of cases (Greenwood, Wildhorn, Poggio,

Strumwasser, and DeLeon, 1976; Katz, 1980). A deputy district attorney must decide within 48 hours of arrest whether or not to file charges. If the deputy does not think that the case should be filed, he can reject it outright, recommend that the district attorney's office handle it as a misdemeanor, refer it to the city attorney for prosecution as a misdemeanor, or suggest that the police investigate further and then resubmit it. Because this initial screening of the charges is a true screening, less than one half of all felony arrests are filed as felonies by the district attorney's office (Greenwood et al., 1976: 16; Katz, 1980: 122–123).

If the case is filed as a felony, it still can be terminated prior to prosecution. The case can be dismissed or reduced to a misdemeanor before or at the preliminary hearing. For example, the court might believe that a felony prosecution is not warranted because there is insufficient evidence to connect the suspect to the crime; the suspect is dead, incarcerated, or otherwise unavailable; the suspect has no prior record or only a minor prior record; or the case seems too trivial to prosecute as a felony. As both Greenwood et al. (1976) and Mather (1979) point out, however, in Los Angeles County only about 10% to 15% of cases are dismissed or reduced to a misdemeanor at this stage. There the initial screening of the charges in the district attorney's office, rather than the preliminary hearing, functions as the major screening point.

PREVIOUS RESEARCH ON REJECTIONS AND DISMISSALS

Only a few studies have analyzed the prosecutor's decision to prosecute fully. Two concluded that the race of the defendant and victim are significant factors. One found that blacks arrested for raping white women in a large midwestern city were more likely to be charged with felonies than either blacks arrested for raping black women or whites arrested for raping white women (LaFree, 1980).[1] Another found that defendants arrested for murdering whites in Florida were more likely to be indicted for first-degree murder than those arrested for murdering blacks (Radelet, 1981).[2]

One researcher has also concluded that sex is a significant factor. Among those arrested for burglary in California who did not have a prior record, women were more likely to have their case dismissed than men (Pope, 1976a). Yet, this relationship did not materialize for men and women with a prior record.

In sum, these studies did uncover a relationship between race or sex and the prosecutor's decision to prosecute a case fully. However, their small number and limited scope minimize their generalizability.

Moreover, some studies concluded that neither race nor sex is a significant factor in the decision to dismiss. These include a study of misdemeanors in New Haven, Connecticut (Feeley, 1979), examination of various felonies in a city in upstate New York (Bernstein, Kelly, and Doyle, 1977; Bernstein et al., 1979), and analysis of the treatment of Indians and whites in a medium-sized city in Canada (Hagan, 1975).

In these studies, race and sex explain a relatively small portion of the variance in the decision to dismiss. One researcher found that they account for considerably less of the variance in this decision than in the decisions to convict and sentence (Myers, 1977). Thus, race and sex do not appear to have a substantial impact on the decision to dismiss. Presumably, the strength of the case weighs more heavily at this stage, since the prosecutor already has weeded out many cases. Yet, researchers have not had information about rejections that occur prior to the preliminary hearing. Before concluding that there is little racial or sexual discrimination by the prosecutor, it is necessary to obtain and analyze such information.

DATA

Data for this project were obtained from the PROMIS data file maintained by the Los Angeles County District Attorney's Office. A complete file of all cases filed with the District Attorney's Office from 1977 to 1980 was available. From this file a random sample of over 70,000 cases was selected. Cases were then eliminated where multiple charges were filed against the defendant.[3] This left about 33,000 cases.

Two dependent variables were used to measure pretrial dispositions. The first focuses on the prosecutor's initial decision to prosecute or not. It is a dichotomous variable (reject = 1; not reject = 0) which reflects the prosecutor's decision to reject a felony charge against the defendant, either by dropping the charge outright or by reducing it to a misdemeanor. The second focuses on the decision to dismiss a felony charge against the defendant after a formal charge has been filed by the prosecutor. It too is a dichotomous variable (dismiss = 1; not dismiss = 0) which reflects whether or not the charge, once filed, was later dismissed, either before or following the preliminary hearing. Use of these two variables allowed testing for ethnic and gender discrimination in the pretrial stages of the criminal justice process.

Six independent variables were used as controls in the analysis. For all analyses, the defendant's age and prior criminal record, the seriousness of the charge against the defendant, and whether or not the defendant used a weapon in committing the crime (yes = 1; no = 0) were controlled for. For the analysis of differences by gender, race was controlled for with two dummy variables: black (black = 1; other = 0); and Hispanic (Hispanic = 1; other = 0). For the analysis of differences by ethnicity, gender was controlled for with a dummy variable for male (male = 1; female = 0).[4]

Two of the independent variables, the seriousness of the charge and the prior criminal record, require elaboration. The seriousness of the charge against the defendant is measured by the offense score, which ranges from 1 to 99,[5] and which is one factor used by the Los Angeles County District Attorney's office to assess the gravity of the charge against the defendant. The score includes such items as the number of victims killed, hospitalized, or treated and released; the number of victims of forcible sexual intercourse; the number of victims threatened by a weapon or by physical force; the number of premises forcibly entered; and so on. Each item is assigned a weight,[6] and the score is calculated by multiplying the weight of the item by the number of times it occurred and then summing these. This score was used as a substitute for and an improvement upon the standard categorization of felonies. Since the score takes various facets of a criminal act into account, it allows one to distinguish between defendants charged with more or less serious versions of the same crime.

The prior record score is used by the district attorney's office to measure the seriousness of the defendant's prior criminal record. Four items are included in the score:

whether or not the defendant had been arrested in the last five years, the number of previous arrests, the number of arrests for crimes against persons, and whether or not the defendant ever used an alias. Each item included in the score is weighted[7] and the scores for each item are summed. This score, then, discriminates among defendants primarily on the basis of their prior arrest records.[8]

Multiple regression was used to analyze rejection and dismissal of charges against Anglo, black, and Hispanic male and female defendants. Since both of the dependent variables were dichotomous, a logit model was also tested as a check on the validity of the regression results.[9] Logit, of course, is designed primarily for variables with only a few values. This technique yielded results nearly identical with those of the regression, so only the regression results will be presented.[10]

FINDINGS

A major problem with studies which examine the decision to prosecute or not is that very few adequately control for the strength of the evidence against the defendant. This factor has been shown to have a strong impact on the decision to prosecute (Miller, 1969; Vera Institute of Justice, 1981). While this study yielded information only on cases rejected, that information (in Table 1) does reveal some similarities among ethnic and gender groups.

This table lists, by ethnicity and gender, the reason given by the district attorney for rejecting or reducing the charge at the initial screening of these Los Angeles felony defendants. The reasons cited are remarkably similar for all groups. Evidence problems (the first three reasons listed) are cited as the primary reason for rejecting the charge against a majority of the defendants in each group; the figures range for 38% for black males to 49% for black females. An examination of the next two reasons, both of which involve victim or witness reluctance to testify, also shows little variation among the groups. Victim or witness problems were given as the reason for rejecting the charge against 4% to 7% of each group.

Thus, for those defendants whose cases are rejected, the reasons are strikingly similar. There is little variation among ethnic groups and between sexes in the decisions to reject. But does that mean that ethnicity and gender are not factors in these decisions?

The effect of race and gender on pretrial dispositions is shown in Table 2, which presents adjusted rates of rejection and dismissal for these defendants.[11] The data reveal a pattern of discrimination in favor of female defendants and against black and Hispanic defendants. The differences are particularly striking for the prosecutor's decision to reject the charge. Parts a and b of column one show that females are much more likely than males, and Anglos more likely than either blacks or Hispanics, to have the charge against them rejected. Part c of Table 2 further clarifies the preferential treatment of women and Anglos. Women in each ethnic group are significantly more likely than their male counterparts to benefit from charge rejection; the differences range from 8% for blacks to 4% for Anglos. Furthermore, the rejection rates for both Anglo men and Anglo women are higher than the rate for any other group.

Table 1.   Reasons Given by District Attorney for Rejecting Charge

Reasons Given[a]	Anglo[b]		Black		Hispanic	
	MALE	FEMALE	MALE	FEMALE	MALE	FEMALE
Insufficent Evidence that a Crime Occurred	19*	19	16	20	17	17
Insufficient Evidence to Connect Suspect to Crime	19	17	17	24	23	24
Evidence Inadmissible–Violation of Search and Seizure Laws	3	4	5	5	2	3
Victim Unavailable or Declines to Testify	3	4	5	5	3	6
Witness Unavailable or Declines to Testify	1	1	1	1	1	1
Interest of Justice[c]	7	6	6	4	5	4
Case Referred to Police for Further Investigation	1	1	2	1	1	1
Pretrial Diversion	0	0	1	0	0	0
Total Rejections	53	52	53	60	52	56
Referred to City Attorney for Prosecution as Misdemeanor	32	33	29	24	31	30
Referred to District Attorney for Prosecution as Misdemeanor	15	15	17	15	15	12

[a] The reason given by the District Attorney for rejecting the charge as felony. Up to four reasons could be entered for each charge, but in 86% of the cases, only one reason was listed. Therefore, the first reason only was used.

[b] For the number of cases in each ethnic/gender combination, see Table 2.

[c] Included here are cases in which the victim requested no further prosecution, in which the suspect was dead or insane, or in which the statute of limitations was applied.

* All table entries are percents.

Prosecutors, then, do appear to take both gender and race into account in deciding whether to charge the defendant.

Table 2 also indicates that gender, but not race, plays a role in the subsequent decision to dismiss the charge filed by the prosecutor. As noted earlier, charges are dismissed either at the request of the prosecutor prior to the preliminary hearing or by order of the judge following the preliminary hearing. Part c of column two in the table reveals that in each racial group, females are more likely than males to have the charge against them dismissed prior to trial. The differences—9% for Hispanics, 7% for Anglos, and 6% for blacks—are large and statistically significant. They indicate that females, who already benefit from more favorable treatment by prosecutors in the decision to charge or not, continue to be treated more leniently as the case moves toward trial.

Why are there ethnic and gender differences in the decision to reject but only gender differences in the decision to dismiss? One reason might be that dismissals are somewhat more visible than rejections. Where rejections are done in the privacy of the prosecutor's office, dismissals must be, at least pro forma, judicial decisions. As the

Table 2.   The Effect of Ethnicity and Gender on the Decisions to Reject or Dismiss Charges against Criminal Defendants

	Adjusted Means[a]				
	Disposition of Charge				
	REJECTED[b]		DISMISSED[c]		PROSECUTED
	%	N	%	N	%
a) Gender					
Female	55	3,693*[d]	41	1,482*	25*
Male	46	29,639	34	16,227	35
b) Ethnicity					
Anglo	59	12,540	34	4,636	25
Black	40	12,666*[e]	36	8,568	39
Hispanic	37	7,126	34	4,505	41
c) Ethnicity and Gender					
Anglo Female	59	1,697*[f]	42	475*	19
Anglo Male	54	10,840	33	4,163	26
Black Female	57	1,547	42	781*	30*
Black Male	46	12,123	34	7,787	39
Hispanic Female	54	450	43	228*	31*
Hispanic Male	46	6,676	33	4,277	42

[a] See note 11 for a description of the way in which adjusted means were calculated. For all analyses the defendant's age and prior criminal record, the seriousness of the charge against the defendant, and whether or not a weapon was used in committing the crime were controlled for. For the analysis of differences by gender, race was also controlled for by entering two dummy variables: black (black = 1, other = 0) and (Hispanic = 1, other = 0). For the analysis of differences by race, gender was also controlled for by using a dummy variable (male = 1, female = 0).

[b] Whether or not the charge brought by the police was rejected by the prosecutor. Analysis includes 33,332 defendants.

[c] Whether or not the charge, once brought by the prosecutor, was later dismissed at the initiation of the prosecutor or the court. Analysis includes only defendants whose charge was not rejected by the prosecutor (n = 17,709).

[d] Test of significance for differences between females and males.

[e] Test of significance for differences between Anglos and blacks or between Anglos and Hispanics.

[f] Test of significance for difference between males and females in each ethnic group.

*p < .01

process becomes more visible, norms against racial discrimination in the process may become more pronounced. There may be a greater acceptance of the idea that racial discrimination is wrong than of the notion that it is wrong to treat women more leniently. Given the responsibilities of many women for child care, there may also be a greater reluctance of both the prosecutor and witnesses to proceed with cases against women, even if initially the prosecutor believed the case was sound.

The existence of gender and ethnic discrimination in pretrial dispositions is further substantiated by the data presented in the third column of Table 2. It is clear that men are more likely than women to be prosecuted (to plead guilty or go to trial). It also is apparent that Hispanics are prosecuted more often than blacks, who are prosecuted more often than Anglos. And in each ethnic group males have a higher rate of prosecution than females. The low rate of prosecution for Anglo females is particularly striking; at 19%, the rate is less than one half the rate for black males (39%) or Hispanic males (42%). In fact, both Anglo men and women are prosecuted at a lower rate than any other group.

Why might there be some ethnic and gender differences in the decision to prosecute? One conceivable explanation is that the prosecutor acts without prejudice, but the police are prejudiced in making arrests. However, this would mean that the police are more likely to arrest Anglos and women on weak evidence than males, blacks, or Hispanics. The prosecutor then adjusts for this tendency by prosecuting fewer women and fewer whites. While possible, this scenario seems unlikely.

If this is unlikely, then one must assume that there is some discrimination in the prosecutor's decision, perhaps in those cases that are most marginal: those that could either be prosecuted or dropped. Presumably, strong cases will be prosecuted no matter what the gender or ethnicity of the defendant, and weak cases will be dropped. But in marginal cases prosecutors may simply feel less comfortable prosecuting the dominant rather than the subordinate ethnic groups. They might feel the dominant groups are less threatening. Or they might believe they can win convictions more often against blacks and Hispanics than against Anglos. There is no evidence that blacks are convicted more often than Anglos. However, if the cases against blacks are on the average weaker (because they include marginal cases that would not be prosecuted against Anglos), then in fact there is some discrimination against blacks at that stage and this presumed assumption of prosecutors is correct.

Similar speculative reasons can be offered for gender differences. It is very plausible that the same paternalistic attitudes occur in prosecutors when deciding whether to prosecute a woman as occur in judges in deciding whether to sentence her to prison. Fears of removing a woman from her dependents or placing her in a brutal environment may guide prosecutors as well as judges. Then, too, crimes may be seen as less heinous when committed by a woman.

SUMMARY

Though social scientists have examined ethnic and gender discrimination in the criminal justice system, they have paid relatively little attention to the prosecutor's decision to prosecute fully. While sometimes they have looked at the decision to dismiss a case, they have largely ignored the initial decision to reject a case.

This study has helped to fill this gap in the understanding of ethnic and gender discrimination. Though few differences were found among the groups examined in the reasons charges are rejected, significant ethnic and gender differences were found in the decision to prosecute. Hispanic males are most likely of all six gender/ethnic groups to be prosecuted. Black males are next, then Anglo males and females of all ethnic groups. The ethnic differences are apparent only at the rejection stage, the gender differences at both the rejection and dismissal stages.

The analysis looked at the question of ethnic and gender discrimination in these pretrial decisions in at least two novel ways. First, treatment of Hispanics as well as of blacks and Anglos was examined. The only previous study that explored the treatment of Hispanics at this stage in the process grouped them with blacks in a "non-Anglo" category because there were not enough to create a separate category (Bernstein et al., 1977; Bernstein et al., 1979). And, though the present study found that both Hispanics and blacks are more likely to be prosecuted than Anglos, there were some differences between Hispanics and blacks. At least in the city studied, Hispanic males were slightly more likely than black males to be prosecuted.

Equally importantly, this study seems to be unique in its examination of not only dismissals but also rejections by the prosecutor. Indeed, it was found that blacks and Hispanics were less likely to have their case rejected at the initial screening, even though they were just as likely as Anglos to have their case dismissed later in the process. This suggests that some previous studies which found no discrimination at the dismissal stage may have overlooked discrimination at the earlier screening.

One factor that could not be examined is the possible effect of the length of time a defendant has served in jail before the preliminary hearing. Earlier work has shown that defendants spending more time in jail have a higher probability of having their cases dismissed (Bernstein et al., 1977). Spending time in jail could also encourage a plea of guilty in order to get out sooner. Either way, time in jail, as a potentially important influence on the probability of dismissal, should be taken into account.

This study suggests that one cannot be too sanguine about the growing number of studies finding little racial discrimination in the criminal justice process. These studies are reassuring about the basic fairness of the formal trial process, perhaps even of the less formal guilty plea process. However, what happens before conviction may not be so reassuring. Indeed, in the one community examined, discrimination against black and Hispanic males was found in the decision to reject the case or not. It was also found that females, especially Anglo females, were treated preferentially. While these findings are certainly not definitive, even for this community, they do call for the kind of scrutiny in the pretrial stages that has been so rightly given to the convicting and sentencing stages.

Notes

*An earlier version of this paper was presented at the 1985 annual meeting of the Midwest Political Science Association. The support of the University of Nebraska at Omaha Committee on Research; the University of Nebraska, Lincoln, Research Council; and the National Institute of Justice are gratefully acknowledged.

1. There were too few whites arrested for raping black women (LaFree, 1980).

2. Though grand juries technically are responsible for indictments, prosecutors generally control grand juries and usually can manipulate grand jurors to issue indictments.

3. It is recognized that prosecutors may file multiple charges in an attempt to induce guilty pleas and that there may be ethnic and/or gender discrimination in the decision to dismiss some of these charges. However, discrimination in the plea-bargaining process is beyond the scope of this paper. The question of interest is who is prosecuted and who is not.

It was decided to limit the analysis to defendants with only one charge against them for several reasons. The PROMIS data did not allow one to disaggregate crime scores for each separate charge. Some cases did have indicators for each separate crime charged, but most cases did not. Given that, it was concluded that the crime score, which measures the severity of the charge against the defendant, would produce misleading results in cases with multiple charges. The crime score aggregates points for the severity of each charge against the defendant into one composite score. Thus, it could give a disproportionately high score to defendants charged with several less serious crimes. A defendant charged with several counts of a crime such as burglary, for example, could receive a score higher than that of a defendant charged with a single count of murder.

Finally, the preliminary analysis revealed few differences in the treatment of defendants with one charge and defendants with multiple charges.

While, as expected, the dismissal rate is higher for those with only one charge, in both groups the *differences* between females and males or between Anglos, blacks, and Hispanics are similar. The differences in the rates for females and males are 10% for those with one charge, 8% for those with multiple charges. The differences in the rates for Anglos and blacks are 1% for those with one charge, 2% for those with multiple charges. For blacks and Hispanics, the comparable figures are 3% and 4%; for Anglos and Hispanics they are 2% and 2%. In short, these similarities, coupled with the potential for the crime score to produce misleading results for defendants with multiple charges, led to limiting the analysis to defendants with only one charge.

4. Other variables—employment, marital status, social class, relationship between the defendant and victim, strength of the evidence—have been shown to affect the decision to prosecute. Some of these variables, such as the defendant-victim relationship and the strength of the evidence, were not available through the PROMIS system. Others, such as employment and marital status, were available only for a small part of the sample.

5. If the computed value of the offense score is greater than 99, it is set at 99.

6. The 11 items included in the score and their weights are as follows: the number of victims killed (26); the number of victims of forcible sexual intercourse (10); the number of victims hospitalized (7); the number of victims treated and released (4); the number of victims threatened or intimidated by display of weapons (4); the number of victims threatened or intimidated verbally or by physical force (2); the number of victims of sex crimes intimidated by any type of weapon (2); the number of motor vehicles stolen (2); the number of premises forcibly entered (1); the dollar value of property stolen, damaged, or destroyed ([less than $10 = 1], [$10–250 = 2], [$251–2,000 = 3], [over $2,000 = 4]); and whether the defendant possessed a firearm or replica of a firearm (5) or another dangerous weapon (1) at the time of arrest.

7. The weights for each item are as follows: an arrest within the last five years (10); the number of previous arrests (5); the number of arrests for crimes against persons (5); and use of an alias (2.5).

8. Because it focuses on a defendant's arrest record, the prior record score may be an imperfect indicator of the seriousness of a defendant's prior record. Research has shown that prior convictions, and especially prior incarcerations, are better predictors of sentence than is the prior arrest record. This may not be true, however, for predicting rejection or dismissal of the charges.

9. To obtain accurate OLS estimates, the error terms must be normally distributed. When the dependent variable has only two values, it is impossible, or nearly so, to have such a normally distributed term. The residuals will vary systematically with the independent variables (for general discussions of this problem, compare Aldrich and Cnudde, 1975; Kritzer, 1978; Swofford, 1980). With large sample sizes, these problems are somewhat mitigated (Stokes, 1967), but nevertheless still remain when one has the extreme cases of a truncated dependent variable, a binary dependent variable.

10. A two-step technique was used to estimate logit coefficients. First, a saturated logit model for dismissal and for rejection was estimated, including the dependent variable and the independent variables. The interval level variables (for example, age) were recoded to three and four category variables to be usable. Once the basic saturated model is fit, the significance of the various terms is computed by examining the chi square fit changes when the effect is excluded from the model. The expected frequencies are then calculated from a reduced logit

model that includes only the terms that were found to reduce the chi square fit by a significant amount. In the reduced model, the interval level variables were restored to their original form.

Estimates of the expected value for each cell were nearly identical to those presented here. For example, with dismissal as a dependent variable, the estimates produced by the regression shown in Table 2 and the logit model are remarkably similar, which led to the conclusion that the original regression model was highly acceptable. This is not surprising, given that the dependent variable is not highly skewed.

11. These adjusted figures were computed in the following way. Dummy variables were created for two of the three racial groups (Hispanics and blacks), for males, and for five of the six race/gender combinations—white females, black males, black females, Hispanic females, and Hispanic males. Regressions were done on each of the two dependent variables using the independent variables as controls. Briefly, the difference between any two categories is equal to the unstandardized regression coefficient for the relevant dummy variable. So, for example, the difference of .03 between rejection rates for blacks and Hispanics (see Table 2) reflects a .03 unstandardized regression coefficient for Hispanics when blacks are the omitted category.

For the analysis of differences by race, adjusted figures for the dependent variables were calculated using the following formulas:

$$b_1 = -[\{(b_2)(prop_2)\} + \{(b_3)(prop_3)\}]$$
$$adjmean_1 = M + b_1$$
$$adjmean_2 = adjmean_1 + b_2$$
$$adjmean_3 = adjmean_1 + b_3$$

Where:

b_1 = the adjusted unstandardized regression weight (b weight) for the omitted category (whites);

b_2, b_3 = the b weights for the two dummy variables in the regression;

$prop_2$, $prop_3$ = the means of the two dummy variables (or the proportion of defendants scoring 1 on the dummy variables);

M = the mean of the dependent variable;

$adjmean_1$, $adjmean_2$, $adjmean_3$ = the adjusted means for each of the three racial groups.

References

Aldrich, John and Charles Cnudde
1975   Probing the bounds of conventional wisdom: A comparison of regression, probit and discriminant analysis. American Journal of Political Science 19: 571–608.

Baab, George William and William Royal Fergesun, Jr.
1967   Texas sentencing practices: A statistical study. Texas Law Review 45: 471–503.

Bernstein, Ilene H., John Cardascia, and Catherine Ross
1979   Defendant's sex and criminal court decisions. In R. Alvarez (ed.), Discrimination in Organizations. San Francisco: Jossey-Bass.

Bernstein, Ilene Nagel, William R. Kelly, and Patricia A. Doyle
1977   Societal reaction to deviants: The case of criminal defendants. American Sociological Review 42: 743–755.

Bishop, Donna M. and Charles E. Frazier
1984   The effect of gender on charge reduction. The Sociological Quarterly 25: 385–396.

Black, Charles L.
1974   Capital Punishment: The Inevitability of Caprice and Mistake. New Haven: Yale University Press.

Boland, Barbara, INSLAW, Inc.
1983   The Prosecution of Felony Arrests. Washington, D.C.: Bureau of Justice Statistics.

Brosi, Kathleen B.
  1979   A Cross-City Comparison of Felony Case Processing. Washington, D.C.: Institute for
            Law and Social Research.
Davis, Kenneth Culp
  1969   Discretionary Justice. Baton Rouge: Louisiana State University Press.
Engle, Charles Donald
  1971   Criminal justice in the city: A study of sentence severity and variation in the
            Philadelphia criminal court system. Unpublished Ph.D. dissertation. Philadelphia:
            Temple University.
Feeley, Malcolm M.
  1979   The Process is the Punishment: Handling Cases in a Lower Criminal Court. New
            York: Russell Sage Foundation.
Green, Edward
  1961   Judicial Attitudes in Sentencing. New York: St. Martins Press.
Greenwood, Peter W., Sorrel Wildhorn, Eugene C. Poggio, Michael J. Strumwasser, and Peter
            DeLeon
  1976   Prosecution of Adult Felony Defendants: A Policy Perspective. Lexington, MA: Lex-
            ington.
Gruhl, John, Susan Welch, and Cassia Spohn
  1984   Women as criminal defendants: A test for paternalism. Western Political Quarterly:
            456–467.
Hagan, John
  1974   Extra-legal attributes and criminal sentencing: An assessment of a sociological
            viewpoint. Law and Society Review 8: 857–884.
  1975   Parameters of criminal prosecution: An application of path analysis to a problem
            of criminal justice. Journal of Criminal Law and Criminology 65: 536–544.
Hagan, John and Kristin Bumiller
  1983   Making sense of sentencing: A review and critique of sentencing research. In
            Alfred Blumstein, Jacqueline Cohen, S. Martin, and Michael Tonry (eds.),
            Research on Sentencing: The Search for Reform, Vol. 2. Washington, D.C.:
            National Academy.
Katz, Lewis R.
  1980   The Justice Imperative: An Introduction to Criminal Justice. Anderson Publishing.
Katzenelson, Susan
  1976   The Female Defendant in Washington, D.C. Washington, D.C.: The Institute for Law
            and Social Research.
Kleck, Gary
  1981   Racial discrimination in criminal sentencing. American Sociological Review 46:
            783–805.
Kritzer, Herbert M.
  1978   An introduction to multivariate contingency table analysis. American Journal of
            Political Science 22: 187–226.
LaFree, Gary D.
  1980   The effect of sexual stratification by race on official reactions to rape. American
            Sociological Review 45: 842–854.
Mather, Lynn M.
  1979   Plea Bargaining or Trial? The Process of Criminal Case Disposition. Lexington,
            MA: Lexington.
Miller, Frank W.
  1969   Prosecution: The Decision to Charge a Suspect with a Crime. Boston: Little, Brown.
Myers, Martha A.
  1977   The effects of victim characteristics in the prosecution, conviction, and sentencing
            of criminal defendants. Unpublished Ph.D. dissertation. Bloomington: Indiana
            University.

Nagel, Stuart and Lenore J. Weitzman
1971 Women as litigants. In Freda Adler and Rita James Simon (eds.), The Criminology of Deviant Women. Boston: Houghton Mifflin.
Pope, Carl E.
1976a The influence of social and legal factors on sentencing dispositions: A preliminary analysis of offender-based transaction statistics. Journal of Criminal Justice: 203–221.
1976b Post arrest release decisions: An empirical examination of social and legal criteria. Presented at the annual meeting of the American Society of Criminology.
Radelet, Michael L.
1981 Racial characteristics and the imposition of the death penalty. American Sociological Review 46: 918–927.
Silberman, Charles E.
1978 Criminal Violence, Criminal Justice. New York: Random House.
Simon, Rita James
1975 Women and Crime. Lexington, MA: Lexington.
Spohn, Cassia, John Gruhl, and Susan Welch
1981– The effect of race on sentencing: A re-examination of an unsettled question. Law
1982 and Society Review 16: 72–88.
Spohn, Cassia, Susan Welch, and John Gruhl
1985 Women defendants in court: The interaction between sex and race in convicting and sentencing. Social Science Quarterly 66: 178–185.
Steffensmeier, Darrell and John H. Kramer
1982 Sex-based differences in the sentencing of adult criminal defendants. Sociology and Social Research 66: 289–304.
Stokes, Donald
1967 Some dynamic elements of contests for the presidency. American Political Science Review 60: 19–28.
Sutton, L. Paul
1978 Variations in Federal Criminal Sentences: A Statistical Assessment at the National Level. Albany, NY: Criminal Justice Research Center.
Swigert, Victoria Lynn and Ronald A. Farrell
1977 Normal homicides and the law. American Sociological Review 42: 16–32.
Swofford, Michael
1980 Parametric techniques for contingency table analysis. American Sociological Review 45: 664–690.
Unnever, James
1981 Institutional racism: Direct and structural discrimination. Presented at the American Sociological Association annual meeting.
Vera Institute of Justice
1981 Felony Arrests: Their Prosecution and Disposition in New York City's Courts. New York: Longman.
Welch, Susan, John Gruhl, and Cassia Spohn
1984 Dismissal, conviction and incarceration of Hispanic defendants: A comparison with Anglos and blacks. Social Science Quarterly 65: 257–264.
Welch, Susan, Cassia Spohn, and John Gruhl
1985 Convicting and sentencing differences among blacks, Hispanics and whites in six localities. Justice Quarterly 2: 67–80.
Zatz, Marjorie
1981 Differential treatment within the criminal justice system by race/ethnicity. Presented at the American Sociological Association annual meeting.
1984 Race, ethnicity and determinate sentencing. Criminology 22: 147–172.

33.   The Impacts of Evidence and Extralegal Factors in Jurors' Decisions*

BARBARA F. RESKIN AND CHRISTY A. VISHER

INTRODUCTION

This study seeks to advance our understanding of how jurors use evidence. Specifically, it addresses three issues: (1) the effects of several measures of evidence on jurors' judgments of a defendant's guilt, (2) whether jurors' judgments are more strongly influenced by the evidence as they recall it or as it is measured by an observer at trial, and (3) whether the effects of extralegal factors on jurors' decisions depend on the strength of the evidence. Our analyses are based on courtroom observations and posttrial interviews with jurors who served in sexual assault trials.

Researchers have examined how both evidence and various extralegal factors influence jurors' judgments (see, e.g., Simon, 1967; Kaplan and Kemmerick, 1974; Saks et al., 1975; Kaplan and Miller, 1978; Myers, 1979; Feild and Bienen, 1980; Loftus, 1981; Tanford and Penrod, 1982; for reviews see Penrod and Hastie, 1979; Kaplan, 1982; Hastie et al., 1983). Many earlier studies have loosely classified evidence as "strong" or "weak" and focused primarily on defendants' characteristics to indicate extralegal variables. Few studies have simultaneously examined the influence of a wide range of both evidence and extralegal factors. Of those that have taken this approach, most included both evidence and extralegal factors in an additive model rather than testing Kalven and Zeisel's (1966) "liberation hypothesis" of the *interactive* relationship between the strength of the evidence and jurors' "sentiments." Studies designed to test explicitly whether the effects of legally irrelevant factors are confined to cases in which the evidence is weak or ambiguous have yielded mixed and nonpersuasive results. Our data provide a stronger test of the liberation hypothesis.

METHODS

Data and Sample

Our data come from a larger study of thirty-eight forcible sexual assault trials held in Marion County (Indianapolis), Indiana, courts between 1978 and 1980.[1] Two observers coded trial data using a detailed coding scheme. We interviewed 331 of the total 456 jurors,[2] yielding a 70.4 percent response rate.[3] In interviews, which were held within several days of each of the trials and lasted about ninety minutes, we questioned jurors about their personal background (age, education, occupation, marital status, and previous jury service), their attitudes about crime, and their reactions to the defendant and alleged victim, using both open and closed items.[4] We then asked them several questions about the evidence (described below), whether before deliberating they believed the defendant was guilty, and whether they agreed with the final verdict. Many variables were precoded; trained coders coded the rest.[5] These data permit us to assess whether jurors' recollections better predict their decisions than the more readily available measures of evidence observed in court.

Variables

Our dependent variable is the individual juror's assessment of the defendant's guilt or innocence at the end of the trial but before deliberating. Response choices included certainly guilty, probably guilty, probably innocent, and certainly innocent. The nineteen jurors who did not answer this question are omitted from the analysis. We chose to analyze the predeliberation "verdict" because our interest is in how individual jurors' assessments of the evidence and trial participants influence their decisions. Unlike the final verdict, the predeliberation verdict varies among jurors within the same trial and thus can covary with independent variables measured at the juror-level. After hearing the evidence and the attorneys' closing arguments, most jurors have reached a tentative decision about the defendant's guilt (Kalven and Zeisel, 1966; Simon, 1980). Since we interviewed jurors after deliberation, the deliberation process may have affected their recollections of their predeliberation judgments. We cannot eliminate this problem, but the jurors' candor about their degree of certainty in the final verdict suggests that recall bias did not seriously threaten the validity of this measure.[6]

Our independent variables include evidence, jurors' perceptions of victims and defendants, and a measure of jurors' attitudes about crime. We do not examine jurors' other personal characteristics such as age, sex, and race in this paper because in several earlier analyses of these data they showed no independent effects on the dependent variable (Visher, 1982; 1985; for similar results see Hepburn, 1980; Sealey, 1981; Hastie et al., 1983).

Measuring Evidence

Legally, all admissible testimony from the witness stand is evidence, and jurors' accounts of the evidence that influenced their decisions reflect the wide range of "data" presented at trial. In recounting what influenced them, jurors cited more than one hundred different factors ranging from victim's testimony to material evidence to inferences about the victim's and defendant's characters. Researchers consider some of these, such as a victim's sexual history and a defendant's employment status or prior criminal record, extralegal factors.

Given the adversarial nature of trials, much evidence is disputed, and in trying the facts jurors must choose which piece of contradictory evidence to believe. However, some evidence, such as a broken arm, a recovered weapon, or the testimony of a disinterested witness such as a passer-by who heard screams, is harder to dispute. For example, the evidence that convinced one juror that an assault had been attempted was a prosecution witness who had helped the victim get away from the attacker: "We couldn't hear him [this witness] very well, but the fact that he was there was what counted."

In recognition of this difference between various types of evidence we sought to distinguish such hard-to-contest evidence (i.e., "hard" evidence) from both evidence that the other side contradicts and extralegal "evidence" such as disputants' personal characteristics or their claims about what occurred. In this paper we classify as hard evidence eyewitness testimony, a recovered weapon, physical injury to the victim, and other physical evidence. Evidence of physical injury came from medical records, photographs, or testimony from doctors who had treated the victim. Physical evidence is material evidence linking the defendant to the crime, such as a book inscribed with the defendant's name that was found in the victim's car or a police report in which the victim's description of her assailant's tatoos matched those visible on the defendant. While the four evidence variables listed above do not capture all hard evidence presented at trials, they represent an advance over the measurement of evidence in most previous studies of jurors.

We measured evidence in two ways: by coding testimony and exhibits presented during the trial and by asking jurors about the evidence. Trial observers recorded the content of each witness's testimony as well as any physical evidence presented in court in testimony or as an exhibit. From their observations we constructed trial-level measures of the four types of hard evidence described: no versus any recovered weapon, no versus any physical injury to victim, no versus any eyewitness testimony, and no versus any other physical evidence (all coded 0, 1).[7] Eyewitnesses testified in six of the thirty-eight trials, a recovered weapon was introduced in ten, evidence that the victim was injured in addition to the assault itself was presented in nine cases, and physical evidence was offered in fourteen.

Our juror interviews were designed to measure the evidence jurors found important. We asked, with respect to each of the legal elements of assault (namely, that sexual contact occurred or was attempted, that the defendant was the perpetrator, that the victim did not consent, and that the assailant used either force or the threat of imminent force), first whether the evidence proved each element and then what specific evidence led them to believe it did or did not. We also asked which evidence had been most influential for their final decision about the defendant's guilt. We constructed dichotomous variables indicating whether the jurors mentioned each of the four types of hard evidence. The trial and juror evidence measures are moderately correlated: for eyewitness testimony, $r = .59$; weapon, $r = .44$; victim injury, $r = .55$; and other physical evidence, $r = .30$. We suspect that the correlations are not stronger partly because the state must offer evidence for each element of the crime regardless of whether it is at issue, while jurors probably emphasized evidence for the element(s) under dispute in their trial (e.g., whether the victim consented or the correct identification of the defendant).

Jurors' Perceptions of Defendants and Victims

Our measures of jurors' sentiments or extralegal factors are based on their comments about or evaluations of the defendants' and victims' personal characteristics or life

Table 1. Description of Variables (N = 331)

Variable (Coding)	Mean	Correlation with Dependent Variable
Juror's perception of defendant's guilt (1 = certainly innocent; 4 = certainly guilty)	3.07	—
Trial-Level Evidence		
Recovered weapon (0, 1)[a]	.58	.30
Victim injured (0, 1)	.52	.28
Eyewitness testimony (0, 1)	.17	.22
Other physical evidence (0, 1)	.38	.28
Jurors' Recollections of Evidence		
Recovered weapon (0, 1)	.31	.31
Victim injured (0, 1)	.25	.23
Eyewitness testimony (0, 1)	.18	.20
Other physical evidence (0, 1)	.30	.21
Extralegal Factors		
Defendant seemed unattractive (1 = attractive; 5 = unattractive)	3.02	.12
Defendant employed (0, 1)	.69	−.26
Victim judged of poor moral character (0, 1)	.22	−.45
Victim seemed careless (1 = careful; 5 = careless)	2.76	−.40
Juror holds tough-on-crime attitude (factor scale)[b]	.00	.16

[a] All dichotomies are coded 0 = no, 1 = yes.
[b] For details see LaFree et al. (1985).

styles. After examining the correlations among a large number of such variables and estimating preliminary equations, we selected four variables for this analysis: (1) assessment of the defendant's attractiveness, (2) any reference to the defendant being employed or unemployed, (3) any negative comment about the victim's moral character,[8] and (4) juror's perception of the extent of the victim's carefulness or carelessness at the time of the assault. We also included a scale measuring jurors' attitudes toward crime. Table 1 shows how we coded these variables.

Analysis

We used ordinary least squares multiple regression to assess the effects of evidence and extralegal factors on jurors' predeliberation judgments of a defendant's guilt. We used statistical significance tests to assess the possibility that observed relationships may stem from random measurement error. We used a conservative one-tailed test (α = .01, t = 2.33).

Table 2.   Regressions of Defendants' Guilt on Evidence Measures

Variable[a]	Equation 1	Equation 2	Equation 3
Trial-Level Evidence			
Recovered weapon	.49	–	.28
	(.24)[b]		(.14)
Victim injury	.37	–	.24
	(.19)		(.12)
Other physical evidence	.38	–	.24
	(.19)		(.12)
Eyewitness testimony	.26[c]	–	.28[c]
	(.10)		(.10)
Jurors' Recollections of Evidence			
Recovered weapon	–	.60	.41
		(.28)	(.19)
Victim injury	–	.50	.29
		(.22)	(.13)
Other physical evidence	–	.29	.19[c]
		(.14)	(.09)
Eyewitness testimony	–	.33	.01[d]
		(.13)	(.02)
Y-intercept	2.41	2.62	2.38
$\bar{R}^2$	.19	.18	.23
N	312	312	312

[a] All variables significant at $p < .01$ except as noted.
[b] Standardized coefficients are in parentheses.
[c] $.01 < p < .05$.
[d] Not significant.

RESULTS

We begin by estimating, in turn, the effects of trial-level evidence measures and jurors' perceptions of the evidence. Next we examine jurors' perceptions of the defendant and victim, adding evidence measures in a second step. This latter specification assumes an additive model, in contradiction to the liberation hypothesis, and our final analyses test that assumption and the liberation hypothesis by estimating separate equations for cases with strong and weak evidence.

Extralegal Variables

As Table 2 indicates, the evidence presented at trial clearly influenced jurors' decisions. The four trial-level measures of evidence – a recovered weapon, victim injury, other physical evidence, and eyewitness testimony – jointly explained almost one-fifth of the variation in jurors' judgments about the defendant's guilt (see Table 2, Equation 1). The most influential variable was a recovered weapon. Not only does a weapon attest to force, one of the legal elements of rape, but it also indicates an assault's seriousness. Kalven and Zeisel (1966) found that jurors were more lenient when they deemed an assault to be nonserious (*de minimis*). Presumably for the same reasons, evidence showing that a victim had been injured increased jurors' propensity to believe that a defendant was guilty. Half of the victims sustained some injury in addition to the sexual assault, but these injuries varied in severity from bumping one's head against a car door to multiple stab wounds. The significant effect of a dichotomous representation (any injury versus no injury) suggests that evidence of an injury probably influenced jurors because it implied the use of force rather than indicating severe harm to the victim.

As we expected, other physical evidence was also influential. In few of the trials we studied was the defendant's guilt or innocence clear-cut, and jurors often had trouble deciding whom to believe, so it is not surprising that concrete evidence linking a defendant to the crime helped convince jurors of his guilt. Finally, an eyewitness's evidence was influential presumably because it bears on several of the legal elements of rape—whether sex occurred or was attempted, whether it was accomplished (or attempted) through force or the imminent threat of force and without the victim's consent, and whether the defendant was the assailant.

Jurors' Perceptions of the Evidence

The results for the four measures of jurors' perceptions of the evidence shown in Table 2, Equation 2 resemble those for the trial-level measures. All are statistically significant, and together they explain 18 percent of the variance in the dependent variable. As in Equation 1, a recovered weapon appeared to influence the jurors most, and eyewitness testimony was least influential.

Measuring evidence exclusively by either what was introduced at trial or what jurors recalled as influential implies the two operationalizations are interchangeable. Although we have seen that jury- and trial-level measures of each of the four kinds of evidence we examined are only moderately correlated, the similar results in Equation 1 and Equation 2 suggest that their covariance captures whatever it is in the evidence that influenced jurors' decisions. Moreover, including both trial evidence and jurors' recollections only slightly improved the explanatory power of either individually (a 4 percentage-point increase in explained variance; see Table 2, Equation 3). Thus, neither operationalization appears to be inherently preferable, and either adequately measures evidence.

Extralegal Variables

We next considered whether the personal characteristics of the two contestants in the trial influenced jurors' decisions by examining the effects of four extralegal variables—defendant's appearance, defendant's employment status, victim's apparent carelessness, and victim's moral character—as well as whether jurors held a tough-on-crime attitude. We began by examining the effects of these factors, without controlling for hard evidence, to provide a benchmark against which we could compare subsequent equations. As Table 3, Equation 1 indicates, all five variables show significant effects. That they jointly explain 31 percent of the variance might suggest that these measures of jurors' sentiments were more important in influencing jurors' decisions than was the evidence. Subsequent analyses required us to withhold such a conclusion.

Equation 2 shows the effects of the sentiment measures net of both trial- and juror-level evidence measures. The characteristics of both a defendant and his accuser affected juror's judgments net of the effects of evidence. If defendants seemed attractive or were employed, jurors were less likely to believe they were guilty.[9] Jurors were also swayed by the character of the woman who testified she had been assaulted. If, in their opinion, she had not exercised sufficient caution or was of poor moral character, they were less likely to believe the defendant was guilty. In fact, these two variables exerted the strongest independent effects on jurors' predeliberation verdicts. The victim's attractiveness did not influence jurors (results not shown tabularly), consistent with Feild (1979) but contrary to Seligman et al. (1977) and Calhoun et al. (1978). We also examined whether jurors' attitudes toward crime influenced their propensity to find the defendant guilty. Net of hard evidence and the defendant's characteristics, jurors who held hard-line anticrime attitudes were more likely to believe in the defendant's guilt.

Including the evidence measures in the equation attenuated the size of the effects of the extralegal variables, although all remained significant. Thus, failing to take evidence into account yields inflated estimates of the importance of extralegal factors. Taking into account both evidence and the extralegal factors moderately improved our ability to explain predeliberation verdicts over an equation with just evidence ($\bar{R}^2$ increased from .23 in Equation 3 of Table 2, to .39 in Equation 2 of Table 3), and the partial effects of every evidence measure—both trial- and juror-level—declined.

Juror Decision-Making in Strong and Weak Cases

The above results are derived from an additive model that assumes that the effects of jurors' impressions of the trial parties are independent of the strength of the evidence. If Kalven and Zeisel's liberation hypothesis is correct, "rule departures"—that is, extralegal effects—are most likely to occur when the evidence is weak. Variation across our trials in the amount of hard evidence the prosecution introduced permitted us to distinguish between weaker and stronger cases. We classified the evidence as "weak" in fifteen trials in which the state presented none or only one of the four types of evidence. In the remaining twenty-three trials in which the state offered at least two of the four kinds of evidence, we classified the evidence as "strong." Not surprisingly, jurors in strong cases were more likely to believe in the defendant's guilt. On a four-point scale on which jurors judged a defendant's guilt (with 1 representing certainly innocent and 4 representing certainly guilty), the means for the strong and weak cases were 3.5 and 2.5, respectively. Moreover, 91 percent of the strong cases resulted in guilty verdicts in contrast to 53 percent of the weak cases.

To test Kalven and Zeisel's hypothesis that the influence of legally irrelevant factors is greatest in weak cases, we compared the effects of jurors' reactions to defendants' and victims' characteristics in strong and weak cases. Including jurors' recollections of evidence in these equations makes it more difficult for extralegal factors to show an effect, which yields a more conservative test for the weak cases. Omitting juror-level evidence measures makes it easier for extralegal factors to show an effect, thus posing a more conservative test for the strong cases. As a result, for both types of cases we estimated equations both with and without the juror-level evidence measures.

Strong Cases.   Our results support the hypothesis that the strength of a case affects whether the jurors consider factors other than hard evidence in arriving at a decision. In cases in which the state presented at least two pieces of hard evidence, jurors tended to ignore the trial parties' personal characteristics (see Table 3, Equation 3a—the more conservative test—and Equation 3b). Only one such variable significantly affected their assessments of the defendant's guilt—whether they thought the victim had failed to exercise sufficient caution. Jurors who made this attribution were more likely to rate the defendant as innocent. Some have argued that equity considerations govern jurors' allocation of responsibility (see, e.g., Scheflin and Van Dyke, 1980; Howard, 1984) and that jurors are more inclined to exonerate defendants if they believed a victim's negligence contributed to her assault (Kalven and Zeisel, 1966).[10]

Note also that two of the juror-level evidence measures show significant effects (Table 3, Equation 3b), even though we partially controlled evidence by considering strong and weak cases separately. Jurors in strong cases who mentioned a recovered weapon or injury to the victim were more likely to judge the defendant guilty than were those who did not mention such evidence.

Weak Cases.   In sharp contrast to these findings stand the results for the fifteen cases in which the state introduced none or only one of the four types of hard evidence. Even when we controlled for evidence (see Table 3, Equation 4b), the jurors' verdicts were still influenced by their attitudes toward crime as well as by the characteristics of the alleged victims and the men they accused. Jurors were more likely to believe in a defendant's guilt if he were unemployed or seemed unattractive to them, and more likely to exonerate him if, by their standards, the victim had behaved carelessly or was of poor moral character. Thus, in weak cases jurors were heavily influenced by their own values and their reactions to victims and defendants.

That the effects of jurors' sentiments depend on the strength of the case supports Kalven and Zeisel's liberation hypothesis. As they said, "The jury does not consciously . . . yield to sentiment in the teeth of the law. Rather it yields to sentiment in the apparent process of resolving doubts as to the evidence" (1966: 165). Thus, the additive equation (Table 3, Equation 2) is misspecified. Its coefficients represent an average of minimal extralegal effects in the strong evidence cases and strong effects in the weak cases.

Table 3. Regressions of Defendants' Guilt on Evidence Measures and Extralegal Variables for All Cases and for Strong and Weak Cases

Independent Variables	All Cases		Strong Cases		Weak Cases	
	EQUATION 1	EQUATION 2	EQUATION 3A	EQUATION 3B	EQUATION 4A	EQUATION 4B
Trial-Level Evidence						
Recovered weapon		$.26^a$		—		—
		$(.13)^b$				
Victim injury		.13		—		—
		(.06)				
Other physical evidence		$.20^c$		—		—
		(.10)				
Eyewitness testimony		.03		—		—
		(.01)				
Jurors' Recollections of Evidence						
Recovered weapon		$.28^a$		$.26^a$		$.35^c$
		(.13)		(.18)		(.12)
Victim injury		.13		$.22^c$		−.04
		(.08)		(.15)		(−.01)
Other physical evidence		.10		.07		−.04
		(.05)		(.05)		(−.01)
Eyewitness testimony		−.01		.12		−.11
		(.00)		(.08)		(−.02)

Independent Variables	All Cases		Strong Cases		Weak Cases	
	EQUATION 1	EQUATION 2	EQUATION 3A	EQUATION 3B	EQUATION 4A	EQUATION 4B
Extralegal Variables						
Juror holds tough-on-crime attitude	$.14^a$	$.12^a$	$.05$	$.06$	$.16^c$	$.16^c$
	$(.12)$	$(.11)$	$(.06)$	$(.08)$	$(.13)$	$(.13)$
Defendant seemed unattractive	$.10^c$	$.10^a$	$.02$	$.01$	$.24^a$	$.24^a$
	$(.11)$	$(.11)$	$(.04)$	$(.01)$	$(.22)$	$(.21)$
Defendant employed	$-.41^a$	$-.38^a$	$-.00$	$-.01$	$-.98^a$	$-.92^a$
	$(-.20)$	$(-.18)$	$(-.00)$	$(-.01)$	$(-.40)$	$(-.37)$
Victim seemed careless	$-.16^a$	$-.11^a$	$-.15^a$	$-.12^a$	$-.13^a$	$-.15^a$
	$(-.22)$	$(-.15)$	$(-.27)$	$(-.22)$	$(-.17)$	$(-.19)$
Victim judged of poor moral character	$-.83^a$	$-.65^a$	$-.10$	$-.08$	$-.72^a$	$-.66^a$
	$(-.35)$	$(-.27)$	$(-.04)$	$(-.03)$	$(-.34)$	$(-.31)$
Y-intercept	3.67	3.01	3.78	3.50	3.29	3.23
$\bar{R}^2$	.31	.39	.06	.14	.42	.41
N	312	312	184	184	128	128

[a] $p < .01$.
[b] Standardized coefficients are in parentheses.
[c] $.01 < p < .05$.

DISCUSSION AND CONCLUSIONS

As Kalven and Zeisel suggested twenty years ago, the facts and values in a trial are intertwined in jurors' decisions. Our analyses document the importance of both. Trial- and juror-level measures of evidence show a moderate effect of facts on jurors' predeliberation judgments, and jurors' sentiments influenced them to varying degrees, depending on the strength of the case. In considering these findings we must bear in mind that our results are based on sexual assault trials. The inclusion in these data of actual jurors' evaluations of both trial parties and evidence well suits them to testing the liberation hypothesis. However, the generalizability of our conclusions to other criminal cases ultimately depends on their replication in other contexts.

What do these results tell us about the processes by which evidence influenced these jurors' opinions about a defendant's guilt? And what are their implications for measuring evidence? These analyses point to four conclusions. First, jurors appropriately used trial evidence in reaching decisions about defendants' guilt. Second, evidence presented at trial and jurors' recollections of that evidence served about equally well to measure evidence. The analysis incorporating both kinds of evidence confirmed that the jurors selectively interpreted the trial evidence—they tended to disregard eyewitness testimony even when it was available and to emphasize instead evidence of force and seriousness of the assault. The reductions in the sizes of the metric coefficients for three of the four trial-level measures (recovered weapon, victim injury, and other physical evidence) when their moderately correlated juror-level counterparts were added to the equation were to be expected, but the continued statistical significance of trial-level measures means that jurors' reports did not wholly mediate trial measures. From this we can conclude that regardless of the reasons, jurors' self-reports are not necessarily preferable to trial data. Third, because the strength of the effects of the evidence measures declined when we took the extralegal factors into account, and vice versa, omitting either measures of evidence or jurors' sentiments would lead to inflated estimates of the effects of the variables examined. Fourth, jurors' sentiments—their reactions to trial parties' personal characteristics and their attitude toward crime—appeared to influence their judgments, but subsequent analyses confirmed Kalven and Zeisel's liberation hypothesis that additive models misspecify juror decision processes. The influences of extralegal factors were largely confined to weak cases in which the defendant's guilt was ambiguous because the prosecution did not present enough hard evidence. In these situations, jurors—forced to arrive at a decision—were apparently swayed by their own values and reactions to the defendants and victims. When the prosecution offered ample hard evidence, jurors were more likely to be convinced of the defendant's guilt without considering the extralegal factors we examined.

Recognizing the relationship between the strength of a case and jurors' values and sentiments is crucial to characterizing juror decision-making accurately. Previous studies, which were mostly experimental, have tended to find effects of extralegal factors; few report evidence-sentiment interactions. Both findings are misleading. In cases with weak evidence, jurors turn to other factors such as the defendant's appearance or the victim's life-style in reaching a decision. But if the state can muster enough hard evidence in the form of disinterested eyewitness testimony or physical exhibits, sentiments play a minor role in jurors' decisions.

Notes

*This research was supported by National Institute of Mental Health Grant No. R01 MH29727, awarded through the National Center for the Prevention and Control of Rape. We gratefully acknowledge the helpful suggestions of Gary LaFree, Polly Phipps, David Rauma, two anonymous reviewers, and the current and past editors of the *Law & Society Review*. We are indebted to Stephanie Sanford for observing trials and helping to prepare the data for analysis, the Linda Copenhaver for arranging the juror interviews, to the Marion County Criminal Courts and Prosecutor's Office for their cooperation, and to the jurors for generously participating in this study. Our greatest debt is to Marie Matthews, who was instrumental in all phases of study design and data collection.

1. Charges included first and second degree rape, first and second degree attempted rape, first and second degree unlawful deviant conduct (anal and oral sodomy), incest, and confinement.

2. We could not always conduct interviews immediately after the trial because jury duty disrupted jurors' schedules; sometimes a week transpired between trial and interview.

3. Respondents did not differ significantly on age, sex, and race from jurors who declined to be interviewed. Comparisons between the respondents and a sample of nonrespondents who consented to a brief telephone interview showed no systematic difference on a wide range of variables. For other information about study design, see Reskin and LaFree, 1981; LaFree et al., 1985.

4. For more detailed description of these measures, see LaFree et al. (1985) or write Barbara Reskin, Department of Sociology, University of Illinois, 222 Lincoln Hall, 702 S. Wright Street, Urbana, IL 61801.

5. Open-ended items were coded by two trained coders. Coders discussed and jointly resolved the few disagreements.

6. Eighty-two percent of the jurors expressed complete certainty with the final verdict, 10 percent were "pretty sure," and 8 percent expressed some doubt.

7. Because the state has the burden of proving each element of the crime, whereas the defense does not have to prove anything, the state was more likely to introduce hard evidence. With the occasional exception of physical evidence, these measures refer to prosecution evidence.

8. We solicited jurors' opinions of the victim's moral character by asking them how they "would describe [her] moral character." We classified responses into positive, neutral, and negative categories and distinguished the last from the first two for this analysis.

9. Other researchers have reported effects of defendant's race (Feild, 1979), socioeconomic status (Gleason and Harris, 1975), and failure to testify (Myers, 1979). In analyses not shown tabularly in which we substituted each of these variables in turn for the defendant's employment status, both race and failure to testify showed significant effects. However, when we included each in the same equation as defendant's employment status, neither showed a significant effect.

10. Our research design does not allow us to rule out the possibility that a belief in the defendant's innocence led some jurors to fault the victim for failing to exercise caution.

References

Calhoun, L., J. Selby, A. Cann, and G.T. Keller (1978) "The Effects of Victim Physical Attractiveness on Social Reactions to Victim of Rape," 17 *Journal of Social and Clinical Psychology* 191.

Feild, H. (1979) "Rape Trials and Jurors' Decisions: A Psycholegal Analysis of the Effects of Victim, Defendant, and Case Characteristics," 3 *Law and Human Behavior* 261.

Feild, H., and L. Bienen (1980) *Jurors and Rape*. Lexington, MA: Lexington Books.

Gleason, J., and V. Harris (1975) "Race, Socioeconomic Status, and Perceived Similarity as Determinants of Judgments by Simulated Jurors," 3 *Social Behavior and Personality* 175.

Hastie, R., S. Penrod, and N. Pennington (1983) *Inside the Jury*. Cambridge, MA: Harvard University Press.

Hepburn, J. (1980) "The Objective Reality of Evidence and the Utility of Systematic Jury Selection," 4 *Law and Human Behavior* 89.

Howard, J. (1984) "Societal Influences on Attribution: Blaming Some Victims More than Others," 47 *Journal of Personality and Social Psychology* 494.

Kalven, H., and H. Zeisel (1966) *The American Jury*. Boston: Little, Brown.

Kaplan, M. (1982) "Cognitive Processes in the Individual Juror," in N. Kerr and R. Bray (eds.), *The Psychology of the Courtroom*. New York: Academic Press.

Kaplan, M., and G. Kemmerick (1974) "Juror Judgment as Information Integration: Combining Evidential and Nonevidential Information," 30 *Journal of Personality and Social Psychology* 493.

Kaplan, M., and L. Miller (1978) "Reducing the Effects of Juror Bias," 36 *Journal of Personality and Social Psychology* 1443.

LaFree, G., B. Reskin, and C. Visher (1985) "Jurors' Responses to Victims' Behavior and Legal Issues in Sexual Assault Trials," 32 *Social Problems* 389.

Loftus, E. (1981) "Reconstructive Memory Processes in Eyewitness Testimony," in B. Sales (ed.), *The Trial Process*. New York: Plenum Press.

Myers, M. (1979) "Rule Departures and Making Law: Juries and Their Verdicts" 13 *Law & Society Review* 781.

Penrod, S., and R. Hastie (1979) "Models of Jury Decision Making: A Critical Review," 86 *Psychological Bulletin* 462.

Reskin, B., and G. LaFree (1981) *Final Report to National Institute of Mental Health on Grant No. R01 MH29727*. Unpublished.

Saks, M., C. Werner, and T. Ostrom (1975) "The Presumption of Innocence and the American Juror," 2 *Journal of Contemporary Law* 46.

Scheflin, A., and J. Van Dyke (1980) "Jury Nullification: The Contours of a Controversy," 43 *Law and Contemporary Problems* 51.

Sealy, A. (1981) "Another Look at Social Psychological Aspects of Juror Bias," 5 *Law and Human Behavior* 187.

Seligman, C., J. Brickman and D. Koulack (1977) "Rape and Physical Attractiveness: Assigning Responsibility to Victims" 45 *Journal of Personality* 554.

Simon, R. (1967) *The Jury and the Defense of Insanity*. Boston: Little, Brown.

Simon, R. (1980) *The Jury: Its Role in American Society*. Lexington, MA: Lexington Books.

Tanford, S., and S. Penrod (1982) "Biases in Trials Involving Defendants Charged with Multiple Offenses," 12 *Journal of Applied Social Psychology* 453.

Visher, C. (1982) "Jurors' Decisions in Criminal Trials: Individual and Group Influences." Ph.D. dissertation, Department of Sociology, Indiana University, Bloomington.

Visher, C. (1985) "Research on Juror Decision Making: Do Experimental Studies Generalize?" Unpublished. Washington, D.C.: National Research Council.

34.   Conducting Presentencing Investigations: From Discourse to Textual Summaries*

J. WILLIAM SPENCER

In recent years the dominant approach to the study of the criminal justice system has focused on identifying causal relationships between decisions made by personnel (outcomes or dependent variables) and variables such as characteristics of the offender and the offense, and features of the system (inputs or independent variables). This has been true especially of research on the courts (Bernstein et al., 1977; Boris, 1979; Cole, 1970). Sentencing decisions have been of major theoretical interest in this research (Chiricos and Waldo, 1975; Cohen and Kluegel, 1978). Some researchers within this tradition have examined the nature and effects on sentencing outcomes of probation officers' (PO) recommendations, especially those made in the context of presentencing investigations (Carter, 1967; Carter and Wilkins, 1967; Hagan, 1975, 1977).

A presentencing investigation (PSI) is an inquiry into the background of a criminal case performed by a PO subsequent to the conviction of the defendant and prior to the sentencing hearing.[1] PSIs are used by judges for gathering information about a case and for obtaining advice from POs in the form of sentence recommendations. They are a partial, yet crucial, element in the sentencing process in two respects. First, much of the information that judges use in sentencing defendants is gathered and interpreted by POs in the course of conducting PSIs. Second, and relatedly, research has shown a consistently strong correlation between the sentence recommendations of the PO and the final disposition made by the judge (Carter and Wilkins, 1967; Hagan, 1977).

The input-outcome approach to the study of PSIs has identified a variety of factors that are correlated strongly with PO recommendations. For example, we know that characteristics of the POs (Dembo, 1972), characteristics of the offense and the offender (Elion and Megargee, 1979; Peterson and Friday, 1975), and characteristics of the bureaucracy (Hagan, 1977) are all related to POs' sentencing recommendations. Unfortunately, we know little about the procedures POs use in routinely processing defendants to arrive at such decisions. In part, this gap in our knowledge of the presentencing *process* results from the very nature of the input-outcome approach. The quantitative analyses typically used in this approach are ill suited for the study of process. Rather, they can only approximate process, by using a "snapshot" approach—by examining process "held still" at various points. In addition, this approach often implicitly conceptualizes the presentencing investigation as a "black box"—ignoring the processes that occur between inputs and outcomes or treating them as of only secondary interest.

Not only is the process of accomplishing PSIs an important research focus in its own right, but an understanding of the process can illuminate and extend some of the findings generated by input-outcome research. For example, while we can be confident that sentence recommendation and final disposition are statistically related in some way, we can only speculate as to *why* this relationship exists. Three alternative explanations suggest themselves. Judges may seriously consider recommendations and use them to guide their decisions (thus recommendations have a causal effect on dispositions). Alternatively, POs may anticipate what the judges' decisions will be and tailor their recommendations accordingly (dispositions have a causal effect on recommendations). Finally, it may be that judges and POs use the same types of information and criteria in making their respective decisions (Carter and Wilkins, 1967). Treating POs' practical accomplishment of PSIs as a research question in its own right is one important way of assessing which alternative seems to explain best the relationship between this particular set of inputs and outcomes.

To address matters of process in conducting PSI, I use data and a conceptual framework that differ from those prevalent in input-outcome research. Specifically, I treat as data material generated by POs in the course of this routine processing—when they interviewed defendants (discourse or conversational data) and when they historicized their decisions and the rationales for these decisions (textual data). In addition, I use systematically collected ethnographic data as an integral part of my research.

I also rely upon an analytical framework that focuses on the POs' routine procedures for processing defendants and that examines outcomes in relation to process (Cicourel, 1968, 1975). Specifically, a critical matter in POs' work in performing PSI arises in their processing of information about cases, especially about defendants and their behavior. This focus on information processing is important because in an impersonal bureaucratic setting such as the criminal justice system, this information is reduced to a written file or dossier and hence is largely divorced from the defendant to whom it refers. Traditionally, this information about defendants and their behavior has been treated as input variables. However, a prior question is how this information (and other types of information and knowledge) is assembled and processed by POs.

POs face three analytically distinct, yet empirically intertwined, tasks in processing information for PSIs—eliciting, interpreting, and utilizing such information. First, as POs process presentencing cases, they *elicit* a variety of types of information from several sources—prosecutors and their case files, arrest records, and so on. While these and other sources of information are important, the single most critical source of information for a PO is the presentencing interview he or she conducts with a defendant. In turn, this discourse event was an important source of data for my analysis of the presentencing process because it revealed the types of information being elicited from defendants as well as the POs' perspectives on these types of information.

Second, as this information is being elicited, it is also being *interpreted*. In the interviews, POs are often faced with an array of diverse, sometimes disjointed information about defendants and their behavior, from which POs must construct meaningful or familiar configurations. They construct these configurations by linking or articulating information about a case with cultural knowledge (Cicourel, 1968, 1975, 1978; Sudnow, 1965). The presentencing interview provided an important source of data concerning these interpretative processes, because it revealed how POs accomplished this articulation. Ethnographic data proved particularly important in providing insights into POs' knowledge categories.

Finally, POs *utilize* information by making and justifying decisions in the form of recommendations about what to do about defendants. POs utilize information selectively in ways that—in accordance with informal and formal bureaucratic protocol—render their decisions rational or reasonable. An important aspect of sentencing recommendations is that they are recorded in formal documents—the presentence report. I will analyze these texts to identify the ways POs construct or provide warrant for these reasonable decisions by selectively incorporating and presenting information in ways that take account of known bureaucratic practices and protocol.

METHOD AND SETTING

The analysis presented in this article draws from data collected during nine months of field research in a county probation department in the midwestern United States. The data consist of ethnographic field notes of observations and in-depth interviews with POs, tape recordings of presentencing interviews between POs and defendants, and copies of presentence reports. In some cases, I also obtained copies of other materials in the presentence case files, such as the prosecutor's file, police report, arrest record, and final deposition. In all, I collected systematic data on 23 cases involving all of the POs in the adult felony and misdemeanor divisions.

The felony and misdemeanor divisions were among four divisions of the probation office where research was conducted. I excluded the other two divisions—juvenile and substance abuse—early in the study; strict confidentiality requirements of the former made research impractical, and the latter had substantially different goals and procedures from standard probation offices. The staff overall consisted of a chief PO, three division heads, six POs, two substance-abuse counselors, and support personnel. The POs and other staff were extremely helpful, allowing me access to most sources of data I sought and providing important ethnographic background. After a short time my presence was taken for granted and I routinely occupied an unused desk in the office when I was not recording interview data. I also occasionally ran errands and answered telephones.

I collected data through the following procedures: I obtained initial permission from the felony and misdemeanor POs to include them in the study. I then spent approximately three months collecting ethnographic material—observing the routine duties of the POs and conducting in-depth interviews. After this phase of the study, I began to tape-record the presentencing interviews. Before each interview I would introduce myself to the defendant and describe my study. After I received permission to record the interview and obtain copies of the contents of the case file, I would move to an unobtrusive corner of the room and begin taping. I also took field notes concerning such aspects of the interview as the nonverbal behaviors of each participant and the defendant's appearance. After the interviews, I discussed with the POs their perceptions of each interview and case. Finally, when the final report had been typed I obtained a copy of it and other contents of the case file.

I used several criteria to choose cases for systematic data collection and analysis. First, I wanted to obtain a more or less equal number of cases for each PO in the study. Within this criterion I randomly chose cases from among all PSI orders received by the department. Second, at various points in the study I selectively chose cases to obtain a representative sample of the kinds of cases processed by the department. For example, after several months, ethnographic data revealed that the misdemeanors POs processed contained a preponderance of shoplifting and alcohol-related offenses, each including a certain range of defendant types. Following the constant comparative method (Glaser and Strauss, 1967), I sought to include a sufficient number of these kinds of cases, covering a representative range of defendant types (university students, repeat offenders, and so on). In this and other instances, I used my ethnographic data to inform both my collection and analysis of the discourse and textual data (Cicourel, 1978; Corsaro, 1982).

ELICITING

POs relied on a variety of sources of information in accomplishing PSIs. Upon receiving a court order for a PSI, POs went to the prosecutor's office and obtained the case file. Most often this file contained the police report on the offense, the defendant's arrest record, and the prosecutor's notes on the case. When the police report or the arrest record was missing, the PO would obtain it from the city or county police department. In addition, information was occasionally obtained from other POs, other court staff (such as court recorders or secretaries), and lawyers who were familiar with the case.

In most cases POs had reviewed at least the police report and the defendant's arrest record prior to the presentencing interview. This information did not affect the structure of the interview significantly, however, because POs usually proceeded according to a standard "interview worksheet." This worksheet was very much like an interview schedule used in survey research in that it contained items of information followed by blanks, which were filled in by POs with defendants' responses. However, police and prosecution records did give the POs something to "work with"—a point of orientation for approaching the interview. For example, they often had some idea about the nature and circumstances of the offense and general information about the criminal history of the defendant.

In their interviews with defendants, POs attended to three major types of information. The first, traditionally termed "legal," comprised prior record and nature and circumstances of the current offense. The second, traditionally termed "extralegal," comprised such information as age, sex, employment history, and defendant's statement or version of the offense. The third type comprised the defendant's subjective orientations toward his or her criminal behavior, including the defendant's accounting for the offense and his or her attitude toward (a) the offense, (b) the consequences of the offense, and (c) changing his or her behavior (Spencer, 1983).

These types of information tended to be elicited at distinct points in the interview. POs attended to much of the legal and extralegal information at the beginning of the interview—the background information phase—when they asked questions about prior record, employment history, and the like. POs elicited information regarding the defendant's version of the offense in the second phase, and subjective orientations were addressed in the final phase.

Background information was ordinarily very basic and unproblematic to POs; in most cases it was unrelated in any direct way to the current offense. In addition, POs viewed most of the PSIs they conducted as routine and as a distraction from the many other duties for which they were responsible (such as supervising probationers). The typical presentencing interview lasted an hour or more, and, as the background information phase constituted the major portion of the interview, POs sought to get through this phase of the interview as quickly and efficiently as possible. They did so by relying heavily on restricted elicitation acts, typically questions focused on eliciting "factually" accurate and complete information and calling for clearly defined responses. For example:

> PO: You go by any nicknames?
> D: Uhm, Bill.
> PO: OK. Before [name of first employer], where were you at?
> D: Uh [name of second employer].
> PO: From when to when?
> D: 1974 to 1980.

POs used information gleaned during the initial background phase of the interview to guide and direct subsequent inquiry and questioning. As background data, for example, prior record and much of the extralegal information were not intended to stand alone. Rather, they provided POs with certain basic information to use in eliciting subsequent information. In one case a defendant had attempted to steal a saw by altering a sales receipt. In the background information phase of the interview the PO learned that the defendant was young (in his early twenties), had no prior offenses, owned a construction company, and was quite concerned about the impact of this conviction upon his future business affairs. From this information, the PO inferred that the defendant was honest and cooperative. The PO later told me that this information allowed her to concentrate subsequent questioning on the defendant's accounting of his offense rather than on, for example, the validity of his version of the offense. In another case, a defendant told the PO during the background information phase that he had an alcohol problem. The PO focused her later questioning on the part alcohol played in the defendant's criminal behavior. In both these instances background information served as an aid in eliciting certain types of information at later points in the interview.

The defendant's version phase exhibited a quite different pattern. POs began this phase with an open elicitation act, generally a statement that instructed the defendant to respond with his or her version of the current offense, but did not restrict the defendant's response within some clearly defined set of parameters. For example:

PO: OK. Why don't you explain to me what happened that ended up in your getting charged with attempted theft.

PO: What I want you to do for me now is go into your version of what happened: how you happened to come across the stolen property.

This open elicitation strategy allowed defendants to choose the ways in which they presented the offense, explaining and contextualizing it in ways they considered appropriate, selecting events and contingencies they felt to be important, and phrasing the account in their own words. This strategy thus provided POs with access to essential information concerning defendants' perspectives, allowing them to grasp the offense not as an isolated phenomenon but as part of a defendant-relevant fabric of antecedent and subsequent behavior, events, and conditions. In this way, POs often were able to make inferences about defendants' attitudes toward their criminal behavior.

Use of this open elicitation strategy at this phase of the interview also served another important end. It is at the point of eliciting the defendant's version of the offense that POs typically first broach the subject of the defendant's guilt. POs generally assume that defendants are guilty of some wrongdoing, even if not exactly the offense for which they were convicted, and the open elicitation strategy is an effective way to probe into the defendant's version of the offense. But, as the prior examples illustrate, POs' initial questions here are usually framed in ways that assume guilt but that present such guilt indirectly, as a neutral, "factual" matter that invites both confirmation and elaboration by the defendant (see the parallels with public defenders' opening questions to clients, as analyzed by Sudnow, 1965).[2]

Finally, the orientation phase exhibits still another pattern of linguistic strategies. In this phase POs used combinations of restricted and open elicitations, but in conjunction with informatives — statements or declaratives that explicitly commented upon the defendants' responses. For example:

D: I realize there's a difference between stealing and a college prank.
PO: Give me another example of a college prank — a legitimate college prank.
D: Another thing people on my dormitory floor have done, which I think is worse than the thing I did, and that's paintin' a bridge outside the front of the dorm, which is not the dorm's property. It's University property. That's permanently defacing it. I would say this is a college prank that was worse than the one I did.
PO: So there's somethin' you would call a college prank that you admitted was wrong. It's probably a criminal offense, yet you think they're mainly college pranks.

In this example the PO and defendant are discussing the latter's attitude toward his offense (stealing a soft-drink cannister from the university football stadium). The PO presents the behavior as a violation of the law warranting serious attention. The defendant, on the other hand, depicts it as nothing more than a college prank. The PO views this attitude as inappropriate and begins an extended negotiation in an attempt to elicit the defendant's agreement with his definition of the offense.

This pattern reveals probation-officer goals in this phase. POs were interested not only in assessing defendants' subjective orientations but also with *negotiating* these orientations—that is, with eliciting responses that at least approximate their notions of acceptability or propriety. Thus POs viewed orientations not only as an important type of information to be elicited, but, if inappropriate, as something to attempt to change. This stance reflects POs' position in the court system. While POs occupy a role of social control agent in their capacity of adviser to the court, they also occupy a role of counselor or social worker (Klockars, 1972; Ohlin et al., 1956). These two roles and goals are intertwined—to the extent that POs could effect a change in orientations conducive to criminal behavior, they could also effect a decrease in the risk of the defendants' recidivism. The strategies they used in this regard were typically indirect. They would use restricted and open elicitations to "guide" defendants to change orientations "on their own," the assumption being that this change "would mean more to them" than if the new orientations were directly presented to them. The POs would then comment on the acceptability of the orientations expressed in the defendants' responses (Spencer, 1983).

INTERPRETING

Even as information was elicited from defendants, POs were actively engaged in the task of interpreting that information by articulating or linking it with established knowledge categories or predicates (Cicourel, 1978, 1980).[3] Perhaps the most critical predicates involved knowledge of "typical" defendants. While characteristics of the offense were important to POs, they were primarily actor or defendant oriented.[4] This focus was due to two factors. Historically, POs were originally charged with the responsibility of supervising offenders placed on probation by the courts. It is only recently that POs have been elevated "to an advisory role in the sentencing process" (Hagan, 1975:622). Thus POs have traditionally been primarily concerned with actors, and in fact, supervision still constitutes a major portion of their work. In addition, recommendations were in large part based on the POs' perceptions of the defendants' risk of recidivism. While risk assessments drew upon characteristics of the offense, they were dominated by characteristics of the defendant. As Emerson (1969:87) notes, risk assessment is a *predictive* concern. For the POs such predictions were better grounded on the characteristics and past history of the defendant than on the characteristics of a single offense. In fact, the offense becomes important for assessing the character and risk of the defendant (Emerson, 1969; Matza, 1964).

POs used a threefold typology of defendants in their work that turned on a consideration of risk (Spencer, 1983). The first category was made up of *high-risk defendants*. These individuals typically had two or more prior offenses that, in most cases, were similar in nature (for instance, theft related). In addition, they were generally of low socioeconomic status, had trouble holding steady jobs, and possessed little formal education. In many cases, they were perceived by POs as having "unstable" marital histories (for example, several divorces, a history of abuse). Often, POs perceived them to be unconcerned about their criminal behavior or its consequences. The second category involved *low-risk defendants*, who generally had no prior record or a small number of "minor" offenses (such as traffic offenses). In addition, these individuals were typically young and attending the university or, if they were older, holding down steady jobs. If they were married, their family lives were generally defined as "stable." They were also perceived by POs as quite concerned about their criminal behavior and its consequences. The third group of defendants was made up of individuals whose risk was seen as *indeterminate* or *problematic*. In many cases, these individuals possessed "contradictory" background characteristics—that is, some of their characteristics were associated with low risk, others with high risk. A defendant with a steady job and stable family life but several prior related offenses is an example of this kind of defendant. Others in this category possessed all the characteristics of low-risk defendants, yet exhibited some "problem"—heavy drinking, recent loss of job, drug problem—that was related to the current offense. In all of these cases, the POs perceived these defendants as possessing the "potential for heading for trouble."

In the process of identifying typical defendants, POs were simultaneously making initial decisions on the nature and severity of the sentences to be recommended in their reports. Within the sentencing range determined by the nature of the offense, low-risk defendants typically received lenient recommendations, and high-risk defendants received more harsh ones. With indeterminate risk defendants POs faced a much tougher task because the appropriate recommendation was less clear-cut. For example, where these defendants exhibited "problems" (such as drug abuse), POs faced the decision of whether to impose recommendations that were punitive (such as incarceration) or more rehabilitative (such as counseling).

Finally, like all bureaucratic personnel, POs were interested not only in making appropriate decisions, but also in doing so in a time-efficient manner. Defendant types made case processing easier. In cases when background information was consistent with a typing of low or high risk, POs made an earlier provisional typing decision that held until subsequent information called it into question. For example, one defendant who possessed background information that included a record showing several theft-related offenses and a prison sentence, was on probation when he committed his current offense, and had a "spotty" employment history and an alcohol problem. The PO described him to me as a "prime example" of a high-risk defendant. Another defendant was determined to possess all the characteristics of a low-risk type: a university student majoring in pre-med, having excellent grades, from an upper-middle-class professional family, and having no prior record.

In these cases, such consistent background information allowed POs to type defendants in lieu of other kinds of information, particularly their orientations, or allowed the POs to address the defendants' orientations in a perfunctory manner. For example, in the case mentioned above of the defendant who had altered a sales receipt, the PO had elicited information congruent with a low-risk typing. After eliciting the defendant's version of the offense, the PO merely sought clarification of his accounting for the attempted theft:

PO: Why did you go ahead and do this? Was it motivated purely by your frustrations in your financial situation?

Here the PO merely sought to verify her perception of an account that was gleaned from the defendant's version of his offense and that "made sense" given her provisional typing of the defendant. In addition, this typing precluded the necessity of negotiating or otherwise seriously addressing the defendant's attitudes – a strong provisional typing of low risk rendered such factors "obvious."

On the other hand, when background information was such that it did not allow for a strong provisional typing of either high or low risk, POs sought more information. Orientations provided one such set of information. Particularly when background information was inconsistent, POs generally made extensive inquiries into defendants' orientations. In turn, prolonged negotiations tended to occur when defendants expressed inappropriate or unacceptable orientations. The POs' goal was twofold – to attempt to modify inappropriate orientations and, concurrently, to assess the defendants' willingness to modify their orientations and adopt acceptable ones. That is, POs were attempting to change a provisional typing of indeterminate risk to one of determinate risk.

For example, in one case a young defendant was holding two steady jobs and was saving money to return to the university (low-risk characteristics). Yet he had also committed several theft-related offenses and a current offense of stealing a motorcycle (high-risk characteristics). The PO characterized the defendant's current offense as incongruous because he did not need the motorcycle and the offense placed "the things he had going for him" in jeopardy. During the interview, the PO conducted extensive negotiations with the defendant concerning his orientation. Consider the following excerpt:

PO: What's to convince us you're not gonna keep stealing? Sounds to me like you got sticky fingers.

D: I know I'm not gonna do it again.

PO: Why not?

D: Cause, ya know, I'm doing too much for myself now. Lots of things I wouldn't want to screw up and friends I admire are trying to teach me things. I'm really tryin' to get out on my own. Even I did these things I really thought about that over the summer.

PO: Didn't the time that you spent a day in jail over the [shoplifting] thing have any impact on you when you decided to steal the motorcycle? Did you think about that at all? Did you think about what might happen if you got caught?

D: To be truthful, as far as I can remember, I didn't even think about that.

PO: You didn't even consider it. Did you realize that you can go to prison for four years?

D: I do now yes.

PO: How does that feel?

D: I wouldn't want that to happen.

PO: Do you realize that that's a possibility?

D: Yes.

PO: Was it worth it?

D: No, not at all.

Here, the PO addresses the defendant's attitude toward changing his behavior and his attitude toward the consequences of his offense. First, the PO challenges the defendant to convince her that he will not offend in the future. The defendant finally provides a seemingly appropriate response—he has a lot going for him now, that this is jeopardized by this and future offenses, and that he has reflected upon his behavior and is concerned about it. In effect the defendant's stance lays claim to a low-risk type. However, as the PO implies, a low-risk defendant would not have committed an offense in the first place after having previously been convicted of and jailed for a similar offense. This leads the PO to address the defendant's failure to consider the consequences of his misconduct. In piecemeal fashion, she addresses his awareness of these possible consequences, his concern about them, and their failure to serve as a deterrent.

In presentencing interviews, orientations tended to become explicit topics for negotiation when defendants' initial responses were deemed inappropriate and/or when they did not make sense given the background information POs had elicited. PO strategies revealed the ways in which they interpreted background information and emergent expressions of orientations by articulating these characteristics with known defendant types.

UTILIZING

The ultimate task confronting POs in conducting PSIs was that of preparing the presentence report. I will focus my analysis on the final section of this text—the summary and recommendation—for several reasons. First, POs constructed the previous sections of the report primarily by transferring information from the interview worksheet onto the final typed form. Second, POs told me that judges typically read only this summary and recommendation part of the report. Finally, formal and informal court protocol required that POs compress information into brief statements. For example, the department's *Policy and Procedures Manual* instructed POs to make the summary and recommendation a "readable summary" and to keep it "succinct." POs knew that many judges not only read just the summary and recommendation, but did so in the few minutes immediately prior to the sentencing hearing. This knowledge precluded POs from presenting anything but the bare essentials necessary for providing a warrant for their recommendations. As a result, this section contains that subset of the total array of information that POs have deemed relevant for the recommendation. It is here that one can see most clearly how POs systematically select and link information to a specific recommendation.[5]

There are two important issues in the construction of the reports: how POs *choose* subsets of information to include in the summary and how this information is *presented* in the text. First, as Cicourel (1975:5) states with regard to textual summaries in a medical setting, "The summary should reveal a concise statement of those elements deemed relevant to a prior or emergent diagnosis." In making recommendations POs chose subsets of information that, as a result of their interpretation, were "deemed relevant" for the recommendation.

These recommendations were oriented to generally recognized yet informal guidelines for sentencing in the court. In lieu of other considerations and within the sentencing range determined by the nature of the offense, typical low-risk defendants received standard recommendations for short terms of incarceration, small fines, and/or more frequent probation. Typical high-risk defendants, in contrast, received standard recommendations for longer terms of incarceration, larger fines, and/or a lesser chance of probation.

The point here is not that POs explicitly tailor their recommendations for judges. Rather, POs were aware of and used the informal guidelines for making their recommendation decisions. Since judges used the same guidelines, POs were aware of what kinds of recommendations would and would not "fly." To paraphrase one PO, you've got to express your feelings about a case, but it is also important to avoid having the judges reject your recommendations all the time. Over time POs learn what it is they can "get done" and typically conform to these guidelines. PO recommendations in line with these informal guidelines included little information beyond the standard background information sufficient to specify the typing work the PO had done. That is, a summary typing was sufficient warrant for the recommendation. For example:

> Defendant is a twenty-six-year-old divorced, self-employed male with no prior criminal record. He changed a receipt at [name of store] in an attempt to get two saws totaling $599.52. Defendant admitted what he had done and has been cooperative. There is no restitution as he never received the saws.
>
> In light of the mitigating circumstances which include that this is his first criminal offense, I recommend that judgment be entered as a misdemeanor. Defendant is a good candidate for probation and can afford a minimum fine. A brief period of incarceration is also a consideration to serve as punishment and deterrent.

In this case the defendant had been convicted of felony attempted theft. The PO, however, recommends that judgment be entered as a misdemeanor, with a small fine and brief period of incarceration—all in line with what the guidelines dictate for a low-risk defendant with a similar offense. Note that only brief reference is made to his orientation; a lengthy consideration is unnecessary because background information and recommendation articulate with a low-risk typing.

In other instances, however, POs needed to include detailed additional information. In some cases POs would decide on recommendations at variance with what the informal guidelines specified for a case showing such background characteristics. In these cases POs provided more extensive documentation of orientations as warrant for this variation. In one such case, a young university student was convicted of misdemeanor theft for possessing stolen university parking permits. During the interview the defendant told the PO that he had bought the permits from someone because of a "parking problem"—that is, he could not find parking close enough to class. In the report, the PO stated:

> Defendant is twenty years old, a university student majoring in psychology with no prior arrests.
>
> Defendant spoke disparagingly of the university administrators and alumni, since they can park anywhere and do not allow students to do so. He justifies illegally parking by stating he may be late and *has* to park near the buildings (illegally). This officer pointed out that leaving earlier would alleviate this problem and defendant admitted that would work, but did not appear willing to do this. Since defendant knew what he was doing was illegal,

> I recommend he serve time in jail [two days to serve, thirteen days suspended]. I recommend he be fined forty dollars as punishment.

In another misdemeanor theft case, the same PO stated:

> Defendant is nineteen years old, a university sophomore, unemployed with no prior convictions.
> Defendant related in the course of the interview that he rarely goes out and spends much time (five to seven hours a day) studying. He would like to become a doctor. Defendant is extremely worried about his future ability to get into medical school with a conviction on his record. Defendant did make a personal apology to the manager [of the store] and is extremely remorseful for his actions. Due to his responsible attitude and lack of prior record I do not recommend defendant serve time in jail. I recommend he be fined ten dollars as a punishment.

In both cases, the defendants possessed background characteristics congruent with a low-risk typing. However, in both cases the recommendations varied from those that would have been in accordance with standard court practice—a day in jail and a $15 to $20 fine. In the first case, the PO used the defendant's inappropriate attitudes as a warrant for the relatively harsh recommendation—two days in jail and a $40 fine. In the second case the PO used the defendant's particularly "responsible" orientation as justification for a lenient recommendation—no jail time and only a $10 fine.

Another aspect of utilization of information concerned POs' strategies of selective presentation of information in the text. That is, information chosen for inclusion in the report was not necessarily merely "copied down." Rather, there was variation in the manner in which that information was presented in the text. This variation reveals not only the typing work accomplished by POs, but also the various macro or structural factors that made possible and constrained their preparation of these reports.

The POs' presentation of defendants' orientations, more so than other information, revealed the various structural factors that constrained their preparation of the reports. I discussed above that POs occupied dual roles in their work—social control agent and counselor—and that both these roles were manifested in the ways in which they handled and negotiated orientational issues while interviewing with defendants. Yet the negotiated character of such orientations was rarely evidenced in the presentence reports: Rather than presenting an overview of the negotiation process, POs presented only a concluding summary statement of the result. Thus orientations appeared in the text much like background information—as "objective" information—masking the fact that this information had been elicited and interpreted in vastly different ways from the other information.

This tendency reflects several factors operative within the POs' organizational milieu. Despite the fact that POs occupied dual roles, it was only their role of social control agent that was salient in their preparation of these reports. Judges were not particularly interested in *how* POs arrived at their assessments of defendants' orientations, only in *what* those assessments were. In effect, orientations were rendered as merely one type of information, among a variety of similar types, that was potentially salient for recommendation decisions. Also, their presentation of orientations as "objective" information reflected a general outlook in the criminal justice system, namely, that personnel should focus their attention on objective factors in making decisions. POs knew that "subjective" interpretations in their reports could provide ammunition for prosecution and/or defense during sentencing hearings. The more their assessments of orientations *appeared* as stable, objective entities, the less assailable their recommendations became in subsequent proceedings.

CONCLUSION

Traditional approaches to the study of presentencing investigations have tended to focus on relationships between inputs and outcomes to the relative neglect of the processes whereby POs routinely accomplish the component tasks associated with these investigations. I have presented an analysis of PSIs that focuses on how POs process presentencing cases by eliciting, interpreting, and utilizing information related to these cases. I have stressed that this process can be examined fruitfully by analyzing discourse and textual data in conjunction with ethnographic data. This analysis has shown the importance of POs' knowledge categories in their accomplishment of this process, especially as this knowledge is articulated with information about a case at each step of the process.

While this way of analyzing PSIs represents an alternative to traditional input-outcome research, it can also complement it by examining the linkages between characteristics of defendants (inputs) and recommendations (outcomes). My analysis also represents an alternative and complement to traditional ethnographic studies of the courts. Much of my study relied upon ethnographic data, but this emphasis was always in conjunction with the systematic collection and detailed analysis of discourse and textual data. In this sense, my analysis represents an attempt to bridge a gap between what has tended to be two different and to some extent opposing approaches to the study of the court system.

Notes

*This is a revised version of a paper presented at the 79th Annual Meeting of the American Sociological Association, San Antonio, Texas, August 1984. I would like to thank Robert M. Emerson, Aaron Cicourel, Kriss Drass, Gary LaFree, Marjorie Zatz, and Peter Whalley for their helpful suggestions and criticisms on earlier drafts.

1. While the majority of PSIs conform to this description, some occur prior to conviction as part of the plea-bargaining process. In these cases, the POs recommend that the judges either accept or reject the plea agreement. In 85% of the states, PSIs are mandatory in felony cases (Allen et al., 1981). In the remainder of the states (and in all states, all misdemeanor cases) PSIs are ordered at the discretion of the judge. In my study, such requests varied with the particular judge involved, the seriousness of the offense, and the complexity of the case.

2. During this phase of the interview, POs would also become interested in eliciting certain basic points of "objective" information. For example, as official versions of the offense (such as the police report) were seldom an all-inclusive source of information, POs often used the defendant's version of the offense to fill in details missing from the official versions and hence to reconstruct the immediate sequence of events leading up to the commission of the offense. This goal was revealed in the POs' use of restricted elicitations. Thus at various points during or after

the defendant's initial response, POs would often use restricted elicitations to obtain or clarify specific points of information. For example:

D: I went to [name of store] and I bought a piece of equipment I needed.
PO: OK. What did you buy?
D: . . . then this security guard started chasing us. We went and hid the [stolen] money and stuff over toward my friend's house.
PO: *At* a friend's house or *near* it?

3. Here I will discuss only POs' interpretive procedures as they occur during the presentencing interviews. Much interpretive work is accomplished after these interiews. For example, my data suggest that in some cases POs reinterpreted information at later points in time—that is, would retype a defendant—when they went back over their information or new information would surface.

4. According to Sudnow (1965), public defenders are oriented toward "normal crimes," that is toward "cases" that include offenses, offenders, and settings or situations. While he talks of "normal crimes" and I talk here of "typical defendants," the process is similar. That is, both sets of personnel use higher-order knowledge predicates to make sense of individual instances. The difference is that public defenders seem to be oriented toward the entire case, while POs are more actor oriented.

5. Previous research has tended to utilize such reports as a resource rather than treating this text as topics of inquiry in its own right; that is, reports are treated as data only to the extent that they contain recommendations and other pieces of information (Gross, 1967). My approach was to treat the accomplishment of the report as problematic (see Cicourel, 1968).

References

Allen, H., P. Friday, J. Roebuck, and E. Sagarin (1981) Crime and Punishment. New York: Free Press.

Bernstein, I.N., W. Kelly, and P. Doyle (1977) "Societal reactions to deviants: the case of criminal defendants." Amer. Soc. Rev. 42 (October):743–755.

Boris, S. (1979) "Stereotypes and dispositions for criminal homicides." Criminology 17, 2:139–158.

Carter, R. (1967) "The presentence report and the decision-making process." J. of Research in Crime and Delinquency 4, 2:203–211.

Carter, R. and L. Wilkins (1967) "Some factors in sentencing policy." J. of Criminal Law, Criminology, and Police Sci. 58 (December):503–514.

Chiricos, T. and G. Waldo (1975) "Socioeconomic status and criminal sentencing: an empirical assessment of a conflict proposition." Amer. Soc. Rev. 40, 6:753–772.

Cicourel, A. (1980) "Three models of discourse analysis: the role of social structure." Discourse Processes 3, 2:102–132.

Cicourel, A. (1978) "Language and society: cognitive, cultural and linguistic aspects of language use." Socialwissenschaftliche Annalen Band 2:B25–B58.

Cicourel, A. (1975) "Discourse and text: cognitive and linguistic processes in the study of social structure." Versus: Quaderni di Studi Semiotica (September/December):33–84.

Cicourel, A. (1968) Social Organization of Juvenile Justice. New York: John Wiley.

Cohen, L. and J. Kluegel (1978) "Selecting delinquents for adjudication: an analysis of intake screening in two juvenile courts." J. of Research in Crime and Delinquency 16:143–163.

Cole, G. (1970) "The decision to prosecute." Law and Society Rev. 4:331–343.

Corsaro, W. (1982) "Something old and something new: the importance of prior ethnography in the collection and analysis of audiovisual data." Soc. Methods and Research 11, 2:145–166.

Dembo, R. (1972) "Orientations and activities of parole officers." Criminology 10, 4:193–215.

Elion, V. and E. Megargee (1979) "Racial identity, length of incarceration, and parole decision-making." J. of Research in Crime and Delinquency 16:232–245.

Emerson, R.M. (1969) Judging Delinquents. Chicago: Aldine.

Glaser, B. and A. Strauss (1967) The Discovery of Grounded Theory. Chicago: Aldine.

Gross, S. (1967) "The prehearing report: probation officers' conceptions." J. of Research in Crime and Delinquency 4, 2:212–217.

Hagan, J. (1977) "Criminal justice in rural and urban communities: a study of the bureaucratization of justice." Social Forces 55, 3:597–612.

Hagan, J. (1975) "The social and legal construction of criminal justice: a study of the presentencing process." Social Problems 22, 5:620–637.

Klockars, C. (1972) "A theory of probation supervision." J. of Criminal Law, Criminology, and Police Sci. 63, 4:550–557.

Matza, D. (1964) Delinquency and Drift. New York: John Wiley.

Ohlin, L., H. Piven, and D. Pappenfort (1956) "Major dilemmas of the social worker in probation and parole." National Probation and Parole Assn. J. 2:211–225.

Peterson, D. and R. Friday (1975) "Early release from incarceration: race as a factor in the use of shock probation." J. of Criminal Law, Criminology, and Police Sci. 66, 1:79–87.

Spencer, J. (1983) "Accounts, attitudes and solutions: probation officer-defendant negotiations of subjective orientations." Social Problems 30, 5:570–581.

Sudnow, D. (1965) "Normal crimes: sociological aspects of the penal code." Social Problems 12, 3:255–276.

35. The Rich Get Richer and the Poor Get Prison: Sentencing

JEFFREY H. REIMAN

SENTENCING

He had a businessman's suit and a businessman's tan, but Jack L. Clark no longer had a business. His nursing home construction company had collapsed in a gigantic stock fraud, leaving shareholders out $200 million and leaving Clark in a federal courthouse, awaiting sentence for stock manipulation. Ten million of the swindled dollars had allegedly gone for Clark's personal use, and prosecutors accused him of stashing away 4 million unrecovered dollars in a retirement nest egg. Out of an original indictment of 65 counts, Clark had pleaded guilty to one charge. He faced a maximum penalty of a $10,000 fine and five years in prison. But the judge, before passing sentence, remembered the "marked improvement" in care for the elderly that Clark's nursing homes had provided. . . . He considered that Clark was a 46-year-old family man who coached little kids in baseball and football. Then he passed sentence. No fine. One year in prison. Eligible for parole after four months.

In another federal courtroom stood Matthew Corelli (not his real name), a 45-year-old, $125-a-week laborer who lived with his wife and kids in a $126-a-month apartment. Along with three other men, Corelli had been convicted of possessing $5,000 of stolen drugstore goods that government prosecutors identified as part of a $63,000 shipment. The judge considered Corelli's impoverished circumstances, his number of dependents, the nature of his crime, and then passed sentence: four years in prison. Or in other words, four times the punishment Clark received for a fraction of the crime.[1]

Jack Greenberg took $15 from a post office; last May in Federal Court in Manhattan he drew six months in jail. Howard Lazell "misapplied" $150,000 from a bank; in the same month in the same courthouse he drew probation.[2]

The first quotation is the opening passage of a magazine article on white-collar crime, aptly titled "America's Most Coddled Criminals." The second quotation is the opening paragraph of a *New York Times* article, more prosaically titled "Wide Disparities Mark Sentences Here." Both, however, are testimony to the fact that the criminal justice system reserves its harshest penalties for its lower-class clients and puts on kid gloves when confronted with a better class of crook.

The system is doubly biased against the poor. First, there is the class bias *between* crimes that we have just seen. The crimes that poor people are likely to commit carry harsher sentences than the "crimes in the suites" committed by well-to-do people. Second, for *all* crimes, the poor receive less probation and more years of confinement than well-off defendants *convicted of the same offense*, assuring us once again that the vast majority of these who are put behind bars are from the lowest social and economic classes in the nation.

The *New York Times* article referred to above reports the results of a study done by the *New York Times* on sentencing in state and federal courts. The *Times* states that "crimes that tend to be committed by the poor get tougher sentences than those committed by the well-to-do," that federal "defendants who could not afford private counsel were sentenced nearly twice as severely as defendants with private or no counsel," and that a "study by the Vera Institute of Justice of courts in the Bronx indicates a similar pattern in the state courts."[3]

Looking at federal and state courts, Stuart Nagel concludes that

> not only are the indigent found guilty more often, but they are much less likely to be recommended for probation by the probation officer, or to be granted probation or suspended sentences by the judge.

And, further, that

> the federal data show that this is true also of those with *no* prior record: 27 percent of the indigent with no prior record were *not* recommended for probation against 16 percent of the non-indigent; 23 percent indigent did *not* receive suspended sentences or probation against 15 percent non-indigent. Among those of both groups with "some" prior record the spread is even greater.[4]

Eugene Doleschal and Nora Klapmuts report as "typical of American studies," Thornberry's analysis of "3,475 Philadelphia delinquents that found that blacks and members of lower socioeconomic groups were likely to receive more severe dispositions than whites and the more affluent even when the appropriate legal variables [i.e., offense, prior record, etc.] were held constant."[5] More recently, applying more sophisticated statistical techniques to the data upon which his Philadelphia study was based,

Thornberry concludes, "When seriousness, prior record and SES [socioeconomic strata] were held constant, blacks were significantly more likely than whites to receive more severe dispositions." Although he finds the effect of socioeconomic status weaker than in the earlier study, Thornberry writes, "When the variable of race was suppressed . . . , SES was found to be significantly related to dispositions such that lower SES subjects were treated more severely than their high SES counterparts."[6]

Studying the experiences of 798 burglary and larceny defendants in North Carolina, Clarke and Koch find that "other things being equal, the low-income defendant had a greater chance than the higher-income defendant of emerging from the criminal court with an active prison sentence. . . . Our tentative conclusion is that most of the influence of income on the likelihood of imprisonment among the defendants studied is explained by the poorer opportunity of the low-income defendant for [release on] bail and his greater likelihood of having a court-assigned rather than a privately retained, attorney."[7] Analyzing data from Chicago trial courts, Lizotte finds that, other things being equal, "laborers and non-whites are. . . twice as likely as proprietors to stay incarcerated between arrest and final disposition [i.e., not be released on bail]. Further, other factors being equal, laborers and non-whites are given longer prison sentences than higher SES groups."[8]

As usual, data on racial discrimination in sentencing exist in much greater abundance than data on class discrimination, but they tell the same story of the treatment of those who cannot afford the going price of justice. Most striking perhaps is the fact that over 44 percent of the inmates of all correctional facilities in the United States — state and federal prisons as well as local jails — are black, while blacks account for a little under one-quarter of all arrests in the nation. Even when we compare the percentage of blacks arrested for serious (i.e., FBI Index) crimes with the percentage of blacks in federal and state prisons (where presumably those convicted of such offenses would be sent), blacks still make up over 46 percent of the inmates but only about 33 percent of the arrestees, which is still a considerable disparity. Furthermore, when we look at federal prisons, where there is reason to believe racial and economic discrimination is less prevalent than in state institutions, we find that the average sentence for a white inmate in 1979 was 98.9 months, as compared to 130.2 months (over 2½ years more!) for nonwhite inmates. The nonwhite inmate serves, on the average, 20 more months for a drug law violation than the white inmate, and almost twice as long for income tax evasion.[9]

Studies have confirmed that black burglars receive longer sentences than do white burglars. And blacks who plead guilty receive harsher sentences than whites who do, although by an act of dubious mercy of which Americans ought hardly be proud, blacks often receive lighter sentences for murder and rape than whites as long as the victim was black as well.[10] According to a recent four-state study of capital sentencing, this dubious mercy extends to the death penalty. In Florida, for example, blacks "who kill whites are nearly forty times more likely to be sentenced to death than those who kill blacks." Moreover, among "killers of whites, blacks are five times more likely than whites to be sentenced to death." This pattern of double discrimination was also evidenced, though less pronouncedly, in Texas, Ohio, and Georgia, the other states surveyed. Together, these four states "accounted for approximately 70 percent of the nation's death sentences" between 1972 and 1977.[11] Note that these discriminatory sentences were rendered under statutes that had passed constitutional muster and were therefore presumed free of the biases that led the Supreme Court to invalidate death penalty statutes in *Furman v. Georgia* in 1972.

Mary Owen Cameron studied the sentencing practices of judges in the Chicago Women's Court during a three-year period. Her findings were as follows:

> Judges found sixteen percent of the white women brought before them on charges of shoplifting to be "not guilty," but only four percent of the black women were found innocent. In addition, twenty-two percent of the black women as compared to four percent of the white women were sent to jail. Finally, of the twenty-one white women sentenced to jail, only two (ten percent) were to be jailed for thirty days or more; of the seventy-six black women sentenced to jail twenty (twenty-six percent) were to be jailed for thirty days or more.[12]

An extensive study by the *Boston Globe* of 4500 cases of armed robbery, aggravated assault, and rape, found that "blacks convicted in the superior courts of Massachusetts receive harsher penalties than whites for the same crimes. . . . The median time served by blacks is nine weeks longer than that served by whites for armed robbery, 13½ months longer for rape and about equal for aggravated assault. . . . The typical minimum sentence for blacks . . . on all three crimes combined is more than a year longer than for whites."[13] The authors of a study of almost 1200 males sentenced to prison for armed robbery in a southeastern state found that "in 1977 whites incarcerated for armed robbery had a greater than average chance of receiving the least severe sentence, while nonwhites had a greater than average chance of receiving a moderately severe sentence."[14] A study of 229 adjudicated cases in a Florida judicial district yielded the finding that "whites have an 18 percent greater chance in the predicted probability of receiving probation than blacks when all other things are equal."[15]

Another study has shown that among blacks and whites on death row, whites are more likely to have their sentences commuted. And blacks or whites who have private counsel are more likely to have their execution commuted than condemned persons defended by court-appointed attorneys.[16]

As I have already pointed out, justice is increasingly tempered with mercy as we deal with a better class of crime. The Sherman Antitrust Act is a criminal law. It was passed in recognition of the fact that one virtue of a free enterprise economy is that competition tends to drive consumer prices down, so agreements by competing firms to refrain from price competition is the equivalent of stealing money from the consumer's pocket. Nevertheless, although such conspiracies cost consumers far more than lower-class theft, price-fixing was a misdemeanor until 1974.[17] In practice, few conspirators end up in prison, and when they do, the sentence is a mere token, well below the maximum provided in the law. Thus, based on the government's track record, there is little reason to expect things to change significantly now that price-fixing is a felony.

In the historic *Electric Equipment* cases in the early 1960s, executives of several major firms secretly met to fix prices on electrical equipment to a degree that is estimated to have cost the buying public well over a billion dollars. The executives involved knew they were violating the law. They used plain envelopes for their communications, called their meetings "choir practice," and referred to the list of executives in attendance as the "Christmas card list." This case is rare and famous because it was one in which the criminal sanction was actually imposed. Seven executives received and served jail sentences. But in light of the amount of money they had stolen from the American public, their sentences were more an indictment of the government than of themselves: *30 days in jail!*

Speaking about the record of federal antitrust prosecution, Clinard and Yeager write that "even in the most widespread and flagrant price conspiracy cases, few corporate executives are ever imprisoned; of the total 231 cases with individual defendants from 1955 to 1975, prison sentences were given in only 19 cases. Of a total of 1027 individual defendants, only 49 were sentenced to prison."[18] There is some (slight) indication of a toughening in the sentences since antitrust violations were made a felony in 1974, and penalties were increased. "In felony cases prosecuted under the new penalties through March 1978, 15 of 21 sentenced individuals (71 percent) were given terms averaging 192 days each."[19] Nevertheless, when the cost to society is reckoned, even such penalties as these are hardly severe.

Indeed, Clinard and Yeager maintain that "There is even more leniency for corporate than for other white-collar offenders. Few members of corporate management ever go to prison, even if convicted; generally they are placed on probation."[20] In their study of 56 corporate executives who were convicted of criminal offenses, 40 either received probation or a suspended sentence. Only 16 were actually sent to prison. These 16 "were sentenced to a total of 594 days of actual imprisonment (an average of 37.1 days each). Of the total days of imprisonment, 360 (60.6 percent) were accounted for by two officers, who received six months each in the same case."[21] The remaining 14 served an average of 16.7 days each.

In general the crimes of the poor receive stiffer sentences than the crimes of the well-to-do. For instance, Marvin Frankel points out, in his book *Criminal Sentences: Law Without Order*, that "of 502 defendants convicted for income tax fraud 95, or 19 percent, received prison terms, the average being three months. Of 3,791 defendants sentenced for auto theft, 2,373, or 63 percent, went to prison, the average term being 7.6 months."[22] More recent figures fit this pattern. A statistical report of the Federal Bureau of Prisons yields information about the average sentences received by inmates of federal institutions and the average time served until parole (see Table 1).

Keep in mind while looking at these figures that *each* of the "crimes of the affluent" costs the public more than *all* of the "crimes of the poor" put together.

A study of sentencing practices in the Southern District of New York, optimistically entitled *Justice in Sentencing*, found

> plain indications that white collar defendants, predominantly white, receive more lenient treatment as a general rule, while defendants charged with common crimes, largely committed by the unemployed and undereducated, a group which embraces large numbers of blacks in today's society, are more likely to be sent to prison. If these indications are correct, then one may conclude that poor persons receive harsher treatment in the Federal Courts than do well-to-do defendants charged with more sophisticated crimes.

Table 1.   Sentences for Different Classes of Crime

	Average Sentence (in months)	Average Time Served until First Release (in months)
Crimes of the poor		
Robbery	131.3	44.4
Burglary	63.4	31.6
Larceny/theft	31.0	17.1
Crimes of the affluent		
Embezzlement	18.8	10.3
Fraud	22.0	11.0
Income tax evasion	15.5	7.9

Source: Federal Bureau of Prisons—Statistical Report, Fiscal Year 1976.

Specifically, the study reports that "during the six-month period covered by the Southern District of New York sentencing study, *defendants convicted of white collar crimes stood a 36% chance of going to prison; defendants convicted of nonviolent common crimes stood a 53% chance of going to prison*; and defendants convicted of violent crimes stood an 80% chance of going to prison."[23] Several things are worthy of note here. First, the study carries forth the distorted conventional wisdom about crime by distinguishing between "white-collar" and "common" crime, when, as we have found, there is every reason to believe that white-collar crime is just as common as the so-called common crimes of the poor. Second, the disparities reported refer only to likelihood of imprisonment *for any length of time,* and so they really understate the disparities in treatment, since the so-called common crimes also receive *longer* prison sentences than the white-collar crimes. But third, and most importantly, the disparities cannot be explained by the greater danger of lower-class criminals because even the perpetrators of *nonviolent "common" crimes* stand a 50 percent greater chance of going to prison than do white-collar crooks.

A graphic illustration of the way the criminal justice system treats the wealthy is provided by Fleetwood and Lubow in their article "America's Most Coddled Criminals." They put together their pick of ten convicted white-collar criminals, comparing their sentences with the crimes they committed. The chart speaks for itself (see Table 2).

Equally eloquent testimony to the merciful face that the criminal justice system turns toward upper-class crooks is found in a *New York Times* report on the fate of 21 business executives found guilty of making illegal campaign contributions during the Watergate scandal:

> Most of the 21 business executives who admitted their guilt to the Watergate Special Prosecutor in 1973 and 1974—especially those from large corporations—are still presiding over their companies. . . .
>
> Only two went to jail. They served a few months and were freed. . . .
>
> Furthermore, the fines of $1,000 or $2,000 that most of the contributors of illegal funds had to pay have not made much of a dent in their style of living. . . .

Table 2. Ten Bandits: What They Did and What They Got

This isn't the Chamber of Commerce list of brightest young businessmen, and it's not the ten best-dressed list. It's a list of ten very respectable criminals. Have any favorites you don't see here? Send them in.

Criminal	Crime	Sentence
Jack L. Clark	President and chairman of Four Seasons Nursing Centers, Clark finagled financial reports and earnings projections to inflate his stock artificially. Shareholders lost $200 million.	One year in prison.
John Peter Galanis	As portfolio manager of two mutual funds, Galanis bilked investors out of nearly $10 million.	Six months in prison and five years probation.
Virgil A. McGowen	As manager of the Bank of America branch in San Francisco, McGowen siphoned off $591,921 in clandestine loans to friends. Almost none of the money was recovered.	Six months in prison, five years probation and a $3,600 fine.
Valdemar H. Madis	A wealthy drug manufacturer, Madis diluted an antidote for poisoned children with a worthless, look-alike substance.	One year probation and a $10,000 fine.
John Morgan	President of Jet Craft Ltd., John Morgan illegally sold about $2 million in unregistered securities.	One year in prison and a $10,000 fine.
Irving Projansky	The former chairman of the First National Bank of Lincolnwood, Ill., Projansky raised stock prices artificially and then dumped the shares, costing the public an estimated $4 million.	One year in prison and two years probation.
David Ratliff	Ratliff spent his 21 years as a Texas state senator embezzling state funds.	Ten years probation.
Walter J. Rauscher	An executive vice-president of American Airlines, Rauscher accepted about $200,000 in kickbacks from businessmen bidding for contracts.	Six months in prison and two years probation.
Frank W. Sharp	The multimillion-dollar swindles of Sharp, a Houston banker, shook the Texas state government and forced the resignation of the head of the Criminal Division of the Justice Dept.	Three years probation and a $5,000 fine.
Seymour R. Thaler	Soon after his election to the New York State Supreme Court, Thaler was convicted of receiving and transporting $800,000 in stolen U.S. Treasury bills.	One year in prison and a fine of $10,000.

Source: Blake Fleetwood and Arthur Lubow, "America's Most Coddled Criminals," *New Times Magazine*, September 19, 1975.

An investigation into the whereabouts and financial status of the 21 executives involved in illegal contributions leads to a conclusion that the higher the position the more cushioned the fall—if indeed there was a fall.[24]

The *Times* report also includes a chart illustrating the fate of these upper-class criminals, who were found guilty of nothing less than participating in schemes that undermine the independence of the electoral process—guilty, that is, of contaminating the very lifeblood of democratic government. Here, again, the chart speaks for itself (see Table 3). As for the government officials themselves (and their hirelings) who were directly responsible for the Watergate crimes, their treatment has also been relatively gentle (see Table 4).

On either side of the law, the rich get richer. . . .

. . . AND THE POOR GET PRISON

At 9:05 A.M. on the morning of Thursday, September 9, 1971, a group of inmates forced their way through a gate at the center of the prison, fatally injured a guard named William Quinn, and took 50 hostages. The Attica uprising had begun. It lasted almost exactly four days, until 9:43 A.M. on the morning of Monday, September 13, when corrections officers and state troopers stormed the prison and killed 10 hostages and 29 inmates.[25] During those four days the nation saw the faces of its captives on television—the hard black faces of young men who had grown up on the streets of Harlem and other urban ghettos. Theirs were the faces of crime in America. The television viewers who saw them were not surprised. Here were the faces of dangerous men who should be locked up. Nor were people outraged when the state launched its murderous attack on the prison, killing many more inmates and guards than did the prisoners themselves. Maybe they were shocked—but not outraged. Neither were they outraged when two grand juries refused to indict any of the attackers, nor when the mastermind of the attack, then-Governor Nelson Rockefeller, was named to be Vice President of the United States three years after the uprising and massacre.[26]

They were not outraged because the faces they saw on the TV screens fit and confirmed their beliefs about who is a deadly threat to American society—and a deadly threat must be met with deadly force. But how did those men get to Attica? And how did Americans get their beliefs about who is a dangerous person? Obviously, these questions are interwoven. People get their notions about who is a criminal at least in part from the occasional television or newspaper picture of who is inside our prisons. And the individuals they see there have been put in prison because people believe that certain kinds of individuals are dangerous and should be locked up.

I have argued in this chapter that this is not a simple process of selecting the dangerous and the criminal from among the peace-loving and the law-abiding. It is also a process of *weeding out the wealthy* at every stage, so that the final picture—a picture like that which appeared on the TV screen on September 9, 1971—is not a true reflection of the real dangers in our society but a distorted image, the kind reflected in a carnival mirror.

Table 3. Convicted Watergate Campaign Contributors

Company	Name	Fine/Prison	Current Status
American Ship Building	George M. Steinbrenner	$15,000	Still chairman at $50,000/year
	John H. Melcher, Jr.	$ 2,500	Discharged; practicing law in Cleveland
Ashland Oil	Orin E. Atkins[a]	$ 1,000	Still chairman at $314,000/year
Associated Milk Producers	Harold S. Nelson	4 months prison	Resigned; now in commodities exports
		$10,000	
	David L. Parr	4 months prison	Resigned
		$10,000	
	Stuart H. Russell	2 years prison[b]	Resigned; now in private law practice
Braniff International	Harding L. Lawrence	$ 1,000	Still chairman at $335,000/year
Carnation	H. Everett Olson	$ 1,000	Still chairman at $212,500/year
Diamond International	Ray Dubrowin	$ 1,000	Still V.P. for public affairs
Goodyear Tire and Rubber	Russell DeYoung	$ 1,000	Still chairman of 2 committees at $306,000/year and pension
Gulf Oil	Claude C. Wild, Jr.	$ 1,000	Consultant in Washington, D.C.
HMS Electric	Charles H. Huseman	$ 1,000	Still president
LBC&W Inc.	William G. Lyles, Sr.	$ 2,000	Still chairman
Lehigh Valley Cooperative Farmers	Richard L. Allison	$ 1,000 (suspended)	Discharged
3M	Harry Heltzer	$ 500	Retired as chairman, does special projects at $100,000/year
Northrop	Thomas V. Jones	$ 5,000	Still chief executive at $286,000/year
	James Allen	$ 1,000	Retired as V.P. with pension est. at $36,000/year
Phillips Petroleum	William W. Keeler	$ 1,000	Retired, with pension est. at $201,742/year
Ratrie, Robbins and Schweitzer	Harry Ratrie	1 month probation	Still president
	Augustus Robbins III	1 month probation	Still executive V.P.
Time Oil	Raymond Abendroth	$ 2,000	Still president

[a]Pleaded no contest.
[b]Under appeal.

Source: Michael C. Jensen, "Watergate Donors Still Riding High," *The New York Times*, August 24, 1975.

Table 4.   The Watergate Roster

Name	Charge/Conviction	Sentence	Served
Richard M. Nixon	Unindicted co-conspirator	Pardoned	
Dwight L. Chapin	Convicted of lying to a grand jury	Sentenced to serve 10 to 30 months	Served 8 months
Charles W. Colson	Pleaded guilty to obstruction of justice	Sentenced to serve 1 to 3 years and fined $5,000	Served 7 months
John W. Dean III	Pleaded guilty to conspiracy to obstruct justice	Sentenced to serve 1 to 4 years	Served 4 months
John D. Ehrlichman	Convicted of conspiracy to obstruct justice, conspiracy to violate civil rights and perjury	Sentenced to serve concurrent terms of 20 months to 8 years	Served 18 months
H.R. Haldeman	Convicted of conspiracy to obstruct justice and perjury	Sentenced to serve 2½ to 8 years	Served 18 months
E. Howard Hunt	Pleaded guilty to conspiracy, burglary and wiretapping	Sentenced to serve 30 months to 8 years and fined $10,000	Served 33 months
Herbert W. Kalmbach	Pleaded guilty to violation of the Federal Corrupt Practices Act and promising federal employment as a reward for political activity	Sentenced to serve 6 to 18 months and fined $10,000	Served 6 months
Richard G. Kleindienst	Pleaded guilty to refusal to answer pertinent questions before a Senate committee	Sentenced to serve 30 days and fined $100	Sentence suspended
Egil Krogh Jr.	Pleaded guilty to conspiracy to violate civil rights	Sentenced to serve 2 to 6 years (all but 6 months were suspended)	Served 4½ months
Frederick C. LaRue	Pleaded guilty to conspiracy to obstruct justice	Sentenced to serve 1 to 3 years (all but 6 months were suspended)	Served 5½ months
G. Gordon Liddy	Convicted of conspiracy, conspiracy to violate civil rights, burglary and wiretapping	Sentenced to serve 6 years and 8 months to 20 years and fined $40,000	Served 52 months

Jeb S. Magruder	Pleaded guilty to conspiracy to obstruct justice, wiretapping and fraud	Sentenced to serve 10 months to 4 years	Served 7 months
John N. Mitchell	Convicted of conspiracy to obstruct justice and perjury	Sentenced to serve 2½ to 8 years	Served 19 months
Donald H. Segretti	Pleaded guilty to campaign violations and conspiracy	Sentenced to serve 6 months	Served 4½ months
Maurice H. Stans	Pleaded guilty to five misdemeanor violations of the Federal Elections Campaign Act	Fined $5,000	
James W. McCord Jr.	Convicted of conspiracy, burglary, wiretapping and unlawful possession of intercepting devices	Sentenced to serve 1 to 5 years	Served 4 months
Bernard L. Barker	Pleaded guilty to conspiracy, burglary, wiretapping and unlawful possession of intercepting devices	Sentenced to serve 18 months to 6 years	Served 12 months
Virgilio R. Gonzalez	Pleaded guilty to conspiracy, burglary, wiretapping and unlawful possession of intercepting devices	Sentenced to serve 1 to 4 years	Served 15 months
Eugenio R. Martinez	Pleaded guilty to conspiracy, burglary, wiretapping and unlawful possession of intercepting devices	Sentenced to serve 1 to 4 years	Served 15 months
Frank A. Sturgis	Pleaded guilty to conspiracy, burglary, wiretapping and unlawful possession of intercepting devices	Sentenced to serve 1 to 4 years	Served 13 months

Source: *The Washington Post*, June 17, 1982.

It is not my view that the inmates in Attica were innocent of the crimes that sent them there. I am willing to assume that they and just about all the individuals in prison in America are probably guilty of the crime for which they were sentenced and maybe more. My point is that people who are equally or more dangerous, equally or more criminal, are not there; that the criminal justice system works systematically, not to punish and confine the dangerous and the criminal, *but to punish and confine the poor who are dangerous and criminal.*

And it is successful at all levels. Of the 7724 inmates of *federal* prisons and reformatories in 1970 who had an income in 1969, 4491 (nearly 60 percent) reported an annual income of under $2000.[27] Of 141,600 persons confined in *local* jails throughout the nation in mid-1972, 61,800 (44 percent) had a pre-arrest annual income of less than $2000 – only 11 percent reported a pre-arrest income of $7500 or more. "The 1972 U.S. median income of $9255 was exceeded by roughly 10 percent of the inmates. Only 6 percent had pre-arrest incomes of more than $10,000."[28] The U.S. Bureau of the Census conducted a nationwide survey of inmates of *state* correctional facilities for the Law Enforcement Assistance Administration in January 1974. They found 191,400 persons confined in state institutions; of these, 98 percent (187,500) were serving sentences – the remainder was made up of persons awaiting trial or drug addicts who "voluntarily" had submitted to treatment in lieu of being sentenced and so on. Sixty-one percent of the sentenced inmates had less than a high school education, as compared with 48 percent of the males age 18 and over in the general population. Of 168,300 state inmates who had held a full-time job after December 1968 or who had been employed during most of the month prior to their arrest, 40,000 (24 percent) reported income of less than $2000 for the year prior to arrest. Sixty percent reported income of under $6000 for the year prior to arrest. The median annual pre-arrest income of these 168,300 state inmates was $4639. About 69 percent of them "had worked most recently as non-farm laborers, operatives, or craftsmen," as compared to 47 percent of employed males age 16 and over in the general population. Of the inmates who were supporting some dependents prior to arrest, 33,300 (38 percent) "reported at the time of the survey that their dependents were on welfare." And finally, of 187,500 sentenced inmates, 179,400 had been represented by legal counsel. Of these, 127,000 (more than 70 percent) had been defended by a court-appointed lawyer or public defender or legal aid attorney. *Less than 30 percent could afford to retain their own lawyer.*[29]

Since the early 1970s, the period from which these figures are taken, there has been an unprecedented growth in the number of persons in state and federal prisons. In 1973, there were 204,211 individuals in state and federal prisons, or 96 prisoners for every 100,000 individuals in the general population. By 1979, state and federal inmates numbered 301,470, or 133 per 100,000. In 1981, the number had grown to 353,167 – 153 prisoners for every 100,000 Americans. And this does not include another 15,605 who are in prisons because they are either awaiting sentencing or have received sentences of under one year.[30] To this, add the 158,394 who were in local jails as of 1978, and we have well over half a million people locked up! They are, of course, still predominantly people from the bottom of society. The median pre-arrest annual income of the 158,394 in local jails was $3714. For those on whom we have the information, 10,659 had no pre-arrest income, 55,118 – over a third – had pre-arrest incomes under $2000. Only 21,393 (about 14 percent) had incomes of $10,000 or more.[31] Of the 274,564 inmates in state institutions as of November 1979, 81,000 were not employed prior to arrest and 27,000 were employed part-time. Of these state inmates, 25,940 were admitted after November 1977. In this group, 5768 (nearly a quarter) had no pre-arrest income. 10,750 (40 percent) had pre-arrest incomes under $3000. And 6457 (a quarter) had incomes of $10,000 or more.[32]

The criminal justice system is sometimes thought of as a kind of sieve in which the innocent are progressively sifted out from the guilty, who end up behind bars. I have tried to show that the sieve works another way as well. It sifts the affluent out from the poor, so it is not merely the guilty who end up behind bars, but the *guilty poor.*

With this I think I have proven the hypotheses set forth in Chapter 2, in the section entitled *Criminal Justice as Creative Art.* The criminal justice system does not simply weed the peace-loving from the dangerous, the law-abiding from the criminal. At every stage, starting with the very definitions of crime and progressing through the stages of investigation, arrest, charging, conviction, and sentencing, the system *weeds out the wealthy.* It refuses to define as "crimes" or as serious crimes the dangerous and predatory acts of the well-to-do – acts that, as we have seen, result in the loss of hundreds of thousands of lives and billions of dollars. Instead, the system focuses its attention on those crimes likely to be committed by members of the lower classes. Among those acts defined as "crimes," the system is more likely to investigate and detect, arrest and charge, convict and sentence a lower-class individual than a middle- or upper-class individual who has committed *the same offense, if not a worse one!*

The people we see in jails and prisons may well be dangerous to society. But they are not *the* danger to society, not *the gravest* danger to society. Individuals who pose equal or greater threats to our well-being walk the streets with impunity. The criminal justice system is a mirror that hides as much as it reveals. It is a carnival mirror that throws back a distorted image of the dangers that lurk in our midst – and conveys the impression that those dangers are the work of the poor.

Notes

1. Blake Fleetwood and Arthur Lubow, "America's Most Coddled Criminals," *New Times* (September 19, 1975), pp. 26–29. *New Times Magazine,* copyright © 1975. Reprinted by permission of *New Times Magazine.*

2. Lesley Oelsner, "Wide Disparities Mark Sentences Here," The *New York Times,* September 27, 1972, p. 1. Stuart Nagel writes, "The reasons for the economic class sentencing disparities, holding crime and prior record constant, are due possibly to the quality of legal representation that the indigent receive and probably to the appearance that an indigent defendant presents before a middle-class judge or probation officer." "Disparities in Sentencing Procedure," *UCLA Law Review,* 14 (August, 1967), p. 1283.

3. Oelsner, p. 1.

4. Nagel, "The Tipped Scales of American Justice," p. 39.

5. Doleschal and Klapmuts, "Toward a New Criminology," p. 613; reporting the findings of Terence Patrick Thornberry, *Punishment and Crime: The Effect of Legal Dispositions on Subsequent Criminal Behavior* (Ann Arbor, Mich.: University Microfilms, 1972); see footnote 23, above.

6. Terence P. Thornberry, "Sentencing Disparities in the Juvenile Justice System," *Journal of Criminal Law and Criminology* 70, No. 2 (Summer 1979), pp. 164–171, esp. p. 170.

7. Steven H. Clarke and Gary G. Koch, "The Influence of Income and Other Factors on Whether Criminal Defendants Go to Prison," *Law and Society Review* (Fall 1976), pp. 57–92, esp. pp. 81, 83–84.

8. Alan J. Lizotte, "Testing the Conflict Model of Criminal Justice," *Social Problems* 25, No. 5 (1978), pp. 564–580, esp. p. 564.

9. *Sourcebook-1981*, pp. 463, 477, 490.

10. Henry Allen Bullock, "Significance of the Racial Factor in the Length of Prison Sentences," in *Crime and Justice in Society*, ed., R. Quinney (Boston: Little, Brown, 1969), p. 425; also, Marvin E. Wolfgang and Marc Riedel, "Race, Judicial Discretion and the Death Penalty," in *Criminal Law in Action*, ed., Chambliss, p. 375.

11. William J. Bowers and Glenn L. Pierce, "Racial Discrimination and Criminal Homicide Under Post-*Furman* Capital Statutes," in H.A. Bedau, ed., *The Death Penalty in America* (New York: Oxford University Press, 1982), pp. 206–224.

12. William J. Chambliss and Robert B. Seidman, "Sentencing and Sentences," in *Criminal Law in Action*, ed., Chambliss, p. 339; reporting the findings of Mary Owen Cameron, *The Booster and the Snitch: Department Store Shoplifting* (New York: Free Press, 1964).

13. "Blacks Receive Stiffer Sentences," *The Boston Globe*, April 4, 1979, pp. 1 and 50f.

14. Randall Thomson and Matthew Zingraff, "Detecting Sentencing Disparity: Some Problems and Evidence," *American Journal of Sociology* 86, No. 4 (1981), pp. 869–880, esp. p. 875.

15. J. Unnever, C. Frazier, J. Henretta, "Race Differences in Criminal Sentencing," *The Sociological Quarterly* 21 (Spring 1980), pp. 197–205, esp. p. 204.

16. Marvin E. Wolfgang, Arlene Kelly, and Hans C. Nolde, "Comparison of the Executed and the Commuted Among Admissions to Death Row," in *Crime and Justice in Society*, ed., Quinney, pp. 508, 513.

17. "Antitrust: Kauper's Last Stand," *Newsweek*, June 21, 1976, p. 70. On December 21, 1974, the "Antitrust Procedures and Penalty Act" was passed, striking out the language of the Sherman Antitrust Act, which made price-fixing a misdemeanor punishable by a maximum sentence of one year in prison. According to the new law, price-fixing is a felony punishable by up to three years in prison. Since prison sentences were a rarity under the old law and usually involved only 30 days in jail when actually imposed, there is little reason to believe that the new law will strike fear in the hearts of corporate crooks.

18. Clinard and Yeager, *Corporate Crime*, pp. 291–292.

19. Ibid., p. 153.

20. Ibid., p. 287.

21. Ibid., p. 291.

22. Marvin E. Frankel, *Criminal Sentences: Law Without Order* (New York: Hill and Wang, 1972), p. 24, footnote.

23. *Justice in Sentencing: Papers and Proceedings of the Sentencing Institute for the First and Second U.S. Judicial Circuits*, eds., Leonard Orland and Harold R. Tyler, Jr. (Mineola, N.Y.: Foundation Press, 1974), pp. 159–160. (Emphasis added.)

24. Michael C. Jensen, "Watergate Donors Still Riding High," *The New York Times*, August 24, 1975, sec. 3, pp. 1, 7. Copyright © 1975 by The New York Times Company. Reprinted by permission.

25. Tom Wicker, *A Time to Die* (New York: Quadrangle, 1975), pp. 311, 314.

26. Ibid., p. 310.

27. *Sourcebook-1974*, p. 470.

28. U.S. Department of Justice, U.S. Law Enforcement Assistance Administration, National Criminal Justice Information and Statistics Service, *Survey of Inmates of Local Jails: Advance Report* (Washington, D.C.: U.S. Government Printing Office, 1974), pp. 3, 4, 16.

29. U.S. Department of Justice, U.S. Law Enforcement Assistance Administration, National Criminal Justice Information and Statistics Service, *Survey of Inmates of State Correctional*

Facilities, 1974, No. SD-NPS-SR-2 (Washington, D.C.: U.S. Government Printing Office, March, 1976), pp. 1, 2, 4, 5, 6, 9, and 25.

30. U.S. Department of Justice, *Bureau of Justice Bulletin: Prisoners 1925–81* (December 1982), pp. 2–3; see also, Kevin Krajick, "Annual Prison Population Survey: The Boom Resumes," *Corrections Magazine* (April 1981), pp. 16–20.

31. *Sourcebook-1981,* p. 463.

32. U.S. Department of Justice, *Bureau of Justice Bulletin: Prisons and Prisoners* (January 1982), p. 2.

36. The Moral Career of an Accused Person

ABRAHAM S. BLUMBERG

We have described the journey of an accused person through the sifting process of the court system as a "career." Sociologists use the term not necessarily to describe conventional notions of occupational careers but to delineate the social-psychological steps in transition from one status to another.[1] Erving Goffman speaks of "the moral aspects of career—that is, the regular sequence of changes that career entails in the person's self and in his framework of imagery for judging himself and others."[2] Goffman elaborates:

> The moral career of a person of a given social category involves a standard sequence of changes in his way of conceiving of selves, including, importantly, his own [self]. . . . Each moral career, and behind this, each self, occurs within the confines of an institutional system, whether a social establishment such as a mental hospital or a complex of personal and professional relationships. The self, then, can be seen as something that resides in the arrangements prevailing in a social system for its members. The self in this sense is not a property of the person to whom it is attributed, but dwells rather in the pattern of social control that is exerted in connection with the person by himself and those around him. This special kind of institutional arrangement does not so much support the self as constitute it.[3]

One can apply Goffman's analysis to the case of the accused person who moves from civilian to criminal, or is convicted. We begin with a complainant, who may be a private individual, a policeman, the district attorney, or an administrative agency. If the gravamen of his complaint is sustained in a lower criminal court of first instance, the individual complained of has become an accused person. Henceforth the accused will be dealt with and processed by a variety of mediators and agencies who will relay him along. But already he has marked the first milestone in his career—he has become an accused person.

He may now face an assistant district attorney who will point to the multiple counts of an indictment and ask whether the accused would rather go to trial than plead to some proposed lesser offense. Even the most obtuse accused will understand the full import of this.

To police administrations, a plea of guilty is a welcome addition to the statistical evidence of their effectiveness, for they correlate a favorable public image and a high conviction rate. Equally important is the fact that valuable police time that would be spent in trial testimony is freed for other activities.

Most police work at every level—federal, state, and local—is conducted on the basis of information furnished by informers and paid agents. Because of the nature of this mode of operation, which encroaches on dearly held ethical values, police work and negotiation with other agencies is best carried on in relative secrecy. Thus the kind of informal negotiations which are conducted by police, district attorney, defense counsel, and judge in connection with a negotiated plea are best performed in virtual secrecy. In bargaining with an accused, the police use the possibility of a negotiated plea as leverage, usually to get further information. Of course, at times they are completely out of bounds in their zeal, making offers of immunity or threats of punishment wholly beyond their authority or function.

The vested interest of the district attorney and the police, and their role as agents, is readily perceived and understood by an accused person. He will have sensed certain negative attitudes toward police and will have internalized them long before he has ever been arrested. The agent-mediator roles of judges, lawyers, probation officers, psychiatrists, and members of his own family are not so easily understood. The accused could reasonably define them as allies.

But some of the same reasons which serve as the basis for the district attorney's actions apply also to the judge. According to the ideology of the law, the judge is required to be not only impartial but active in seeking out and preserving the rights of all offenders. Nevertheless, he also has a vested interest in a high rate of negotiated pleas. He shares the prosecutor's earnest desire to avoid the time-consuming, expensive, unpredictable snares and pitfalls of an adversary trial. He sees an impossible backlog of cases, with their mounting delays, as possible public evidence of his "inefficiency" and failure. The defendant's plea of guilty enables the judge to engage in a social-psychological fantasy—the accused becomes an already repentant individual who has "learned his lesson" and deserves lenient treatment. Indeed, as previously indicated, many judges give a less severe sentence to a defendant who has negotiated a plea than to one who has been convicted of the same offense after a trial.[4]

The lawyer, whether a public defender or a privately retained defense counsel, is subject to pressures peculiar to his role and organizational obligations. But ultimately he is also concerned with strategies leading to a plea. Again, impersonal elements prevail—the economics of time, labor, expense, and the commitment of the defense counsel to the rationalistic values of the court organization; the accused who expects a personal, affective relationship with his lawyer is likely to be disappointed. The lawyer regulars of Metropolitan Court are frequently former staff members of the prosecutor's office. They utilize the charisma, "know-how," and contacts of their former affiliation as part of their stock in trade. An accused and his kin, as well as others outside the court community, are unable to comprehend the nature and dimensions of the close relations between the lawyer "regular" and his former colleagues in the prosecutor's office. Their continuing colleagueship is based on real professional and organizational needs of a quid pro quo, which goes beyond the limits of an accommodation one might ordinarily expect in a seemingly adversary relationship. Indeed, adversary features are for the most part muted and exist in their attenuated form largely for external consumption. The principals—lawyer and assistant district attorney—rely upon each other's cooperation for their continued professional existence, and so the bargaining between them usually is "reasonable" rather than fierce.

In his relations with his counsel, the accused begins to experience his first sense of "betrayal." He had already sensed or known that police and district attorneys were adversaries, and perhaps even a judge might be cast in such a role, but he is wholly unprepared for his counsel's performance as an agent or mediator.

It is even less likely to occur to an accused that members of his own family may become agents of the court system. Upon the urging of other agents or mediators, relatives may believe they are really helping an accused negotiate the best possible arrangement under the circumstances. Usually the lawyer will activate next of kin in this role, his ostensible motive being to arrange for his fee. But soon counsel will suggest that they appeal to the accused to "help himself" by pleading. *Gemeinschaft* sentiments are to this extent exploited by a defense lawyer (or even at times by a district attorney) to achieve specific secular ends, to conclude the matter with all possible dispatch.

Sooner or later the probation officer becomes an agent in an accused's processing, depending upon when his services are invoked by judicial requisition. In his role as an agent-mediator there is a fundamental theme—the professional self-conception of a "case worker in an authoritative setting." Probation officers and psychiatrists in the court must, according to established procedures, accept as a "given" the facts of a defendant's case as they are presented by the police and the district attorney. This has specific consequences in their relations with an accused. In other words, they view important aspects of a defendant's social biography in terms and meanings defined for them by agents hostile to the accused. Thus they see him, whether before or after he has pleaded, as already "in treatment."

The accused is usually unable to understand that he does not enjoy the worker-client or doctor-patient relationship with these functionaries. On the contrary, their professional services are preempted by the court organization, and they tend to impute primacy to the organization for the content and meaning of their roles. Usually, a defendant speaks much more freely and reveals a good deal more about himself to psychiatrists and probation officers than he would to other agent-mediators. But he can also reveal too much; he overlooks the lack of real confidentiality present in his relationship with them, and this too has consequences in terms of his ultimate disposition. The court organization may rely heavily on probation and psychiatric reports, especially in those cases where there are no other firm compelling legal, political, personal, or other criteria to use as a basis for disposing of a case. Bear in mind that the justifications and rationales employed by these agents are grounded in a stock of knowledge about the accused that is precast by police and prosecutor, whose objectivity may be problematic. So, to a large extent, probation and psychiatric reports reaffirm and recirculate the same knowledge about the accused originally furnished by police and prosecutor—refurbished in the patois and argot of social work and psychiatry.

The probation officer has an important function as an agent-mediator, especially after the accused has pleaded and has begun to have second thoughts about the matter. This function may be best described as "cooling the mark out." The phrase was originally used to describe that part of a confidence game in which the operatives leave one of their number behind to discourage the victim from going to the police and to help him accept his new social situation. The victim of, let us say, a swindle must be furnished with a set of apologia or rationales so that he can redefine himself in suitable and defensible terms, instead of going to the police to complain. His embarrassment and defeat are assuaged by the operative who is "cooling him." In similar fashion, on other social matrices, losers and defeated persons must be somehow "cooled out" in order to avoid some sort of social explosion. Erving Goffman furnishes an illustration in which one spouse "decourts" another by maneuvering the marital partner into a divorce without incurring undue hostility. Or in the case of a dying person, the cooling role is assumed by a doctor or priest.[5] Helping an accused person to accept defeat is another aspect of the agent-mediator role which is thus of great significance. The lawyer, probation officer, psychiatrist, and next of kin perform important "cooling out" functions. Even the police, prosecutor, and judge may occasionally find it necessary to perform such a function as an accused is processed toward a reconceptualization of self, in the course of changing his initial plea of "not guilty" to one attesting guilt.

We have previously noted that the short-term jail which houses defendants awaiting disposition is frequently crowded to double the intended capacity. Although this is a state of affairs not deliberately created, the discomforts occasioned thereby are employed as a weapon against the accused by the prosecutor and judge. A recalcitrant accused can be socialized relatively quickly by an extended sojourn in the remand jail, including setting bail at a level high enough so that he cannot meet it. The common refrain heard in the remand jail, from those who have been there for an extended period, is a desire to plead quickly and get sentenced, so that they can be moved to a more commodious prison. The greatly crowded conditions, while unintended and unforeseen, are used as part of the process of reducing an accused's resistance to the various agent-mediators.

While it is true that efforts have been made to simplify and develop less onerous bail procedures,[6] most defendants are still subject to the usual difficulties connected therewith. The bail-or-jail feature of the system is not the crucial one in terms of an accused's defeat; it is only one feature in the total array of structure and personnel in the prosecutor's arsenal of weapons.

Although many accused persons are never confronted with the problem, their alleged wrongdoing being unsung in the press, there are instances in which the news media serve in an agent-mediator role. Obviously this is not their intention, for they desire to serve publics and ends of their own. But it is virtually impossible for an accused to receive a fair trial by an "impartial jury," should he elect to do so, because an "impartial jury" could never be constituted if the press, radio, and television have established for weeks in advance of his "trial" that a defendant is guilty.

In summary, the accused is confronted by definitions of himself which reflect the various worlds of the agent-mediators—yet are consistent for the most part in their negative evaluation of him. The agent-mediators have seized upon a wholly unflattering aspect of his biography to reinterpret his entire personality and justify their present attitude and conduct toward him. Even an individual with considerable personal and economic resources has great difficulty resisting pressures to redefine himself under these circumstances. For the ordinary accused of modest personal, economic, and social resources, the group pressures and definitions of himself are simply too much to bear. He willingly complies with the demands of agent-mediators, who in turn will help "cool him out."

Figure 1 . . . does not spell out the interrelationships of the various agent-mediators, but it depicts the accused's ultimate situation. Of course, he does not initially assume that all these pressures are allied against him.

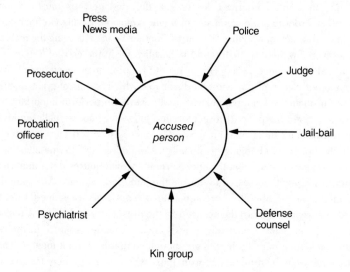

Figure 1. The Accused vis-à-vis His Agent-Mediators.

One of the major requisites of due process is a "public trial," but justice by negotiation avoids public scrutiny. Technically, it may meet the minimum requirements of due process (the defendant having waived jury trial), but whether it meets the ideological and historical criteria of due process is at least an open question.

The court, unlike most other formal organizations, functions as a genuinely "closed community" in that it successfully conceals the true nature of its routine operations from the view of outsiders — and sometimes even from some of the participants themselves. It socializes its members and participants toward compliance with specific objectives which are not part of the official goals of justice and due process.

But the usual organizational use of ideological goals and internal discipline are inadequate in the court situation. They must be augmented and implemented. In dealing with this problem the court is unique in a number of respects, and organizational solutions that have been elaborated are calculated to overcome not only the resistance of the accused but the possible reluctance and work alienation of his accusers.

Notes

1. Erving Goffman, *Asylums* (New York: Doubleday, 1961), pp. 127–169. See also a most recent example of the use of the "career" concept by a sociologist whose basic focus is the tuberculosis patient, but who also employs it in an analysis of prisoners, airline pilots, and business executives. Julius A. Roth, *Timetables: Structuring the Passage of Time in Hospital Treatment and Other Careers* (New York, 1963).

2. Ibid., p. 128.

3. Ibid., p. 168.

4. Lloyd E. Ohlin and Frank J. Remington, "Sentencing Structure: Its Effects upon Systems for the Administration of Criminal Justice," *Law and Contemporary Problems* 23 (Summer 1958): 495–507.

5. Erving Goffman, "On Cooling the Mark Out: Some Aspects of Adaptation to Failure," in Arnold M. Rose, ed., *Human Behavior and Social Processes* (Boston, 1962), pp. 482–505.

6. See, for example, one major effort in this direction which is summarized in Charles E. Ares, Anne Rankin, and Herbert Sturz, "The Manhattan Bail Project: An Interim Report on the Use of Pre-Trial Parole," *New York University Law Review* (January 1963): 67–95.

PART 6

CHANGING CRIME AND
THE CRIMINAL

The idea that the subject of crime can be viewed most productively from an *interactional-organizational* frame of analysis, that is, through an examination of how individual traits articulate with organizational components and processes to produce crime, has been stressed throughout this volume. Hence, several of the readings have focused on the ways in which criminal careers and identities are *structured* and *maintained*.

In this final part we turn to the manner by which various factors may operate to alter the nature and extent of crime – alterations that have implications for other criminological concerns, such as the efforts to define and explain crime. We also look at the *transformation* of criminal identities. The selections include a discussion of some of the important theoretical issues in the area of crime correction; a look at how correctional institutions are organized, as well as how they can impact on guards and inmates; an analysis of some data on recidivism rates; and finally, a presentation of specific tactics that could be employed to change the roots and picture of crime.

ISSUES IN CORRECTIONS

It has been shown how individuals may not only be tagged as criminals but may come to view themselves as criminals. People respond differently to labeling, however; some may accept or reject a criminal label, while others may attempt to ignore it. Predicting the response of actors is, therefore, frequently difficult.

In "Theoretical Justifications for Prison: Retribution, Deterrence, and Isolation," Leonard Orland provides substance to this contention. Orland argues that the three justifications named in the title are at the core of any policy of criminal justice. Two of them – deterrence and isolation – purport to reduce crime: the first, by causing people to abstain from crime because of the threat of punishment; the second, by keeping wrongdoers "off the street." The trouble, Orland says, is that both theories suffer from a lack of empirical evidence. It is difficult to demonstrate that more people would commit crimes if they thought they would go unpunished, and studies have shown that even the experts cannot accurately predict which criminals will commit further crimes. Punishment, then, may or may not be an effective way to deal with criminals. Nevertheless, Orland argues, the fact remains that punishment, and not rehabilitation, is the guiding principle of our justice system.

Elliott Currie, in "The Limits of Imprisonment," examines the issue of deterrence in greater detail. The extent to which punishment can actually deter crime, he notes, is one of the oldest and most difficult questions facing the criminologist. Stated most simply, the evidence on this issue is far from settled. What type of punishment, for example, works the best? A related question concerns the issues of who does the actual punishing and where should the sanctioning occur? Also, do more severe punishments, as well as the consistent application of punishments, deter any better than less severe ones? Finally, if punishing does work, how *well* does it work? "And," Currie asks, "'Well' compared to what?" He notes that social policy has been based on a set of choices about such questions, and that formal punishment, particularly imprisonment, has been increasingly the sanction of choice. Moves have also been made to increase the severity of punishment. Such recent changes in policies seem to flow from the view that attempts at crime prevention have failed. He continues by analyzing how various assumptions underlying the deterrence model actually stack up against what he terms the "liberal argument." Currie draws upon both existing theory and research in his evaluation. A portion of the evidence reviewed suggests that if punishment has a deterrent effect, it probably is more apt to come from the imposition of "informal" sanctions. For example, the potential loss of community respect, or loss of esteem in the eyes of peers and family, seems to be a more influential deterrent than the threat of sanctioning by the formal system of justice. He notes, too, that when sources of informal sanctions become disrupted, the task of sanctioning becomes the burden of the formal system.

CHANGING THE CRIMINAL: INSTITUTIONS, GUARDS, AND INMATES

As noted by Currie, imprisonment is frequently used as a formal sanction. Leo Carroll, in "Race, Ethnicity, and the Social Order of the Prison," examines the impact that race and ethnicity have on the social structure of the prison. After reviewing some of the early studies of the prison culture, Carroll notes that "prisoners are sharply divided along racial and ethnic lines." He then proceeds to explore such topics as "black prisoners and discrimination" and "Latin prisoners and family." Carroll observes, for example, that the Latin prisoners are strongly concerned with family. Specifically, separation from family poses threats to their identity and self-esteem. The culture of the barrio, moreover, has a bearing on how such prisoners adapt to imprisonment, with ties to the barrio extending into the prison. In a sense, the street gang serves as a family surrogate while one is imprisoned. Carroll describes briefly how Chicano gangs have moved into the heroin market, and he then contends that involvement in the heroin trade may help to account for the high degree of violence and conflict associated with adult Chicano prisoners, particularly in California and certain areas of the Southwest. In fact, the level of violence in prisons is extremely high. Carroll elaborates on this by describing the various types of victimization (e.g., sexual aggression) that occur—often along racial and ethnic lines—within the prison. He comments on institutions for females and then concludes by outlining some steps that could be taken to reduce existing racial tension and hostility (e.g., eliminating racial discrimination, and recruiting and retaining black and brown staff).

James W. Marquart, in "Prison Guards and the Use of Physical Coercion as a Mechanism of Prisoner Control," takes a look at how social control mechanisms operate in the prison. He comments initially that most studies of social control have focused on the formal means used for maintaining prison control (rules, regulations, "write-ups," and the like). By contrast, there have been only a few studies of the informal control system, with the evidence indicating that social order is based on such factors as "trade-offs," "illegitimate awards," and guard accommodations with selected inmate elites. No research, however, had examined how, in particular, physical coercion may be used to maintain the prison's internal institutional order. Marquart conducts such a study. He is concerned with examining how guards may use unofficial physical force as a routine tactic of informal social control. His data are based on a 19-month study of a large maximum security prison in Texas. The facility housed some 3,000 inmates (47 percent black, 36 percent white, and 17 percent Hispanic). In his data analysis, Marquart describes the various types of intimidation and physical coercion employed by the guards. For example, the first type of unofficial physical coercion was termed a "tune-up," "attitude adjustment," or "counselling." These acts of physical force were not only of a minor nature (e.g., a slap, shove, or kick) but served primarily as "attention getters." Inmates who violated more serious rules (e.g., challenging an officer's authority) were subjected to a more severe form of physical coercion known as "ass whippings." In these exchanges, and even though weapons such as blackjacks and batons were frequently used, the inmate-victim usually did not require extensive medical treatment or hospitalization. The third type of force involved the severe beating. Such beatings, although rare, were administered to those inmates who violated "sacred" rules (e.g., attacking an officer or inciting a riot). These beatings frequently produced serious physical injury and hospitalization. The use of force, Marquart observes, was not a random occurrence. Rather, coercion was "a socially structured and highly organized form of guard behavior," and it served to (1) maintain control and order, (2) maintain status and deference, (3) facilitate promotions, and (4) build guard solidarity. He concludes by analyzing how the existing organizational structure actually helps to promote guard aggression. For example, the lack of organizational controls was associated with a great deal of autonomy for the guards; this allowed the guards to exercise great discretion in the handling of their charges. And as a result, physical force not only became the preferred method of inmate control, but the use of coercion became an entrenched feature of the guard subculture.

Will imprisonment deter an individual from committing a future crime, or will he or she recidivate by committing the same or a different crime? This, it will be recalled, is one of the central concerns addressed by Currie. A. Nicholas Groth, Robert E. Longo, and J. Bradley McFadin offer an interesting twist to the study of recidivism by incorporating a direct concern for *undetected* recidivism. In "Undetected Recidivism among Rapists and Child Molesters," the authors comment on the prevailing notion that sexual assault is a crime that is situational in nature and thus not apt to be repeated. They also review research suggesting, in a more specific sense, that dangerous sex offenders, particularly rapists and child molesters, are not serious recidivists. The researchers not only challenge such views and evidence, but they offer some new information on this subject, drawing upon data obtained from a study of 83 rapists and 54 child molesters incarcerated in a mental-health facility and a maximum security prison. Some interesting patterns emerge. For example, in terms of prior convictions, a frequently used measure of recidivism, two-thirds or 65 percent of the combined sample of rapists had at least one prior conviction for sexual assault; this compares to 37 percent for the combined sample of child molesters. The information on the number of undetected sexual assaults is equally revealing, with the average number of undetected rapes for one sample being 5.9 and 4.2 for the other. Significant, too, is the observation that rapists and child molesters begin at an early age. The modal age (i.e., the most frequently occurring age) for each group of offenders, combined, is 16. The researchers conclude their data analysis and then move to a discussion of some of the implications of their findings. For example, using recidivism rates (e.g., probation or parole violations, or reconvictions for the same or similar crimes) to measure a rehabilitation program's effectiveness is unreliable and may also be misleading, especially in view of the evidence indicating that much of an offender's recidivism may go undetected.

CHANGING CRIME: STRUCTURES, LAWS, AND ENFORCEMENT STRATEGIES

Not only have correctional programs ignored societal conditions or situational determinants that may lead to crime, but they have paid scant attention to the nature of crime itself, particularly its definitional components and presumed causative factors. If, however, crime is a matter of public definition, then changing definitions (or laws) must produce changes in the picture of crime. And if negative experiences and "failure" labels, both within socializing and social control institutions, can give rise to adult criminal careers, then some changes are called for in schools and other institutions. Similarly, if blocked opportunity leads either directly or indirectly to criminal activities, then manipulation of opportunity structures will affect the overall volume of crime. The point is that any serious effort to alter the picture of crime must deal not only with individual criminals but also with those societal and structural conditions that have played a role in shaping an actor's attitudes and behavior. Samuel Walker, in "Reform Society: Provide Opportunity," echoes some of these same concerns. He notes that many have looked to such factors as poverty, racial discrimination, limited opportunities, and the like to explain involvement in criminal activity. Others of a different persuasion give little credence to such influences. A central question that must be asked, however, is: How can one explain the fact that the greatest increase in crime occurred during one of the most sustained periods of economic prosperity? Walker suggests four possible answers to this question: (1) the theories that look to social and economic deprivation as the principal causes or "roots" of crime may have been wrong; (2) the theory may be correct, but the programs that flow from it may have been flawed; (3) the programs may be effective but have not been instituted on a large enough scale to make a substantial difference; and (4) the government programs employed may, in view of the massive economic dislocation that has occurred, have been irrelevant. Walker makes the comment here that a total restructuring of economic opportunity may be in order, and he then proceeds to examine these possible explanations in light of selected theories (e.g., Cloward and Ohlin's theory in Part 2) and existing evidence. Most insightful is his discussion of the emergence of a new permanent *underclass*, a new stratum of people who have become permanently trapped at the bottom of the social and economic heap. A moving economic force behind the creation of this class has been the steady shrinkage of manufacturing jobs over the last 30 some years; this, in turn, has produced a steady rise in teenage unemployment, with black teenagers bearing the brunt of this phenomenon. Walker goes on to weave connections among the underclass, unemployment, and crime. He contends that the underclass, trapped as it is, will probably continue to be "a generator of predatory crime." Walker ends by outlining briefly the economic reconstruction that must, if crime is to be reduced at all, be implemented. Social tinkering (e.g., offering job training for a few thousand people), Walker argues, will not begin to impact on the underclass. He calls for the creation of a massive number of jobs.

Some selections in this book have explored the topic of corporate or business crime. One of the messages offered has been that even though the cost of corporate crime is many times greater than that of street and ordinary crime, relatively little direct empirical attention has been given to the subject. Obviously, if corporate crime becomes more tightly regulated (e.g., through the passage of laws and more stringent enforcement policies), then the nature and extent of crime will exhibit different patterns. The last selection by James William Coleman, "The Criminal Elite," touches upon issues such as these. He begins by noting how organizational structures and subcultures can pressure individuals into conforming to their expectations. This has prompted calls for ethical reforms. Coleman argues that ethical standards will change "only when the structural rewards for unethical behavior change." Increasing the civil and criminal penalties would probably help to accomplish this end. Coleman proceeds to outline some of the enforcement reforms that have been advanced (e.g., giving enforcement agencies more resources, levying stiffer fines and penalties on individuals, and enacting laws requiring the licensing of corporate executives). Coleman concludes with a discussion of some of the specific reforms, structural (e.g., adding public representatives to boards of directors) and political (e.g., changing the system of campaign financing), that could be implemented to regulate and control corporate offenders.

37. Theoretical Justifications for Prison: Retribution, Deterrence, and Isolation

LEONARD ORLAND

RETRIBUTION

The ancient justification for punishment was moral and retributive. The function of criminal law was to exact vengeance on one who deserved vengeance. The Old Testament called for an eye for an eye. The infliction of terrible punishment on the wrongdoer was seen as a moral good. "Who does evil will have evil done to him" (*Qui malum fecit, malum ferat*) is an early theological theme.

The doctrine of retribution justice, however, is not merely a relic of theological antiquity. Kant, in the eighteenth century, took a similar approach: "Juridical Punishment can never be administered merely as a means for promoting another Good either with regard to the Criminal himself or to Civil Society, but must in all cases be imposed only because the individual on whom it is inflicted *has committed a Crime.*" According to Kant, only the law of retribution (*lex talionis*) can determine exactly the kind and degree of punishment.[1]

Pope Pius XII, in 1954, addressed himself to the continuing viability of this doctrine. The man who commits a criminal act, Pius declared, "rejects" and "refuses to obey" the demand to be good and rather "accepts the evil." Criminal acts are directed not just against a thing or a person, but also against higher authority, and "therefore in the end always against the authority of God." Since "every criminal act is an opposition to God Himself," the "author of the [criminal] act becomes deserving of punishment (*reatus poenae*)." Punishment "accomplishes its purpose . . . inasfar as it compels the criminal, because of the act performed, to suffer, that is it deprives him of good and imposes upon him an evil."[2]

It is significant, as Nigel Walker reminds us, that the genuine retributive penologist believes that "the enforcement of atonement is a proper aim of penal systems whether or not his enforcement reduces the incidence of the offenses in question, and whether or not it protects the offender against unofficial retaliation." Indeed, the retributivist must be prepared to argue that "the penal system should enforce atonement even if by so doing it increases the frequency of the offense in question (as imprisoning some homosexuals is said to do), and even if it renders the offender more exposed to unofficial retaliation (as the pillory did)."[3]

This seemingly strange viewpoint was defended by the Victorian jurist Sir James Stephen, who, in a classic statement, concluded that the legal infliction of punishment gives expression and ratification to the hatred excited by the commission of crime. The criminal law proceeds on the principle "that it is morally right to hate criminals," and justifies that sentiment by inflicting punishment on criminals. Moreover, it is "desirable that criminals should be hated," and that punishment continue to be inflicted in order to give expression to and justify hatred of criminals.[4]

While Stephen's language is unusually blunt, Herbert Packer observes that it does not express a pure revenge theory. Rather, it proceeds on the closely related but distinguishable notion that "punishment is justifiable because it provides an orderly outlet for emotions that, denied it, would express themselves in socially less acceptable ways."[5] That idea was classically expressed by Émile Durkheim and restated by Jackson Toby. Toby tells us that for Durkheim, punishment was not "mere vindictiveness." Durkheim felt that unpunished deviance would tend to demoralize the conformist, the "upright people," while punishment would "heal the wounds made upon the collective sentiments of upright people."[6]

The rationale for punishment, according to Durkheim's disciples, is not that it deters and not that punishment of the evildoer is a good in itself; rather, punishment of the criminal reinforces the collective sentiments of the majority that crime is bad, and that he who commits a criminal act should be punished.

DETERRENCE

A familiar justification for punishment is that it deters crime. The problem with general deterrence theory is that its validity depends on our knowing what might have happened in the absence of the deterrent. How does one go about empirically demonstrating that a given punishment is effective in deterring crimes on the part of people who would otherwise commit them? Do people forgo criminal opportunities because of the mere *threat* of sanction? Shall we remove that threat and find out?

Despite these difficulties, the theory of general deterrence, popular in the eighteenth century, appears to be enjoying a rebirth. The original notion stems from the eighteenth-century utilitarianism of Bentham and Beccaria. Deterrence theory is derived directly from the hedonistic calculus of Bentham, who believed that the potential criminal would be prevented from performing a criminal act if the pain of punishment exceeded the pleasure expected from the act. To Bentham, "everyone, even the madman, calculates pleasures versus pain."[7] The same approach is evident in the works of Cesare Beccaria.[8] The purpose of punishment is not to torment the criminal nor to undo a crime already committed, but rather "to prevent the criminal from inflicting new injuries on . . . citizens and to deter others from similar acts." Accordingly, "for a punishment to attain its end, the evil which it inflicts has only to exceed the advantage derivative from the crime." In this excess of evil, Beccaria included the certainty of punishment and the loss of the good which the crime might have produced. Moreover, he felt that punishment would be more just and useful if it closely followed the commission of a crime.

The most forceful contemporary restatement of classical deterrence theory comes from Andenaes.[9] He refers to "general prevention," which he defines as the restraints which emanate from criminal law. This differs from simple deterrence in that it also includes the "moral or socio-pedagogical" influence of punishment (and is therefore closer to Durkheim's concept of punishment). To Andenaes, general prevention may depend on the deterrent effects of punishment, but it also involves the ability of criminal law to evoke other inhibitions in the public. The idea is that punishment "helps to form and strengthen the public moral code and thereby create both conscious and unconscious inhibitions against the commission of crimes." According to Andenaes, punishment serves a threefold function: to deter, to strengthen moral inhibitions, and to stimulate habitual law-abiding conduct. Andenaes readily acknowledges that the problem with his theory is that it cannot be validated, simply because the deterrent effects of punishment cannot be measured.

This lack of empirical validation for deterrence theory is but part of the larger problem—the lack of empirical validation for *any* theory of punishment. A recent evaluation of punishment literature by Bailey and Smith observes that deterrence research has typically been quite limited in scope, concerned for the most part with one offense, homicide, and one punishment, capital punishment.[10] These studies tell us little, if anything, about deterring noncapital crimes. Moreover, deterrence studies are sharply limited in that they fail to validate empirically the theoretical assumption that maximum deterrence is achieved if punishment is severe and certain.

Deterrence, Nigel Walker observes, "has become a dirty word in penological discussion, partly because it has so often been the battle-cry of those who support capital or corporal punishment," partly because it is more "fashionable," "enlightened," and "scientific to talk about rehabilitation."[11] The shortcoming of deterrence theory, as Packer has noted, is that deterrence, to the extent it is effective, deters those who are subject to socializing influences. But deterrence cannot threaten those beyond the point of hope. It cannot improve the morality of those whose value system is closed. And, even if deterrence is possible, it may work only at too great a price—by cruel and rigorous enforcement and by widespread suppression of individual freedom.

ISOLATION

The theory of general deterrence is closely related to another theoretical justification for punishment: isolation, or "keeping them off the streets."

Isolation is a fairly straightforward notion: for as long as a man is locked up in a cell, he is unable to commit another crime. This appears, at first blush, to be a self-evidently sound basis for the punishment of offenders. But the problem is again one of prediction. Isolation theory assumes that it is possible to predict that the person actually isolated for a specific crime is likely to commit other crimes. Does the incarcerated criminal in fact have a tendency to commit other crimes? In order words, will he recidivate?

Unfortunately, our knowledge is not advanced to the point where we can predict human behavior with any degree of confidence, let alone predict that a convicted burglar will, if released, commit another burglary. The logic of isolation theory is that it permits criminals to be locked up for a long period of time even though there is no basis for reliably predicting that they will recidivate. Pushed to its logical extreme, it permits imprisonment for life for relatively minor offenses if the offender is perceived to be a recidivist.

Our profound inability to predict recidivism is underscored by three recent efforts to appraise our capacity to predict violence. In 1972, a sophisticated California social science group headed by Dr. Ernst A. Wenk attempted to identify felons who upon release would commit further violent acts. The results are dramatic evidence of our inability to predict: 86 percent of those identified by the research group as dangerous did not commit a violent act on parole.[12]

Similar failures were reported by a group headed by Dr. Harry L. Kozol. Employing all the diagnostic tools currently available, including independent examinations by two psychiatrists and a social worker, Kozol attempted to predict dangerousness among high-risk prison offenders in Massachusetts. The Kozol group compared the behavior of patients released on its recommendation with the behavior of those who were released against its advice. The results: thirty-two of the forty-nine inmates released against the advice of the psychiatric team did not commit any serious unsolved crimes in the five years following their release.[13]

A third key study was that reported by Dr. Henry Steadman, based on observation of patients held as criminally insane at New York's Dannemora and Matteawan institutions. In 1966, the United States Supreme Court had ruled that it was unconstitutional for the New York institutions to confine such patients beyond the maximum of their original criminal sentence without new proceedings that met constitutional guarantees of due process.[14] As a result of the decision, 967 patients were either released or transferred to civil mental hospitals. Dr. Steadman's four-year follow-up of these patients concludes: "Between 1966 and 1970, barely 21 of the 967 Baxstrom patients returned to Matteawan or Dannemora. All the findings seriously question the legal and psychiatric structures that retained these 967 people an average of thirteen years in institutions for the criminally insane."[15]

The implications of these data are direct and inescapable: neither the best trained of psychiatrists or social scientists nor the best intentioned of judges or parole boards is capable of accurately predicting violent recidivism.

The theories of retribution, deterrence, and isolation—often conflicting rationalizations for punishment—are at the core of any policy of criminal justice. We would be better served by facing the existence of these core theories, with all their inadequacies, than by continuing to deceive ourselves with the pious—and unrealistic—rhetoric of rehabilitation.

Notes

1. Kant, *The Philosophy of Law* (1887, Hastie, tr.), pp. 194–201.
2. Pope Pius XII, "Crime and Punishment," *Catholic Lawyer* 92 (1960) 6.
3. Walker, *Sentencing in a Rational Society* (1969), p. 5.
4. Stephen, II *History of Criminal Law* (1883), p. 8.
5. Packer, *The Limits of the Criminal Sanction* (1968), p. 37.
6. Toby, "Is Punishment Necessary?" *Journal of Criminal Law, Criminology and Police Science* 332 (1964) 55.
7. Bentham, *Principles of Penal Law* (1843), p. 396.
8. Beccaria, *On Crimes and Punishments* (1963), pp. 42–44.
9. Andenaes, "The General Preventive Effects of Punishment," 114 *U. Pa. L. Rev.* (1966) 949. See also Andenaes, *Punishment and Deterrence* (1974).
10. Bailey and Smith, "Punishment: Its Severity and Certainty," *Journal of Criminal Law,*

Criminology and Police Science (1972) 63. See also Zimring and Hawkins, *Deterrence: The Legal Threat in Crime Control* (1973).

11. Walker, *supra*, p. 56, n. 3.

12. Wenk, Robison, and Smith, "Can Violence Be Predicted?" 18 *Crime and Delinquency* (1972), p. 393.

13. Kozol, Boucher and Garofalo, "The Diagnosis and Treatment of Dangerousness," *Crime and Delinquency* 371 (1972), 18.

14. Baxstrom *v.* Herold, 383 U.S. 107 (1966).

15. Steadman and Keveles, "The Community Adjustment and Criminal Activity of the Baxstrom Patients: 1966–70," *American Journal of Psychiatry* 304 (1972) 129.

38. The Limits of Imprisonment

ELLIOTT CURRIE

The extent to which punishment deters crime is one of the oldest and least settled questions in criminology. On the surface, the issue seems simple enough. What is sometimes rather grandiosely called the *deterrence doctrine* holds that—other things being equal—people will be less inclined to break the law if they think they are likely to be punished for it. On that very general level, the argument isn't really controversial; but neither is it very helpful. For it is a long way from this relatively innocuous "doctrine" to the more specific argument that we can deter much crime by sending more criminals to prison.

If we wish to make reasonable judgments about the role of punishment in an intelligent strategy against crime, we need to know more. To begin with, we must specify what kind of punishment—or *sanction*—we mean. Do we mean spanking, fines, prison, losing a hand? The anger of one's parents, the loss of a job, the electric chair? Without some specifics, the general idea that punishment deters is useless for guiding social policy, since depending on which kinds of punishment work best, we will be moved toward drastically different approaches to crime prevention.

Then there is the related issue of who does the punishing, and where. Most of the sanctions a society imposes to influence behavior are administered informally—at home, on the job, among peers. Indeed, only comparatively recently did *formal* punishments—particularly imprisonment—take on the major role they now play. (The penitentiary itself is a creation of the late eighteenth and early nineteenth centuries.)

Even within the sphere of formal punishments, we must answer more questions before we can begin to think in practical terms about the uses of the criminal-justice system in deterring crime in the real world. For example, do more severe punishments, say longer prison sentences, deter any better than less severe ones? Or is it the consistent application of punishment—its "certainty"—that is most important? Each emphasis requires a different strategy. And even if we have settled, at least theoretically, the question of what kind and level of punishment deters crime most effectively, there remains the equally important practical question of how—or whether—the criminal-justice system can actually provide it. And there is still another complication: formal punishment may deter some people but not others; it may even make some offenders worse than before.

A final question, related but distinct and especially crucial for translating the general idea of deterrence into sensible social policy, looms in the background. If punishing criminals does indeed "work," how *well* does it work? And "well" compared to what? After all, many things besides punishment may also deter crime, ranging from steady work to religious conviction, from moral exhortation to marriage. Social policy is necessarily made up of choices among alternatives; hence, even in the barest cost-benefit terms, it is important to have evidence not just that formal punishment has *some* deterrent effect, but that it has a *superior* deterrent effect.

Recent American social policy has been based, at least tacitly, on a set of choices about each of these questions. It has emphasized formal punishment administered through the criminal-justice system, and imprisonment as the punishment of choice. And in practice, it has relied mainly on increasing the severity of punishment rather than its certainty. In part, these policies are a response to the widespread belief that other approaches to crime prevention—social programs, rehabilitation—had failed, a view that was part of a broader conservative critique of the more activist public policy of the sixties. The then-dominant liberal criminology was decidedly lukewarm, if not hostile, to the idea that the threat of formal punishment (especially imprisonment) could do much to deter serious crimes. Liberal criminologists did not necessarily deny that some deterrent effect existed, but they granted it only a secondary status. (The term *deterrence*, for example, does not even appear in the index of the 1967 Report of the President's Commission on Law Enforcement and Administration of Justice.)

The liberal argument had several levels, both theoretical and empirical. At the most general level, many criminologists felt that the deterrence model was based on a severely limited conception of the mainsprings of human behavior and motivation. Most liberal criminologists took their bearings from sociological and social-psychological theories that held that people behaved as they did because of a complex interplay of values and norms learned in their cultural and institutional settings, from family to workplace. The idea that criminals (or anyone else) could be understood as simply atomized, rational calculators of costs and benefits, carefully weighing the gains of crime against the risks of punishment, seemed grossly inadequate. It might fit some criminals, under certain conditions; but as a model of criminal behavior in general, it strained the imagination. Criminologists were well aware that many crimes took place in the heat of passion (including many homicides and assaults between family members) or under the influence of alcohol or drugs.[1] Others, like much youth-gang violence, reflected a quest for "manhood," status, or street level "glory"—which, given the values prevalent on the street, might even be enhanced by a stint behind bars. These points remain valid. We don't have much research on what goes on in the minds of criminals before they commit crimes, but what we do have suggests that rational planning is the exception rather than the rule, even for crimes involving material gain.[2] The enormous role of drugs and alcohol in serious crimes has likewise been reaffirmed in recent Department of Justice findings.

This emphasis on the psychological and social context of crime led many criminologists to believe that, if a general deterrent effect of punishment existed at all, it was much more likely to come from "informal" sanctions than from the fear of formal punishment. The desire for the respect of society and the local community, the need for the esteem of family and peers, the power of religious or other institutions to include individuals within the pale or to exclude them, were felt to be far more influential deterrents than the threat of punishment by a formal and distant justice system. Once again, recent research bears this out.

In 1972, the sociologists Charles Tittle and Charles Logan, reviewing the research on deterrence, concluded that it was impossible to say anything stronger about general deterrence than that "sanctions apparently have some deterrent effect under some circumstances." In 1978, after intensive research, the National Academy of Sciences reviewed the accumulating evidence and concluded that it was "woefully inadequate for providing a good estimate of the magnitude of whatever effect may exist." Three years later, another noted specialist on deterrence, the sociologist Jack P. Gibbs, declared that "only incorrigible partisans regard the evidence as compelling one way or the other."[3]

Virtually all this research affirms that if a general deterrent effect of punishment exists, it is produced primarily by informal communal institutions. By implication, when these sources of informal sanctioning are badly disrupted and the task of deterrence falls by default to the formal justice system, the task is likely to be accomplished poorly, if at all. As Charles Tittle concluded in a 1980 study, the ability of communities to exercise "social control" is apparently "rooted almost entirely in how people perceive the potential for negative reactions from interpersonal acquaintances"; formal sanctions are "largely irrelevant." A more recent series of studies by Raymond Paternoster, Linda Saltzman, Gordon Waldo, and Theodore Chiricos similarly concludes that "extra-legal influences"—especially the fear that their parents, best friends, or lovers might disapprove of them—are a particularly strong deterrent against theft and drug use among the students they surveyed, while perception of the risks of formal punishment "plays virtually no role."[4]

To whatever extent formal punishment deters crime, it may be largely because it has an *indirect* effect on these more personal, informal relationships. Tittle discovered, for example, that among his subjects "any apparent general deterrent effect" of formal sanctions "seems to be a function of the person's perception of interpersonal respect loss"—that is, potential offenders feared the criminal-justice system mainly because arrest might provoke the disrespect of family and peers. Similarly, in a six-year study of drug dealers, Sheldon Ekland-Olson and his coworkers at the University of Texas found that the risks of arrest and imprisonment deterred the dealers' activities mainly by disrupting or threatening to disrupt their relations with family, friends, and other dealers.[5]

Another kind of evidence for the central importance of informal sanctions comes from the few studies that shed light on why most people who get involved in crime at some point in their lives *stop*. Most young Americans do things in the course of growing up that could land them in court, but most don't go on to a deepening criminal "career": if they did, American society would be altogether uninhabitable. But why don't they? The evidence suggests that most youths desist from crime less because they are afraid of being caught and locked up than because the rewards of becoming valued and productive members of a community and earning the approval of family and peers begin to outstrip the lures of delinquency. In a long-term study in Racine, Wisconsin, Lyle Shannon found that most of the young men he interviewed reported having committed crimes serious enough to merit arrest, but that most of them had stopped by the age of 18.[6] Why? Fewer than 8 percent said they had quit because they were afraid of being caught and punished. Most had reappraised their behavior on their own in light of the trouble it caused them with families, friends, or school and of the effect it would have on their future in the community.

The importance of informal sanctions has vital—though unduly neglected—implications for social policy.[7] It suggests that the best deterrent to crime is the creation and maintenance of stable communities in which people may reasonably expect that good behavior will lead to esteemed and rewarding social roles.

In the abstract, even many conservative criminologists would probably agree, but they would counter with two related arguments. The first is that conscious social action cannot do much to build and maintain such communities—a central theme in the conservative attitude toward crime. The second is that, even if formal punishments don't work as well as informal sanctions in deterring crime, that doesn't mean they don't work at all; hence, in the absence of strong communal bulwarks against crime, we have little choice but to invoke harsher or more frequent prison sentences.

Yet the evidence that increasing imprisonment can markedly deter serious crime is murky at best. The lack of interest in deterrence among liberal criminologists in the 1950s and 1960s was based in part on their awareness that in the United States an extraordinarily high crime rate had historically gone along with a notoriously punitive penal system. (Indeed, those places with the most punitive penal systems—notably parts of the South—also tended to have the worst rates of criminal violence.) This constituted a substantial prima facie case that if indeed imprisonment "worked" in some marginal sense, it didn't work very well.

More recently, criminologists have studied the question from a variety of angles, but none have offered strong or consistent support for the general deterrent effect of imprisonment. To begin with, although we would expect increases in incarceration rates to be followed by declines in crime (and lower rates, by increases), that isn't what the evidence shows. Consider the recent American experience again: though imprisonment rates have risen *faster* than crime rates since the early seventies, the latter have stubbornly failed to oblige by falling in reasonable proportion. This crude, but fundamental, observation is supported by more elaborate studies using what statisticians call a *time-series analysis*, which allows a much more precise calculation of any possible relationships, over time, between levels of imprisonment and levels of crime.

In one such study, the American criminologist Lee Bowker charted crime and imprisonment in the United States between 1941 and 1978.[8] He found that the rates for crime and for imprisonment were negatively related—crime went down when imprisonment went up, and rose when imprisonment fell—for *part* of the period he studied, but not for all of it. Indeed, increases in the imprisonment rate were associated with *increases* in the crime rate during some of the earlier years studied.

Bowker concluded that the widely varying relationships between imprisonment and crime rates probably meant that the connection between them is tenuous—and that therefore (as liberal criminologists had long argued) it was "impossible to construct policies about the use of imprisonment as a social sanction based on its presumed relationship with the crime rate."

The Australian criminologist David Biles confirmed Bowker's conclusion in a study comparing crime and imprisonment rates in England and in Australia from 1960 to 1979.[9] Disconcertingly, the trends in crime were very similar in the two countries, while the trends in imprisonment were almost exactly opposite. In both countries, reported crime went up during the sixties and seventies—by 177 percent in England and Wales and by a remarkably similar 180 percent in Australia. But during the same years, the British were greatly increasing their incarceration rate, while the Australians were slightly decreasing theirs. On the whole, Biles discovered, the Australian incarceration rate tended to go down when the crime rate rose; but this decrease in imprisonment had no effect on the crime rate in ensuing years. Biles concluded that a rising number of offenders in custody has "no measurable effect on the level of public safety."

On the other hand, several studies since the early seventies—mostly by economists trained in the Chicago school of neoclassical economics—have compared crime rates in states with stricter versus more lenient penal policies and have come up with at least moderate support for the supposition of a deterrent effect of imprisonment (mainly, it should be noted, for the certainty but not necessarily the severity of sentences).[10] But such findings must be taken with a heavy dose of skepticism.

For one thing, there are at least equally convincing findings in the opposite direction. In a study of the United States, Canada, and Australia, David Biles found that the relationships between crime rates and levels of imprisonment were *positive*—that is, other things being equal, the more imprisonment, the more crime.[11] This distressing result didn't necessarily mean that imprisonment *caused* crime; more likely it meant that, although rising imprisonment was a predictable *response* to rising crime, it had little effect of its own on crime rates.

A second reason for skepticism is that these cross-sectional studies are beset with such formidable methodological problems that it is difficult to know what to make of them.[12] One problem is that a host of factors other than a state's penal policy influence its crime rate, and they are very difficult to isolate—to "control" statistically—while estimating the effect of punishment itself. Suppose we discover that state x has a lower robbery rate than state y, and that x also puts robbers in prison more often than y. Does this mean that greater use of imprisonment reduces the robbery rate? Maybe; but it may also mean that some other aspect of life in state y produces more robbers— or more energetic ones. It may be an economic factor (like higher unemployment among youth), a demographic one (like a bigger proportion of youth in the state's population), or a social one (like a greater degree of residential mobility). Or it may be that y is a richer state and therefore that more is stolen simply because there is more to steal. Since all these factors, and a great many more, have been held to influence robbery rates, we must control for the potential effects of all of them in order to be sure that any apparent effect of putting more robbers in prison isn't an illusion. But without knowing all these other relevant factors, and fitting them into our equations, we cannot eliminate their potentially biasing influence, no matter how mathematically sophisticated those equations are.

This problem bedevils even the most technically sophisticated cross-sectional research. Over and over, the only really consistent finding has been that whether or not increased imprisonment (or other variations in criminal-justice policy, such as increased spending on police) shows a deterrent effect depends almost entirely on what assumptions are made about these other potentially relevant variables—as the language of econometrics puts it, on *how the model is specified*.

Another source of uncertainty in this kind of deterrence research comes from the nature of the criminal-justice system itself. The deterrence argument is based on the assumption that what happens in the criminal-justice system influences the crime rate; but it usually ignores the less obvious fact that the influence runs both ways. Suppose, once again, that state x puts many robbers in prison and has a low robbery rate, while state y puts proportionately fewer robbers behind bars and has a higher rate. Does this mean that the lower risk of imprisonment in y is responsible for its higher robbery rate? Perhaps; but it could also mean that the high robbery rate in y makes it hard to apprehend and convict robbers in the first place, and also makes it less feasible to send them, once convicted, to already overcrowded and volatile prisons. So the crime rate isn't simply a response to criminal-justice policies; to an important extent, the crime rate itself influences the effectiveness of the system. And since these occur simultaneously, it is difficult to isolate and measure the effect of either one by itself.

The research, in short, shows at best only an uncertain deterrent effect of increases in imprisonment. A similar uncertainty surrounds studies of the deterrent impact of specific efforts to "get tough" on criminals in the courts—for example, mandatory prison sentences. Traditionally applied to "habitual" offenders or to crimes accompanied by special circumstances, like gun use, mandatory sentences have been increasingly established for lesser offenses as well. By 1983, only two states in the Union had no mandatory minimum sentences at all. Such penalties are often easy to legislate and popular with the public, because they promise that by reducing the discretion of the courts they will increase the certainty and severity of punishment and thereby lower the crime rate. But is this what happens in practice?

Apparently not—at least not consistently. Several careful studies of the effects of mandatory sentencing have been made, and though there is debate about how to interpret the results, they can't be described as encouraging. These studies do not disprove the abstract notion that more certain punishment deters crime. But they do show that accomplishing this, within the limitations of the justice system, is harder in practice than in theory—a point so important that it is worth considering in some detail.

One of the best-known recent experiments in self-consciously "tough" mandatory sentencing was New York State's drug law of 1973, often known as the "Rockefeller drug law" and widely billed as the "nation's toughest" drug legislation. This law mandated draconian penalties for many drug offenses, on the untested theory that cracking down on drug use and sales would indirectly cut drug-related crime. The minimum sentence for possessing two ounces of heroin, for example, was fifteen to twenty-five years; the maximum, life. A repeat conviction for possessing any stimulant or hallucinogen "with intent to sell" carried a mandatory minimum of one to eight and a half years, a maximum of life imprisonment. Probation and other alternatives to prison were prohibited under most circumstances, as was plea bargaining to lesser charges. Though it took a while, in the end the drug law did substantially increase the number of drug offenders in the prisons of New York and lengthen their sentences.

The law accordingly became one source of the state's serious prison overcrowding. The proportion of convicted drug felons sentenced to prison more than doubled between 1972 and 1975; the proportion given maximum sentences of more than five years shot from 57 percent in 1974 to 91 percent in 1975.

That increase was costly, economically and otherwise. New York poured tens of millions of dollars into the court system to handle the added load; nevertheless the courts quickly became clogged – in part because defendants responded to the threat of harsher penalties by demanding more trials. The average time between arrest and disposition in drug cases doubled from 173 days in 1973 to 340 in 1976 – an outcome hardly encouraging to those who thought mandatory sentences would increase the swiftness as well as the certainty and severity of punishment.

Yet, for all this, the drug law's impact on crime (or, for that matter, on drug use) is unclear. Certainly it did not hold back the big increases in burglary and robbery, frequently drug-related crimes, that hit New York in the late seventies. According to an analysis by Kenneth Carlson, the proportion of people charged with felonies who were identifiable drug users did decrease slightly just after the drug law was passed; but it had already been dropping before that. On careful inspection, the proportional decrease turned out to be the result of a *growing* number of non-drug users in the arrested population, not a shrinking number of drug users. It wasn't clear that the law had much impact even on drug sales and use, much less the hoped-for impact on other serious crimes. (Recognizing all this, the state legislature moved, in the late seventies, to modify some of the law's mandatory imprisonment provisions).[13]

The drug law's unanticipated effect of overloading the courts with demands for formal trials had parallels in Massachusetts. There, a 1974 law mandated a one-year minimum prison term, without possibility of parole, for anyone caught illegally carrying a gun. Although the aim was to increase the certainty as well as the severity of penalties for the illegal possession of guns, in practice the law probably *reduced* certainty, while increasing severity for those ultimately convicted. The tougher mandatory penalty apparently spurred defendants to go to trial to seek acquittal (rather than accepting a lighter penalty in exchange for a guilty plea). Accordingly, there were more verdicts of not guilty, more dismissals, more appeals, and more new trials. As Kenneth Carlson concludes, "For most defendants at most stages of the process the effect was to increase the chance of outcomes favorable to the defendant."[14] As a result, before the law was passed, about half of gun-violation defendants were released without conviction, but two years afterward, *four-fifths* got off free.

Once again, the results in terms of crime prevention were ambiguous. Homicides in Boston fell after the law was passed, but the rates were falling well beforehand. Assaults with guns also dropped, but they followed a pattern that is difficult to interpret. Gun assaults had risen sharply in the early seventies, reaching a peak in 1974. They declined over the following two years, but not enough to bring them down to their level before that sudden rise. It's impossible to tell, therefore, whether the drop was connected with the gun law or whether, for unknown and unrelated reasons, the rates were merely once again approaching their usual level.

Similar ambiguities appear in an evaluation of a 1977 Michigan statute, the "Felony Firearm" law, which mandated an extra two years in prison for criminals using guns while committing felonies, besides the sentence for the original crime. The statute was popular with the state legislature, which passed it overwhelmingly, and with the public. In Detroit, the county prosecutor was an avid supporter and mounted a vigorous, highly visible campaign—complete with bumper stickers and billboards warning potential gun-wielders that "one with a gun gets you two"—to let it be known that the law would be enforced. He also prohibited plea bargaining in the Detroit courts. All things considered, it was a tough law, seriously pursued. Did it deter gun-related felonies?

According to an analysis by Colin Loftin, David McDowall, and Milton Heuman, it did not. Some gun-related crimes decreased in Detroit shortly after the passage of the gun law, but not, apparently, because of it. The drop in crime began well before the passage of the statute; moreover, the rate of *non*-gun felonies dropped as much as that of felonies with guns—all to the good, of course, but making it unlikely that the drop in crime resulted from a law aimed solely at the use of firearms. Armed robberies fell, but so did unarmed robberies. Gun homicides fell—but not just killings during planned robberies and other murders that might reasonably be prevented by the threat of an added two-year sentence; unplanned murders (as in lovers' quarrels) fell as well. Serious crime, furthermore, increased sharply in the city a few years later. Whatever caused Detroit's happy (though, as it turned out, short-lived) slump in crime, it apparently wasn't the Felony Firearm law.

Why? The first hypothesis that comes to mind is that the law wasn't really enforced. Not surprisingly, the courts in Detroit did not act exactly as the law prescribed (courts rarely do); they didn't uniformly impose the two-year sentence in all possible cases. Sometimes, apparently, with serious offenders who would probably have received tough sentences anyway, the courts "absorbed" the mandatory sentence by reducing the original sentence, thus arriving at a relatively steady "going rate" for specific kinds of crimes. In less serious cases, some judges and prosecutors may have felt uncomfortable with long prison sentences for, say, first offenders, and gotten around the gun law by charging the original cases as misdemeanors, not felonies.

But the researchers argued that none of these maneuvers really altered the law's genuine toughness or—perhaps more importantly—the way it was perceived in the community and by potential felons. "This was a tough law," they write.

> There were no major loopholes in its formulation and the Wayne County prosecutor was aggressive in his policy of charging the law and resisting attempts to circumvent it. Our interviews indicate that, in spite of some cynicism about the impact of the law, many defendants were concerned that they might get caught in its rigid flat time provisions. A strong message was sent to the community that gun offenders would be dealt with sternly.[15]

To believe that potential gun-wielding robbers would have figured out that, by means of complex and subtle mechanisms barely teased out by these experienced researchers, they might escape the clutches of the gun law requires us to grant the average street criminal some very sophisticated analytical abilities indeed. It's more plausible, Loftin and his colleagues argue, that the law's deterrent impact on crime was intrinsically limited, largely because it realistically affected only a narrow range of offenders. For robbers planning serious crimes where they were likely to meet armed resistance, the inducement to carry guns was likely to be too strong to be much influenced by mere two-year additions to what were already sure to be stiff potential sentences. The law was therefore likely to have a strong impact only on those robbers who had no compelling reason to use a gun in the first place but *might* have used one if there were no law—and that can't be a very substantial group.

The apparent inability of the Michigan statute to deter gun crime doesn't mean there aren't other arguments—moral and philosophical—for inflicting special punishment on people who use guns while committing crimes. It *does* suggest, however, that we have no strong reason to believe that such laws will markedly reduce gun-related crime.

More generally, it affirms that we are unlikely to gain much more deterrence through the simple expedient of restricting the discretion of the courts, for the crucial reason that the courts' "discretion" is not the main part of the problem—usually not even a very significant part.

Those who believe that we could cut crime dramatically if only we would "get tough" with criminals in the courts often quote dramatic figures on how few crimes, proportionately, result in prison sentences. The figures are real enough. But what they show is that most of the "slippage" between crime and punishment—between the commission of a crime and the realistic "costs"— takes place at the "front end" of the criminal-justice process: in the difficulty of catching and, to a lesser degree, of convicting criminals, not in the leniency of the courts once they've been convicted. According to the Rand Corporation's survey of repeat felons in the California prisons, for example, almost nine out of ten of those arrested for robbery were convicted; of these almost nine out of ten were imprisoned.[16]

To be sure, criminal cases do get "lost" between arrest and conviction. But despite widespread belief in the pernicious effects of laws protecting the civil liberties of criminals, a growing body of evidence shows that not many serious criminals, especially violent criminals, go free because the courts are "handcuffed" by rules that favor criminals over the welfare of the public at large. Probably the most criticized of the constraints on the justice system is the *exclusionary rule*, which requires courts to disregard evidence in criminal cases that is illegally acquired by the police. Critics argue that the rules circumscribing the ways police may conduct searches or seize evidence cause the "loss" of vast numbers of criminal cases, drastically lower the conviction rate, and therefore undercut the deterrent effect of the criminal-justice system.[17] Periodically there has been a great outcry, recently taken up by the Reagan administration, to modify (if not eliminate) the exclusionary rule. But careful studies of the exclusionary rule's real effects do not support this rather apocalyptic view. The United States General Accounting Office concluded in the late seventies that in the federal courts, less than eight felony arrests in a thousand were "lost"—either screened out by prosecutors or dismissed by the court—because of the exclusionary rule. A similar study of urban courts by the Institute for Law and Social Research found that less than 1 percent of felony arrests were rejected because of illegal searches. In 1982, a National

Institute of Justice study in California claimed to have found more substantial effects of the rule in causing prosecutors to reject felony cases; but on closer inspection, the results mainly confirm those of earlier research. Less than 5 percent of all felony cases in California rejected by prosecutors involved the exclusionary rule; therefore less than 1 percent of *all* felony arrests were rejected because of violations of the rule and something over 2 percent of felony cases were lost at *any* stage of the court process because of illegal searches. Even these minor effects were concentrated in one kind of crime — felony drug offenses — and were still smaller in the most serious crimes of violence.[18]

Several recent studies give a more complex view of what usually happens as criminal cases wend their way through the courts. Researchers at the Vera Institute of Justice found that two factors in particular — the relationships between offenders and victims, and the offenders' prior records — explained a substantial proportion of variation in the risks of conviction and incarceration in New York City courts.[19] If victims and offenders knew each other, the cases were often dismissed because the victims didn't press charges, either because they had become reconciled with the offender or because they were afraid of retaliation. Cases involving strangers much more often resulted in conviction and incarceration. Moreover, 84 percent of convicted felony defendants with criminal records (versus just 22 percent of those without them) were given prison sentences. Another recent study similarly finds that prosecutors' decisions about which cases to try and which to dismiss or plead downward to lesser charges are usually governed by "rational and consistent" guidelines.[20] Thus the cases prosecutors are willing to take to trial on the most serious charges are, predictably, those in which the evidence is strong, the offense is grave, and the perpetrator has a prior criminal history.

To be sure, none of this research tells us that the courts are uniformly efficient at putting serious offenders away. No one can deny that some awful people are let off with a slap on the wrist or that the process of justice can be arbitrary, chaotic, and frustrating. Specialists can fruitfully debate the precise consequences of particular rules and regulations — such as the exclusionary rule or the frequent practice of discouraging the use of juvenile-court records in adult-court proceedings — on the courts' effectiveness. We should certainly continue to do whatever we can to increase the courts' efficiency.[21] But no one has demonstrated that their inefficiency can be blamed for America's uniquely high rate of criminal violence, or that we can achieve significantly more deterrence by making the courts work better between arrest and conviction.

There are exceptions to this general point, of which the most important is the courts' ambiguous and often lenient treatment of domestic violence. . . . Another is drunken driving, taken much more seriously as a potentially violent offense in some countries — Sweden, for example — that are otherwise far less harsh in their penal policies than the United States.[22] (Close to a third of Sweden's relatively small prison population consists of inmates convicted of drunken driving.) Indeed, some of the strongest evidence for a general deterrent effect of punishment comes from studies of "crackdowns" on drunken driving — but this exception helps prove the rule, for drunken driving so rarely meets with serious sanctions that crackdowns by courts and police represent a dramatic change in the risks of punishment. If the courts were likewise routinely lenient with murderers and robbers, a better argument might be made that getting "tougher" would dramatically deter murder and robbery. But that simply isn't what the evidence shows. As the Vera Institute of Justice concluded in their study of the processing of felony arrests in New York, "Where crimes are serious, evidence is strong, and victims are willing to prosecute, felons with previous criminal histories ended up with relatively heavy sentences." If criminals are indeed "getting away with it," they argued, "they may be getting away with it more on the streets than in the courtrooms."[23]

They *are* often "getting away with it" on the streets. The same Rand Corporation survey showing that nine out of ten convicted robbers were incarcerated in California also noted that the chances of their being arrested in the first place for any given robbery were only a shade over one in ten.[24] The risks of arrest were slightly less for a burglary and just one in twenty-five for an auto theft. Even for armed robberies, the Rand researchers estimated that the chance of being caught for any particular crime was about one in eight.

As these facts suggest, the best place to improve the certainty of punishment is at the stage of apprehension. Apprehending criminals, of course, is mainly a function of the police, and whether we can improve their ability to carry it out remains an unsettled question. It's all too easy to blame the police for the frustratingly low proportion of crimes that result in solid arrests, easy to wax indignant over their inefficiency or their oversensitivity to the rights of offenders. But to argue that changes in police behavior or attitudes would markedly increase the certainty of punishment requires us to show that the police are now, *in general*, markedly inefficient in ways we know how to improve. The evidence for that position is scanty at best. The little we know about what factors affect the ability of police to "clear" crimes suggests that the most important of them is one that cannot be affected by changes in policy: the nature of the crimes committed. Some crimes are simply easier to "clear" than others.[25] A murder in the family or a robbery with witnesses produces reasonably identifiable suspects; "stranger" crimes, especially if there are no witnesses, much more rarely result in arrests that hold up in court. Whether there are ways to improve the ability of the police to make inroads on stranger crimes is a complicated (and unresolved) question. . . . The essential point here is that increases in general deterrence, if we can achieve them at all, will come primarily through our increased capacity to catch offenders in the first place, not by adopting an even harsher approach to those who have arrived at the stage of sentencing.

Notes

1. Almost a third of state prison inmates reported having had four or more ounces of alcohol just before committing the crime that put them in prison. The use of alcohol was especially heavy among repeat offenders and inmates convicted of rape, assault, and burglary; U.S. Bureau of Justice Statistics, *Prisoners and Alcohol* (Washington, D.C., 1983). The same survey found that a third of inmates were under the influence of some illegal drug while committing the crime for which they'd most recently been convicted; drug use was particularly common among robbers, burglars, and repeat offenders. *Justice Assistance News*, April 1983.

2. See especially Edna Erez, "Planning of Crime and the Criminal Career: Official and Hidden Offenses," *Journal of Criminal Law and Criminology* 71, no. 11 (Spring 1980).

Interviewing Philadelphia delinquents now in their twenties, Erez found that only 21 percent of all offenses had been planned rather than essentially "impulsive," according to the respondents; the "impulsive" offenders, moreover, committed twice as many crimes as the "planners." Other research supports this point. A Rand Corporation survey of California prison inmates found that their perceptions of the certainty of arrest had little bearing on the amount of crime they committed; Mark A. Peterson, Harriet B. Braiker, and Suzanne Polich, *Doing Crime: A Study of California Prison Inmates* (Washington, D.C.: National Institute of Justice, 1980), p. xii.

3. Deterrence quotations: Charles Tittle, *Sanctions and Social Deviance* (New York: Praeger, 1980), p. 4; Alfred Blumstein, Jacqueline Cohen, and Daniel Nagin, eds., *Deterrence and Incapacitation: Estimating the Effects of Criminal Sanctions on Crime Rates* (Washington, D.C.: National Academy of Sciences, 1978), p. 9; and Jack P. Gibbs, *Norms, Deviance, and Social Control* (New York: Elsevier, 1981), p. 143.

4. Tittle quotation: *Sanctions and Social Deviance*, p. 320. Paternoster et al. quotation: Raymond Paternoster, Linda Saltzman, Gordon Waldo, and Theodore Chiricos, "Perceived Risk and Social Control: Do Sanctions Really Deter?" *Law and Society Review* 17, no. 3 (1983): 478. A good general review of recent deterrence research is Sheldon Ekland-Olson, William Kelly, and Michael Supancic, "Sanction Severity, Feedback, and Deterrence," in *Evaluating Performance of Criminal Justice Agencies*, ed. Gordon P. Whitaker and Charles David Phillips (Beverly Hills: Sage Publications, 1983), pp. 129–164.

5. Tittle quotation: *Sanctions and Social Deviance*, p. 320. Drug dealers: Ekland-Olson et al., "Sanction Severity," p. 155.

6. Lyle W. Shannon, *Assessing the Relationship of Adult Criminal Careers to Juvenile Careers: A Summary* (Washington, D.C.: U.S. Office of Juvenile Justice and Delinquency Prevention, 1982), p. 10.

7. It should be noted that the tendency of conservative writers in particular to support formal deterrence—despite the paucity of supporting evidence—seems especially peculiar given the traditional emphasis in conservative thought on the integrative role of smaller-scale social institutions in achieving social order. In theory, that emphasis ought to lead neoconservatives to promote sanctions at the level of family and local community. With some exceptions..., many conservatives instead push for precisely those sanctions that most decisively separate individuals from their surrounding communities and lodge the most power in the hands of that arch-villain of conservative rhetoric, the state.

8. Lee H. Bowker, "Crime and the Use of Prisons in the United States: A Time-Series Analysis," *Crime and Delinquency*, April 1981, p. 211.

9. David Biles, "Crime and Imprisonment: A Two-Decade Comparison Between England and Wales and Australia," *British Journal of Criminology* 23, no. 2 (April 1983): quotation at 171.

10. Econometric studies: see especially Isaac Ehrlich, "Participation in Illegitimate Activities: A Theoretical and Empirical Investigation," *Journal of Political Economy* 81, no. 3 (May–June 1973). For an excellent discussion of the difficulties of this research generally, see Thompson et al., *Employment and Crime*, chap. 2.

11. David Biles, "Crime and the Use of Prisons," *Federal Probation* 43, no. 2 (1979).

12. Problems in "cross-sectional" research: for discussion, see especially Blumstein et al., *Deterrence and Incapacitation*; and Alfred Blumstein, "Research on Sentencing," *Justice System Journal* 7, no. 3 (1982):314–315.

13. Drug law findings: Kenneth Carlson, *Mandatory Sentencing: The Experience of Two States* (Washington, D.C.: National Institute of Justice, 1982); and Prison Association of New York, *The Prison Population Explosion in New York State* (New York, 1982), pp. 59, 114–119.

14. Carlson quotation: *Mandatory Sentencing*, p. 8.

15. "Tough law": Milton Heumann, Colin Loftin, and David McDowall, "Federal Firearms Policy and Mandatory Sentencing," *Journal of Criminal Law and Criminology* 73, no. 3 (Fall 1982):1055.

16. Rand survey: Joan Petersilia, Peter Greenwood, and Marvin Lavin, *Criminal Careers of Habitual Felons* (Washington, D.C.: National Institute of Law Enforcement and Criminal Justice,

1978), p. 38. For similar findings, see Peter Greenwood, "The Violent Offender in the Criminal Justice System," in *Criminal Violence*, ed. Marvin Wolfgang and Neil Alan Weiner (Beverly Hills: Sage Publications, 1982), pp. 325–330.

17. For example, Edwin Meese, "Improving the Criminal Justice System," *Christian Science Monitor*, December 2, 1982.

18. Studies of exclusionary rule: cited in Thomas Y. Davies, "A Hard Look at What We Know (and Still Need to Learn) About the 'Costs' of the Exclusionary Rule," *American Bar Foundation Research Journal* (Summer 1983):611–624. Cf. Shirley Melnicoe et al., *The Effects of the Exclusionary Rule: A Study in California* (Washington, D.C.: National Institute of Justice, 1982).

19. Vera Institute of Justice, *Felony Arrests: Their Prosecution and Disposition in New York City's Courts* (New York: Vera Institute, 1977). See also Hans Zeisel, *The Limits of Law Enforcement* (Chicago: University of Chicago Press, 1982).

20. Joan E. Jacoby et al., *Prosecutorial Decisionmaking: A National Study* (Washington, D.C.: National Institute of Justice, 1982).

21. For example, though the evidence so far is mixed, many feel that the "Career Criminal" programs inaugurated in recent years, which provide greater resources to prosecutors to try the most hardened repeat offenders, have made a difference in conviction rates—and hence, presumably, to deterrence. For a less sanguine evaluation, see E. Chelimsky and J. Damaan, *Career Criminal Program National Evaluation, Final Report* (Washington, D.C.: National Institute of Justice, 1981); for a positive one, California Office of Criminal Justice Planning, *Career Criminal Prosecution Program: Second Annual Report to the Legislature* (Sacramento: Office of Criminal Justice Planning, 1980).

22. Drunken driving evidence: see, for example, the review in Ekland-Olson et al., "Sanction Severity," p. 139; Harold L. Votey, "Control of Drunken Driving Accidents in Norway," *Journal of Criminal Justice* 11, no. 2 (1983); and H. Laurence Ross, "Interrupted Time Series Studies of Deterrence of Drinking and Driving," in *Deterrence Reconsidered*, ed. John Hagan (Beverly Hills: Sage Publications, 1982).

23. *Felony Arrests*, p. 134.

24. Petersilia et al., *Criminal Careers*, pp. 36–37.

25. Clearance rates: see especially John Burrows and Roger Tarling, *Clearing Up Crime* (London: Home Office Research Unit, 1982); also John M. Stevens and Brian Stipak, "Factors Associated with Police Apprehension Productivity," *Journal of Police Science and Administration* 10, no. 1 (1982). Note that the crucial relation of apprehension to deterrence is well understood by offenders themselves. The Rand survey of California repeaters found that half those inmates said that *nothing* could deter them from further crimes after release; the remaining half reported that certainty of apprehension, not the threat of longer sentences, would have the most deterrent influence. As the researchers note, this "reflects their awareness of a fairly high probability of conviction and incarceration once arrested." Petersilia et al., *Criminal Careers*, p. xiii.

39. Race, Ethnicity, and the Social Order of the Prison

LEO CARROLL

Racial and ethnic minorities have always been overrepresented in American prisons. As far back as 1833, de Beaumont and de Tocqueville (1833, p. 61) observed that "in those states in which there exists one negro to thirty whites, the prisons contain one negro to four white persons." After the Civil War, prisons in the South became overwhelmingly black, while those in the North were populated mainly by first- and second-generation immigrants from Europe (Sellin, 1976, pp. 140–144). Thus, the great "manual labor school," the Massachusetts State Prison in Charlestown, with its largely immigrant population, stood in sharp contrast to the "South Carolina Penitentiary, almost entirely black, with its chain gangs, field hands, work songs and white overseers" (Hindus, 1980, pp. 175–178, 243).

Despite the high visibility and probable significance of these statistical facts, scholars have until recently ignored the impact of race and ethnicity on the culture and social structure of the prison. Clemmer (1940/1958), in his pioneering study of the prison community, notes that about one-fourth of the prisoner population at Menard at the time of his observations were black. However, despite numerous references to race in the remarks and observations of his informants, Clemmer makes no attempt to analyze race relations either among the prisoners or between staff and inmates. Sykes (1958, p. 81), in his classic study of the New Jersey State Prison in Trenton, observes at one point that "the inmate population is shot through with a variety of ethnic and social cleavages which sharply reduce the possibility of continued mass action," but he makes no mention of these cleavages in the rest of his analysis. The same inattention to ethnicity characterizes every major prison study prior to 1970.

Whatever reasons there may be for this inattention to the role of race and ethnicity in the prison,[1] the fact remains that we know little about its influence. Today, however, in many prisons "racial politics set the background against which all prisoner activities are played out" (Jacobs, 1979, p. 14). Indeed, the contemporary crisis in corrections is largely "attributable to the changing pattern of race relations" (Jacobs, 1979, p. 7). The black challenge to the traditional pattern of white dominance, which extended into the prison in the early 1960s, plunged prisons into a turmoil from which they have yet to emerge.

TOTAL INSTITUTION OR SLUM?

Following Goffman (1961, pp. 14–48), it has been common to view the prison as a total institution. From this perspective the prison is seen as set off from the larger society and impervious to its influence. Upon entry, prisoners are stripped of their pre-prison identities and, through a ritual series of defilements, confirmed in a new identity, that of the convict. Through their interaction within the walls, prisoners are said to develop a subculture designed to alleviate the pains of imprisonment, and interaction is seen to be structured in terms of the normative prescriptions of an inmate code of solidary opposition to staff (Sykes and Messinger, 1960).

As plausible as this view is, conceptualizing the contemporary prison as a slum community would seem to be as valid, and perhaps more so, than characterizing it as a total institution. Over half the residents of the contemporary prison are drawn from racial and ethnic minority groups, and most were residents of ghettos prior to their incarceration. Many slum dwellers have been characterized as untrustworthy and perhaps dangerous in the eyes of others; this is true of all prison inmates. Slums provide a cheap source of labor to marginal enterprises in the service economy and are characterized by high levels of unemployment and underemployment. Prison industries are prohibited from competing with private industry and produce goods at low cost for use by the state; there is a high level of unemployment in the prison, and wages for the employed are abysmally low. Of course, slums are not typically surrounded by walls, though ghettos in the Middle Ages were. Thus this obvious physical difference might be interpreted as a reversion to an earlier form of ghettoization because of the proven disreputability of the residents of the particular slums we call prisons.

Suttles (1968), in his analysis of the Addams area of Chicago, portrays the social order of a slum community as one of "ordered segmentation." Cultural differences and the fact that many peers are known to share disreputable characteristics produce a high degree of mistrust and suspicion. In the absence of trust, people withdraw into small territorial groupings segregated first by ethnicity and then by sex and age.

Despite their seemingly common status, prisoners are sharply divided along racial and ethnic lines. In a recent study of federal youth institutions, Slosar (1978, pp. 86, 111) found race to be the most important determinant of friendship and leadership choices. White inmates chose white friends and leaders 2 to 6 times more often than would be expected by chance. Blacks exhibited even greater ethnocentricity, choosing black friends and leaders between 19 and 35 times more frequently than chance. Self-segregation by race appears even in small residential units with as few as 3 minority group inmates; an equal ratio of minorities in a cottage with 30 residents results in virtually separate and parallel racial subcultures (Feld, 1977, pp. 181–188). Administrative policy may make for a high degree of demographic integration in cell and work assignments, but biracial interaction cannot so easily be compelled. In those areas subject to formal controls, it is rare; it is nonexistent in areas of life beyond the boundary of administrative policy. Certain areas in the cell blocks, break areas in the industrial buildings, and select spots in the yard become identified with particular cliques and are used only by them. As the cliques are almost always racially and ethnically homogeneous, the prison is thereby balkanized (Carroll, 1974, pp. 147–172; Moore, 1978, pp. 109–110).

It is hard to imagine a convict code of solidarity spanning the social distance that prisoners of different races place between themselves. One recent study reports the existence of racially specific norms encouraging the exploitation and victimization of outgroup members (Bartollas et al., 1976, pp. 62–67); Irwin (1980, p. 184) observes that "loyalty to other prisoners has shrunk to loyalty to one's clique or gang." Loyalty, however, was probably always coterminous with primary group cohesion, and the inmate code has probably always been more fiction than fact. Like public morality in the slum, the code may be "not so much the heartfelt sentiments of people as much as a set of defensive guarantees demanded by various minority members . . . a means of protecting themselves from one another" (Suttles, 1968, p. 4). The increased heterogeneity of the contemporary prison has made it more difficult to create and maintain personalized relations between and among groups that undergird the public fiction. To comprehend the social order of today's large prison we must therefore understand the diverse cultural orientations of prisoners, how these define the experience of imprisonment, and how they shape adaptations to its pains.

BLACK PRISONERS AND DISCRIMINATION

In *The Society of Captives*, Sykes (1958, p. 64) delineates five "pains of imprisonment" — "deprivations or frustrations of prison life today . . . which the free community deliberately inflicts on the offender for violating the law [and] . . . the unplanned . . . concomitants of confining large groups of criminals for prolonged periods." In delineating these pains, Sykes was emphasizing what he perceived as the "hard core consensus" among those confined, though he recognized the fact that there was diversity among prisoners in the saliency of those concerns. In today's prisons, the diversity stands in sharper relief than the consensus.

Through three centuries of oppression in the United States, black Americans have developed a sensitivity to discrimination and victimization. Expecting whites to victimize them, lower-class blacks are inclined to view every use of power with skepticism. This tendency is reinforced by their experience with the criminal justice system. Researchers may debate the existence of discrimination in arrest and sentencing (see, for example, Hagan, 1974; Kleck, 1981; Zatz, 1981), but from the perspective of many black prisoners the evidence is clear and compelling. The rate of incarceration for blacks is nearly 10 times that for whites, 544 versus 65 per 10,000. Black males, who constitute but 5.4 percent of the population, make up 45.7 percent of the prisoner population (Christianson, 1981, pp. 364–368).[2] It is scarcely surprising that in the minds of many black males prison "simply looms as the next phase in a sequence of humiliations" (Jackson, 1970, p. 9).

The very structure of the prison — its walls and bars, its rigid hierarchy, its whiteness — seems designed to foster an image of a racist conspiracy. At Attica at the time of the riot in 1971, there were only 2 minority employees on a staff of over 500, with a prison population that was 63.5 percent black and 9.5 percent Puerto Rican (New York State Special Commission on Attica, 1972, pp. 24, 490).[3] The commission made the following observation regarding race relations:

> There was no escape within the walls from the growing mistrust between white middle America and the residents of urban ghettos. Indeed, at Attica, racial polarity and mistrust were magnified by the constant reminder that the keepers were white and the kept were largely black and Spanish-speaking. The young black inmate tended to see the white

officer as the symbol of a racist, oppressive system which put him behind bars [New York State Special Commission on Attica, 1972, p. 4].

While affirmative action policies have increased the number of minorities employed in corrections since 1971, the observations of the Attica Commission remain accurate with respect to most prisons today. A report on a recent disturbance at the Brushy Mountain State Penitentiary, for instance, notes that 55 percent of the prisoners are black but 100 percent of the officers are white; among the staff there is only 1 black, a teacher (Rawls, 1982a).

The sense of discrimination is confirmed through the daily round of discretionary decisions to which prisoners are subject. Research suggests that black prisoners are more likely to be seen as dangerous and threatening by white custodians. As a result, they are kept under closer surveillance than white prisoners. Their visitors and cells are more likely to be searched, they themselves are more likely to be denied passes to go from one part of the prison to another, and small groups of them are likely to be told to "break it up." Black prisoners are written up for disciplinary offenses in significantly larger numbers than white prisoners, particularly in those categories in which the guards have the greatest discretion (Carroll, 1974, pp. 115–143; Held et al., 1979). There is also some evidence that black prisoners, at least in some jurisdictions, are subject to discrimination in consideration for release on parole (Carroll and Mondrick, 1976; Clark and Rudestine, 1974, p. xx; Peterson and Friday, 1975).

All minority prisoners are concerned with discrimination, but for blacks it is the most salient concern. Johnson (1976) reported the results of clinical interviews with 325 men who had either mutilated themselves or attempted suicide in confinement and with a random sample of 146 prisoners used as a comparison group. Black prisoners in the comparison group were strikingly different from Hispanic and white prisoners in their concern with being victims of inequity and abuse by the criminal justice system and in tending to express fear of being unable to control their anger and resentment at this perceived victimization (Johnson, 1976, pp. 74–77). Much the same inference can be drawn from the work of Toch (1977). He identified eight environmental concerns of prisoners; the most prominent for blacks was freedom: "A concern about the circumscription of one's autonomy; a need for minimal restriction and for maximum opportunity to govern one's conduct" (Toch, 1977, p. 17). Prisoners exhibiting a high degree of concern with freedom are those who see themselves as placed in childlike roles, deprived of their due respect, continually harassed in both serious and petty ways, and tending to experience anger at their lack of autonomy and perhaps rage at their inability or fear of expressing resentment (Toch, 1977, pp. 97–104).

The debasement and degradation of being an inmate pose serious threats to self-esteem. Black prisoners in the late 1960s and early 1970s were able to protect themselves from these threats by using the perspectives of black nationalism to integrate their role as blacks with their role as prisoners in such a way as to place themselves in the vanguard of a worldwide revolutionary movement against oppression (Carroll, 1974, pp. 95–98). Undoubtedly this prison-reinforced ideology affected the concerns of black prisoners and is reflected in the findings of Johnson and Toch. Nationalism, however, was superimposed and to some degree in conflict with more enduring strains of black culture, strains that extol perseverance rather than revolution (Carroll, 1974, pp. 95–98; Johnson and Dorin, 1978; Dorin and Johnson, 1979). Pervasive victimization gives rise to a view of life as a jungle, an almost paranoid suspiciousness of one's environment and the motives of others (Grier and Cobbs, 1969, p. 172). Both cunning and toughness are highly valued and assiduously cultivated. The concern for safety and the instability of the family gives rise to a strong peer group orientation that is also indispensable to the maintenance of self-esteem, providing an audience to validate the young ghetto male's claims of masculinity and personal worth (Anderson, 1978; Liebow, 1967). This orientation is also the source of special relations of mutual aid and affection, which are frequently given the status of kinship, as in "going for cousins" (Anderson, 1978, p. 21). The appraisal of one's future as being filled with trouble, failure, and despair results in a "present-time orientation," the absence of a delayed gratification pattern (Liebow, 1967, pp. 64–71).

The adaptiveness of the black ghetto subculture to the prison was evident in the social organization of black prisoners in Rhode Island in the early 1970s (Carroll, 1974, pp. 98–113). Virtually every black inmate in Rhode Island's small prison was a member of an Afro-American Society. The organization was begun by some "revolutionaries" who saw it as a means to convert their "brothers." Most black prisoners remained semi-converts, however. They were "half-steppers," "talking the talk" of nationalism but not "walking the walk." This produced continual strain and conflict between the public leaders of the group and their presumed followers. The operative basis of black unity, however, was not the leaders' political ideology, but cohesive, personalized relations among cliques. Most black prisoners had several "partners," inmates whom they knew well, with whom they could rap easily, and who would go "all the way" for them. Some of these peers were "street partners" and others were "jail house partners" but, regardless of the origin of the relationship, the obligations of partnership remained. In consequence, the entire black population was bound together by an interlocking structure of diffuse relationships of mutual aid and obligation.[4]

Relationships similar to those between "partners" have been described as the building blocks of a black street gang (Keiser, 1969, pp. 13–14, 18), and in large prisons they may also provide the foundation for a larger structure. Jacobs (1977, ch. 6) has documented the development of street gangs in Stateville Penitentiary following a crackdown on gang activity in the streets of Chicago. In his view, the intrusion of the gangs changed the very principles by which inmates sought to "do time"—from "doing your own time" to "doing gang time"—and transformed the nature of the inmate social system as gangs gained a monopoly over the sub rosa economy.[5]

> When the gangs emerged at Stateville in 1969, they placed the old con power structure in physical and financial jeopardy. For the first time those convicts with the good jobs were not necessarily protected in their dealings, legitimate or illegitimate. Seeing strength in numbers, the gang members attempted to take what they wanted by force. . . . For the first time in history the old cons who "knew how to do time" found their lives disrupted and in danger. Gang members moved in to take over the "rackets." One informant described one instance where a half dozen "gang bangers" simultaneously put knives to his throat. Rather than cut the gangs in, many of the dealers went out of business [Jacobs, 1977, pp. 157–158].

Gang members also used their numbers to gain considerable freedom from custodial control. Jacobs (1977, pp. 161–162) describes how gang members at Stateville confronted officers attempting to discipline one of their members, with the result that the officers frequently backed down. In one case a gang leader negotiated his appearance at a disciplinary court with two captains. The same pattern of group-based confrontation existed in Rhode Island, even in the absence of street gangs (Carroll, 1974, p. 130). The result was a contradictory pattern of enforcement in which the guards were more inclined to keep the black inmates under surveillance but less inclined to punish them severely.

There exists a fair amount of research to support the hypothesis that black prisoners are more resilient to the stresses of confinement than are prisoners from other ethnic backgrounds. Harris (1975, 1976), for instance, found black prisoners to have higher levels of self-esteem than white prisoners. He also found that while the number of months imprisoned was related to a significant decrease in the self-esteem of white inmates, it was unrelated to any change in self-esteem among the blacks. Consistent with this finding are those of several studies of psychological distress. Jones (1976, pp. 70–71, 80–83) reports that among inmates at the Tennessee State Penitentiary a much lower percentage of black prisoners than white prisoners reported symptoms of general psychological distress, and that while one-third of the white prisoners have considered suicide, only 3 percent of the black prisoners have. In his more focused study of self-injury in New York's correctional system, Johnson (1976, pp. 41–55) found black prisoners to be grossly underrepresented among those who had experienced psychological crises and breakdowns. This relationship between race and breakdown remained unaltered when a wide variety of variables were held constant, which adds support to a cultural interpretation. Blacks apparently also feel safer in prison than do whites. Nearly 40 percent of the white prisoners in Jones's (1976, p. 164) study believed they could be the next victim of a random knife attack, as compared to only 12.5 percent of the blacks.

It is plausible to infer that the subculture of the black urban ghetto is functional for survival in the walled ghetto of the prison. The ghetto inhabitants' sense of themselves as victims, reinforced daily by the facts of their existence, provides a rationale that shifts responsibility for their acts from themselves to the system. Having been raised to be cunning and tough, they feel less vulnerable, and through their extensive involvement in peer groups they are able to monopolize the available goods and services and, to some degree, can counter the power of the guards. Moreover, their "present-time orientation" inclines them to do "easy time" by absorbing themselves in the prison rather than trying to "live with their heads on the streets while their bodies are in jail."

LATIN PRISONERS AND FAMILY

In a recently published study that examines the continuities and parallels between life in the barrio of East Los Angeles and life in prison, Moore (1978, p. 103) echoes the words of George Jackson: "In actual experience, pintos [Chicano prisoners] can see their lives as a set of recurrent, accelerating interactions with Anglo institutions that inevitably climaxed in the disaster of prison." True as this may be, it nonetheless appears that the subculture of the barrio does not insulate Latin prisoners from the stresses of confinement to the same degree that the ghetto subculture insulates black inmates. Indeed, in certain respects the core values of Latin culture may increase prison stress.

Latin prisoners are distinctive in the saliency of their concern with family. In Johnson's (1976, pp. 71–75, 170) clinical interviews, the most common theme expressed by his random sample of Latins (70.8 percent of them) was self-linking, defined as "a protest against intolerable separation from significant others [usually family], against perceived abandonment by them, or against inability to function as a constructive group member." Moore (1978, p. 111), in a survey of Chicanos who were members of prisoner self-help groups, confirms this finding; she finds that family is mentioned as the greatest worry by some 60 percent of the Chicano prisoners.

These concerns are a direct reflection of the familistic basis of Latin culture. Latins view the world in terms of extended kinship networks and "even with respect to identification the Chicano self is likely to take second place after the family" (Murillo, 1971, p. 99). Even *machismo*, the Latin ideal of masculinity, is a derivative of familism. *Macho* connotes virility, aggressiveness, fearlessness, and risk-taking, but not independent self-sufficiency. The *macho* male is bound to his family by complex ties of duty and dependency. A man provides for his wife and children; he is deferential and respectful to his elders. In return he is heavily dependent upon his family, especially his wife and/or his mother, for nurturance and emotional support. This dependency perpetuates a sense of adult masculinity which, by Anglo standards, has a "curious childlike quality" (Mintz, 1973, p. 75).

Separation from family thus poses a serious threat to the identity and self-esteem of many Hispanic prisoners. Moore (1978, pp. 100–106) describes how a Chicano prisoner may become morbidly preoccupied with the well-being of his family as a result of a missed visit or a delay in the mail. Johnson (1976, pp. 81–93) traces the complex and circuitous route by which such concerns lead to self-injury. (Self-injury and attempted suicide are comparatively common among Latin prisoners [Beto and Claghorn, 1968] and disproportionately high in comparison to their numbers in prison [Johnson, 1976].) Crisis-prone Latin inmates, overwhelmed with anxiety about family, seek to place staff in the role of parental surrogates. Non-Latin staff are inclined to view such concerns and tactics as unmanly and perhaps as manipulations to gain special treatment. Self-mutilation may be an attempt by the prisoner to convince the staff that he is, in fact, a man and that his requests are serious and urgent (Johnson, 1976, pp. 89–93).

In other ways, however, the culture of the barrio can be functional, and Latin adaptations to imprisonment may be seen as "variants of adaptations to the streets" (Moore, 1978, p. 98). Of particular importance, again, is the street gang. Moore's description of Chicano gangs in East Los Angeles in many ways parallels Suttles's (1968) description of Italian and Mexican gangs in Chicago. Barrio gangs are territorially based to the extent that *"mi barrio"* refers equally to neighborhood and gang. Gangs are also age graded. New cohorts are formed every few years as the result of conflicts between teenage boys from different barrios. While territoriality decreases with time, the gang remains a primary reference group into adulthood, being reinforced by marriage to female relatives of fellow gang members and by ritual kinship ties such as godparent-hood (Moore, 1978, pp. 35–36). The strength of barrio ties extends deeply into the prison. Even after years in prison, Chicano prisoners spend much of their time with friends from their neighborhoods, and turn to them for aid in dealing with personal problems and stresses of prison life (Moore, 1978, pp. 119–121). In a sense, the gang becomes a family surrogate that extends its support into the prison (Davidson, 1974, p. 84).

Although Chicano gangs arise from conflict and remain fighting gangs, they are also heavily involved in the marketing of heroin. As described by Moore (1978, pp. 88–92), the heroin market in Los Angeles is more decentralized than it is in other areas, and suppliers and dealers go into and out of business with relative frequency. A number of factors account for this. Of primary importance is the closeness of sources of supply, the poppy fields in northwestern Mexico. Extended kinship ties often mean that a distributor can gain a supply on credit, and the relative impurity of Mexican heroin means that the organizational chain cannot be very long, as there cannot be too many cuts made. Organizational relation-ships are not those of a bureaucratic hierarchy, but those of kinship and friend-ship among a group of men who are from the same gang or perhaps have done time together.

Encounters with the Anglo system of criminal justice have provided a basis for coalescence among Chicano gangs in prison. Since 1967, the dominant Chicano groups in California prisons have been two super-gangs that, while resembling street gangs, had their origins inside the prison in conflicts over the control of the narcotics trade. The "Mexican Mafia" originated as a gang of "state-raised youths" with ties to Southern California who attempted to organize the drug traffic in San Quentin by strong-arming Chicano loners who were mostly from small towns in central and north-ern California. *La Nuestra Familia* emerged in response to these attacks. For years conflict between the two gangs was responsible for a spiraling wave of violence in the California prisons.[6] Prison officials have been able to stem this tide only by segregating the gangs into different institutions, sending Mafia members to San Quentin and Folsom, and Familia members to Soledad or Tracy (Irwin, 1980, pp. 189–191; Moore, 1978, pp. 114–116).

The high degree of conflict and violence associated with Chicano prisoners in California and other areas of the Southwest is perhaps due to their involvement in the narcotics trade and to conflicts between territorial groups outside the prison. It is not typical of other areas, nor even of youth institutions in California, where Chicanos appear to form the most cohesive and solidary group. Jacobs (1977, pp. 148, 156) found the Latin Kings to be the best organized and most disciplined of the gangs at Stateville and to pose few control problems for the staff, and Dishotsky and Pfeffer-baum (1981, p. 1060) observe that at the Karl Holton School "only the Chicanos were sufficiently cohesive to develop an institutionwise, clandestine organization with a sin-gle leader coordinating policy aims." Moreover, Chicanos seem to be little involved in interethnic conflict in prisons.

WHITE PRISONERS AND SAFETY

Judging by reports of psychological distress, suicidal ideation, rates of self-injury, and completed suicides, incarceration today seems more painful for white prisoners than for their black and Latin counterparts (Johnson, 1976, pp. 42–49; Jones, 1976, pp. 69–85). The stress for whites does not seem to be related to any single focal concern. Like Hispanics, white inmates show great concern for their separation from significant others, and like blacks, a goodly number see themselves as victims of unjust treatment. But in addition to these stresses, there are several distinctive concerns expressed by white prisoners. In comparison to blacks and Hispanics, white prisoners are more prone to express a disinterest in day-to-day prison life and to direct their anger and resentment at themselves rather than at the system (Johnson, 1976, pp. 75–79). As Jacobs (1977, pp. 17–18) has observed, "'Whiteness' simply possesses no ideological or cultural significance in American society." Lacking in class or ethnic consciousness, white prisoners lack a group-supported rationale to deflect blame from themselves. Forced by their incarceration to take a personal inventory, many white inmates develop a view of their lives as devoid of value and of themselves as despicable and inadequate. They are also particularly vulnerable to threats to their external relations, which are probably less secure than those of Latin prisoners. Unlike blacks, many whites seem to make a "quasi-psychotic attempt to reside physically in the prison while living psychologically in the free (real) community" (Johnson, 1976, p. 122).

Another theme found by Johnson (1976, pp. 68–71) to be more common among white prisoners than others is "fate avoidance," fear that one is unable to stand up to prison pressure, especially the pressure generated by threats from other inmates. Confirming this, Toch (1977, p. 127) found safety to be the second most common concern of white inmates; it was mentioned in 44 percent of prisoner interviews and was the primary theme in 20 percent.[7] Quite possibly, the backgrounds of white prisoners have not provided them an equal opportunity with ghetto and barrio dwellers to develop the skills functional for survival in the prison. To some extent, these concerns with safety may also reflect common white stereotypes of ethnic minorities and a consequent exaggerated fear of life in an institution where minorities are the numerical majority. The concern is, however, also based on a realistic, albeit somewhat self-fulfilling, perception of their fate.

Whatever solidarity may have developed among white convicts in the past was presumably a product of their common deprivation in prison. As this deprivation has decreased with humanitarian reforms of the prison, so apparently has the sense of solidary opposition to staff. White prisoners today are not an organized collectivity so much as a congeries of small cliques with diverse orientations to the prison and the outside (Carroll, 1974, p. 85). Similar observations have been made in both juvenile and adult facilities in all regions of the country (see, for example, Bartollas et al., 1976; Davidson, 1974; Dishotsky and Pfefferbaum, 1979, 1981; Feld, 1977; Jacobs, 1977). Irwin (1980, p. 147) compares the withdrawal of the white prisoners to the tactics of slum residents who, as depicted by Suttles (1968), restrict the range of their interaction to their households and close relatives. Toch (1977, pp. 179–205) describes the retreat of many white prisoners into subsettings within the larger prison in which the inmate can relax with a small number of others of similar interests and orientations. For a disproportionately large number of white inmates, however, the only avenue of retreat is protective custody, where they may be kept in a cell for 23 hours a day. In the mid-1970s at Coxsackie, a youth prison in New York, 90 percent of those in protective custody were white; these prisoners accounted for one-fourth of the white prisoner population (Lockwood, 1980, p. 73). These figures reflect a national trend.

In some institutions, most notably in California but also in Illinois and elsewhere (Jacobs, 1979, p. 18), the threat posed to white inmates by minority numbers and solidarity has produced counterorganizations along the lines of the Ku Klux Klan and the American Nazi Party. Generally small, these groups tend to make up for lack of numbers with their high cohesion and virulent racism. In the youth institution studied by Dishotsky and Pfefferbaum (1979, 1981), for example, 17 percent of the white residents belonged to a neo-Nazi group. However, members of this group, which was the most internally cohesive and displayed the highest level of cross-ethnic hostility, accounted for over half the white inmates designated as leaders. In this institution and others there seems to be the potential of replacing convict solidarity, rooted in opposition to staff, with a similarly defensive solidarity rooted in racial and ethnic hatred.

INTERGROUP RELATIONS

The level of violence in the contemporary prison is exceedingly high, whether judged by the standards of the outside or by those of prisons in the past. . . . Using anonymous prisoner reports, Fuller et al. (1977) estimate that approximately 77 of every 100 prisoners in North Carolina are assaulted every year,[8] and in state prisons the annual homicide rate is at least double that in the nation as a whole (Bowker, 1980, p. 27). Much of this violence crosses racial and ethnic lines. Of the incidents documented by Fuller et al. (1977), 40 percent were interracial; of these, 82 percent involved a black aggressor and a white victim. The black victimization rate was 45 percent lower than the rate for whites.

This pattern of victimization is quite common. Indeed, in some institutions, blacks seem to dominate whites totally. In a juvenile institution in Columbus, Ohio, with equal numbers of black and white residents, Bartollas et al. (1976, pp. 53–81) found that a boy's status was determined by and inversely proportional to the level of exploitation to which he permitted himself to be subjected. The status hierarchy is described as an "exploitation matrix" and its racial composition is portrayed as follows:

> At the top is normally a black leader called a "heavy." He is followed closely by three or four black lieutenants. The third group, a mixture of eight to sixteen black and white youths, do the bidding of those at the top. This group is divided into a top half of mostly blacks, known as "alright guys," with the bottom half comprised mostly of whites, designated as "chumps." One or two white scapegoats make up the fourth group in each cottage. These scapegoats become the sexual victims of the first three groups [Bartollas et al., 1976, p. 72].

This degree of dominance seems unusual by comparison to other studies (for example, Carroll, 1974; Feld, 1977) and may have been related to a rather active cooperation of the staff in maintaining black hegemony (see Bartollas et al., 1976, pp. 106–125).[9] The sexual domination of whites by blacks in prison is, however, a matter of general agreement, with a number of studies reporting that somewhere in the vicinity of two-thirds of all sexual assaults involve black aggressors and white victims (Carroll, 1974, 1977; Davis, 1968; Jones, 1976; Lockwood, 1980; Scacco, 1975). Most researchers have seen this pattern as indicative of racial antagonism. Lockwood (1980, pp. 106–107), however, in what is the most detailed study of the problem, reports that

> neither aggressors nor their peers emphasized racial antagonism in interviews. The idea also fails to explain the significant number of blacks becoming targets and victims of aggressors. We should also consider that most rape victims of black aggressors in the street are black. If sexual aggression were primarily motivated by racial animosity, we would expect to find the same victim-aggressor pattern on the street as we find in prison.

Lockwood (1980, ch. 6) argues that the root cause of the problem is the threat that incarceration poses to the sexual identity of young males and results from the response to that problem on the part of some males who have been socialized into a subculture of violence. True as this may be, racism still must remain an important element. How else can we explain why "most informants reported young slender white men were the highest object of desire" and that "the white target brings the highest status to the aggressor" (Lockwood, 1980, p. 32). Moreover, Lockwood's comment on the difference in the racial composition of sexual assaults overlooks the symbolism of the penitentiary for blacks.[10] As we have seen, to many blacks the prison represents white dominance and oppression. In raping a white inmate, the black aggressor may in some measure be assaulting the white guard on the catwalk.[11]

Sexual aggression is only one dimension, however, of the conflict and violence in the prison. There has always existed an illegal economy through which inmates have sought to meet their needs for desirable food, good coffee, and cigarettes, not to mention alcohol and drugs. In the past twenty years, the affluence of the surrounding society has spilled over the walls and created a more visible and pronounced stratification within. In some institutions, prisoners who can afford them are permitted luxuries such as televisions, stereos, musical instruments, virtually unlimited supplies of food and books, even street clothing. And, as the result of more liberal visiting policies and the power and connections of gangs, drugs, alcohol, and cash have become more readily available. All of this has stimulated increased economic competition and conflict. . . . In the larger prisons, well-organized gangs struggle to control a share of the sub rosa economy, and in all prisons small cliques, usually differentiated by race, prey upon one another (Irwin, 1980, pp. 206–212).

Unlike sexual aggression, the violence surrounding economic conflict tends to be instrumental, and leaders attempt to control and moderate it. Jacobs (1977, pp. 155–156) describes how the leaders of rival gangs at Stateville reached an accommodation by pledging to abide by a set of "international rules." A similar agreement was arrived at between a white "Mafia" clique and black leaders in Rhode Island (Carroll,

1974, pp. 188–190). Due to the mistrust that surrounds such arrangements, they tend to be tenuous and are heavily dependent upon the personal relations between the leaders who enter into them and their ability to control the behavior of their followers. The release or transfer of a leader, any challenges to his position within the gang, or independent actions by small cliques can prove sufficient to destroy the precarious equilibrium and can plunge the prison into violence.

For a brief period of time in the early 1970s, it appeared that prisoners might bridge racial and ethnic cleavages. Black and white inmates, politicized by the civil rights and antiwar movements, came to see racism as a facet of the prison administration's efforts to divide and conquer prisoners. A series of unity strikes at San Quentin, followed by a number of other dramatic prison-related events across the country, focused attention on the prison and drew groups as diverse as the American Friends Service Committee and the Black Panthers into coalitions with prisoner organizations. Reform was pursued both through the courts and by direct action of strikes and nonviolent demonstrations in prisons from California to Massachusetts. While some significant victories were won, notably in the area of disciplinary procedures and minimum health and safety standards, the diversity of goals and tactics made common action tenuous, and the movement ultimately collapsed in the face of a strong custodial reaction. Leaders were segregated or transferred, followers were harassed, and political organizations, in the most generic sense of the term, were banned. Irwin (1980) argues that this movement, though indirectly causing an increase in violence against staff, afforded the only possibility to develop a new and peaceful order in the prison. He argues that in repressing this movement "the administrators stopped the development of alternative group structures that could have prevented the rise of hoodlum gangs involved in rackets, formed on racial lines, and engaged in extreme forms of prisoner-to-prisoner violence" (Irwin, 1980, p. 151).

Whether or not Irwin is right in his speculation, it is clear that the resurgence of custody has not been accompanied by a decrease in violence and rapacity. In the late 1970s, in the words of a long-term observer of prisons, *"anarchy within the walls replaced unity; atavism replaced ideology; prisoners destroyed their own"* (Dinitz, 1981, p. 9; emphasis in original).

A NOTE ON INSTITUTIONS FOR FEMALES

Females constitute only about 3 percent of the adult prisoner population in the United States (Hindelang et al., 1981, Table 6-21) and institutions for females have been studied infrequently. What is known of race relations in these institutions, however, suggests a much different order than is found among males.

In an early article on the sub rosa life of residents at a girls' training school, Otis (1913) noted that lesbian[12] relationships are common and usually interracial. Most recently, Carter (1973, p. 40) has reported that

the single most important factor determining this distribution (between sex roles) is race. Within the institution, race becomes a highly visible constant for imagined sex differentiation. Blacks, grossly disproportionate to their numbers . . . become butches, and whites, equally disproportionately, become femmes. The most common and desirable arrangement is a relationship consisting of a black butch and a white femme.

Giallombardo (1966, pp. 174–184), while not discussing the role of race in the family structures she details, does present two prison "family" kinship diagrams in which the race of the participants is indicated. Nearly three-fourths of the make-believe kinship relations are interracial, including five of seven marriages.

On the basis of such descriptions, it would seem that race relations among female prisoners may be characterized by intimacy and warmth rather than tension and hostility.[13] Carter (1973, p. 40) makes the interesting observation that when racial segregation does occur it seems to be an indirect result of segregation by sex roles— when butches want to discuss things femmes should not hear—but that the high correlation of race and sex role makes it difficult to determine which axis is primary. This is certainly an area in which more research is needed.

CONCLUDING REMARKS

Racial tension and hostility, although exacerbated by the pain of prison life, is endemic to American society. It is unrealistic to expect to cure in the prison what is one of society's most serious and persistent problems. Nevertheless, some measures can be taken to moderate the current high level of racially tinged antagonism in our prisons. Some of these steps may be relatively minor, such as classifying prisoners according to their environmental concerns as assessed by Toch's (1977) Prison Preference Inventory and placing them in congruent environments. Especially vulnerable prisoners could be placed in sheltered environments or niches. . . . Such classification could have a major impact in some institutions, particularly where minorities are not a numerical majority. In most cases, however, improving race relations will require major changes in the organization of the prison.

There is an extensive body of research in the field of race relations that rather uniformly concludes that, under certain conditions, interracial contact reduces racial prejudice even among highly prejudiced persons (see Carroll, 1974, p. 217, n. 12). The situation in most contemporary prisons is the antithesis of these conditions, but where it is not there is evidence to suggest that contact reduces prejudice among black and white prisoners (Foley, 1976).[14] Attempts at intervention need to focus on those features of the prison's physical and social structure that impinge on these conditions.

The first condition to be met is that the contact situation must be one in which the participants are defined as equals and in which the social climate favors interracial association and egalitarian attitudes. Obviously, prison inmates cannot be defined as the equal of officers, but more could be done to minimize status distinctions, as is being attempted at the new Minnesota Correctional Facility (Rawls, 1982b). More important is the elimination of racial discrimination. Among other things, this will require that prisons be lawful. There must be reasonable rules, clearly stated and firmly enforced in a manner consistent with minimum guarantees of due process.

Disciplinary decisions must be subject to review, and there must be a grievance system for both staff and inmates so that meaningful action on complaints may be taken in advance of serious problems. Parole eligibility guidelines should be developed and implemented, and inmates denied parole should be informed of the reasons for denials in specific terms. These procedures, and others, must be seen as legitimate. Ultimately, legitimacy can be gained only by efficacious implementation, which depends on continual, credible communication among staff and between staff and inmates.

Minority prisoners may never entirely suspend their belief in racial discrimination, but they certainly will not become less bitter as long as those who keep them in prison are almost entirely white and Anglo. Active efforts must be made and, where they are being made, must be increased to recruit minorities into staff positions at all levels. Recruitment is not enough, however. The little research that exists suggests that black officers may be subject to rather severe discriminatory practices by their largely rural white superiors (Jacobs and Grear, 1977; Jacobs and Kraft, 1978). Affirmative action must be accompanied by continuing staff training that focuses on interracial understanding and cooperation among the staff members themselves. Moreover, it is to be emphasized that minority staff are not needed primarily to understand minority prisoners any more than white staff are needed primarily to understand white prisoners. The primary needs are for a racially and ethnically integrated staff to serve as a model of effective cooperation, to promote a climate that encourages interracial understanding, and to ensure that all prisoners are defined and treated as equals.

The recruitment and retention of black and Hispanic staff will be greatly facilitated by relocating prisons nearer cities in which large numbers of black and Hispanic people live. With so many prisons overcrowded, decrepit, and obsolete, and with the necessary public support emerging,[15] we appear to be entering a new era of prison construction. These new facilities should be near larger population centers, not on abandoned military posts in remote rural areas. Moreover, they should be smaller, housing perhaps no more than 300–400 prisoners in relatively autonomous living units of 15 to 20 prisoners. This will facilitate security and order maintenance, of course; it will also facilitate credible communication between staff and inmates.

A second characteristic of contact situations that reduces prejudice is that they require, or at least encourage, mutually interdependent relationships to promote interaction that is personal, intimate, and of sufficient duration to overcome stereotypes. The most obvious issue that could draw prisoners into such association is that of meaningful sharing of power. In suggesting this, I am under no illusions about the amount of support that exists for inmate self-government. But it seems that the failure of such experiments has usually been a self-fulfilling prophecy. Initiated under pressure from prisoners or by a lone administrator with a vision, fragile arrangements have been doomed to failure. Where prisoners have been unopposed they have achieved some notable successes, as when a biracial organization of convicts ran the Walpole prison in Massachusetts for three months during a guard strike in 1973 (Irwin, 1980, p. 246). Even programs now branded as failures seem to have had some beneficial effects. A study at Walla Walla, for example, found that participants in the inmate self-government system established in the early 1970s showed significant increases (over a nine-month period) in self-esteem, self-confidence, acceptance of others, and acceptance of law and order—the last two showing the biggest gains (Regens and Hobson, 1978). With respect to racial antagonism, Feld (1977, pp. 186, 204–205) found that collaborative decision-making concerning the establishment of rules and the imposition of sanctions was particularly useful in defusing racial violence, which became translated instead into verbal aggression. Collaborative efforts may also be used to reduce the antagonism that sometimes spills over into sexual violence. . . .

Ideally, the construction of smaller facilities, and the renovation of existing prisons to create smaller and more autonomous units, will make prisoner participation in decision-making less threatening to custodians and administrators. We can then experiment with different types and degrees of collaboration to determine which are most feasible. (Collaboration in service of voluntary treatment programs is one possible agenda. . . .) Only through collaborative efforts do we have a chance to reduce racial hostility and violence; the result may be prisons that are reasonably stable, safe, and possibly even constructive living environments. Our only other choice is to repress conflict, maintaining order by a reign of terror. This is an unacceptable and unworkable option and, in the long run, we will all suffer its consequences.

Notes

1. Jacobs (1979, pp. 19–20) speculates that the oversight may have been due to the general acceptance of segregation and discrimination against which prison relations may have appeared normal or even progressive, and/or to theoretical "blindness" due to the concepts dominating the discipline at the time and thus filtering perceptions. Fascinating as the second explanation may be, I find it hard to accept in light of the intense interest in race and ethnic relations in American sociology back to the 1920s and before. Another factor of possible importance is the overpowering fascination with the prison as an institution that tempts all observers to see other influences on prison behavior as subsidiary.

2. Blacks constitute about 47 percent of the prisoner population and are a majority in 17 states and the District of Columbia. This percentage has been rising steadily (see Christianson, 1981). The percentage of prisoners who are Hispanic is difficult to estimate because they are counted as white. Those states with majority black prisoner populations are: District of Columbia (95.8), Maryland (75.7), Mississippi (66.7), New Jersey (61.5), Alabama (59.8), Georgia (59.8), Virginia (59.5), Illinois (57.9), South Carolina (56.8), Delaware (56.3), Michigan (56.1), Pennsylvania (54.5), North Carolina (54.2), New York (53.6), Ohio (52.3), Arkansas (51.9), Florida (51.4), Missouri (50.0) (Hindelang et al., 1981, Table 6-19).

3. De jure racial segregation in prisons continued in the 1970s. Jacobs (1979, p. 5) presents a list of cases in which racial segregation in prisons was held to be unconstitutional. The most recent was Battle v. Anderson, 376 F Supp. 402 at 410 (E.D. Oklahoma, 1974).

4. Davidson (1974, p. 55) presents a rather negative view of black prisoners at San Quentin. Noting that their private behavior is frequently at odds with their public displays of unity, he concludes that "they are concerned for themselves, not for any group." While agreeing that the public demonstrations of unity are often only a veneer, I find his conclusion slights the real sense of mutual obligation found among "partners."

5. Of the four gangs at Stateville, three are black—the Black P. Stone Nation, the Devil's Disciples, and the Vice Lords—and one is Hispanic, the Latin Kings. During the 1960s the black gangs had been politicized, at least to the degree that they realized that black nationalist symbolism and ideology could be used to gain money and power. They continued to use this tactic within the prison but never allied with other groups such as the Black Panthers, who

regarded the gangs as counterrevolutionary (Jacobs, 1977, p. 155). This is the same tension I found in Rhode Island, but on a larger scale.

6. In 1969 the rate of violent incidents in the California prison system was 1.08 per 100 prisoners per year. By 1974 the rate had risen to 4.3. Much of this increase was due to the feud between the Chicano gangs (Park, 1976).

7. By way of comparison, safety was mentioned as a concern by 30.7 percent of the black prisoners, but was the primary theme in only 4.1 percent of the interviews (Toch, 1977, p. 127).

8. The rate based on official records was much lower, 6.8 per 100.

9. Bartollas and Sieverdes (1981), in a recent study in another state, report a similar pattern but note that it does not exist to the same degree.

10. Hispanic prisoners, as I have discussed, probably suffer sexual identity problems more than others; yet only 14 percent of the aggressors identified by Lockwood (1980, p. 27) were Hispanic. This is perhaps due to their comparative lack of anger and resentment at being victimized. It is not apparently due to a lack of participation in homosexual activity (see Davidson, 1974, pp. 74–77).

11. Not all white inmates succumb to threats of sexual aggression or retreat to protective custody. Some retaliate. In nearly one-fifth of the homicides in prison, homosexuality is the primary motive (Sylvester et al., 1977, p. 48). These homicides often involve a young white aggressor and an older black victim (Jones, 1976, p. 151–152).

12. There is some question about how frequently these relations involve genital sex. Many, perhaps most, seem to be symbolically sexual, involving emotional intimacy and displays of affection, but not physical sex.

13. Bartollas and Sieverdes (1981) have recently presented evidence to the contrary. They found a stronger association between race and victimization among females than among males in six coeducational facilities for juveniles.

14. It should be noted, however, that this study has a number of methodological flaws. Many of the requisite conditions (such as equal status, cooperation, intimacy) are not observed but are assumed to exist. The living units compared (dormitories, two-man cells, and eight-man cells) are radically different, and it is quite possible, indeed likely, that the prisoners in the different units were quite different from each other despite random assignment with respect to race. The retest occurred after only three weeks, nearly one-third refused the retest, and many who took it had to be coaxed by the researcher.

15. A recent Gallup (1982) poll shows that 57 percent of the American people believe their states need more prisons and 49 percent are willing to pay more taxes to build them.

References

Anderson, E. *A place on the corner.* Chicago: University of Chicago Press, 1978.

Bartollas, C., Miller, S.J., and Dinitz, S. *Juvenile victimization: The institutional paradox.* New York: Halsted, 1976.

Bartollas, C., and Sieverdes, C.M. The victimized white in a juvenile correctional system. *Crime and Delinquency*, 1981, 27, 534–543.

Beto, D., and Claghorn, J. Factors associated with self-mutilation within the Texas Department of Correction. *American Journal of Corrections*, January/February 1968, pp. 25–27.

Bowker, L. *Prison victimization.* New York: Elsevier, 1980.

Carroll, L. *Hacks, blacks and cons: Race relations in a maximum security prison.* Lexington, MA: D.C. Heath, 1974.

Carroll, L. Humanitarian reform and biracial sexual assault in a maximum security prison. *Urban Life*, 1977, 5, 417–437.

Carroll, L., and Mondrick, M.E. Racial bias in the decision to grant parole. *Law and Society Review*, 1976, 11, 93–107.

Carter, B. Race, sex and gangs: Reform school families. *Society*, 1973, 11, 36–43.

Christianson, S. Our black prisons. *Crime and Delinquency*, 1981, 27, 364–375.

Clark, R., and Rudestine, D. *Prison without walls: Report on New York parole.* New York: Praeger, 1974.

Clemmer, D. *The prison community.* New York: Holt, Rinehart and Winston, 1958. (Originally published, 1940.)

Davidson, R.T. *Chicano prisoners: The key to San Quentin.* New York: Holt, Rinehart and Winston, 1974.

Davis, A.J. Sexual assaults in the Philadelphia prison system and sheriff's vans. *Transaction*, 1968, 6, 8–16.

de Beaumont, G., and de Tocqueville, A. [*On the penitentiary system in the United States and its application in France*](F. Lieber, trans.). Philadelphia: Carey, Lea and Blanchard, 1833.

Dinitz, S. Are safe and humane prisons possible? *Australian and New Zealand Journal of Criminology*, 1981, 14, 3–19.

Dishotsky, N.I., and Pfefferbaum, A. Intolerance and extremism in a correctional institution: A perceived ethnic relations approach. *American Journal of Psychiatry*, 1979, 136, 1438–1443.

Dishotsky, N.I., and Pfefferbaum, A. Racial intolerance in a correctional institution: An ecological view. *American Journal of Psychiatry*, 1981, 138, 1057–1062.

Dorin, D., and Johnson, R. The premature dragon: George Jackson as a model for the new militant inmate. *Contemporary Crises*, 1979, 3, 295–315.

Feld, B.C. *Neutralizing inmate violence.* Cambridge, MA: Ballinger, 1977.

Foley, L.A. Personality and situational influences on changes in prejudice: A replication of Cook's Railroad Game in a prison setting. *Journal of Personality and Social Psychology*, 1976, 34, 846–856.

Fuller, D., Orsagh, T., and Raber, D. *Violence and victimization within the North Carolina prison system.* Paper presented at the meeting of the Academy of Criminal Justice Sciences, 1977.

Gallup, G. Most Americans receptive to wholesale prison reform. *Providence Sunday Journal*, April 4, 1982, p. A-11.

Giallombardo, R. *Society of women: A study of a women's prison.* New York: John Wiley, 1966.

Goffman, E. *Asylums: Essays on the social situation of mental patients and other inmates.* Garden City, NY: Doubleday, 1961.

Grier, W.H., and Cobbs, P.M. *Black rage.* New York: Bantam, 1969.

Hagan, J. Extra-legal attributes and criminal sentencing: An assessment of a sociological viewpoint. *Law and Society Review*, 1974, 8, 357–383.

Harris, A.R. Imprisonment and the expected value of criminal choice: A specification and test of aspects of the labelling perspective. *American Sociological Review*, 1975, 40, 71–87.

Harris, A.R. Race, commitment to deviance and spoiled identity. *American Sociological Review*, 1976, 41, 432–441.

Held, B.S., Levine, D., and Swartz, V.D. Interpersonal aspects of dangerousness. *Criminal Justice and Behavior*, 1979, 6, 49–58.

Hindelang, M.J., Gottfredson, M.R., and Flanagan, T.J. (Eds.). *Sourcebook of criminal justice statistics–1980.* U.S. Department of Justice, Bureau of Justice Statistics. Washington, D.C.: Government Printing Office, 1981.

Hindus, M.S. *Prison and plantation: Crime, justice and authority in Massachusetts and South Carolina, 1767–1878.* Chapel Hill: University of North Carolina Press, 1980.

Irwin, J. *Prisons in turmoil.* Boston: Little, Brown, 1980.

Jackson, G. *Soledad brother: The prison letters of George Jackson.* New York: Bantam, 1970.

Jacobs, J.B. *Stateville: The penitentiary in mass society.* Chicago: University of Chicago Press, 1977.

Jacobs, J.B. Race relations and the prisoner subculture. In N. Morris and M. Tonry (Eds.), *Crime and justice: An annual review of research* (Vol. 1). Chicago: University of Chicago Press, 1979.

Jacobs, J.B., and Grear, M. Drop-outs and rejects: An analysis of the prison guard's revolving door. *Criminal Justice Review*, 1977, 2, 57–70.

Jacobs, J.B., and Kraft, L.J. Integrating the keepers: A comparison of black and white prison guards in Illinois. *Social Problems*, 1978, 25, 304–318.

Johnson, R. *Culture and crisis in confinement*. Lexington, MA: D.C. Heath, 1976.

Johnson, R., and Dorin, D. Dysfunctional ideology: The black revolutionary in prison. In D. Szabo and S. Katzenelson (Eds.), *Offenders and corrections*. New York: Praeger, 1978.

Jones, D.A. *The health risks of imprisonment*. Lexington, MA: D.C. Heath, 1976.

Keiser, R.L. *The Vice Lords: Warriors of the streets*. New York: Holt, Rinehart and Winston, 1969.

Kleck, G. Racial discrimination in criminal sentencing: A critical examination of the evidence with additional evidence on the death penalty. *American Sociological Review*, 1981, 46, 783–804.

Liebow, E. *Tally's corner: A study of Negro streetcorner men*. Boston: Little, Brown, 1967.

Lockwood, D. *Prison sexual violence*. New York: Elsevier, 1980.

Mintz, S. An essay on the definition of national culture. In F. Cordasco and E. Bricchione (Eds.), *The Puerto Rican experience*. Totowa, NJ: Rowan and Littlefield, 1973.

Moore, J.W. *Homeboys: Gangs, drugs and prison in the barrios of Los Angeles*. Philadelphia: Temple University Press, 1978.

Murillo, N. The Mexican-American family. In N. Wagner and M. Haur (Eds.), *Chicanos: Social and psychological perspectives*. St. Louis: Mosby, 1971.

New York State Special Commission on Attica. *Attica: The official report*. New York: Bantam, 1972.

Otis, M. A perversion not commonly noted. *Journal of Abnormal Psychology*, 1913, 8, 112–114.

Park, J. The organization of prison violence. In A.K. Cohen, G.F. Cole, and R.G. Bayley (Eds.), *Prison violence*. Lexington, MA: D.C. Heath, 1976.

Peterson, D.M., and Friday, P.C. Early release from incarceration: Race as a factor in the use of "shock probation." *Journal of Criminal Law and Criminology*, 1975, 66, 79–87.

Rawls, W., Jr. Fortress prison harbors violence that erupted in death of 2 blacks. *New York Times*, February 9, 1982, p. 15 (a)

Rawls, W., Jr. Prison in Minnesota, considered best ever built, opens to first convicts. *New York Times*, March 25, 1982, p. A-16. (b)

Regens, J.L., and Hobson, W.G. Inmate-self-government and attitude change: An assessment of participation effects. *Evaluation Quarterly*, 1978, 2, 455–479.

Scacco, A. *Rape in prison*. Springfield, IL: Charles C. Thomas, 1975.

Sellin, J.T. *Slavery and the penal system*. New York: Elsevier, 1976.

Slosar, J.A., Jr. *Prisonization, friendship and leadership*. Lexington, MA: D.C. Heath, 1978.

Suttles, G.D. *The social order of the slum: Ethnicity and territory in the inner city*. Chicago: University of Chicago Press, 1968.

Sykes, G.M. *The society of captives: A study of a maximum security prison*. Princeton, NJ: Princeton University Press, 1958.

Sykes, G.M., and Messinger, S.M. The inmate social system. In R.A. Cloward et al., *Theoretical studies in social organization of the prison*. New York: Social Science Research Council, 1960.

Sylvester, S.F., Reed, J.H., and Nelson, D.O. *Prison homicide*. New York: Spectrum, 1977.

Toch, H. *Living in prison: The ecology of survival*. New York: Free Press, 1977.

Zatz, M.S. Differential treatment within the criminal justice system by race/ethnicity: A dynamic model. Paper presented at the annual meeting of the American Sociological Association, Toronto, August 1981.

40.   Prison Guards and the Use of Physical Coercion as a Mechanism of Prisoner Control*

JAMES W. MARQUART

In the past 40 years, the study of social control in prisons has generated a consider-able body of research. Most of these studies have primarily focused on the formal prisoner control structure wherein internal order is achieved through such mechan-isms as official rules and regulations (Clemmer, 1940; McCleery, 1960; Goffman, 1961; Cressey, 1968); formal disciplinary procedures involving "write-ups" and adjudication before disciplinary courts (Carroll, 1974; Gobert and Cohen, 1981); and the prison staff's use of such punishments as loss of privileges or solitary confine-ment (Cloward, 1960; Wright, 1973; Hawkins, 1976; Berkman, 1979). In addition, other researchers have examined the staff's official use of inmate elites as convict guards to maintain order (Mouledous, 1962; Marquart and Crouch, 1984).

Although most prisoner control research centers on formal measures, several studies have been conducted on the informal system. This line of inquiry typically shows that order is based on "trade-offs"; illegitimate rewards; guard accommodations with inmate elites (Cloward 1960; Carroll, 1974; Davidson, 1974; Jacobs, 1977); or concessions in which the staff overlook minor inmate rule violations (Sykes, 1958; Thomas, 1984). No research, to date, however, has examined the internal institutional order that is based on the guards' use of physical coercion.

In theory, the threat of force by guards is always present, but the literature lacks any systematic analysis of violence as a mechanism of social control in this setting. This neglect leaves an unbalanced picture of the structure and process of prisoner control. The present research documents with participant observation data how and why guards in one Texas penitentiary utilized unofficial physical force as a routine mechanism of informal social control.[1] The research shows that the guards' use of coercion does not result from personality defects or the brutalizing nature of the institutional environment (Zimbardo, 1972). Neither did their use of coercive power precipitate any mass dis-order or widespread retaliation from the prisoners (Sykes, 1958; Hepburn, 1985). Instead, this paper demonstrates that the guards' use of force was a socially structured tactic of prisoner control that was well entrenched in the guard culture.

RESEARCH STRATEGY

Data for this paper were collected at the Johnson Unit (a pseudonym), a large maxi-mum security facility within the Texas Department of Corrections. The author entered the penitentiary, with the warden's permission, as a guard to collect data on social con-trol and order for 19 months (June 1981 through January 1983), worked throughout the institution (for example, cell blocks, shops, dormitories), and observed how the guards meted out official and unofficial punishments, coopted inmate elites to act as "convict guards," cultivated snitches, and other guard work activities. Formal and informal interviews, documents and records, and direct observations were used (Lofland, 1971; Wax, 1971). In addition, over 20 key informants were cultivated among the guards and inmate elites or leaders who assisted in analyzing control and order as daily phenomena. Close relationships were developed with these informants, and their "expert" knowledge about prison life and prisoner control was essential throughout the fieldwork (Jacobs, 1974; Marquart, 1986). Most importantly, the daily routine of prison events (work, school, counts, cell and body searches, the administration of punishment) as well as various unexpected events (fights, stabbings, suicide attempts, escapes) were observed and noted.

After a time, the author became privy to guard violence and observed and simply noted 30 incidents wherein the guards physically punished inmates for various rule violations. Key guard informants also described an additional 20 force situations. These 50 cases occurred between December 1981 and November 1982. At this point, a general description of the incidents was written up and the altercations were discussed at great length with 7 guard and 15 inmate key informants. The guard informants consisted of 3 supervisors (sergeant, lieutenant, captain) and 4 hall officers – a highly regarded slot for nonranking guards. All 15 convict informants were called building tenders. These inmates were used by the guards to maintain control in the living areas. Most had violent records and many years of prison experience. These 22 informants were extremely reliable because of their positions, sympathy with the research effort, and consistency in providing accurate information. Essentially, these 50 cases served as a base to further develop a systematic method of data collection and analysis. Then, after reviewing the literature on social control in prison and social control theory in general (as well as the police use of force), the author developed a systematic strategy to catalogue and code four functions of the guards' use of unofficial force. This analytic strategy was then applied to 30 cases of observed and informant-reported guard violence that occurred between December 4, 1982, and January 28, 1983. These latter 30 cases serve as the data base and will be examined at length throughout this paper.

THE RESEARCH SETTING

The Johnson Unit is a large maximum security institution housing, in 1981, nearly 3,000 inmates (47% black, 36% white, 17% Hispanic) and is located on 14,000 acres of farmland. Inmates assigned to this prison were classified by the Texas Department of Corrections as recidivists over the age of 25, all of whom had been in prison (excluding juvenile institutions) three or more times. Johnson had a system-wide reputation for tight disciplinary control and housed a large number of inmate troublemakers from the Texas prisons. Structurally, the prison had 18 inside cell blocks (or tanks) and 12 dormitories which branched out from a single central hall – a telephone pole design. The hall was the main thoroughfare of the prison and was almost one quarter of a mile long, measuring 16 feet wide by 12 feet high.

The staff at the prison numbered around 235 officers (85% white, 10% black, 5% Hispanic). This all-male security force was divided into two forces—building and field. The interest in this investigation lies with the building force that numbered nearly 145 officers. They were distributed between the three shifts.[2] The apex of the organizational structure was the warden, and beneath him were two assistant wardens. Although the wardens were the prison's chief security officers, they served primarily as administrators. The actual management and supervision of the daily security measures and convict "business" was the responsibility of the Building Major. The Major supervised two captains who in turn supervised four lieutenants. Last, there were eight sergeants who helped the lieutenants manage the shifts.

Between the ranking staff and the line prison guards was a group of nearly 25 guards called hall officers. At Johnson, all officers began their careers working in the cell blocks or tanks. Officers who demonstrated they could "work a tank" were defined as "good officers" and were selected by their supervisors (lieutenants and sergeants) to become hall officers. Properly "working a tank" involved keeping correct inmate counts, breaking up fights, the maintenance of discipline in a "cool manner" without yelling and arguing with inmates or constantly writing disciplinary reports. Although counting ability and "common sense" (the ability to manage inmates in ordinary situations) were musts, the willingness and initiative to break up fights with inmates, not backing down in confrontations with inmates, and the inclination to actually fight inmates were the critical factors leading to selection for a hall "boss" slot. As one supervisor stated, "I don't want him (as a hall officer) if he doesn't have nuts." These officers were regarded as the best of the line prison officers, and selection for this position was regarded as a promotion, a status symbol, and a sign of a promising future within this prison system. The remaining officers staffed the cell blocks, dormitories, gun towers, dining halls, and other security-related jobs and were rarely promoted. This latter group supplied the rapid turnover cadre that characterizes all prisons.

INTIMIDATION AND PHYSICAL COERCION

To control the inmates at Johnson, the guard staff employed both rewards and punishments. In the official control structure, the guards used a privilege system (for example, good time, furloughs, improved job and living quarters) that provided the majority of prisoners with enough incentive to follow the rules most of the time. Failure to comply typically resulted in the loss of privileges and usually solitary confinement. Because Johnson was so highly regimented, the fear of getting caught and losing privileges deterred most inmates from serious rule infractions. However, those who frequently broke the rules or engaged in serious violations (for example, assaulted staff, fomented rebellion, or stabbed other inmates) were unofficially controlled by the guards through verbal intimidation and various degrees of physical punitive force.

Verbal Intimidation

Inmates who challenged an officer's authority (for example, by insubordination, cursing at him, or "giving him a hard time") usually received verbal assaults from ranking officers or supervisors (sergeants, lieutenants, and captains). Verbal assaults, though physically harmless, induced humiliation and were used to cripple or demean the erring inmate's self concept. In addition, this control tactic intimidated, ridiculed, or destroyed the "face" of the offending inmate and often involved racial epithets, name calling, derogation, threats, and scare tactics. The following verbal assault by one ranking officer upon an inmate illustrates a typical humiliation ceremony. "You stupid nigger, if you ever lie to me or any other officer about what you're doing, I'll knock your teeth in." On another occasion the researcher observed a supervisor make this frequently heard threat: "Say, big boy, you're some kind of mother fucker, aren't you? I ought just go ahead and whip your ass here and now. If you think you're man enough let's do it."

Verbal assaults such as these were daily occurrences. In some cases, inmates were threatened with extreme physical injury ("you'll leave here [the prison] in an ambulance") or even death ("nobody cares if a convict dies in here, we'll beat you to death"). Essentially, verbal assaults alluding to physical force were scare tactics meant to deter inmates from future transgressions. Those who failed to "internalize" the message and repeatedly violated the rules were roughed up as a matter of course.

Types of Coercion

The first type of unofficial physical coercion was called (by inmates and officers alike) a "tune up," "attitude adjustment," or "counselling." These force displays were used for minor officer-inmate offenses (for example, refusing to obey an order, swearing at or arguing with an officer, belligerence, and the expression of a flippant and negative attitude) and rarely involved serious physical injury. "Tune ups" consisted of verbal humiliation, shoves, kicks, and head and body slaps.

This type of coercion functioned as an "attention getter" and was meant to scare and intimidate the inmate-victim. The following account, related to the researcher by an officer eyewitness, illustrates the circumstances that led to most "tune ups."

> I [hall officer] had a hard time in the North Dining Hall with an inmate who budged in line to eat with his friend. Man, we had a huge argument right there in the food line after I told him to "Get to the back of the line." I finally got him out [of the dining hall] and put him on the wall.[3] I told my supervisor about the guy right away. Then the inmate yelled "Yea, you can go ahead and lock me up [solitary] or beat me if that's how you get your kicks." Me and the supervisor brought the guy into the Major's office.[4] Once in the office, this idiot [inmate] threw his chewing gum in a garbage can and tried to look tough. One officer jumped up and slapped him across the face and I tackled him. A third officer joined us and we punched and kicked the shit out of him. I picked him up and pulled his head back by the hair while one officer pulled out his knife and said "You know, I ought to just go ahead and cut your lousy head off."

Besides being roughed up, this inmate was indeed scared. He had actually believed that the officers would not hit him. I saw this inmate, who had several lumps and bruises on his face, standing "on the wall" by the Major's office and asked him what happened. He said "Man, I didn't think you got fucked up for smarting off." Although this inmate had been at Johnson for six months, he stated to the author that he knew the guards would use force, but he also believed they would not hit him for such a "petty ass" violation.

Many "tune ups" also took place after disciplinary court. One reliable officer informant told the researcher about two "tune ups" following the court procedure.

> The first inmate was tried for refusing to work. The tape recorder was shut off[5] and a supervisor said, "You're going to work from now on, you understand?" After this, the supervisor slapped him on the head, kicked him in the ass, and literally threw him out the door. The next inmate came in and was tried and found guilty of self-mutilation. He ingested numerous razor blades. One supervisor yelled at him, "It's hard enough for me to keep the rest of these inmates in razor blades to shave with around here, let alone having you eat them all the time." The inmate stuttered and a supervisor slapped him twice across the face.

Inmates "tuned up" after court were the victims of multiple punishments. That is, they received both official (loss of privileges or solitary confinement) and unofficial forms of punishment.

The second form of physical coercion was dubbed "ass whippings" and befell inmates who broke more serious rules such as challenging an officers's authority, threatening an officer, totally defying an officer's authority, or fighting back during a "tune up." Further, these were force situations where the officers employed various types of weapons, such as blackjacks,[6] riot batons, fist loads, or aluminum-cased flashlights. Although weapons were employed, the inmate-victims were not brutalized enough to require hospitalization or other extensive medical treatment. A noteworthy example occurred when a newly arrived inmate, who was in the Major's office for an initial interview retorted, "I can see I'm going to have trouble making it on this farm [prison]." Several officers immediately attacked the inmate and threw him to the floor. While one officer literally stood on the inmate's head (called a "tap dance"), another hit him on the buttocks and thighs with a riot baton, and several others kicked him. During this event, a supervisor was heard yelling, "Hurt him, hurt him" and even encouraged the other officers by saying "Go on, get you some of that ass."

The third type of force used at Johnson was the severe beating. Such beatings occurred infrequently and were reserved for inmates who violated certain "sacred" rules through such actions as attacking staff members, inciting work strikes or mob action, or escaping. The purpose of a beating was intentional physical injury and in some cases hospitalization. For example, while making a routine check of the inmates in a solitary confinement area, the author observed an inmate who had struck an officer earlier in the day; he was beaten so severely that he could not stand up. In this particular case, the inmate was forcibly dragged from the hall into the Major's office and beaten, and then beaten again while being locked in a solitary cell.

Beatings, like the latter two types of coercion, were primarily backstage events and conducted in closed settings to avoid witnesses. However, "public" beatings were occasionally staged to set an example. A good illustration of a "front-stage" beating occurred in the hall near a spot adjacent to the Major's office and was reported by an officer eyewitness.

I was sitting at the Searcher's desk and Rick [convict] and I were talking and here comes Joe [convict] from 8-block. Joe thinks he knows kung fu, hell he got his ass beat about four months ago. He comes down the hall and he had on a tank top, his pants were tied up with a shoe lace, gym shoes on, and he had all his property in a large sack. As he neared us, Rick said, "Well, Joe's fixing to go crazy again today." He came up to us and Rick asked him what was going on and Joe said they [staff] were fucking with him by not letting him have a recreation card. I told him, "Well, take your stuff and go over there to the Major's office" and there he went. Officer A went over and stood in front of Joe, so did Officer B who was beside Joe, Officer C was in back of Officer A, and two convicts stood next to Officer A. Inmate James, an inmate who we tuned up in the hospital several days before, stood about ten feet away. All of a sudden Joe took a swing at Officer A. Officers A and B tackled Joe. I ran over there and grabbed Joe's left leg while a convict had his right leg and we began kicking his legs and genitals. Hell, I tried to break his leg. At the same time Officer B was using his security keys, four large bronze keys, like a knife. The security keys have these points on their ends where they fit into the locks. Well, Officer B was jamming those keys into Joe's head. Joe was bleeding all over the place. Then all of a sudden another brawl broke out right next to us. Inmate James threw a punch at Officer D as he came out of the Major's office to see what was going on. James saw Joe getting beat and he decided to help Joe out. I left Joe to help Officer D. By the time I got there (about two seconds), Officer D and about six convicts were beating the shit out of James. Officer D was beating James with a blackjack. Man, you could hear that crunch noise every time he hit him. At the same time a convict was hitting him in the stomach and chest and face. These other inmates were kicking him and stomping him at the same time. It was a wild melee, just like being in a war. I got in there and grabbed James by the hair and Officer D began hitting him on the head and face with a blackjack. I mean he was hitting him, no love taps. He was trying to beat his brains out and yelling, "You mother fucker, you think you're bad, you ain't bad, you mother fucker, son of a bitch, you hit me and I'll bust your fucking skull." I think we beat on him alone for ten minutes. I punched him in the face and head. Then Officer D yelled, "Take him [James] to the hospital." Officer C and me had to literally drag him all the way to the hospital. Plus we punched and stomped him at the same time. At the hospital, Officer D began punching James in the face. I held his head up so Officer D could hit him. Then Officer D worked James over again with a blackjack. We then stripped James and threw him on a bed. Officer D yelled at James, "I'm going to kill you by the time you get off this unit." Then Officer D began hitting him in the shins and genitals with a night stick. Finally, we stopped and let the medics take over. James had to leave via the ambulance. Joe required some stitches and was subsequently put in solitary.[7]

This gruesome event occurred in the full view of many inmates in the hall and hospital. In addition, the screams of the inmate-victims were heard throughout the building and for several days after this event, the entire prison operated smoothly with few officer-inmate confrontations. This beating was the talk of the prison and many officers used the incident as a scare tactic. In others words, "If you don't do what I say you'll get what Joe and James got and worse."

Beatings such as these were not restricted specifically to serious altercations between officers and inmates. In early August 1982, during breakfast in the South

Dining Hall, three inmates fatally stabbed another inmate. Seven officers armed with riot batons and baseball bats led the aggressors, weapons in hand, out of the dining hall to a spot near the Major's office. A supervisor ordered the inmates to throw down their weapons, but they refused. The supervisor made his plea one more time and the inmates still refused. At this point, two hall officers attacked the inmates with aluminum baseball bats. The inmates immediately dropped their weapons and were stripped, escorted to the Major's officer, and beaten severely. The staff was outraged at this homicide and made examples of the culprits.[8]

The Legitimation of Violence

These latter examples of guard violence were obviously illegal and violated written departmental policy as well as civil and criminal law. The informal norms of the guard staff justified violence that violated legal and administrative policy in certain instances. The use of unofficial force was so common in the institution under study that the guards viewed it as an everyday operating procedure and legitimized its use. Further, Johnson was not an anomaly with regard to punitive force. Although this researcher did not observe the use of force in other Texas prisons, the trial proceedings from a prison reform case documented numerous (and quite similar) incidences of guard coercion in seven other state prisons. The Court found that the guards' use of punitive force was not an isolated phenomenon but constituted a routine (and rampant) guard activity (Ninth Monitor's Report to the Special Master, 1983).

In almost every situation where a staff member struck an inmate at Johnson, post facto explanations were manufactured (Van Maanen, 1978). Due to the intervention in recent years of the Federal courts into prisoner discipline, inmates frequently sued officers for various types of civil rights violations, particularly for brutality. In light of this fact, the staff involved in such force situations got together after the fact and wrote statements to the effect that the inmate-victim assaulted a staff member and force was needed to subdue the inmate (similar to "throw downs"). The more force used against an inmate, the more the inmate was said to have "fought back." The officers involved generally used a "covering charge" of striking an officer to justify physical coercion (Manning, 1977). For most "tune ups," statements were not made. However, "ass whippings" and beatings were quickly followed up with statement and disciplinary report writing sessions. Many times inmates filed civil suits concerning excessive force and brutality against the officers. These civil suits were routinely investigated by the Federal Bureau of Investigation but were quashed due to the weight of the staffs' evidence. In short, no medical reports were made to verify physical damage and, in the end, it was the word of one inmate against two, three, or more officers and sometimes several prostaff inmate witnesses as well.

FINDINGS AND ANALYSIS

The use of punitive force by the guards was not a random activity or directed against any particular prisoner for any particular reason. Instead, coercion was a socially structured and highly organized form of guard behavior. To understand why the guards relied on force, it is necessary to first describe the setting for this behavior. Then four reasons for the use of coercion are analyzed. These are: (1) coercion maintains control and order; (2) coercion maintains status and deference; (3) coercion facilitates promotions; and (4) coercion builds guard solidarity.

The Setting for Coercion

Twenty-eight of the force situations occurred in the Major's office and two in a solitary confinement area. These areas were private settings free from the eyes of other inmates. Physically coercing or "adjusting an inmate's attitude" in private reduced the chances of the inmate-victim securing witnesses for a civil action. In this way, the victim's ability to win a brutality case was virtually impossible. The "hidden" force situation was difficult for the FBI or Department of Justice to investigate. If a suit was filed and investigated (and several were), the guards implicated simply denied knowledge of the event or else read a manufactured report that claimed self-defense, which in turn led to a dismissal of the inmate's claim of brutality.

The application of force was always done in the presence of more than one officer. Hall officers and ranking guards always carried out the physical punishment of inmates. In all 30 incidents, between 2 and 6 of these guards were present. Further, it was an unwritten rule that at least 2 staff members must be present, for safety and evidentiary reasons, whenever an inmate was physically punished. Most coercive situations were initiated by a ranking guard and then the other officers moved in and finished the episode. It was not uncommon for 4, 5, or even 6 officers to be involved in a "tune up" or other force situations.

Coercion Maintains Control and Order

The guards regarded force as an important means to achieve tight disciplinary control and punish recalcitrant inmates. Of the observed force situations, the majority (n = 21) involved inmates who challenged the guards' authority or disrupted the well-defined prison order (for example, refusing to obey an order, swearing at or threatening officers). On one occasion, for example, a guard ordered an inmate to quit talking while standing in line to receive some medicine. The inmate then stated, "I can talk to anybody I please and I sure as hell can talk as loud as I want." This inmate was immediately escorted to the Major's office where the officer made his report about the incident. The inmate was allowed to make a statement and then was slapped across the face and kicked in the buttocks by several ranking officers. Although these episodes were not serious, they were defined by the guards as mutinous and not to be tolerated.

The guards argued that these latter offenses undermined prison discipline and control and inmate violators had to be retaliated against. As guards, they also maintained that the prison was their domain and internal order was their paramount goal. These beliefs therefore justified their use of force, at least to themselves. They firmly believed that coercion was a legitimate mechanism of social control. Further, new officers at Johnson were constantly reminded, as well as placated, by ranking guards with the maxim, "We don't tolerate officers getting jumped on or talked crazy to around here, they'll [inmates] ride the ambulance if they try it."

Punitive force was not always directed against inmates who openly challenged the guards' authority. In some cases, inmates were "tuned up" for inmate-on-inmate offenses. For the most part, the guards did not consider minor inmate-on-inmate incidents (such as gambling, tattooing, stealing) as malicious or as undermining their authority or as serious breaches of prison order. However, for serious inmate-inmate rule infractions such as fighting with weapons, sexual attacks, or threatening other inmates, the guards generally took action. Nine of the 30 cases of force involved these latter offenses. Of these 9 cases, 3 were for homosexual threats, 4 for physical threats, and 2 for continuous fighting (these 2 inmates had several fights at work and in their cell). For example, a small black inmate told the staff that a larger, "stronger" black inmate was "talking sex stuff" to him and making other threatening advances. The aggressive inmate was called to the Major's office and confronted with the complainant's accusation. Although the aggressor denied the threats, he was slapped across the face several times and pushed around by one guard. During this episode, 6 other staff members repeatedly derogated and threatened the aggressor with severe bodily harm if he continued to make homosexual or any other kind of threats against other inmates.

Coercion Maintains Status and Deference

The data indicate that inmate deportment and race were critical elements in the guards' decision to use or not use force. After being confronted with a rule violation, those inmates who responded in an antagonistic or nondeferential attitude towards the staff typically provoked a physical response from the guards. Of the 30 force situations, 23 were directed against inmates who offered increased resistance, lied to, antagonized, or exhibited disrespect toward an officer either at the time of apprehension for a violation or at a later stage during interrogation. For example, on December 4, 1982, inmate Sims lied to an officer about the loss of his work boots. Sims concocted a story to obtain a new pair of boots by saying his old pair were stolen while he was bathing. The officer issued Sims a permit to procure new boots. One hour later, an inmate informer told the officer that Sims merely threw his old boots away in the cell block's trash can. The shoes were retrieved and Sims was "tuned up" for lying to the officer. On another occasion, an officer instructed several prisoners in a cell block dayroom (television room) to "Hold the noise down" whereupon inmate Warren retorted, "Shut up yourself and stay the hell out of the dayroom." Warren was ordered out of the dayroom, escorted to the Major's office where he was punched, kicked, and blackjacked by several officers.

These inmate-victims were physically coerced solely for not showing the officers proper deference and demeanor—passivity, civility, and politeness (Goffman, 1956; Manning, 1977). This finding parallels Reiss's (1971), Sykes and Clark's (1975), and Friedrich's (1983) research on police use of force against "disrespective" citizens. The finding is also similar to the research by Piliavin and Briar (1964), who argued that a juvenile's demeanor was an important determinant in the disposition of the case. Essentially, prisoners who failed to embrace their role or identity as subordinates were more likely to be coerced than "properly" behaved inmates. In sum, the guards used coercion to protect their superior status and the lack of deference or respect for an officer greatly affected the outcome of guard-inmate encounters.

Racial Factors. The inmate's race also played an important role in the guards' willingness to use coercion to maintain social status. The inmates at Johnson were mostly urban blacks while the guards were primarily rural whites who viewed the black inmates as basically antiauthority, inferior, disrespectful, aggressive, and, most of all, nondeferential. Twenty-four of the force situations involved black prisoners. Only one Hispanic and five white inmates were physically punished. For the white guards, black prisoners represented troublesome, hostile, and rebellious prisoners who occasionally "needed" physical coercion to "keep them in their place." Racial prejudice was common, and this factor helped facilitate the belief on the part of the guards that black inmates were impolite and troublesome.

Coercion as a Route of Upward Mobility

All new officers began their careers in the cell blocks, which familiarized them with the prison routine and served as a type of character test. Cell block duty was often mentally taxing due to the constant interaction with the inmates, counting, and relaying messages. Those officers who "ran a good tank" and had "snap" were sometimes selected as hall officers. Working in the hall was regarded as a reward because it freed the officer from cell block duty, and it also put him in greater proximity to the ranking guards. Contact with supervisors was a plus and often paved the way for promotions. In fact, it was quite common for shift supervisors to personally groom three or four promising hall officers.

This process was actually a form of tutelage wherein the supervisor played the role of mentor and taught the "pupil" about, among other things, writing disciplinary reports, developing inmate snitches, and searching cells for contraband. More importantly, these "teachers" taught their officers about when, where, and how to use physical force. If an officer used "inappropriate" force (for example, "tuning up" an inmate in the hall, using too much force, beating up older inmates), then the supervisor warned the officer about unwanted investigations. On one occasion, a hall officer slapped an inmate in the inmate dining hall. He lost his hall officer position and was reassigned to an inmate housing unit. In another instance, a hall officer "tuned up" an inmate with a history of heart trouble as well as without other guard witnesses. He was reprimanded for his behavior and forbidden from using coercion. In short, coercion was subject to rules and those who used it in deviant ways were sanctioned.

It was at the level of hall officer that the guards began to learn about the use of force. For example, a new hall officer may be called upon to take part in a Disciplinary Court hearing and might observe a "tune up" or a new hall officer might see a "tune up" while helping to escort an inmate to a solitary confinement cell. In these situations the hall officer was expected to participate in the force display. If the neophyte participated, he also learned how to construct covering charges and post-facto explanations of the event. Fifteen guards were involved in the 30 incidents and 7 were hall officers, 4 were sergeants, 3 were lieutenants, and 1 was a captain. Line prison officers, or those working in cell blocks and other security areas, were not involved in a single case of unofficial coercion.

Becoming a hall officer did facilitate upward mobility, but the willingness of an officer to fight inmates was the primary variable affecting his acceptance by other hall officers and ranking guards. In the guard culture at Johnson, fighting an inmate ("getting on one" or "frapping his ass") was a measure of an officer's manhood or "nuts." Excessive or compulsive masculinity more commonly referred to as machismo was a highly valued personality trait (Toby, 1966). A cult of male honor prevailed in which personal violence was obligatory to establish the officer's reputation and status within the guard subculture (Reider, 1984). As one ranking guard stated, "You have to make a convict fear you or respect you or you won't make it here." Another ranking guard said, "Hell, some of these officers are crazier and meaner than the convicts." Those who embraced these subcultural tenets were labeled as good officers and were confirmed as members in the ruling clique of officers—hall officers and all ranking guards. Fighting an inmate was the equivalent of a rite of passage because this event solidified the perception of an officer as a person who could be trusted.

Personal toughness and "acting like a man" were the critical factors ranking guards employed to evaluate all employees. Specifically, officers who exhibited the "proper" traits were usually rewarded in the form of better duty assignments or promotions. The ranking officers viewed force as a legitimate control tactic and tacitly approved of this behavior. Hall officers were expected to use force when the situation arose, and those who could not or would not were quickly discovered, labeled weak or unloyal, and in some cases reassigned back to cell block duty. Earning a reputation as weak or cowardly was a personal disaster for the officer and parallels the spoiled identity concept commonly found in the deviance literature. In addition, exceptional hall officers were often promoted due to their past performances, thus enhancing their organizational careers. Excluding the 3 wardens, all 18 ranking officers of the building force were hall officers either at Johnson or at another of Texas's many correctional institutions. Promotion of hall officers ensured that this important subcultural value would be passed on to other officers.

Age Factors.   It should also be noted that the officers who were most likely to use force were young and had relatively few years of guard experience. Six of the 15 guards involved were between the ages of 18 and 24, while 7 were between 25 and 29. The remainder were over the age of 33. In addition, 5 of the officers had less than 1 year of experience, 5 had between 1 and 3 years, 4 had between 4 and 9 years, and only 1 had more than 10 years of prison experience. These data underscore the point that those guards most likely to employ force were young hall officers with little experience. These young men were also quite eager to make guardwork a career. It was precisely this group of officers who were being tailored or groomed for promotion by ranking guards. The primary reason older ranking guards were less likely to be involved was that they had already established themselves and did not have to continuously reaffirm their reputation. It was the younger officers who were under pressure to "perform," and their close proximity to ranking officers provided the push to employ force (Milgram 1965). Indeed, upward mobility within the organization hinged on the acceptance and performance of physical coercion as a mechanism of control. This system or structure of unofficial prisoner control determined the content of guard socialization.

Racial Factors. The race of the officer was also an important factor in the use of force. White guards, like their police counterparts (Friedrich, 1983), were more likely to use force than black or Hispanic guards. Twelve of the guards involved were white, 2 were black, and 1 was Hispanic. Minority officers were not trusted by the predominantly white ruling (administrative) elite, and they were rarely promoted and frequently terminated for "collaborating with the enemy" (Jacobs and Grear, 1977). Minority officers were generally concentrated in cell block duty far away from the settings where inmates were unofficially disciplined.

Of the 15 officers involved, 12 were white and 10 of these were born and raised near the institution, which was located in a rural area of the state. It is also important to note that almost half (47%) of the inmates in the prison were black. In addition, 68% of the inmates in this particular department of corrections were from urban areas. These data underscore the conclusion that rural white guards were using physical coercion against urban black inmates. The white guards at the prison under study openly expressed racial prejudice and tendencies toward discrimination. For example, one day the author of this paper entered the Major's office and found a hall officer punching a black inmate in the kidneys. As the inmate writhed and moaned on the floor, the officer stated nonchalantly, "I told the captain I was going to whip a nigger today."

Coercion Builds Solidarity

The use of coercion by the hall officers and ranking guards induced solidarity among this group. Only this group of officers participated in physical punishment, and those officers who were accepted by this group were deemed "successful." That is, they internalized and justified the use of coercion. These officers formed the "hard core" of the guard culture. Indeed, they were members of a primary group and social circle that had daily face-to-face interaction. These officers also associated with each other off the job. In addition, there was low turnover and high morale among this group. Ironically, this system created high turnover and low morale among the other line guards who refused, could not, or did not accept force as a tactic of control. The ruling elite viewed the nonforce group as "bodies," people needed to open and close doors. These "unsuccessful" guards either quit or eventually transferred to other Texas correctional institutions.

Secrecy was another factor enhancing solidarity. As a new hall officer became privy to force incidents, he also learned about the code of secrecy. A similar norm exists among police (Westley, 1970). There was an unwritten rule that hall and ranking officers refrain from talking about force displays with the lower-ranking guards. Being privy to this information as well as keeping "one's mouth shut" was an important norm that facilitated acceptance by the ruling clique of guards. It was not uncommon for low-ranking guards to ask hall officers about force situations. However, their queries were closed off with the standard answers, "I don't know what you're talking about" or "I wasn't here that day." These standard responses were also employed during FBI investigations into illegal use of force. In short, the ruling clique of guards represented a primary group that sustained a high degree of camaraderie (on and off the job) which in turn produced group loyalties and fostered group cohesion (Shils and Janowitz, 1948).

GUARD COERCION AND ORGANIZATIONAL STRUCTURE

Any inquiry into the dynamics of force within an institutional setting must concern itself with organizational structure. Police departments, for example, are highly centralized with numerous formalized policies that govern police-citizen encounters. Police organizations emphasize training and professionalism in which widespread abuse of citizens is not tolerated. Furthermore, these agencies frequently have an internal affairs division to investigate citizen claims about police misuse of force. This latter factor alone has without doubt severely curtailed the arbitrary use of force (and discretion) by police officers.

Although there appear to be no studies on the relationship between guard coercion and the prison's organizational structure, the research under discussion found that organizational structure affects guard aggression. The prison under study was part of a large bureaucracy. Rules, records, various departments, and accountability were present, but rarely did these bureaucratic elements affect the daily operation of Johnson. This prison, like the other Texas prisons, enjoyed a great deal of autonomy from the central administration. Moreover, there was a low level of interdependence between the various institutions. Specifically, the security staff at Johnson was permitted to carry out control activities with little or no interference from the main administration. Therefore, the guards possessed enormous discretion to control their charges as they saw fit. As a mechanism of social control, physical force became the cornerstone for inmate control. The use of coercion not only maintained order, but it also functioned as a means of cohesion and was an important element within the guard culture. This pattern emerged because of the lack of strong organizational controls unlike, for example, police departments.

On the one hand, it may be argued that in prison organizations characterized by decentralization and unit autonomy, the specter of coercion will always be present. Furthermore, the statuses and roles of the keepers and kept will be institutionalized, like a caste system, as superiors and inferiors. Inmates will be treated as social inferiors or as objects who enjoy few civil or due process rights. Physical coercion in these organizations will be employed as a control device (an instrumental need) as well as to maintain status, build cohesion, and facilitate upward mobility.

On the other hand, those prison organizations based on centralization and formalization (with little autonomy and discretion), such as the California system or the Federal Bureau of Prisons, will not support an inmate control system predicated on coercion and fear. Most of these latter systems have formalized inmate grievance procedures and some (such as the Virginia Department of Corrections) have a department of internal affairs to investigate inmate claims of guard brutality. Physical coercion in these latter organizations serves neither instrumental nor symbolic purposes but is the idiosyncratic and unstructured behavior of a "bad guard"–paralleling the "bad cop" in police organizations. In sum, guard violence is an open area of research, and future inquiries should look at force and its relation to organizational structure in order to better understand prisoner control structures.

CONCLUSION

This paper has demonstrated that guard violence was not idiosyncratic nor a form of "self-defense" and was relatively unprovoked. Instead, force was used against inmates as a means of physical punishment by a small but significant percentage of the guards. These officers were primarily hall officers and sergeants with relatively low-ranking positions in the guard hierarchy. It also demonstrated that force served not only as a control mechanism, but it also induced group cohesion, maintained status and deference, and facilitated promotions. Like Mischel (1968) and Milgram (1965), it was found that guard violence was not the sole result of sadistic or power-hungry motives, but was shaped by powerful social and situational forces. Officers learned violence from their peers and were rewarded by their superiors for their behavior. They also did not physically coerce inmates at random or for no reason. Punitive force was directed against inmates, particularly blacks, who refused (or appeared to refuse) the guards' definition of the situation. Indeed, any challenges to their authority were met with quick, calculated physical responses. The guards managed the penitentiary with an iron hand and inmates who upset the regimen were literally beaten into submission.

The correspondence of these findings with other state maximum security institutions is unknown. As a consequence, numerous research questions exist and future studies should address violence as a mechanism of social control in prison and extra-prison settings. One line of research might examine the effects of the organizational culture and its impact on guard socialization processes and outcomes, values, and resultant guard personality traits. Research, particularly comparative research between northern and southern prison systems, would provide data and make an important contribution to the areas of social control theory, the sociology of violence, and the study of prison organizations.

Notes

*Revised version of a paper delivered at the annual meeting of the American Sociological Association, 1984. The assistance of Julian B. Roebuck, Bradley Anderson, and Sheldon Ekland-Olson in reading earlier drafts is gratefully acknowledged. I also appreciate the Social Science Research Center for support during the preparation of this draft.
1. Unofficial force is defined as force not related to the protection of life and property.
2. The morning shift was from 5:45 A.M. to 1:45 P.M., the evening shift 1:45 to 9:45 P.M., and the night shift 9:45 P.M. to 5:45 A.M. The researcher was fortunate enough to work on all three shifts.
3. The "wall" was the wall area near the Major's office. Practically every time a hall officer had a problem with an inmate, the inmate was instructed to "catch the wall." Once "on the wall,"

the inmate waited until the officer or his supervisor talked over the problem. It was not uncommon for inmates to "stand on the wall" for hours, or even days.

4. The Major's office was the place where all disciplinary measures against inmates were meted out.

5. Disciplinary court procedures deemed as major cases were tape recorded.

6. One old-time convict was the staff's blackjack "connection." This inmate routinely made and repaired blackjacks for the "right" staff members.

7. The inmates who helped the staff in this fight were called building tenders and turnkeys. These inmates were violent criminals who were coopted by the staff with special privileges to help in controlling the ordinary inmates, especially in the cell blocks. For a more in-depth analysis of these inmates, see Marquart and Crouch (1984) and Marquart (1983).

8. Killing of any sort at the prison was a rare phenomenon. This was the second inmate murder by other inmates since 1972. However, one officer, a major, died in 1979 of a heart attack during a fight with an inmate.

References

Berkman, Ronald
    1979   Opening the Gates: The Rise of the Prisoners' Rights Movement. Lexington, MA: Lexington.
Carroll, Leo
    1974   Hacks, Blacks, and Cons: Race Relations in a Maximum Security Prison. Lexington, MA: Lexington.
Clemmer, Donald
    1940   The Prison Community. New York: Holt, Rinehart and Winston.
Cloward, Richard A.
    1960   Social control in the prison. In Donald Cressey (ed.), Theoretical Studies in Social Organization of the Prison. New York: Social Science Research Council.
Cressey, Donald
    1968   Contradictory directives in complex organizations: The case of the prison. In Lawrence Hazelrigg (ed.), Prison within Society. Garden City, NY: Anchor.
Davidson, Theodore
    1974   Chicano Prisons: The Key to San Quentin. New York: Holt, Rinehart and Winston.
Friedrich, Robert
    1983   Police use of force: Individuals, situations, and organizations. In Carl B. Klockars (ed.), Thinking About Police. New York: McGraw-Hill.
Gobert, James J. and Neil P. Cohen
    1981   Rights of Prisoners. Colorado Springs, CO: Shephard's/McGraw-Hill.
Goffman, Erving
    1956   The nature of the deference and demeanor. American Anthropologist 58: 473–501.
    1961   Asylums. Chicago: Aldine.
Hawkins, Gordon
    1976   The Prison, Policy and Practice. Chicago: University of Chicago Press.
Hepburn, John
    1985   The exercise of power in coercive organizations: A study of prison guards. Criminology 23: 145–164.
Jacobs, James
    1974   Participant observation in prison. Urban Life and Culture 3: 221–240.
    1977   Stateville: The Penitentiary in Mass Society. Chicago: University of Chicago Press.
Jacobs, James and Mary Grear
    1977   Drop-outs and rejects: An analysis of the prison guard's revolving door. Criminal Justice Review 2: 57–77.

Lofland, John
1971   Analyzing Social Settings. Belmont, CA: Wadsworth.
Manning, Peter K.
1977   Police Work: The Social Organization of Policing. Cambridge, MA: MIT Press.
Marquart, James W.
1983   Cooptation of the kept: Maintaining control in a southern penitentiary. Unpublished
        doctoral dissertation. College Station: Texas A & M University.
1986   Outsiders as insiders: Participant observation in the role of a prison guard. Justice
        Quarterly 3: 15–32.
Marquart, James W. and Ben M. Crouch
1984   Coopting the kept: Using inmates for social control in a southern prison. Justice
        Quarterly 1: 491–509.
McCleery, Richard
1960   Communication patterns as a basis of systems of authority. In Theoretical Studies
        in Social Organization of the Prison. New York: Social Science Research Council.
Milgram, Stanley
1965   Some conditions of obedience and disobedience to authority. Human Relations
        18: 57.
Mischel, Walter
1968   Personality and Assessment. New York: Wiley.
Mouledous, Joseph C.
1962   Sociological perspectives on a prison social system. Unpublished master's thesis.
        Baton Rouge: Louisiana State University.
Ninth Monitor's Report of Factual Observations to the Special Master
1983
Piliavin, Irving and Scott Briar
1964   Police encounters with juveniles. American Journal of Sociology. 37: 73–82.
Reider, Jonathan
1984   The social organization of vengeance. In Donald Black (ed.), Toward a General
        Theory of Social Control II: Fundamentals. New York: Academic Press.
Reiss, Albert
1971   The Police and the Public. New Haven, CT: Yale University Press.
Shils, Edward and Morris Janowitz
1948   Cohesion and disintegration of the Wehrmacht in WW II. Public Opinion and
        Quarterly 12: 280–315.
Sykes, Gresham
1958   The Society of Captives. Princeton, NJ: Princeton University Press.
Sykes, Richard E. and John P. Clark
1975   A theory of deference exchange in police-civilian encounters. American Journal of
        Sociology 81: 584–600.
Thomas, James
1984   Some aspects of negotiated order, loose coupling and meso-structure in maximum
        security prisons. Symbolic Interaction 4: 213–231.
Toby, Jackson
1966   Violence and the masculine ideal: Some qualitative data. The Annals 364: 19–27.
1982   Fieldwork on the beat. In John Van Maanen (ed.), Varieties of Qualitative Research.
        Beverly Hills: Sage.
Van Maanen, John
1978   The asshole. In Peter K. Manning and John Van Maanen (eds.), Policing: A View
        from the Street. Santa Monica, CA: Goodyear.
Wax, Rosalie H.
1971   Doing Fieldwork: Warnings and Advice. Chicago: University of Chicago Press.
Westley, William
1970   Violence and the Police. Cambridge, MA: MIT Press.

Wright, Erik
  1973   The Politics of Punishment. New York: Harper & Row.
Zimbardo, Phillip G.
  1972   Pathology of imprisonment. Society 9: 4, 6, 8.

41. Undetected Recidivism among Rapists and Child Molesters

A. NICHOLAS GROTH, ROBERT E. LONGO, AND J. BRADLEY McFADIN

Recidivism is generally a critical variable for assessing the risk of an offender to the community and for measuring the success of efforts to rehabilitate him. One of the prevailing attitudes with regard to sexual assault is that, for the most part, the crime is situational in nature and not likely to be repeated. The state of New Jersey's Commission on the Habitual Sex Offender reported that

> Sex offenders have one of the lowest rates as "repeaters" of all types of crime. Among serious crimes homicide alone has a lower rate of recidivism. Careful studies of large numbers of sex criminals show that most of them get into trouble only once. Of those who do repeat, a majority commit some crime other than sex. Only 7 percent of those convicted of serious crimes are arrested again for a sex crime. Those who are recidivists are characteristically minor offenders—such as peepers, exhibitionists, homosexuals—rather than criminals of serious menace.[1]

Similar observations have been reported by Tappan,[2] Kupperstein,[3] Sadoff,[4] and the majority of researchers reviewed by Karpman.[5] Their general conclusion is that the dangerous sexual offender, the rapist or child molester, is not a serious recidivist. Clinical experience, however, suggests otherwise. In our professional work with convicted sexual offenders we find it not at all uncommon that they have committed many more sexual assaults than appear on record. The aim of this study is to assess the rate of recidivism among offenders incarcerated for sexual assault.

STUDY SAMPLE

Our sample of offenders was drawn from two different populations: men who were convicted of sexual assault but were committed to a security treatment center for rehabilitation before sentencing, the North Florida Evaluation and Treatment Center in Gainesville; and men who were serving time for a sexual assault in a maximum security prison, the Connecticut Correctional Institution at Somers. The subjects for this study not only come from different regions of the country, but also were in two different types of settings: one a mental health facility designed exclusively for sexual offenders, and the other a traditional correctional facility in which the sexual offenders were housed in the general population with other adult male felons. Of those in the Florida center, 90 (100 percent) agreed to participate in this study; 49 of these men had sexually assaulted adult victims and 41 had sexually assaulted children. Of the first 50 inmates screened at the Connecticut institution in regard to their sexual offense, 47 (94 percent) agreed to cooperate: 34 had sexually assaulted adults and 13 had sexually assaulted children. This produced a combined sample of 83 rapists and 54 child molesters, for a total of 137 subjects. All the participants were males between the ages of 16 and 57, with the average age being 29; 21 (15 percent) of the men were black; 79 (58 percent) were unmarried, 33 (24 percent) were married, and 25 (18 percent) were either divorced, separated, or widowed.

DESIGN

Each subject was administered a confidential, five-item questionnaire, instructed not to put his name on the answer sheet, and informed that the information obtained would not be identified with him or appear in his records or files. The following five questions appeared in our survey:

1. How old were you at the time of your *first* sexual assault or attempted assault, regardless if you were caught for this or not?
2. How many sexual assaults have you been convicted of, to date? (Include attempted sexual assaults, homicide, etc.)
3. How many sexual assaults have you attempted or committed for which you were *never* apprehended or caught?
4. How many sexual offenses (assaults or attempted assaults) have you been acquitted for, which, in fact, you *did* do?
5. How many offenses (assaults or attempted assaults) have you been found guilty of, which, in fact, you *did not* do?

Upon completion of the questionnaires by the respondents, the individual responses were tallied and total scores were computed separately for each type of subject at each institution.

FINDINGS

Recorded Recidivism

In order to assess the known recidivism rate for our subjects, we asked them how many sex-related offenses they had been convicted of to date. A study was then made of their presentence investigation reports to confirm independently the convictions on record. Table 1 summarizes the number of convictions for sexual assault in the records of our subjects.

Table 1. Known Recidivism Rates

	Florida Sample	Connecticut Sample	Combined
Rapists			
n	49	34	83
Range	1–20	1–10	1–20
Mean	2.7	3.1	2.8
Offenders committing			
more than 1 offense	24 (48.9%)	30 (88.2%)	54 (65%)
Child molesters			
n	41	13	54
Range	1–8	1–7	1–8
Mean	1.4	2	1.7
Offenders committing			
more than 1 offense	13 (31.7%)	7 (53.8%)	20 (37%)

The number of known sexual offenses by the rapists in the Florida sample ranged from 1 to 20, with an average of 2.7. In the Connecticut sample the range was from 1 to 10, with an average of 3.1. About half (48.9 percent) of the rapists in the Florida center and almost 90 percent (88.2 percent) of those in the Connecticut institution had at least one prior conviction for sexual assault. Overall, for the combined sample of rapists, two-thirds (65 percent) of these offenders had at least one prior conviction, and the average number of known offenses for this group was 2.8.

For the offenders in the Florida sample who had sexually molested children, the number of known convictions ranged from 1 to 8, with an average of 1.4; convictions of the Connecticut sample ranged from 1 to 7, with an average of 2 offenses on record. About one-third (31.7 percent) of the Florida sample and a little over half (53.8 percent) of the Connecticut sample had been convicted of more than 1 such offense. Overall, for the combined group, about two-fifths (37 percent) of the offenders had at least one prior conviction, and the average number of known offenses for this group was 1.7.

Undetected Recidivism

It would be erroneous to assume, however, that conviction data accurately reflect the actual recidivism rate of sexual offenders; and the "first offender" designation may only reflect first conviction, not first offense. Therefore, our subjects were asked how many sexual assaults they had attempted or committed for which they were never apprehended.

The number of undetected sexual assaults reported by our subjects ranged from 0 to 250. A tally of their responses made it clear that there were a number of subjects for whom the incidence of undetected offenses was extremely high. Therefore, so as not to bias the overall estimations, we excluded from the calculations any subject who reported 50 or more such undetected offenses. Nine offenders (6 rapists in the Florida center, 1 rapist in the Connecticut institution, and 2 child molesters in

Table 2. Undetected Recidivism

	Florida Sample	Connecticut Sample	Combined
Rapists			
n	43	33	76
Range	0–30	0–27	0–30
Mean	5.9	4.2	5.2
Offenders committing			
more than 1 offense	35 (81.4%)	16 (48.5%)	51 (67.1%)
Child molesters			
n	39	13	52
Range	0–27	0–30	0–30
Mean	3.4	6	4.7
Offenders committing			
more than 1 offense	19 (48.7%)	7 (53.8%)	26 (50%)

Florida), or 7 percent of our total sample, were excluded. The results for the remaining 128 subjects are summarized in Table 2.

The number of undetected rapes in the Florida sample ranged from 0 to 30, with an average of 5.9. In the Connecticut sample it ranged from 0 to 27, with an average of 4.2. More than three-quarters (81.4 percent) of the rapists in the first group and about half (48.5 percent) in the second admitted to 1 or more undetected offenses, with an average number for the combined sample of 5.2 undetected rapes.

The number of undetected sexual assaults against children in the Florida sample ranged from 0 to 27, with an average of 3.4. In the Connecticut sample it ranged from 0 to 30, with an average of 6, producing a combined average of 4.7. In the case of child molesters, these figures reflect the number of different victims whom the offender molested without being caught rather than the number of sexual contacts, for it is characteristic of many child molesters to have repeated sexual contacts with the same victim over an extended period of time, which would distort the data. About half the Florida (48.7 percent) and the Connecticut (53.8 percent) samples admitted to one or more undetected involvements with children.

As a point of interest, if the nine subjects who were excluded from the calculations had been included, the estimate would advance to an average of fourteen undetected involvements for the rapist and eleven undetected involvements for the child molester.

Age at Time of First Offense

It would appear that our subjects got away with two to five times as many sexual offenses as resulted in apprehension. Our subjects were, for the most part, relatively young men. A question that seemed appropriate was how old they were when they began committing their crimes. Their responses to this question are summarized in Table 3.

The age at first offense for the rapists in the Florida center ranged from 11 to 47, with an average age of 19.6 and a modal age of 18. For the rapists in the Connecticut

Table 3. Age at Time of First Offense

	Florida Sample	Connecticut Sample	Combined
Rapists			
n	49	34	83
Range	11–47	9–35	9–47
Mean	19.6	17.6	18.78
Mode	18	16	16
Child molesters			
n	41	13	54
Range	8–50	16–33	8–50
Mean	23.7	24	23.8
Mode	13, 35	16, 31	16

institution, it ranged from 9 to 35, with an average of 17.6 and a mode of 16. The age at first offense for the child molesters in Florida ranged from 8 to 50, with an average age of 23.7 and two modal ages: 13 and 35. For the child molesters in the Connecticut sample, it ranged from 16 to 33, with an average of 24 and two modes: 16 and 31. In studying these data, the mode appears to have more significance than does the mean in reflecting the onset of sexual assaultiveness, since it will take many subjects below the mean to balance out a lower number above the mean. Therefore, the finding of greatest significance is that the modal age for both groups of offenders in the combined sample is 16. The bimodal results for the child molesters can be understood to reflect, respectively, the early onset of behavior among fixated offenders for whom the sexual orientation toward children results from arrested sociosexual development, and the later onset of behavior among regressed offenders for whom the sexual involvement with children results from sudden or progressive deterioration of emotionally meaningful or gratifying adult relationships.[6]

False Conviction

When working with convicted sex offenders, one often hears the inmate allege that he is the victim of false accusation or misidentification. In our combined survey, eighteen (21.7 percent) of the rapists and six (11.1 percent) of the child molesters claimed that they had, at some point, been convicted of a charge of which they were innocent. Overall, the average number of allegedly false convictions was .46 for the rapists and .11 for the child molesters.

False Acquittals

Interestingly, the results with regard to false convictions are comparable to the reported number of acquittals for sexual offense charges of which the subjects were in fact guilty, these data revealing an average of .48 acquittals for the rapists and .30 for the child molesters. Seventeen (20.5 percent) of the rapists and 12 (22.2 percent) of the child molesters acknowledged having escaped conviction at some prior point.

RESULTS

For the most part, the results of our investigation into the recidivism of dangerous sexual offenders are remarkably similar in both the comparisons of the North Florida Evaluation and Treatment Center and Connecticut Correctional Institution samples, and the comparisons of the rapists and the child molesters. The findings suggest that, contrary to the impression yielded by the general literature, such offenders are serious recidivists. It would appear from this study that sexual offenders avoid detection approximately twice as often as they are apprehended for their crimes. The rapists, who had an average of three rape convictions on record, and the child molesters, who averaged two convictions on record, admitted to an average of five similar offenses for which they were never apprehended. It can reasonably be assumed that this is at best a very *conservative* estimate of the actual undetected recidivism among these inmates. One of the characteristic traits of sexual offenders is their mistrust of other adults, particularly those in positions of authority; although anonymity was assured in regard to their responses, a number of the respondents may have believed that their answers could be traced and that admitting to their undetected crimes could make them liable for prosecution or jeopardize their chances for parole or community release. Then, too, such offenders frequently misperceive their own behavior or misinterpret that of their victims, so what they acknowledge to constitute an assault, as opposed to what an objective observer would view as an offense, may differ significantly. In addition, a number of offenders stated that they could not remember committing the offense for which they were serving time; they did not claim innocence, but attributed their memory lapse to intoxication. If this is true, then there is a possibility that other similar events occurred for which they were not apprehended and which they cannot recall. Finally, it is more characteristic for sexual offenders to minimize their wrongdoing than it is for them to exaggerate their criminal activity. There is no status recognition or reward for being a sexual offender, either in the community or in an institutional setting. Given these considerations, it may be that a more accurate approximation of the true incidence of undetected recidivism among rapists and child molesters is reflected in the unaltered calculations for this sample, which estimate an average of fourteen undetected sexual offenses for the rapists and an average of eleven undetected sexual offenses for the child molesters. This produces an undetected recidivism rate for sexual assaults that is comparable to the rates for other, nonsexual crimes.

The amassing of considerable assault histories by offenders who were, for the most part, still young men may appear surprising. It is more easily understood when one realizes that, for the majority of men, this pattern of behavior began in their adolescent years. Unfortunately, all too frequently sexual offenses by juveniles are dismissed as merely adolescent sexual curiosity or experimentation. Since such offenses go unrecognized by the criminal justice and mental health systems, they are not addressed. No intervention occurs until the offender is an adult; by then, many sexual assaults and victimizations may have occurred which might otherwise have been prevented.

Although the results are consistent for both samples, it is evident that the Florida group had more "first offenders" than did the Connecticut sample. This is understandable since apparent first offenders would probably be regarded as having a better prognosis for rehabilitation than would persistent offenders, who would more likely be sent to prison.

DISCUSSION

The finding that offenders who commit serious sexual offenses (rape and child molestation) do, in fact, have a significant history of recidivism has a number of important implications. First, it indicates that such behavior is a chronic problem, the extent of which will not be apparent from the offender's record of conviction. Second, it suggests that sexual assault is more psychologically than situationally determined. Third, it emphasizes the necessity to concentrate on the needs of juvenile sexual offenders, in order to detect this problem early and prevent or reduce later victimization. Fourth, it shows that the use of recidivism as a measure of a program's effectiveness in rehabilitating rapists and child molesters is unreliable.

It is generally true that most criminals get away with more crimes than they are convicted of, but it would appear that this is especially true of offenders who commit sexual assaults. The low recidivism rate generally attributed to such offenders can be understood to be due to the low visibility of such offenses. Although the sexual offender's behavior is repetitive, most of his recidivism goes undetected. This may be attributable in part to how recidivism is defined. Usually, recidivism refers to parole or probation violation or reconviction for similar criminal acts within a specified period of time. In Florida and Connecticut, this period is two years. Consequently, a person may be convicted twice of sexual assault, but if the convictions are separated by a space of more than two years he will not technically be regarded as a recidivist. More important, however, very many sexual aggressors commit their initial offenses as juveniles—typically, such sex offenses are dismissed as insignificant. Arrest records can be misleading, because many juvenile records are destroyed. This practice, intended to avoid lengthy stigmatization of juvenile offenders, can also mean that their adult records for sexual offenses omit serious crimes they committed as juveniles.

Then, too, there is a wide variety of factors that serve to deter many victims of sexual assault from reporting their victimization. Even if the offense is reported, in the majority of cases, no suspect is apprehended; few of the cases in which a suspect is apprehended reach trial level, and still fewer result in conviction.[7] Then, too, in some cases the victim is rescued or escapes from the assailant before being sexually assaulted and the offender is convicted of a nonsexual offense, such as kidnapping, unlawful restraint, battery, or aggravated assault, when the offense was in fact a sex-related crime. Finally, the procedure of plea bargaining, in which the offender is permitted to enter a guilty plea to a nonsexual charge in exchange for the dismissal of the sexual offense charge, serves to mask still further the recidivism of the sexual offender. If we are to deal effectively and meaningfully with the problem of sexual assault, we must recognize that it is a repetitive pattern of behavior, most of which is undetected.

Notes

1. State of New Jersey, Commission on the Habitual Sex Offender, *Final Report* (1950), cited in *Federal Probation*, September 1966, p. 55.

2. Paul W. Tappan, *The Habitual Sex Offender* (Trenton, N.J.: New Jersey Commission on the Habitual Sex Offender, 1950).

3. Lenore R. Kupperstein, *An Analysis of Sex Offenses Committed in Philadelphia during 1962* (Philadelphia: Pennsylvania Prison Society, 1963).

4. Robert L. Sadoff, "Quiz: Criminal Sexual Behavior," *Medical Aspects of Human Sexuality*, February 1979, p. 108.

5. Benjamin Karpman, *The Sexual Offender and His Offenses* (New York: Julian Press, 1954), pp. 276–78.

6. Ann W. Burgess et al., *Sexual Assault of Children and Adolescents* (Lexington, Mass.: Lexington Books, 1978), pp. 6–9.

7. A. Nicholas Groth, with H. Jean Birnbaum, *Men Who Rape: The Psychology of the Offender* (New York: Plenum Press, 1979), pp. 222–33.

42. Reform Society: Provide Opportunity

SAMUEL WALKER

Liberals have traditionally emphasized the social and economic influences on criminal activity. The bulk of criminological research since the 1920s has focused on the criminogenic effect of poverty, inadequate educational opportunities, racial discrimination, broken families, and the cultural values of low-income peer groups. The policy implications are simple: expand social and economic opportunities for disadvantaged people and we will reduce their tendency to commit crimes.

The liberal social policies of the 1960s reflected this view of crime. The War on Poverty and many of the recommendations of the President's Crime Commission were attempts to expand legitimate opportunities for disadvantaged youths, to reduce the stigmatizing effect of the criminal justice system on those who did fall into the hands of the law, and to assist convicted offenders in establishing productive, law-abiding lives through community-based rehabilitation programs. At the same time, improvement in the criminal justice system would reduce the criminogenic effect of discriminatory arrest, prosecution, and punishment. Social reform was only one part of a crime-reduction package that included diversion, correctional treatment, and system improvement. All were based on the same assumptions about the causes of crime.[1]

It is fashionable among conservatives today to mock the liberal view of crime. James Q. Wilson points out that the great social experiments of the 1960s coincided with the greatest increase in crime in American history. He dismisses the entire mainstream of American criminology with a wave of the hand, saying he never saw a "root cause" of crime. The challenge thrown down by Wilson and other conservatives is a serious one. Why did the greatest increase in crime in our history go hand in hand with our most concerted effort yet to eliminate the causes of crime? The 1960s also represented the most sustained period of prosperity in this century. How do we explain what Wilson calls the "paradox" of crime amidst prosperity?[2]

Four explanations are possible. First, the theory may be wrong: social and economic deprivation may not be the principal cause of crime. Second, the theory may be sound but the programs it inspired were flawed and did not fulfill their goals. The third possibility is that some of the programs were effective but were not implemented on a broad enough scale to make a significant difference. Finally, government programs to help individuals may be irrelevant in the face of massive economic dislocation. What may be needed is a truly radical restructuring of economic opportunity. Somewhat surprisingly, even the conservative James Q. Wilson leans toward this view. Referring to Marxist criminologists, he observes that "in a sense, the radical critics of America are correct. If you wish to make a big difference in crime rates, you must make a fundamental change in society."[3]

SOCIAL THEORY AND SOCIAL POLICY

Where exactly did the ambitious social programs of the 1960s go wrong? We should begin by examining their theoretical roots, which can be found in a 1960 book titled *Delinquency and Opportunity*, by Richard Cloward and Lloyd Ohlin.[4] This enormously influential book summarized the dominant themes in American theoretical criminology. Appropriately, the authors dedicated it to Robert K. Merton and Edwin H. Sutherland, two giants in the field of social theory and criminology. *Delinquency and Opportunity* inspired most of the War on Poverty and many of the recommendations of the President's Crime Commission. Ohlin had ample opportunity to put his ideas into practice as one of the four associate directors of the Crime Commission.

As the title of their book suggests, Cloward and Ohlin found the primary causes of delinquency in lack of social and economic opportunity. They began with Robert Merton's argument that deviant behavior results from "a breakdown in the relationship between goals and legitimate avenues of access to them." Delinquents are not abnormal or sick people. They share the same values and aspirations as other people. In the United States, most people aspire to "success," measured by material well-being. People who cannot achieve success through legitimate means turn to illegitimate means. Elliot Liebow's classic study of ghetto life, *Tally's Corner*, also painted a picture of people continually trying to fulfill the conventional values of successful Americans (job, family, etc.) but repeatedly failing.[5]

Refining Merton's ideas, Cloward and Ohlin identified three delinquent subcultures, each reflecting a different choice of illegitimate means. The *criminal* subculture involves illicit activity as a career, often through organized criminal syndicates. The individual is socialized into a relatively disciplined, though illegal, lifestyle. The *conflict* subculture involves violent antisocial behavior as a way of life. Unlike members of the criminal subculture, the delinquents in this group lead lives that are highly disorganized. The *retreatist* subculture involves absorption in drug use and a retreat from any purposive behavior (criminal or otherwise) not related to drugs.

Cloward and Ohlin's point is that delinquents begin with normal and legitimate values and aspirations (although by the time they fall into the hands of the law they may be very seriously damaged). It is the lack of legitimate opportunities, not some inherently "sick" personality or willful free choice, that leads them into delinquency and lives of crime. The solution to this problem is obvious: expand the opportunities for legitimate advancement. The specific policies include reducing unemployment, expanding educational opportunities, and eliminating the barriers of racism.

CRIME AND UNEMPLOYMENT

Not everyone accepts the basic premise that unemployment causes predatory street crime. Liberals, noting that predatory crime is concentrated in low-income neighborhoods and that most offenders have marginal employment records at best, regard the premise as self-evident fact, while conservatives question it. James Q. Wilson points out the paradox of rising crime during the great prosperity of the 1960s. Conservatives find somewhat more self-evident the failure of the criminal justice system to deter criminals effectively through meaningful punishment. Just as we have examined this conservative assumption, so we should take a close look at the liberal view that unemployment generates crime.

Research on the relationship between crime and unemployment resembles research on the death penalty in two respects. First, the proposition is inherently difficult to test scientifically, given the multitude of factors that influence human (and thus criminal) behavior. Even though the economic formulas are increasingly sophisticated, we may never be able to isolate the critical variables with precision. Second, the findings of the research to date are highly ambiguous. Some researchers claim to find a direct relationship between crime and unemployment, while others do not.

Oddly enough, Isaac Ehrlich has made one of the stronger cases for the connection between crime and unemployment by using the same approach he subsequently took in his research on the deterrent effect of the death penalty. (Ehrlich's work poses a dilemma for liberals. If his death-penalty research is deeply flawed, mustn't they reject his research on crime and unemployment as well?) Ehrlich's article "Participation in Illegitimate Activities" is one of the cornerstones of the econometric theory of crime. It begins with the assumption that individuals make rational choices, weighing the relative costs and benefits of each action. Thus, if the risks of punishment are slim and the relative monetary gains are high, people will be more inclined to commit crimes. (Despite the apparent differences, Ehrlich's perspective is remarkably similar to the Merton-Cloward-Ohlin view. They too see people choosing crime as a rational alternative in the face of blocked legitimate alternatives.) The costs and benefits will differ with a person's circumstances. The unemployed person has more to gain by a successful robbery than the employed person and less to lose in social status by apprehension and conviction.[6]

Analyzing cross-sectional data on crime, income levels, and unemployment for the years 1940, 1950, and 1960, Ehrlich found a correlation between economic status and crime. His data indicate "that the rates of all felonies, particularly crimes against property, are positively related to the degree of a community's income inequality." The higher the level of unemployment and the greater the proportion of people below the median income level, the higher the crime rate. In the same analysis, however, Ehrlich found that the risk of punishment was also correlated with crime: the lower the risk, the higher the crime rate. Given the economic view of human behavior, these two factors are opposite sides of the same coin. One measures relative gain, the other relative cost.

Sheldon Danziger and David Wheeler also concluded that economic opportunity and deterrence are interrelated. They examined the rates of aggravated assault, burglary, and armed robbery between 1949 and 1970, in conjunction with cross-sectional data on urban areas in 1960. Their variables included the unemployment rate, the distribution of income, the percentage of the population in the crime-prone ages of fifteen to twenty-four, the probability of imprisonment, and the expected sentence for those imprisoned. They concluded that crime could be reduced either by an increase in the level of punishment or by a reduction of economic disparities. According to their data, however, income redistribution produced the greater reduction in crime.[7]

The research on crime and unemployment suffers from the same problems that plague the death-penalty research. Aggregate data on income, unemployment, crime, and other variables inevitably mask the behavior of individuals. We simply may not be able to specify the impact of the relevant variables on the crime-prone individuals who are our primary concern. Furthermore, there are serious problems with the data. As we saw earlier, the official data on crime rates are highly suspect, and the further back in time we extend our analysis, the more suspect they become. Without a reliable estimate of the amount of crime, we cannot accurately measure the risks of apprehension, conviction, and imprisonment. Our economic data are not much better. The official unemployment rate is as fictitious as the FBI's crime rate. The official figures grossly understate unemployment among teenagers, and among black teenagers in particular—precisely the groups we are most concerned with in our efforts to understand the sources of crime.

Given these problems, other analysts have concluded that the evidence in support of the idea that unemployment causes crime is weak at best. In a skeptical review of the subject, Thomas Orsagh and Anne Witte point out that aggregate data on income, unemployment, and crime conceal fundamental differences among types of offenders. They identify four distinct categories of criminals, each with a different relation to economic status. Some offenders, by definition, must be employed in order to commit their offenses (employee theft and embezzlement, for example). Other offenders combine employment with crime, while a third group moves back and forth between full-time employment and full-time criminal activity. Finally, there is a group of offenders who are only marginally employed at best and commit offenses at a very high rate.[8] The fourth group, the marginally employed, is the proper object of our attention, and we may gain a better understanding of the relationship between crime and unemployment if we think of this group as an "underclass."

Orsagh and Witte's findings have broad implications. They set out to determine the extent to which different kinds of offenders would respond to rehabilitation programs. Their conclusions are relevant to other crime control strategies as well. Just as some kinds of offenders are more amenable to rehabilitation programs, so offenders respond dissimilarly to the deterrent threat posed by prosecution and imprisonment. The traditional discussions of rehabilitation, deterrence, and incapacitation are flawed by the habit of regarding criminal offenders as an undifferentiated group. A more sensible approach is to recognize that different kinds of people will respond positively, in varying degrees, to alternative crime control strategies.

THE UNDERCLASS

The most disturbing economic trend in the United States is the emergence of a permanent underclass. The sociologist William Julius Wilson, in an illuminating discussion of the subject, prefers to call this group "the truly disadvantaged." Whatever the term we use, we are concerned here with a group of people who are enmeshed in a set of interrelated social and economic problems. The critical new factor is not the incidence or degree of poverty and unemployment; we have experienced both throughout our history. The new phenomenon is a condition that permanently traps people at the bottom of the social heap. The result is the emergence of a class line unlike any we have known before in American history.[9]

The idea of an underclass is closely associated with the concept of the "culture of poverty." Unfortunately, this concept has been grossly misunderstood and applied in a way that leads us far from its original point. It originated with the anthropologist Oscar Lewis, who argued that the special conditions of advanced capitalist societies trap some of the poor at the bottom of the social heap and reinforce attitudes and behavior that make it difficult or impossible for those individuals to escape from poverty.[10] Some analysts, instead of being encouraged to examine the larger economic system, transformed his idea by focusing on the attitudes and behavior of the poor themselves. This is a classic instance of the phenomenon of "blaming the victim."

The driving force behind the creation of the underclass in the United States has been the steady disappearance of manufacturing jobs and, in particular, of entry-level jobs. Between 1953 and 1984 New York City lost nearly 600,000 manufacturing jobs. It gained 700,000 white-collar service jobs, but those are beyond the reach of young people at the bottom of society. Over the same period, Philadelphia lost 280,000 manufacturing jobs and St. Louis lost 127,000. Virtually every industrial city in the Northeast and Midwest had the same experience.[11] The best index of this development is the steady rise of teenage unemployment, as Table 1 indicates. Black teenagers have always borne the brunt of the unemployment problem. White teenage unemployment rose slightly between 1950 and 1979, while black teenage unemployment more than doubled. Throughout the course of the past thirty years, black unemployment has been consistently double the rate for whites, and the gap between white and black teenagers has been growing. Moreover, the data in the table do not reflect the devastating impact on both races of the 1980–1982 recession.

These figures shed some light on the so-called paradox of crime in the 1960s. Although the economy as a whole was prosperous, young blacks did not share in the prosperity and in fact were becoming steadily worse off in relation to young whites. The baby boom only aggravated the long-term economic trends. Not only were there more kids in the high-crime age group but their economic condition was far worse than that of any previous teenage group.

The researchers who examined crime and unemployment may have been looking in the wrong place. Fluctuations in the unemployment rate measure the number of people moving in and out of employment. As far as crime is concerned, most of these people are not our primary concern. Middle-management executives and sales representatives who lose their jobs do not become career criminals. The fluctuating unemployment rate does not reflect the true size or nature of the underclass. The unemployment rate was cut in half between the 1982 recession and 1987 (from 10 percent to 5 percent), yet this economic achievement had only a marginal effect on the underclass. Crime continued to decline, but not at a rate equal to the reduction in unemployment. The economic boom of the mid-1980s left the criminogenic milieu of the underclass untouched.

The emerging underclass was not totally unaffected by the civil rights movement. In *Criminal Violence, Criminal Justice*, Charles Silberman tackles the sensitive question

Table 1. Unemployment Rates, White and Black Males, 1950–1979 (Percent)

	Total, 16 Years and Over		16 and 17 Years		18 and 19 Years		20 to 24 Years	
	WHITE	BLACK	WHITE	BLACK	WHITE	BLACK	WHITE	BLACK
1950	4.7	9.4	13.4	12.1	11.7	17.7	7.7	12.6
1951	2.6	4.9	9.5	8.7	6.7	9.6	3.6	6.7
1952	2.5	5.2	10.9	8.0	7.0	10.0	4.3	7.9
1953	2.5	4.8	8.9	8.3	7.1	8.1	4.5	8.1
1954	4.8	10.3	14.0	13.4	13.0	14.7	9.8	16.9
1955	3.7	8.8	12.2	14.8	10.4	12.9	7.0	12.4
1956	3.4	7.9	11.2	15.7	9.7	14.9	6.1	12.0
1957	3.6	8.3	11.9	16.3	11.2	20.0	7.1	12.7
1958	6.1	13.8	14.9	27.1	16.5	26.7	11.7	19.5
1959	4.6	11.5	15.0	22.3	13.0	27.2	7.5	16.3
1960	4.8	10.7	14.6	22.7	13.5	25.1	8.3	13.1
1961	5.7	12.8	16.5	31.0	15.1	23.9	10.0	15.3
1962	4.6	10.9	15.1	21.9	12.7	21.8	8.0	14.6
1963	4.7	10.5	17.8	27.0	14.2	27.4	7.8	15.5
1964	4.1	8.9	16.1	25.9	13.4	23.1	7.4	12.6
1965	3.6	7.4	14.7	27.1	11.4	20.2	5.9	9.3
1966	2.8	6.3	12.5	22.5	8.9	20.5	4.1	7.9
1967	2.7	6.0	12.7	28.9	9.0	20.1	4.2	8.0
1968	2.6	5.6	12.3	26.6	8.2	19.0	4.6	8.3
1969	2.5	5.3	12.5	24.7	7.9	19.0	4.6	8.4
1970	4.0	7.3	15.7	27.8	12.0	23.1	7.8	12.6
1971	4.9	9.1	17.1	33.4	13.5	26.0	9.4	16.2
1972	4.5	8.9	16.4	35.1	12.4	26.2	8.5	14.7
1973	3.7	7.6	15.1	34.4	10.0	22.1	6.5	12.6
1974	4.3	9.1	16.2	39.0	11.5	26.6	7.8	15.4
1975	7.2	13.7	19.7	39.4	17.2	32.9	13.2	22.9
1976	6.4	12.7	19.7	37.7	15.5	34.0	10.9	20.7
1977	5.5	12.4	17.6	38.7	13.0	36.1	9.3	21.7
1978	4.5	10.9	16.9	40.0	10.8	30.8	7.6	20.0
1979	4.4	10.3	16.1	34.4	12.3	29.6	7.4	17.0

Source: Adapted from U.S. Department of Labor, *Handbook of Labor Statistics, 1980* (Washington, D.C.: U.S. Government Printing Office, 1981), pp. 63–64.

of black crime in an imaginative and thought-provoking manner. The extremely high rates of criminal violence among blacks cannot be ignored. Although crime increased in all groups in the 1960s, much of that increase was produced by a veritable explosion of violence among black Americans. And since violent crime is overwhelmingly an intraracial phenomenon, most of the victims were black as well. In 1972, deaths of black males by homicide in the United States reached the astounding level of 83.1 per 100,000. This was ten times the rate for white males (8.2) that year and more than 100 times higher than the national rate for England and some other European countries. Murder was the leading cause of death among young black men.[12]

Silberman explains the explosion of violence by reference to the history of blacks in this country. Racial oppression not only generated powerful sources of anger but turned that anger inward, in the direction of self-hatred and intergroup violence. The civil rights movement challenged and dismantled the structure of power that had created and focused black anger. As the constraints fell, that anger poured out in all directions. Much of it was channeled into organized political protest, particularly the mass protests of the early 1960s. Some of it found expression in the riots of the mid-1960s. And much of it took the form of aggressive criminal violence. Silberman's point is that criminal violence in the United States cannot be understood solely as an outgrowth of poverty. The history of racism has given the black component of criminal violence an especially volatile character. The deteriorating economic condition of the black teenage underclass added further fuel to this explosive situation.

The nature of the underclass also suggests that there are limits to the decline in criminal violence which can be expected to flow from demographic trends. I have already argued that the aging of the baby-boom generation and the relative decline in the proportion of people in the fourteen-to-twenty-four-year-old age group is probably the major reason for the fall in crime rates since the mid-1970s. Aggregate population figures, however, mask important distinctions. The overall birth rate declined through the 1960s and even approached zero population growth in the early 1970s. The decline was greatest among middle-class whites. Among low-income people, and low-income blacks in particular, the birth rate dropped only moderately and thus remained substantially higher than that of middle-class whites. The number of low-income, inner-city males between fourteen and twenty-four has declined as well, but not so much as the national average. One can argue that the modest decline that is occurring in this group is offset by the continuing deterioration of its economic prospects. All indicators suggest that unemployment and family breakdown are increasing rather than improving for people in the underclass. This segment of our population, permanently trapped at the bottom of our society, will probably remain as significant a generator of predatory crime as before. Demographic trends do not offer the relief from crime that some observers have anticipated.

One final comment on economic trends is in order. It is now obvious that the American economy is in the midst of a historic transition, one that rivals the Industrial Revolution 150 years ago. Manufacturing jobs have been moving to the Third World (first to Japan and now to Korea, Singapore, etc.). There has been an enormous and perhaps permanent erosion of jobs in the basic industries of steel, automobiles, and machine tool production. Service industries have been the major source of new jobs since the 1970s. The social impact of these developments on the industrial cities of the Northeast is still uncalculated. With the collapse of the basic industries, thousands of blue-collar workers have become economically irrelevant. Not only have they lost their own jobs but their children can no longer expect to step into similar jobs, as they themselves once took their places in the factories next to their parents, older siblings, and other relatives. In short, what happened to black teenagers in the 1950s is now happening to white adults in the 1980s. Both groups are rendered economically superfluous by long-term economic trends.

From the Dangerous Class to the Underclass: A Historical Note

At this point the skeptic (and most conservatives) may well raise a serious objection to the underclass argument. Haven't we been through this before? Didn't we always have an urban underclass consisting of the most recent arrivals to the city? And didn't they all eventually succeed in achieving upward mobility? Isn't it really just a matter of time?

Almost exactly one hundred years ago, the social reformer Charles Loring Brace published a widely read book titled *The Dangerous Classes.* Brace's account has a familiar ring: the inner city was filled with a new and "dangerous" element, people mired in poverty whose lives were characterized by alcoholism, unemployment, family breakdown, and crime. Worse, many of the young men seemed to be completely amoral, with no respect for law and order.[13] Sound familiar? The people Brace was talking about were primarily Irish immigrants. Fifty years later, other reformers would write the same things about the new Italian and Jewish immigrants. Yet each of these groups has managed to be assimilated by the mainstream of American society. Their communities are no longer characterized by the cycle of unemployment and crime.

The idea that every immigrant group encountered difficulty at first but then succeeded is extremely attractive. It was first advanced more than twenty years ago by Nathan Glazer and Daniel Moynihan (the current senator from New York) in *Beyond the Melting Pot.* Black Americans are simply the latest in a long line of immigrant groups and they too will eventually succeed. More recently, the noted black conservative economist Thomas Sowell has made the same argument in *Ethnic America.*[14]

There are several problems with this view, however. First, and most important, it ignores the structural changes occurring in the American economy. Previous immigrant groups arrived at a time of extraordinary industrial growth. There was a demand for unskilled labor. Today we face a serious shrinkage of those same kinds of jobs. This process began slowly in the 1950s and, as Table 1 indicates, had a devastating effect on black teenage employment. Second, it ignores the special quality of American racial discrimination. The historian Herbert Gutman has challenged the popular view that the problems of the black family can be traced back to slavery. His research indicates that the black family emerged from slavery in remarkably strong condition. The current problems with the black family are a result of more recent economic conditions in the urban North. Finally, Moynihan himself repudiated the central thesis of *Beyond the Melting Pot* twenty years later. In a remarkable act of intellectual courage, he admitted he had been wrong. The experience of the previous immigrant groups was not a viable model for our current problems. Moynihan now claims that since the 1960s the gap between rich and poor has been dramatically widening. We are closer to becoming a truly class-divided society now than at any earlier time in our history.[15]

In short, the combination of new economic forces and long-standing racial discrimination has led us into a historically unique situation. The so-called lessons of the past about other immigrant groups do not apply.

ECONOMIC RECONSTRUCTION

Virtually everyone agrees that in the long run, economic opportunity will reduce crime by allowing ordinary people to establish productive lives and stable families. The real dispute between liberals and conservatives is over the means to achieve that end. Conservatives put their hopes in a marketplace free of government intervention. Liberals, on the other hand, want the government to assume an active role both in stimulating growth and in providing assistance to people in need.

The social programs of the 1960s failed because they did not address the need to create massive numbers of jobs. The Vietnam War did that job better by stimulating production and channeling hundreds of thousands of young men out of the work force and into military service. But even the war-induced prosperity failed to stem the rising tide of teenage unemployment and the growth of the underclass. The education and job-training programs of the War on Poverty were irrelevant in the face of the structural changes in the economy. The criticisms published in *The Public Interest* and other neoconservative journals are probably fair: the programs never demonstrated their effectiveness and many were counterproductive. But those criticisms are beside the point. Even if the programs had been effective, they would not have served enough people to reduce unemployment significantly and certainly would not have halted the steady erosion of entry-level jobs and the growth of the underclass.

If in fact unemployment breeds crime, we will not solve that problem by social tinkering. Job training for a few thousand unemployed, or a 30 percent or even 50 percent reduction in the official unemployment rate, will not in any way touch the underclass, which is the core of our predatory crime problem. Yet neither liberal Democrats nor conservative Republicans have offered a realistic program for the creation of massive numbers of jobs.

BEYOND RACE?

William Julius Wilson makes a persuasive argument about the kinds of social programs that are politically feasible in today's political environment. The problems of unemployment, family breakdown, and crime are disproportionately concentrated in a relatively small group—the truly disadvantaged, the underclass, call it what you want. In the political arena, however, the majority will not support programs designed just for this group. To obtain the necessary political support, effective programs will need to be presented as beneficial to all racial and economic groups. As Wilson puts it, "The hidden agenda is to improve the life chances of groups such as the ghetto underclass by emphasizing programs in which the more advantaged groups of all races can positively relate." In short, the fate of the underclass is tied up with the fate of all the rest of us. To deal with crime we should target not just the hard-core career criminals, Wolfgang's famous 6 percent, but the social policies that affect society as a whole.[16]

Notes

1. Samuel Walker, *Popular Justice: A History of American Criminal Justice* (New York: Oxford University Press, 1980), pp. 232–239.

2. James Q. Wilson, *Thinking about Crime*, rev. ed. (New York: Basic Books, 1983), chap. 1.

3. James Q. Wilson, "Thinking about Crime," *Atlantic Monthly*, September 1983, pp. 86, 88.

4. Richard A. Cloward and Lloyd E. Ohlin, *Delinquency and Opportunity* (New York: Free Press, 1960), p. 83.

5. Elliot Liebow, *Tally's Corner* (Boston: Little, Brown, 1967).

6. Isaac Ehrlich, "Participation in Illegitimate Activities: A Theoretical and Empirical Investigation," *Journal of Political Economy*, May–June 1973, pp. 521–565.

7. Sheldon Danziger and David Wheeler, "The Economics of Crime: Punishment or Income Distribution," *Review of Social Economy* 33 (October 1975): 113–131.

8. Thomas Orsagh and Anne D. Witte, "Economic Status and Crime: Implications for Offender Rehabilitation," *Journal of Criminal Law and Criminology* 72 (1981): 1055–1071.

9. Ken Auletta, *The Underclass* (New York: Vintage, 1983); William Julius Wilson, *The Truly Disadvantaged: The Inner City, the Underclass, and Public Policy* (Chicago: University of Chicago Press, 1987).

10. Oscar Lewis, *Five Families: Mexican Case Studies in the Culture of Poverty* (New York: Basic Books, 1959), and *The Children of Sánchez* (New York: Random House, 1961).

11. Wilson, *Truly Disadvantaged*, pp. 157–158.

12. Charles Silberman, *Criminal Violence, Criminal Justice* (New York: Random House, 1978).

13. Charles Loring Brace, *The Dangerous Classes of New York* [3rd ed., 1880] (New York: Patterson Smith, 1967).

14. Nathan Glazer and Daniel Patrick Moynihan, *Beyond the Melting Pot* (Cambridge: MIT Press, 1963); Thomas Sowell, *Ethnic America: A History* (New York: Basic Books, 1981).

15. Herbert G. Gutman, *The Black Family in Slavery and Freedom, 1750–1925* (New York: Pantheon, 1976); Moynihan, *New York Times*, November 9, 1985.

16. Wilson, *Truly Disadvantaged*, p. 120.

43. The Criminal Elite

JAMES WILLIAM COLEMAN

WHAT CAN BE DONE?

Crime, as Emile Durkheim pointed out long ago, is inevitable in modern societies. The function of criminal law is to create crime by branding certain people and certain behaviors as deviant. A law that no one broke would be an unnecessary law. Thus, a certain amount of white-collar crime is inevitable in any society that bases its legal system on standards that apply to all social strata. But as we have seen, the incidence of white-collar crime goes far beyond this inevitable minimum. No other kind of crime—

and indeed, few problems of any sort—can even approach the hundreds of thousands of lives and billions of dollars lost every year through white-collar crime.

The aim of this final section is to explore some of the ways of dealing with this pressing problem. Although its conclusions are based on the preceding analysis, a crystal ball is not part of the standard inventory of sociological tools. The sociology of deviance has shown the unexpected damage done by past efforts to deal with such problems as drug use and prostitution through criminal law,[1] and there are no guarantees that any of the following proposals would have the desired effects. Yet there is good reason to believe that the growing body of research into the problem of white-collar crime can help us avoid the mistakes of the moral crusaders of the past.

Ethical Reforms

One of the most common reactions to the news of some heinous crime is to ask, "What kind of a person would do such a thing?" and to blame the crime on the moral failings of the criminal. Sociologists have long opposed such one-sidedly individualistic explanations, and they are especially suspect when applied to white-collar crime. Organizations and occupational subcultures generate powerful pressures on employees to conform to their expectations, and any effort to deal with the problem of white-collar crime on this level must be aimed at changing the "ethical climate" within the corporations and the government. DeFleur argued that "because it is impossible to police everyone . . . a reduction in illegal corporate behavior depends on the development of stronger codes of ethics in business."[2] But how can that be done? He recommended three ways in which those goals might be met: (1) courses in ethics should be made mandatory in business schools, (2) trade associations should establish uniform ethical codes for each industry, and (3) individual corporations should make systematic efforts to develop ethical codes and instill them in their employees.[3]

To more structurally oriented sociologists, however, such proposals appear extremely naive. It is hard to imagine that a single college class, or even a series of them, would be likely to stimulate achievement-oriented young managers to defy the expectations of the organizations on whose approval their futures depend. It is equally difficult to imagine that an industry trade association would promulgate any standards of behavior that ran counter to the financial interests of its members, or that the members would follow the standards if they did. High sounding codes of ethics may make for good public relations, but by themselves they are unlikely to have any effect on the "ethical climate" of the government or the business world. After a careful statistical comparison of corporations with codes of ethics with explicit penalties, corporations with codes but without penalties, and corporations with no codes at all, Marilynn Mathews concluded that: "It just didn't make a difference."[4]

A structural analysis suggests that ethical standards will change only when the structural rewards for unethical behavior change. What is necessary, then, is some way to make ethical behavior more rewarding than criminal behavior. The most obvious course of action would be to increase the civil and criminal penalties for such offenses. . . . Christopher Stone, Donald Cressey, and others have proposed another approach—the creation of a public award given to corporations that maintain proper ethical standards.[5] Such awards would be highly publicized, and corporations would be encouraged to use them in advertising campaigns. Corporations that fail to meet ethical standards would then face negative publicity, especially since their competitors would be free to advertise their ethical superiority. This proposal still leaves many unanswered questions concerning the nature of those ethical standards and the best ways to evaluate corporate performance, but it does merit further study. A similar proposal made by W. Brent Fisse would also use publicity as a sanction against corporate offenses, but instead of a public award, he calls for new legislation requiring convicted corporate offenders to pay for advertising that would inform the public of their offenses.[6]

Because occupational criminals are not supported by large impersonal organizations, individual ethical standards are probably more important in controlling their behavior. Tougher punishments would once again be helpful, but there are limits to the effectiveness of even a well-organized and well-financed criminal justice system. As long as the culture of competition remains a central part of our culture, the level of occupational crime is likely to remain high. There are, of course, alternative value systems, both religious and secular, that stress the ethics of cooperation. But a significant weakening of the culture of competition would have to be accompanied by changes in the structural relations that support it. Such a change is by no means impossible—and perhaps not even unlikely—but cultural evolution of this sort tends to be a painfully slow process.

Enforcement Reforms

Of all the reforms discussed here, the idea that white-collar criminals must be more severely punished is probably the most widely accepted. But there are many different proposals, and none of them has won universal acceptance by experts and political activists. Foremost among these suggestions are the calls for greater resources and new priorities for enforcement agencies, a greater effort to isolate those agencies from outside political pressures, and legislation that is less ambiguous and easier to enforce.

The data given in chapter 5 clearly show the need for greater resources. Regulatory agencies and prosecutors are often hopelessly outmatched by their corporate opponents, who command larger and more skilled legal staffs and much greater financial support. There are too few government inspectors to detect more than a small fraction of the pollutants illegally released into the environment, and the same is true of occupational health and safety hazards and dangerous consumer products. The regulatory agencies even lack the resources to test most potentially dangerous substances so that appropriate regulations can be promulgated. To remedy this situation, regulatory and enforcement agencies must be given very substantial increases in their budgets. Certainly, funding at five or ten times the current levels would not be out of line with the importance of the problem. The most pressing needs are for larger research budgets to permit regulatory agencies to actively search out threats to public health and safety before disaster strikes; for substantial increases in the ranks of the investigators and prosecutors; and for higher pay for the legal, medical, and scientific personnel who now are often lured away to higher-paying jobs in private industry.

Greater support is also needed for the local agencies that bear the primary responsibility for dealing with occupational crimes.

An increase in resources must be accompanied by a greater effort to insulate enforcement agencies from undue political pressure. Although there appears to be no certain way to achieve that end, several possibilities have been suggested. First of all, along with an increase in pay, the employees of regulatory agencies could be required to sign an agreement, backed up by explicit legal penalties, promising never to work for any of the firms that fall under their regulatory jurisdiction. Currently, there is a two-year moratorium on such employment changes, but many people believe that a longer time period is necessary and that the regulatory agencies would be better off without an employee who would refuse to sign such an agreement. Secondly, in order to defuse the threat of punitive budgetary cutbacks for agencies that offend powerful special interests, as well as to lighten the financial burden on the public, enforcement and regulatory agencies could be made more self-supporting. This could be accomplished by legislation requiring that convicted offenders pay the full cost of the government's investigation and prosecution. This money, along with any punitive fines, would then be turned over to the agencies involved in the case.

The current system of fines and penalties needs restructuring for another reason as well. Far too often, penalties do not even equal the profits made from an organizational crime, much less pose a credible deterrent. To resolve this problem, the laws could be rewritten to require that convicted corporate offenders automatically pay a penalty at least equal to the amount of profit they made from their illegal activities. The judge or hearing officer would also be given the authority to impose additional punitive fines as appropriate. Where violent offenses are involved, much stiffer financial penalties are called for — perhaps based on the severity of the injuries and the number of deaths the offenders caused.

Many criminologists believe that even large fines have little impact on organizational crime, because corporate offenders merely pass them on to their customers in the form of higher prices. This is indeed a problem in some cases, but it is not always so. In a competitive industry, a corporate offender may be unable to pass on the cost of the fines to its customers, thus resulting in lower profits and trouble for top management. Fines are likely to have less impact in more oligopolistic industries, but if the penalties were sufficiently large and were assessed on only a single member of the oligopoly, they might still have the desired effect.

Other critics have charged that the imposition of large financial penalties may force some offenders into bankruptcy, thus punishing the innocent along with the guilty. There is little doubt that financial penalties based on a realistic estimate of the damage done by organizational crime would indeed cause some firms to go bankrupt. But there are good grounds for believing that such an event would ultimately work to the public good. Although some workers might lose their jobs, the assets of bankrupt firms do not vanish, they are purchased by other businesses. Most of the workers probably would be quickly rehired — hopefully, by a more reputable employer. If necessary, new legislation could be enacted mandating the bankruptcy courts to take special action to protect the interests of the workers in such cases. Stockholders would suffer a more permanent loss, but that is part of the risk investors take when they buy stocks rather than invest in more secure investments such as insured bank accounts. The example of a major corporation being forced into bankruptcy because of the penalties for its criminal behavior would certainly pose a powerful deterrent to other offenders and might also spur stockholders to monitor the activities of management more closely.

Another promising approach focuses on prevention rather than punishment. The idea here is to penetrate the organizational shell of the corporate offender by placing enforcement agents in a position to make it impossible for a corporation to repeat its crimes. For example, a firm that has committed repeated environmental violations would be required to pay the cost of hiring enough government inspectors to continually monitor the firm's compliance with the law. In order for such a system to function effectively, it would probably be necessary to rotate the inspectors periodically to prevent them from becoming too closely identified with a single firm.

There are also a number of ways in which current laws could be changed to improve the effectiveness of the enforcement effort. A simple modification of the laws concerning mergers could greatly strengthen the government's antitrust efforts. Instead of the current requirement that the government prove that a proposed merger would tend to restrain trade or create a monopoly, new legislation could simply forbid all mergers by the nation's five hundred or so largest corporations. Specific exemptions might then be granted if the firms involved could show that the proposed merger would have beneficial economic and social effects.

Under a bill introduced by Senator Edward Kennedy in 1979, corporations with over $2.5 billion in sales or $2 billion in assets would have been prohibited from merging, no matter how different their lines of business. Corporations with $350 million to $2.5 billion in sales and $200 million to $2 billion in assets would have had to prove that the proposed merger would lead to greater efficiency and more competition. Not only would such legislation simplify the current enforcement procedures and encourage competition, but it could be expected to yield other economic benefits as well. By reducing the tendency of big corporations to simply buy up an existing firm when they want to enter a new line of business, laws of this kind would encourage U.S. firms to build new plants and buy new equipment.

Lawyers associated with Ralph Nader have drawn up a much broader piece of legislation that has been proposed for adoption in several states. Were this model legislation, entitled "The Corporate Deviance Act," enacted by a significant number of states, it would certainly strike a forceful blow at corporate criminality. Among other things, it would make it a felony for a corporation to conceal any product or process that might cause death or injury, and it would also make it a crime to retaliate against "whistleblowers" seeking to inform the public about such activities. A business license would be made contingent on the "good character" of the corporation and could be denied if the state found a consistent pattern of unethical or illegal activities. The legislation would require corporations to provide workers, consumers, and the public with all available information about any hazards their activities may create.[7]

Another approach would be to enact legislation mandating the licensing of executives of the major corporations, in the same way we license other professionals. Such a license need not be difficult to obtain. A simple test on the legal and ethical requirements of corporate management would be sufficient. The main value of this licensing system would be to create a mechanism for disbarring corporate officers who violate their ethical obligations. A special regulatory agency might be established to hear the cases against individual executives. If the evidence warranted, the hearing officer would be empowered to prohibit an offender from working for any major corporation for a fixed number of years. Although many disbarment cases would undoubtedly be appealed to the federal courts, such a procedure would provide a means of sanctioning executive misconduct without having to prove criminal intent.

One largely untapped resource in the battle against organizational crime can be found in the outside auditors whom publicly traded firms must hire to examine their financial reports. These auditors are obviously in an excellent position to uncover many types of corporate illegalities. However, the American Institute of Certified Public Accountants, along with most individual practitioners, has traditionally held that "the normal audit arrangement is not designed to detect fraud and cannot be relied upon to do so."[8] Outside auditors face a built-in conflict of interest, for although their employer is an independent firm, it is still paid by the corporation whose books they are examining. Hence, a firm that gains a reputation for "overzealousness" in checking for corporate illegalities might find itself losing many important clients. The attitude of most accounting firms is reflected in the following statement by one member of a major firm: "We are not required to audit below the normal levels of materiality in search for illegal payments. *Our responsibility in this connection is to our clients.* It does not extend to informing the SEC about immaterial payments if we find them. We are not police for the commission."[9]

Auditors may not be policemen, but they are in a unique position to assist law enforcement, and a few basic reforms could greatly enhance their role in protecting the public from corporate fraud. Auditors could be legally required to search out fraud and deception in corporate financial statements and to report any suspected illegalities to enforcement agencies. But in order to carry out this new role, the accounting firms would have to be insulated from their clients' financial pressures. To achieve this goal, major corporations could be required to pay an audit fee to a government clearinghouse, which would then select the firm to do the actual audit. Thus, the auditors would feel no undue pressure to compromise the integrity of their report.

Honest employees who refuse to accept the idea that illegal activities are necessary to get the job done can be another important ally in the fight against white-collar crime. But to win their help, a strong new law protecting the whistle-blowers who report the crimes of their employers is needed. Such legislation would make it a crime to retaliate against whistle-blowers in any way and require that substantial punitive damages be paid to the victim of such an action.

According to the polls discussed in chapter 5, the public is most concerned about white-collar crimes that cause direct physical harm to people. It therefore makes sense to give such crimes as environmental pollution, occupational safety violations, and the manufacture of unsafe products a high priority in the enforcement effort. Those same polls show that the public believes that such violent white-collar crimes deserve punishments as severe as those given for violent street crimes. A much more vigorous effort is therefore needed to investigate, prosecute, and imprison violent white-collar offenders. For example, a greater volume of cases is necessary to establish clear legal precedents for the prosecution of negligent corporate executives for criminal manslaughter and to make such legal actions a routine and expected response to violent organizational crime.

"Supply side" economists have taken a very different approach to enforcement reform, arguing that the government ought not to be involved in economic regulation at all. They would write most white-collar crimes out of existence and allow the economic system to operate on its own. Advocates of this position have argued that consumers can regulate unsafe products by refusing to buy them, that workers can regulate occupational safety by refusing to work at unsafe jobs, and so on. In this view, environmental pollution could be controlled through some system of taxation on emissions, so that corporations can decide whether or not to install antipollution devices on economic grounds. Although such a program of deregulation would eliminate many white-collar crimes by legal fiat, it is hard to imagine how it could help resolve the underlying problems that led to the creation of those laws. If it were true that an unfettered market naturally takes care of such problems, those laws would never have been enacted in the first place.

Another attack on the regulatory system came from President Reagan in February 1981, when he issued an executive order requiring a special cost/benefit analysis before any regulation is put into effect. The goal of this cost/benefit analysis is to reduce "'regulatory unreasonableness' and the burden the latter allegedly places on American business."[10] Our previous analysis has shown, however, that the regulatory process has always been most sensitive to the interests of the businesses being regulated, and that regulatory inaction is a much greater problem than regulatory unreasonableness. The imposition of one more level of review to the already cumbersome rule-making procedure only aggravates the failures of the enforcement process.[11]

Structural Reforms

Criminologists have long held that the best way to deal with any kind of crime is to attack it at the source rather than to rely on the criminal justice system to punish the offenders after the fact, and that is exactly what proposals for structural reforms try to do. Yet these proposals are highly controversial, both because they have strong ideological implications and because they threaten powerful vested interests. Nevertheless, this approach offers some of the most promising avenues for achieving long-range solutions to the problem of white-collar crime.

Many proposals for dealing with organizational crime involve basic changes in corporate structure to reduce the incentives for illegal activities, or at least to make them more difficult. Christopher Stone has proposed that public representatives be added to the boards of directors of all the major corporations.[12] These directors would have their own staffs and be charged not only with representing the public interest in the boardroom but also with supervising corporate behavior, hearing complaints, and uncovering corporate illegalities. In a variation on this idea, several European nations, including Sweden and West Germany, now require worker representation on corporate boards. Such workers' representatives might well be combined with Stone's public representatives to further broaden the spectrum of interests participating in corporate decision-making.

How effective would these new board members be at making corporations more responsible? Studies of the European experience have shown that worker representation on corporate boards has not brought radical changes in corporate policies, for the new board members' main concerns have been in the areas of job security and working conditions.[13] Thus, there is reason to doubt that, in itself, worker representation in corporate decision-making would do much to improve the integrity of the business, discourage environmental pollution, or encourage safer products. Impetus for such reforms must come from public representatives. But as long as stockholders continue to dominate corporate boards, the likelihood of major internal reforms is obviously limited. If, however, the worker representatives and the public representatives worked together, and their combined votes exceeded those of the stockholders, some fundamental changes might well occur.

Ralph Nader's Corporate Accountability Research Group has argued that much stricter standards of corporate accountability can be imposed by means of the chartering process.[14] But if an individual state tried to impose tough new standards under the current chartering system, major corporations would simply move their headquarters to other states that gave them a better deal. The Nader group therefore proposed a system of federal chartering that would prevent corporations from playing one state off against another. Under the Nader proposal, the federal chartering agency would require corporate boards to take a much more active role in guiding firms. The boards also would be expanded to include worker representatives, and the corporations would be required to give the public much greater access to their records on such things as product safety research, plant emissions, and plans for factory closings.

However it is achieved, a freer flow of information among top management, corporate directors, regulatory agencies, and the general public would help discourage corporate crime and make the enforcement agencies' job an easier one. Too often, top managers and directors are able to cultivate selective ignorance about the criminal activities of their subordinates, the dangerous emissions of their plants, or the hazards of their products. Today, corporate spokesmen who make false public statements that cause serious harm to others can avoid criminal liability for fraud simply by claiming that they honestly believed their statements to be true.

One way to deal with this problem would be to require corporate decision-makers to review explicit reports on such things as product safety research, environmental pollution, and unethical practices. As those reports moved up the chain of command, officials at each level would be required to describe their effort to conform to legal regulations and to report any knowledge they have of possible illegalities. After the reports had been signed by the corporate board, they would be given to an appropriate federal agency for legal review. In addition to alerting enforcement agencies to possible problems, such a reporting system would make it impossible for top managers to claim that they were unaware that, for example, the statements made by the sales division were contrary to the findings of the research department.

John Braithwaite has proposed a similar program. Whether by new legislation, by court order, or by voluntary corporate reform, Braithwaite argued that those assigned the responsibility for keeping a corporation in compliance with the law must be given greater strength within the corporation. Among other things, he suggested that: compliance personnel be given a more professional status; a high-level ombudsman be established to hear complaints; reports be made directly to the chief executive officer in writing (thus "tainting" him or her with the knowledge of potential criminal activities); and corporate decisions about ethical and legal matters be written down to create a kind of "corporate case law" that would then provide a guide for employees who must make a difficult decision.[15]

A different approach to the control of corporate crime would be the selective nationalization of firms that have long records of criminal violations. Nationalization may sound like an extreme measure, but it is a common practice in many nations around the world. All the government would have to do is buy up enough stock to gain a controlling interest in the criminal firm. The old management would then be replaced by a new group of managers, who would be instructed to reform and restructure the corporation. After the reforms had been effected and the corporation was operating in a responsible manner, the government could either sell its stock and return the firm to private ownership, or continue to operate it as a public trust.

A program of nationalization might also focus on industries rather than on individual firms. The rationale behind this approach is that some industries (petroleum, for example) have such a long history of antitrust violations that they clearly are no longer regulated by the free market, and the government therefore needs to step in to protect the public interest. This could be done in several ways. All the firms in the industry could be nationalized—but that, of course, would produce even less competition, albeit with public instead of private control. Another alternative would be to nationalize a single large firm and to use it to reintroduce competition into the oligopolistic industry. A third alternative would be to start an entirely new, government-owned firm to compete with the existing oligopoly.

On the whole, occupational crimes are not as amenable to structural solutions as are organizational crimes. But there are two important exceptions—occupational crimes among government employees (discussed in the next section) and occupational crimes in the health care professions. Our previous analysis showed that the fee-for-service technique of payment is a major cause of crime in the health care industry. The motivation for performing unnecessary tests and treatments, for example, comes from the fact that physicians and laboratories are paid for each service they perform; thus, they are rewarded for "overdoctoring." If the health care system paid professionals on the basis of a salary rather than on the volume of services performed, the motivation for many offenses would be eliminated. This approach has already proven successful in private health maintenance organizations, as well as in nationalized health care systems such as the one in Great Britain.

Political Reforms

White-collar crime differs from most other types of crimes in that there are so many promising proposals for dealing with it. There is little doubt that, if some reasonable combination of the proposals discussed above were vigorously applied to the problem, the incidence of white-collar crime would decline. The difficulty in dealing with white-collar crime lies not so much in discovering viable responses but in winning their implementation. In other words, this is primarily a political problem that can be solved only by reforming the political process.

The most urgent need is for radical changes in the present system of campaign financing. The fact that most politicians have to rely on campaign contributions from well-endowed special interests clearly has had a paralyzing effect on the battle against white-collar crime. An aide to former Senator Gary Hart, during his campaign to win the 1988 presidential nomination, revealed exactly what the problem was when he was asked about his candidate's position on corporate crime: "No Democratic presidential candidate has ever made corporate crime an issue," he said, because "the money will dry up."[16]

The simplest way to resolve this problem would be to create a system of federal and state financing for election campaigns. The current provision for matching funds in presidential elections is certainly an improvement over the old system, but it is only a halfway measure for a single office. It would be far better to provide complete government funding for all major elections. Each candidate would naturally be given the same amount of money to spend, and large blocks of free television and radio time would be set aside for the candidates to discuss the issues.

The main difficulty in formulating such a system is to create a fair way to determine who is to receive government funds. On the one hand, a large number of frivolous candidates might run for office if no cost were involved. But on the other hand, the large, established parties currently in power might well write the campaign financing legislation in such a way as to exclude small-party candidates. Nonetheless, some fair system could certainly be worked out. One promising approach would be to require petitions with a minimum number of signatures to qualify for funding in the primary, and then use the primary returns as the basis for funding eligibility in the general election.

Another essential step toward reform is the provision of stronger protections for individual civil rights and the freedom of political expression. As we have seen, the government has not only established systematic programs for the surveillance of those who challenge the political interests of the elite, but it has actually taken direct covert action to repress such political activities. It would be helpful to have a new federal law explicitly criminalizing any activities on the part of government agents that interfere with the freedom of expression. Although most such activities are already illegal, such a law would still have an important symbolic value.

A more difficult problem is to get the government to enforce existing laws that regulate the behavior of its agents. Many observers have suggested the creation of a permanent special prosecutor's office, similar to the temporary one first created during the Watergate scandals. This office, equipped with its own investigative force, would have unrestricted access to all government records, files, and reports. The selection of the head of this office would best be left up to the Supreme Court or some prestigious, nonpartisan group. With such a strong institutional base, the effort to control the government's abuse of power would seem to stand a much better chance of success than it has in the past.

But because there is some question about how effectively the government can ever police itself, it is crucial that the public be given access to the broadest possible range of information about the government's activities. When a government agency begins an investigation of a political group, it should be required to notify the group of that fact. The activities of all government agents, operatives, and informants involved in such political cases should be periodically reviewed by a panel of federal judges to make sure that the government is staying within the bounds of the law and the standards of ethical conduct. Individuals should be given speedy access to all files kept on them by public or private organizations, without having to take costly legal action. All citizens should also be able to get inaccurate information removed from their files and have the right to sue for any damages caused by the dissemination of false information. . . .

Notes

1. See, for example, James William Coleman, "The Myth of Addiction," *Journal of Drug Issues* 6 (Spring 1976): 135–141; Troy Duster, *The Legislation of Morality* (New York: The Free Press, 1970); Edwin M. Schur, *Crimes Without Victims* (Englewood Cliffs, N.J.: Prentice-Hall, 1965).

2. Melvin L. DeFleur, *Social Problems in American Society* (Boston: Houghton Mifflin, 1983), 352.

3. Ibid.

4. Quoted in Paul Richter, "Big Business Puts Ethics in Spotlight," *Los Angeles Times*, 19 June 1986, I: 28; also see Marilynn Cash Mathews, "Codes of Ethics: Organizational Behavior and Misbehavior" in William C. Frederick (ed.), *Research in Corporate Social Performance and Policy* (Greenwich, Conn.: JAI, 1987). For a discussion of corporate codes of ethics, see Donald R. Cressey and Charles A. Moore, *Corporation Codes of Ethical Conduct* (New York: Report to the Peat, Marwick, and Mitchell Foundation, 1980).

5. Christopher D. Stone, *Where the Law Ends: The Social Control of Corporate Behavior* (New York: Harper & Row, 1975), 243.

6. W. Brent Fisse, "The Use of Publicity as a Criminal Sanction Against Business Corporations," *Melbourne University Law Review* 8 (June 1971): 113–130.

7. *Corporate Crime Reporter* 1 (27 April 1987): 5–60.

8. C. David Baron, Douglas A. Johnson, D. Gerald Searfoss, and Charles H. Smith, "Uncovering Corporate Irregularities: Are We Closing the Expectation Gap?," *Journal of Accountancy* (October 1977): 56.

9. Walter Guzzardi, Jr., "An Unscandalized View of Those 'Bribes' Abroad," *Fortune* (July 1978): 178. Italics added.

10. See, for example, Eugene Bardach and Robert A. Kagan, *Going by the Book: The Problem of Regulatory Unreasonableness* (Philadelphia: Temple University Press, 1982).

11. See, for example, Mark Green and Norman Waitzman, *Business War on the Law: An Analysis of the Benefits of Federal Health/Safety Enforcement*, rev. 2nd ed. (Washington, D.C.: The Corporate Accountability Research Group, 1981).

12. Stone, *Where the Law Ends*.

13. See Martin Carnoy and Derek Shearer, *Economic Democracy: The Challenge of the 1980s* (White Plains, N.Y.: M.E. Sharpe Inc., 1980), 249–257.

14. Ralph Nader, Mark J. Green, and Joel Seligman, *Taming the Giant Corporation* (New York: Norton, 1976).

15. John Braithwaite, *Corporate Crime in the Pharmaceutical Industry* (London: Routledge & Kegan Paul), 290–388.

16. *Corporate Crime Reporter* 1 (13 April 1987): 50.

Acknowledgments (continued from p. iv)

William Wilbanks, "Is Violent Crime Intraracial?" From *Crime and Delinquency*, 31:1, pp. 117–128, copyright 1985 by William Wilbanks. Reprinted by permission of Sage Publications, Inc. and the author.

Carol A. Whitehurst, "Women and the Commission of Crime: A Theoretical Approach." From *Deviant Behavior*, Second Edition, by Delos H. Kelly (editor). Copyright © 1984 by St. Martin's Press, Inc.

Murray A. Straus and Richard J. Gelles, "Societal Change and Change in Family Violence from 1975 to 1985 as Revealed by Two National Surveys." From the *Journal of Marriage and the Family*, 48:3, pp. 465–479 (August 1986). Copyrighted 1986 by the National Council on Family Relations, 3989 Central Ave. NE, Minneapolis, MN 55421.

Delos H. Kelly and William T. Pink, "School Crime and Individual Responsibility: The Perpetuation of a Myth?" from *The Urban Review*, 14:1, Spring 1982, pp. 47–63. Reprinted by permission.

C. Ronald Huff, "Historical Explanations of Crime: From Demons to Politics." Reprinted with permission from C. Ronald Huff. From *Crime and the Criminal Justice Process* by Inciardi-Haas. Copyright © 1978 by Kendall/Hunt Publishing Company, Dubuque, Iowa.

Emile Durkheim, "The Normal and the Pathological." Reprinted with permission of The Free Press, a Division of Macmillan, Inc. from Emile Durkheim, *The Rules of Sociological Method*, translated by Sarah A. Solovay and John H. Mueller, edited by George E. G. Catlin. Copyright © 1938 by George E. G. Catlin, renewed 1966 by Sarah A. Solovay, John H. Mueller, George E. G. Catlin.

Raymond J. Michalowski, "A Critical Model for the Study of Crime." From *Order, Law and Crime* by Raymond J. Michalowski, Random House (1985), pp. 21–38. Copyright © 1985 by McGraw-Hill, Inc.

Travis Hirschi, "A Control Theory of Delinquency." Reprinted from *Causes of Delinquency* by Travis Hirschi. Copyright © 1969 by The Regents of the University of California; reprinted by permission of the University of California Press.

Gresham M. Sykes and David Matza, "Techniques of Neutralization: A Theory of Delinquency," *American Sociological Review*, vol. 22, 1957, pp. 666–670.

Walter B. Miller, "Lower Class Culture as a Generating Milieu of Gang Delinquency." From the *Journal of Social Issues*, Vol. XIV, no. 3, pp. 5–19. Reprinted by permission of The Society for the Psychological Study of Social Issues.

Robert K. Merton, "Social Structure and Anomie," *American Sociological Review*, vol. 3, 1938, pp. 672–682.

Richard A. Cloward and Lloyd E. Ohlin, "Differential Opportunity and Delinquent Subcultures." Reprinted with permission of The Free Press, a Division of Macmillan, Inc. from *Delinquency and Opportunity* by Richard A. Cloward and Lloyd E. Ohlin. Copyright © 1960 by The Free Press.

Delos H. Kelly and Robert W. Balch, "Social Origins and School Failure: A Reexamination of Cohen's Theory of Working-Class Delinquency." From *Pacific Sociological Review*, 14:4, October 1971, pp. 413–430. Reprinted by permission of JAI Press, Inc.

Frank Tannebaum, "Definition and the Dramatization of Evil." From *Crime and Community* by Frank Tannenbaum. Copyright © 1938 by Columbia University Press. Used by permission.

John Rosecrance, "The Stooper: A Professional Thief in the Sutherland Manner." From *Criminology*, 24:1, 1986, pp. 29–40. Reprinted by permission of The American Society of Criminology and Marion F. Rosecrance (spouse under Durable Power of Attorney).

David F. Luckenbill, "Criminal Homicide as a Situated Transaction." Copyright © 1977 by the Society for the Study of Social Problems, Inc. Reprinted from *Social Problems*, vol. 25, no. 2, December 1977, pp. 176–186, by permission.